FUTURES

A N D

OPTIONS

THEORY AND APPLICATIONS

HANS R. STOLL
Owen Graduate School
of Management
Vanderbilt University

ROBERT E. WHALEY
The Fuqua School of Business
Duke University

**CURRENT
ISSUES IN**

Sponsoring Editor: James M. Keefe
Production Editor: Susan C. Williams
Production House: Graphic Typesetting Service
Cover Design: Graphica
Internal Designer: Ann Scheid
Marketing Manager: Scott D. Person

FD60AA

Library of Congress Cataloging-in-Publication Data

Stoll, Hans R.
    Futures and options : theory and applications / Hans R. Stoll,
Robert E. Whaley.
        p.   cm.
    Includes bibliographical references.
    ISBN 0-538-80115-8
    1. Futures. 2. Options (Finance)   I. Whaley, Robert E.
II. Title.
HG6024.A3S76   1993   91-45058
332.64′5—dc20   CIP

1 2 3 4 5 6 7 8 9   D   0 9 8 7 6 5 4 3 2

Printed in the United States of America

ABOUT THE AUTHORS

HANS R. STOLL

Hans R. Stoll is The Anne Marie and Thomas B. Walker, Jr. Professor of Finance and Director of the Financial Markets Research Center at the Owen Graduate School of Management, Vanderbilt University.

A recognized authority on financial markets, including futures and options markets, Professor Stoll has published more than fifty articles and monographs on subjects ranging from the forward foreign exchange market to stock market structure and volatility. His work with Professor Whaley on program trading and the "triple witching hour" is frequently cited. He is a consultant to industry and government and speaks frequently at academic and industry conferences. Professor Stoll is a member of the recently formed Shadow Securities and Exchange Commission, serves as a director of the American Finance Association and the Financial Management Association, and is president-elect of the Western Finance Association.

He is an associate editor of the *Journal of Financial Economics, The Journal of Finance, The Journal of Financial and Quantitative Analysis,* and serves on the editorial boards of *Financial Management,* the *Journal of Financial Research,* and *The Review of Futures Markets.*

Prior to coming to Vanderbilt in 1980, Professor Stoll taught at the Wharton School of the University of Pennsylvania. He has also held visiting positions at the Board of Governors of the Federal Reserve System, at the Institutional Investor Study of the Securities and Exchange Commission, at the University of Chicago, and as a Senior Fulbright-Hays Visiting Lecturer in France.

He received an A.B. degree from Swarthmore College and M.B.A. and Ph.D. degrees from the Graduate School of Business, University of Chicago.

ROBERT E. WHALEY

Robert E. Whaley is Professor of Finance, Finance Area Coordinator, and Director of the Futures and Options Research Center at the Fuqua School of Business, Duke University.

Professor Whaley is recognized as an expert in the area of option valuation. His research in this area includes developing option valuation models and approximations and testing pricing performance. His experience includes working in the futures and options industry as well as acting as consultant to investment houses, futures, option and stock exchanges, governmental agencies, and accounting and law firms concerning the pricing and use of derivative contracts. Together with Professor Stoll, he has published a number of widely-cited studies concerning the market effects of stock index futures and options and program trading. In 1987, one of their joint studies on program trading and expiration day effects received a "Graham and Dodd Award" for excellence in financial writing.

Professor Whaley has published dozens of articles in academic and practitioner journals, has authored several books and monographs, and has made presentations on futures and options to academic and practitioner audiences in the U.S., Canada, and Europe. He currently serves as associate editor of *The Journal of Finance* and the *Journal of Financial Economics,* as co-editor of *The Review of Futures Markets,* and as referee of numerous journals and granting agencies. Professor Whaley has also served on the faculties of Vanderbilt University, the University of Alberta, and the University of Chicago.

Professor Whaley received his bachelor's degree from the University of Alberta, and his M.B.A. and Ph.D. degrees from the University of Toronto.

THE CURRENT ISSUES IN FINANCE SERIES

Finance, as a field of study and research, has attained a level of development that makes it increasingly difficult to present the latest ideas in a single textbook. *The Current Issues in Finance Series* provides a mechanism for publishing specialized volumes that cover important subjects in greater detail than is possible in a general finance text. Advanced material is covered in considerable depth, yet presented in a readable fashion. A guiding principle of the series is that the books be written by recognized experts who are in a position to provide balanced coverage and in-depth analysis of a particular subject matter.

Books in the *Current Issues in Finance Series* are intended primarily for upper-level undergraduate courses and MBA courses. They may be used as the principal text in specialized courses or as a supplementary text in courses with broader coverage. Books in the series will also be suitable for practitioners who want to become more informed on a particular topic.

The first book in the series, *Futures and Options* by Stoll and Whaley, deals with a subject that has undergone dramatic developments in theory and in practice and one that has attracted the interest of students and practitioners. The book provides coverage of both futures and options in an integrated framework. Coverage includes not only derivative contracts on traditional commodities, but also the newer financial derivatives.

I salute South-Western Publishing, and especially Elizabeth Waters and Jim Keefe, for conceiving the series and supporting its development. Students of finance stand to benefit from South-Western's commitment to the series and can look forward to the publication of additional volumes on important finance topics.

Hans R. Stoll
Consulting Editor, *Current Issues in Finance Series*

PREFACE

This book, *Futures and Options*, the first volume in the *Current Issues in Finance Series*, covers an area of finance that has had unparalleled development in the last 20 years, both in practice and in theory. Trading of futures and options contracts has exploded at the same time that academic analysis and understanding of the valuation of these contracts has made monumental strides forward. In no area of finance is the interface between academic theory and real-world practice as close as in the case of futures and options.

Most remarkable in the growth of derivatives' trading in the 1980s was the development of futures and option contracts on new underlying assets. Futures contracts, traditionally reserved for physical commodities like corn or copper, were developed on underlying assets such as bonds and stock index portfolios. Option contracts, traditionally reserved for common stocks, were developed for bonds, stock indexes and for physical commodities. Our aim in this book is to provide, for the first time, an integrated approach to understanding the relations between futures, options, and their underlying assets.

Chapters 1 and 2 of the book define futures and option contracts, explain their economic purpose, and provide information on the markets in which these contracts trade.

Chapters 3 to 9 focus on futures contracts. Chapter 3 covers the structure of futures prices—basically the cost-of-carry model. Chapter 4 shows how futures are used for hedging and develops the concept of an optimal hedge ratio. Chapter 5 discusses risk and return in futures markets. Chapters 6 to 9 apply the principles developed in chapters 3 to 5 to futures on physical commodities, stock indexes, debt instruments, and currencies, respectively.

Chapters 10 to 16 focus on option contracts. Chapter 10 describes the structure of option prices imposed by arbitrage between puts, calls, futures, and the underlying commodity. Chapter 11 shows how options on any underlying commodity are valued. A risk-neutral valuation approach is used to develop a generalized version of the Black-Scholes model appropriate for the valuation of options on any type of underlying commodity. Sections of Chapters 10 and 11 are quite technical. Less technically-oriented students can skip the derivations of the pricing relations without harm to understanding the basic determinants of option values or arbitrage links. Chapter 12 shows how options are used in various trading strategies. Position diagrams are used to illustrate outcomes of various strategies. In addition, the chapter shows how to calculate expected gains from trading strategies, how to simulate long-term options with short-term options, and how to manage portfolio risk and return dynamically. In chapters 13 to 15, options on common stocks, on stock indexes, and on debt instruments are examined in turn. Chapter 16 examines exchange-traded options on other assets such as currencies and physical commodities. In addition, valuation equations are provided for many exotic options that trade in over-the-counter markets.

This book attempts to distill the many important research contributions that define modern-day derivative security valuation and risk management. More technically-oriented readers may gather further insights by studying the original research articles upon which we have based this book. Most of these articles appear in *Selected Readings on Futures Markets: Interrelations Between Futures, Option and Futures Option Markets*, R.E. Whaley (editor), Chicago: Chicago Board of Trade, 1992.

Finally, many individuals played important roles in the development of this book and need to be recognized formally. First, the students in our classes at Vanderbilt University and Duke University, who used earlier drafts of the book, gave valuable input. Our colleagues, Cam Harvey, Jay Muthuswamy, and Tom Smith, provided useful comments and suggestions. Bill Fung was instrumental in identifying the exotic option contracts discussed in Chapter 16. Shirley Edmond and Pat Scott provided secretarial support in putting together the final manuscript. Barbara Bennett Ostdiek, Jeff Fleming, and Marshall Howard carefully scrutinized last drafts of the chapters. Susan Williams of South-Western provided diligent editorial oversight of the final manuscript. To all of these individuals (and to all of those who we may have overlooked), our heartfelt thanks.

We dedicate this book to our wives and to our children for whom we hope it is evidence that we are doing something with our time.

Hans R. Stoll
Owen Graduate School of Management, Vanderbilt University

Robert E. Whaley
Fuqua School of Business, Duke University

CONTENTS

PART

INSTITUTIONAL BACKGROUND

1

1 INTRODUCTION TO FUTURES AND OPTIONS

A look at the business pages of the newspaper reveals a bewildering array of price quotations for futures and options. While futures contracts on agricultural commodities have been with us since the mid-1800s, futures trading in financial assets—such as bonds, currencies, and stock indexes—were introduced as recently as 1975 and have grown at an explosive rate since that time. Likewise, trading of options on financial and agricultural commodities is a relatively recent event, dating to the founding of the Chicago Board Options Exchange in April 1973. Today, call options trade on five U.S. exchanges in nearly 400 common stocks. Moreover, options also trade on bonds, foreign currencies, stock indexes, and traditional agricultural commodities.

While futures and options contracts on a variety of underlying commodities[1] have been developed, certain principles of valuation and price behavior are common across all commodities. For example, the essence of the price relation between the futures contract and its underlying commodity is captured by a simple arbitrage argument, even though the types of commodities range from agricultural to purely financial.

In this book, we emphasize the principles that determine the value of a futures contract, an option contract, and a futures option contract relative to the value of its underlying commodity. For example, consider the S&P 500 stock index to be

---

[1] In this book, the term "commodity" is defined as being something of value. The commodity may be a foodstuff such as wheat, a currency such as the Japanese yen, or a stock index such as the S&P 500.

the underlying commodity. The index is a value-weighted stock portfolio consisting of 500 large common stocks that trade predominantly on the New York Stock Exchange. The Chicago Mercantile Exchange lists a futures contract on the S&P 500, as well as an option contract on the futures, while the Chicago Board Options Exchange lists an option contract on the index itself. In other words, for this particular commodity—the S&P 500 stock index portfolio—the four markets depicted in Figure 1.1 trade simultaneously. Inextricable linkages exist among prices in these four markets, and, in this book, we identify the nature of these price linkages and the implications they have for expected return/risk management. In this chapter, we begin by defining futures, options, and futures options.

1.1   WHAT ARE FUTURES CONTRACTS?

A *futures contract* is a contract to buy or sell an underlying commodity at a future time, at a price—the *futures price*—specified today. Payment for the underlying commodity is not made unless, and until, delivery of the underlying commodity is taken. In organized futures markets, contracts can be reversed before expiration by taking a position of opposite sign but equal magnitude in the same futures contract. Someone who buys futures takes a long position and gains to the extent that the futures price at which that position is reversed (the terminal futures price) is above the initial futures price. Someone who sells futures takes a short position and gains if the terminal futures price is below the initial futures price.

The profit from a long futures position initiated at price F_0 is plotted in Figure 1.2a. For every dollar price rise above F_0, the investor makes one dollar. For every

FIGURE 1.1   Interrelations Between Commodity Market and Markets for the Commodity's Derivative Instruments

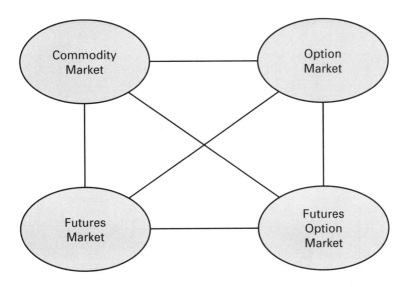

FIGURE 1.2   Profit Diagrams for Futures Position Held to Expiration

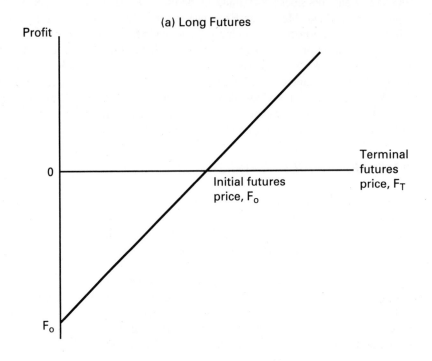

(a) Long Futures

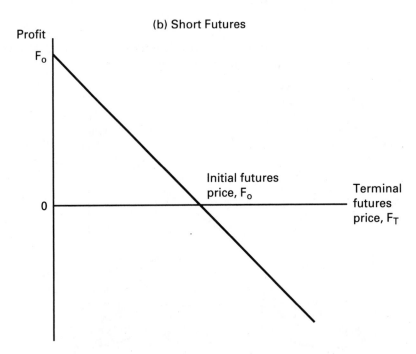

(b) Short Futures

dollar decline below F_0, the investor loses one dollar. The profit from a short position initiated at the futures price, F_0, is shown in Figure 1.2b.

As an example, suppose someone buys the July 1992 wheat futures contract listed in Table 1.1. At the close of trading on November 13, 1991, the futures price (F_0) is reported to be $3.21 per bushel. The denomination of this wheat futures contract is 5,000 bushels. Suppose further that the individual reverses his position on the following February 6 by entering into a contract to sell July wheat. If the price of the July wheat futures (F) is $4.00 on February 6, the individual earns a profit of ($4.00 − $3.21) × 5,000 = $3,950.00. Alternatively, if the futures price on February 6 is $3.00, the individual earns a profit of ($3.00 − $3.21) × 5,000 = −$1,050.00. Most futures contracts are, in fact, reversed in this manner prior to expiration.

Futures contracts are a means for reducing risk or assuming risk in the hope of profit, not a means of taking possession of the underlying commodity. Users of the underlying commodity generally prefer a grade and delivery location of the underlying commodity that are different from the grades and locations allowed under the terms of the futures contract.

As a second example, consider the March 1992 S&P 500 index futures reported in Table 1.2. Suppose someone buys this contract at the close of trading on November 13, 1991, at the reported price (F_0) of $400.35. The contract size for the S&P 500 futures is 500 times the price or $400.35 × 500 = $200,175. Suppose the position is reversed on February 6 when the futures price (F) is, say, $410.00. In this case, the individual earns a profit of ($410.00 − $400.35) × 500 = $4,825.00. If, instead, the index falls to, say, $390.00, the individual has a loss of ($400.35 − $390.00) × 500 = $5,175.00.

Every futures contract entered into has two sides: a willing buyer and a willing seller. If one side of the contract makes a profit, the other side must make a loss. All futures markets participants taken together can neither lose nor gain—the futures market is a zero-sum game.

TABLE 1.1   Prices of wheat futures contracts at the close of trading on Wednesday, November 13, 1991.

						Lifetime		Open
	Open	High	Low	Settle	Change	High	Low	Interest
—GRAINS AND OILSEEDS—								
WHEAT (CBT) 5,000 bu.; cents per bu.								
Dec	347½	352¾	347½	352½	+ 5¼	369¼	272½	19,480
Mr92	349½	353¾	348	353½	+ 5¾	367	279	23,394
May	334	338½	334	338	+ 5¼	352½	280½	5,174
July	317½	321	316¾	321	+ 4¾	337½	279	8,067
Sept	326	326	326	326	+ 5	341	292	690
Dec	333½	335	332	335	+ 4¾	351	329½	703
Est vol 15,500; vol Tues 11,502; open Int 57,508, −149.								

TABLE 1.2   Prices of S&P 500 stock index futures contracts at the close of trading on Wednesday, November 13, 1991.

FUTURES

S&P 500 INDEX (CME) 500 times index

	Open	High	Low	Settle	Chg	High	Low	Open Interest
Dec	395.00	398.50	394.30	398.30	+ 1.00	401.50	316.50	139,341
Mr92	396.80	400.50	396.50	400.35	+ 1.00	404.00	374.70	7,544
June	398.30	402.35	398.30	402.20	+ 1.10	407.00	379.00	1,102

Est vol 42,125; vol Tues 41,413; open int 148,048, +916.
Indx prelim High 397.42; Low 394.01; Close 397.42 +.68

Source: Reprinted by permission of *Wall Street Journal,* © (November 14, 1991) Dow Jones & Company, Inc. All Rights Reserved Worldwide.

1.2 WHAT ARE OPTIONS?

An *option contract* conveys the right to buy or sell an underlying commodity at a specified price within a specified period of time. The right to buy is referred to as a *call option*; the right to sell is a *put option*. Options are generally described by the nature of the underlying commodity. An option on a common stock is said to be a *stock option*; an option on a bond, a *bond option*; an option on a foreign currency, a *currency option*; an option on a futures contract, a *futures option*; and so on. The specified price at which the underlying commodity may be bought (in the case of a call) or sold (in the case of a put) is called the *exercise price* or the *striking price* of the option. To buy or sell the underlying commodity pursuant to the option contract is to exercise the option. Most options may be exercised at any time, up to and including the expiration date. These are called *American options*. If an option can only be exercised at expiration, it is termed a *European option*.

The buyer of an option pays the option writer (seller) an amount of money called the *option premium* or *option price*. In return, the buyer receives the privilege, but not the obligation, of buying (in the case of a call) or selling (in the case of a put) the underlying commodity for the exercise price. In the case of a call option, if the price of the commodity exceeds the exercise price, the call option is said to be *in-the-money*; and the call option buyer could exercise the option, thereby earning the difference between the two prices—the *exercise value* or *intrinsic value*. On the other hand, if the price of the commodity is below the exercise price, the call option is *out-of-the-money* and will not be exercised. Its intrinsic value is zero. In the case of a put option, if the price of the commodity is below the exercise price, the put option is said to be *in-the-money*. The put option buyer could exercise the option to earn the difference between the exercise price and the price of the commodity. A put option is said to be *out-of-the-money* when the commodity price exceeds the exercise price.

The profits from various option positions held to expiration are plotted in relation to the price of the underlying commodity in Figures 1.3 and 1.4. The illustrations assume that options are held to the expiration date, T. The price of the underlying commodity at the option's expiration is denoted as S_T.

The position of a call buyer—a long call position—is profitable if the price of the underlying commodity, S_T, exceeds the exercise price, X, by more than the initial price of the call option, C_0. This is depicted in Figure 1.3a. On the other hand, if S_T is below X at expiration, the call option is not exercised. The maximum gain to the call buyer is unlimited because the exercise value of the option increases directly with increases in the value of the underlying commodity, which is unlimited in principle. The maximum loss to the option buyer is C_0.

The position of a call seller or call writer—a short call position—is depicted in Figure 1.3b. The position is the reverse image of the long call position. A call seller faces the possibility of large losses if the price of the underlying commodity increases, because, in that case, the call will be exercised, and the call seller will be requested to purchase the underlying commodity at S_T and deliver it to the call buyer at X. The maximum gain to the call seller is C_0. It is evident from Figures 1.3a and 1.3b that the sum of the profits of the call buyer and call seller at any terminal price, S_T, is zero. As in the case of futures markets, the option market is also a zero-sum game.

The position of a put buyer—a long put position—depicted in Figure 1.4a is profitable if the price of the underlying commodity falls below the exercise price by more than P_0, the initial price of the put. If the price exceeds the exercise price at expiration ($S_T > X$), the put is not exercised. The maximum loss to the put buyer is P_0 and the maximum profit is $X - P_0$.

The position of the put seller—the short put position—depicted in Figure 1.4b is the reverse image of the put buyer's position. The put seller has a maximum gain of P_0 and a maximum loss of $X - P_0$.

Option buyers may choose to realize profits by exercising their options as we have just discussed. More frequently, however, option positions are closed out by selling the option. At expiration, an option may be sold for its exercise value. Before expiration, options usually sell for more than their exercise value. As a result, it is usually, but not always, preferable to close out an option position prior to expiration by selling the option rather than by exercising it. The gain or loss on the option is then just the change in the price.

An example using S&P 100 index options will, perhaps, make this discussion more concrete. Table 1.3 contains the closing prices of S&P 100 index options on November 13, 1991. The S&P 100 option contract size is 100 times the index value. The December call with an exercise price of $370 has a reported price of $7.375. This means that a call option buyer would pay a premium of $7.375 \times 100 = $737.50 for the right to "buy" the S&P 100 stock index at $370 \times 100 = $37,000 any time before the expiration date.[2] If the index level rises from $371.21 on

---

[2] S&P 100 index options are American-style and expire on the Saturday following the third Friday of the contract month.

FIGURE 1.3   Profit Diagrams for Call Option Positions Held to
Expiration

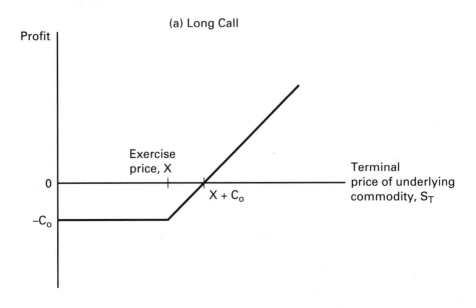

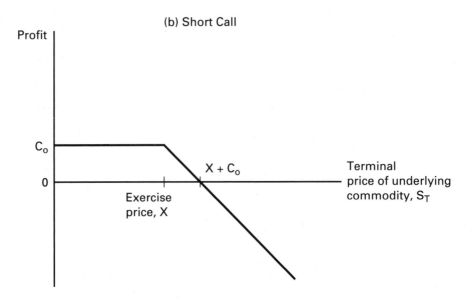

FIGURE 1.4   Profit Diagrams for Put Option Positions Held to Expiration

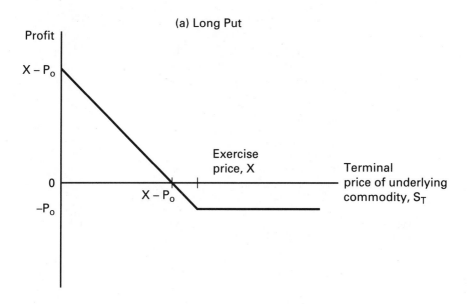

(a) Long Put

Profit

$X - P_0$

Exercise price, X

Terminal price of underlying commodity, S_T

0

$X - P_0$

$-P_0$

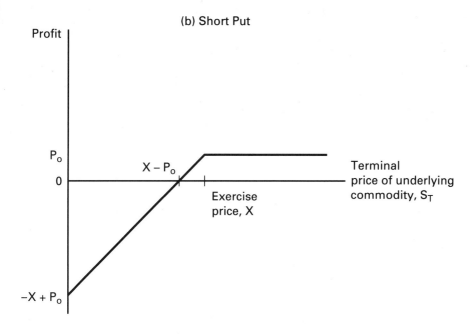

(b) Short Put

Profit

P_0

$X - P_0$

0

Exercise price, X

Terminal price of underlying commodity, S_T

$-X + P_0$

TABLE 1.3 Prices of S&P 100 stock index option contracts at the close of trading on Wednesday, November 13, 1991.

Wednesday, November 13, 1991

OPTIONS

CHICAGO BOARD

S&P 100 INDEX-$100 times index

Strike	Calls—Last			Puts—Last		
Price	Nov	Dec	Jan	Nov	Dec	Jan
335	....	....	....	1/16	....	....
340	30	31½	31¼	1/16	⅝	1½
345	23	27	28	1/16	⅞	2⅛
350	21½	21⅛	....	1/16	1 3/16	3
355	16⅜	19	19⅝	1/16	1¾	3⅞
360	11¼	14¾	17	⅛	2½	4½
365	6⅜	10⅝	13½	5/16	3⅝	6
370	2 5/16	7⅜	10½	1 1/16	5¼	7¾
375	⅜	4⅜	7⅜	4⅛	7⅝	10⅞
380	1/16	2 7/16	5⅛	9¼	10⅞	13¾
385	1/16	1¼	3⅛	....	15¼	....
390	1/16	⅝	1⅞	18⅝	20	20¾

Total call volume 142,982 Total call open int. 387,114
Total put volume 128,390 Total put open int. 421,693
The index: High 371.22; Low 367.54; Close 371.21, +0.92

Source: Reprinted by permission of *Wall Street Journal,* © (November 14, 1991) Dow Jones & Company, Inc. All Rights Reserved Worldwide.

November 13 to, say, $400.00 on November 30, the call option buyer can exercise her option to earn a profit of ($400.00 − $370.00 − $7.375) × 100 = $2,262.50. Alternatively, the option buyer can reverse her position by selling an option contract with the same terms. Suppose that on November 30 the price of the call is $32.00. If the buyer of the option on January 16 chooses to sell the same option, she realizes a profit of ($32.00 − $7.375) × 100 = $2,462.50. Note that closing the position by selling the option as opposed to exercising it yields an additional profit of $2,262.50 − $2,462.50 = $200.00.

The fact that the option can be sold for more in the marketplace than the intrinsic value reflects the time value of the option. On November 13, the 370 call can be sold for $7.375 and yet, if that same option is exercised on November 13, its value is $371.21 − $370.00 = $1.21. The difference between the two values is called the time value of the option and reflects the probability that the stock index will rise significantly from its current level by the third Friday in February. The factors affecting the level of option premiums for different striking prices and different maturities are described later in the book.

The price of the 370 December put option in Table 1.3 is reported to be $5.25. This option is out-of-the-money since the current value of the stock index exceeds 370. Someone who buys this put option on November 13 earns a positive profit if the index level falls below $370.00 − $5.25 = $364.75 before the third Friday in December 1992.

It is important to recognize that the option writer (seller) faces payoffs exactly opposite those of the buyer. If, for example, a call option is in-the-money at expiration, the option writer must deliver a commodity worth more than the exercise price received by the writer. In terms of the call option example above, when the buyer of the option chooses to exercise, the option seller in effect has to purchase the index at $400.00 and deliver it to the option buyer at $370.00. This loss is offset in part by the premium, $7.375, that the writer collected at the outset. The net loss to the writer equals the option buyer's net profit. On the other hand, if the index level stays below the exercise price of the call until expiration, the option will not be exercised, and the option writer keeps the premium collected from the buyer when the option contract was written. This time the writer makes a positive profit, but, again, it is equal to the buyer's loss.

1.3 ECONOMIC PURPOSE OF FUTURES AND OPTIONS

Traditional financial instruments such as stocks and bonds are a mechanism for channeling funds from savers to investors as well as a means for spreading risks. (Of course, most trading in stock and bond markets is trading in the secondary market which does not directly allocate new funds to new investment opportunities.) Futures and options facilitate the channeling of funds but are not savings devices. They are primarily a means for dealing with uncertainty. At the same time, they serve to maintain the liquidity and the reliability of underlying commodity prices, which are important for the proper allocation of new investment funds.

The economic benefits of futures and options arise along three dimensions.[3] First, futures and options are a means for allocating risk more efficiently. Second, futures and options provide price information that is useful in allocating resources in the economy to their best uses. Third, futures and options may lower transaction costs of trading in financial markets below the costs associated with trading in existing financial instruments.

Allocation of Risk

Futures and options provide an efficient mechanism for allocating risk from those who wish to avoid risk to those who are interested in bearing the risk. Futures contracts tend to arise when the underlying commodity is costly or cumbersome to trade. For example, futures on agricultural commodities allow an investor to bear the risk associated with holding an agricultural commodity without the troublesome details of trading in the actual commodity. In this manner, processors of the underlying commodity can pass on price risk to investors and retain the economic function of processing the underlying commodity.

Options provide an additional benefit in allocating risk because the profit function for options is different from the profit function for the underlying com-

---

[3]For an extended discussion of the economic purposes of futures and options, see Carlton (1984), Jaffe (1984), Peck (1985), Silber (1985), and Stoll and Whaley (1988).

modity or for a futures contract. As is evident from Figures 1.3 and 1.4, the profit from options positions are asymmetric. Such an asymmetric payoff pattern is useful, for example, in dealing with situations that involve both quantity and price risk. Consider a farmer who is interested in avoiding the risk associated with a drop in the price of the commodity that he grows. Before the harvest, the farmer does not know the size of the crop or the price. Selling futures against the crop would hedge the farmer against a price decline if the harvest were known, but a futures hedge would expose him to risk if the harvest failed and prices increased, because then the farmer would not have the wheat that he had committed to sell in the futures market. The farmer would take a loss in acquiring the wheat to deliver against the futures contract. Buying a put option on the underlying commodity provides a more effective hedge against price and quantity risk than selling futures. If prices fall, the put is exercised (or liquidated at a profit). If prices rise, the put option expires worthless, and the farmer realizes the revenues from his crop, regardless of the size of the harvest. The cost of this one-sided protection for the farmer is the put option premium. Similar examples exist for other underlying commodities. In addition to this hedging use, options are also a useful portfolio management tool. For example, index put options can be used to limit the down-side risk of stock portfolios while retaining part of the upside potential.

Price Information

Some trading in futures and options markets, as in other financial markets, arises not because individuals have a desire to shift risk, but because they have different information and disagree about the correct price of the underlying commodity. This kind of informational trading is termed *speculative trading*. Society benefits from speculative trading because the analysis and search for information on which it is based cause the prices of futures and options and underlying commodities to correspond more closely to their correct values. Even if an underlying commodity is traded, futures and options on that commodity are likely to increase the interest and the number of judgments bearing on the underlying commodity's price. Because futures and options prices are related to the price of the underlying commodity by an arbitrage relation, factors affecting futures and option prices tend to be conveyed to the price of the underlying commodity; conversely, factors affecting the price of the underlying commodity tend to be conveyed to option and futures prices. Thus, to the extent that futures and option trading increase the total interest in an underlying commodity, the commodity's price will be more broadly based and less likely to be influenced by only a few judgments.

Futures and option markets encourage increased research and analysis. If financial markets are like other markets, this leads to greater efficiency in the production of information. Insofar as increased analysis and increased interest improves the quality of prices, resources will be allocated more efficiently. The price signaling benefit of futures and options is most evident in the case of agricultural futures. For example, the daily newspaper prints futures prices for wheat deliverable many months in the future. That price is the price someone has paid to receive delivery of a particular grade of wheat in the future. Producers or storers of wheat can use this price as a signal for production and storage decisions. If the price is high relative to their costs, more wheat will be produced and stored. If the price is low relative to their costs, less wheat will produced and stored. In this way, the proper amount of wheat will be allocated for future consumption. Of course, if the futures price is wrong—because it is manipulated or for other reasons—resources will be misallocated. Futures markets depend on the presence of many knowledgeable participants to avoid this. One of the benefits of the introduction of futures is the fact that futures trading increases competition. Producers interested in entering into contracts for delayed delivery are no longer compelled to deal with relatively few users of a commodity.

As we shall see later, option prices depend primarily on the projected volatility of the commodity underlying the option. As a result, option prices quoted in the newspaper provide information on the future price uncertainty of an underlying commodity. Processors and users of the underlying commodity therefore have information not only on the expected price of the underlying commodity but also on the price uncertainty in the future.

Transaction Costs

It is sometimes argued that futures and options are *redundant securities* because any futures or option position is achievable by trading the underlying commodity. For example, a long position in wheat futures has the same profit or loss potential as a long position in the wheat itself. A long position in stock index futures can also be achieved by buying a diversified stock portfolio. The payoff to a Treasury bond futures contract can be replicated by a position in the underlying T-bonds. Similarly, option positions can be replicated by appropriate trading strategies in the underlying commodity.

An important benefit of futures and options, however, is that they reduce transaction costs of achieving certain risk return positions compared with the cost of trading the underlying commodity. It is certainly much less costly to trade wheat futures than to trade wheat itself. But the lower trading cost in futures markets also exists with respect to financial instruments. For example, the transaction costs associated with trading index futures contracts are estimated to be 1/15 of the costs associated with trading the corresponding underlying stocks. Index futures are therefore a less expensive means of trading claims on a portfolio of stocks.

1.4 SUMMARY

In this chapter, payoffs to long and short positions in futures and options are illustrated. The economic purposes of futures and options—risk transfer, price discovery, and reduced transaction costs—are discussed.

2 FUNCTIONING OF FUTURES AND OPTION MARKETS

In the last chapter, we defined the nature of futures and option contracts. In this chapter, we describe the nature of the markets in which they trade. In section one, the two types of futures and option markets are described—exchange-traded markets and over-the-counter markets. Section two contains a discussion of the elements of futures and option contract design. Trading procedures in futures and option markets are described in section three, and the role of the clearing house in exchange-traded markets is described in section four.

2.1 EXCHANGE MARKETS VERSUS OTC MARKETS

This book deals primarily with organized exchange markets in futures and option contracts, which are to be distinguished from over-the-counter (OTC) markets. In exchange markets, contracts are standardized, and a clearing house stands between the buyer and seller and guarantees contracts. The clearing house is the buyer to every seller of a contract and the seller to every buyer. Under this arrangement, secondary market trading is possible because a buyer of a contract who wishes to liquidate the position need not find the original seller of the contract but may negotiate a transaction with any individual. Organized exchange markets thus facilitate trading between strangers.

In OTC markets, contracts are tailored to the needs of the transacting parties, and no clearing house exists. As a result, a futures contract or an option contract is a contract between the two parties whose names are on the contract and who make their own arrangements for guaranteeing the contract's financial integrity.

Secondary market trading is very inefficient in OTC markets because a buyer who wishes to liquidate a position must seek an agreement with the original seller of the contract. The term "forward contract" is frequently used to designate OTC contracts that have the form of futures contracts except that they may lack standardization or the presence of a liquid secondary market.

OTC markets usually precede organized exchange markets in futures and options. For example, prior to the start of wheat futures trading in the late 1800s, forward contracts were used by grain elevator operators to purchase wheat from farmers. Prior to the inception of the Chicago Board Options Exchange in 1973, over-the-counter options on common stocks were arranged by put and call dealers.

Organized futures and option markets began in order to provide a means for temporarily hedging a position in the underlying commodity without giving up its control. In OTC markets, delivery is usually implied. The secondary market trading made possible by organized exchange markets allows participants to temporarily hedge their positions without making a commitment to relinquish control of the underlying commodity. Optimal transactions in the underlying commodity can then be arranged either for spot (immediate) delivery or for forward (delayed) delivery. Once the transaction in the underlying commodity is complete, the position in the futures or option market can be liquidated.

The recent growth in organized futures and option markets does not mean that OTC markets have declined in importance, however. Forward contracts in most tangible underlying commodities (such as wheat or oil) are frequently used. Such contracts are the means by which specific grades of the underlying commodity are sold to particular buyers of the commodity. In recent years, OTC market trading in derivative financial instruments has grown dramatically alongside organized markets in these instruments. This reflects the fact that OTC forward and option contracts can be tailored directly to the needs of a customer. Institutions create OTC forward or option contracts tailored to the needs of their retail customers and then use organized markets to offset their OTC market positions. For example, suppose a corporation needs Japanese yen on a particular future date, and the date does not correspond to the maturity of any available Japanese yen futures contract. In this case, the corporation is likely to go to a bank that is willing to design a forward contract to the corporation's needs.

2.2 CONTRACT DESIGN

Futures and options are contracts to do something at a later date. The obligation of the buyer and seller are defined in the contract. Only the price and number of contracts are negotiated at the time of transaction.

Two opposing forces influence contract design: standardization versus market depth. Market participants would prefer the commodity underlying a futures or option contract to be clearly and narrowly defined. However, a narrowly defined contract, while useful to certain participants, may fail to attract sufficient participants to provide a deep and liquid market. A deep and liquid market is desirable for two reasons: first, to permit secondary market trading "in size" to be carried out with relatively little impact on price; and, second, to limit the possibility of corners or short squeezes.[1]

A corner or short squeeze arises when sellers of a futures or option contract cannot acquire the underlying commodity for delivery. If the commodity is narrowly defined, it is possible for someone to monopolize the supply of the commodity. If that individual also purchases futures or option contracts on the commodity, a corner results—the individual owns or has a claim on more of the commodity than is available. If the contract is broadly defined to allow delivery of various related underlying commodities, control of the deliverable supply is much more difficult, and corners and squeezes are much less likely. If a narrowly defined underlying commodity is in large supply, the futures and option contracts can be narrowly defined. However, if the supply of a single grade is not large enough or if a single delivery location is not convenient enough, futures and option contracts are broadly defined to allow delivery of several grades at several locations.

Most futures and option contracts must make provisions for the following features: (a) maturity months; (b) contract size; (c) method of contract settlement; (d) grade of deliverable commodity; (e) point of delivery; (f) time of settlement at maturity; and, in the case of options, (g) the number of exercise prices.

Maturity Months

Too many maturity months reduce the depth and liquidity in any one month. Too few maturity months reduce the usefulness of a contract. How these conflicting objectives are balanced depends on the underlying commodity. For example, in wheat, five maturity months (March, May, July, September, December) are traded at any time, reflecting the harvesting and marketing cycles for wheat. In silver, sufficient volume exists to warrant the trading of ten different maturity months extending one and a half years into the future. In Eurodollar futures, twelve maturity months extending three years into the future are traded.

It is worth noting that the number of days until maturity of a particular futures contract is changing as the maturity date is approached. This is in contrast to various forward contracts, the prices of which are quoted in the newspaper. For example, the newspaper may quote the three-month forward price of silver or the three-month forward price of a currency. These quotes are for new contracts originated on that day. The secondary market for these contracts after they are originated is not very active, so price quotes of existing contracts do not appear in the newspaper.

Contract Size

Contract sizes vary considerably and are chosen to meet the needs of the users of the contract. In many of the grains, the standard contract size is 5,000 bushels, or approximately $15,000 at the current price of the commodities. Contract sizes are considerably larger in some of the financial futures. For example, futures on Treasury bills and Eurodollars have contract sizes of $1 million.

---

[1]For more analysis of contract design and the success and failure of futures contracts, see Black (1986), Carlton (1984), Johnston and McConnell (1989), and Stoll and Whaley (1985).

Method of Contract Settlement at Maturity

Most futures and option contracts are settled by delivery at maturity. Should a contract be carried into the delivery month, certain rules and procedures govern delivery. With futures contracts, the seller of futures (the short) may make delivery of the underlying commodity during a time in the maturity month specified by exchange regulation. Delivery of tangible commodities may be made at any time during an extended period, such as two weeks, and usually takes the form of warehouse receipts giving claim to the commodity, which is stored at an approved location. Delivery of financial commodities is usually more narrowly defined, with delivery taking place through an approved bank. The buyer of futures (the long) is obligated to take delivery if called upon to do so. The assignment of delivery notices by the exchange takes various forms. In some markets, the oldest long is assigned the delivery notice. In other markets, delivery notices are assigned randomly. Futures contracts differ as to the flexibility remaining to the long after the receipt of a delivery notice. In some cases, usually in the tangible commodities, the long has the opportunity to pass the notice on to someone else and to liquidate the futures contract. The shorts usually have the greatest flexibility because they can choose the particular grade of underlying commodity that will be delivered as well as the exact timing of delivery.

With American-style call options, the buyer may request delivery—exercise the options—at any time during the option's life. The seller of the call is then obligated to make delivery. With European-style call options, delivery may be requested only on the expiration date. Options tend not to be written on underlying tangible commodities that may be difficult and cumbersome to deliver. Instead, options on such commodities are written on the futures contract on those commodities. Exercising a call option on corn, for example, is a request for the option seller to deliver the long futures position in corn. When the long futures position is received, the position may be held to maturity if delivery of the corn is desired. The exercise of a put option on corn is a request for the option seller to deliver a short futures position in corn. Options on many financial instruments, such as options on individual common stocks, call for delivery of the underlying financial instrument.

Certain futures and option contracts call for cash settlement rather than delivery at maturity. The buyer of a cash settled futures contract, holding the position until expiration, receives the difference between the final settlement price of the futures contract and the price at which the contract was purchased.[2] The final settlement price of the futures contract is the cash price of the underlying commodity. The seller of the futures contract receives a profit exactly opposite that received by the buyer. In the case of cash settlement call options, the exercise of a call option results not in the delivery of an underlying commodity, but rather in a profit equal to the difference between the price of the underlying commodity and the exercise price of the option.

---

[2]Technically, this statement applies to forward contracts only. The futures contract holder has accumulated over the life of the contract an amount equal to the difference between the final settlement price and the price at which the futures was purchased. In the interest of clarity, we defer detailed discussion of the distinction between forward and futures contracts to Chapter 3.

Cash settlement is particularly useful when the underlying commodity is difficult to deliver. In U.S. markets, stock index futures and options are cash settled because it is difficult to deliver a large portfolio of many different common stocks. Municipal bond futures and futures on the consumer price index are also cash settled, because, in these cases, the underlying commodity is impossible to deliver. In the case of municipal bond futures, the price of the underlying commodity is actually an average of dealer quotations in municipal bonds.

Grade of Underlying Commodity

When the underlying commodity has differing characteristics, the futures or option contract specifies the standard grade of the deliverable commodity as well as the other grades that may be delivered. For example, the Chicago Board of Trade (CBT) wheat contract calls for the delivery of No. 2 soft red wheat, however certain other grades are also deliverable. Another example is the CBT's T-bond futures contract. Nominally, the contract calls for the delivery of an eight-percent coupon bond with a maturity of at least fifteen years. However, T-bonds with other coupons and with maturities in excess of fifteen years are also acceptable for delivery.

The choice for a particular grade of an underlying commodity to be delivered against a futures contract is left to the short, and the short naturally chooses the "cheapest to deliver." For example, if both soft red wheat and hard red winter wheat are deliverable against the wheat futures contract, but hard red winter wheat is selling in the marketplace at a lower price than soft red wheat, the person with a short position will choose to deliver hard red winter wheat because it is the cheapest to deliver. Indeed, the futures price at maturity reflects the price of the cheapest to deliver grade of wheat, not necessarily the grade specified as standard in the futures contract. In T-bond futures, it is sometimes desirable to deliver a low-coupon, long-maturity bond and at other times desirable to deliver a high-coupon, short-maturity bond. The eight-percent coupon bond specified as standard in the contract is usually not the bond being priced by the futures contract.

The cheapest-to-deliver commodity may change during the futures contract life. The exchange specifies the price relation between the deliverable grades prior to the start of the contract. As market conditions change, some grades go to a premium or discount relative to the standard grade.

Point of Delivery

An important feature of futures contracts on tangible commodities is the number and location of delivery points. Transportation of tangible commodities to the delivery location may be costly. As a result, an increase in the number of delivery locations benefits the shorts who are obligated to deliver. To see this, suppose a wheat futures contract calls for delivery only in approved warehouses in Chicago. If wheat is in relatively short supply in Chicago, it is possible for someone to buy up most of the remaining supply while at the same time buying wheat futures contracts. Such an individual would have engineered a corner if the market did not have sufficient time to ship wheat to the Chicago delivery location. As a result, it is sometimes desirable to specify several delivery locations in a contract, thereby making it difficult to corner the available supplies at all the delivery points.[3]

Time of Contract Settlement at Maturity

Most futures contracts on tangible commodities and certain financial futures and option contracts allow a period of time in the maturity month during which delivery may be made. In the case of wheat futures, for example, delivery may be made at any time in the maturity month, at the option of the seller. In the case of futures on tangible commodities, the seller usually has the option of when to deliver, what grade to deliver, and where to deliver it. These features provide protection for the seller against the danger that someone may corner the available supply of the underlying commodity which must be delivered. When delivery is easy and the danger of a corner of the underlying deliverable supply is small, as in many financial instruments, the time of delivery and other features, such as grade and location, are more narrowly prescribed.

Exercise Price

In the case of options, a feature is required that is not required in futures contracts— namely, the number of exercise prices which should be available. It would be possible, for example, to have only one exercise price for each option maturity. This is not done because the usefulness of an option is greatest when the exercise price is close to the price of the underlying commodity. As a result, additional options with new exercise prices are created whenever the underlying commodity's price moves by a prespecified amount. For example, a stock selling at $40 might have an option with an exercise price of $40. If the stock price increases to $45, a new option with an exercise price of $45 would be initiated. The $5 increment at which a new option with a new exercise price is initiated is determined by the exchange.[4] All the options on a particular underlying commodity with the same maturity are called an *option series*. The number of options in an option series is determined by the price volatility of the underlying commodity and the price increment at which additional exercise prices will be set. If the price increment is small, many options, each with relatively little liquidity, will be created. If the price increment is large, few options will be created.

2.3 TRADING PROCEDURES

Public customers wishing to trade futures or options open an account with a brokerage firm. In the futures industry, a brokerage firm is sometimes called a *futures commission merchant* (FCM). Futures and futures option contracts are traded in a

---

[3] A recent book by Pirrong, Haddock, and Kormendi (1991) provides a detailed analysis of delivery terms for agricultural commodities.

[4] Stock option exercise prices at $25 or above have $5 increments. Below $25, the increments are $2.50.

commodity account, and options written directly on financial instruments are traded in securities accounts. These two types of accounts are subject to Commodity Futures Trading Commission (CFTC) oversight and Securities and Exchange Commission (SEC) oversight, respectively.[5]

Types of Orders

In trading futures and options, as with other securities, investors can place a variety of orders. A *market order* instructs the broker to trade at the best price currently available. A *limit order* instructs the broker to buy or sell at a specific price. Naturally, the price given for a limit order to buy is below the current market price, and the price given for a limit order to sell is above the current market price. A *stop-loss order* is an order to sell below the market or to buy above the market. A *spread order* instructs the broker to buy one contract and sell a related contract. In a maturity or calendar spread, for example, the trader buys a contract in one maturity month and sells a contract in the same commodity for a different maturity month. In an intercommodity spread, the trader purchases a contract in one commodity and sells a contract in a different commodity. An almost unlimited array of spread transactions is available in futures and option markets, and these will be discussed in later chapters of this book. An important point to remember is that the trader in a spread transaction is interested in favorable changes in the price differential between two contracts.

Types of Markets

Orders placed by customers with their brokers are transmitted through the brokerage firms' back offices to the floor of the appropriate exchange for execution. The mechanics by which such orders are executed differ between options on securities and futures. Futures and futures option contracts are traded in a pit in an "open outcry" format. Generally, one pit or ring is assigned to each commodity traded on an exchange. Traders stand on the steps around the pit and trade pair-wise with each other. Certain actively traded futures contracts, such as T-bond futures or S&P 500 index futures, attract in excess of 400 traders in the pit. Orders are received on the trading floor by telephone and transmitted to the appropriate trading pit by messengers. Unlike the stock market where trading in a particular stock occurs sequentially in time at a particular location on the floor, many transactions can occur simultaneously in an active futures contract. Futures markets do not therefore guarantee the same degree of price and time priority that stock markets guarantee because of the possibility that two simultaneous transactions might occur in different parts of the trading pit at different prices or because limit orders held by a particular broker may for some reason not be exposed to all other brokers in the crowd. Such price differences within the ring are, however, infrequent and small because many traders on each side of the market are each searching for the best

---

[5]The Chicago Board of Trade (1989) provides useful information on trading procedures and other aspects of futures markets.

price. Competition among floor traders thereby reduces any price deviations within the pit and also provides tremendous liquidity for orders flowing in from the public.

Options on financial instruments are traded according to two different procedures. Options on securities exchanges such as the American Stock Exchange and the Philadelphia Stock Exchange are traded using the specialist system. In a specialist system, market orders are usually traded at the bid or ask price quoted by the specialist on his own behalf or on the behalf of limit orders previously left with the specialist, although there is an opportunity for other traders in the crowd to better the specialist's price. Limit orders are left with the specialist to be executed when the market price reaches the limit price. (In futures markets, each floor broker has his or her own "deck" of customer limit orders.) The specialist system has been criticized because only a single specialist makes a market in each option. As a result, investors do not have an opportunity to shop for better prices from other market-makers.

The Chicago Board Options Exchange (CBOE) system combines elements of futures markets and the specialist system of stock markets. An Order Book Official (OBO) maintains the book of limit orders but does not trade for his own account. At the same time, many professional floor traders are prepared to trade for their own accounts to absorb temporary imbalances and maintain market liquidity. More so than either the futures market system or the specialist system, the CBOE floor trading system represents what many have called for in the stock market: a system that combines competition among market-makers with full exposure of all limit orders through the open book of the OBO.

Types of Traders

Floor traders in futures and option markets can be divided into two general classifications: floor brokers and professional traders. *Floor brokers* are agents who execute transactions for public customers such as processors of tangible commodities or portfolio managers of financial instruments. *Professional traders* buy and sell for their own accounts. Professional traders are sometimes called speculators because they take on varying amounts of risk. Professional traders in futures markets are often classified into position traders, day traders, and scalpers. *Position traders* take on risks and positions that are held for longer periods of time—days or weeks. *Day traders* have a short horizon and take on positions that are usually liquidated at the end of the day. *Scalpers* have a very short horizon and make their income primarily from short-term, minute-by-minute transactions. Scalpers provide liquidity to other investors by buying at the bid price when public customers desire to sell and by selling at the ask price when public customers desire to buy.

In stock exchanges, the major type of professional trader is the specialist. The specialist's role in the stock market is similar to the scalper's role in the futures market. Both are responsible for maintaining market liquidity, and profit from the spread between bid and ask prices. In a specialist system, however, there is only one specialist for each security. In futures markets, many scalpers compete in each contract. In securities markets, there are relatively few professional traders other than the specialist. Most position traders and day traders in options and stocks submit orders from off the exchange through brokerage firms. By contrast, in futures markets, a great deal of volume is the result of trading by professional traders on the floor.

Trading Costs

The costs of trading options and futures consist of two components: the commission charges of the broker and the price concession that may be necessary to execute the transaction. The price concession reflects the fact that sales are made at the bid price of professional traders on the floor (scalpers or the specialist) and purchases are made at the higher ask price of professional traders on the floor. In addition, the broker carrying out a customer transaction is compensated by a commission. Commissions on futures and option exchanges are competitively determined and vary from broker to broker. Commissions cover the back-office services of the broker as well as the charges for floor brokerage and the clearing of transactions.

Price Reporting

On stock exchanges, the price and size of each transaction is reported on the ticker tape immediately after the transaction occurs. In futures markets, not every transaction is reported because many transactions occur simultaneously. Instead, price reporters in the trading pit report each different transaction price and each different bid or ask price in the pit. Systems for price reporting differ among the futures exchanges. Some record prices manually on a price board above the exchange floor. The prices are then entered into computer terminals for transmission worldwide. Others enter price information directly into computer terminals, and then the information is automatically displayed on the exchange floor and is transmitted worldwide. In futures markets, statistics on the volume of trading are not available on a real time basis. Instead, such statistics are compiled at the end of the day on the basis of transactions clearing data.

2.4 THE CLEARING HOUSE

Futures and option contracts are "created" instruments. When a buyer and a seller meet, a contractual agreement containing the specific rights and obligations of each party is created. The number of such contracts that are created is not limited, unlike stock markets where the supply of stock is limited to the number of shares that the firm has issued. *Open interest* is the number of futures or option contracts outstanding at any one time.

The clearing house is critical to the trading of futures and option contracts because it settles and guarantees the contracts. After a contract is agreed to, the clearing house interposes itself between buyer and seller and, in effect, becomes the party to whom delivery is made and from whom delivery is taken. Since the number of buyers always equals the number of sellers, the clearing house always has a zero net position.

Secondary markets in exchange-traded futures and options are made possible by two considerations: (a) the clearing house and (b) the standardized contract design. A buyer who does not wish to hold a position until maturity enters into another contract of identical terms but on the opposite side prior to maturity. Since the individual is now buyer and seller of the same contract, the clearing house nets out the position. Most futures and options positions are not held to maturity but are offset in this manner prior to maturity.

In OTC markets, secondary market trading is not possible for two reasons. First, there is not a clearing house. This means that the buyer must negotiate with the particular seller with whom the contract was first arranged in order to undo the contract before maturity. This is cumbersome and also puts the party that seeks to reverse its position at a competitive disadvantage. Second, contracts in the OTC market are not standardized. Thus, even if a clearing house existed, it would be difficult to find traders on the other side willing to trade in a very specific instrument. OTC futures and options exist because the tailored contracts are sufficiently attractive to particular investors to offset the disadvantages of an absence of a secondary market.

Each of the futures exchanges has its own clearing organization. Options traded on SEC-regulated securities exchanges (NYSE, AMEX, Philadelphia Exchange, Pacific Exchange and the NASD) are issued and guaranteed by the Options Clearing Corporation (OCC).

Margin

Aside from its clerical role of accounting for all contracts and overseeing delivery, the clearing house maintains the financial integrity of markets as guarantor of all contracts. Clearing members post margin deposits to guarantee the transactions carried out through that clearing member. Not all members of a futures or option exchange are members of the clearing house. Firms that are not members of the clearing house clear through member firms. The ultimate guarantor of the contract is the clearing house and its members. Most exchanges establish a guarantee fund that protects clearing members and therefore the customers of those clearing members. In futures markets, the clearing house imposes margin requirements on its clearing members. Customer margins are established by individual brokerage firms and are at least as high as the margins imposed by the clearing house. Margins on futures and futures option contracts are not set by any regulatory authority. Margins on stocks and stock options are regulated by the Federal Reserve Board and the SEC.

It is important to distinguish margins on futures and options from margins on common stocks. The margin on a common stock represents the percentage of the total purchase price paid by the investor. The remainder is borrowed. Currently, the minimum initial margin on common stocks, set by the Federal Reserve Board, is 50 percent. Margins on futures contracts represent a performance guarantee. When a futures contract is entered into, no credit is extended, no asset changes hands, and no payment is made by the buyer to the seller. Full payment (part of which could be borrowed at that time) is required only if delivery is made. Both the buyer and seller of a futures contract deposit margin, which may be in the form of interest-earning securities rather than cash. Positions in futures contracts are settled daily as the futures price changes. Traders are required to make up losses, if any, or are permitted to withdraw profits, if any, each day. These payments from losers to gainers are called *variation margin* and must be in cash.

Options have some features of common stocks and some features of futures contracts. As in the case of common stocks, a payment is made when the option contract is entered into. The buyer of an option pays a premium for an insurance service rendered by the seller of an option. For example, the buyer of a call option has the right to purchase the underlying asset at a known exercise price and is insured against any losses should the underlying asset price fall below the exercise price. Although no asset changes hands when an option contract is entered into, payment for the "insurance service" is made, and money changes hands. Under current margin procedures for futures options as well as securities options, the buyer of the call or put pays 100 percent of the premium. The seller of the option is required to post margin as a performance guarantee, and the margin must be at least as great as the current market value of the seller's obligation. In this way, the clearing house is assured that the seller's obligations will be carried out.

Trading and Settlement Example

Secondary market trading in futures and the role of the clearing house is perhaps best illustrated with the help of a simple example presented in Table 2.1. Suppose that A and B agree to trade one wheat futures contract (5,000 bushels at $3.00 per bushel) on day 1. The volume of trading in day 1 is one contract, and open interest at the end of the day—the number of contracts outstanding—is also one. But, A does not settle profits and losses directly with B. The clearing house becomes buyer to B and seller to A. No money is paid by A to B. Instead, both A and B post margin with the clearing house. In the case of wheat, the margin is $750 per contract for each party to the transaction and may be pledged in T-bills.

On day 2, A decides to sell. The clearing house becomes buyer to A and seller to a new entrant into the market, C. Since A is now a buyer and seller of the same contract on the books of the clearing house, A's position is closed out by the clearing house. In effect, C replaces A as the offset long to B's short position (without B's knowledge). At the end of day 2, cumulative volume of trading is two contracts, and open interest remains at one.

The price of the wheat futures rose from $3.00 to $3.03 from day 1 to day 2. The value of A's position therefore rose by $150, so A makes $150. Since B was a seller and prices rose, the value of B's position falls by $150, and, even though B did not enter into any transaction, B is required to pay $150 in variation margin to the clearing house. Futures markets require the daily settlement of all positions whether or not a transaction is entered into. In forward contracts, profits and losses are realized only when an offsetting transaction is entered into or at maturity. Forward contracts therefore rely much more heavily on the adequacy of margins or other forms of guaranteeing the contract. In futures markets, the margin deposit is needed to protect only against the delay in collecting the variation margin from losers.

On day 3, C buys a second contract from D. The cumulative volume of trading through day 3 is three contracts, and open interest increases to two. The price of the wheat futures has fallen from $3.03 to $2.96, so B gains $350 and C loses

TABLE 2.1   Example of trading in futures and associated cash flows.

Time	Buyer	Seller	Cum. Contract Volume	Open Interest	Futures Price	Contract Value	Daily Profit or Loss				Margin Cash Flow[a]			
							A	B	C	D	A	B	C	D
1	A	B	1	1	3.00	15000					-750	-750		
2	C	A	2	1	3.03	15150	150	-150			750		-750	
3	C	D	3	2	2.96	14800		350	-350				-750	-750
4	B	C	4	1	2.96	14800						750	750	
5	D	C	5	0	3.00	15000			200	-200			750	750
Total							150	200	-150	-200	0	0	0	0

a. Margin deposits are required from both the buyer and the seller. We assume a constant margin deposit of $750 (5%).

$350. On day 4, *B* buys one contract and *C* sells one. Since these transactions offset previous positions established by *B* and *C*, open interest declines by one contract. Since the price did not change, no profits or losses are realized by any remaining participants in the market. On day 5, *C* sells one more contract, and *D* buys one. Since these transactions offset previously established positions, open interest declines to zero.

Futures trading is a zero-sum activity, as is reflected in the example by the fact that the sum of profits of the four traders is zero each day. On balance, *A* and *B* gain; *C* and *D* lose. To the extent that margin is pledged in cash, there is a net loss to traders in the form of foregone interest on the funds pledged as margins. However, if the margin is pledged in the form of interest earning assets such as U.S. Government Securities, this loss is avoided.

Table 2.2 presents a corresponding example of trading and settlement in call options on a common stock. The underlying contract is for 100 shares of the stock which on day 1 is selling for $30. The option premium is assumed to be 10 percent of the contract value. The structure of the example is similar to the futures market example but there are some important differences. First, an option transaction requires the payment of a premium by the option buyer to the option seller. Thus, on day 1, *A* pays $300 to *B*. Second, only sellers of options are required to post margin. Buyers of options pay the full premium and meet all their obligations at the time the premium is paid. Third, profits and losses arising from changes in the option price are not settled daily. The buyer of an option can realize gains only by entering into a transaction. Such gains are not transferred by a daily settlement procedure. Sellers of options do, in effect, realize gains and losses daily because they are required to adjust their margin positions by the amount of the gain or loss in the option. That is, their margin is marked-to-market daily. Thus, individual *B* must post an additional $10 of margin on day 2 to guarantee the ability to purchase the underlying stock and deliver it.

2.5 SUMMARY

In this chapter, we first discuss the difference between over-the-counter (OTC) option and futures markets and organized exchange markets. In OTC markets contracts can be tailored to the particular needs of customers, but secondary market trading is difficult. In organized markets, contracts are standardized so that secondary market trading is facilitated. Another key distinction between organized futures and option exchanges and OTC markets is the existence of a clearing house. The clearing house is central to the operation of organized futures markets. It interposes itself between buyer and seller and guarantees contracts. It sets margins for clearing members and settles profits and losses daily. In contrast, in OTC markets, no clearing house exists. The parties make their own arrangements for guaranteeing the contract's financial integrity.

Next, the factors that must be considered in designing futures and option contracts are discussed. The design of contracts balances the benefits of a narrowly

TABLE 2.2   Example of trading in options and associated cash flows.

Time	Buyer	Seller	Cum. Contract Volume	Open Interest	Contract Value	Option Premium	Premium Cash Flow				Margin Cash Flow[a]			
							A	B	C	D	A	B	C	D
1	A	B	1	1	3000	300	-300	300				-1300		
2	C	A	2	1	3100	310	310		-310			-10		
3	C	D	3	2	2800	280			-280	280		30		-1280
4	B	C	4	1	2800	280		-280	280			1280		
5	D	C	5	0	3000	300			300	-300				1280
Total							10	20	-10	-20	0	0	0	0

a. Margin is required of the seller only. Margin requirements are complex and vary across contracts and exchanges. We assume a margin deposit of $1000 plus the current value of the option.

and clearly defined contract against the benefits of a broadly defined contract that is less susceptible to manipulation and is more liquid.

Trading procedures are examined next. The basic types of orders that may be used are similar across markets, but trading procedures differ quite markedly and range from the open outcry procedures of futures markets to the specialist system used on certain option exchanges. Types of traders, trading costs, and price reporting procedures are also discussed.

PART

2

FUTURES

3 STRUCTURE OF FUTURES PRICES

Futures contracts intermediate between the present and the future. Futures prices are observed today but refer to transactions to be carried out in the future. As such, futures prices must reflect expectations about the future. The relation between the futures price and the expected spot price in the future is called the *intertemporal structure of futures prices*. In this chapter, we assume that the futures price on a contract maturing at time T, $F_t(T)$, equals the expected spot price of the underlying asset at time T, $E(\tilde{S}_T)$. The subscript, t, indicates the time at which the futures price is observed and the expectation is formed. In other words, we assume that $F_t(T) = E(\tilde{S}_T)$ for all t, as depicted in Figure 3.1. The relation between the futures price and the expected spot price is investigated in detail in Chapter 5.

Even if the futures price equals the expected spot price on average, the actual paths of the futures price and the spot price are erratic because new information entering the market causes investors to revise expectations and hence prices. Holders and processors of the commodity underlying the futures contract use the futures contract to guard against unanticipated price fluctuations. They hedge their positions in the underlying commodity by taking an offsetting position in the futures contract. The role of hedging and the effectiveness of hedging strategies are examined in Chapter 4.

In this chapter, the focus is on the relation between the current futures and spot prices, represented by the leftmost vertical line segment joining the commodity and futures markets in Figure 1.1. In terms of Figure 3.1, we investigate the relation of observable prices at time t. At any time t, we can observe a spot price for an underlying commodity and several futures prices for different maturity dates. The difference between $F_t(T)$ and S_t shown in Figure 3.1 is that $F_t(T)$ refers to the price

FIGURE 3.1   Structure of Futures Prices

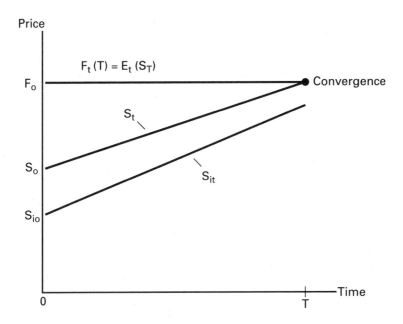

at time t of the underlying commodity to be delivered at time T and S_t is the price at time t of the underlying commodity for immediate delivery. If the underlying commodity is being stored and if it costs something to store it between t and T, the spot price will be less than the futures price as shown in the figure. Sometimes the spot price exceeds the futures price. This occurs when new supplies of the underlying commodity, as in a crop harvest, are expected in the future.

Frequently, futures contracts are written on commodities that are not uniquely definable. For example, there may be different grades of wheat, or wheat may be held in different locations. In other words, there may be many different spot prices, $S_{1t}, S_{2t}, S_{3t}, \cdots S_{nt}$. Because of transportation costs and grade differences, the spot price of a particular grade or at a particular location may be more or less than the spot price of the commodity defined in the futures contract. Sometimes the term *cash price* rather than spot price is used to refer to the price of a particular grade at a particular location, and *spot price* refers to the commodity defined by the futures contract. Processors and holders of the underlying commodity usually deal at the cash price and use the futures market as a way to hedge fluctuations in the cash price. We use S_t to denote the spot price at time t of the commodity defined by the futures contract and S_{it} to denote the cash price of a particular grade or location i at time t.

For some underlying commodities (typically, financial instruments), the distinction between the cash price and the spot price is not important. In the case of a foreign currency, for example, there is only one grade of the underlying commodity and there are no important differences in deliverability by location.

3.1 THE BASIS

The total basis is the difference between the current futures price and the cash price, $F_t - S_{it}$. The total basis contains two components:

$$\text{Total basis} = \text{Time basis} + \text{Space and grade basis}$$

or, algebraically,

$$F_t - S_{it} = (F_t - S_t) + (S_t - S_{it}). \tag{3.1}$$

Since there are many grades and delivery points in some commodities, the space and grade basis, $S_t - S_{it}$, can take on many values depending on transportation costs and grade differences. This component of the total basis is not considered until Chapter 4. We return to it when we consider hedging effectiveness of futures contracts on particular commodities, since the hedging effectiveness of a futures contract depends on how closely futures price movements correspond to price movements in the cash commodity being hedged.

    The lack of costless arbitrage opportunities in a rational, frictionless market determines the equilibrium relation between the contemporaneous futures and spot prices, F_t and S_t, and hence the time basis, $F_t - S_t$. Arbitrage depends on the convergence of F_t and S_t at the maturity of the futures contract, T. At maturity, the futures price of the expiring contract must be the same as the spot price, $F_T = S_T$, or a riskless arbitrage opportunity would exist. If the futures price at maturity were less than the spot price at maturity, arbitrageurs would purchase futures contracts, take delivery, and sell the delivered commodity at the spot price. On the other hand, if the futures price at maturity were greater than the spot price at maturity, arbitrageurs would sell futures, buy the spot commodity, and make delivery against the futures contract. These opportunities are avoided only if, at the last moment of the contract's life, the futures price equals the spot price of the underlying commodity.

    At times prior to maturity, a similar arbitrage is possible. If the underlying commodity is available, one can purchase the commodity at time t at the price S_t and hold it until maturity for delivery against the futures contract. Such a strategy is profitable if F_t exceeds S_t by more than the cost of carrying the commodity to maturity. In such a case, arbitrageurs would sell futures contracts at F_t, buy the underlying commodity at S_t, and carry the commodity to maturity for delivery against the futures contract. If such costless arbitrage opportunities do not exist, the relation between the futures price and the spot price is

$$F_t \leq S_t + B, \tag{3.2}$$

where B is the cost of carrying the commodity until maturity of the futures contract.

The relation (3.2) limits the amount by which the futures price can exceed the spot price. This limit results from the fact that it is always possible to acquire the commodity for future delivery by buying it today and holding it rather than by purchasing a futures contract.

For certain commodities such as financial instruments, arbitrageurs can make profits if the futures price falls too low relative to the spot price by engaging in reverse arbitrage, namely selling the spot commodity and purchasing a futures contract. Reverse arbitrage is possible only if sufficient supplies of the underlying commodity are available. The underlying commodity must be sold by its owner who can replace it with a futures position or it must be loaned to someone else who sells it and buys futures. The sale of the loaned commodity is a *short sale*. The short seller has the obligation to return the commodity on demand. In agricultural commodities, reverse arbitrage is not possible during that part of the crop year in which the commodity is used up or nearly used up. At such times, few people are willing to sell the underlying commodity or lend it out to short sellers. In such cases, the futures price may fall far below the spot price, as a new crop is anticipated. There is no way to make arbitrage profits, however, since there is not enough current supply of the old crop that can be sold to drive down the current spot price.

In most financial instruments, reverse arbitrage is not a problem because a large stock of the cash commodity is on hand. For example, suppose the futures price of the British pound were too low relative to its spot price. Arbitrageurs would, purchase futures and short sell the underlying commodity, the pound. When reverse arbitrage is possible, equilibrium requires

$$F_t = S_t + B. \tag{3.3}$$

The relation (3.3) holds for agricultural commodities only while the commodity is being stored or "carried." Consequently, the relation is often called the *cost of carry relation*. Unless specified otherwise, we shall assume a carrying charge market in which the equality (3.3) holds.

3.2 BASIS ARBITRAGE IN DETAIL

The exact form of the cost of carry relation (3.3) depends on how B is expressed, how profits and losses accrue on the futures contract, when storage costs are paid, and the level of transaction costs. We turn now to a detailed examination of basis arbitrage in which these issues are considered and the arbitrage is explained more precisely. Throughout our discussion, we assume that the transaction costs of buying and selling the spot commodity and the futures contract are zero.

Carrying Costs
The cost of carrying a commodity usually consists of two components—interest and storage. The interest cost is common to all commodities. If a commodity is held in inventory, the opportunity cost of the funds tied up in holding the inventory

is incurred. Over and above interest, however, there may be storage costs. For the agricultural commodities, these costs include warehouse rent, insurance, and spoilage. On the other hand, for some commodities, storage costs are zero or negative. For example, T-bills have negligible storage costs, and T-bonds and stock index portfolios have storage costs that are negative in the sense that coupon yield or dividend yield accrues to holders of these assets.

In this section, we assume that the basis arbitrageur sets aside just enough money to pay for storage costs over the life of the position. If the interest rate and storage costs are known, the amount of money or, alternatively, the size of the "storage cost fund" can always be established today. If interest rates and storage costs were not known with certainty, the appropriate size of the fund would be unclear; and, as a result, the basis arbitrage would have some risk arising from this uncertainty. The exact size of the storage cost fund depends on when and how storage costs are paid.

Storage Costs Paid at Maturity. A simple assumption is that storage costs, $B - r^*S_t$, are paid at maturity, where r^* is the riskless rate of interest over the life of the futures contract. Table 3.1 illustrates the basis arbitrage that, under this assumption, leads to relation (3.3). At time t, the arbitrageur buys one unit of the spot commodity for S_t. When the futures contract matures at time T, the commodity value is $\tilde{S}_T$ and the storage costs, $B - r^*S_t$, are paid. To account for the impending storage cost payment, an amount of money, $(B - r^*S_t)/(1 + r^*)$, is set aside in a storage cost fund. This amount is simply the present value of the storage costs to be paid at time T. The fund is invested at the certain rate of interest, r^*, to guarantee that the necessary amount is available at maturity. The arbitrageur borrows enough to cover the initial cost of the spot commodity and the storage fund. Finally, the arbitrageur takes a short futures position. No cash payment is required in order to establish a futures position so long as collateral to guarantee adherence to the futures contract is deposited. We assume that the spot commodity position provides such collateral. The terminal value associated with each of these initial transactions is shown in the last column of the table. The uncertain commodity price is $\tilde{S}_T$, the necessary storage cost payment is exactly covered by the balance of the storage fund, the face amount of the loan to be repaid at maturity is $S_t(1 + r^*) + (B - r^*S_t) = S_t + B$, and the uncertain value of the short futures position is $F_t - \tilde{S}_T$.

The initial cost of setting up the arbitrage position is zero, as indicated by the sum of the initial value column in Table 3.1. Since the net terminal value is certain, the absence of costless arbitrage opportunities in a rationally functioning market requires that the sum of the terminal value column, $F_t - S_t - B$, also be zero. If the net terminal value were positive, arbitrageurs would store the cash commodity as the table indicates and make a riskless profit with no initial investment. If the net terminal value in Table 3.1 were negative, arbitrageurs would try to reverse the transactions shown in the table in order to make a riskless profit with no initial investment. Reverse arbitrage is possible in financial futures such as T-bonds and stock index futures. In such cases, arbitrageurs would short sell the financial instrument, invest the proceeds at the riskless rate, and buy futures. These arbitrage forces bring about the equilibrium price relation, $F_t = S_t + B$.

TABLE 3.1   Arbitrage transactions for establishing the relation between futures and spot prices, $F_t = S_t + B$.

Position	Initial Value	Terminal Value
Buy one unit of spot commodity	$-S_t$	$\tilde{S}_T - (B - r^*S_t)$
Create storage fund	$-(B - r^*S_t)/(1 + r^*)$	$+(B - r^*S_t)$
Borrow	$S_t + (B - r^*S_t)/(1 + r^*)$	$-(S_t + B)$
Sell futures contract	0	$F_t - \tilde{S}_T$
Net portfolio value	0	$F_t - S_t - B$

The arbitrage presented in Table 3.1 underlies the cost of carry relation (3.3). In subsequent chapters, we also rely on a slightly different form of the cost of carry relation,

$$F_t = S_t(1 + b^*), \qquad\qquad \textbf{(3.4)}$$

where b^* is the cost of carrying the underlying commodity expressed as a proportion of the commodity price, $b^* = B/S_t$. This rate (like the riskless interest rate, r^*) corresponds to the life of the futures contract. The arbitrage underlying this relation is shown in Table 3.2. Note that we have dropped the direct investment in the storage fund at time t as well as the borrowings to set up the fund, since they are offsetting transactions. At time T, the commodity is delivered against the short futures position, eliminating the presence of the $\tilde{S}_T$ terms and the risk of the arbitrage position. The interest terms $S_t r^*$ also cancel. The terminal value of the position is $F_t - S_t(1 + b^*)$, which must be zero in the absence of costless arbitrage opportunities.

Storage and Interest Costs Incurred Continuously. We shall frequently assume that: (a) individuals can borrow or lend risklessly at a compounded rate of interest, r; and (b) the costs of carrying the commodity underlying the futures contract are paid out at a known, continuously compounded rate, b. The interest cost of carrying the commodity is included in b. Both the cost of carry rate, b, and the interest rate, r, are now expressed per unit of time (e.g., annual rates) as opposed to rates over the life of the futures contract to facilitate handling cash flows at different points in time. The use of continuously compounded interest and storage costs simplifies certain arbitrage relations that we examine in this book and takes into account the fact that such costs are often paid during the storage period, not just at maturity.

Under the assumption that storage costs are paid at the continuous rate, b, the appropriate size of the storage cost fund at time zero is $S_0 e^{(b-r)T} - S_0$. We assume the fund is invested in the underlying commodity being stored. As storage costs (for warehouse rent, insurance, and so forth) are incurred, some of the commodity

TABLE 3.2   Arbitrage transactions for establishing the relation between futures and spot prices, $F_t = S_t(1 + b^*)$.

Position	Initial Value	Terminal Value
Buy one unit of spot commodity	$-S_t$	$\tilde{S}_T - S_t(b^* - r^*)$
Borrow S_t	S_t	$-S_t(1 + r^*)$
Sell futures contract	0	$-(\tilde{S}_T - F_t)$
Net portfolio value	0	$F_t - S_t(1 + b^*)$

is sold to pay for these costs. A reduction in the amount of the commodity also occurs if the commodity deteriorates while in storage. The storage cost fund is not used to pay the interest costs of holding the commodity and therefore the term $b - r$, representing carrying costs net of interest, appears in the expression for the fund. Interest costs are treated separately and are assumed to accrue continuously and be paid at time T. For example, suppose that b is 0.0006 per day, r is 0.0002 per day, 100 days remain to maturity, and the spot price is 50. The current value of the storage cost fund is $S_0(e^{(b-r)T} - 1) = 50(e^{(.0006-.0002)100} - 1) = 2.04$.

The initial fund may be negative if the underlying commodity has an income yield. For example, if the underlying commodity is a stock index portfolio that pays a constant dividend rate, d, the cost of carry rate is $b = r - d < r$, which causes the storage fund to be negative. Each day the fund grows to reflect the dividend yield that accrues over the day. Suppose that $b = r - d = 0.0002 - 0.0001 = 0.0001$ per day and other features of the example remain the same. Then the initial fund is $50(e^{.01-.02} - 1) = -0.50$. A negative storage fund is a short position in the underlying commodity that is covered as dividend payments are received. A detailed examination of how the fund changes through time is contained in Appendix 3.1.

Table 3.3 illustrates the basis arbitrage when storage costs are paid continuously. When the portfolio is formed, the net investment cost equals zero, since the cost of acquiring the commodity is completely financed with riskless borrowing. As a result, the futures position in Table 3.3 requires zero initial outlay and has a zero initial value. At the expiration of the futures contract, the one unit of the commodity on hand is delivered against the short futures position, and the net terminal value of the portfolio is $F_t - S_t e^{b(T-t)}$. This term cannot be positive, otherwise costless arbitrage profits would be possible. And, if $F_t - S_t e^{b(T-t)} \leq 0$,

$$F_t \leq S_t e^{b(T-t)}. \tag{3.5}$$

The relation (3.5) limits the amount by which the futures price can exceed the spot price. Again, this limit results from the fact that it is always possible to

TABLE 3.3   Arbitrage transactions for establishing the relation between futures and spot prices, $F_t \leq S_t e^{b(T-t)}$.

Position	Initial Value	Terminal Value
Buy one unit of commodity in spot market	$-S_t$	$\tilde{S}_T$
Create storage fund[a]	$-[S_t e^{(b-r)(T-t)} - S_t]$	0
Borrow $S_t e^{(b-r)(T-t)}$	$S_t e^{(b-r)(T-t)}$	$-S_t e^{b(T-t)}$
Sell futures contract	0	$F_t - \tilde{S}_T$
Net portfolio value	0	$F_t - S_t e^{b(T-t)}$

a. Carrying costs are assumed to be paid in units of the commodity each day during the arbitrage. The storage fund has $e^{(b-r)(T-t)} - 1$ units on hand on day t and is reduced on each subsequent day. In general, the number of units of the commodity in the fund on day τ is $e^{(b-r)(T-\tau)} - 1$, so the number of units on day τ is $e^{(b-r)(T-T)} - 1 = 0$.

acquire the commodity for future delivery by buying it today and holding it rather than by buying a futures contract. When reverse arbitrage is possible, as in the case of financial futures, the equilibrium price relation is

$$F_t = S_t e^{b(T-t)}. \tag{3.6}$$

While the basis is frequently defined as the absolute dollar difference between the futures price and the spot price, it is often preferable to define the basis in proportional terms as F_t/S_t. Under this definition, the basis does not depend on the absolute price level of the commodity, and comparisons across commodities are possible. We see from equation (3.6) that the proportional basis must equal the proportional carrying cost in equilibrium:

$$\frac{F_t}{S_t} = e^{b(T-t)}. \tag{3.7}$$

The basis and the basis behavior are examined in greater detail when individual commodities are considered in Chapters 6 through 9.

3.3 TERM STRUCTURE OF FUTURES PRICES

At any time, several futures contracts with different times to maturity are outstanding. The relation between the futures prices and the time to maturity is called the *term structure of futures prices*. The relation between two futures prices is determined by the same factors that determine the relation between the futures price and the spot price. That makes sense because we are simply looking farther out in time. Let $F_t(T_1)$ be the time t futures price on a contract maturing at time T_1, and $F_t(T_2)$ be the time t futures price on a contract maturing at time T_2, where $T_1 < T_2$.[1] The lack of costless arbitrage opportunities in the futures market ensures that

$$F_t(T_2) \leq F_t(T_1)e^{b(T_2-T_1)}. \tag{3.8}$$

If $F_t(T_2)$ exceeds the value specified by (3.8), arbitrageurs would sell the distant futures at $F_t(T_2)$ and buy near-term futures at $F_t(T_1)$, take delivery at time T_1, and hold the commodity until T_2. If short selling of the spot commodity is possible, condition (3.8) would hold as the equality,

$$F_t(T_2) = F_t(T_1)e^{b(T_2-T_1)}. \tag{3.9}$$

Reverse arbitrage would maintain the equality by the following strategy: If $F_t(T_2)$ were too low, arbitrageurs would buy futures at $F_t(T_2)$ and sell at $F_t(T_1)$. At time T_1, the arbitrageurs would borrow the underlying commodity and deliver it against the futures contract.

The difference between the futures prices of two maturities is called a *spread*. Individuals who buy one maturity and sell another maturity are called *spreaders*. Spreaders usually liquidate their position before delivery is required. They hope that the basis relation between the two maturities will be re-established before the expiration of the "short leg" of the spread.

3.4 FORWARD AND FUTURES CONTRACTS

In Chapter 2 we saw that futures contracts require daily settlement of profits and losses. A forward contract is identical to a futures contract in all respects, except that, with a forward contract, profits and losses are realized only at maturity or when the forward position is reversed.[2] Thus, it is possible for the buyer of a futures contract to suffer short term losses (due to decline in the futures price) even if the contract is not liquidated, while the buyer of a forward contract would not incur those same losses unless he liquidates his forward contract position. The difference between futures contracts and forward contracts lies in the fact that gains (losses) can be invested (financed) at the short-term interest rate, while gains or losses on forward contracts are not recognized until the contract matures or is liquidated. At maturity, the futures and forward contracts have claims on the same amount of the commodity, so that the differences between these contracts have to do with the timing of gains and losses.

---

[1] In general, we talk about a single futures contract written on a single underlying commodity, so we suppress the contract maturity notation in parentheses.

[2] In this section, we assume that there is no difficulty or cost in reversing a forward position before maturity.

The difference in the pattern of cash flows of the forward and futures positions means that the value of a forward contract position is slightly different from the value of a futures contract position. This difference is explained in detail in the first part of Appendix 3.2. However, if the short-term interest rates are constant, the price of a forward contract equals the price of the futures contract, as the second part of Appendix 3.2 shows. The difference between the value of a futures position and a forward position is reflected in a difference in the number of units of the commodity held and not in a difference between the futures and forward prices. Appendix 3.2 also shows how the number of units of a futures contract can be adjusted to make the terminal values of the forward and futures positions equal.

For expositional purposes, we shall assume that a futures contract is the same as a forward contract. While the two are equivalent only if interest rates are known and appropriate adjustments are made in contract size (as shown in Appendix 3.2), the assumption simplifies the presentation considerably.

3.5 SUMMARY

In this chapter, the arbitrage process that links the spot price and futures price is described. Since the underlying commodity can be purchased and held for future delivery, the futures price cannot exceed the spot price by more than the cost of carrying the commodity to the maturity of the futures contract. Similarly, so long as supplies of the commodity exist, the futures price cannot fall below the cost of carry equilibrium price; for if it did, arbitrageurs would short-sell the spot commodity and buy futures. When storage and interest costs are incurred continuously, the relation of the futures and spot prices is given as

$$F_t = S_t e^{b(T-t)}, \tag{3.10}$$

where b is the cost of carrying the commodity, including interest, $T - t$ is the time to maturity of the futures contract, and F_t and S_t are the futures and spot prices at time t, respectively. The term structure of futures prices is defined, and the difference between futures and forward contracts is explained.

APPENDIX 3.1

THE STORAGE COST FUND

In this chapter, as well as many of the futures and options chapters to follow, we use the concept of a storage cost fund. This fund is established to (a) pay the costs (other than interest) of carrying a commodity over the storage period or (b) receive any income earned on the underlying commodity. The fund is invested in the underlying commodity being stored. Each day the number of units held in the storage cost fund is changed slightly to reflect that day's storage cost or income. In the basis arbitrage context, the storage cost fund begins at the end of day 0 with an investment of $e^{(b-r)T} - 1$ units. During each subsequent day, the commodity position is reduced (increased) by the factor $e^{-(b-r)}$ if $b > r$ ($b < r$). The reduction in the commodity position, assuming $b > r$, reflects the payment of carrying costs other than interest. In the case of an agricultural commodity, for example, warehouse rent, insurance, or natural deterioration of the stored commodity must be paid while the commodity is held. On the other hand, if the underlying commodity is, say, a stock index portfolio that pays a dividend so that $b < r$, the storage fund, which starts as a negative amount (a short position in the commodity), is increased each day to reflect the dividend yield that accrued over the day. Using such a scheme ensures that the storage cost fund is zero and exactly one unit of the commodity is held when the futures contract expires at time T, as is shown in Table 3.1a.

We refer to the sum of the commodity position and the position in the storage fund as the *rollover position* in the commodity. The number of units in the rollover position changes as the commodity is sold off to pay storage costs.

To clarify the storage cost fund concept, consider a case where the cost of carry rate, b, is 0.01 per day, the riskless rate of interest, r, is 0.005, and the holding period is ten days. The amount in the storage cost fund at the end of day 0 is therefore $e^{(.01-.005)10} - 1 = 0.051271$ units, as is shown in Table 3.1b; and the number of units in the rollover position is 1.051271. If the commodity price is 100, the total value of the rollover position is 105.1271. On day 1, the total number of units in the commodity is reduced from 1.051271 by the factor $e^{-(.01-.005)} = 0.995012$. Thus, the total number of units of the commodity remaining is $1.051271 \times 0.995012 = 1.046028$, with a total value of $97 \times 1.046028 = 101.4647$. Day after day, the number of units is reduced. With the cost of carry rate, the interest rate, and the holding period known, exactly one unit of the commodity remains on hand at the end of day T.

TABLE 3.1a   End-of-day positions in the commodity and the storage cost fund required to guarantee one unit of the commodity on hand at maturity assuming constant cost of carry and interest rates, b and r.

Day	Units of Commodity	Units of Commodity in Storage Fund[a]	Total Value of Commodity Position
0	1	$e^{(b-r)T} - 1$	$S_0 e^{(b-r)T}$
1	1	$e^{(b-r)(T-1)} - 1$	$\tilde{S}_1 e^{(b-r)(T-1)}$
2	1	$e^{(b-r)(T-2)} - 1$	$\tilde{S}_2 e^{(b-r)(T-2)}$
$\vdots$	$\vdots$	$\vdots$	$\vdots$
t	1	$e^{(b-r)(T-t)} - 1$	$\tilde{S}_t e^{(b-r)(T-t)}$
$\vdots$	$\vdots$	$\vdots$	$\vdots$
T	1	0	$\tilde{S}_T$

a. Each day, storage costs are assessed by reducing the total number of units of the commodity by the factor $e^{-(b-r)}$. Thus, at the end of day 1, the total number of units on hand equals the total number of units on hand on day 0, $e^{(b-r)T}$, times the factor, $e^{-(b-r)}$, or $e^{(b-r)(T-1)}$, and so on.

TABLE 3.1b   End-of-day positions in the commodity and the storage cost fund required to guarantee one unit of the commodity on hand at maturity assuming constant daily cost of carry and interest rates, $b = .01$ and $r = .005$, respectively, and a holding period of $T = 10$ days.

Day	Units of Commodity	Units of Commodity in Storage Fund[a]	Commodity Price	Total Value of Commodity Position
0	1	0.051271	100	105.1271
1	1	0.046028	97	101.4647
2	1	0.040811	95	98.8770
3	1	0.035620	98	101.4907
4	1	0.030455	102	105.1064
5	1	0.025315	99	101.5062
6	1	0.020201	101	103.0403
7	1	0.015113	104	105.5718
8	1	0.010050	106	107.0653
9	1	0.005013	105	105.5263
10	1	0	107	107.0000

a. Each day, storage costs are assessed by reducing the total number of units of the commodity by the factor $e^{-(.01-.005)}$. Thus, at the end of day 1, the total number of units on hand equals the total number of units on hand on day 0, 1.051271, times the factor, 0.995012, or 1.046028, and so on.

APPENDIX 3.2

FORWARD AND FUTURES CONTRACTS[1]

The Difference Between Forward and Futures Positions

To understand the distinction between a long position in a forward contract and a long position in a futures contract, we need to establish the value of the contract positions at some arbitrary point in time t prior to the contracts' maturity, $t < T$.[2] Let f_t be the price at time t of a forward contract maturing at time T, and consider the following course of events. Suppose an individual buys a forward contract at time 0 and lets some time elapse. Now, suppose that the individual unwinds her position at time t (where $t < T$) by selling a different forward contract that also matures at time T. These transactions are summarized in Table 3.2a. Note that the two transactions produce a certain net terminal value (at time T) equal to $f_t - f_0$. The time t value of the forward position established at time 0 must therefore equal the present value of the terminal amount $f_t - f_0$, that is,

$$(f_t - f_0)e^{-r(T-t)}, \tag{A3.1}$$

otherwise costless arbitrage opportunities would exist. That is, the buyer of the forward contract at time t must be indifferent between a new contract priced at f_t for which no payment is required and the existing contract for which payment $(f_t - f_0)e^{-r(T-t)}$ is necessary. At maturity, the difference $f_t - f_0$ will be realized. The value at time t is just the present value of that amount.

The value at time t of a futures contract position established at time 0 is the sum of the daily gains and losses on the futures position carried forward to t at interest rate r, that is,

$$\sum_{\tau=1}^{t}(F_\tau - F_{\tau-1})e^{r(t-\tau)} = \sum_{\tau=1}^{t}(F_\tau - F_{\tau-1})e^{-r(T-t)}e^{r(T-\tau)}, \tag{A3.2}$$

as is shown in Table 3.2b. Each day the gain or loss is posted and carried forward to t. The futures contract is then rewritten at the new futures price.

The expressions (A3.1) and (A3.2) reveal exactly why a long forward position is different from a long futures position. The difference arises because the daily gains or losses on the futures position are taken forward at the riskless interest rate,

---

[1] The analysis in this section is drawn from Stoll and Whaley (1986), pp. 25–62.

[2] We assume that both positions were formed at time 0, where $0 < t$, and that the forward and futures contracts are written on the same underlying commodity and have the same time to expiration.

TABLE 3.2a   Transactions for establishing the value of an existing forward contract position.

Position	Initial Value (0)	Intermediate Value (t)	Terminal Value (T)
Buy forward contract at time 0	0		$\tilde{S}_T - f_0$
Sell forward contract at time t		0	$-(\tilde{S}_T - f_t)$
Net forward position			$f_t - f_0$

while the daily gains or losses on the forward contract are not recognized and therefore are implicitly carried forward with no interest. At any point in time after the futures and forward positions are entered, the value of a futures position will, in general, be different from the value of a forward position, unless, of course, the interest rate is zero. If futures and forward prices have increased on average since the positions were taken, the value of a long futures position will exceed the value of a long forward position because of accumulated interest. On the other hand, if futures and forward prices have decreased on average since the positions were taken, the value of the forward position will be greater.

Forward and Futures Prices Are Equal If the Interest Rate Is Known

Although the values of the two contract positions differ, the prices of the forward and futures contracts are equal (i.e., $f = F$) if the gains and losses on the futures

TABLE 3.2b   Value of an existing futures contract, assuming constant interest rate, r.

Day	Futures Price	Daily Profit	Profit at Time t
0	F_0		
1	$\tilde{F}_1$	$(\tilde{F}_1 - F_0)$	$(\tilde{F}_1 - F_0)e^{r(t-1)}$
2	$\tilde{F}_2$	$(\tilde{F}_2 - \tilde{F}_1)$	$(\tilde{F}_2 - \tilde{F}_1)e^{r(t-2)}$
$\vdots$	$\vdots$	$\vdots$	$\vdots$
t	$\tilde{F}_t$	$\tilde{F}_t - \tilde{F}_{t-1}$	$\tilde{F}_t - \tilde{F}_{t-1}$
Total value at time t			$\sum_{\tau=1}^{t}(F_\tau - F_{\tau-1})e^{r(t-\tau)}$

TABLE 3.2c   Terminal value of a long rollover position in futures, assuming constant interest rate, r.

Day	No. of Contracts at End of Day[a]	Futures Price at End of Day	Daily Profit	Accumulation Factor	Daily Profit at Maturity
0	e^{-rT}	F_0			
1	$e^{-r(T-1)}$	$\tilde{F}_1$	$e^{-r(T-1)}(\tilde{F}_1 - F_0)$	$e^{r(T-1)}$	$\tilde{F}_1 - F_0$
2	$e^{-r(T-2)}$	$\tilde{F}_2$	$e^{-r(T-2)}(\tilde{F}_2 - \tilde{F}_1)$	$e^{r(T-2)}$	$\tilde{F}_2 - \tilde{F}_1$
$\vdots$	$\vdots$	$\vdots$	$\vdots$	$\vdots$	$\vdots$
t	$e^{-r(T-t)}$	$\tilde{F}_t$	$e^{-r(T-t)}(\tilde{F}_t - \tilde{F}_{t-1})$	$e^{r(T-t)}$	$\tilde{F}_t - \tilde{F}_{t-1}$
$\vdots$	$\vdots$	$\vdots$	$\vdots$	$\vdots$	$\vdots$
T	1	$\tilde{F}_T$	$\tilde{F}_T - \tilde{F}_{T-1}$	1	$\tilde{F}_T - \tilde{F}_{T-1}$
		Value of rollover futures position at maturity			$\tilde{F}_T - F_0$

a. Each day, the number of futures contracts is increased by the factor e^r. Thus, at the end of day 1, the total number of futures contracts equals the total number of futures contracts on day 0, e^{-rT}, times the factor, e^r, or $e^{-r(T-1)}$, and so on.

position accumulate interest at *known* rates.[3] Here, we invoke a stronger assumption than is necessary to demonstrate the equivalence of the forward and futures prices. We assume that the short-term interest rate is constant during the contract lives. To see that the futures price equals the forward price, we establish a portfolio that consists of a long rollover position in the futures and a short position in the corresponding forward.[4] The rollover position adjusts for the daily profits and losses in the futures contract and is shown in Table 3.2c. The rollover position in the futures begins at the end of day 0 with e^{-rT} futures contracts purchased. On each subsequent day, the futures profits/losses are recognized, and the number of futures contracts is increased by a factor of e^r. On the last day of the futures' life, exactly one futures contract is held. Assuming the daily gains or losses are invested or financed at the riskless rate of interest r, the terminal value of the long rollover position in the futures equals $\tilde{F}_T - F_0$, as is shown in Table 3.2c.

   To illustrate the concept of a rollover futures position, consider Table 3.2d. In the table, the riskless rate of interest is assumed to be 0.005 per day. At the end

---

   [3] See Cox, Ingersoll, and Ross (1981).
   [4] Naturally, the futures and forward contracts used in this analysis are written on the same underlying spot commodity and have the same maturity date.

TABLE 3.2d   Terminal value of a long rollover position in futures, assuming constant daily interest rate of $r = 0.005$ and a holding period of $T = 10$ days.

Day	No. of Contracts at End of Day[a]	Futures Price at End of Day	Daily Profit	Accumulation Factor	Daily Profit at Maturity
0	0.951229	80			
1	0.955997	83	2.867992	1.046028	3
2	0.960789	84	0.960789	1.040811	1
3	0.965605	79	−4.828027	1.035620	−5
4	0.970446	81	1.940891	1.030455	2
5	0.975310	83	1.950620	1.025315	2
6	0.980199	85	1.960397	1.020201	2
7	0.985112	84	−0.985112	1.015113	−1
8	0.990050	87	2.970150	1.010050	3
9	0.995012	88	0.995012	1.005013	1
10	1	90	2	1	2

Value of rollover futures position at maturity	10

a. Each day, the number of futures contracts is increased by the factor $e^{.005}$. Thus, at the end of day 1, the total number of futures contracts equals the total number of futures contracts on day 0, 0.951229, times the factor, 1.005012, or 0.955997, and so on.

of day 0, $e^{-.005(10)} = 0.951229$ futures contracts are purchased. At the end of day 1, the position is increased by a factor of $e^{.005} = 1.005012$, so the number of contracts held is 0.955997, and so on. Note that the profits/losses from the rollover position each day correspond exactly to the gain/loss on the futures for that day, once the profit/loss is taken forward to time T. At time T, the daily profits/losses plus all interest accumulated/paid on the daily profits/losses sum exactly to the futures price change over the ten-day period, 10. Note that the rollover position in futures is different from the rollover position in the commodity presented in Tables 3.1a and 3.1b. The futures rollover position adjusts for the daily settlement cash flows, while the commodity rollover position adjusts for the daily storage cost payments.

Table 3.2e shows the initial and terminal values of the portfolio consisting of the long rollover futures position and the short forward contract. The initial values are both assumed to be zero since no margin deposit is required. At the expiration of the contracts, both the terminal price of the futures, $\tilde{F}_T$, and the terminal price of the forward, $\tilde{f}_T$, must equal the underlying commodity price, $\tilde{S}_T$, so the net terminal value of the portfolio is $f_0 - F_0$. This value is certain and requires no investment outlay. In equilibrium, the only allowable outcome for a riskless, costless

TABLE 3.2e   Arbitrage transactions for establishing the equivalence of forward and futures prices, $f_0 = F_0$.

Position	Initial Value	Terminal Value
Buy rollover position in futures	0	$\tilde{F}_T - F_0 = \tilde{S}_T - F_0$
Sell forward contract	0	$-(\tilde{f}_T - f_0) = -(\tilde{S}_T - f_0)$
Net portfolio value	0	$f_0 - F_0$

investment portfolio is zero, otherwise costless arbitrage profits can be earned. If the net portfolio value is zero, the futures price must equal the forward price, that is, $f_0 = F_0$, and, since the initial time 0 can be any time, $f_t = F_t$ for all t.

The above arbitrage argument showing the equality of forward and futures prices requires a known riskless rate of interest and the implementation of a rollover strategy. In practice, perfect equality of forward and futures prices may not be possible because interest rates are uncertain and because the rollover futures strategy is difficult to implement.

HEDGING WITH FUTURES CONTRACTS

A *hedger* uses the futures markets to reduce or eliminate the risk of adverse price fluctuations in the cash commodity. The *short hedger* sells short in the futures market against a long position in the underlying commodity. A typical short hedger is someone who, in the normal course of business, holds inventory of an underlying commodity—a stock portfolio manager, for example. The *long hedger* is long the futures contract and is short the underlying commodity. A short position in the underlying commodity means that the hedger has a fixed-price future commitment to deliver the underlying commodity or something highly correlated in price with the underlying commodity. An example of a long hedger is an exporter who has promised to deliver wheat at a fixed price but does not yet possess the wheat. The exporter buys a wheat futures contract to lock in the price at the time of delivery and then goes about acquiring the wheat for delivery. Detailed hedging examples are provided in later chapters when particular cash markets are examined. In this chapter, the basic principles of hedging are discussed.

4.1 A TRADITIONAL HEDGE

The hedger is concerned with unexpected changes in the price of the underlying commodity in which the hedger has a position. Figure 4.1 illustrates such unexpected changes in prices. Figure 4.1 is similar to Figure 3.1 except that a particular path of futures, spot, and cash prices is plotted. The path deviates from the expected path illustrated in Figure 3.1 because the futures price falls. As a result, spot and cash prices also fall. If traders had anticipated a fall in futures prices at time t, however, the futures price would have been lower at that time. Hedgers trade in

FIGURE 4.1   Paths of Spot and Futures Prices

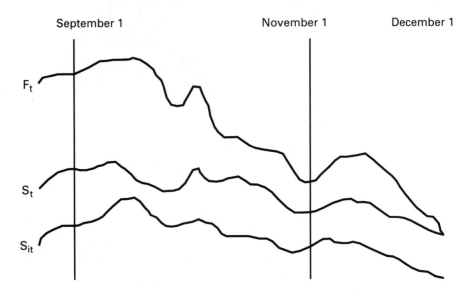

The lines in this figure represent one possible path of F, S, and S_i through time.

the futures market to protect against losses from unexpected price movements in order that they may concentrate on their principal business activity, which may be, for example, processing a commodity or managing a security portfolio.

A hedger with a position in an underlying commodity wants to take a position in the futures market that guards against a price decline of the type shown in Figure 4.1. Hedging is effective if the cash price of the underlying commodity moves in the same way as the futures contract on the commodity. Another way of saying the same thing is that there is no unexpected change in the basis, $F_t - S_t$.

Table 4.1 contains a simple numerical illustration of a short hedge for someone in the business of storing wheat. In Table 4.1, we assume that the storer buys a bushel of wheat on September 1 and hedges it by selling a December 1 futures contract. On November 1, the inventory is sold and the hedge is lifted by an offsetting purchase of futures. Table 4.1 considers the value of this hedge portfolio at the two points in time illustrated by the two vertical lines in Figure 4.1.

On September 1, the bushel of wheat is acquired at \$3.00, and a December futures contract on the bushel of wheat is sold at \$3.09. We assume the futures price obeys the basis relation (3.2) developed in Chapter 3. We also assume that carrying costs (including a normal profit for the storer) are \$.03 per bushel per month at the time the hedge is established, or \$.09 for the three-month period.

TABLE 4.1   Profit results from a short hedge, assuming constant basis per month.

Date	Cash Market Transaction	Price	December Futures Transaction	Price
September 1	Buy 1 bushel at	3.00	Sell futures at	3.09
November 1	Sell 1 bushel at	2.70	Buy futures at	2.73
Gain		−0.30		0.36
Net gain				0.06
Net gain less storage costs of $.03 per month				0.00

After two months, on November 1, wheat prices have fallen dramatically and the wheat is sold at $2.70, causing a loss of $.30 in the cash market. Futures prices, however, have also fallen to $2.73, resulting in a gain of $.36. The difference between the futures price and the cash price has narrowed from $.09 to $.03, but the basis per month remains at $.03 since just one month remains to expiration of the futures contract. Since the hedger was short in the futures market, the gain there of $.36 more than offsets the loss of $.30 in the cash market. This gain reflects the fact that the total basis, $F_t - S_t$, narrows as one approaches maturity to reflect the reduced time over which the commodity must be carried. The hedger, however, carried the underlying commodity for two months and incurred storage costs, which we have assumed to be $.06 per bushel. As a result the $.06 net gain from changes in futures and cash prices is offset by the $.06 cost of carrying the underlying commodity. Table 4.1 illustrates the case in which the hedge is fully effective in the sense that the hedger suffers no losses and makes no gains.

4.2 BASIS RISK

The hedge is not fully effective if the difference between the futures price and the price of the underlying commodity does not converge smoothly at the carrying cost rate during the life of the futures. Basis risk arises if the difference, $F_t - S_t$, deviates from a constant basis per month. In general, if the basis unexpectedly widens (or "weakens"), the short hedger loses. If the basis unexpectedly narrows (or "strengthens"), the short hedger gains. The total gain depends on the carrying costs paid by the hedger. If carrying costs are not fixed, gains from the hedge may be offset by higher storage costs, and losses may be offset by lower storage costs.

These points are illustrated in Table 4.2 by assuming alternative futures prices on November 1. Suppose that all things are identical to Table 4.1, except that the futures price falls only to $2.75. In other words, by November 1, the basis has weakened to a level of $.05 per month. In that case the hedger gains only $.04,

TABLE 4.2   Profit results from a short hedge with basis risk.

| Date | Cash Market | | December Futures | |
	Transaction	Price	Transaction	Alternative Prices
September 1	Buy 1 bushel at	3.00	Sell futures at	3.09 3.09
November 1	Sell 1 bushel at	2.70	Buy futures at	2.75 2.71
Gain		−0.30		0.34 0.38
Net gain				0.04 0.08
Net gain less storage costs of $.03 per month				−0.02 0.02

which is not sufficient to cover storage costs for the preceding two months. If the hedger holds a commodity deliverable against the futures contract, however, the hedger can choose not to sell the commodity on November 1. Instead, the hedger can continue to hold the commodity until December 1 and deliver it against the futures contract. In the case of deliverable commodities, convergence of futures and cash prices guarantees a gain of $.09, which equals the basis when the hedge was established.

If storage costs for the remaining month remain at $.03 a bushel, an excess profit of $.02 will be earned in the last month, which is sufficient to offset the loss of $.02 in the first two months. On the other hand, if storage costs rise to $.05, as is implied by the basis on November 1, the loss on November 1 is unavoidable. The loss arises not from the ineffectiveness of the hedge, but rather from the hedger's failure to lock-in storage costs over the entire three-month period.

This is just another way of saying that the holder of inventory faces two sources of risk: (a) fluctuations in the price of the commodity and (b) fluctuations in the cost of holding the commodity. Futures markets may be perfectly effective in hedging the first risk, but ineffective in hedging the second.

The second case illustrated in Table 4.2 is a decline in the futures price to $2.71, which implies a narrowing or strengthening of the basis. In this case, there is a net gain of $.08 which more than covers the storage costs of $.06 in the first two months. The basis has changed in a favorable direction in this example. As long as the hedger has not contracted for storage facilities in the last month, this gain is real. However, if the hedger has borrowed funds and paid for a grain elevator to carry wheat for the entire three month period, a storage cost will be incurred in the third month whether or not wheat is stored. In that case the gain is not real. If the storage cost of $.03 will be incurred anyway, it pays to hold the wheat for an additional month to earn the basis of $.01, which offsets in part the storage cost of $.03.

The above illustrations and the implications listed below are predicated on the assumption that *the hedger has a position in the commodity underlying the futures contract*. Hedging non-deliverable commodities is discussed in the next section. A summary of the implications of the illustrations in this section (that is, examples where the hedger holds the deliverable commodity and hedges using the futures) follows under two headings:

Commodity Price Risk

Hedging with futures contracts can eliminate commodity price risk.

Carrying Cost Risk

a. Failing to lock in the carrying costs of the commodity over the life of the futures contract causes the short hedger to incur the risk that the costs will increase above the planned or expected amount. Conversely, the short hedger will gain if carrying costs fall below the expected amount.

b. Locking in the carrying costs eliminates the basis risk from the hedge. In terms of Tables 4.1 and 4.2, if the hedger can guarantee storage costs of $.03 per month, and if the underlying wheat is deliverable on December 1 at a futures price of $3.09, a net gain of $0.00 will be earned. There is no risk in this (unrealistic) example because all prices are preset on September 1.

c. Establishing the costs of carrying a commodity in advance may not be possible. As a result, holders of the commodity are subject to some amount of basis risk arising from uncertain carrying costs.

d. The only source of basis risk when the commodity is deliverable against the futures contract is carrying cost risk.

4.3 HEDGING NON-DELIVERABLE COMMODITIES

In addition to carrying cost risk, the hedger also faces commodity price risk when the commodity being hedged is not deliverable against the futures contract. If the commodity being hedged is non-deliverable, commodity price risk cannot be fully eliminated because the cash price and the futures price need not converge at the maturity of the futures contract. Figures 4.1 and 3.1 illustrate this point by the gap between S_i and F at maturity. In effect, on September 1, the hedger buys the underlying commodity and enters into a futures contract to sell another (albeit related) commodity. It is known on September 1 that there is no guarantee that the bushel of wheat can be sold for $3.09 if held to maturity.

The term *cross-hedging* is used to describe situations in which futures contracts are used to hedge non-deliverable commodities. In practice, most hedging is cross-hedging. A storer of wheat in Oklahoma may possess a deliverable grade of wheat, but the transportation costs of getting the wheat to a deliverable location are sufficiently high to make the wheat non-deliverable against the futures contract. This means that the price of wheat in Oklahoma and in Chicago do not converge. Furthermore, the difference between the price of wheat in Oklahoma and in Chicago may be uncertain because of uncertain demand conditions in the two markets. Other examples of cross-hedging include using (a) silver futures to hedge a position in platinum, (b) stock index futures to hedge a position in a single stock, (c) Treasury bond futures to hedge a position in corporate bonds, and (d) Chicago wheat futures to hedge wheat stored in France.

When cross-hedging is undertaken, it is unlikely that unexpected changes in the value of the underlying position will be matched in magnitude by changes in the futures price. For example, a 1-percent change in platinum prices might be accompanied by a 1.5-percent change in silver prices. To the extent that such relations are stable over time, one can adjust the size of the hedge to provide a better cross-hedge. We now turn to a method of determining the optimal amount to hedge and of assessing hedging effectiveness.

4.4 OPTIMAL HEDGING—MEAN/VARIANCE APPROACH

An individual wanting to reduce the price risk of a position in an underlying commodity must choose the size of the position to take in the futures contract. In the preceding examples, we assumed that the futures market position is of the same size as the cash market position, but this is not always optimal. In particular, when the futures price changes by less than the cash price, a larger futures position than cash position is optimal. On the other hand, if the futures price changes by more than the cash price, a smaller futures than cash position is optimal. To determine the optimal number of futures contracts to use, we develop a formal model.

Notation
The notation used in the development of the optimal hedge ratio is as follows:

S_0 = initial cash price. (This variable corresponds to the first entry in the cash market column of Table 4.1, that is, the value $3.00.) We are omitting the subscript i indicating the cash price.

F_0 = initial futures price. (This value corresponds to the first entry in the futures market column of Table 4.1, that is, the value $3.09.)

$\tilde{S}_T$ = uncertain cash price at future time T. (This variable corresponds to the value on November 1 in the cash column of Table 4.1, which is only one of many possible outcomes at that time.)

$\tilde{F}_T$ = uncertain futures price at future time T. (This variable corresponds to the value on November 1 in the futures column of Table 4.1, which is only one of many possible outcomes at that time.)

n_S = number of units of the cash commodity held. (n_S is positive for long positions and is negative for short positions.)

n_F = number of futures contracts held. (n_F is positive for long positions and is negative for short positions.)

Hedge Portfolio Profit
The uncertain gain, $\tilde{\pi}_h$, of the hedger who holds n_S units of the commodity and hedges using n_F futures contracts is

$$\tilde{\pi}_h = (\tilde{S}_T - S_0)n_S + (\tilde{F}_T - F_0)n_F. \qquad \textbf{(4.1)}$$

The term $\tilde{S}_T - S_0$ is the (random) price change per unit of commodity over the life of the hedge, and the term $\tilde{F}_T - F_0$ is the (random) price change of the futures contract over the life of the hedge.

The expected gain to the hedger over the life of the hedge is

$$E(\tilde{\pi}_h) = [E(\tilde{S}_T) - S_0]n_S + [E(\tilde{F}_T) - F_0]n_F. \qquad \textbf{(4.2)}$$

Expression (4.2) provides a convenient way of illustrating two ideas. First, if we assume that the current futures price is an unbiased predictor of the futures price at time T as implied by Figure 4.1, that is, if

$$F_0 = E(\tilde{F}_T), \qquad \textbf{(4.3)}$$

the last term of equation (4.2) drops out. The expected profit on the hedge portfolio depends only on the expected change in the cash price. In a carrying cost market, the difference between the current cash price and the expected future cash price represents storage costs. Second, if the commodity is deliverable and is held to maturity, convergence ensures that

$$E(\tilde{S}_T) = E(\tilde{F}_T). \qquad \textbf{(4.4)}$$

Combining (4.2), (4.3), and (4.4) implies

$$E(\tilde{\pi}_h) = (F_0 - S_0)n_S. \qquad \textbf{(4.5)}$$

In other words, the expected profit on the hedge is directly proportional to the initial basis as indicated in Table 4.1. In general, the overall outcome depends on the carrying costs incurred by the hedger which are not incorporated in equation (4.1). Even if the commodity is not deliverable, the expected gain equals the basis, as long as the expected difference between the spot price and the cash price in Figure 3.1 remains constant.

Realized futures and cash prices deviate from expected prices; therefore, realized gains are greater than or less than expected gains. This is true, in particular, for cross-hedging in which case the opportunity to deliver the underlying commodity is not available. The optimal cross-hedge is the hedge that minimizes the deviation from the expected gain. We turn now to a derivation of the optimal hedge amount based on this criterion.

Optimal Hedge Ratio

To derive the optimal number of futures contracts to sell, first write equation (4.1) in terms of price changes per unit of the underlying commodity, that is,

$$\frac{\tilde{\pi}_h}{n_S} = (\tilde{S}_T - S_0) + (\tilde{F}_T - F_0)\frac{n_F}{n_S}. \qquad (4.6)$$

Now define price change terms, $\tilde{\Delta}_S \equiv \tilde{S}_T - S_0$ and $\tilde{\Delta}_F \equiv \tilde{F}_T - F_0$, and substitute these terms into (4.6),

$$\frac{\tilde{\pi}_h}{n_S} = \tilde{\Delta}_S + h\tilde{\Delta}_F. \qquad (4.7)$$

The hedge ratio, $h \equiv \dfrac{n_F}{n_S}$, is the number of futures contracts per unit of the underlying commodity.

Since a hedger is concerned with minimizing risk,[1] use (4.6) to write the variance of the hedge portfolio profit,

$$\sigma_h^2 = \sigma_S^2 + h^2\sigma_F^2 + 2h\sigma_{SF}, \qquad (4.8)$$

where σ_h^2 is the variance of the hedge portfolio profit per unit of commodity; σ_S^2 is the variance of cash price change; σ_F^2 is the variance of futures price change; and σ_{SF} is the covariance between the cash and futures price changes. The value of h that minimizes σ_h^2 is found by taking the derivative of (4.8) with respect to h and setting it equal to zero:

$$\frac{d\sigma_h^2}{dh} = 2h^*\sigma_F^2 + 2\sigma_{SF} = 0.$$

Solving for h^*, the optimal hedge ratio is

$$h^* = -\frac{\sigma_{SF}}{\sigma_F^2}. \qquad (4.9)$$

The optimal hedge ratio, h^*, thus depends on the covariance between the cash and futures price changes relative to the variance of the futures price change. It is interesting to note that the expression for the optimal hedge ratio, $\sigma_{S,F}/\sigma_F^2$, is the slope coefficient in an ordinary least squares (OLS) regression of the cash price change, $\tilde{\Delta}_S$, on the futures price change, $\tilde{\Delta}_F$. The OLS regression approach to estimating the optimal hedge ratio is described next.

---

[1]The mean-variance hedge ratio framework developed here is similar to that developed in Ederington (1979). In this framework, the hedger is assumed to be interested only in minimizing his risk exposure. In a more general framework, the hedger would be allowed to consider not only price change variance but also expected price change in determining the optimal hedge ratio.

4.5 OPTIMAL HEDGING—OLS REGRESSION APPROACH

Ordinary least squares regression[2] provides an alternative way to derive the optimal hedge ratio. Consider the following regression equation:

$$\tilde{\Delta}_S = \alpha_0 + \alpha_1 \tilde{\Delta}_F + \tilde{\epsilon}, \tag{4.10}$$

where α_0 and α_1 are regression parameters, $\tilde{\epsilon}$ is a random disturbance term with $E(\tilde{\epsilon}) = 0$. Equation (4.10), which is plotted in Figure 4.2, shows that the cash price change, $\tilde{\Delta}_S$, has three components: (a) a constant non-random price change component, α_0, the intercept in the figure; (b) a random component that is systematically related to the futures price change, $\alpha_1 \tilde{\Delta}_F$, and (c) a unique random component, $\tilde{\epsilon}$, that is uncorrelated with the futures price change and is represented by the vertical distances between the line and points off the line in Figure 4.2.

Expected Return

The intercept term, α_0, captures any expected change in the cash price unaccompanied by an expected change in the futures price. From Figure 3.1, we know that, if $E(\tilde{\Delta}_F) = 0$, the expected cash price change equals the basis, that is, $E(\tilde{\Delta}_S) = E(\tilde{S}_T) - S_0 = F_0 - S_0$. The regression model states that the expected cash price

FIGURE 4.2   Cash Price Change Versus Futures Price Change

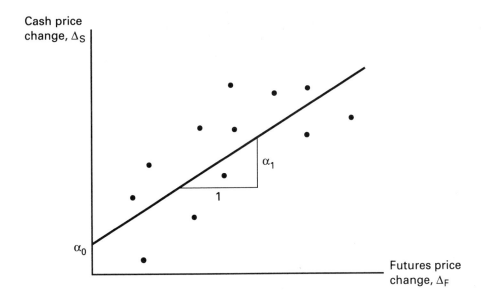

change equals α_0 under the assumption that $E(\tilde{\Delta}_F) = 0$ (and that $E(\tilde{\epsilon}) = 0$), thus the intercept term in (4.10) represents the basis. The basis, in turn, reflects the storage costs which a storer of the assets must recover by price appreciation. The term, $\alpha_1\tilde{\Delta}_F$, reflects the fact that random changes in the futures price will be reflected in the cash price according to the slope coefficient, α_1. The term $\tilde{\epsilon}$ reflects basis risk, which arises from the fact that certain random changes in $\tilde{\Delta}_S$ are unique to the cash commodity and uncorrelated with the futures price change.

Optimal Hedge Ratio

The original expression for hedge portfolio profit (4.7) can be rewritten by substituting the regression equation (4.10) for $\tilde{\Delta}_S$, that is,

$$\frac{\tilde{\pi}_h}{n_S} = \alpha_0 + \alpha_1\tilde{\Delta}_F + \tilde{\epsilon} + h\tilde{\Delta}_F$$

$$= \alpha_0 + (\alpha_1 + h)\tilde{\Delta}_F + \tilde{\epsilon}. \qquad \textbf{(4.11)}$$

Equation (4.11) shows clearly that the profit on the hedge portfolio, $\tilde{\Delta}_h$, can be made independent of movements in cash and futures prices by setting $h = -\alpha_1$. If $\alpha_1 = 1$, a one-dollar change in the cash price is matched by a one-dollar change in the futures price. This implies that futures and cash prices move in tandem. In this case, the optimal hedge is $h = -1$, or a 100 percent hedge. If $\alpha_1 = 0.0$, futures and cash prices are unrelated and there is no point in hedging and the optimal hedge ratio, h, is zero.

Hedging Effectiveness

A hedge is fully effective only if futures and cash price changes are perfectly correlated. This means that the random error term, $\tilde{\epsilon}$, in (4.10) is always zero. Although it may be optimal to hedge 100 percent, the hedge may not be fully effective because deviations from that average relation, represented by points lying off the line in Figure 4.1, may arise.

In order to measure the effectiveness of a hedge, first measure the ineffectiveness of a hedge. The ineffectiveness of a hedge is measured by the ratio of the variance of the price change of the hedged portfolio (σ_h^2) to the variance of the price change of the unhedged portfolio (σ_h^2 when $h = 0$). From equation (4.8), the variance of the price change without hedging is σ_S^2. From (4.11), the variance of the price change for the optimally hedged portfolio ($h = -\alpha_1$) is σ_ϵ^2, that is, the variance of the residual term, ϵ, in the regression model. The ratio measuring the ineffectiveness of the hedge is therefore $\sigma_\epsilon^2/\sigma_S^2$; this ratio can vary between 0 and 1. Since the effectiveness of the hedge is merely the complement of the ineffectiveness, the effectiveness of the hedge can be measured as

$$\rho^2 = 1 - \frac{\sigma_\epsilon^2}{\sigma_S^2}. \qquad \textbf{(4.12)}$$

Coincidentally, expression (4.12) is the definition of the *adjusted R-squared* for the OLS regression (4.10). If the independent variable, $\tilde{\Delta}_F$ explains 100 percent of the variance in $\tilde{\Delta}_S$, $\sigma_\epsilon^2 = 0$ and $\rho^2 = 1$. In this case, the hedge is perfectly effective. If the independent variable $\tilde{\Delta}_F$ explains none of the variance in $\tilde{\Delta}_S$, $\rho^2 = 0$. In this case, $\sigma_\epsilon^2 = \sigma_S^2$, and the hedge is perfectly ineffective.

If $0 < \rho^2 < 1$, hedging is only partially effective in the sense that some of the movements in the cash price are reflected in futures prices, but some movements are unique. Hedging is effective in eliminating the systematic movements also reflected in futures price. Hedging is not effective in eliminating unique price risk that shows up in the random term $\tilde{\epsilon}$.

Hedging with Several Futures Contracts

The OLS regression approach can be generalized very easily to handle cases where two or more different futures contracts are used to hedge the cash position. The value of a corporate bond portfolio, for example, is sensitive to both interest rate risk and stock market risk. To hedge the value of such a portfolio, hedges against movements in both interest rates and the stock market level are required. Treasury bond futures and the S&P 500 index futures contracts are probably best suited for simultaneously hedging the two types of risk exposure of this portfolio.

To hedge against multiple sources of price risk, the cash price change is regressed on the price changes of several futures contracts in the form,

$$\tilde{\Delta}_S = \alpha_0 + \alpha_1 \tilde{\Delta}_{F,1} + \alpha_2 \tilde{\Delta}_{F,2} + \cdots + \alpha_n \tilde{\Delta}_{F,n} + \tilde{\epsilon}. \qquad \textbf{(4.13)}$$

The estimated regression coefficients $\hat{\alpha}_1$ through $\hat{\alpha}_n$ are the respective hedge ratios for each of the n futures contracts. To hedge against all sources of risk, set $h_i = -\hat{\alpha}_i$ for all futures contracts. To hedge against only selected risk exposures, set $h_i = -\hat{\alpha}_i$ for the futures contracts corresponding to the selected risks.

4.6 ESTIMATING THE HEDGE RATIO

In this section, two illustrations of the optimal hedge ratio framework are provided. In the first, a stock portfolio manager uses stock index futures to hedge price risk, and, in the second, the value of a corporate bond is hedged using stock index and Treasury bond futures. Before describing the two applications, however, some subtle issues regarding price change measurement and regression estimation must be discussed.

Price Changes, Price Change Intervals, and Other Issues

An important decision facing the analyst who is attempting to estimate the optimal hedge ratio is the decision about the length of the time interval over which price changes should be measured. The time-series regression model,

$$\tilde{\Delta}_{S,t} = \alpha_0 + \alpha_1 \tilde{\Delta}_{F,t} + \tilde{\epsilon}_t, \qquad \textbf{(4.14)}$$

gives some indirect guidance on this matter. The error term, ϵ_t, in (4.14) is governed by the following assumptions: $E(\epsilon_t) = 0$, $E(\epsilon_t \Delta_{F,t}) = 0$, $E(\epsilon_t^2) = \sigma_\epsilon^2$, and $E(\epsilon_t \epsilon_{t-1}) = 0$. The price change interval should be chosen such that none of these regression assumptions is violated.

The most frequently used price change intervals are daily, weekly, and biweekly. Holding the length of the estimation period constant (say, one year of data), one would imagine that the more frequent the price observations, the more information that is being gathered about the covariability of cash and futures price changes. But, very frequent price observations also give rise to other problems. For example, transaction prices are generally either at bid or ask levels. The shorter the time interval, the more the random movement between bid and ask prices contributes to price change variability and the less reliable the regression results become. This bid/ask price effect introduces negative serial correlation in the security price change series and an errors-in-the-variables problem in estimating (4.14).

A second problem with price changes measured over short time intervals is that if the cash commodity and the futures contract are not traded with equal frequency, the price changes of the two instruments may not reflect the same set of market information. This problem may manifest itself through non-zero serial correlation in the error term, that is, $E(\epsilon_t \epsilon_{t-1}) \neq 0$.

A third problem has to do with seasonality in security price changes. French (1980) and Gibbons and Hess (1981), for example, have documented a day-of-the-week effect in stock returns and returns of certain Treasury instruments. This day-of-the-week seasonality will cause the homoscedastic error term assumption, $E(\epsilon_t^2) = \sigma_\epsilon^2$, to be violated when daily price changes are used in the estimation.

To illustrate the effects of different price change interval measurement assumptions, we estimate the regression (4.14) using daily, weekly, and biweekly price changes for the S&P 500 index and the S&P 500 index futures contracts during the calendar year 1989. In 1989, there were 252 trading days, so 251 daily price changes are computed. The 251 days produce 51 weekly price changes, and 25 biweekly price changes. The weekly and biweekly price changes are measured from Wednesday to Wednesday because there are fewer Wednesday holidays than holidays on other days of the week. Partial weeks at the beginning and the end of the daily price change series are not used. The futures price changes are for the nearby futures contract. On the expiration of the nearby contract, the futures price change series is spliced from the nearby contract to the next nearby contract.[3] The regression results are reported in Table 4.3.

---

[3]For 1989, the prices of the March 1989, June 1989, September 1989, December 1989, and March 1990 S&P 500 index futures contracts are used to generate the futures price change series. The March 1989 contract is used until its last day of trading on March 16, 1989. On that day, the prices of both the March 1989 and the June 1989 contract are recorded. The March contract price is used in combination with its previous day's price to compute the March 16 futures price change. The June contract price is used in combination with its price on the following day to compute the futures price change for March 17. This "splicing" procedure allows the futures price change series to be continuous throughout the year.

TABLE 4.3   Summary of hedge ratio coefficient estimates using daily, weekly, and biweekly S&P 500 index and S&P 500 index futures price changes[a] during the calendar year 1989.

$$\tilde{\Delta}_{S,t} = \alpha_0 + \alpha_1 \tilde{\Delta}_{F,t} + \tilde{\epsilon}_t$$

Interval	n	$\hat{\alpha}_1$	$s(\hat{\alpha}_1)^b$	95 Percent Confidence Interval		Range	$\bar{R}^2$
				Lower	Upper		
Daily	251	0.8034	0.0226	0.7589	0.8478	0.0889	0.8352
Weekly	51	0.9914	0.0163	0.9586	1.0241	0.0673	0.9867
Biweekly	25	1.0013	0.0170	0.9662	1.0365	0.0703	0.9928

a. The price changes of the S&P 500 index and the S&P 500 futures contract are computed as $\Delta_{S,t} = S_t - S_{t-1}$ and $\Delta_{F,t} = F_t - F_{t-1}$, respectively.

b. s($\cdot$) is the estimated standard error of the regression coefficient.

A number of interesting results emerge from Table 4.3. The first is that the slope coefficient estimated using daily price changes, 0.8034, is dramatically different from those using weekly and biweekly price changes, 0.9914 and 1.0013, respectively. This difference results from the problems noted above. For example, the bid/ask price effect introduces an errors-in-the-variables problem in the daily price change regression, which tends to bias the estimated coefficients downward.

Another interesting comparison in Table 4.3 is of the confidence intervals. Holding other factors constant, the range of the confidence interval (the standard error) on α_1 *should* get larger as the price change interval increases from daily to weekly to biweekly because more and more information is being lost. However, that is not the pattern that appears in Table 4.3. The standard error and the confidence interval range is smaller for the weekly and biweekly price change regressions than for the daily price change regression. Again, this result reflects the problems associated with using daily price changes.

The comparison of the weekly and biweekly results also favors the use of weekly data in the estimation procedure. The coefficient magnitudes are very close, and yet the standard error and confidence interval range are smaller for the weekly regression. The lower standard error reflects the fact that twice as much price change information is impounded in the weekly regression as in the biweekly regression.

Related to the selection of the appropriate price change interval is the time horizon of the hedge. The hedge framework developed in this chapter is for a single period. In principle, when the hedge ratio is estimated through the regression analysis, the estimation of the hedge ratio is independent of the distance between price observations used in the regression. The intercept term, however, will grow larger as the length between price observations increases because it is an estimate of the basis between the futures and cash over the length of the observation interval.

Finally, to end the discussion, it is also important to note that the parameter estimate $\hat{\alpha}_1$ is produced from a regression on historical data and that the hedge that we are constructing is for a future period (i.e., estimates of α_1 are *ex post* but hedging decisions are *ex ante*). In applying this procedure, we are implicitly invoking an assumption of stationarity in the relation between cash and futures price changes. *A priori*, we must be comfortable that such an assumption is reasonable.

Hedging with a Single Futures Contract

To illustrate how the optimal hedge for a stock portfolio may be determined, consider a portfolio manager who has $50 million in a stock portfolio similar in composition to the S&P 500 index at the end of 1989. Fearing that the stock market will fall over the next two months, the manager wants to hedge his price risk by selling S&P 500 futures contracts. How many futures contracts should be sold?

The regression results reported in Table 4.3 are useful in estimating the optimal number of contracts to sell. The estimated slope coefficient (hedge ratio) from the regression of weekly, S&P 500 index price changes on the price changes of the S&P 500 index futures contract is 0.9914. In other words, a one-dollar change in the futures price elicits a 0.9914 change in the price of the stock index portfolio, or, alternatively, the optimal number of futures contracts to sell for each unit invested in the stock portfolio is 0.9914. To determine the number of units invested in the stock portfolio, divide the portfolio value by the S&P 500 index level. At the end of 1989, the S&P 500 index was at 353.40. The number of units of the stock portfolio is therefore 141,482.74. In addition, the S&P 500 futures contract is denominated as 500 times the index level, so the number of units of the stock portfolio expressed in the denomination of the futures contract is 141,482.74/500 = 282.97. If the optimal hedge ratio were one, we should sell 282.97 futures contracts to hedge the $50 million stock portfolio. Since the optimal hedge ratio is 0.9914, however, the optimal number of contracts to sell is (0.9914)(282.97) = 280.54.

It is worthwhile to emphasize that the regression produces only an *estimate* of the optimal hedge ratio. In this case, the relatively high coefficient of determination of 0.9867 indicates that the estimate and the effectiveness of the hedge appear to be quite good. Nevertheless, there is still potential error in the best guess that the optimal hedge ratio is 0.9914. The 95 percent confidence interval says that the true ratio is somewhere between

$$0.9586 \leq \alpha_1 \leq 1.0241.$$

This range implies that we are 95 percent confident that the optimal number of futures contracts to sell is between 271.26 and 289.79.

Hedging with Two Futures Contracts

To illustrate hedging with two futures contracts, consider hedging $10,000,000 worth of Mobil Oil's $8\frac{1}{2}$ percent coupon bond maturing in the year 2001. Corporate bonds have both long-term interest rate and stock market exposure, so the weekly price changes of Mobil's bond are regressed on the price changes of the CBT's T-bond futures contract and the CME's S&P 500 index futures contract for the year 1989. Again, we assume that the hedge is being formed at the end of December 1989. The regression results are reported in Table 4.4. Also reported are the regression results when the T-bond futures and the S&P 500 futures price changes are used separately as independent variables.

The results in Table 4.4 indicate that the T-bond futures contract explains more of the variance in the price changes of Mobil's bond than the S&P 500 futures

TABLE 4.4   Summary of hedge ratio coefficient estimates using weekly price changes[a] for Mobil Oil's 8 1/2 percent bond maturing in the year 2001 (MO), the CBT's Treasury bond futures contract (TBF), and the CME's S&P 500 futures contract (SPF) during the calendar year 1989.

$$\tilde{\Delta}_{MO,t} = \alpha_0 + \alpha_1 \tilde{\Delta}_{TBF,t} + \alpha_2 \tilde{\Delta}_{SPF,t} + \tilde{\epsilon}_t$$

n	$\hat{\alpha}_1$	$s(\hat{\alpha}_1)$[b]	$t(\hat{\alpha}_1)$[c]	$\hat{\alpha}_2$	$s(\hat{\alpha}_2)$	$t(\hat{\alpha}_2)$	$\bar{R}^2$
T-bond and S&P 500 futures:							
51	0.4473	0.0407	10.98	0.0159	0.0091	1.75	0.7651
T-bond futures only:							
51	0.4756	0.0382	12.46				0.7553
S&P 500 futures only:							
51				0.0554	0.0154	3.59	0.1920

a. Price changes are computed as $\Delta_{i,t} = I_t - I_{t-1}$, where I represents Mobil Oil's bond, the T-bond futures contract, or the S&P 500 futures contract.

b. s($\cdot$) is the estimated standard error of the regression coefficient.

c. t($\cdot$) is the t-value of the regression coefficent under the null hypothesis that $\alpha = 0$.

contract does. When the single variable regression results are considered, the hedging effectiveness of the T-bond futures contract is 0.7553 and the hedging effectiveness of the S&P 500 futures is 0.1920. But, if Mobil's bond has both interest rate and stock market exposures, the multiple regression results should be used when setting the hedge. In fact, when the multiple regression results are considered, the hedging effectiveness, 0.7651, is greater than either contract used by itself.

The optimal number of T-bond futures contracts to sell is 0.4473 and the optimal number of S&P 500 futures contracts to sell is 0.0159 for each dollar invested in the Mobil bonds. Again, the contract denominations must be taken into account. The T-bond futures has a denomination of $100,000, so the number of units of the spot commodity in terms of the T-bond futures is 100. The S&P 500 index level was at 353.40 at the end of 1989 and the denomination of the S&P 500 futures contract is 500 times the index, so the number of units of the spot commodity in terms of the S&P 500 futures is 56.59. Using the coefficient estimates reported in Table 4.4, the optimal number of T-bond futures to sell is 100 $\times$ 0.4473 $=$ 44.73, and the optimal number of S&P 500 futures to sell is 56.59 $\times$ 0.0159 $=$ 0.90.

4.7 SUMMARY

This chapter begins with an explanation of a traditional short hedge in which the owner of a commodity takes a short position in futures to guard against a decline in the commodity price. A short hedger locks in the basis, $F_t - S_t$. Short hedgers face the risk that the basis may change through time. In the case of hedgers of deliverable commodities, basis risk represents the risk of an increase in the costs of holding the commodity. In the case of hedgers of commodities not deliverable against the futures contract (cross-hedgers), basis risk also represents the risk of changing relative prices of the commodity and futures contract.

A framework for hedging under basis risk is developed in this chapter under standard mean/variance portfolio analysis and also within an ordinary least squares regression framework. The optimal hedge ratio is defined, and measurement of hedging effectiveness is discussed. The optimal hedge framework is then applied in the context of stock portfolio and bond portfolio risk management, with careful consideration given to the nature of security price data and regression estimation.

5 RISK AND RETURN IN FUTURES MARKETS

Hedgers enter the futures market to reduce or eliminate the risk of a commodity position. Conceivably, the futures market could consist solely of hedgers. For example, farmers may want to sell wheat futures, while processors of wheat may want to buy wheat futures. Both these parties are hedgers and could have futures transactions that exactly offset each other. But usually the transactions of the long and short hedgers are not exactly offsetting. Liquid and active futures markets typically require the participation of speculators. Speculators analyze information concerning futures contracts and their underlying commodities in the hope of identifying, and profiting from, futures contract mispricings.

5.1 ROLE OF SPECULATORS

Speculators are willing to *bear risk* that others—hedgers—wish to avoid. Consequently, society benefits. Speculators also help determine futures prices that more accurately reflect underlying economic conditions. This is sometimes called the *price discovery* function of futures markets. Speculators help "discover" the right price by analyzing underlying economic conditions and trading based upon their analyses. If the futures price is too low, speculators buy futures, and, if the futures price is too high, they sell. In equilibrium, the futures price is a consensus estimate of what speculators think the future price of the underlying commodity ought to be. If speculators are wrong, they lose money. If they are right, they make money. As in any financial market, the profit motive causes prices to be good estimates of true economic values.

Many different types of speculators and speculative strategies are possible. Sometimes a speculator concentrates on a particular commodity and, based upon his analysis, concludes that the price will go up (or down). In this case, a naked long (or naked short) position is appropriate. At other times, a speculator may conclude that a particular futures contract will increase in price relative to another futures contract. In this case, the speculator buys one contract and sells the other, thereby becoming a "spreader." A spreader benefits only from a favorable change in the difference between two futures prices, whereas a naked speculator benefits from a change in a particular futures price.

5.2 IS THE FUTURES PRICE AN UNBIASED ESTIMATE OF THE EXPECTED SPOT PRICE?

The expected spot price, $E_t(\tilde{S}_T)$, is the market's expectation at time t of the spot price when the futures contract expires (time T). At any given time t prior to contract maturity, the expectation is likely to be wrong. Unexpected events after time t cause the actual spot price to be different from what was expected. Over a long period of time and many futures contract cycles, however, expectations should, on average, be realized, that is, $E_t(\tilde{S}_T) = \text{avg } S_T$. In other words, the average spot price at maturity ought to reflect the expectation at some prior time.

In order for speculators to make money, futures prices must trend upward toward the expected spot price when speculators are long futures, and futures prices must trend downward when speculators are short futures. A market in which futures prices trend upward [i.e., where $F_t < E_t(\tilde{S}_T)$] is said to exhibit *normal backwardation*. This situation is illustrated as the upward sloping line in Figure 5.1. A market

FIGURE 5.1 Normal Backwardation

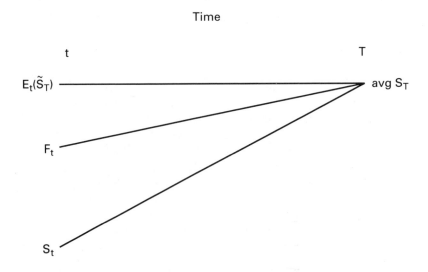

FIGURE 5.2   Contango

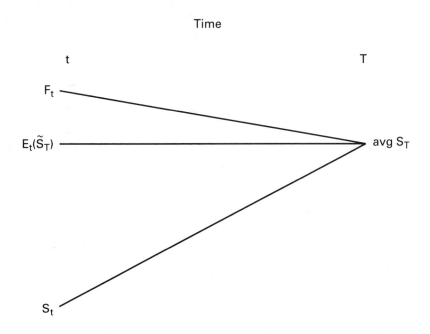

in which futures prices trend downward [i.e., where $F_t > E_t(\tilde{S}_T)$] is said to exhibit *contango*. This situation is depicted in Figure 5.2 as the downward sloping line. If there is no trend in the futures price, the futures price is an unbiased estimate of the expected spot price, that is, $F_t = E_t(\tilde{S}_T)$.

Students of futures markets have long discussed whether or not speculators as a group make money. Some, like Keynes (1930), Hicks (1939), and Cootner (1960a, 1960b) argue that speculators make money because they bear risk and must be compensated for their risk-bearing services. They usually argue that speculators tend to be long futures because hedgers tend to be short.[1] Sales by hedgers force the futures price below the expected spot price and lead to the situation of normal backwardation shown in Figure 5.1. Speculators make money on the upward trend in futures prices.

Others, particularly Telser (1958, 1960), argue that speculators as a group are not risk-averse and do not require compensation for risk. This is possible if there are different categories of speculators. Professional speculators have to make money. Otherwise, they would be unable to support themselves. But amateur speculators could lose money to professional speculators, so speculators as a group just break even. Amateur speculators consist of two categories—gamblers and fools.

---

[1] That is, on balance, there are more short hedgers than long hedgers.

Gamblers enjoy the risks of small futures positions. They know the risks and the fact that there is a house-take, but they enjoy the game. Fools believe they have a successful strategy. They think they know how to make money in futures, but do not. Fools tend to lose money and then withdraw from the market. The supply of fools is replenished by *Barnum's Law*. (There's a sucker born every minute!) Telser thus argues that speculators as a group do not make money even though they bear risk. If Telser's argument is true, hedgers are better off because they are provided insurance at no cost.

Finally, some argue that the amount of risk actually borne by speculators is small, if risk is properly measured. Dusak (1973) takes this position. In modern finance theory, the appropriate measure of risk is the amount of risk that cannot be diversified away. In other words, risk is measured in a portfolio context. Dusak argues that commodity risk can be diversified away so that the systematic risk of a commodity is zero. That means that speculators do not require a risk premium. Competition among speculators for futures contracts will then drive the futures price to a point such that the futures price equals the expected spot price. To the extent that the systematic risk of futures contracts is negative, speculators might be willing to accept losses. For example, suppose futures were a good inflation hedge. In such a situation, speculators would be willing to lose money in futures as a way to reduce the risk in other parts of their portfolio.

5.3 THE CAPITAL ASSET PRICING MODEL FOR FUTURES CONTRACTS

The most familiar form of the Sharpe (1964)–Lintner (1965) capital asset pricing model (CAPM) is the security market line relation,

$$E(\tilde{R}) = r + [E(\tilde{R}_M) - r]\beta, \tag{5.1}$$

where r is the riskless rate of interest, $\tilde{R}_M$ is the rate of return on the market portfolio, and β is the asset's *beta* or *relative systematic risk coefficient*. Equation (5.1) says that the expected rate of return on a risky asset, $E(\tilde{R})$, equals the riskless rate of return, r, plus a market risk premium equal to the market price of risk, $[E(\tilde{R}_M) - r]$, times the asset's relative systematic risk level, β. Assume that the entire asset return is derived from price appreciation (depreciation), that is, $\tilde{R} = (\tilde{V}_T - V_0)/V_0$, where V is the asset price. Then equation (5.1) may be rearranged to derive an expression for the current asset price:

$$V_0 = \frac{E(\tilde{V}_T) - \gamma \left[\frac{\text{Cov}(\tilde{V}_T, \tilde{R}_M)}{\sigma^2(\tilde{R}_M)} \right]}{1 + r}, \tag{5.2}$$

where $\gamma \equiv [E(\tilde{R}_M) - r]$. Equation (5.2) says that the value of an asset today is the difference between expected terminal value of the asset and an appropriate risk adjustment discounted to the present at the riskless rate of interest.

To see how the capital asset pricing model applies to futures contracts, recognize that the terminal value of a long futures position is

$$\tilde{V}_T \equiv \tilde{F}_T - F_0, \tag{5.3}$$

where F_0 is the futures price when the contract is negotiated and $\tilde{F}_T$ is the uncertain futures price when the contract expires.[2] Substituting (5.3) into (5.2) yields

$$V_0 = \frac{E(\tilde{F}_T) - F_0 - \gamma \left[\frac{\mathrm{Cov}(\tilde{F}_T - F_0, \tilde{R}_M)}{\sigma^2(\tilde{R}_M)} \right]}{1 + r}. \tag{5.4}$$

However, the value of a futures position when the contract is first entered into is zero (i.e., the futures position involves no initial investment outlay). Setting $V_0 = 0$ in (5.4) and rearranging yields

$$E(\tilde{F}_T) - F_0 = \gamma \left[\frac{\mathrm{Cov}(\tilde{F}_T - F_0, \tilde{R}_M)}{\sigma^2(\tilde{R}_M)} \right]. \tag{5.5}$$

Dividing both sides of (5.5) by the initial futures price F_0,

$$E(\tilde{R}_F) = \gamma \left[\frac{\mathrm{Cov}(\tilde{R}_F, \tilde{R}_M)}{\sigma^2(\tilde{R}_M)} \right], \tag{5.6}$$

where $\tilde{R}_F$ is the futures return, that is, $\tilde{R}_F = (\tilde{F}_T - F_0)/F_0$. Simplifying, equation (5.6) can be written as

$$E(\tilde{R}_F) = [E(\tilde{R}_M) - r]\beta_F, \tag{5.7}$$

where β_F is the futures contract *beta*.

Figure 5.3 contrasts the expected return/risk relation for assets with the expected return/risk relation for futures contracts. The two lines depicted in Figure 5.3 have the same slope, however the line corresponding to assets has an intercept equal to the riskless rate of interest while the line corresponding to futures contracts goes through the origin. Since asset positions require an investment outlay, an expected rate of return of at least the riskless rate is earned on the asset position. Since futures positions require no investment outlay, the minimum expected return for a futures contract is zero. In equilibrium, the expected rate of return on futures

---

[2] In (5.3), the daily settlement feature of futures is ignored. The interest earned or paid on daily settlements ought to be a part of the profit or loss on the futures position. Usually the interest amount is very small. In addition, we have shown in Chapter 3 that, if interest rates are known and transaction costs are zero, futures market positions can be adjusted so that expression (5.3) is an appropriate measure of profit on a futures contract.

FIGURE 5.3   The Capital Asset Pricing Model and Alternative Views of the Returns to Speculators

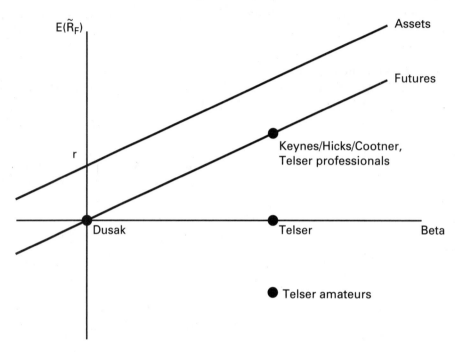

equals only a market risk premium equal to the market price of risk times the futures contract beta.

In the preceding section, we discussed three alternative views of the expected return to holding futures contracts. Under the Keynes/Hicks/Cootner view, speculators earn a positive risk premium. That view is reflected in Figure 5.3 as a position along the futures pricing line with a positive level of systematic risk. The positive return is earned from the upward drift in futures prices when speculators are long. An alternative view is that of Dusak, who argues that futures contracts have no systematic risk. In other words, the beta of a futures contract is zero. In that case, futures contracts are also on the futures contract pricing line but at the point where the line crosses the origin and where beta equals zero. Under the Dusak view, there is no upward drift in futures prices because no compensation for risk is necessary. Under the third view, that of Telser, speculators in the aggregate earn no risk premium, even though risk exists. The Telser position in Figure 5.3 is an average of the position of professionals and amateurs in the figure. Professionals earn a normal risk premium and are on the futures pricing line. However, gamblers and fools earn negative returns as shown in the figure. The average of these two points is the Telser position—positive risk but no return.

The empirical evidence on risk and return in futures markets is ambiguous and makes it difficult to distinguish among these three alternative views. Telser and

Cootner debated vehemently in the 1960's as to the meaning of the data for corn, wheat, and cotton. Cootner maintained that an upward drift in futures prices was observable, while Telser argued it was not.

In a comprehensive investigation using semi-monthly price data for corn, wheat, and soybean futures during the period May 1952 through November 1967, Dusak (1973) concludes that the expected futures returns equal zero. To support her conclusions, she estimates (a) the mean realized futures return and (b) the systematic risk coefficient for each of the futures contract months of the three underlying commodities. The systematic risk coefficients are estimated using the OLS regression,

$$\tilde{R}_{F,t} = \alpha_F + \beta_F(\tilde{R}_{M,t} - r_t) + \tilde{\epsilon}_t, \qquad \text{(5.8)}$$

where the proxy for the market return, $\tilde{R}_{M,t}$, is the price appreciation on the S&P 500 stock portfolio, and the proxy for the riskless rate, r_t, is the return on a T-bill with fifteen days to maturity. The results are reported in Table 5.1.

In Table 5.1, note first that in only two of the sixteen cases reported is the mean realized return significantly different from zero (i.e., twice its standard error), and in both of those cases the realized return is negative. These results are further corroborated by the estimates of the systematic risk coefficients. In only one of the sixteen cases is the beta of the futures contract significantly different from zero. The lack of covariation of the futures returns with the market return is also reflected through the low R^2 values reported in the table.

All in all, the Dusak results appear to support the position that futures prices are unbiased predictors of expected spot prices, however, the generality of the results is not known. Other investigators have found different results as far as agricultural and metal futures markets are concerned.[3] A broader range of underlying commodities and longer time series of daily or weekly prices are among the experimental improvements necessary to determine which of the competing theories is best supported.

5.4 EQUILIBRIUM OF HEDGERS AND SPECULATORS

The CAPM indicates that speculators could receive a risk premium for holding futures contracts. Obviously, some other group would have to pay a risk premium, since futures are a zero-sum game. Hedgers may be willing to pay a risk premium to eliminate the risk of holding the commodity. The situation is more complicated than that described in Chapter 4 because a hedger would consider not only the

---

[3] Bodie and Rosansky (1980), for example, analyze futures prices for the period 1949 and 1976 and conclude that futures contracts on average have a positive return. Unfortunately, the Bodie/Rosansky results are suspect given that they use annual data (and, hence, very few time-series observations) in their statistical analyses.

TABLE 5.1   Summary of regression test results from Dusak (1973).

Contract	Number of Obs.	$\bar{R}_F$	$s(\bar{R}_F)^a$	$\hat{\beta}_F$	$s(\hat{\beta}_F)$	R^2
Wheat:						
Jul.	302	−.00164	.00126	.048	.051	.003
Mar.	302	.00060	.00139	.098	.049	.013
May	302	.00096	.00142	.028	.051	.001
Sep.	319	−.00194	.00127	.068	.051	.006
Dec.	319	.00044	.00134	.059	.048	.005
Corn:						
Jul.	301	−.00158	.00116	.038	.046	.002
Mar.	301	−.00381	.00138	−.009	.050	.000
May	301	−.00268	.00120	−.027	.048	.001
Sep.	320	−.00243	.00128	.032	.048	.001
Dec.	320	−.00212	.00147	.007	.047	.000
Soybeans:						
Jan.	287	−.00025	.00146	.019	.058	.000
Mar.	287	−.00029	.00152	.100	.065	.008
May	287	.00038	.00148	.119	.068	.011
Jul.	287	.00006	.00158	.080	.076	.004
Sep.	287	−.00105	.00157	.077	.065	.005
Nov.	287	−.00071	.00137	.043	.058	.002

a. $s(\cdot)$ is the estimated standard error of the regression coefficient.

correlation between the futures price and the price of the underlying commodity but also the relation between the futures and the hedger's entire portfolio of all assets.[4]

Figure 5.4 shows how hedgers and speculators interact to determine a futures price in relation to the expected spot price and the current spot price. The figure assumes homogeneous expectations on the part of hedgers and speculators. Hedgers are distinguished from speculators because they have a position in the underlying commodity. The HH schedule in Figure 5.4 depicts the futures market position that hedgers as a group would like to hold for alternative futures prices. Note that the HH schedule crosses the vertical axis below the expected spot price. That means that hedgers would sell futures at prices below the expected spot price because of the attractiveness of risk transfer. The position of the HH schedule depends on the

---

[4] See Stoll (1979) for a more detailed discussion of this point.

FIGURE 5.4   Equilibrium Futures Price

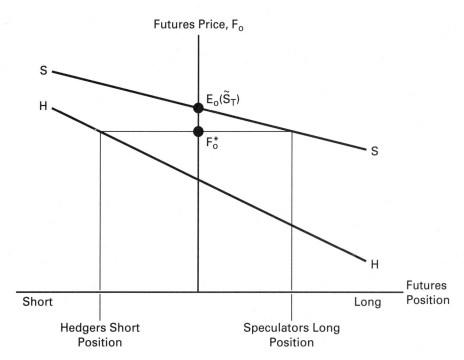

nature and size of the underlying commitment. The slope of the schedule depends on the amount of price risk of the underlying commodity and the degree of risk aversion of hedgers.

The SS schedule depicts the futures market positions that speculators would accept for alternative futures prices. The SS schedule is downward sloping and intersects the vertical axis at the expected spot price. When the futures price equals the expected spot price, the speculator has no incentive to take a futures position—either long or short. When the futures price falls below the expected spot price, speculators earn a risk premium by taking a long position; and when the futures price is above the expected spot price, speculators earn a risk premium by taking a short position. The downward sloping SS schedule implies that a larger risk premium is required to induce speculators to take a larger position.[5]

In Figure 5.4, the equilibrium futures price, F_0^*, is determined such that the short position taken by hedgers equals the long position taken by speculators. Speculators expect to receive a risk premium of $E_0(\tilde{S}_T) - F_0^*$, and hedgers expect to pay that risk premium. Hedgers hold real assets (like wheat or common stocks) and sell futures to avoid risk. Speculators accept the risk; and, in return, earn a risk pre-

---

[5] Such an increase in risk premium as a function of position size is not modeled in the standard one-period capital asset pricing model.

mium. Figure 5.4 is consistent with the Keynes/Hicks/Cootner view and a capital asset pricing model in which the underlying commodity has systematic risk.

Under the Telser and Dusak views of speculators, the SS schedule would be perfectly horizontal and would cross the vertical axis at $E_0(\tilde{S}_T)$. In such a case, hedgers would receive insurance at no cost, and speculators would, as a group, not earn a risk premium.

It is possible that the risk premium is time-varying, particularly in agricultural commodities, which have a seasonal harvest cycle. In the case of a commodity like wheat, for example, hedgers might be long wheat and short wheat futures in the fall after the harvest has come in, and they might be short wheat and long wheat futures in the spring when handlers of wheat make commitments to deliver wheat that they do not yet have in hand. In terms of Figure 5.4, such a seasonal pattern would imply an HH schedule below the SS schedule in the fall and an HH schedule above the SS schedule in the spring. In the fall, speculators are long futures and $F_0 < E_0(\tilde{S}_T)$; and in the spring, speculators are short futures and $F_0 > E_0(\tilde{S}_T)$. Futures prices would display normal backwardation in the fall when speculators indirectly bear the risk of the long positions in the commodity that has been harvested. In the spring, futures prices would display contango when speculators indirectly bear the risk of the short positions in the underlying commodity assumed by hedgers.

5.5 SUMMARY

In this chapter, the role of speculators and the returns speculators can expect in an efficient market are discussed. Some researchers argue that futures prices are unbiased estimates of subsequent spot prices, which means that futures prices do not trend up or down over time. In that case, speculators as a group do not make profits. The absence of speculative profits is possible if amateur speculators lose to professional speculators so that speculators as a group do not make profits. The absence of profits is also possible if the risk of holding futures contracts is fully diversifiable. If the risk can be diversified away, no risk premium is required to induce speculators to hold futures contracts.

On the other hand, some researchers argue that futures prices trend up (normal backwardation) or trend down (contango). If futures prices have a trend, speculators as a group make profits commensurate with the level of risk that they assume from hedgers.

This chapter also derives the expected return to speculators under the Sharpe–Lintner capital asset pricing model. Since futures contracts require no investment, the expected return of a futures contract equals only the futures contract's market risk premium (no riskless return is earned). The last section of the chapter contains a model in which hedgers and speculators interact and determine an equilibrium futures price.

FUTURES CONTRACTS ON PHYSICAL COMMODITIES

Organized futures markets began in response to the risks associated with the marketing of seasonal commodities such as wheat and corn. Farmers would enter into forward contracts with users to dispose of their harvests, and futures markets arose to provide users and farmers a financial instrument to hedge risks while forward contracts were being negotiated. The principal U.S. futures markets are in Chicago because, at one time, Chicago was the key location for grain elevators and the transportation point for shipments to the East. Today, futures contracts are traded not only on seasonal agricultural products, but also on other real commodities such as metals and various industrial materials. The greatest expansion in futures trading has occurred in the 1970s and 1980s with the advent of financial futures.

This chapter focuses on physical commodities. We begin with a discussion of why futures markets arise in certain physical commodities and not in others. We then focus on the seasonal patterns of inventories and prices, on hedging by storers and producers, on the behavior of the basis, on returns to speculators and other issues.

6.1 FUTURES CONTRACTS ON PHYSICAL COMMODITIES

The most actively traded futures contracts on physical commodities are listed in Table 6.1 by major category—grains and oil seeds, livestock, food and fiber, metals, and petroleum. The oldest futures contracts are those for the grains, which began trading in 1859. The livestock contracts date to the 1960s. The most recent additions to the list are the petroleum products. Crude oil and heating oil began trading in the 1970s and gasoline futures began in 1981.

TABLE 6.1   Physical commodity futures contracts specifications (most active contracts in U.S. markets).

Commodity (Exchange)	Trading Hours	Contract Months[a]	Units/ Minimum Price Change	Last Day of Trading
Grains and Oil Seeds				
Corn (CBT)	9:30–1:15 (CST)	12,3,5,7,9	5,000 bushels/ 1/4($12.50)	7 business days before last business day of month
Oats (CBT)	9:30–1:15 (CST)	12,3,5,7,9	5,000 bushels/ 1/4($12.50)	7 business days before last business day of month
Soybeans (CBT)	9:30–1:15 (CST)	9,11,1,3,5, 7,8	5,000 bushels/ 1/4($12.50)	7 business days before last business day of month
Soybean meal (CBT)	9:30–1:15 (CST)	1,3,5,7,8, 9,10,12	100 tons 10($10)	7 business days before last business day of month
Soybean oil (CBT)	9:30–1:15 (CST)	1,3,5,7,8, 9,10,12	60,000 pounds $0.0001($6)	7 business days before last business day of month
Wheat (CBT)	9:30–1:15 (CST)	7,9,12,3,5	5,000 bushels 1/4($12.50)	7 business days before last business day of month

a. The notation used in this column corresponds to the month of the calendar year (e.g., 1 is January, 2 is February, and so on).

TABLE 6.1

Livestock

Live cattle (CME)	9:05-1:00 (CST)	2,4,6,8,9, 10,12	40,000 pounds $0.00025($10)	20th calendar day of contract month
Hogs (CME)	9:10–1:00 (CST)	2,4,6,7,8, 10,12	30,000 pounds $0.00025($7.50)	20th calendar day of contract month
Pork bellies (CME)	9:10–1:00 (CST)	2,3,5,7,8	40,000 pounds $0.00025($10)	business day before last 5 business days of contract month

Food and Fiber

Cocoa (CSCE)	9:30–2:15 (EST)	12,3,5,7,9	10 metric tons $1($10)	
Coffee (CSCE)	9:15-1:58 (EST)	3,5,7,9,12	37,500 pounds $0.0001($3.75)	
Sugar(world) (CSCE)	10:00–1:43 (EST)	1,3,5,7,10	112,000 pounds $0.0001($11.20)	last business day of month preceding delivery month
Cotton (CTN)	10:30–3:00 (EST)	current + 17 suc.	50,000 pounds $0.0001($5)	
Orange juice (CTN)	10:15-2:45 (EST)	1,3,5,7,9, 11	15,000 pounds $0.0005($7.50)	

continued

TABLE 6.1

Commodity (Exchange)	Trading Hours	Contract Months[a]	Units/ Minimum Price Change	Last Day of Trading
Metals				
Copper (CMX)	9:25-2:00 (EST)	1,3,5,7,9, 12,1,3,5,7, 9,12+ cur.3	25,000 pounds $0.0005($12.50)	3rd to last business day of maturing delivery month
Gold (CMX)	8:20–2:30 (EST)	2,4,6,8,10, 12,cur.+ 2	100 troy ounces 10 cents($10)	
Platinum (NYM)	8:20–2:30 (EST)	1,4,7,10 incl.cur.3	50 troy ounces 10 cents($5)	
Silver (CMX)	8:25-2:25 (EST)	1,3,5,7,9, 12,cur.+ 2	5,000 troy ounces 1/10 cent($5)	
Petroleum				
Crude oil (NYM)	9:45-3:10 (EST)	18 cons.mos. begin w/cur.	1,000 barrels 1 cent($10)	
Heating oil (NYM)	9:50–3:10 (EST)	15 cons.mos. begin w/cur.	42,000 US gal. $0.0001	
Gasoline (NYM)	9:50–3:10 (EST)	15 cons.mos. begin w/cur.	42,000 US gal. $0.0001	

Source: Various futures exchange publications.

Futures contracts on physical commodities call for delivery at the option of the short sometime in the delivery month. The first day on which delivery may be made is the first notice day. In many commodities, the long that receives a notice of delivery has the opportunity to sell his futures contract and redeliver the notice; but once futures trading is ended, all outstanding longs have no choice other than taking delivery. In practice, only a small fraction of the futures contracts entered into ever results in delivery.

The trading activity in various futures contracts varies as customer needs change and as competing contracts arise. At the end of 1989, 121 futures contracts on physical commodities were approved by the CFTC.[1] Some of these have never

[1]Commodity Futures Trading Commission *Annual Report 1989.*

been successful. Some had once been successful and are now dormant. Others are traded but are very inactive. We turn now to the factors that give rise to futures markets in physical commodities and that determine their success or failure.

6.2 WHY DO FUTURES MARKETS IN PHYSICAL COMMODITIES ARISE?

Uncertainty

Since the principal purpose of futures markets is to hedge risks, futures markets do not arise if the price of the commodity is not uncertain. If agricultural price supports determine the price of wheat, no wheat futures market will arise. Currency futures would not exist in a system of fixed exchange rates. Coffee futures trading dies out when the international coffee cartel "stabilizes" the price of coffee at a fixed level. Uncertainty about prices arises from uncertainty about the supply of commodities and uncertainty about the demand for commodities. The relative amount of supply side and demand side uncertainty varies by commodity type.

Even though most seasonally produced agricultural commodities are grown during some part of the year around the world, supply is uncertain because the size of harvest is greatly affected by weather conditions. On the other hand, overall demand for most agricultural foodstuffs and oils is reasonably stable since final consumption patterns do not change dramatically from period to period. Demand uncertainty may arise, however, even after a crop is harvested because the supply of a substitute commodity may be uncertain. A bumper harvest of corn, for example, can adversely affect the price of wheat.

Commodities in continuous production—such as petroleum, gas, lumber, and certain metals—face uncertainty from both the demand side and the supply side. Strikes and unexpected increases in costs affect the supply. At the same time, demand uncertainty is greater than in the agricultural commodities because the commodities in continuous production tend to be industrial materials that are subject to the business cycle.

A few physical commodities, namely gold and silver, are in nearly fixed supply in the sense that the outstanding stock of these commodities is large relative to annual production. As a result, price uncertainty arises primarily from the demand side. Gold is like many financial instruments that are also in nearly fixed supply. The prices of gold and of financial instruments depend on interest rates, inflation, and other macroeconomic factors.

Large and Competitive Market

Futures markets do not succeed if the market for the underlying commodity is small, because there is insufficient futures trading to maintain market liquidity. Furthermore, Telser and Higgonbotham (1977, p. 998) make the point that "an organized futures market facilitates trade among strangers." In small markets, producers and users of the commodity find it preferable to deal directly with each other rather than have someone incur the expense of setting up a futures market.

A liquid futures market arises only if the market in the underlying commodity is one in which a large number of units of a standard commodity are available. The automobile market is large, but the units are not standard. Commodity futures markets arise only for commodities that can be standardized and thus easily traded. For some commodities, such as gold, standardization is easy to achieve. For others, standardization is more difficult. For example, standardizing live cattle (traded on the CME) requires a complex contract specification. Even commodities like corn and wheat have a considerable range of grades. As we noted in Chapter 2, futures contracts are designed to allow delivery of a variety of grades at a variety of delivery points so that the danger of a corner is limited, but broadening the definition of the commodity in this way reduces its standardization. The success of the market depends on the degree to which the various grades of the commodity are correlated. A market is large if the prices of a large number of units are strongly correlated with the price of the futures contract.

Futures contracts are unlikely to succeed in non-competitive markets where production of the underlying commodity is monopolized or where buyers of the commodity are few. In such markets, the danger is too great that the cash price can be manipulated to produce artificial gains on the futures contract (as in a corner). At the same time, futures markets can enhance competition in a market that is not fully competitive. For example, crude oil futures trading gives users the opportunity to lock in the future price of oil without negotiating long term contracts with producers. The futures market provides an alternative to dealing directly with the producer. As a result, the producer is compelled to sell in the cash market where he loses control of the supply. For this reason, producers often oppose introduction of futures markets. The most famous example of producer opposition to the introduction of futures markets is the opposition by onion growers to the introduction of onion futures, which resulted in a congressional ban against onion futures trading in 1958.

Storability and Deliverability

Physical commodities on which futures contracts are written are storable either directly or indirectly. Storability has usually been considered a necessity for a successful futures contract on the grounds that the contract calls for delivery of the commodity at a later date, and delivery can only be made if the commodity can be carried over to the delivery date. If the commodity can be produced for delivery, however, storability would not seem necessary. Thus, a futures contract on fresh eggs exists, yet eggs are clearly not storable in the usual sense. Deliverability is not a problem because future availability of the eggs can be assured by having the chickens. The eggs are stored indirectly, as it were, in the chickens. Similarly, live cattle are not storable in the usual sense; yet they clearly can be stored (and fed) for later delivery. Thus, in this broader sense, the requirement of storability and deliverability are met by all physical commodities.

6.3 INVENTORY AND PRICE PATTERNS

Commodities in Seasonal Supply

The pattern of inventories of commodities in seasonal supply can be represented by the saw tooth pattern in Figure 6.1. The high points reflect the harvests when

FIGURE 6.1   Seasonal Inventory Pattern in Agricultural Commodities

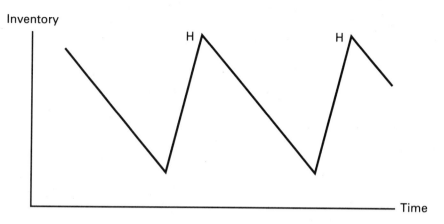

inventories are replenished, and the low points represent the fact that the old crop is used up just before the harvest. The downward sloping line represents the gradual consumption of the commodity out of inventory. Of course, the simple and regular pattern of Figure 6.1 is unrealistic for a number of reasons. First, harvests do not occur all at once but over a period of time. For example, the U.S. harvest of wheat begins in the Southwest in May, when winter wheat planted in the preceding fall is harvested, and continues in the northern states into September, when spring wheat planted in early spring is harvested. The peak inventories in the U.S. usually occur in September. The gradual harvest smooths out the peaks and valleys in the figure. Second, harvest quantities are not the same in each year as is implied by the regularity of the pattern in Figure 6.1. Some years are better than others, with the result that some peaks are higher than others. In some years, the new crop is so small that the old crop is carried over to the next year.

The pattern of the spot price, S, that corresponds to the inventory pattern is shown in Figure 6.2. As might be expected, it is simply the reverse—low prices when inventory is high and high prices when inventory is low. Actual spot prices do not follow this simple stereotype since harvests occur over a period of time. Peaks and troughs in spot prices will be attenuated just as peaks and troughs in inventory are attenuated.

At a time before the harvest, such as t in Figure 6.2, a futures price for a contract maturing at time $H - 1$ just before the harvest and for a contract maturing at a time, $H + 1$, just after the harvest typically exist. These futures prices are forecasts of spot prices at the respective maturities of the two futures contracts. The basis at time t for the futures contract maturing before the end of the old crop year, $F_t(H-1) - S_t$, represents a *carrying charge market* and is typically positive to reflect storage costs. The basis at time t for the futures contract maturing immediately after the new crop, $F_t(H+1) - S_t$, represents an *inverted market* because the new crop is expected to lower prices below the level at time t.

The figures are useful for identifying the three major sources of risk in seasonal commodities. For an individual farmer, the most important risk is quantity

FIGURE 6.2   Seasonal Price Pattern in Agricultural Commodities

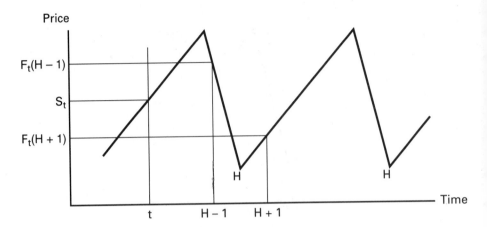

risk, that is, risk relating to the size of the crop at the seasonal harvest. Because of the weather and other factors, the farmer does not know the amount of the crop that will be harvested.

The second risk is price risk, which is present not only at the harvest point but also during the rest of the year. Around the harvest, variability of prices reflects uncertainty about the aggregate harvest. Price risk and quantity risk are related. If the aggregate crop is poor, the price will be higher than normal. If the aggregate crop is good, the price will be lower than normal. The farmer whose harvest is representative of the aggregate will find that price and quantity are negatively correlated—a poor crop is associated with higher-than-normal prices, and a good crop is associated with lower-than-normal prices. This negative association collectively mitigates the price and quantity risks. The harvest of each farmer, however, is not perfectly correlated with the aggregate harvest since weather conditions in different parts of the country vary. The farmer who has a poor crop when other farmers have good crops is in particularly bad shape because the price of the crop is low at the same time she has little to sell. Correspondingly, a farmer with a bumper crop profits greatly when other farmers have a poor crop. After the harvest, price risk still remains because demand for the commodity is uncertain. Commodity demand is uncertain because the supply of substitutes is uncertain and because final consumer demand may fluctuate.

Once the harvest is in, the crop is supplied out of storage. As already noted, most of the risk during this part of the cycle comes from the demand side. However, a third source of risk—storage risk—is also present. Storage costs include warehouse rent, the interest cost of funds tied up in the commodity, insurance, labor and handling, and spoilage. Fluctuations in these costs affect the profitability of storage and the price of the commodity in the period between harvests.

Futures markets can be used to hedge commodity price risk, but futures markets are less well suited to hedge quantity risk or storage cost risk. The discussion of hedging that follows, therefore, emphasizes commodity price risk.

Non-Seasonal Commodities

Non-agricultural commodities such as metals and oils are produced continuously. For all except the precious metals, inventories are small relative to consumption and do not fluctuate seasonally as do the inventories of agricultural commodities. Inventories, however, can be quickly depleted if production is interrupted. For example, a copper miners' strike can halt production of copper and cause copper inventories to be depleted. Similarly, restrictions on the production of crude oil by OPEC can deplete petroleum inventories. In such cases, the spot price can be dramatically affected. In the case of the precious metals gold and silver, inventories are large relative to production, and prices are determined mostly by demand factors. Interruption of production of precious metals takes a longer time to affect inventories.

The pattern of prices of natural resources was first analyzed by Hotelling (1931), and most recently, by Miller and Upton (1985). In a world of certainty, the Hotelling Principle states that the profit margin from mining a natural resource— the price of the extracted resource, S_T, net of per unit marginal production costs, C_T—increases at the rate of interest, r^*:

$$(S_T - C_T) = (S_0 - C_0)(1 + r^*), \tag{6.1}$$

where T refers to a future period and 0 refers to the present period.[2] Intuitively, the idea is that the profit margin must increase to cover the cost of funds tied up in the reserves of the natural resource. If the profit margin in the future period, T, is less than the amount specified by (6.1), producers would increase production at time 0 rather than waiting to produce at T. The profit margin could be invested at r^* to yield more at T than if production had been delayed until tomorrow. That action depresses S_0 and lowers the profit margin at time 0 until condition (6.1) is met. Conversely, if the profit margin at T is greater than the amount specified by (6.1), the present value of what the producer could earn tomorrow would exceed today's profit margin. The producer would be better off restricting production today and producing more tomorrow. He could borrow against tomorrow's profit to give a present amount that exceeds the profit margin at time 0. The process of producing more tomorrow depresses S_T until condition (6.1) is again met. In a world with uncertainty, a modified version of the Hotelling Principle continues to hold in which the expected values of $\tilde{S}_T$ and $\tilde{C}_T$ are used and r^* is a risk-adjusted, expected rate of return.

If there is a futures market, (6.1) holds with $\tilde{F}_T$ substituted for $\tilde{S}_T$. With that substitution and some manipulation, (6.1) can be written as

$$\tilde{F}_T = S_0(1 + r^*) + \tilde{C}_T - C_0(1 + r^*). \tag{6.2}$$

---

[2] Again, we adopt the convention of using an asterisk to denote a rate applied over the futures contract life or the hedge period.

If there are no production costs either in the present or the future, the futures price is above the spot price by the interest cost of the funds tied up in the commodity. This is the same as the cost-of-carry model discussed in Chapter 3. The cost-of-carry model says the futures price on a contract maturing at T exceeds the spot price by the cost of carrying the commodity. In the absence of storage cost other than the interest cost, that means $\tilde{F}_T = S_0(1 + r^*)$. This simple equilibrium is appropriate for a commodity like gold that exists in large quantities in refined form.

Equation (6.2) also shows why the futures price for natural resources may be temporarily below the spot price. This can happen if the current production cost, C_0, is abnormally high, as in the case of a strike or a disruption of supply. In the Kuwait crisis of 1990–91, the spot oil price rose dramatically relative to the futures price, reflecting a rise in C_0 relative to $\tilde{C}_T$. Over time, as current production costs returned to normal, the oil futures price returned to its normal premium over the oil cash price.

6.4 HEDGING COMMODITY PRICE RISK

Storer's Short Hedge

Commodities are often held by storers for resale to users. The storer's hedging decision was analyzed in Chapter 4, and the example of Chapter 4 is repeated in Table 6.2. On September 1, the storer decides to store grain for three months and sell December futures because the three-month basis of nine cents per bushel covers the storage costs of three cents a month. The success of the hedge depends in part on the eligibility of the commodity for delivery against the futures contract. Assume first that the commodity is deliverable. If the position is held to maturity, the storer can simply deliver the grain against the futures contract and lock in a gain of nine cents that covers storage costs. The only risk is that storage costs turn out to be greater than expected. For example, if storage costs turn out to be 3.5 cents per month, the storer makes a loss of 1.5 cents by purchasing the commodity at $3.00 on September 1 and delivering it against the futures contract for $3.09 on December 1. The only way to protect against this risk is to contract forward for storage costs, something that may not always be possible. If all storage costs are locked in before hand, the storer is in the position of having a riskless return (assuming no default risk). In practice, it is unlikely that storers lock in all costs.

Table 6.2 analyzes the outcome of the storer's hedge if the commodity is sold to a customer on November 1, one month before maturity of the futures contract. The price of the cash commodity on November 1 is assumed to be $2.70, a thirty-cent decline from September 1. By selling futures, the storer has eliminated the risk of such adverse moves in the price of the commodity. Basis risk, however, remains. As we noted in Chapter 4, basis risk is the same as storage cost risk if the commodity is deliverable. The effect of basis risk is illustrated by assuming three alternative futures prices on November 1—$2.73, $2.75, $2.71—each implying a different basis. An increase in the basis (weakening) to five cents results when the futures price falls to $2.75 rather than to $2.73. This produces a net loss of two

TABLE 6.2   Profit results from a short hedge.

	Cash Market			December Futures		
Date	Transaction	Price	Transaction	Alternative Prices		
Sept 1	Buy bushel at	3.00	Sell futures at	3.09	3.09	3.09
Nov 1	Sell bushel at	2.70	Buy futures at	2.73	2.75	2.71
Gain		−0.30		0.36	0.34	0.38
Net gain				0.0	0.04	0.08
Net gain less storage costs of $.03 per month				0.0	−0.02	0.02

cents. The storer has the option to store again on November 1 to earn a basis of five cents per month, but that is profitable only if storage costs are locked in at a lower level. If storage costs are not locked in, the increase in the basis reflects a market-wide increase in storage costs which will likely affect the particular storer analyzed in Table 6.2. On the other hand, a narrowing (strengthening) of the basis to one cent results in a net gain of two cents for the storer, assuming she has no obligation to pay storage costs for the month of November.

Assume now that the commodity is not deliverable against the futures contract. In this case, basis risk reflects price risk of the commodity as well as storage cost risk. In the absence of deliverability, the cash and futures prices need not converge at maturity. For example, the storer of wheat in Oklahoma cannot at reasonable cost deliver his wheat against the futures contract in Chicago. As a result the price of Oklahoma wheat can fall relative to the price of the futures contract, albeit the differential fall can be no greater than transportation costs. A short hedge is therefore not fully effective. The more distant the cash commodity in grade and in space, the greater the possibility that the cash price and the futures price will move in different directions between the time of the hedge and the maturity of the futures contract. As shown in Chapter 4, the effectiveness of the hedge will depend on the degree of correlation between the cash price and the futures price.

Merchandiser's Long Hedge
A long hedge involves the purchase of futures to protect against an increase in the price of a commodity. A typical situation is that of an exporter who, on September 1, enters into a forward contract to sell 500,000 bushels of corn for delivery in New Orleans in three months. The exporter does not possess the corn and must make arrangements to acquire it and ship it to New Orleans. To protect against increases in the price of corn while making those arrangements, the exporter buys 100

December futures contracts. If the price of corn goes up, the gain on the futures contract offsets the loss on the export contract. As the particular grade of corn is acquired and shipped to New Orleans, the exporter lifts the futures position.

Producer's Hedge

A producer transforms an input, such as wheat, into an output, such as flour, that is sold to her customers. The producer maintains an inventory of raw materials (wheat) and an inventory of finished goods (flour). She must also acquire raw materials and market the final product to customers. The optimal futures market hedge for the producer depends on whether she wishes to hedge inventory risk, like the storer, or whether she wishes to protect against an increase in the cost of the commodity, like the merchandiser, or both.

Producer's Short Hedge. The producer is in the same position as the storer with respect to finished goods inventory and raw materials inventory if the final product price and the commodity price are positively correlated. Because of the positive correlation, a drop in the price of the final product is like a drop in the price of the commodity, resulting in a loss with respect to the cost of both inventories. A short futures market position hedges inventory risk of this type, and the effectiveness of the hedge depends on the basis risk for the raw materials or finished goods inventory. If the final product price is uncorrelated with the futures price, the producer can still use a short futures hedge to limit raw materials inventory risk, but the futures market provides no hedge against adverse changes in the final product price.

Unlike storers, producers may be willing to hold the commodity even if the basis is zero or negative. For example, suppose that on February 1 the May futures price and the spot price of wheat are both $3.00, while the marginal storage costs are nine cents. A terminal elevator operator would not store the wheat because the revenue from storage is zero, while the costs are positive. The producer, however, may store the wheat because the convenience of having the wheat and maintaining production more than offsets the fact that he has locked in a net loss. The amount by which marginal storage costs exceed the basis is called the *convenience yield*— nine cents in the above example. The producer may choose to lock in a net loss of nine cents to guard against the possibility of an even greater loss if the price of the commodity should fall below $3.00.

Producer's Long Hedge. A producer enters into a long hedge in order to lock in the price of future supplies of the commodity. A flour miller, for example, may wish to guard against increases in the cost of wheat. A long hedge is optimal if the producer has negotiated a price for the final product and wishes to fix costs. If the final product price is uncertain, however, it is not a hedge to lock in a fixed price for inputs. The product price could fall to a point that makes it difficult to cover the cost of the inputs locked in by the futures contract.

The term *anticipatory hedge* is used to describe a futures market purchase in the absence of a fixed price for the final product. An anticipatory hedge is no hedge at all if the final product price is uncertain. An anticipatory hedge can also be a mistake because the price of the commodity might be even lower later. On the other hand, a knowledgeable purchasing agent may be able to predict the likely future cost of the commodity.

Natural Hedge Versus Futures Market Hedge

Producers incur costs for inputs and receive revenues from the sale of the final product. If the cost of inputs is correlated with the price of the final product, a natural hedge exists. For example, a flour miller may find that increases in the price of wheat are generally accompanied by increases in the price of flour. If that is the case, the profit margin is maintained, and hedging does not reduce risk. For example, if the miller locks in the price of wheat with a futures contract and wheat and flour prices fall, he suffers a loss because of the decline in the price of the output while the input price is fixed at the original higher level by the hedge. Had he not hedged the cost of the input, wheat, he would have been better off because the decline in flour prices would have been offset by the decline in the price of the input. On the other hand, if wheat and flour prices rise, hedging the price of wheat produces an overall gain because the price of the output rises while the input price is fixed by the hedge. This example, which assumes that input and output prices are correlated, is summarized in Table 6.3.

TABLE 6.3   Effect of hedging on profits if input and output prices are correlated.

	Hedge	Do Not Hedge
Prices fall	Loss	No effect
Prices rise	Gain	No effect

It is evident that "hedging"—by which we mean locking in the price of the input—actually *increases* the variability of profits in this case. If input and output prices are not correlated, however, hedging would tend to reduce risk.

Many producers face this kind of problem. Candy manufacturers must determine whether to hedge the price of sugar, cocoa, and other raw materials. Cereal producers may wish to hedge grain costs. Producers of electrical wiring may wish to hedge the cost of copper. Cattle ranchers may wish to hedge the price of feed. In each case, the desirability of locking in the price of the input must be determined. Further, if locking in the prices of inputs is desirable, the producer can choose forward contracts with suppliers or futures market hedging.

A more precise formulation of optimal hedging when output and input prices are uncertain is now presented. The formulation is a modification of the optimal hedging discussion presented in Chapter 4 to allow for uncertainty concerning the price of the producer's output as well as the price of commodity inputs.

The notation used in this section is as follows:

$\tilde{P}_T$ = uncertain price of a unit of output at future time T.

Q_P = number of units of the product to be sold.

$\tilde{S}_T$ = uncertain cash price of the input at future time T. We assume one input, although additional inputs could easily be included.

Q_S = number of units of the input required to produce Q_P units of the product.

F_0 = futures price at time 0.

$\tilde{F}_T$ = uncertain futures price at future time T.

n_F = number of futures contracts held. (n_F is positive for a long position and is negative for a short position.)

K = fixed costs incurred in the manufacturing process.

The uncertain profit, $\tilde{\pi}_h$, of a producer who sells Q_P units, uses Q_S units as inputs, and hedges n_F units in the futures market is

$$\tilde{\pi}_h = \tilde{P}_T Q_P - \tilde{S}_T Q_S + (\tilde{F}_T - F_0) n_F - K \qquad \text{(6.3)}$$

By dividing through by Q_P, the equation may be restated in terms of profit per unit of output:

$$\frac{\tilde{\pi}_h}{Q_p} = \tilde{P}_T - \tilde{S}_T \frac{Q_S}{Q_P} + (\tilde{F}_T - F_0) \frac{n_F}{Q_P} - \frac{K}{Q_P} \qquad \text{(6.4)}$$

We now define one unit of the input as the size of the futures contract. In other words, if the input is sugar, we define one unit of sugar as 112,000 pounds, which is one futures contract. We also define one unit of output as the amount produced by the number of units contained in the futures contract. Thus, if 112,000 pounds of sugar are used in producing 1,000,000 candy bars, one unit of output is 1,000,000 candy bars. That means $Q_S/Q_P = 1.0$.[3] Given these conventions, the equation may be written as

$$\frac{\tilde{\pi}_h}{Q_p} = \tilde{P}_T - \tilde{S}_T + (\tilde{F}_T - F_0)h - \frac{K}{Q_P},$$

---

[3] It should be noted that this firm has a fixed input/output ratio and that it plans to produce a fixed number of units, all of which will be sold. In actuality, firms have some flexibility in how they combine factors of production, and they may not be able to sell everything they produce.

where $h = n_F/Q_P$ is the hedge ratio. To be consistent with Chapter 4, we write the equation in price changes by adding and subtracting $P_0 - S_0$ on the right-hand side:

$$\frac{\tilde{\pi}_h}{Q_p} = c + \tilde{\Delta}_P - \tilde{\Delta}_S + h\tilde{\Delta}_F, \tag{6.5}$$

where

$$c = P_0 - S_0 - \frac{K}{Q_P}.$$

Following the procedure of Chapter 4, the variance of the per unit profit can be calculated as

$$\sigma_h^2 = \sigma_P^2 + \sigma_S^2 + h^2\sigma_F^2 - 2\sigma_{PS} + 2h\sigma_{PF} - 2h\sigma_{SF}. \tag{6.6}$$

If the producer does not hedge with futures so that $h = 0$, the risk is

$$\sigma_h^2 = \sigma_P^2 + \sigma_S^2 - 2\sigma_{PS}. \tag{6.7}$$

Note that $\sigma_{PS} = \rho_{PS}\sigma_P\sigma_S$, where ρ is the correlation coefficient. If the price change of the input and the output are perfectly correlated, $\rho_{PS} = 1.0$, which implies $\sigma_h^2 = 0.0$, assuming the variances of the price changes of the input and output are the same. This is the case of a perfect natural hedge. If the price of the output and the input are not perfectly correlated, however, hedging with futures may be desirable. In that case, the problem is to find the hedge ratio that minimizes the variance of the producer's per unit profit.

The value of h that minimizes σ_h^2 in (6.6) is found by taking the derivative of σ_h^2 with respect to h and setting it equal to zero:

$$\frac{d\sigma_h^2}{dh} = 2h^*\sigma_F^2 + 2\sigma_{PF} - 2\sigma_{SF} = 0.$$

Solving for h^*, the optimal hedge ratio, gives

$$h^* = \frac{\sigma_{SF} - \sigma_{PF}}{\sigma_F^2}. \tag{6.8}$$

Note that $\sigma_{SF}/\sigma_F^2 \equiv b_S$ is the slope coefficient of a regression of $\tilde{\Delta}_S$ on $\tilde{\Delta}_F$ and that $\sigma_{PF}/\sigma_F^2 \equiv b_P$ is the slope coefficient of a regression of $\tilde{\Delta}_P$ on $\tilde{\Delta}_F$. Another way of writing the optimal hedge is, therefore,

$$h^* = b_S - b_P. \tag{6.9}$$

If both the input and output react in the same way to a change in the futures price, that is, if the regression coefficients are equal, $h^* = 0.0$, the case of the perfect natural hedge.

For some producers, output prices may be very stable or may be fixed by long-term contracts so that $b_P = 0.0$. In this case, the optimal hedge is determined by b_S, the sensitivity of the input price to the futures price. The producer would purchase futures to lock in the cost of inputs. For other producers, the input price might be stable or fixed by long-term contracts so that $b_S = 0.0$. In this case, the producer would sell futures to protect against a decline in the output price.

As noted in Chapter 4, the optimal hedge can also be developed by starting with the regression equations that relate the output and input prices to the futures price:

$$\tilde{\Delta}_P = a_P + b_P \tilde{\Delta}_F + \tilde{e}_P, \tag{6.10}$$

$$\tilde{\Delta}_S = a_S + b_S \tilde{\Delta}_F + \tilde{e}_S, \tag{6.11}$$

where a and b are the intercept and slope terms, respectively, and e is a random disturbance term. Substituting these equations in the equation for the per unit profit (6.5) yields

$$\frac{\tilde{\pi}_h}{Q_p} = c + a_P - a_S + (b_P - b_S + h)\tilde{\Delta}_F + \tilde{e}_P - \tilde{e}_S. \tag{6.12}$$

It is clear that the per unit profit can be made independent of movements in input and output prices by setting $h^* = b_S - b_P$, the result derived above by minimizing the variance.

The effectiveness of the hedge depends on the extent to which the residual errors, $\tilde{e}_P$ and $\tilde{e}_S$, are eliminated. The variance of the per unit profit remaining after the hedge is the variance of (6.12). When $h = b_S - b_P$, this equals $\text{Var}(\tilde{e}_P - \tilde{e}_S)$.

Estimating the Hedge Ratio

The optimal hedge requires an estimate of b_S and b_P in equations (6.10) and (6.11). As noted in Chapter 4, the usual procedure is to estimate these parameters using historical time-series data. To illustrate the amount to hedge when an input and output price are correlated, we consider the case of an oil refiner who produces gasoline from crude oil. Suppose that one barrel of crude oil produces thirty gallons of gasoline. For the purposes of equation (6.4), the price of the output, $\tilde{P}_T$, refers to thirty gallons of gasoline; and the price of the input, $\tilde{S}_T$ refers to one barrel of crude oil. The hedging vehicle is the crude oil futures contract traded on the New York Mercantile Exchange, the price of which is quoted in dollars-per-barrel. Weekly price data (Tuesdays) were collected for 53 weeks in the period November 1988 to November 1989 for unleaded gasoline sold in New York, for West Texas "sour" crude oil, and for "light sweet" crude oil futures.

The following regressions were estimated:

$$\tilde{\Delta}_P = a_p + b_P \tilde{\Delta}_F + \tilde{e}_p, \tag{6.13}$$

and

$$\tilde{\Delta}_S = a_s + b_S \tilde{\Delta}_F + \tilde{e}_s. \tag{6.14}$$

In regression analysis, the assumptions governing the error term are that $E(\tilde{e}) = 0$, $E(\tilde{e}\tilde{\Delta}_F) = 0$. We also assume that successive error terms in time are independent. The regression results are provided in Table 6.4.

TABLE 6.4   Summary of regression estimates for weekly "sour" crude oil, "light sweet" crude oil futures, and unleaded gasoline futures price changes during November 1988 to November 1989.

No. of observations = 53	
$\overline{\Delta}_P = -0.0312$ dollars	$\hat{\sigma}_P = 0.9000$ dollars
$\overline{\Delta}_S = 0.1161$ dollars	$\hat{\sigma}_S = 0.7994$ dollars
$\overline{\Delta}_F = 0.2580$ dollars	$\hat{\sigma}_F = 0.6370$ dollars
$\hat{a}_P = -0.1985$	$s(\hat{a}_P) = 0.1187$
$\hat{b}_P = 0.6487$	$s(\hat{b}_P) = 0.1741$
$\overline{R}^2 = 0.1956$	$\hat{\sigma}_{e_p} = 0.6516$
$\hat{a}_S = -0.1351$	$s(\hat{a}_S) = 0.0748$
$\hat{b}_S = 0.9738$	$s(\hat{b}_S) = 0.1098$
$\overline{R}^2 = 0.5944$	$\hat{\sigma}_{e_s} = 0.2592$

a. $\overline{\Delta}$ denotes the mean weekly price change and $\hat{\sigma}$ is the standard deviation estimate. $s(\cdot)$ is the standard error of coefficient estimate. $\hat{\sigma}_e$ is the standard error of the regression.

The estimate of the optimal hedge ratio is

$$\hat{h}^* = \hat{b}_S - \hat{b}_P = 0.9738 - 0.6487 = .3251.$$

In other words, for every thirty gallons of gas that the refinery produces, it should purchase futures contracts on only .3251 barrels of oil even though it takes one barrel to produce thirty gallons of gas. The reason that only .3251 barrels of oil futures are purchased is that the refinery has a partial natural hedge arising from the fact that the price received for gas offsets part of any price change in the oil used to produce the gas.

The small values of the $\bar{R}^2s$ imply that the effectiveness of the hedge is not great. Changes in oil futures prices explain only 19.56 percent of the variation in gas prices and only 59.44 percent of the variation in Texas crude oil prices. Thus, a hedge ratio of 0.3251 may prove to be incorrect after the fact. For example, suppose the estimate $\hat{b}_s$ is one standard error below its true value and the estimate $\hat{b}_p$ is one standard error above its true value. Then

$$h^* = (0.9738 + 0.1098) - (0.6487 - 0.1741) = 0.6090,$$

which is nearly twice the estimated hedge ratio.

6.5 SUPPLY OF STORAGE AND DEMAND FOR STORAGE

We showed in Chapter 3 that the futures price cannot exceed the spot price by more than the cost of storing the commodity:

$$F_t \leq S_t + B_t. \tag{3.1}$$

Another way to express this relation is to say that the basis cannot exceed the cost of storage: $F_t - S_t \leq B_t$. Storers will hold a commodity only if the basis, which can be thought of as the price of storage, covers storage costs. It should be noted that the storage cost, B_t, is the marginal cost of storage for the time period in question. Another bushel of wheat will be stored if the marginal cost, B_t, of storing that bushel is less than the price received, $F_t - S_t$, for storing that bushel.

The individual storer takes the price of storage as given, but in the aggregate the price of storage depends on the interaction of the demand for and the supply of storage. The solid line in Figure 6.3 plots the aggregate supply curve of storage for agricultural commodities like wheat, corn, and soybeans. The curve is based on actual data showing how much is stored at each value of the basis, $F - S$. To the left of point A, the out-of-pocket marginal cost of storage, B, represented by the dotted line, exceeds the basis.[4] To the right of point A, the supply curve of storage is coincident with the marginal cost of storage, B. The extended horizontal segment of the supply curve means that storage costs are constant over this range. To the left of point A, positive quantities are stored even when the basis is less than the marginal cost of storage, B, because producers derive a convenience yield from

---

[4] The dotted line slopes upward on the assumption that the marginal costs of storage of the producers that store are higher when small amounts are stored; in other words, there are economies of scale up to point A.

FIGURE 6.3   Supply Curve of Storage

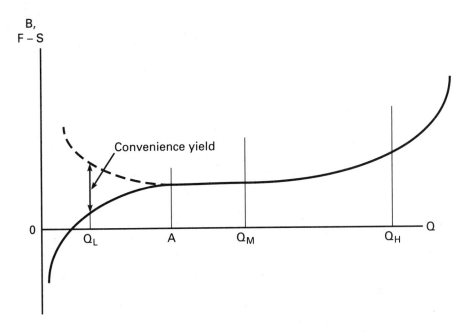

having the commodity. The smaller the amount of the commodity in existence, the greater the convenience yield must be to offset the fact that the price received for storage is less than the marginal cost of storage. The producer presumably passes on the cost of storage in the final price of the product.

The demand for storage varies over the crop year. It is greatest immediately after the harvest and declines thereafter as the crop is used up. The vertical line at Q_H represents the demand for storage after a bumper crop. It intersects the supply curve where marginal storage costs are rising, which reflects the fact that inefficient, high-cost storage facilities must be used to handle the bumper crop. Later in the storage season, the demand curve shifts left to a point like Q_M, and the basis falls.

Finally, near the end of the storage season and just before a new harvest is due, the demand curve is at a point like Q_L. At this point, the basis is small or negative in anticipation of the new crop, and marginal storage costs exceed the basis. Thus, over the storage season, the one-month basis would normally decline as storage facilities are used less and less.

At the beginning of the storage season, storers and producers can use futures prices to decide how much to store for how long. The term structure of futures prices provides an estimate of the basis for different future periods. For example, Table 6.5 lists soybean futures prices in October 1989, and calculates a monthly basis from the difference in successive futures prices. Thus, the implied basis between November and January is 5.88 cents. The peak storage demand appears to occur from November to March and then declines. Storage costs appear to be lower in March to April and in May to July. After July, the basis becomes negative

TABLE 6.5   Soybean futures prices and the implied monthly basis in October, 1989.

Contract Maturity	Soybean Price in Cents	Monthly Basis[a]
November '89	552.5	
January '90	564.25	5.88
March '90	576.00	5.88
May '90	586.00	5.00
July '90	592.25	3.13
August '90	590.00	−2.25
September '90	573.00	−17.00
November '90	572.00	−0.50

a. The basis is calculated as the difference between adjacent futures contract prices divided by the number of months separating the contract maturities.

in anticipation of the new crop to be harvested. To the extent that storage facilities can be used for several crops, the pattern of the expected basis in soybeans depends not only on the supply and demand for soybean storage but also on the supply and demand for storage of other crops. This means it is not perfectly accurate to relate the basis pattern in soybeans to the harvest cycle in soybeans. The matter is actually more complicated. But for the storer of different commodities, the implied basis derived from the term structure of futures prices provides useful guidance in planning what commodities to store, when to store them, and for how long. In general, high-cost storers will store when the demand for storage is high, whereas low-cost storers will store for a longer period of time.

The supply of storage for non-seasonal commodities such as oil, copper, and so forth would have a similar shape. The demand for storage, however, would not have the predictable seasonal pattern that is typical for agricultural commodities. Overproduction of oil would put demand pressure on storage facilities (a movement to the right on the supply of storage function) and cause an increase in the basis. A labor strike in copper production would reduce the demand for storage and cause a movement to the left on the supply of storage function, perhaps even to a point where the basis is negative. As in agricultural commodities, a negative basis means that an increase in production is anticipated, in this case, when the strike ends.

6.6 RETURNS TO SPECULATORS

Unlike hedgers who try to avoid commodity price risk, speculators take risk in the hopes of profit. The riskiest position a speculator can take is simply to go long or short a commodity. A less risky position is to do a spread—to buy (sell) one futures contract and sell (buy) a related contract. For example, a meteorologist who anticipates a drought in Kansas may decide she can profit handsomely by buying corn futures. If she is wrong, she can lose a great deal. A spread is less risky because the futures prices tend to move together. Typical spreads are made up of one maturity against another maturity in the same commodity or one commodity against a related commodity. For example, the drought may affect corn prices differently than wheat prices. In this case, it might be desirable to buy corn futures and sell wheat futures. If corn and wheat futures prices go down together, there is no loss. Only if corn declines more than wheat is there a loss for the speculator.

Speculators in commodity futures, as in other investment vehicles, decide what to buy or sell on the basis of *fundamental* or *technical analysis*. Fundamental analysts examine the supply and demand for a commodity and try to predict future supply and demand and thereby future price changes. In agricultural commodities, the weather is an important factor in supply. In other commodities, political factors or the likelihood of labor disputes may be important. Technical analysis focuses on the pattern of past prices in hopes of predicting future price changes. Technicians chart the behavior of prices and trading volume and look for patterns that will predict futures price changes.

In an efficient market, neither the technician nor the fundamental analyst can expect to make abnormal profits. As in the stock market, the evidence for commodity futures markets is that they are efficient. Studies of the efficiency of the futures markets in physical commodities have taken different approaches. As we noted in Chapter 5, one approach has been to ask whether speculators as a group earn a risk premium. As also noted there, little evidence exists to show that speculators as a group make profits. That may be because the risk taken by speculators is fully diversifiable, which, under the capital asset pricing model, means no risk premium need be paid. Or it may mean that a certain class of speculators—gamblers and fools—lose money to professional speculators so that speculators as a group do not earn abnormal returns.

A second approach has been to analyze the time-series pattern of futures prices to see if any dependencies exist that may be exploited for profit. In the stock market, Fama (1970) has dubbed such tests "weak form" tests of market efficiency since they seek to determine whether a "weak" information set—the past sequence of prices—can predict future price changes. If the market is efficient, the futures price at *t* reflects all available information at that point, including the past history of prices. The past history of prices therefore cannot be used to generate a positive profit in the period t to $t + 1$. A simple empirical implication of efficient markets is that today's futures return should not be correlated with tomorrow's futures return, that is, $\rho(R_t, R_{t+1}) = 0.0$. Several investigators have examined the correlation of successive futures returns. See, for example, Smidt (1965) and Stevenson and Bear (1970). They find that serial correlation is not economically significant. When serial dependence is observed, it is not large enough to overcome the transaction costs incurred in trying to profit from it.

An alternative form of time-series investigation is to simulate a trading rule based on the past sequence of prices. For example, such a rule might be to buy after the futures price has increased by three percent, hold until the price decreases by three percent, at which time the position is sold and a short position is taken, and so forth. If markets are efficient and the normal return is zero, such a technical trading rule should not be profitable. Empirical tests conclude that such rules are not profitable. In carrying out such tests, one must be careful to specify the rule in advance before seeing the data since one can always find some rule that will make money if applied to a particular sequence of historical prices.

A further implication of efficient markets is that fundamental analysis also cannot yield abnormal returns if that analysis is based solely on public information available to all analysts. In efficient markets, all public information is reflected in the current price. In other words, public information available at t cannot be used to predict the price at $t + 1$. Presumably, resources are spent in gathering information in the hopes of discovering information that is not general knowledge, so abnormal returns may be periodically earned. In an efficient market, such abnormal returns should not, on average, exceed the cost of acquiring the special information that yields those abnormal returns.

A third approach to testing the efficiency of commodity futures markets is to examine subgroups of investors, such as professional traders and investment advisers, to see if they can earn abnormal returns. What is a normal return now requires discussion. It is unlikely that the normal return of professional traders and advisers is zero; for if it were, how would they feed their families? One would expect professional investors, those who spend time and resources in analysis, to generate positive trading profits or to charge fees. In the stock market, a popular subgroup to examine is mutual funds. The finding there is that the typical mutual fund does not outperform the market, although they charge fees that allow portfolio managers to feed there families (sometimes very handsomely). The findings in the physical futures markets are consistent with efficient markets. Papers by Rockwell (1967) and Houthakker (1957) examine returns to large hedgers, large speculators and to small traders in physical futures markets. These studies conclude that large speculators do make profits, which is consistent with the idea that professional speculators should make a profit. The studies disagree on whether other speculators make or lose money. Under the null hypothesis of zero expected returns to speculators, gains by one group of speculators should be offset by losses of the remaining speculators. Rockwell argues that this is the case. Houthakker argues that small speculators also make money, which means he rejects the null hypothesis of zero return to speculators.

Elton, Gruber, and Rentzler (1987, 1989) have recently examined the investment performance of commodity funds for the period 1979 to 1985. Commodity funds are the analog of mutual funds in the stock market in that they are professionally managed. Over the six years analyzed, the average annual holding period return is -0.0007. This return does not reflect all the transaction costs that investors are required to pay. Thus, commodity funds underperformed other much less risky investment instruments such as government securities. The performance of commodity funds does not support the idea that professional managers can earn positive profits. Indeed, the performance is so bad, Elton, Gruber, and Rentzler (1989) question the rationality of investors in the funds.

6.7 INTERNATIONAL PRICE LINKS: THE LAW OF ONE PRICE

Most physical commodities are actively traded internationally. The United States is an important exporter of agricultural products. Crude oil produced in the Middle East is imported by Europe and by the United States. Cocoa and coffee are produced in Africa and imported by other countries. It is important, therefore, to specify the relation of the prices of the same commodity denominated in different currencies and to determine if it is possible to use futures contracts traded in the United States and denominated in dollars to hedge positions in a commodity in a different country.

In the absence of transportation costs and transaction costs, the dollar price, S_d, of a commodity must equal the foreign price, S_f, of the same commodity adjusted for the exchange rate, X:

$$S_d = X S_f. \tag{6.15}$$

The exchange rate is defined as the dollar price of the foreign currency. The above relation, known as the *Law of One Price* (*LOP*), holds because of commodity arbitrage. If the dollar price of a commodity were to exceed the cost of buying the commodity in a foreign country, an arbitrageur would purchase the commodity in the foreign country and import it to the United States, thereby depressing prices in the United States and raising prices in the foreign country. Conversely, if the U.S. price were too low, the commodity would be exported from the U.S. to the foreign country. Suppose, for example, that the price of a bushel of wheat in Britain is 2.00 pounds; the exchange rate is 1.60 dollars per pound; and the U.S. price of a bushel of wheat is 3.10 dollars. An arbitrageur could buy a bushel for 3.10 in the U.S., sell the bushel in Britain for 2.00 pounds and convert the pounds into $(1.6)(2) = 3.20$ dollars, which yields a profit of 10 cents per bushel. Such arbitrage raises the price of wheat in the U.S. and lowers it in Britain until the *LOP* is re-established.

In practice, the *LOP* does not hold exactly because commodity arbitrage is costly. Transportation costs and other transaction costs lead to spatial differences in price across countries. Just as the price of wheat is different in Kansas and New

York City, so the price of wheat stated in dollars may differ across countries. In addition, comparisons of prices, even of narrowly defined commodities, do not usually fully account for grade differences in the commodities.

The *LOP* can also be defined for futures prices:

$$F_{d,t}(T) = F_t^X(T)F_{f,t}(T),$$ (6.16)

where $F_{d,t}(T)$ and $F_{f,t}(T)$ are respectively the domestic and foreign futures prices for commodity contracts maturing at T, and $F_t^X(T)$ is the futures price of the foreign currency contract with maturity T. The *LOP* should hold more closely for futures or forward prices because optimal arrangements for transport can be made over the time until maturity.

Table 6.6 presents evidence, taken from Protopapadakis and Stoll (1983), on deviations from the *LOP* for certain spot, forward, and futures prices. Under the *LOP*, the mean and the standard deviation of deviations from the *LOP* would be zero because the *LOP* is a non-stochastic arbitrage relation. The average deviation is small for most of the commodities, particularly for a commodity like silver that is precisely defined. The large mean deviations in coffee and wheat can be ascribed to special factors. The U.S. coffee futures price was high relative to the British futures price because of a manipulation of the New York coffee futures contract by the South American coffee cartel in 1977–80. The U.S. wheat futures price was low in comparison to the British futures price because agricultural price supports in Britain and the EEC artificially maintained a high price.

6.8 CORNERS AND SHORT SQUEEZES

A corner or short squeeze arises if someone gains control of the deliverable supply of a commodity and concurrently holds a long futures position. At maturity, shorts can either liquidate their futures position by trading with a long; or they can deliver the commodity. In a short squeeze, both options are closed off. The short position in the futures market cannot be liquidated because the long refuses to sell, and the commodity cannot be delivered because the long also controls ownership of the deliverable supply and refuses to sell. Shorts usually attempt to cover their futures market short position by buying futures, thereby driving up the futures price. The rise in the futures price in the delivery month relative to other futures prices and to the cash price usually signals the presence of a short squeeze. In the absence of intervention by exchanges or regulators, the long would refuse to sell until the futures price rose substantially. Today, exchanges and the CFTC usually intervene when a short squeeze is suspected and require the person or firm undertaking the squeeze to liquidate futures contracts.

The most recent example of a near short squeeze was the attempt by an Italian grain trading firm, Ferruzzi Finanziaria S.p.A., to corner the July 1989 soybean contract. The July contract expired on July 19. At the beginning of July, Feruzzi

TABLE 6.6   Deviations from the Law of One Price for U.S. and British commodities' prices.[a]

Commodity	$lnS_d - lnS_f - lnX$	
	Mean	Standard Deviation
Silver spot	0.0005	0.0200
Silver 3 month forward	−0.0050	0.0146
Copper spot	0.0038	0.1959
Copper 3 month forward	0.0116	0.0258
Coffee futures	0.1991	0.0941
Cocoa futures	−0.0386	0.0795
Wheat futures	−0.2305	0.2023

a. Commodity price and exchange rate observations are weekly. The period covered is 1972–1980 for most of the commodities. Wheat data are for the period 1976–79.

Source: Protopapadakis and Stoll (1983).

held more than half of the net long July futures positions, which was double the deliverable supply, and owned 85 percent of the soybeans in deliverable position. The shorts would have to move massive amounts of soybeans to the approved delivery points (Chicago and Toledo) in order to make delivery on their futures contracts, an impossibility in the short time remaining to expiration. In reaction to the potential corner, the Chicago Board of Trade ordered those holding futures positions in excess of three million bushels to liquidate. This meant that Feruzzi had to sell much of its long position to the shorts, thereby avoiding a short squeeze. July soybean futures prices, which had risen in reaction to the developing short squeeze, fell back to normal levels.[5]

Futures markets try to guard against a corner by broadening delivery terms to several grades and locations (Chicago and Toledo, in the case of soybeans); but in the event that supplies of the commodity are still monopolized, it is quite appropriate for the exchange to take actions such as forced liquidation to break the short squeeze.

---

[5]Details of the attempted short squeeze are in Chicago Board of Trade (1990).

6.9 SUMMARY

In this chapter, the major futures contracts on physical commodities are identified, and the factors giving rise to futures markets in physical commodities are discussed. Inventory and price patterns for commodities in seasonal supply and for non-seasonal commodities are analyzed.

The use of futures contracts as a hedging tool by commodity storers, by commodity merchandisers, and by producers is explained and modeled. A producer often has uncertain input and output prices, something that makes the hedging problem more difficult than if uncertainty about only one commodity price exists. A framework for optimal hedging in this situation is presented, and calculation of the optimal hedge is illustrated.

The basis in physical commodities depends on the amount of the commodity that must be stored. After a harvest, the demand for storage is high, which causes a movement along the supply curve of storage to a higher cost of storage and a higher basis. When the demand for storage declines, the basis also declines.

Speculators in futures on physical commodities have a difficult time making profits, just as they do in other markets. The evidence implies that futures markets are efficient in the sense that abnormal profits are not consistently achievable. Technical trading rules are not found to be profitable (after trading costs). Professionally managed commodity funds underperform the market. The fact that speculators do not seem to make profits implies that hedgers are provided risk-bearing services at very low cost.

Commodity futures contracts are used by hedgers and speculators in many countries. This chapter shows how prices of the same commodity are linked in terms of different currencies. The chapter ends with a discussion of corners and short squeezes.

7 STOCK INDEX FUTURES CONTRACTS

Arguably, the most exciting financial innovation of the 1980s has been the introduction of stock index futures contracts. These contracts, written on the value of various stock index portfolios, provide important benefits to stock portfolio managers. The uses and benefits of these contracts are described in this chapter. We begin with a description of the history of stock index futures contracts in the U.S. and an explanation of current contract designs. The second section details the composition of the stock indexes that underlie currently traded index futures contracts. Section 3 describes the index arbitrage that holds the cost of carry relation in alignment and explains the concept of "program trading." In section 4, the intraday price behavior of the index and its futures contracts is investigated to see how well the price movements in the two markets are synchronized. The chapter concludes with an illustration of hedging with stock index futures contracts.

7.1 STOCK INDEX FUTURES MARKETS

The first stock index futures contract was introduced in February 1982 by the Kansas City Board of Trade. This contract, the Value Line futures contract, is written on the Value Line Composite Index, a stock index that consists of approximately 1700 stocks from the New York, American, and OTC stock markets.[1] The Chicago Mercantile Exchange quickly followed suit in April 1982 with a futures contract on the S&P 500 stock index, and then the Chicago Board of Trade in July 1984 followed with a futures contract on the Major Market Index. Other stock index

---

[1] The composition of the various stock indexes is discussed in the next section.

futures on over-the-counter stocks have been introduced, but most have failed. Table 7.1 contains the contract specifications of the five stock index futures contracts currently active in the U.S.

By far the most active stock index futures contract is that on the S&P 500 index. Table 7.1 shows that this contract trades at the Chicago Mercantile Exchange from 8:30 AM to 3:15 PM (CST). On a given day, S&P 500 futures contracts extending out four different maturities may trade. The contract maturities will be the following March, June, September, and December. The last trading day of the S&P 500 futures contract is the third Thursday of the contract month. Cash settlement of the contract takes place at the opening prices of the index stocks on Friday.[2] The contract denomination is 500 times the futures price. On November 13, 1991, for example, the December 1991 futures price was $398.30, so the stock equivalent of the futures is $398.30 $\times$ 500 or $199,150. The minimum price increment for changes in the futures price is $.05 $\times$ 500 or $25. As of April 1991, the initial speculative margin for the S&P 500 contracts was $22,000,[3] and the maintenance margin was $9,000.

The specifications of the other index contracts are also shown in Table 7.1. Next to the S&P 500, the most active markets are for the futures contracts on the NYSE Composite Index and the Major Market Index. The Value Line futures contracts have never been particularly active relative to their counterparts on the other futures exchanges, probably because of the way in which the index level is computed.[4] The only difference between the Value Line and Mini Value Line index futures contracts is that the latter contract is one-fifth the size of the former.

Table 7.2 contains a clipping from the *Wall Street Journal* showing prices for the various index futures contracts as of the close of trading on Wednesday, November 13, 1991. Only the three nearby S&P 500 futures contracts were active on November 13—the December 1991 and the March and June 1992 contracts. The estimated trading volume on that day was 42,125 contracts. The implied dollar stock equivalent of this volume of trading is at least $398.30 $\times$ 500 $\times$ 42,125 or $8.39 billion. As is usually the case, the nearby futures contract is the most active, as is reflected through the higher open interest figure for the December contract. The underlying S&P 500 index level, 397.42, is also reported in the table, just below the futures price summary.

7.2 COMPOSITION OF STOCK INDEXES

The indexes underlying the futures contracts contained in Tables 7.1 and 7.2 fall into one of three general categories: (a) value-weighted arithmetic stock indexes;

---

[2] In June 1987, the Chicago Mercantile Exchange and the New York Futures Exchange changed the settlement of their S&P 500 and NYSE index futures contracts from the close of trading to the open in an attempt to mitigate concern about occasional abnormal stock price movements in the "triple witching hour." The futures contracts on the Major Market and Value Line indexes continue to settle at the close. For an analysis of the effects of this change, see Stoll and Whaley (1991).

[3] Margins are adjusted when the risk of the underlying index changes perceptibly. Prior to the October 19, 1987, stock market crash, speculative margin on the S&P 500 futures contract was $6,000. Immediately following the crash, speculative margins were set as high as $20,000.

[4] The index composition is described later in this chapter.

TABLE 7.1   Contract specifications of stock index futures contracts trading in the U.S.

Index (Exchange)	Trading Hours	Contract Months[a]	Units/ Minimum Price Fluctuation	Last Day of Trading[b]
S&P 500 (CME)	8:30–3:15 (CST)	3,6,9,12	500 x index/ .05 ($25)	Third Thursday
NYSE Index (NYFE)	9:30–4:15 (EST)	3,6,9,12	500 x index/ .05 ($25)	Thursday preceding third Friday
Major Market Index (CBOT)	8:30–3:15 (CST)	3 current months plus 3,6,9,12	250 x index/ .05 ($12.50)	First business day prior to Saturday following third Friday
Value Line Index (KC)	8:30–3:15 (CST)	3,6,9,12	500 x index/ .05 ($25)	Third Friday
Mini Value Line Index (KC)	8:30–3:15 (CST)	3,6,9,12	100 x index/ .05 ($5)	Third Friday

a. The notation used in this column corresponds to the month of the calendar year (e.g., 1 is January, 2 is February, and so on).

b. All stock index futures contracts are cash settled.

(b) price-weighted arithmetic indexes; and (c) equal-weighted geometric indexes. The term *arithmetic* refers to the fact that the market values or returns of the individual stocks are "added up." The term *geometric* refers to the case where the values or returns are "multiplied." The S&P 500 and NYSE Composite indexes are in the first category; the Major Market Index falls in the second; and the Value Line Index falls in the third.

Value-Weighted Arithmetic Indexes

The "value" of the common stocks in a value-weighted index refers to the total market capitalization of the firm's outstanding shares, that is, the number of shares outstanding ($n_{i,t}$) times the current price per share ($p_{i,t}$). The total market value of the index at time t is therefore

$$\text{Total market value of index}_t = \sum_{i=1}^{N} n_{i,t} p_{i,t}, \qquad \text{(7.1)}$$

TABLE 7.2   Stock index futures contract prices at the close of trading on Wednesday, November 13, 1991.

FUTURES

S&P 500 INDEX (CME) 500 times index

	Open	High	Low	Settle	Chg	High	Low	Open Interest
Dec	395.00	398.50	394.30	398.30	+ 1.00	401.50	316.50	139,341
Mr92	396.80	400.50	396.50	400.35	+ 1.00	404.00	374.70	7,544
June	398.30	402.35	398.30	402.20	+ 1.10	407.00	379.00	1,102

Est vol 42,125; vol Tues 41,413; open int 148,048, +916.
Indx prelim High 397.42; Low 394.01; Close 397.42 +.68

NIKKEI 225 Stock Average (CME)−$5 times NSA

Dec	24690.	24700.	24600.	24700.	− 340.	28900.	22380.	10,869
Mr92	25250.	25250.	25170.	25230.	− 340.	26725.	23000.	2,423

Est vol 1,107; vol Tues 1,132; open int 13,292, +467.
The index: High 24814.35; Low 24416.23; Close 24416.23 − 251.50

NYSE COMPOSITE INDEX (NYFE) 500 times index

Dec	218.00	220.10	217.75	220.05	+ .70	220.10	175.50	5,026
Mr92	218.80	221.00	218.80	221.00	+ .80	221.00	207.60	746
June	....	....	....	222.00	+ .80	220.10	208.90	172
Sept	....	....	....	223.00	+ .80	221.00	217.50	123

Est vol 5,057; vol Tues 5,996; open int 6,067, +344.
The index: High 219.37; Low 217.64; Close 219.37 +.37

MAJOR MKT INDEX (CBT) $500 times index

Nov	323.70	327.40	323.25	327.25	+ 1.55	327.40	315.20	2,819
Dec	323.50	327.70	323.50	327.70	+ 1.50	327.70	315.75	746

Est vol 2,500; vol Tues 1,163; open int 3,598, +122.
The index: High 327.25; Low 323.58; Close 327.25 +1.28

MGMI BASE METAL INDEX (FOX) 100 times index

Nov	....	....	....	134.50	....	140.50	132.50	2,246
Dec	....	....	....	134.80	....	182.70	133.00	8,662
Ja92	....	....	....	134.90	....	137.10	132.30	120
Mar	....	....	....	135.30	....	160.20	132.60	2,643
June	....	....	....	136.00	....	155.90	134.50	962
Sept	....	....	....	136.80	....	146.60	134.60	149

Est vol 0; vol Tues 0; open int 14,712, .
The index: High 134.52; Low 133.58; Close 134.03 +.81

OTHER FUTURES

Settlement price of selected contract. Volume and open interest of all contract months.

KC Mini Value Line (KC)−100 times Index
   Dec 328.60 +.85; Est. vol. 100; Open Int. 254
KC Value Line Index (KC)−500 times Index
   Dec 328.30 +.70; Est. vol. 250; Open Int. 1,722
   The index: High 326.47; Low 324.48; Close 326.47 +.24
CRB Index (NYFE)−500 times Index
   Dec 214.90 +.35; Est. vol. 206; Open Int. 1,221
   The index: High 214.43; Low 213.94; Close 214.20 +.26

   CBT−Chicago Board of Trade. CME−Chicago Mercantile Exchange. KC−Kansas City Board of Trade. NYFE−New York Futures Exchange, a unit of the New York Stock Exchange.

where N is the number of stocks in the index. This market value is then scaled by a divisor so that the index in period t is

$$S_t = \frac{\sum_{i=1}^{N} n_{i,t} p_{i,t}}{\text{Divisor}_t}. \tag{7.2}$$

The divisor represents what the stocks currently in the index would have been worth in a base period. In the base period, the divisor is the market value of the stocks in the index,

$$\text{Divisor}_0 = \sum_{i=1}^{N} n_{i,0} p_{i,0}. \tag{7.3}$$

Over time, the numerator of (7.2) changes because stocks enter or leave the index or because shares are issued or repurchased by companies. Because such changes do not reflect a change in the value of the stocks, an adjustment to the divisor is made on the day that a change in the index composition occurs. The new divisor on day t is just the old divisor on day t adjusted by the ratio of the market value of the new index composition on day t divided by the market value of the old index composition on day t,

$$\text{new divisor}_t = \left(\frac{\text{market value new}_t}{\text{market value old}_t} \right) \text{old divisor}_t. \tag{7.4}$$

Both the S&P 500 and NYSE Composite indexes are value-weighted. The S&P 500 consists of 500 common stocks, the majority of which trade on the NYSE, although about fifty stocks trade on the American Exchange and in the OTC market. The index was designed by Standard & Poors' to contain stocks from a broad variety of industry groupings. The market value for the base period of the S&P 500 is based on the average market values of the component stocks during the years 1941 through 1943. At that time, the index was set equal to 10. The NYSE Composite contains all common stocks traded on the NYSE, slightly more than 1,500 in number. The base period for the NYSE index is December 31, 1965, at which time the index was set equal to 50. As Table 7.2 shows, the values of the S&P 500 and NYSE Composite stocks indexes were 397.42 and 219.37, respectively, at the close of trading on November 13, 1991, reflecting percentage gains of 3,874 percent and 339 percent, respectively, from their base periods.

Price-Weighted Arithmetic Indexes

A price-weighted arithmetic index is like a value-weighted arithmetic index, except that the number of shares outstanding does not play a role. The price-weighted arithmetic index is computed as

$$S_t = \frac{\sum_{i=1}^{N} p_{i,t}}{\text{Divisor}_t}. \qquad \textbf{(7.5)}$$

In a price-weighted index, the divisor in the base period equals the sum of the prices of the stocks in the base period, that is,

$$\text{Divisor}_0 = \sum_{i=1}^{N} p_{i,0}. \qquad \textbf{(7.6)}$$

Like a value-weighted index, the divisor of a price-weighted index is adjusted to reflect stock splits and stock dividends so that the index level remains unchanged during the stock split/stock dividend process [i.e., in the manner of (7.4)]. Unlike the value-weighted index, however, the divisor of the price-weighted index is unaffected by new stock issues or share repurchases.

The best known price-weighted arithmetic index is the Dow Jones Industrial Average (DJIA), which consists of thirty "blue-chip" stocks. In an attempt to create an index that mimics the price movements of the DJIA, the American Exchange created the Major Market Index (MMI). This price-weighted index contains twenty stocks, seventeen of which are also members of the DJIA. Table 7.2 shows that the value of the MMI at the close of trading on November 13, 1991, was 327.25.

Equal-Weighted Geometric Indexes

An equal-weighted geometric index is somewhat peculiar. To compute it, a geometric average of the rates of return of the individual stocks within the index over a period ($R_{i,t}$) is taken, that is,

$$R_{S,t} = \sqrt[N]{\prod_{i=1}^{N}(1 + R_{i,t})} - 1. \qquad \text{(7.7)}$$

This return is used to update the index from the previous period,

$$S_t = S_{t-1}(1 + R_{S,t}). \qquad \text{(7.8)}$$

Currently, the only equal-weighted geometric index is the Value Line Index. It consists of approximately 1,700 stocks. Approximately ninety percent of the Value Line index capitalization is from shares traded on the NYSE, one percent from AMEX, and nine percent OTC. The Value Line index and its futures contracts are of limited interest for two reasons. First, the index weights all stocks equally so small stocks have as much impact on the index movements as large stocks. For an index to track the behavior of the "market," much greater weight should be placed on large capitalization issues. Second, geometric averaging causes the rate of return on the index to be less than the rate of return that would be earned by an equal-weighted investment in each of the 1,700 stocks. As a result, price movements (returns) of the Value Line index are not as strongly correlated with most stock portfolios as are other indexes, which makes the Value Line futures contract less useful for hedging purposes. Table 7.2 shows that the open interest of the Value Line futures is much lower than the futures contracts on the other indexes. The Value Line index closed at 326.47 on November 13, 1991.

Stock Index Simulations

The arithmetic versus geometric averaging of the various stock indexes warrants further discussion, and the discussion is best facilitated through a numerical example. Assume that there are two stocks, A and B, in the marketplace. Both are priced at $20 per share, and both have 100 shares outstanding. Neither stock pays dividends. Table 7.3 shows sample paths for the prices of each stock over a twelve-month period. Alongside of the stock prices are: (a) a value-weighted arithmetic index, (b) a price-weighted arithmetic index, and (c) an equal-weighted geometric index corresponding to these two stocks. All the indexes are created to have a base value of 100 at time 0. The index values are computed using equations (7.2), (7.5), and (7.8), respectively.

In Table 7.3, note two things. First, the value-weighted and price-weighted arithmetic indexes have identical values. This is because the simulation begins with equal investments in both stocks (the stocks' market capitalizations and prices per share are equal). The price movements of these indexes are perfectly positively correlated with any equal-weighted portfolio of these two common stocks formed at time 0. Second, the equal-weighted geometric index has a terminal value considerably below the terminal values of the other two indexes, 134.16 versus 140.00. This is the downward bias discussed earlier. The price movements of a geometric index in general do not correspond to price movements in a stock portfolio, so

TABLE 7.3   Simulation of value-weighted arithmetic, price-weighted arithmetic, and equal-weighted geometric stock index values created using two stocks.

Time t	Stock A	Stock B	Value-Weighted Arithmetic Index[a]	Price-Weighted Arithmetic Index[b]	Equal-Weighted Geometric Index[c]
0	20	20	100.00	100.00	100.00
1	25	16	102.50	102.50	100.00
2	30	20	125.00	125.00	122.47
3	33	22	137.50	137.50	134.72
4	27	20	117.50	117.50	116.19
5	36	15	127.50	127.50	116.19
6	40	16	140.00	140.00	126.49
7	36	18	135.00	135.00	127.28
8	38	21	147.50	147.50	141.24
9	40	18	145.00	145.00	134.16
10	38	21	147.50	147.50	141.24
11	40	22	155.00	155.00	148.32
12	36	20	140.00	140.00	134.16

a. The value-weighted arithmetic index consists of 100 shares of Stock A and 100 shares of Stock B. At time 0, the market capitalization is 4,000, which is adjusted to an index level of 100.

b. The price-weighted arithmetic index at time 0 equals the sum of the share prices of Stock A and Stock B divided by the divisor.

c. The equal-weighted geometric index equals 100 in the base period. The value at time 1 equals the time 0 index value times the square root of the product of one plus the rate of return on Stock A and one plus the rate of return on Stock B.

futures contracts on a geometric index are of less value for hedging purposes than are futures contracts on an arithmetic index.

Correlation Among Index Returns

Still more intuition about the different stock indexes can be gathered by examining actual weekly rates of price appreciation in selected U.S. stock indexes. Table 7.4 contains the means and standard deviations of the percentage rates of price appreciation of six different stock indexes. Also included in the table are estimated contemporaneous correlation coefficients between each pair of return series. Weekly returns are computed using closing index levels each Wednesday during the calendar year 1989. Several interesting results appear in the table.

First, note that the standard deviation of the rate of return for the arithmetic indexes is highest for MMI—1.7453 percent per week. This result is not surprising

TABLE 7.4   Summary statistics of weekly percentage rates of price appreciation in five U.S. stock indexes during the calendar year 1989.[a]

Means and Standard Deviations of Index Returns

Index	Mean Return	Standard Deviation
DJIA	0.4537	1.6640
MMI	0.5072	1.7453
S&P 500	0.4481	1.5825
VL	0.1809	1.3180
NYSE	0.4127	1.4916

Contemporaneous Correlations Between Pairs of Index Returns

Index	MMI	S&P 500	VL	NYSE
DJIA	.9779	.9774	.8880	.9750
MMI		.9497	.8104	.9403
S&P 500			.9137	.9972
VL				.9337

a. Rates of price appreciation are computed on the basis of the closing index
levels each Wednesday during 1989. Cash dividends paid on index stocks are
not considered.

considering that the MMI has the fewest stocks of any of the indexes examined.
The reduction in standard deviation from the MMI to the DJIA to the S&P 500,
and, finally, to the NYSE reflects increasingly higher degrees of diversification. The
DJIA has 30 stocks, the S&P 500 has 500, and the NYSE has more than 1500. The
standard deviation of the return of the Value Line index reflects both diversification
and a downward bias due to the way in which the index is computed. (Recall the
geometric averaging discussed earlier in this section.)

Second, note that the correlation between pairs of return series is highest for
the S&P 500 and the NYSE indexes—0.9972. Both of these indexes are value-
weighted and are highly diversified. The rates of return of the two stock indexes
are virtually perfectly positively correlated.

Third, the returns of the MMI and the DJIA are also strongly positively correlated—0.9779. One would expect this to be the case given that seventeen of the
stocks in the MMI are also in the DJIA. The fact that these indexes are not well-
diversified, however, attenuates to a small degree the correlation between the
returns of these two indexes.

Finally, while the correlation among the returns of any pair of arithmetic
indexes is very high (approximately 0.93 or higher), the correlation between the

returns of the Value Line index and any of the other indexes is relatively much lower. The geometric averaging of the returns of the stocks in the Value Line index portfolio and the inclusion of many small companies undermines the index's co-movements with other indexes.

7.3 INDEX ARBITRAGE AND PROGRAM TRADING

The cost of carry relation (3.6) from Chapter 3 applies to the relation between the stock index futures price and the price of the underlying index under the assumption that the dividend yield rate d is a constant, continuous proportion of the index price level. Active stock index arbitrage ensures that

$$F_t = S_t e^{(r-d)(T-t)}, \tag{7.9}$$

where F_t and S_t are the time t prices of the futures contract and the underlying stock index, respectively. Note that the derivation of this relation in Chapter 3, as it applies to stock index arbitrage, implies that the cash dividends, as they accrue through time, are being reinvested in the stock index portfolio.

Assuming that cash dividends are a constant, continuous proportion of the index level may be inappropriate, particularly for a narrow-based index like the MMI, where the small number of stocks in the index portfolio implies an obvious discreteness and seasonality of cash dividend payments.[5] In such a case, an assumption that the amount D_i and the timing t_i of the discrete cash dividends paid during the futures contract life (i.e., between time t and time T) are known is usually used. Furthermore, rather than assuming that the dividends are being reinvested in the stock index portfolio, dividends are assumed to be reinvested at the riskless rate of interest until the futures contract expires.

Under these assumptions, stock index arbitrage involves the transactions shown in Table 7.5a. The long position in the index portfolio provides a terminal value equal to the uncertain index price $\tilde{S}_T$ plus a known aggregate dividend income (plus accrued interest) $\sum_{i=1}^{n} D_i e^{r(T-t_i)}$. The stock portfolio position is financed completely with riskless borrowings, which are repaid at time T at a cost $S_t e^{r(T-t)}$. The short futures position has a terminal value $-(\tilde{S}_T - F_t)$. Since the arbitrage portfolio involves a zero investment outlay and has no risk, the net terminal value of the portfolio must equal zero for the market to be in equilibrium. Thus, under the assumption of known discrete dividends, the cost-of-carry relation is

$$F_t = S_t e^{r(T-t)} - \sum_{i=1}^{n} D_i e^{r(T-t_i)}. \tag{7.10}$$

---

[5]Harvey and Whaley (1992) show pronounced seasonality in the cash dividends of the S&P 100 index, which contains approximately forty percent of the market value of the S&P 500 index. In particular, during the period 1983 through 1989, dividends tend to be highest in the months of February, May, August and November.

TABLE 7.5a   Index arbitrage transactions for establishing the relation between index futures and underlying index prices, assuming known discrete cash dividends.

$$F_t = S_t e^{r(T-t)} - \sum_{i=1}^{n} D_i e^{r(T-t_i)}$$

Position	Initial Value	Terminal Value
Buy index portfolio	$-S_t$	$\tilde{S}_T + \sum_{i=1}^{n} D_i e^{r(T-t_i)}$
Borrow S_t	S_t	$-S_t e^{r(T-t)}$
Sell futures contract	0	$-(\tilde{S}_T - F_t)$
Net portfolio value	0	$F_t - S_t e^{r(T-t)} + \sum_{i=1}^{n} D_i e^{r(T-t_i)}$

A simple version of the cost-of-carry relation arises if one assumes dividends and interest are paid at the end of the period corresponding to the life of the futures contract. Table 7.5b presents arbitrage transactions for this case and shows that this simple cost-of-carry relation is

$$F_t = S_t(1 + r^* - d^*), \tag{7.11}$$

where r^* is the rate of interest and d^* is the dividend yield over the remaining life of the futures contract.

Violations of the cost-of-carry relation (7.9), (7.10), or (7.11) signal profitable index arbitrage opportunities. If, for example, the observed futures price is above the theoretical futures price as implied by the right-hand side of (7.9), (7.10), or (7.11), arbitrageurs sell futures and buy the underlying stocks, driving the price of the futures down and the prices of stocks up. The arbitrage becomes unprofitable when the futures price reflects the cost of carrying the underlying stocks, that is, the interest cost less the cash dividends.

Unlike typical basis arbitrage, the underlying commodity is a precisely weighted *portfolio* of common stocks, rather than a single asset. For example, engaging in index arbitrage with the S&P 500 index requires a mechanism for buying or selling quickly and simultaneously all 500 stocks in the S&P 500 index portfolio. Since the simultaneous purchase or sale of the stocks in a precisely weighted and timely fashion is beyond human capability, computers and computer programs are usually used to place transaction orders as well as to assist in the execution of those orders. For this reason, trading of portfolios of stocks is called *program trading*, although program trades can also be done by manually preparing order tickets for each stock. NYSE statistics define a program trade as any order for a portfolio of 15 or more stocks.

TABLE 7.5b   Index arbitrage transactions for establishing the relation between index futures and underlying index prices, assuming dividends and interest are paid at maturity.

$$F_t = S_t(1 + r^* - d^*)$$

Position	Initial Value	Terminal Value
Buy index portfolio	$-S_t$	$\tilde{S}_T + d^* S_t$
Borrow S_t	S_t	$-S_t(1 + r^*)$
Sell futures contract	0	$-(\tilde{S}_T - F_t)$
Net portfolio value	0	$F_t - S_t(1 + r^* - d^*)$

Treasury Bill Substitute

Technically speaking, one thinks of "index arbitrage" as being conducted by professional index arbitrageurs who establish offsetting positions in the manner shown in Table 7.5a. However, deviations from the cost of carry relation also offer opportunities for investors, such as pension funds, to structure an investment with index futures that offers a higher return than an investment of equivalent risk in another market. For example, if the futures price is high relative to the cost-of-carry equilibrium, fund managers can generate a riskless investment with a rate of return higher than the return on a Treasury bill of a maturity comparable to the index futures by selling index futures and buying the index portfolio. Such a strategy is called a *Treasury bill substitute.*

To understand how this strategy works, suppose that the current S&P 500 index level is 348.60 and that the nearby S&P 500 futures contract has a price of 354.50 and a time to expiration of 73 days. Suppose also that the future value of the S&P 500 dividends over the next 73 days is $2.79 and that a 73-day Treasury bill will provide a rate of return of 1.6 percent over its life. Using (7.11), the implied riskless rate of interest, r^*, on a 73-day investment involving selling the index futures and buying the stock index portfolio is determined by solving

$$354.50 = 348.60(1 + r^*) - 2.79.$$

The interest rate from the Treasury bill substitute strategy, r^*, is 2.5 percent. In other words, a pension fund that might ordinarily invest $3,486,000 in T-bills to earn 1.6 percent over 73 days could invest the same amount of money in a Treasury bill substitute to earn 2.5 percent over 73 days. To do so, the $3,486,000 is invested in the index portfolio (i.e., 10,000 units of the index are purchased) and twenty index futures contracts are sold (recall each index futures is 500 times the index value). Over the 73-day period, the index portfolio will generate $27,900 in cash dividends, and the index level will appreciate by 5.90 relative to the futures (because the futures price and index level converge at the end of 73 days), for a total price appreciation of $59,000. The overall rate of return on the Treasury bill substitute position is (27,900 + 59,000)/3,486,000 or 2.5 percent.

Stock Replacement

A second example of how index futures may be used to generate a higher return than an investment with equivalent risk is a *stock replacement strategy*. When the actual futures price is below the theoretical futures price, an arbitrageur enacts a short arbitrage—the short sale of stocks and the purchase of futures contracts. But stock portfolio managers, too, can profit from such an opportunity by selling their stock portfolios and using the proceeds to buy index futures and Treasury bills, that is, by engaging in stock replacement.

To illustrate a stock replacement strategy, consider the previous example in which the current S&P 500 index level is 348.60, the time to expiration of the nearby S&P 500 futures contract is 73 days, the rate of return on a 73-day T-bill over the next 73 days is 1.60 percent, and the future value of the cash dividends on the S&P 500 over the next 73 days is $2.79. However, this time, assume the nearby S&P 500 futures price is $350.25. On the basis of these figures, the theoretical futures price is

$$F = 348.60(1.0160) - 2.79 = 351.39.$$

Since the observed futures price, $350.25, is less than its theoretical value, a stock replacement strategy can be used to generate a rate of return that will exceed the rate of return on a direct investment in the S&P 500 index portfolio without assuming more risk. A portfolio manager with $50,000,000 in the S&P 500 index portfolio will have a portfolio value of

$$\tilde{V}_{\text{S\&P 500},T} = \left(\frac{50,000,000}{348.60}\right)(\tilde{S}_T + 2.79)$$
$$= 143,430.87\tilde{S}_T + 400,172$$

in 73 days. On the other hand, if he liquidates his S&P 500 stock portfolio and buys T-bills and the nearby S&P 500 futures contract, the portfolio value for the stock replacement strategy (SRS) will be

$$\tilde{V}_{\text{SRS},T} = \left(\frac{50,000,000}{348.60}\right)(\tilde{S}_T - 350.25) + 50,000,000(1.016)$$
$$= 143,430.87\tilde{S}_T - 50,236,662 + 50,800,000$$
$$= 143,430.87\tilde{S}_T + 563,338.$$

Note that the stock replacement strategy is certain to have a terminal value $163,166 higher than the stock portfolio strategy. The fact that this incremental value is certain reflects the fact that, while each strategy's terminal value is uncertain, both strategies have equal risk. If the observed futures price is below its theoretical level, however, the stock replacement strategy will dominate.

Practical Considerations in Index Arbitrage

In practice, there are several reasons why deviations from the cost of carry relation do not ensure that arbitrage profits can be earned. First, and most important, are the transaction costs involved in trading the underlying index stocks. These include the commissions and the market impact costs of buying stocks at the ask price or selling stocks at the bid price. Procedures for trading portfolios of stock have improved dramatically in recent years and frequently involve the use of the NYSE computer entry system, DOT (Designated Order Turnaround). Nevertheless, these costs can be substantial, particularly if a number of portfolio transactions are hitting the market at the same time. Stock index arbitrageurs estimate the total round-trip transaction costs to be on the order of 0.5 to 0.75 percent of the underlying portfolio value.[6]

Second, the dividends in the cost-of-carry relation are assumed to be known with certainty. In general, this assumption is reasonable since firms tend to pay regular, constant, or constantly-increasing quarterly dividends. Any uncertainty about the anticipated dividend payments on the underlying stocks, however, introduces uncertainty about the return of the index arbitrage and can therefore limit arbitrage somewhat.

Third, certain types of arbitrage may involve risk. In some cases, arbitragers do not trade all the underlying stocks in the index. Instead, they buy or sell a representative basket of stocks because of the difficulty and the cost associated with transacting, say, all 500 of the stocks in the S&P 500 index. If the representative basket fails to move exactly like the underlying index, the arbitrage is risky.

Fourth, certain rules and regulations can impede arbitrage. For example, "circuit breakers" are now used to suspend index futures trading when the DJIA moves by more than a pre-specified amount in a given trading day. On such days, apparent arbitrage opportunities may be only illusory in the sense that the futures leg of the arbitrage may not be executable. Another example of an instance where a rule impedes arbitrage is when the arbitrage requires stocks to be sold and futures to be purchased. Since the index portfolio must be sold short, the *short-sale rule* comes into play. Under the short-sale rule, a stock is required to uptick before it may be sold short. When an entire portfolio of stocks must be sold, the time delay in waiting for an uptick in each stock makes the short arbitrage difficult to implement, so the futures price may tend to be less than or equal to its theoretical value. It is worthwhile to note that stock sales conducted by portfolio managers using stock

---

[6] See Stoll and Whaley (1987, p. 18).

replacement strategies, however, are not subject to the uptick rule, and this will tend to limit the amount by which the futures price will fall below its theoretical price.[7]

Fifth, arbitrage is sometimes limited by the lack of capital. Brokerage firms may be limited by net capital requirement rules and the availability of higher yielding alternative fund uses. Moreover, many institutional investors may not be authorized to engage in index arbitrage.

The efficacy of the index arbitrage process has been examined in a number of theoretical and empirical papers.[8] In general, these papers find that observed futures prices can deviate from the theoretical futures price specified by arbitrage conditions by more than normal transaction costs. This is particularly the case for deviations of the futures price below the theoretical price. Such deviations may be difficult to arbitrage though because of the short sale restrictions and because of the lack of a sufficient number of institutions willing to engage in stock replacement strategies.

7.4 INTRADAY BEHAVIOR OF RETURNS

In perfectly efficient and continuous futures and stock markets absent transaction costs, riskless arbitrage profit opportunities should not appear so the cost-of-carry relation (7.9),

$$F_t = S_t e^{(r-d)(T-t)},$$

should be satisfied at every instant t during the futures contract life. If such is the case, the instantaneous rate of price appreciation in the stock index equals the net cost-of-carry of the stock portfolio plus the instantaneous relative price change of the futures contract. To see this, take the natural logarithm of (7.9) at time t and at time $t - 1$:

$$\ln S_t = -(r - d)(T - t) + \ln F_t, \tag{7.12}$$

---

[7] In August 1990, the NYSE implemented a rule requiring a downtick on each stock in an index arbitrage program purchase if the DJIA rose by 50 points or more and an uptick on each stock in an index arbitrage program sale (short or from a long position) if the DJIA declined by 50 points. This rule is counter productive because it impedes index arbitrage.

[8] Cornell and French (1983), Figlewski (1984a), Gastineau and Madansky (1983), Modest and Sundaresan (1983), Peters (1985), Stoll and Whaley (1986b), MacKinlay and Ramaswamy (1988), Kleidon (1991), Kleidon and Whaley (1991), and Miller, Muthuswamy, and Whaley (1991) examine the arbitrage process and consider possible explanations for observed deviations from theoretical prices. Other papers, notably Garcia and Gould (1987), Gould (1988), and Brennan and Schwartz (1990), analyze strategies for trading on mispricing.

and

$$\ln S_{t-1} = -(r - d)(T - t + 1) + \ln F_{t-1}, \tag{7.13}$$

and then subtract (7.13) from (7.12),

$$R_{S,t} = (r - d) + R_{F,t}, \tag{7.14}$$

where $R_{S,t} = \ln(S_t/S_{t-1})$ and $R_{F,t} = \ln(F_t/F_{t-1})$.

Several implications follow from (7.14) under the assumptions that the short-term interest rate and the dividend yield rate of the stock index are constant and that the index futures and stock markets are efficient and continuous:

a. The expected rate of price appreciation on the stock index portfolio $E(\tilde{R}_{S,t})$ equals the net cost of carry $(r - d)$ plus the expected rate of return on the futures contract $E(\tilde{R}_{F,t})$.

b. The standard deviation of the rate of return on the futures contract equals the standard deviation of the rate of return of the underlying stock index.

c. The contemporaneous rates of return of the futures contract and the underlying stock portfolio are perfectly positively correlated.

d. The rates of return of the futures contract and of the underlying stock index portfolio are serially uncorrelated.[9]

e. The noncontemporaneous rates of return of the futures contract and the underlying stock portfolio are uncorrelated.

Naturally, all of the above implications are based on the assumption that the cost-of-carry relation (7.9) holds at all points in time. It has been shown, however, that (7.9) does not hold exactly; indeed, one of the puzzles in stock index futures is the frequency with which deviations from the cost-of-carry relation are observed. Stoll and Whaley (1986b, Table 23A), for example, report frequent violations of the cost-of-carry relation in excess of transaction costs using hourly S&P 500 index and index futures data during the period April 1982 through December 1985. The frequency of violation is nearly eighty percent for the June 1982 futures contract. For more recent contract maturities, however, the frequency falls below fifteen percent. MacKinlay and Ramaswamy (1988, Table 6) report similar results for the S&P 500 futures contracts expiring in September 1983 through June 1987. Using fifteen-minute price data, they find that the cost-of-carry relation is violated 14.4 percent of the time on average.

Violations of the cost-of-carry relation may appear for a variety of reasons. Some, like transaction costs, were discussed in the last section. The presence of

---

[9]Technically speaking, more than an assumption of market efficiency is needed to ensure serially uncorrelated rates of return. It must also be the case that the expected rates of return of the futures and stock index are constant. [See Fama (1976, pp. 149–151).] Such an assumption is reasonable since the rate of return series that we will examine below are intraday.

transaction costs tends to introduce noise in the rate of return relation (7.14). An important reason not mentioned in the last section is the infrequent trading of stocks within the index. Markets for individual stocks are not perfectly continuous. Consequently, stock index prices, which are averages of the last transaction prices of component stocks, lag actual developments in the stock market. Fisher (1966) describes this phenomenon. Cohen, *et al.* (1986, Ch. 6) give a more general discussion of serial correlation of stock index returns in terms of delays in the price adjustment of securities. Lo and MacKinlay (1988) model the effects of infrequent trading on index returns under certain restrictive assumptions. Assuming that the index futures prices instantaneously reflect new information, observed futures returns should be expected to lead observed stock index returns because of infrequent trading, even though there is no economic significance to this behavior whatsoever.

Stoll and Whaley (1990b) use five-minute, intraday rate of return data for the S&P 500 index and the nearby S&P 500 futures contracts to (a) model and purge the effects of infrequent trading in the stock index portfolio, and (b) assess the degree of simultaneity between returns in the index futures and stock markets. The effects of infrequent trading are shown in Table 7.6. Note that, while the S&P 500 futures contract returns have virtually no serial correlation, the returns of the S&P 500 index portfolio are strongly positively serially correlated. The first-order serial correlation in the S&P 500 index returns exceeds 0.5. Because not all stocks within the S&P 500 index portfolio trade in every five-minute interval, a market movement within this interval may not be recorded in the price of less actively traded stocks until some time later when the stock finally trades. The effect of this phenomenon is positive serial correlation in the portfolio return series. The serial correlation does not disappear until lag 4 or 5 using five-minute returns.

The effects of infrequent trading on observed stock index returns are modeled theoretically and estimated empirically in Stoll and Whaley (1990b). The residuals (return innovations) from the estimated model are examined to assess the degree of any remaining positive serial correlation. The last pair of columns in Table 7.6 show these results. With the effects of infrequent trading modeled and purged, the return innovations of the S&P 500 index are virtually white noise. None of the estimated serial correlation coefficients exceed 0.02 in absolute magnitude.

Finally, to assess the degree of simultaneity between the S&P 500 index futures and stock market returns, the return innovations of the S&P 500 index are regressed on lag, contemporaneous, and lead futures returns,

$$\epsilon_{S,t} = \alpha + \sum_{k=-3}^{3} \beta_k R_{F,t-k} + u_t. \tag{7.15}$$

The regression results are shown in Table 7.7. In addition, for purposes of comparison, the regression results of observed S&P 500 index returns regressed on lag, contemporaneous, and lead futures returns are also reported.

The return innovation regression results in Table 7.7 indicate that the dominant relation between the two markets is contemporaneous. The estimated coefficient of the contemporaneous futures return, $\hat{\beta}_0$, in the return innovation regression is 0.1338, higher than any of the leading or lagged coefficients. The estimated coef-

TABLE 7.6   Estimated serial correlation coefficients of observed returns of the S&P 500 index (R_S^o) and the S&P 500 index futures contract (R_F^o) for the 1249-day period April 21, 1982, through March 31, 1987^a.

		$\rho_k(R_{S,t}^o, R_{S,t-k}^o)$		$\rho_k(R_{F,t}^o, R_{F,t-k}^o)$			$\rho_k(\epsilon_{S,t}, \epsilon_{S,t-k})$	
Lag k	No. of obs.^{b}	$\hat{\rho}_k^c$	$t(\hat{\rho}_k)^d$	$\hat{\rho}_k^c$	$t(\hat{\rho}_k)^d$	No. of obs.^{e}	$\hat{\rho}_k^c$	$t(\hat{\rho}_k)^d$
1	86,952	0.5117	175.61	0.0229	6.77	84,454	0.0071	2.06
2	85,703	0.2654	80.60	0.0265	7.76	83,205	0.0053	1.52
3	84,454	0.1312	38.46	0.0015	0.45	81,956	0.0068	1.95
4	83,205	0.0759	21.96	−0.0137	−3.96	80,707	0.0050	1.41
5	81,956	0.0460	13.17	−0.0222	−6.36	79,458	0.0052	1.48
6	80,707	0.0199	5.64	−0.0108	−3.06	78,209	−0.0042	−1.18
7	79,458	0.0077	2.18	−0.0087	−2.46	76,960	−0.0119	−3.30
8	78,209	0.0154	4.32	−0.0015	−0.42	75,711	0.0017	0.46
9	76,960	0.0195	5.42	0.0039	1.07	74,462	−0.0005	−0.15
10	75,711	0.0110	3.04	−0.0030	−0.83	73,213	−0.0082	−2.22
11	74,462	0.0018	0.49	0.0047	1.29	71,964	−0.0163	−4.37
12	73,213	0.0019	0.51	0.0002	0.07	70,715	−0.0067	−1.77

a. The numbers in this table are taken from Stoll and Whaley (1990, Tables 1 and 3).

b. The number of observations used in the computation of the serial correlation coefficient. Note that as the lag k is incremented by one, the number of observations lost equals the number of days in the sample period. This reflects the loss of one return each day of the sample. The serial correlation coefficient estimates are, therefore, not contaminated by using returns from adjacent days.

c. The estimated lag k serial correlation coefficient across all five-minute returns in all days of the period, excluding overnight returns and the first two returns each trading day.

d. The t-ratio corresponding to the null hypothesis that ρ_k equals zero.

e. The number of observations drops by 2,498 as a result of fitting an $ARMA(2,3)$ regression model to observed returns.

ficient of the lag one futures return, $\hat{\beta}_1$, is 0.1015, showing that there is a tendency for the futures market to lead the stock market. All other coefficients in the return innovation regression are indistinguishably different from zero in an economic sense. When stock index returns are used as the dependent variable, the leading effect of the futures market appears considerably longer, but most of this is illusion attributable to infrequent trading in the stock market. Overall, the evidence supports the notion that futures markets tend to play a price discovery role in the marketplace.

TABLE 7.7   Parameter estimates from regressions of S&P 500 index returns/return innovations on lag, contemporaneous, and lead nearby S&P 500 futures returns for the 1249-day period April 21, 1982 through March 31, 1987[a].

$$\text{Returns:}\quad R_{S,t} = \alpha + \sum_{k=-3}^{3} \beta_k R_{F,t-k} + u_t$$

$$\text{Return innovations:}\quad \epsilon_{S,t} = \alpha + \sum_{k=-3}^{3} \beta_k R_{F,t-k} + u_t$$

	Returns		Returns Innovations	
No. of Obs.	78,209			78,209
R^2	0.4730			0.2132
	Parameter estimate[b]	t-ratio[c]	Parameter estimate[b]	t-ratio[c]
$\hat{\alpha}$	−0.0001	−1.08	−0.0002	−1.73
$\hat{\beta}_{-3}$	−0.0077	−6.57	−0.0094	−8.04
$\hat{\beta}_{-2}$	−0.0158	−13.48	−0.0153	−13.04
$\hat{\beta}_{-1}$	0.0213	18.10	0.0194	16.54
$\hat{\beta}_0$	0.1690	142.93	0.1338	113.50
$\hat{\beta}_1$	0.2032	171.14	0.1015	85.72
$\hat{\beta}_2$	0.1330	111.45	0.0153	12.87
$\hat{\beta}_3$	0.0798	66.50	0.0059	4.92

a. The numbers in this table are taken from Stoll and Whaley (1990b, Table 5).
b. Parameter estimates obtained from times series regression across all five-minute returns in all days of the period, excluding overnight returns and the first two returns each trading day.
c. The t-ratio corresponding to the null hypothesis that the respective coefficient equals zero.

7.5 HEDGING MARKET RISK

Stock index futures contracts are useful in a variety of risk management situations. In this section, we examine an important one—hedging market risk. Assume you are responsible for managing a $50,000,000 stock portfolio. This portfolio has a systematic risk coefficient (β_p) of 1.20 relative to the S&P 500 index and a total risk (σ_p) of forty percent on an annualized basis. The future value of the promised dividends on this stock portfolio over the next three months is $400,000, or 0.8 percent of the current portfolio value. At the same time, the S&P 500 stock index portfolio has a total risk level (σ_s) of twenty-five percent annually and promises cash dividends over the next three months amounting to one percent of the current index value. The current S&P 500 index value is 373.63 and the price of the nearby, three-month S&P 500 futures contract is 375.50. A three-month T-bill promises a 1.5 percent rate of return. This illustration assumes the cost of carry relation (7.11) holds, that is, $375.50 = 373.63(1 + .015 - .01)$.

Suppose that your research director has informed you that the market (as reflected by the S&P 500) will drop by sixteen percent over the next three months. You have a great deal of confidence in his prediction so you decide to hedge the market risk of your portfolio. One option that you have is to liquidate the stock portfolio and buy T-bills, however this strategy would not allow you to capture the non-market returns that your portfolio of "winners" is expected to earn over the next three months. Selling S&P 500 futures contracts, on the other hand, allows you to hedge the market risk of the stock portfolio without selling your stocks.

Forming the Hedge Portfolio

The optimal number of futures contracts to sell in this instance can be obtained indirectly using the stock portfolio beta. $\beta_p = 1.20$ implies that the stock portfolio is expected to earn 1.2 times the gain/loss of the S&P 500 index per dollar invested. The stock portfolio beta is defined as

$$\beta_p \equiv \frac{\text{Cov}(\tilde{R}_p, \tilde{R}_S)}{\text{Var}(\tilde{R}_S)},$$

where $\tilde{R}_p$ and $\tilde{R}_S$ are the random rates of return on the stock portfolio and the market index (in this case, the S&P 500), respectively. To understand the relation between the stock portfolio beta and the optimal hedge ratio, we need to establish the relation between the futures and stock index returns over the hedge period, which is equal to the futures contract life in this illustration. Over the hedge period, the stock index return is

$$\tilde{R}_S = \frac{\tilde{S}_T - S_0}{S_0},$$

and the futures return is

$$\tilde{R}_F = \frac{\tilde{F}_T - F_0}{F_0}.$$

Using (7.11) to substitute for F_0,

$$
\tilde{R}_F = \frac{\tilde{S}_T - S_0(1 + r^* - d^*)}{S_0(1 + r^* - d^*)}
$$

$$
= \frac{\tilde{R}_S}{1 + r^* - d^*} - \frac{r^* - d^*}{1 + r^* - d^*}.
$$

Rearranging to isolate $\tilde{R}_S$, we get

$$
\tilde{R}_S = \tilde{R}_F(1 + r^* - d^*) + r^* - d^*.
$$

Substituting for the stock index return, the expression for the stock portfolio beta becomes

$$
\beta_p = \frac{\text{Cov}[\tilde{R}_p, \tilde{R}_F(1 + r^* - d^*) + r^* - d^*]}{\text{Var}[\tilde{R}_F(1 + r^* - d^*) + r^* - d^*]}
$$

$$
= \frac{\text{Cov}(\tilde{R}_p, \tilde{R}_F)}{\text{Var}(\tilde{R}_F)(1 + r^* - d^*)}.
$$

The remaining step in showing the relation between the stock portfolio beta and the hedge ratio involves substituting the relations between returns and price changes. These relations are $\tilde{R}_p \equiv \tilde{\Delta}_p/p_0$ and $\tilde{R}_F \equiv \tilde{\Delta}_F/F_0$. Hence, the stock's rate of return beta β_p is

$$
\beta_p = \frac{\text{Cov}(\tilde{\Delta}_p/p_0, \tilde{\Delta}_F/F_0)}{\text{Var}(\tilde{\Delta}_F/F_0)(1 + r^* - d^*)}
$$

$$
= \frac{\frac{1}{p_0 F_0} \text{Cov}(\tilde{\Delta}_p, \tilde{\Delta}_F)}{\frac{1}{F_0^2} \text{Var}(\tilde{\Delta}_F)(1 + r^* - d^*)}
$$

$$
= \frac{\text{Cov}(\tilde{\Delta}_p, \tilde{\Delta}_F)F_0}{\text{Var}(\tilde{\Delta}_F)(1 + r^* - d^*)p_0}.
$$

Using the definition of the optimal hedge ratio given in Chapter 4 and assuming the cost-of-carry relation, (4.9), β_p can be written as

$$
\beta_p = -h^* \frac{S_0}{p_0}.
$$

Finally, the initial investment in the stock portfolio and the cash index with respect to which β_p is calculated are the same, so $p_0 = S_0$. This implies that

$$
\beta_p = -h^*.
$$

In other words, the optimal hedge ratio is the negative of the stock portfolio beta. In the case of the example, the optimal hedge ratio is

$$h^* = -1.2.$$

The optimal number of futures contracts to sell is therefore the stock portfolio beta times the number of units of the stock portfolio,

$$1.2 \left[\frac{50,000,000}{373.63(500)} \right] = 321.17.$$

Assessing Hedging Effectiveness

The information indicates that the variance of the unhedged stock portfolio return is $.40^2 = .16$. If the stock portfolio investment is one dollar, the *price change* variance of the unhedged portfolio is also $.16$. In Chapter 4, we learned that hedging effectiveness is measured by the adjusted R-squared of the regression of cash price changes on futures price changes. The R-squared, in turn, is closely related to the correlation of cash price changes with futures price changes (i.e., $R^2 = \rho_{p,F}^2$). To find the effectiveness of the S&P 500 hedge in our illustration, therefore, we focus on the correlation coefficient between the stock portfolio price changes and the futures price changes. Over the life of the futures contract, the futures and stock index price changes are perfectly correlated and the standard deviation of the futures price change equals the standard deviation of the stock index price change, so the correlation coefficient may be written

$$\rho_{p,F} = \rho_{p,S} = \frac{\sigma_{p,S}}{\sigma_p \sigma_S}.$$

Also, we know that $\beta_p = \sigma_{p,S}/\sigma_S^2$, so

$$\rho_{p,F} = \beta_p \frac{\sigma_S}{\sigma_p}.$$

On the basis of the given values ($\beta_p = 1.20$, $\sigma_S = 0.25$ and $\sigma_p = 0.40$); the correlation coefficient, $\rho_{p,F}$, is 0.75. The R-squared is thus 0.5625, and the proportion of the stock portfolio return variance that is unrelated to the return variance of index futures is $1 - .5625$ or 0.4375. The remaining variance of the rate of price change on the hedged portfolio is therefore

$$\sigma_h^2 = 0.4375(.16) = .07.$$

Decomposing the Hedge Portfolio Return

Suppose that the S&P 500 index drops by twenty percent over the three-month period after the hedge portfolio is formed. Over the same time, your stock portfolio drops to a value of $40,000,000, excluding dividends. Find the overall rate of return on your hedged portfolio, and decompose the overall return into its riskless rate

TABLE 7.8   Hedging market risk of a stock portfolio that has a $\beta = 1.2$ and a three-month dividend yield of 0.8 percent.

| | Cash Market | | December Futures | | |
	Index Level	Value of Stock Portfolio	Futures Price	Value of Futures Position[a]	Value of Hedged Portfolio
Sept 15	373.63	50,000,000	375.50	−60,300,000	
Dec 15	298.90	40,400,000[b]	298.90	−48,000,000	
Gain		−9,600,000		12,300,000	2,700,000
Return(%)	−20.00	−19.20[c]	−20.40	−24.60[c]	5.40[c]

a. The optimal hedge involves selling 321.17 futures contracts, with each contract valued at 500 times the index futures price.

b. Includes dividends of $400,000.

c. Dollar gain divided by the initial stock portfolio value, $50,000,000.

and abnormal return components. Table 7.8 provides such a decomposition for a hedge established on September 15 and liquidated on December 15, when the futures contract is assumed to expire.

The overall rate of return on the unhedged portfolio can be measured easily by focusing on the price appreciation and dividend yield components of total return, that is,

$$R_p = \left(\frac{40,000,000}{50,000,000} - 1\right) + \left(\frac{400,000}{50,000,000}\right) = -19.20\%.$$

To find the hedged portfolio return, we must also compute the rate of return on the futures. At the outset, the S&P 500 index level was 373.63 and the three-month S&P 500 futures price was 375.50. If the S&P 500 index level fell by twenty percent over the three-month period, the new index level and futures price (recall that futures had three months to expiration when they were sold) are 373.63(.80) or 298.90. The rate of return on the index futures over the period was therefore

$$R_F = \frac{298.90}{375.50} - 1 = -20.40\%.$$

Thus, the total return of the hedged portfolio over the three-month period is

$$R_h = R_p + h\left(\frac{F_0}{S_0}\right) R_F$$

$$= -0.1920 - 1.2\left(\frac{375.50}{373.63}\right)(-0.2040)$$

$$= 5.40\%.$$

The alternative to hedging in this example is to liquidate the stock portfolio and buy three-month T-bills. Such an action would have produced a 1.5 percent return, given our assumption that the T-bill rate is 1.5 percent. The riskless rate and abnormal performance components of the hedge portfolio return in this illustration are therefore 1.5 percent and 3.9 percent, respectively. In other words, the 3.9 percent return was the abnormal or extra-market rate of return arising from the fact that the portfolio of "winners" outperformed the market on a risk-adjusted basis.

The hedged portfolio would also have earned 1.5 percent if the stock portfolio had declined exactly according to its beta of 1.20, without an abnormal return. In that case, the return would have been

$$R_p = r^* + (R_m - r^*)\beta_p = 0.015 + (-0.19 - 0.015)1.2 = -0.231,$$

where R_m is the return on the stock index including the dividends, or -0.19. That implies a value for the stock portfolio, including dividends, of \$38,450,000, instead of the value of \$40,400,000 shown in Table 7.8. The values in Table 7.8 for the cash index and the futures market would remain the same. The dollar gain on the hedged portfolio becomes \$750,000, and the hedged return becomes 1.5 percent, exactly the same as the riskless rate.

It is worth noting that the hedged stock portfolio has basis risk because the portfolio's return is not perfectly correlated with the index futures return. If, for example, the stock portfolio had a negative abnormal return, the hedged portfolio would have earned less than the riskless rate.

7.6 SUMMARY

In this chapter, stock index futures contracts and the composition of stock indexes underlying futures contracts are described. The cost-of-carry relation for stock indexes is derived, and the role of index arbitrage in maintaining the link between stock index futures and cash prices is explained. Evidence on the short-run behavior of the returns of index futures and of the cash index is presented. Finally, the use of stock index futures to hedge the market risk in a stock or a portfolio of stocks is illustrated in detail.

8 INTEREST RATE FUTURES CONTRACTS

Like stock index futures contracts, interest rate futures have been extremely successful financial futures contracts. Interest rate futures provide a means of trading future loan commitments and are important and useful risk management tools for fixed-income portfolio managers. This chapter begins with a description of interest rate futures markets and the specifications of the contracts traded in those markets. Section 2 analyzes the instruments underlying interest rate futures contracts. In section 3, a key measure of interest rate risk, duration, is explained. In section 4, the term structure of interest rates is examined. We focus on the effect of the term structure on the value of coupon and non-coupon bonds. Spot rates, forward rates, and yield to maturity are defined. Examples illustrate most of the important concepts. Sections 5 and 6 describe, in detail, the interest rate futures contracts corresponding to short-term and long-term interest rates. The most active short-term interest rate futures contracts in the U.S. are the Chicago Mercantile Exchange's Treasury bill and Eurodollar contracts, while the most active long-term interest rate futures contract is the Chicago Board of Trade's Treasury bond contract. Contracts in the intermediate-term range, the CBT's five-year and ten-year Treasury note futures, are also discussed. Section 7 describes the cost-of-carry equilibrium in the T-bond futures market. Section 8 contains three illustrations of the use of interest rate futures contracts, and section 9 contains a summary.

8.1 INTEREST RATE FUTURES MARKETS

Table 8.1 contains the contract specifications of the most active interest rate futures contracts traded in the U.S. Of the contracts listed in Table 8.1, the CME's T-bill

TABLE 8.1   Interest rate futures contracts specifications (most active contracts in U.S. markets).

Security (Exchange)	Trading Hours	Contract Months[a]	Units/ Minimum Price Fluctuation	Last Day of Trading	Deliverable Grade[b]
T-Bond (CBT)	8:00–2:00 (CST)	3,6,9,12	$100,000/ 1/32 ($31.25)	Seven business days prior to last business day of month	Nominal 8% coupon with 15 years to maturity or first call date
10-yr. T-Note (CBT)	8:00–2:00 (CST)	3,6,9,12	$100,000/ 1/32 ($31.25)	Seven business days prior to last business day of month	Nominal 8% coupon with 6.5 to 10 years to maturity
5-yr. T-Note (CBT)	8:00–2:00 (CST)	3,6,9,12	$100,000/ 1/32 ($31.25)	Seven business days prior to last business day of month	Any of the four most recently auctioned 5-year Treasury notes
91-day T-Bill (CME)	7:20–2:00 (CST)	3,6,9,12	$1,000,000/ .01 ($25.00)	Business day preceding issue date of new 91-day T-bill	Any of the three T-bills 91-days from maturity
Eurodollar Time Deposit (CME)	7:20–2:00 (CST)	3,6,9,12 plus current month	$1,000,000/ .01 ($25.00)	Second London business day before third Wednesday	Cash settled

a. The notation used in this column corresponds to the month of the calendar year (e.g., 1 is January, 2 is February, and so on).
b. All interest rate futures contracts other than the Eurodollar contract call for delivery of the underlying security.

futures contract is the oldest, with trading beginning in January 1976. The CBT had introduced a futures contract on GNMA pass-through certificates in the fall of 1975, but it was later delisted.

Unlike stock index futures contracts, most interest rate futures contracts call for the delivery of the underlying interest rate instrument. The CBT's T-bond futures contract, for example, requires the delivery of a nominal eight-percent coupon, $100,000 face value, U.S. Treasury bond. Delivery may take place at any time during the delivery month, at the discretion of the short. The last day of trading of the futures contract is the eighth-to-last business day of the contract month.

Table 8.2 shows prices of these contracts as of the close of trading on November 13, 1991. The open interest figures in Table 8.2 show that the T-bill, Eurodollar, and T-bond futures contracts are the most active interest rate futures contracts pres-

TABLE 8.2   Interest rate futures contract prices.

INTEREST RATE INSTRUMENTS

FUTURES

TREASURY BONDS (CBT)–$100,000; pts. 32nds of 100%

	Open	High	Low	Settle	Chg	Yield Settle	Chg	Open Interest
Dec	101-04	101-05	99-15	100-03	− 29	7.991	+ .091	280,722
Mr92	100-08	100-10	98-20	99-07	− 30	8.079	+ .095	31,420
June	99-12	99-12	97-30	98-10	− 30	8.173	+ .097	10,197
Sept	98-13	98-13	97-06	97-14	− 31	8.264	+ .101	2,717
Dec	97-19	97-19	96-10	96-20	− 31	8.350	+ .102	4,487
Mr93	96-00	96-05	95-28	95-28	− 32	8.430	+ .107	511

Est vol 370,000; vol Tues 245,191; op int 330,091, +8,975.

TREASURY BONDS (MCE)–$50,000; pts. 32nds of 100%

	Open	High	Low	Settle	Chg	Yield Settle	Chg	Open Interest
Dec	101-02	101-02	99-15	100-04	− 32	7.987	+ .100	13,542

Est vol 6,600; vol Tues 6,396; open int 13,641, −132.

T−BONDS (LIFFE) U.S. $100,000; pts of 100%

	Open	High	Low	Settle	Chg			
Dec	101-02	101-03	99-21	100-05	− 0-23	101-03	96-24	5,443

Est vol 2,273; vol Tues 4,086; open int 5,480, +721.

GERMAN GOV'T. BOND (LIFFE)
250,000 marks; $ per mark (.01)

	Open	High	Low	Settle	Chg			
Dec	86.23	86.25	86.02	86.19	+ .02	86.44	83.73	75,176
Mr92	n.a.	n.a.	n.a.	n.a.	n.a.	86.70	85.39	6,879

Est vol 47,392; vol Tues 51,218; open int 82,055, −2,487.

TREASURY NOTES (CBT)–$100,000; pts. 32nds of 100%

	Open	High	Low	Settle	Chg	Yield Settle	Chg	Open Interest
Dec	103-23	103-23	102-18	103-06	− 14	7.540	+ .061	86,289
Mr92	102-29	102-29	101-26	102-13	− 14	7.651	+ .062	12,194
June	....	....	....	101-18	− 13	7.772	+ .058	418

Est vol 30,000; vol Tues 25,215; open int 98,902, +4,714.

5 YR TREAS NOTES (CBT)–$100,000; pts. 32nds of 100%

	Open	High	Low	Settle	Chg	Yield Settle	Chg	Open Interest
Dec	04-275	104-28	104-12	04-215	− 5.5	6.880	+ .040	91,919
Mr92	04-015	04-015	103-19	03-275	− 6.0	7.071	+ .045	10,105

Est vol 19,429; vol Tues 16,648; open int 102,024, +2,602.

2 YR TREAS NOTES (CBT)–$200,000, pts. 32nds of 100%

	Open	High	Low	Settle	Chg	Yield Settle	Chg	Open Interest
Dec	103-26	103-26	103-17	03-255	− ¼	....	....	13,800
Mr92	103-11	103-11	03-057	03-105	− ½	....	....	3,553

Est vol 1,500; vol Tues 885; open int 17,353, +153.

30-DAY INTEREST RATE (CBT)-$5 million; pts. of 100%

	Open	High	Low	Settle	Chg	Yield Settle	Chg	Open Interest
Nov	95.14	95.14	95.13	95.14	− .01	4.86	+ .01	1,254
Dec	95.12	95.12	95.08	95.09	− .05	4.91	+ .05	1,232
Ja92	95.16	95.17	95.15	95.17	− .05	4.83	+ .05	1,100
Feb	95.23	95.27	95.23	95.26	− .04	4.74	+ .04	962
Mar	95.18	95.21	95.18	95.21	− .05	4.79	+ .05	570
Apr	95.20	95.20	95.20	95.20	− .05	4.80	+ .05	107
June	95.10	95.11	95.10	95.11	− .04	4.89	+ .04	189

Est vol 725; vol Tues 529; open int 5,464, +185.

TREASURY BILLS (IMM)–$1 mil.; pts. of 100%

	Open	High	Low	Settle	Chg	Discount Settle	Chg	Open Interest
Dec	95.38	95.38	95.31	95.34	− .03	4.66	+ .03	21,996
Mr92	95.52	95.52	95.42	95.50	− .02	4.50	+ .02	29,371
June	95.23	95.34	95.23	95.32	− .03	4.68	+ .03	3,892
Sept	95.09	95.09	95.05	95.08	− .02	4.92	+ .02	338
Dec	94.64	94.64	94.64	94.64	....	5.36	....	156

Est vol 6,328; vol Tues 5,830; open int 55,771, +261.

LIBOR-1 MO. (IMM)–$3,000,000; points of 100%

	Open	High	Low	Settle	Chg	Yield Settle	Chg	Open Interest
Nov	95.05	95.05	94.98	95.02	− .04	4.98	+ .04	6,950
Dec	94.60	94.60	94.50	94.55	− .10	5.45	+ .10	7,336
Ja92	95.11	95.11	95.02	95.08	− .05	4.92	+ .05	9,651
Feb	95.01	95.08	94.99	95.06	− .05	4.94	+ .05	2,515
Mar	94.96	95.01	94.94	95.00	− .05	5.00	+ .05	1,390
Apr	....	....	....	95.01	− .04	4.99	+ .04	163

Est vol 1,577; vol Tues 2,063; open int 28,005, +300.

MUNI BOND INDEX (CBT)-$1,000; times Bond Buyer MBI

	Open	High	Low	Settle	Chg	High	Low	Open Interest
Dec	95-23	95-23	95-01	95-08	− 15	95-25	88-16	12,542
Mr92	95-04	95-04	94-07	94-13	− 19	95-04	88-00	827

Est vol 2,500; vol Tues 2,607; open int 13,370, +850.
The index: Close 95-09; Yield 6.82.

EURODOLLAR (IMM)–$1 million; pts of 100%

	Open	High	Low	Settle	Chg	Yield Settle	Chg	Open Interest
Dec	94.85	94.86	94.75	94.80	− .07	5.20	+ .07	242,049
Mr92	94.99	94.99	94.84	94.94	− .05	5.06	+ .05	252,314
June	94.77	94.78	94.62	94.74	− .04	5.26	+ .04	145,943
Sept	94.48	94.50	94.34	94.46	− .03	5.54	+ .03	100,739
Dec	93.94	93.96	93.83	93.93	− .03	6.07	+ .03	71,656
Mr93	93.76	93.77	93.65	93.74	− .03	6.26	+ .03	55,423
June	93.46	93.46	93.36	93.43	− .02	6.57	+ .02	44,243
Sept	93.17	93.19	93.09	93.17	− .01	6.83	+ .01	31,658
Dec	92.79	92.82	92.72	92.82	+ .02	7.18	− .02	21,132
Mr94	92.76	92.81	92.71	92.80	+ .03	7.20	− .03	27,888
June	92.50	92.58	92.46	92.57	+ .05	7.43	− .05	17,956
Sept	92.28	92.37	92.23	92.35	+ .06	7.65	− .06	11,828
Dec	91.97	92.06	91.92	92.05	+ .07	7.95	− .07	9,816
Mr95	91.96	92.05	91.93	92.04	+ .07	7.96	− .07	7,178
June	91.84	91.93	91.82	91.92	+ .07	8.08	− .07	6,868
Sept	91.69	91.78	91.67	91.77	+ .07	8.23	− .07	6,419

Est vol 283,796; vol Tues 130,709; open int 1,053,277, +4,629.

EURODOLLAR (LIFFE)–$1 million; pts of 100%

	Open	High	Low	Settle	Change	Lifetime High	Low	Open Interest
Dec	94.86	94.87	94.75	94.83	− .02	94.94	90.58	17,546
Mr92	94.97	94.99	94.85	94.96	....	95.06	90.60	10,098
June	94.77	94.78	94.66	94.75	....	94.83	90.97	5,226
Sept	94.49	94.49	94.47	94.46	....	94.53	90.97	2,724
Dec	93.97	93.97	93.95	93.93	....	94.00	91.54	614
Mr93	93.80	93.80	93.78	93.74	+ .02	93.80	91.55	545
June	....	....	....	93.43	− .23	93.44	92.60	405
Sept	....	....	....	93.17	+ .08	93.09	92.82	137

Est vol 3,771; vol Tues 4,227; open int 37,295, +327.

STERLING (LIFFE)–£500,000; pts of 100%

	Open	High	Low	Settle	Change	High	Low	Open Interest
Dec	89.79	89.82	89.78	89.81	+ .02	90.35	86.52	52,369
Mr92	90.25	90.29	90.24	90.28	+ .04	90.49	86.68	45,849
June	90.34	90.37	90.33	90.36	+ .03	90.46	87.45	34,626
Sept	90.31	90.33	90.29	90.32	+ .02	90.41	87.46	10,853
Dec	90.22	90.23	90.20	90.23	+ .02	90.32	87.55	6,664
Mr93	90.07	90.10	90.07	90.09	+ .02	90.16	87.50	4,548
June	89.97	89.97	89.97	89.98	+ .02	90.09	87.58	2,095
Sept	89.93	89.95	89.93	89.95	+ .02	90.08	88.20	1,746
Dec	89.88	89.90	89.88	89.92	+ .04	90.02	88.95	1,641

Est vol 20,529; vol Tues 20,507; open int 160,391, −1,238.

LONG GILT (LIFFE)–£50,000; 32nds of 100%

	Open	High	Low	Settle	Chg	High	Low	Open Interest
Dec	95-17	95-23	95-09	95-17	+ 0-03	97-17	89-10	43,299
Mr92	95-24	95-24	95-18	94-22	+ 0-05	96-06	94-18	2,524

Est vol 24,368; vol Tues 23,953; open int 45,823, +1,160.

OTHER INTEREST RATE FUTURES

Settlement prices of selected contracts. Volume and open interest of all contract months.

Mortgage-Backed (CBT)–$100,000, pts. & 64ths of 100%
Nov Cpn 8.5 102-04 −6; Est. vol. 0; Open Int. 90
5-Yr. Int. Rate Swap (CBT)–$25 per ½ b.p.; pts of 100%
Dec 92.770 −.010; Est. vol. 50; Open Int. 707
3-Yr. Int. Rate Swap (CBT)–$25 per ½ b.p.; pts of 100%
Dec 93.490 −.010; Est. vol. 0; Open Int. 456
Treas. Auction 5 Yr (FINEX)–$250,000, 100 minus yield
Dec 93.22 −4.0; Est. vol. 100; Open Int. 4

CBT–Chicago Board of Trade. FINEX–Financial Instrument Exchange, a division of the New York Cotton Exchange. IMM–International Monetary Market at Chicago Mercantile Exchange. LIFFE–London International Financial Futures Exchange. MCE–MidAmerica Commodity Exchange.

ently trading. These contracts are the focus of the dominant part of this chapter. The T-bill and Eurodollar futures contracts are on short-term debt instruments and are discussed first. The T-bond (and T-note) futures are written on long-term interest rates and are discussed second. Prior to beginning either discussion, however, it is useful to review the pricing mechanics of the fixed-income securities that underlie these futures contracts.

8.2 UNDERLYING BONDS

Two types of interest rate or fixed-income securities underlie interest rate futures contracts. One type is a *zero-coupon* or a *discount bond*. A discount bond provides no explicit interest payments. It is traded at prices below the face value or par value of the security. Security income results from price appreciation. The other type of fixed-income security is a *coupon-bearing bond*. Like a discount bond, a coupon-bearing bond pays the face or par value at the end of the bond's life. In addition, a coupon-bearing bond has prespecified coupon interest payments at regular intervals throughout the bond's life.

Zero-Coupon or Discount Bonds

The price of a discount bond, B_d, is computed by taking the present value of the promised payment of face value, F_n, at the end of the bond's life, n periods from now, that is,

$$B_d = \frac{F_n}{(1+y)^n},$$ (8.1)

where y is the yield to maturity or rate of return on the bond.

U.S. Treasury bills are discount bonds. T-bills are short-term debt instruments issued by the U.S. Government. New 91-day and 182-day bills are issued every Thursday. New 364-day bills are issued every fourth Thursday. The minimum face value of a T-bill is $10,000.

T-bill quotes are unusual in that their prices are not reported directly. Table 8.3 contains market information about the T-bills that were active on November 13, 1991. Note that, in this table, bid and ask "discounts" appear. These are *bank discount price quotations*. The definition of a bank discount is

$$\text{Bank discount} = (360/n)(100 - B_d),$$ (8.2)

where n is the number of days to maturity of the bill, and B_d is the bill's price expressed as a percentage of par. (Traditionally, bankers have assumed a 360-day year.) To compute the price of the T-bill, simply rearrange equation (8.2) to isolate B_d, that is,

$$B_d = 100 - \text{Bank discount}(n/360).$$ (8.3)

TABLE 8.3 Treasury bond, note, and bill prices.

TREASURY BONDS, NOTES & BILLS

Wednesday, November 13, 1991

Representative Over-the-Counter quotations based on transactions of $1 million or more.

Treasury bond, note and bill quotes are as of mid-afternoon. Colons in bid-and-asked quotes represent 32nds; 101:01 means 101 1/32. Net changes in 32nds. n-Treasury note. Treasury bill quotes in hundredths, quoted on terms of a rate of discount. Days to maturity calculated from settlement date. All yields are to maturity and based on the asked quote. Latest 13-week and 26-week bills are boldfaced. For bonds callable prior to maturity, yields are computed to the earliest call date for issues quoted above par and to the maturity date for issues below par. *-When issued.

Source: Federal Reserve Bank of New York.

U.S. Treasury strips as of 3 p.m. Eastern time, also based on transactions of $1 million or more. Colons in bid-and-asked quotes represent 32nds; 101:01 means 101 1/32. Net changes in 32nds. Yields calculated on the bid quotation. ci-stripped coupon interest. bp-Treasury bond, stripped principal. np-Treasury note, stripped principal. For bonds callable prior to maturity, yields are computed to the earliest call date for issues quoted above par and to the maturity date for issues below par.

Source: Bear, Stearns & Co. via Street Software Technology Inc.

GOVT. BONDS & NOTES

Rate	Maturity Mo/Yr	Bid	Asked	Chg.	Ask Yld.
$6\frac{1}{2}$	Nov 91n	100:00	100:02	....	0.00
$8\frac{1}{2}$	Nov 91n	100:00	100:02	....	0.00
$14\frac{1}{4}$	Nov 91n	100:01	100:03	....	0.00
$7\frac{3}{4}$	Nov 91n	100:04	100:06	....	3.06
$7\frac{5}{8}$	Dec 91n	100:11	100:13	....	4.24
$8\frac{1}{4}$	Dec 91n	100:14	100:16	....	4.10
$11\frac{5}{8}$	Jan 92n	101:03	101:05	– 1	4.43
$8\frac{1}{8}$	Jan 92n	100:22	100:24	– 1	4.40
$6\frac{5}{8}$	Feb 92n	100:13	100:15	....	4.65
$9\frac{1}{8}$	Feb 92n	101:01	101:03	....	4.59
$14\frac{5}{8}$	Feb 92n	102:13	102:15	– 1	4.48
$8\frac{1}{2}$	Feb 92n	101:01	101:03	....	4.61
$7\frac{7}{8}$	Mar 92n	101:03	101:05	– 1	4.69
$8\frac{1}{2}$	Mar 92n	101:11	101:13	....	4.63
$11\frac{3}{4}$	Apr 92n	102:25	102:27	– 2	4.72
$8\frac{7}{8}$	Apr 92n	101:26	101:28	....	4.68
$6\frac{5}{8}$	May 92n	100:27	100:29	....	4.77
9	May 92n	102:00	102:02	– 1	4.78
$13\frac{3}{4}$	May 92n	104:11	104:13	– 1	4.73
$8\frac{1}{2}$	May 92n	101:28	101:30	– 1	4.83
$8\frac{1}{4}$	Jun 92n	102:01	102:03	– 1	4.82
$8\frac{3}{8}$	Jun 92n	102:03	102:05	....	4.84
$10\frac{3}{8}$	Jul 92n	103:16	103:18	....	4.88
8	Jul 92n	102:02	102:04	– 1	4.92
$4\frac{1}{4}$	Aug 87-92	98:13	99:13	– 1	5.07
$7\frac{1}{4}$	Aug 92	101:18	101:22	....	4.94
$7\frac{7}{8}$	Aug 92n	102:00	102:02	– 1	5.04
$8\frac{1}{4}$	Aug 92n	102:09	102:11	– 1	5.03
$8\frac{1}{8}$	Aug 92n	102:11	102:13	– 1	4.99
$8\frac{1}{8}$	Sep 92n	102:18	102:20	– 1	5.02
$8\frac{3}{4}$	Sep 92n	103:03	103:05	– 1	5.02
$9\frac{3}{4}$	Oct 92n	104:04	104:06	– 1	5.02
$7\frac{3}{4}$	Oct 92n	102:12	102:14	– 1	5.11
$7\frac{3}{4}$	Nov 92n	102:15	102:17	– 1	5.12
$8\frac{3}{8}$	Nov 92n	103:02	103:04	– 1	5.13
$10\frac{1}{2}$	Nov 92n	105:04	105:06	– 1	5.11
$7\frac{3}{8}$	Nov 92n	102:06	102:08	– 1	5.13
$7\frac{1}{4}$	Dec 92n	102:06	102:08	....	5.17
$9\frac{1}{8}$	Dec 92n	104:06	104:08	– 1	5.19
$8\frac{3}{4}$	Jan 93n	103:28	103:30	– 2	5.23
7	Jan 93n	101:30	102:00	– 1	5.27
4	Feb 88-93	96:22	97:22	– 1	5.94
$6\frac{3}{4}$	Feb 93	101:22	101:26	– 1	5.24
$7\frac{7}{8}$	Feb 93	103:00	103:04	– 1	5.26
$8\frac{1}{4}$	Feb 93n	103:15	103:17	– 1	5.30
$8\frac{3}{8}$	Feb 93n	103:20	103:22	– 1	5.29
$10\frac{7}{8}$	Feb 93n	106:19	106:21	– 2	5.31
$6\frac{3}{4}$	Feb 93n	101:22	101:24	– 2	5.33
$7\frac{1}{8}$	Mar 93n	102:08	102:10	– 2	5.36
$9\frac{5}{8}$	Mar 93n	105:17	105:19	– 1	5.35
$7\frac{3}{8}$	Apr 93n	102:20	102:22	– 1	5.38
7	Apr 93n	102:05	102:07	– 1	5.40
$7\frac{5}{8}$	May 93n	103:02	103:04	....	5.43
$8\frac{5}{8}$	May 93n	104:15	104:17	....	5.44

Rate	Maturity Mo/Yr	Bid	Asked	Chg.	Ask Yld.
$8\frac{1}{2}$	Jul 97n	107:07	107:09	– 5	6.92
$8\frac{5}{8}$	Aug 97n	107:26	107:28	– 6	6.94
$8\frac{3}{4}$	Oct 97n	108:16	108:18	– 4	6.96
$8\frac{7}{8}$	Nov 97n	109:04	109:06	– 7	6.97
$7\frac{7}{8}$	Jan 98n	104:06	104:08	– 7	7.01
$8\frac{1}{8}$	Feb 98n	105:13	105:15	– 6	7.03
$7\frac{7}{8}$	Apr 98n	104:06	104:08	– 5	7.04
7	May 93-98	100:16	100:24	....	6.47
9	May 98n	109:27	109:29	– 8	7.07
$8\frac{1}{4}$	Jul 98n	105:30	106:00	– 7	7.10
$9\frac{1}{4}$	Aug 98n	111:04	111:06	– 8	7.13
$7\frac{1}{8}$	Oct 98n	100:09	100:11	– 5	7.06
$3\frac{1}{2}$	Nov 98	97:24	98:24	+24	3.70
$8\frac{7}{8}$	Nov 98n	109:09	109:11	– 6	7.15
$8\frac{7}{8}$	Feb 99n	109:09	109:11	– 6	7.20
$8\frac{1}{2}$	May 94-99	105:00	105:08	– 4	6.20
$9\frac{1}{8}$	May 99n	110:23	110:25	– 7	7.24
8	Aug 99n	104:08	104:10	– 6	7.26
$7\frac{7}{8}$	Nov 99n	103:15	103:17	– 6	7.28
$7\frac{7}{8}$	Feb 95-00	102:15	102:19	– 1	6.97
$8\frac{1}{2}$	Feb 00n	107:01	107:03	– 9	7.34
$8\frac{7}{8}$	May 00n	109:06	109:08	–12	7.39
$8\frac{3}{8}$	Aug 95-00	104:18	104:22	– 3	6.93
$8\frac{3}{4}$	Aug 00n	108:12	108:14	–13	7.42
$8\frac{1}{2}$	Nov 00n	106:27	106:29	–13	7.43
$7\frac{3}{4}$	Feb 01n	101:31	102:01	–11	7.44
$11\frac{3}{4}$	Feb 01	128:14	128:18	–10	7.43
8	May 01n	103:22	103:24	–10	7.44
$13\frac{1}{8}$	May 01	138:04	138:08	–13	7.44
$7\frac{7}{8}$	Aug 01n	102:29	102:31	–14	7.44
8	Aug 96-01	103:19	103:23	–15	7.07
$13\frac{3}{8}$	Aug 01	140:16	140:20	– 8	7.44
$7\frac{1}{2}$	Nov 01n*	100:19	100:20	–11	7.41
$15\frac{3}{4}$	Nov 01	157:21	157:25	–10	7.45
$14\frac{1}{4}$	Feb 02	147:25	147:29	–14	7.48
$11\frac{5}{8}$	Nov 02	130:10	130:14	–13	7.51
$10\frac{3}{4}$	Feb 03	123:31	124:03	–12	7.54
$10\frac{3}{4}$	May 03	124:06	124:10	–12	7.55
$11\frac{1}{8}$	Aug 03	127:04	127:08	–15	7.58
$11\frac{7}{8}$	Nov 03	133:07	133:11	–23	7.59
$12\frac{3}{8}$	May 04	137:30	138:02	–29	7.60
$13\frac{3}{4}$	Aug 04	149:07	149:11	–29	7.63
$11\frac{5}{8}$	Nov 04	132:02	132:06	–23	7.67
$8\frac{1}{4}$	May 00-05	104:10	104:14	– 8	7.53
12	May 05	135:23	135:27	–26	7.69
$10\frac{3}{4}$	Aug 05	125:12	125:16	–19	7.71
$9\frac{3}{8}$	Feb 06	114:14	114:18	–18	7.68
$7\frac{5}{8}$	Feb 02-07	99:20	99:24	–16	7.65
$7\frac{7}{8}$	Nov 02-07	101:14	101:18	–16	7.66
$8\frac{3}{8}$	Aug 03-08	104:28	105:00	–12	7.72
$8\frac{3}{4}$	Nov 03-08	107:19	107:23	–19	7.75
$9\frac{1}{8}$	May 04-09	110:21	110:25	–24	7.76
$10\frac{3}{8}$	Nov 04-09	120:28	121:00	–24	7.78
$11\frac{3}{4}$	Feb 05-10	132:10	132:14	–25	7.78

Mat.	Type	Bid	Asked	Chg.	Bid Yld.
Nov 99	np	55:03	55:07	– 7	7.59
Feb 00	ci	53:28	54:00	– 8	7.64
Feb 00	np	53:22	53:27	– 9	7.68
May 00	ci	52:28	53:00	– 7	7.64
May 00	np	52:22	52:27	– 7	7.68
Aug 00	ci.	51:26	51:30	– 7	7.66
Aug 00	np	51:23	51:27	– 7	7.68
Nov 00	ci	50:24	50:28	– 8	7.68
Nov 00	np	50:24	50:28	– 7	7.68
Feb 01	ci	49:14	49:19	– 7	7.76
Feb 01	np	49:09	49:13	– 8	7.80
May 01	ci	48:14	48:18	– 8	7.78
May 01	np	48:08	48:12	– 9	7.82
Aug 01	ci	47:16	47:21	– 9	7.78
Aug 01	np	47:11	47:15	– 8	7.82
Nov 01	ci	46:20	46:24	– 7	7.78
Feb 02	ci	45:09	45:13	– 12	7.88
May 02	ci	44:11	44:15	– 11	7.90
Aug 02	ci	43:12	43:17	– 12	7.92
Nov 02	ci	42:15	42:19	– 11	7.94
Feb 03	ci	41:16	41:21	– 12	7.97
May 03	ci	40:21	40:26	– 12	7.98
Aug 03	ci	39:27	39:31	– 11	7.99
Nov 03	ci	39:00	39:05	– 12	8.00
Feb 04	ci	38:04	38:08	– 11	8.03
May 04	ci	37:09	37:13	– 12	8.05
Aug 04	ci	36:16	36:21	– 12	8.06
Nov 04	ci	35:24	35:28	– 12	8.07
Nov 04	bp	35:23	35:27	– 11	8.08
Feb 05	ci	34:31	35:03	– 11	8.09
May 05	ci	34:08	34:12	– 11	8.10
May 05	bp	34:09	34:13	– 11	8.09
Aug 05	ci	33:18	33:22	– 11	8.10
Aug 05	bp	33:19	33:24	– 12	8.09
Nov 05	ci	32:29	33:01	– 11	8.10
Feb 06	ci	32:05	32:10	– 12	8.12
Feb 06	bp	32:04	32:08	– 11	8.13
May 06	ci	31:17	31:21	– 11	8.12
Aug 06	ci	30:29	31:01	– 11	8.12
Nov 06	ci	30:10	30:14	– 11	8.12
Feb 07	ci	29:16	29:20	– 12	8.17
May 07	ci	28:29	29:01	– 12	8.17
Aug 07	ci	28:11	28:15	– 12	8.17
Nov 07	ci	27:25	27:29	– 12	8.17
Feb 08	ci	27:03	27:07	– 11	8.20
May 08	ci	26:15	26:19	– 11	8.22
Aug 08	ci	25:30	26:02	– 11	8.22
Nov 08	ci	25:14	25:18	– 10	8.22
Feb 09	ci	24:25	24:29	– 11	8.25
May 09	ci	24:10	24:13	– 10	8.25
Aug 09	ci	23:26	23:30	– 10	8.25
Nov 09	ci	23:11	23:15	– 10	8.25
Nov 09	bp	22:30	23:02	– 9	8.35
Feb 10	ci	22:28	23:00	– 10	8.25
May 10	ci	22:13	22:17	– 10	8.25
Aug 10	ci	21:30	22:01	– 10	8.26
Nov 10	ci	21:15	21:19	– 11	8.26
Feb 11	ci	21:02	21:05	– 10	8.26
May 11	ci	20:20	20:24	– 10	8.26
Aug 11	ci	20:07	20:11	– 10	8.26
Nov 11	ci	19:26	19:30	– 10	8.26
Feb 12	ci	19:12	19:16	– 10	8.27
May 12	ci	19:00	19:03	– 9	8.27
Aug 12	ci	18:20	18:23	– 9	8.27
Nov 12	ci	18:08	18:11	– 9	8.27
Feb 13	ci	17:28	17:31	– 9	8.27
May 13	ci	17:16	17:20	– 10	8.27
Aug 13	ci	17:05	17:09	– 9	8.27
Nov 13	ci	16:26	16:30	– 9	8.27
Feb 14	ci	16:15	16:19	– 9	8.27
May 14	ci	16:05	16:08	– 9	8.27
Aug 14	ci	15:26	15:30	– 9	8.27
Nov 14	ci	15:16	15:20	– 9	8.27
Feb 15	ci	15:06	15:10	– 9	8.27
Feb 15	bp	15:07	15:11	– 8	8.26
May 15	ci	14:29	15:00	– 8	8.27

TABLE 8.3   continued

Coupon	Maturity	Bid	Asked	Chg.	Yld.
10 1/8	May 93n	106:18	106:20	− 2	5.46
6 3/4	May 93n	101:26	101:28	− 1	5.47
7	Jun 93n	102:08	102:10	− 1	5.49
8 1/8	Jun 93n	103:31	104:01	− 1	5.50
7 1/4	Jul 93n	102:21	102:23	− 1	5.52
6 7/8	Jul 93n	102:02	102:04	− 1	5.56
7 1/2	Aug 88-93	100:20	100:24	+ 2	7.04
8	Aug 93n	103:30	104:00	....	5.57
8 5/8	Aug 93	104:30	105:02	....	5.55
8 3/4	Aug 93n	105:05	105:07	....	5.58
11 7/8	Aug 93n	110:11	110:13	....	5.56
6 3/8	Aug 93n	101:09	101:11	....	5.58
6 1/8	Sep 93n	100:27	100:29	− 1	5.61
8 1/4	Sep 93n	104:19	104:21	− 1	5.60
7 1/8	Oct 93n	102:21	102:23	− 1	5.61
6	Oct 93n	100:21	100:23	....	5.61
7 3/4	Nov 93n	103:27	103:29	− 1	5.66
8 5/8	Nov 93	105:15	105:19	+ 1	5.63
9	Nov 93n	106:05	106:07	− 1	5.67
11 3/4	Nov 93n	111:10	111:12	− 1	5.65
7 5/8	Dec 93n	103:24	103:26	− 1	5.70
7	Jan 94n	102:15	102:17	− 2	5.74
6 7/8	Feb 94n	102:09	102:11	....	5.75
8 7/8	Feb 94n	106:10	106:12	− 3	5.81
9	Feb 94	106:18	106:22	− 2	5.79
8 1/2	Mar 94n	105:24	105:26	− 2	5.84
7	Apr 94n	102:19	102:21	− 1	5.81
4 1/8	May 89-94	96:24	97:24	− 3	5.09
7	May 94n	102:17	102:19	− 2	5.87
9 1/2	May 94n	108:06	108:08	− 3	5.90
13 1/8	May 94n	116:17	116:19	− 3	5.89
8 1/2	Jun 94n	106:03	106:05	− 1	5.93
8	Jul 94n	104:30	105:00	− 2	5.95
6 7/8	Aug 94n	102:08	102:10	− 2	5.95
8 5/8	Aug 94n	106:16	106:18	− 2	6.00
8 3/4	Aug 94	106:25	106:29	− 2	5.99
12 5/8	Aug 94n	116:17	116:19	− 2	5.99
8 1/2	Sep 94n	106:12	106:14	− 1	6.03
9 1/2	Oct 94n	109:00	109:02	− 2	6.06
6	Nov 94n*	100:00	100:01	− 2	5.99
8 1/4	Nov 94n	105:27	105:29	− 2	6.07
10 1/8	Nov 94n	110:28	111:00	− 3	6.06
11 5/8	Nov 94n	114:31	115:01	− 2	6.07
7 5/8	Dec 94n	104:10	104:12	− 2	6.07
8 5/8	Jan 95n	106:30	107:00	− 2	6.16
3	Feb 95	97:00	98:00	− 3	3.66
7 3/4	Feb 95n	104:17	104:19	− 3	6.17
10 1/2	Feb 95	112:10	112:14	− 3	6.22
11 1/4	Feb 95	114:17	114:19	− 5	6.22
8 3/8	Apr 95n	106:08	106:10	− 4	6.29
8 1/2	May 95n	106:24	106:26	− 2	6.30
10 3/8	May 95	112:14	112:18	− 3	6.32
11 1/4	May 95	115:03	115:05	− 4	6.35
12 5/8	May 95	119:14	119:18	− 2	6.31
8 7/8	Jul 95n	107:28	107:30	− 4	6.41
8 1/2	Aug 95n	106:24	106:26	− 4	6.43
10 1/2	Aug 95n	113:07	113:09	− 4	6.46
8 5/8	Oct 95n	107:08	107:10	− 4	6.48
8 1/2	Nov 95n	106:28	106:30	− 4	6.50
9 1/2	Nov 95n	110:10	110:12	− 6	6.51
11 1/2	Nov 95	117:12	117:16	− 4	6.47
9 1/4	Jan 96n	109:18	109:20	− 5	6.57
7 1/2	Jan 96n	103:09	103:11	− 5	6.58
7 7/8	Feb 96n	104:18	104:20	− 5	6.61
8 7/8	Feb 96n	108:07	108:09	− 6	6.61
7 1/2	Feb 96n	103:07	103:09	− 5	6.61
7 3/4	Mar 96n	104:03	104:05	− 5	6.64
9 3/8	Apr 96n	110:08	110:10	− 5	6.64
7 5/8	Apr 96n	103:22	103:24	− 5	6.64
7 3/4	May 96n	102:22	102:24	− 5	6.66
7 5/8	May 96n	103:21	103:23	− 5	6.66
7 7/8	Jun 96n	104:18	104:20	− 5	6.70
7 7/8	Jul 96n	104:19	104:21	− 6	6.70
7 7/8	Jul 96n	104:23	104:25	− 5	6.68
7 1/4	Aug 96n	102:06	102:08	− 5	6.69
7	Sep 96n	101:06	101:08	− 5	6.70
8	Oct 96n	105:06	105:08	− 5	6.73
6 7/8	Oct 96n	100:26	100:28	− 5	6.66
7 1/4	Nov 96n	102:04	102:06	− 5	6.73
8	Jan 97n	105:04	105:06	− 5	6.79
8 1/2	Apr 97n	107:07	107:09	− 5	6.87
8 1/2	May 97n	107:07	107:09	− 5	6.89

Coupon	Maturity	Bid	Asked	Chg.	Yld.
10	May 05-10	118:15	118:19	− 23	7.75
12 3/4	Nov 05-10	141:24	141:28	− 29	7.79
13 7/8	May 06-11	152:06	152:10	− 30	7.79
14	Nov 06-11	154:08	154:12	− 31	7.79
10 3/8	Nov 07-12	122:13	122:17	− 25	7.87
12	Aug 08-13	137:25	137:29	− 30	7.88
13 1/4	May 09-14	150:07	150:11	− 36	7.89
12 1/2	Aug 09-14	143:13	143:17	− 34	7.90
11 3/4	Nov 09-14	136:27	136:31	− 35	7.87
11 1/4	Feb 15	135:01	135:05	− 36	7.92
10 5/8	Aug 15	128:19	128:23	− 33	7.92
9 7/8	Nov 15	120:23	120:25	− 30	7.93
9 1/4	Feb 16	113:30	114:00	− 33	7.94
7 1/4	May 16	92:21	92:23	− 27	7.93
7 1/2	Nov 16	95:07	95:09	− 28	7.94
8 3/4	May 17	108:25	108:27	− 31	7.94
8 7/8	Aug 17	110:05	110:07	− 31	7.94
9 1/8	May 18	113:00	113:02	− 32	7.94
9	Nov 18	111:21	111:23	− 32	7.94
8 7/8	Feb 19	110:09	110:11	− 32	7.94
8 1/8	Aug 19	101:31	102:01	− 30	7.94
8 1/2	Feb 20	106:06	106:08	− 32	7.94
8 3/4	May 20	109:02	109:04	− 32	7.94
8 3/4	Aug 20	109:02	109:04	− 30	7.94
7 7/8	Feb 21	99:07	99:09	− 30	7.94
8 1/8	May 21	102:04	102:06	− 31	7.93
8 1/8	Aug 21	102:09	102:11	− 30	7.92
8	Nov 21*	101:12	101:13	− 28	7.88

U.S. TREASURY STRIPS

Mat.	Type	Bid	Asked	Chg.	Bid Yld.
Feb 92	ci	98:26	98:26	+ 1	4.87
May 92	ci	97:18	97:19	− 1	4.99
Aug 92	ci	96:11	96:11	− 1	5.04
Nov 92	ci	95:04	95:05	− 2	5.05
Feb 93	ci	93:19	93:20	− 1	5.38
May 93	ci	92:08	92:09	− 1	5.46
Aug 93	ci	90:26	90:27	− 3	5.59
Nov 93	ci	89:13	89:15	− 2	5.68
Feb 94	ci	87:24	87:26	− 1	5.89
May 94	ci	86:13	86:15	− 1	5.93
Aug 94	ci	84:30	85:00	− 3	6.03
Nov 94	ci	83:12	83:15	− 3	6.15
Nov 94	np	83:08	83:11	− 3	6.20
Feb 95	ci	81:18	81:20	− 4	6.37
Feb 95	np	81:24	81:26	− 4	6.30
May 95	ci	80:02	80:05	− 5	6.45
May 95	np	80:01	80:03	− 4	6.47
Aug 95	ci	78:20	78:22	− 4	6.52
Aug 95	np	78:14	78:17	− 5	6.58
Nov 95	ci	77:08	77:11	− 5	6.56
Nov 95	np	77:02	77:05	− 5	6.62
Feb 96	ci	75:14	75:17	− 5	6.74
Feb 96	np	75:09	75:12	− 5	6.79
May 96	ci	74:04	74:07	− 5	6.77
May 96	np	74:01	74:05	− 6	6.79
Aug 96	ci	72:19	72:22	− 5	6.86
Nov 96	ci	71:14	71:17	− 6	6.84
Nov 96	np	70:10	70:13	− 3	7.17
Feb 97	ci	69:20	69:23	− 4	7.02
May 97	ci	68:07	68:10	− 3	7.08
May 97	np	68:05	68:09	− 4	7.09
Aug 97	ci	66:27	66:31	− 4	7.13
Aug 97	np	66:26	66:29	− 3	7.14
Nov 97	ci	65:24	65:28	− 1	7.11
Nov 97	np	65:18	65:22	− 4	7.16
Feb 98	ci	63:31	64:02	− 8	7.28
Feb 98	np	63:23	63:27	− 4	7.34
May 98	ci	62:24	62:28	− 4	7.30
May 98	np	62:16	62:20	− 4	7.36
Aug 98	ci	61:15	61:19	− 8	7.34
Aug 98	np	61:06	61:10	− 4	7.41
Nov 98	ci	60:12	60:16	− 8	7.34
Nov 98	np	60:05	60:09	− 7	7.39
Feb 99	ci	58:19	58:23	− 7	7.55
May 99	ci	57:14	57:18	− 7	7.53
May 99	np	57:09	57:13	− 8	7.57
Aug 99	ci	56:07	56:11	− 7	7.57
Aug 99	np	56:04	56:08	− 7	7.59
Nov 99	ci	55:06	55:10	− 8	7.57

Mat.	Type	Bid	Asked	Chg.	Yld.
Aug 15	ci	14:19	14:22	− 9	8.27
Aug 15	bp	14:20	14:23	− 8	8.26
Nov 15	ci	14:10	14:13	− 8	8.27
Nov 15	bp	14:11	14:14	− 7	8.26
Feb 16	ci	14:00	14:04	− 9	8.27
Feb 16	bp	14:03	14:06	− 8	8.25
May 16	ci	13:23	13:27	− 9	8.27
May 16	bp	14:00	14:03	− 8	8.19
Aug 16	ci	13:15	13:18	− 8	8.27
Nov 16	ci	13:06	13:09	− 8	8.27
Nov 16	bp	13:12	13:15	− 6	8.21
Feb 17	ci	12:31	13:02	− 8	8.26
May 17	ci	12:22	12:25	− 8	8.26
May 17	bp	12:26	12:29	− 8	8.22
Aug 17	ci	12:14	12:17	− 8	8.26
Aug 17	bp	12:18	12:21	− 8	8.22
Nov 17	ci	12:05	12:08	− 8	8.27
Feb 18	ci	11:31	12:02	− 8	8.25
May 18	ci	11:24	11:26	− 7	8.25
May 18	bp	11:27	11:30	− 8	8.21
Aug 18	ci	11:16	11:19	− 8	8.25
Nov 18	ci	11:09	11:12	− 7	8.25
Nov 18	bp	11:12	11:15	− 9	8.21
Feb 19	ci	11:03	11:06	− 8	8.23
Feb 19	bp	11:08	11:11	− 8	8.18
May 19	ci	10:29	11:00	− 8	8.22
Aug 19	ci	10:22	10:25	− 8	8.22
Aug 19	bp	10:27	10:30	− 7	8.17
Nov 19	ci	10:16	10:19	− 8	8.21
Feb 20	ci	10:11	10:13	− 7	8.20
Feb 20	bp	10:14	10:17	− 7	8.16
May 20	ci	10:05	10:08	− 7	8.19
May 20	bp	10:08	10:10	− 7	8.16
Aug 20	ci	9:30	10:01	− 7	8.19
Aug 20	bp	10:02	10:05	− 9	8.15
Nov 20	ci	9:26	9:28	− 7	8.17
Feb 21	ci	9:20	9:22	− 7	8.17
Feb 21	bp	9:23	9:26	− 8	8.13
May 21	ci	9:16	9:19	− 7	8.14
May 21	bp	9:19	9:21	− 7	8.11
Aug 21	ci	9:19	9:21	− 7	8.04
Aug 21	bp	9:18	9:20	− 9	8.05
Nov 21	bp	9:19	9:22	− 6	7.97

TREASURY BILLS

Maturity	Days to Mat.	Bid	Asked	Chg.	Ask Yld.
Nov 21 '91	6	4.68	4.58	−0.02	4.65
Nov 29 '91	14	4.54	4.44	−0.01	4.52
Dec 05 '91	20	4.41	4.31	−0.03	4.39
Dec 12 '91	27	4.36	4.26	−0.08	4.34
Dec 19 '91	34	4.39	4.35	−0.05	4.43
Dec 26 '91	41	4.40	4.36	−0.04	4.45
Jan 02 '92	48	4.43	4.39	−0.02	4.49
Jan 09 '92	55	4.50	4.46	−0.02	4.57
Jan 16 '92	62	4.55	4.53	−0.01	4.63
Jan 23 '92	69	4.57	4.55	−0.01	4.67
Jan 30 '92	76	4.57	4.55	−0.01	4.67
Feb 06 '92	83	4.62	4.60	....	4.73
Feb 13 '92	90	4.63	4.61	....	4.73
Feb 20 '92	97	4.62	4.60	....	4.74
Feb 27 '92	104	4.62	4.60	....	4.74
Mar 05 '92	111	4.64	4.62	....	4.76
Mar 12 '92	118	4.66	4.64	+0.01	4.79
Mar 19 '92	125	4.66	4.64	+0.01	4.79
Mar 26 '92	132	4.64	4.62	....	4.78
Apr 02 '92	139	4.66	4.64	....	4.80
Apr 09 '92	146	4.69	4.67	....	4.84
Apr 16 '92	153	4.69	4.67	+0.01	4.84
Apr 23 '92	160	4.72	4.70	....	4.88
Apr 30 '92	167	4.68	4.66	....	4.84
May 07 '92	174	4.72	4.70	+0.02	4.89
May 14 '92	181	4.70	4.68	−0.01	4.87
Jun 04 '92	202	4.65	4.63	+0.02	4.82
Jul 02 '92	230	4.71	4.69	+0.01	4.89
Jul 30 '92	258	4.74	4.72	+0.03	4.93
Aug 27 '92	286	4.74	4.72	+0.02	4.94
Sep 24 '92	314	4.73	4.71	+0.04	4.94
Oct 22 '92	342	4.75	4.73	+0.03	4.98

To illustrate the bank discount convention, consider the T-bill in Table 8.3 that matures on February 13, 1992. If this bill is purchased, it would be at the ask price,[1] as reflected by the ask discount of 4.61. The number of days to maturity of this bill is 92. Therefore, the ask price of the bill is

$$B_d = 100 - 4.61(92/360) = 98.822$$

percent of par. If the par value is $10,000, the price of the T-bill is $9,882.20.

To compare the rate of return on the T-bill with the rate of return on other instruments, the *effective annual rate of return* is often computed. If the price of a 92-day T-bill is 98.822, the effective annual rate of return compounded on a daily basis[2] is

$$r = (100/98.822)^{365/92} - 1 = 4.81\%.$$

Eurodollar certificates of deposit (CD's) are also discount bonds. Eurodollar deposits are U.S. dollar deposits in any foreign bank, although Eurodollar deposits are most typically thought of as being U.S. dollar deposits in London. The rate on these CD's is referred to as the *London Interbank Offer Rate* (LIBOR). The usual denomination of Eurodollar CD's is $1,000,000. The usual maturities are in the three- to six-month range, however, maturities as long as five years are not uncommon. Simple interest on Eurodollar deposits is calculated for the actual number of days on a 360-day year basis and is paid at maturity on deposits with terms of less than one year. For longer-term deposits, interest is paid annually.[3]

Sample Eurodollar rates are contained in Table 8.4. The rates reported are averages of the rates quoted by five major banks in London. The three-month rate, for example, is reported to be 5⅛ percent. That implies that a $1,000,000 Eurodollar deposit on November 13, 1991, will be worth $1,000,000 + 1,000,000(.05125)(90/360), or $1,012,812.50, on February 11, 1992.[4] The effective annual rate of return on this investment may be computed as follows:

$$r = (1,012,812.50/1,000,000)^{365/90} - 1 = 5.30\%.$$

Note that although this Eurodollar deposit has approximately the same maturity as the T-bill in the previous example, the effective annual rate of return is 49 basis

---

[1] The bid/ask spread is the cost of immediate trade execution. A market-maker stands ready to buy immediately at her bid price and sell immediately at her ask price. The bid/ask spread is her compensation for providing market liquidity.
[2] The effective annual return compounded continuously is $r = \ln(100/98.822)(365/92) = 4.70\%$.
[3] For more information on Eurodollar certificates of deposit, see Stigum (1990).
[4] The number of days from November 13, 1991, to February 11, 1992, is 90.

TABLE 8.4 Money market rates.

MONEY RATES

Wednesday, November 13, 1991

The key U.S. and foreign annual interest rates below are a guide to general levels but don't always represent actual transactions.

PRIME RATE: 7½%. The base rate on corporate loans at large U.S. money center commercial banks.

FEDERAL FUNDS: 5⅛% high, 2% low, 2% near closing bid, 2½% offered. Reserves traded among commercial banks for overnight use in amounts of $1 million or more. Source: Babcock Fulton Prebon (U.S.A.) Inc.

DISCOUNT RATE: 4.50%. The charge on loans to depository institutions by the Federal Reserve Banks.

CALL MONEY: 6¾% to 7%. The charge on loans to brokers on stock exchange collateral.

COMMERCIAL PAPER placed directly by General Electric Capital Corp.: 4.85% 15 to 36 days; 4.70% 37 to 59 days; 4.93% 60 to 89 days; 4.90% 90 to 149 days; 4.87% 150 to 179 days; 4.70% 180 to 189 days; 4.87% 190 to 270 days. Commercial Paper placed directly by General Motors Acceptance Corp.: 4.85% 30 to 44 days; 4.80% 45 to 59 days; 5% 60 to 270 days.

COMMERCIAL PAPER: High-grade unsecured notes sold through dealers by major corporations in multiples of $1,000: 5% 30 days; 5.10% 60 days; 5.02% 90 days.

CERTIFICATES OF DEPOSIT: 4.48% one month; 4.61% two months; 4.60% three months; 4.62% six months; 4.98% one year. Average of top rates paid by major New York banks on primary new issues of negotiable C.D.s, usually in amounts of $1 million and more. The minimum unit is $100,-000. Typical rates in the secondary market: 4.90% one month; 5% three months; 5% six months.

BANKERS ACCEPTANCES: 4.80% 30 days; 5.03% 60 days; 4.91% 90 days; 4.87% 120 days; 4.85% 150 days; 4.81% 180 days. Negotiable, bank-backed business credit instruments typically financing an import order.

LONDON LATE EURODOLLARS: 5% - 4⅞% one month; 5¼% - 5⅛% two months; 5 3/16% - 5 1/16% three months; 5 3/16% - 5 1/16% four months; 5 3/16% - 5 1/16% five months; 5⅛% - 5% six months.

LONDON INTERBANK OFFERED RATES (LIBOR): 4 15/16% one month; 5⅛% three months; 5⅛% six months; 5¼% one year. The average of interbank offered rates for dollar deposits in the London market based on quotations at five major banks. Effective rate for contracts entered into two days from date appearing at top of this column.

FOREIGN PRIME RATES: Canada 8.50%; Germany 11.50%; Japan 7%; Switzerland 10%; Britain 10.50%. These rate indications aren't directly comparable; lending practices vary widely by location.

TREASURY BILLS: Results of the Tuesday, November 12, 1991, auction of short-term U.S. government bills, sold at a discount from face value in units of $10,000 to $1 million: 4.64% 13 weeks; 4.71% 26 weeks.

FEDERAL HOME LOAN MORTGAGE CORP. (Freddie Mac): Posted yields on 30-year mortgage commitments. Delivery within 30 days 8.54%, 60 days 8.60%, standard conventional fixed-rate mortgages; 6%, 2% rate capped one-year adjustable rate mortgages. Source: Telerate Systems Inc.

FEDERAL NATIONAL MORTGAGE ASSOCIATION (Fannie Mae): Posted yields on 30 year mortgage commitments for delivery within 30 days (priced at par): 8.47%, standard conventional fixed rate-mortgages; 6.10%, 6/2 rate capped one-year adjustable rate mortgages. Source: Telerate Systems Inc.

MERRILL LYNCH READY ASSETS TRUST: 4.90%. Annualized average rate of return after expenses for the past 30 days; not a forecast of future returns.

Source: Reprinted by permission of *Wall Street Journal,* © (November 14, 1991) Dow Jones & Company, Inc. All Rights Reserved Worldwide.

points higher.[5] This reflects the higher default risk of these deposits vis-à-vis U.S. government securities.

T-bills and CD's are short-term discount bonds. Table 8.3 also contains prices of Treasury strips, which are long-term discount bonds. Strips get their name from the fact that, for each year, coupons of several government coupon bonds are "stripped" from the principal and combined to create a discount bond that makes only one payment. Table 8.3 provides the prices and yields to maturity for these bonds.

Coupon Bonds

The price of a coupon-bearing bond, B, is computed by summing the present values of the fixed periodic coupon payments, C_t, and the present value of the terminal face value, F_n, that is,

$$B = \sum_{t=1}^{n} \frac{C_t}{(1+y)^t} + \frac{F_n}{(1+y)^n}. \tag{8.4}$$

In general, the coupon payments are the same fixed amount each period, so the bond price may also be written as the present value of an annuity plus the present value of the final amount:

$$B = (C/y)[1 - (1+y)^{-n}] + F(1+y)^{-n}. \tag{8.5}$$

The Treasury bonds and notes in Table 8.3 are coupon-bearing bonds. Treasury notes are issued with maturities of two to ten years and Treasury bonds with maturities longer than ten years. The denominations of bonds and notes range from $1,000 to $1 million. Their prices are quoted as a percentage of par, so a reported price of 96:00 for a $100,000 face-value bond is actually 96 percent of $100,000 or $96,000. In addition, the decimal part of a T-bond or T-note price is the number of 32nds, so a reported price of 94:8 is actually $94\frac{8}{32}$, or 94.25 in decimal form. Finally, all T-bonds and T-notes have semiannual coupon payments. The "9s of November 2018" in Table 8.3, for example, pay coupon interest at a rate of 4.5 percent of par in May and November of each year. The last coupon is paid with the repayment of the face value in November 2018.[6]

The fact that Treasury bonds pay semiannual coupons implies that the yield to maturity, y, in (8.4) and (8.5) is an effective rate over a six-month period. To annualize this rate, the *effective annual yield to maturity*, y_A, may be computed as

---

[5] A basis point is 1/100 of one percent.

[6] Fabozzi and Fabozzi (1989, pp. 83–84) provide a summary of the various types of bill, note, and bond issues of the U.S. government.

$$y_A = (1+y)^2 - 1. \tag{8.6}$$

While (8.6) is technically correct, some people prefer to use the *bond equivalent yield*, which is simply $2 \times y$, to measure of the expected annual rate of return on the bond.[7]

One last convention about Treasury bonds and notes must be discussed. The bond price reported in the financial press (i.e., the *quoted bond price*) excludes the *accrued interest* of the current coupon period. The price that you would pay for the bond if you decided to buy it would be the quoted price plus the coupon interest that has accrued on a straight-line basis during the current coupon period. That is, accrued interest equals the proportion of the current coupon period that has elapsed times the amount of the coupon,

$$AI = C \left(\frac{\text{number of days since last coupon was paid}}{\text{total number of days in current coupon period}} \right). \tag{8.7}$$

To illustrate, consider the 9s of November 2018, whose price is reported in Table 8.3. The bond is reported to have a bid price of 111:21 and an ask price of 111:23. Treasury bonds pay coupon interest every six months and do so on the 15th of the month. For the 9s of November 2018, coupon interest of 4.5 percent of par is paid on May 15th and November 15th. On November 13, 1991, the number of days since the last coupon payment is 182. The total number of days from May 15, 1991, to November 15, 1991, is 184. The accrued interest on this bond as of November 13 is, therefore, 4.5(182/184) or 4.45. If this bond were bought at the ask price, we would pay the reported ask price of $111^{23}\!/\!32$ plus accrued interest of 4.45, or a total amount 116.17.

To verify that 116.17 is actually the ask price of the 9s of November 2018, compute the present value of the promised coupons and face value as of November 13, 1991, using the reported bond equivalent yield of 7.94 percent. We cannot apply the bond valuation formulas (8.4) and (8.5) directly because those formulas assume that the next coupon payment is in exactly six months. For the 9s of November 2018, we are part way through the coupon period, so the bond valuation formula needs to be modified:

$$B = \frac{1}{(1+y)^p} \left[\sum_{t=0}^{n-1} \frac{C_t}{(1+y)^t} + \frac{F_n}{(1+y)^{n-1}} \right], \tag{8.8}$$

where p is the ratio of the number of days remaining in the current coupon period to the total number of days during the current coupon period. The term in brackets

---

[7] Yet others rely on *coupon yield*, which is simply the annual coupon amount divided by the bond price.

represents the present value, just prior to the next coupon, of all future payments to the bondholder. This amount is then discounted back p coupon periods to the current date. Substituting the example parameters,

$$B = \frac{1}{(1.0397)^{2/184}} \left[\sum_{t=0}^{54} \frac{4.50}{(1.0397)^t} + \frac{100}{(1.0397)^{54}} \right] = 116.17.$$

Subtracting the accrued interest yields the quoted ask price of the bond reported in Table 8.3.

Finally, some Treasury bonds do not have a fixed maturity date. The issues denoted by the hyphenated maturity date in Table 8.3 are *callable bonds,* which the Treasury has the right to "call," or redeem, at any time during a prespecified period in the future. The 11¾ of August 2009-14, for example, are callable bonds which may be redeemed during the period November 2009 through 2014. Callable bonds may be delivered on certain futures contracts, as long as they satisfy some minimum amount of time before the first call date.

8.3 INTEREST RATE RISK

Bondholders (lenders) face the risk that interest rates will rise, causing a decline in the value of their bonds. Bond issuers (borrowers) face the risk that interest rates will fall, causing an increase in the value of their debt obligation. Interest rate risk is a key concern of all financial institutions that operate in the debt markets. These include banks, pension funds, and insurance companies. In this section, we analyze the risk of the default-free fixed income securities (such as U.S. Treasury securities) that these institutions hold.[8]

Duration
One measure of a fixed income security's interest rate risk is its *duration.* Duration specifies the sensitivity of the bond price to movements in yield. A specific formula for computing duration may be obtained by taking the derivative of B with respect to y in equation (8.4). First, for the sake of mathematical convenience, rewrite (8.4) as

$$B = \sum_{t=1}^{n} C_t(1+y)^{-t}. \tag{8.9}$$

---

[8] Default risk is also an important consideration in fixed-income security risk management. Recall that in Chapter 4, we showed how to hedge both the interest rate and default risk exposure of Mobil Oil bonds using T-bond and stock index futures contracts.

Under this specification, we let $C_t = C$ for $t = 1, \cdots, n - 1$ and $C_t = C + F_n$ for $t = n$. Now, take the derivative of B with respect to y,

$$\frac{dB}{dy} = -\sum_{t=1}^{n} tC_t(1+y)^{-t-1}. \tag{8.10}$$

Multiply (8.10) by $(1 + y)$,

$$(1+y)\frac{dB}{dy} = -\sum_{t=1}^{n} tC_t(1+y)^{-t}. \tag{8.11}$$

Finally, divide (8.11) by B,

$$\frac{dB/B}{dy/(1+y)} = -\sum_{t=1}^{n} t\left[\frac{C_t(1+y)^{-t}}{B}\right] = -\sum_{t=1}^{n} tw_t \equiv -D, \tag{8.12}$$

where $w_t = C_t(1 + y)^{-t}/B$ and where duration is defined as

$$D \equiv \sum_{t=1}^{n} tw_t. \tag{8.13}$$

Equations (8.12) and (8.13) tell us two important things about duration. First, as the left-hand side of (8.12) indicates, minus duration, $-D$, can be interpreted as the percentage change in the bond price, dB/B, induced by a change in the bond's yield to maturity, dy, scaled by $1/(1 + y)$. Second, duration is the *weighted average time to maturity* of a bond, where the weights, w_t, are the present values of the payments in each period.[9] For coupon bonds, duration is less than time to maturity because some of the bond payments—the coupons—are received in years prior to maturity of the bond. For non-coupon bonds, duration equals time to maturity.

The scale factor $1/(1 + y)$ on the left-hand side of (8.12) is cumbersome to account for. Most fixed income portfolio managers prefer to use a measure of dura-

---

[9]Note that by virtue of equation (8.9), the weights, w_t, sum to one, that is,

$$\sum_{t=1}^{n} w_t = \sum_{t=1}^{n} \frac{C_t(1+y)^{-t}}{B} = \frac{B}{B} = 1.$$

tion that is simply the percentage change in bond price, dB/B, induced by a change in yield, dy. To find this expression, divide (8.12) by $(1 + y)$,

$$\frac{dB/B}{dy} = -\sum_{t=1}^{n} tw_t/(1+y) = -D/(1+y) \equiv -D_m. \qquad \textbf{(8.14)}$$

D_m is called *modified duration* and is more commonly used in interest risk management strategies. It is simply the duration, as defined in (8.13), divided by $(1 + y)$. We use modified duration in a hedging application later in this chapter. We now turn to a numerical example that uses the duration formulas (8.13) and (8.14).

EXAMPLE 8.1

What is the duration and the modified duration of an 8 percent, ten-year, $1000 bond, assuming annual coupon payments and a required yield to maturity of 7 percent?

From equation (8.4), we know the bond price is

$$B = \sum_{t=1}^{10} \frac{80}{(1.07)^t} + \frac{1,000}{(1.07)^{10}} = \$1,070.24.$$

This present value consists of the present value of 10 payments. In tabular form,

t	C_t	$(1+y)^{-t}$	$C_t(1+y)^{-t}$	w_t	tw_t
1	80.00	0.9346	74.77	0.0699	0.0699
2	80.00	0.8734	69.88	0.0653	0.1306
3	80.00	0.8163	65.30	0.0610	0.1831
4	80.00	0.7629	61.03	0.0570	0.2281
5	80.00	0.7130	57.04	0.0533	0.2665
6	80.00	0.6663	53.31	0.0498	0.2989
7	80.00	0.6227	49.82	0.0466	0.3259
8	80.00	0.5820	46.56	0.0435	0.3480
9	80.00	0.5439	43.51	0.0407	0.3659
10	1080.00	0.5083	549.02	0.5130	5.1299
Total			1,070.24	1.0000	7.3466

The duration of the bond is 7.3466, and the modified duration is 7.3466/1.07 = 6.8660.

The modified duration figure computed in the example predicts that if interest rates increase by 100 basis points, the bond price will change by

$$dB/B = -D_m \times dy = -6.8660 \times .01 = -6.8660\%.$$

Conversely, a decrease in yield of 100 basis points implies a 6.8660% increase in bond price.

The formula for the duration of a bond shows that duration—price sensitivity—depends on the maturity of the bond, on the coupon level, and on the yield to maturity. First, the greater the maturity, the greater the duration, holding constant other characteristics of the bond. Second, the larger a bond's coupon, the smaller the duration. Coupon payments cause weight to be put on the early years in the duration formula. In the case of a zero-coupon bond, duration equals maturity. Third, duration decreases with increases in the yield to maturity. This is because an increase in the yield has a greater effect on the present value of a distant coupon than on the present value of a nearby coupon.

Convexity

Modified duration is only an approximation of the percentage change in bond price for a given change in yield. In fact, it is accurate only for *infinitesimal* shifts in yield. To assess the degree of error that may be introduced, reconsider the results of Example 8.1. The level of modifed duration predicts that the bond price will increase to $1,070.24(1.068660) = $1,143.72 if the yield drops to 6 percent. By using the bond valuation formula (8.4), however, we know that the bond value is exactly $1,147.20 at a yield of 6 percent. The difference between these prices is attributable to the fact that bond price is a nonlinear function of yield to maturity.

Figure 8.1 illustrates the approximation error in this example. At a yield of 7 percent, the bond's price is $1,070.24. Modified duration depends on the derivative, dB/dy, evaluated at 7 percent. The derivative is depicted in the figure by the straight line tangent to the bond price curve at 7 percent. To estimate the change in bond price due to a 100 basis point drop in yield, we draw a vertical line from 6 percent on the horizontal axis to the straight line depicting the derivative, and then draw across horizontally to the vertical axis. The estimated value of the bond based on modified duration is $1,143.72. If the vertical line is continued upward to the bond price curve, we find the exact value of the bond at a 6-percent yield, $1,147.20. The pricing error, $3.48, is attributable to the failure of modified duration to account for the convex nature of the bond pricing function.

We can achieve greater precision in measuring the bond's responsiveness to yield shifts by also accounting for the bond's convexity. To understand convexity, expand the bond price as represented by (8.9) into a Taylor series:

$$dB = \frac{dB}{dy}dy + \frac{1}{2}\frac{d^2B}{dy^2}(dy)^2 + \epsilon. \tag{8.15}$$

FIGURE 8.1   Bond Price as a Function of Yield

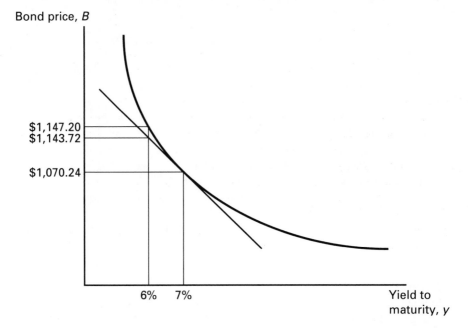

The error term, ϵ, recognizes the fact that we have used only the first two terms of the Taylor series expansion. Hence, our approximation for bond price changes will remain only approximate. Now, we drop the error term and divide both sides by B,

$$\frac{dB}{B} = \frac{dB/B}{dy}dy + \frac{1}{2}\frac{d^2B}{dy^2}\frac{1}{B}(dy)^2. \qquad \textbf{(8.16)}$$

We now define *convexity* as

$$\text{Convexity} \equiv \frac{1}{2}\frac{d^2B}{dy^2}\frac{1}{B}, \qquad \textbf{(8.17)}$$

and rewrite (8.16), the percentage change in bond price, using (8.14) and (8.17), as

$$\frac{dB}{B} = -D_m dy + \text{Convexity}(dy)^2. \qquad \textbf{(8.18)}$$

The value of the second derivative of the bond price with respect to a change in yield is

$$\frac{d^2 B}{dy^2} = \sum_{t=1}^{n} t(t+1) \left[\frac{C_t}{(1+y)^{t+2}} \right].$$ (8.19)

EXAMPLE 8.2

What is the convexity of an 8 percent, ten-year, $1000 bond, assuming annual cou-
pon payments and a required yield to maturity of 7 percent?

From Example (8.1), we know the bond price is $1,070.24. The components
of convexity (8.19) are

t	$t(t+1)$	$\frac{C_t}{(1+y)^{t+2}}$	$\frac{t(t+1)C_t}{(1+y)^{t+2}}$
1	2	65.3038	130.61
2	6	61.0316	366.19
3	12	57.0389	684.47
4	20	53.3074	1,066.15
5	30	49.8200	1,494.60
6	42	46.5607	1,955.55
7	56	43.5147	2,436.82
8	72	40.6679	2,928.09
9	90	38.0074	3,420.67
10	110	479.5329	52,748.62
Total			67,231.77

The value of $d^2 B/dy^2$ for this bond is 67,231.77, so the convexity is ½ × 67,231.77
× 1/1,070.24 = 31.4098.

To complete our illustration, we now use convexity in conjunction with modified duration to arrive at a more accurate estimate of the percentage change in bond
price attributable to a 100 basis point fall in yield.

$$\frac{dB}{B} = -D_m dy + \text{Convexity}(dy)^2$$

$$= -6.8662 \times (-.01) + 31.4098 \times (-.01)^2 = -7.180\%.$$

In other words, based upon modified duration and convexity, the bond price is
expected to rise to $1,147.08 if yield falls by 100 basis points. Note that the error
in prediction has been reduced from $3.48 to $0.12 by accounting for convexity.

All bonds with fixed payment schedules plot as convex curves in y, as shown
in Figure 8.1, although different bonds have different degrees of convexity. Mortgage backed securities (MBS's), however, sometimes exhibit "negative convexity."
That is, they plot as curves that are concave to the origin. This is because their

payment schedules are uncertain. The underlying mortgages have the option to pre-pay before maturity, and they will choose to prepay just when it is most incon-venient for the holder of the MBS. When interest rates fall, mortgages are prepaid, so the duration and price sensitivity of the MBS are reduced. Consequently, while fixed-payment bonds increase in price, the price of MBS's increases little and may even decline. When interest rates rise, mortgage prepayments slow, resulting in duration and price sensitivity increases for the MBS. Consequently, the price decline resulting from an increase in interest rates is relatively greater for a MBS than for a fixed-payment bond.

8.4 TERM STRUCTURE OF INTEREST RATES

Up to this point in the chapter, we have assumed that all cash flows of a fixed-income security are discounted at a single rate—the yield to maturity. This assump-tion may be inappropriate since lenders may demand different rates on short-term loans than on long-term loans. The relation between the level of interest rates and the time to maturity of the loan is the focus of this section.

Yield Curve
The simplest way to consider the relation between expected bond return and time to maturity is to plot the yield to maturity of U.S. Treasury obligations versus the term to maturity (making sure that the bonds have the same default risk, no imbed-ded options such as callability, and no differential tax privileges). This relation is referred to as the *yield curve*. The yield curve is usually plotted using Treasury bonds and notes. The yield to maturity differs by maturity because expected future interest rates are different for different maturities and because risk premia differ by maturity.

The yield to maturity of a coupon-bearing bond can be a misleading reflection of its expected rate of return, however. To see this, consider the following situation. Suppose there exist two discount Treasury bonds, one with a one-year maturity and a price of 90.91, and the other with a two-year maturity and a price of 81.16. Assuming each of these bonds is redeemed at a par value of 100 at their respective maturities, the expected yield on the one-year bond is

$$100/90.91 - 1 = 10.00\%,$$

and the expected yield on the two-year bond is

$$(100/81.16)^{1/2} - 1 = 11.00\%.$$

Note that if the Treasury decided to issue other one- and two-year discount bonds, they must have the same prices as the existing issues, otherwise, costless arbitrage profits could be earned.

Now, suppose that the Treasury also has a two-year, 12-percent coupon bond. The 12-percent issue pays 12 at the end of one year, and 112 at the end of two years. The price of this coupon-bearing Treasury bond has to be

$$B = \frac{12}{1.10} + \frac{112}{(1.11)^2} = 101.81,$$

otherwise, costless arbitrage profits are possible.[10] But, if the two-year coupon-bearing bond has a price of 101.81, its yield to maturity is 10.94 percent, that is, the solution to

$$101.81 = \frac{12}{1+y} + \frac{112}{(1+y)^2}.$$

On the surface, it might appear that the two-year coupon bond expected yield to maturity of 10.94 percent conflicts with the two-year discount bond expected yield to maturity of 11 percent. However, arbitrage profits are not possible. The discrepancy between the rates arises because the two-year coupon bond has an "actual" term to maturity of less than two years. If you buy the coupon bond, you will receive 12 at the end of one year and 112 at the end of two years; so, in essence, you have a portfolio of two discount bonds. The first discount bond is worth

$$B_{d_1} = \frac{12}{1.10} = 10.91,$$

and the second discount bond is worth

$$B_{d_2} = \frac{112}{1.11^2} = 90.90.$$

The average term to maturity of the bond portfolio (or the coupon-bearing bond) is, therefore,

$$\text{Average term to maturity} = \left(\frac{10.91}{101.81}\right)1 + \left(\frac{90.90}{101.81}\right)2 = 1.893 \text{ years.}$$

---

[10] Note that buying .12 units of the one-year discount bond and 1.12 units of the two-year discount bond produces a cash flow stream exactly the same as the two-year coupon-bearing bond at a cost of .12(90.91) + 1.12(81.16) = 101.81.

The 10.94-percent yield is not an expected return on a bond with two years to maturity, but rather on a bond with a maturity of approximately 1.893 years.

Two principles underlie this discussion. First, to value coupon-bearing bonds precisely, all cash flows of the bond should not be discounted at the same rate. Instead, each cash flow should be discounted at the zero-coupon or discount bond rate, r_t, which coincides with the timing of the cash flow,

$$B = \sum_{t=1}^{n} \frac{C_t}{(1 + r_t)^t} + \frac{F_n}{(1 + r_n)^n}. \tag{8.20}$$

The rate r_t is called the *spot rate of interest* on a t-period loan. Second, to estimate the relation between expected bond returns and time to maturity, only zero-coupon or spot rates of interest should be used. The yields to maturity on coupon bonds should *not* be used because the term to maturity of the bond overstates its true "economic life." The economic life of a coupon bond is a weighted average life of its constituent discount bonds, that is,

$$\text{Average term to maturity} = \sum_{t=1}^{n} \left(\frac{\frac{C_t}{(1+r_t)^t}}{B} \right) t + \left(\frac{\frac{F_n}{(1+r_n)^n}}{B} \right) n. \tag{8.21}$$

Note that this weighted average term to maturity is the same as the bond's duration defined in (8.12).[11]

In practice, the relation between zero-coupon or spot rates of interest and time to maturity is referred to as the *zero-coupon yield curve*. In this section, we refer to the relation as the *term structure of interest rates*. The term structure can be read directly from the yields to maturity of Treasury strips. For example, Table 8.3 shows that the term structure was upward sloping on November 13, 1991. The one-year, two-year, five-year, and ten-year spot rates were 5.05, 5.68, 6.84, and 7.78, respectively.

The shape of the term structure of spot rates affects the relative values of bonds with different coupons. We have already illustrated this point when we showed that a two-year coupon bond would yield 10.94 percent to maturity while a two-year discount bond yielded 11 percent. In general, for bonds of the same maturity, when the term structure is upward sloping, the yield to maturity decreases as the coupon payment increases; when the term structure is downward sloping, the yield to maturity increases with a larger coupon. This result can be explained in two ways. First, a coupon bond has a duration that is less than its maturity. Its

---

[11]Duration and maturity are the same only for a discount bond because the coupon terms, C_t, in the summation of (8.21) are zero.

yield to maturity corresponds to its duration, not its maturity. Second, when the term structure is upward sloping, investors prefer coupon bonds because it is expected that the coupon payments can be invested at higher future rates. They, therefore, bid up prices of coupon bonds and lower their yield to maturity. Correspondingly, when the term structure is downward sloping, investors prefer low-coupon bonds because it is expected that the coupons can be invested only at lower future rates. Only when the term structure of interest rates is flat do all bonds have the same yield to maturity.

Spot Rates and Forward Rates

Spot rates of interest are rates observable today. The spot rate on a three-month, default-free security is the rate of return promised on a three-month T-bill. The notation that we use to describe the spot rate on a t-period bond is r_t. *Forward rates of interest* are interest rates on loans in the future and are implied from the current term structure of spot rates. The forward rate on a t-period loan in period n, denoted $_nf_t$, is computed using

$$(1 +_n f_t)^t = \frac{(1 + r_{n+t})^{n+t}}{(1 + r_n)^n}.$$ (8.22)

The forward rate on a one-year loan today, for example, is computed as

$$(1 +_0 f_1)^1 = (1 + r_1)^1,$$

and the forward rate on a one-year loan in three years is

$$(1 +_3 f_1)^1 = \frac{(1 + r_{3+1})^{3+1}}{(1 + r_3)^3}.$$

EXAMPLE 8.3

Suppose the one-year spot rate of interest is 10 percent and the two-year spot rate is 11 percent. What is the implied one-year forward rate in one year?

Substituting the parameters of the example into equation (8.22), we find that

$$1 +_1 f_1 = \frac{(1 + r_2)^2}{(1 + r_1)} = \frac{(1.11)^2}{(1.10)},$$

or

$$_1 f_1 = 12.01\%.$$

EXAMPLE 8.4

Using the values reported in Table 8.3, find the 91-day forward rate implied by selling the December 19, 1991 T-bill and buying March 19, 1992 T-bill. The effective annual rate of return of the December 19th T-bill is

$$r = \left[\frac{100}{100 - 4.39(36/360)} \right]^{365/36} - 1 = 4.562\%.$$

The effective annual rate of return of the March 19th T-bill is

$$r = \left[\frac{100}{100 - 4.64(127/360)} \right]^{365/127} - 1 = 4.858\%.$$

Given these two spot rates of interest, the implied forward rate of interest on a 91-day T-bill in 36 days is the solution to

$$(1 +_{36} f_{91})^{91/365} = \frac{(1.04858)^{127/365}}{(1.04562)^{36/365}}.$$

The implied forward rate of interest is 4.975 percent.

8.5 SHORT-TERM INTEREST RATE FUTURES CONTRACTS

The most actively traded short-term interest rate futures contracts are the Chicago Mercantile Exchange's T-bill and Eurodollar futures contracts. The *Treasury bill futures contract* requires the delivery of a $1,000,000 face value T-bill with 91-days to maturity. The contract expires the business day before the date on which the new 91-day T-bill is issued. The newly issued 91-day T-bill, the seasoned 182-day, and the seasoned 364-day T-bills are eligible for delivery on this futures contract.

The price of a T-bill futures contract is an index value based on the bank discount. The price reported for the December 1991 T-bill futures in Table 8.2, for example, is 95.34. This does not mean that the futures buyer will pay 95.34 percent of par when she buys the T-bill at the futures maturity. The index price, 95.34, implies that the bank discount on the bill is $100 - 95.34 = 4.66$ on an annualized basis. Since the futures contract requires the delivery of a 91-day T-bill, the annualized discount is adjusted to a 91-day period using the banker's convention of a

360-day year. The 91-day discount is 4.66(91/360) = 1.178. Thus, if we bought the December 1991 T-bill futures contract on November 13, 1991, at the reported price of 95.34, we would be entering into a commitment to buy a 91-day, $1,000,000 T-bill on March 19, 1992, at a price of 98.822 percent of the face value of the T-bill or $988,220. The implied forward rate of interest on this T-bill is

$$\left(\frac{100}{98.822} \right)^{365/91} - 1 = 4.868\%.$$

It is interesting to note that the implied forward rate of interest from the futures contract, 4.868 percent, is less than the 4.975 percent rate implied by the T-bills in Example 8.4. Both rates apply to the 91-day period beginning on December 19, 1991. If one could borrow at 4.868 percent and lend at 4.975 percent, an arbitrage profit could be earned. In effect, this can be done by the following arbitrage transactions: (a) sell the December 19, 1991 T-bill for $9,956.10; (b) buy the March 19, 1992 T-bill for $9,836.31; and (c) sell the December 1991 T-bill futures contract at $9,882.20. Transactions (a) and (b) have the net effect of lending money over the period December 19, 1991 to March 19, 1992; transaction (c) commits the investor to borrowing money for the same period. The borrowing and lending, however, may never occur because the transactions can be closed out on December 19, 1991. On that date, the arbitrageur covers the short position in the maturing December 19 T-bill by paying $10,000, thereby incurring a cost of $43.90. The March 19 T-bill purchased on November 13 now has 91 days to maturity and can be delivered against the futures contract for $9,882.20, a net gain of $45.89. Finally, the net proceeds from the T-bill transactions on November 13, 1991, $119.79, have earned interest at, say, 5 percent and, after 36 days, are now worth $120.37. The arbitrage profit realized on December 19, therefore, totals

$$\$120.37 + \$45.89 - \$43.90 = \$122.36.$$

The *Eurodollar futures contract* is a commitment to transact a $1,000,000, three-month Eurodollar deposit. Delivery never takes place since a Eurodollar futures contract is cash settled. Cash settlement occurs on the second London business day before the third Wednesday of the contract month.

The settlement price of the Eurodollar futures contract on the expiration day is computed in such a way as to minimize the variation in the quoted Eurodollar deposit rates. During the last day of trading, a random sample of approximately twelve rates are taken from the twenty-plus approved banks in the London Eurodollar market. The rates are then ranked from highest to lowest, and the highest and lowest rates are discarded. The remaining ten rates are averaged, and the average rate is subtracted from 100 to determine the settlement price.

As noted in the previous paragraph, quoted Eurodollar futures prices are actually index values, that is, the value reported in the financial press is 100 less the Eurodollar interest rate. Thus, if we buy the March 1992 Eurodollar futures at the price reported in Table 8.2, 94.94, the implicit agreement that we are entering into is to buy a $1,000,000 three-month Eurodollar certificate of deposit on March 16, 1992 (the second London business day before the third Wednesday of the futures contract month), where the stated interest rate on the deposit is $100 - 94.94$, or 5.06 percent. The effective three-month forward interest rate on such a deposit is, therefore,

$$r = \left[\frac{100 + 5.06(\frac{92}{360})}{100} \right]^{365/92} - 1 = 5.23\%.$$

Note that the three-month interval from March 16, 1992, through June 16, 1992, has 92 days.

8.6 LONG-TERM INTEREST RATE FUTURES CONTRACTS

The most active long-term interest rate futures contract is the T-bond contract on the Chicago Board of Trade.[12] The CBT's *Treasury bond futures contract* is a commitment to deliver a nominal 8 percent, $100,000 face-value U.S. Treasury bond with a least fifteen years to maturity or to first call date, whichever comes first. The seller of the futures contract has the option to deliver any of the eligible issues on any date during the delivery month. Whether an 8-percent coupon issue is available for delivery is unimportant since the futures contract allows for the delivery of any T-bond with a long enough maturity. To remove the effects of different bonds having different coupon rates, the CBT designed a system of conversion factors.

Conversion Factor and Invoice Price

To understand the CBT's system of conversion, recall first that the lower the coupon rate, the lower the bond's price, other factors being held constant [see equation (8.4)]. Since the seller of the T-bond futures contract can deliver *any* U.S. Treasury bond with at least fifteen years to maturity or to the first call date, a method of conversion is needed to offset the economic incentive to deliver the lowest coupon bond. The CBT's system adjusts the futures price, which is based on an 8-percent coupon, to a price that corresponds to the coupon of the issue being delivered. To illustrate the principle underlying the conversion, consider the price of an 8-percent, fifteen-year bond with annual coupons and a yield to maturity of 8 percent. Using equation (8.4), the bond price is

---

[12]For an interesting analysis of why this contract supplanted the earlier GNMA contract, see Johnston and McConnell (1989).

$$B = \sum_{t=1}^{15} \frac{8}{(1.08)^t} + \frac{100}{(1.08)^{15}} = 100.00.$$

Now, consider the price of a 12-percent, fifteen-year bond with fifteen years to maturity and the same 8-percent yield. The bond price is

$$B = \sum_{t=1}^{15} \frac{12}{(1.08)^t} + \frac{100}{(1.08)^{15}} = 134.24.$$

Note that the only difference between the two bonds is that the second bond has higher coupon payments. Owning the 12-percent coupon bond is like owning 1.3424 8-percent bonds. Since the futures price is based on an 8-percent coupon bond, the futures price is multiplied by a conversion factor of 1.3424 to compute the amount paid (delivery price) by the long to the short if the short delivers the 12-percent coupon issue.

The actual formula for computing the conversion factor is slightly more complex than what is demonstrated in the above example because coupons are paid on a semi-annual basis, and, in general, the next coupon payment is made in less than six months (i.e., we are part of the way through the current coupon period). The actual formula for the conversion factor, CF, is

$$CF = (1+y/2)^{-X/6} \left(\frac{C}{2} + \left\{ \frac{C}{y} \left[1 - (1+y/2)^{-2n} \right] + (1+y/2)^{-2n} \right\} \right)$$
$$- \frac{C}{2} \frac{(6-X)}{6}, \tag{8.23}$$

where C is the annual coupon rate of the bond in decimal form, y equals 0.08, n is the number of whole years to first call, if the bond is callable, or the number of years to maturity, and X is the number of months that the maturity exceeds n, rounded down to the nearest quarter (e.g., $X = 0, 3, 6, 9$). Note that if $X = 0, 3, 6$, the formula (8.23) is used directly. If $X = 9$, set $2n = 2n + 1$, $X = 3$, and calculate as above.[13] Computer programs are available to perform the computation (8.23). The values in Table 8.5, for example, were generated using a program called OPTVAL. Alternatively, the CBT and others publish and distribute conversion factor tables.

---

[13] Note that if $X = 0$ the formula (8.23) reduces to

$$CF = \left\{ \frac{C}{y} \left[1 - (1+y/2)^{-2n} \right] + (1+y/2)^{-2n} \right\}.$$

TABLE 8.5 Conversion factors for the U.S. Treasury Bonds eligible for delivery on the CBT's T-bond futures contract. These factors convert different coupon issues to yield 8 percent.

Years-Months	9%	$9\frac{1}{8}\%$	$9\frac{1}{4}\%$	$9\frac{3}{8}\%$	$9\frac{1}{2}\%$	$9\frac{5}{8}\%$	$9\frac{3}{4}\%$	$9\frac{7}{8}\%$
25-0	1.1074	1.1208	1.1343	1.1477	1.1611	1.1745	1.1880	1.2014
25-3	1.1075	1.1210	1.1345	1.1479	1.1614	1.1749	1.1883	1.2018
25-6	1.1081	1.1216	1.1351	1.1486	1.1621	1.1756	1.1892	1.2027
25-9	1.1082	1.1217	1.1353	1.1488	1.1624	1.1759	1.1895	1.2030
26-0	1.1087	1.1223	1.1359	1.1495	1.1631	1.1767	1.1903	1.2039
26-3	1.1088	1.1225	1.1361	1.1497	1.1633	1.1770	1.1906	1.2042
26-6	1.1094	1.1230	1.1367	1.1504	1.1640	1.1777	1.1914	1.2051
26-9	1.1094	1.1232	1.1369	1.1506	1.1643	1.1780	1.1917	1.2054
27-0	1.1100	1.1237	1.1375	1.1512	1.1649	1.1787	1.1924	1.2062
27-3	1.1100	1.1238	1.1376	1.1514	1.1652	1.1789	1.1927	1.2065
27-6	1.1105	1.1244	1.1382	1.1520	1.1658	1.1796	1.1935	1.2073
27-9	1.1106	1.1245	1.1383	1.1522	1.1660	1.1799	1.1937	1.2076
28-0	1.1111	1.1250	1.1389	1.1528	1.1666	1.1805	1.1944	1.2083
28-3	1.1111	1.1251	1.1390	1.1529	1.1668	1.1807	1.1947	1.2086
28-6	1.1116	1.1256	1.1395	1.1535	1.1675	1.1814	1.1954	1.2093
28-9	1.1117	1.1257	1.1396	1.1536	1.1676	1.1816	1.1956	1.2096
29-0	1.1121	1.1262	1.1402	1.1542	1.1682	1.1822	1.1963	1.2103
29-3	1.1122	1.1262	1.1403	1.1543	1.1684	1.1824	1.1965	1.2105
29-6	1.1126	1.1267	1.1408	1.1549	1.1690	1.1830	1.1971	1.2112
29-9	1.1127	1.1268	1.1409	1.1550	1.1691	1.1832	1.1973	1.2114
30-0	1.1131	1.1273	1.1414	1.1555	1.1697	1.1838	1.1980	1.2121
30-3	1.1131	1.1273	1.1415	1.1556	1.1698	1.1840	1.1981	1.2123
30-6	1.1136	1.1278	1.1420	1.1562	1.1704	1.1846	1.1988	1.2130
30-9	1.1136	1.1278	1.1420	1.1562	1.1705	1.1847	1.1989	1.2131

To illustrate the use of the conversion factor system, suppose that we are considering delivery of the 9s of November 2018 on the March 1992 T-bond futures contract. This bond is eligible for delivery because on March 1, 1992, it has more than fifteen years to maturity. Specifically, on March 1, 1992, the 9s of November 2018 have 26.50 years to maturity (rounded down to the nearest quarter). Using Table 8.5, the conversion factor of this bond is 1.1094. In other words, in place of delivering the hypothetical 8-percent, fifteen-year bond on the March 1992 futures contract, we can deliver the 9s of November 2018, but the buyer is going to have to pay 1.1094 times the prevailing futures price.

On the delivery date, the seller of the T-bond futures delivers an eligible T-bond to the buyer of the T-bond futures contract. In return, the buyer must pay the *invoice price* to the bond seller. The amount of the invoice price will be the sum of the futures price times the conversion factor of the delivered bond and the accrued interest on the delivered bond. For example, suppose that on March 15, 1992, the March 1992 futures contract is priced at 96-18. Like the underlying bonds, the decimal part of the price is the number of 32nds, so the futures price is 96.5625. If we sell the futures and promptly deliver the 9s of November 2018 to the futures contract buyer, the invoice price paid by the buyer equals .965625 (the futures price in decimal form) times 100,000 (the denomination of the futures contract) times 1.1094 (the conversion factor of the 9s of November 2018 as of March 1, 1992), or $107,126.44, plus the accrued interest on the 9s of November 2018 as of March 15, 1992, $2,991.76 [i.e., .045(121/182)(100,000)]. The total invoice price is

$$\$107,126.44 + \$2,991.76 = \$110,118.20.$$

Cheapest to Deliver
In principal, the system of conversion factors is intended to make the short indifferent about which bond he delivers. This means that if we are at time T—the end of the futures contract life—the profits from selling the futures and buying and delivering bond i, computed as

$$\pi_{i,T} = F_T(CF_i) + AI_{i,T} - B_{i,T} - AI_{i,T} = F_T(CF_i) - B_{i,T},$$

where $F_T(CF_i) + AI_{i,T}$ is the invoice price received from delivering bond i and $B_{i,T} + AI_{i,T}$ is the price paid for the purchase of bond i, should equal zero.

In practice, however, one of the eligible delivery bonds is "cheapest to deliver" because the system of conversion factors is not exact. Each bond will have a different value of $\pi_{i,T}$. The bond with the highest $\pi_{i,T}$ is the cheapest to deliver. Its value of $\pi_{i,T}$, however, will be equal to zero. If it were positive, costless arbitrage profits could be earned by the short at the expense of the long. If it were negative, costless arbitrage profits could be earned by the long at the expense of the short. The computed profits for all other deliverable bonds will be negative. However, negative profits for these bonds do not imply arbitrage opportunities. To capture these "gains," the long would need to take delivery of a bond issue that is not the cheapest to deliver. Since it is not rational for the short to deliver any issue other than the cheapest to deliver, no arbitrage gains are possible.

A cheapest-to-deliver issue arises because the conversion factors are derived by discounting the cash flows of all bonds at 8 percent. Using 8 percent assumes that coupon payments can be reinvested at 8 percent. If the average future interest rate at which the coupons can be reinvested exceeds 8 percent, however, investors prefer high-coupon bonds over low-coupon bonds (when each bond is valued by discounting at 8 percent). The cheapest-to-deliver bond is, therefore, the low-coupon bond. If the average future interest rate at which coupons can be reinvested is less than 8 percent, investors prefer low-coupon bonds over high-coupon bonds, so the cheapest to deliver is the high-coupon bond. Only when the term structure of interest rates is flat at 8 percent, will all bonds be equally desirable for delivery. If the yield curve is above 8 percent, low-coupon bonds are the cheapest to deliver, and if the yield curve is below 8 percent, high-coupon bonds are the cheapest to deliver.

8.7 COST-OF-CARRY RELATION

Under the assumptions that the cheapest-to-deliver bond issue i is known and that it does not change through time, the cost-of-carry relation between the futures price and the cheapest-to-deliver bond may be written

$$F_0 = \frac{(B_{i,0} + AI_{i,0})e^{rT} - AI_{i,T} - \sum_{t=0}^{T} C_{i,t}e^{r(T-t)}}{CF_i}. \tag{8.24}$$

The left-hand side of the equation is the futures price at time 0. The maturity of the futures contract is T periods hence. The first term in the numerator of the right-hand side of the equation, $(B_{i,0} + AI_{i,0})e^{rT}$, is the time 0 cost of the bond taken forward to time T at the riskless rate of interest (i.e., the bond purchase is financed at the short-term riskless interest rate). The second and third terms in the numerator represent interest earned on the bond—accrued interest, $AI_{i,T}$, received when the bond is delivered against the futures contract and the future value of the coupons received (if any), $\sum_{t=0}^{T} C_{i,t}e^{r(T-t)}$. The conversion factor CF_i in the denominator "converts" bond i into the hypothetical 8-percent coupon issue upon which the futures contract is designed.

Prior to discussing the cost-of-carry relation in more detail, it is worth noting that the "short-term riskless rate of interest" used to finance the purchase of bonds required in the arbitrage transactions that drive (8.24) is usually the rate on a *repurchase agreement* or "repo." Repurchase agreements are collateralized loans. They involve a commitment to sell and then later to buy back a specific bond issue (presumably at the maturity of the futures contract).[14] The agreement specifies the date on which the bond will be repurchased,[15] as well as the interest rate that will be paid on the loan. The dollar interest paid on the loan is computed as

---

[14] Repurchase and reverse repurchase agreements are discussed at length in Stigum (1990).

[15] When the term of the loan is one day, it is called an *overnight repo*. Terms of greater than one day are *term repos*.

$$\text{Interest} = \text{Principal amount} \times \text{Repo rate} \times \frac{\text{Days repo is outstanding}}{360}.$$

Note that, under this arrangement, the lender has commited to consummating actions opposite the borrower, that is, the lender has entered into an agreement to buy and then later to sell the underlying bond. For this reason, the lender is said to have a *reverse repurchase agreement*, a "reverse repo" or, simply, a "reverse." Both the borrower and lender gain from these agreements. The borrower gets a lower rate than he might otherwise get at the bank, and the lender gets a higher rate than he might otherwise get on short-term, highly liquid investments.

Before maturity, as at maturity, the futures price is based on the price of the cheapest to deliver, and the cheapest to deliver is determined by finding the bond with the highest "cash and carry" portfolio profit,

$$\pi_{i,0} = F_0(CF_i) + AI_{i,T} + \sum_{t=0}^{T} C_{i,t}e^{r(T-t)} - (B_{i,0} + AI_{i,0})e^{rT}. \qquad \textbf{(8.25)}$$

Again, the highest value of profit equals zero; otherwise arbitrage profits are possible. This identifies the cheapest-to-deliver issue. All other profits will be less than zero. In other words, the futures price will be less than in (8.24) for all bonds other than the cheapest to deliver.

Although (8.25) allows us to identify which bond is cheapest to deliver at time 0, there is no assurance that this bond will also be cheapest to deliver at time T. Since the identity of the cheapest to deliver at time T is uncertain, (8.24) does not hold as an equality, even for the bond that is currently cheapest to deliver. Indeed, the short has a valuable *quality option* that gives him the right to choose which bond to deliver at time T. Although the short may have entered a cash-and-carry position when bond i was cheapest to deliver, if, at maturity, bond j is cheapest, the short can profit by selling bond i, buying bond j, and then delivering bond j on his short futures commitment. Because this option to switch bonds is valuable, the investor doing cash-and-carry arbitrage is willing to sell futures at a price below the price specified by the cost of carry on the right-hand side of (8.24), that is,

$$F_0 < \frac{(B_{i,0} + AI_{i,0})e^{rT} - AI_{i,T} - \sum_{t=0}^{T} C_{i,t}e^{r(T-t)}}{CF_i}, \qquad \textbf{(8.26)}$$

or, alternatively,

$$F_0 = \frac{(B_{i,0} + AI_{i,0})e^{rT} - AI_{i,T} - \sum_{t=0}^{T} C_{i,t}e^{r(T-t)}}{CF_i} - \text{Quality option}, \qquad \textbf{(8.27)}$$

where bond i is the current cheapest to deliver. The value of the quality option embedded in the T-bond futures contract is estimated in Chapter 11.

The short futures also has a *timing option* that allows a choice about when during the contract month to deliver. The most valuable element in the timing option is called the *wildcard option*. In the delivery month, the futures price at which delivery is made is the settlement price established when the market closes at 2:00 PM. The short has until 8:00 PM to declare delivery. Obviously, if news arrives that justifies a decline in bond prices, the short will choose to make delivery at the already established settlement price.

8.8 HEDGING WITH INTEREST RATE FUTURES CONTRACTS

Short-Term, Long Hedge

Interest rate futures can be used to lock in forward interest rates. Suppose, for example, that on November 13, 1991, a company anticipates a cash inflow of $1,000,000 on March 16, 1992. The cash, when it is received, will be placed in a three-month certificate of deposit until summer when it will be used to partially finance a major capital expenditure that the firm plans. Suppose also that the company's financial analyst expects three-month CD rates to fall to a level of 4 percent by March, while the current implied three-month forward rate of the March 1992 Eurodollar futures, based on its reported price of 94.94, is 5.06 percent. What can the company do to lock in the higher rate of interest?

A simple solution to this problem is to buy the March 1992 Eurodollar futures contract at the reported price of 94.94. When the $1,000,000 is received on March 16, 1992, the price of the Eurodollar futures will be approximately the same as the spot Eurodollar rate since the futures is near expiration. Assume that our analyst is correct in her prediction, and the spot rate is 4 percent. When we sell the futures position, our profit is (9600 − 9494) basis points times $25, or $2,650. The Eurodollar deposit on March 16, 1992, is, therefore, $1,002,650, which, at a 4-percent rate implies a deposit balance of $1,012,787.91 on June 15, 1992. Thus, in spite of the fact that the nominal rate is lower, the earned interest income amounts to a nominal rate of 1.2788(360/91), or 5.06 percent, exactly the desired result. Note that it does not matter what the spot rate is on March 16, 1992—the 5.06-percent rate is locked in regardless.

Long-Term, Short Hedge

Earlier we developed the concept of modified duration to assess the interest rate risk of a bond. Recall that modified duration is an approximation for the percentage change in bond price with respect to a change in yield. From a fixed-income security portfolio risk management standpoint, it is useful to recognize that the duration of a portfolio of bonds or fixed-income securities is simply the market-value-weighted average of the durations of the constituent bonds. It is also useful to know that, in the absence of the options imbedded in the T-bond futures contract, the duration of the T-bond futures is approximately equal to the duration of the cheapest-to-deliver T-bond.

To develop a framework for using T-bond futures to manage the risk of a fixed-income security portfolio, define the following notation:

$D_P \equiv$ modified duration of fixed-income security portfolio P.
$D_F \equiv$ modified duration of T-bond futures contract.
$D^* \equiv$ modified desired duration exposure for fixed-income portfolio.
$P \equiv$ current market value of fixed-income portfolio.
$F \equiv$ current futures price.
$h \equiv$ optimal number of futures contracts to buy (sell).

Under this notation, the dollar change in the value of the unhedged fixed-income portfolio is $D_P P$ times the interest rate change. If we buy h futures contracts against this fixed-income investment, the dollar change in the overall portfolio is $(D_P P + hD_F F)$ times the interest rate change, which we equate to the dollar change in the hedged portfolio at the desired duration level, D^*P, that is,

$$D^*P = D_P P + hD_F F, \qquad \textbf{(8.28)}$$

in order to determine the optimal hedge ratio. Rearranging to isolate h, we get

$$h = \frac{P(D^* - D_P)}{D_F F}. \qquad \textbf{(8.29)}$$

EXAMPLE 8.5

Suppose that the cheapest-to-deliver bond (and hence the T-bond futures) has a duration of 12.50. Suppose also that the duration of the bond portfolio that we are managing is 10.00 and that the market value of the portfolio is $50,000,000. If today's date is November 13, 1991, and we wish to hedge completely against movements in the level of long-term rates until the end of February 1992, how many March 1992 T-bond futures contracts should we sell?

Substituting the example values into equation (8.29), we get

$$h = \frac{50,000,000(0 - 10.00)}{12.50 \times .9921875 \times 100,000} = -403.15.$$

Asset Allocation

At its most basic level, portfolio management involves a decision concerning what types of assets should be purchased. For example, a fund manager might choose to invest 40 percent of the fund in stocks, 40 percent in bonds, and 20 percent in real estate. Deciding what proportion of fund wealth to place in each asset category is called the *asset allocation decision.*

Once the asset allocation decision is made and fund wealth is invested, dramatic changes to the allocation are usually avoided because the transaction costs of liquidating assets in one category and buying assets in another are excessive. Instead, fund managers use futures contracts to change the asset allocation indirectly.

To demonstrate, assume that a fund consists of S in stocks and B in bonds, for a total value of $V = S + B$. Now, suppose the fund manager wants to change the amount invested in long-term bonds from B to B^*. The bond portfolio has a modified duration of D_B. Rather than selling (buying) stocks to buy (sell) bonds, the portfolio manager can effectuate the change by buying (selling) T-bond futures contracts. She wants her bond portfolio to have income $D_B B^*$ if interest rates fall 1 percent. She plans on generating that amount with income from the current bond portfolio, $D_B B$, and income from a T-bond futures position, $h D_F F$, that is,

$$D_B B^* = D_B B + h D_F F. \tag{8.30}$$

Rearranging (8.30) to isolate h, we get

$$h = \frac{D_B(B^* - B)}{D_F F}. \tag{8.31}$$

Note that if the dollar investment in bonds is to be reduced (i.e., $B^* < B$), T-bonds futures contracts are sold, and, if the dollar investment in bonds is to be increased (i.e., $B^* > B$), T-bond futures contracts are purchased. Presumably, the reduction (increase) in bond investment is then transferred to stocks through buying (selling) stock index futures contracts.

EXAMPLE 8.6

A fund manager currently has $50,000,000 in a stock portfolio whose composition matches the S&P 500 and $50,000,000 in a bond portfolio whose modified duration is 12.00. Believing that stocks are going to do extraordinarily well over the next three months, the fund manager wants to take advantage of the impending stock market rise and to eliminate his interest rate risk exposure. Unfortunately, liquidating bonds and buying stocks is expensive, particularly if, at the end of the three months, the manager wants to return to his fifty-fifty portfolio mix. How can the fund manager use T-bond and S&P 500 futures to carry out his plans? Assume that the cheapest-to-deliver bond (and hence the T-bond futures) has a duration of 9.00 and that the price of a three-month T-bond futures contract is 96.00. Also, assume that the three-month S&P 500 futures is priced at 325.

First, with respect to eliminating the interest rate exposure, the number of T-bond futures to sell is 694.44:

$$h = \frac{12.00(0 - 50,000,000)}{9 \times .96 \times 100,000} = -694.44.$$

This action is tantamount to liquidating the bond investment. Second, to take a long position of $50,000,000 in stocks using the S&P 500 futures, the number of contracts to buy is

$$h = \frac{50,000,000}{325.00 \times 500} = 307.69.$$

8.9 SUMMARY

Following an introduction to the particular interest rate futures markets in the U.S., specific pricing and yield conventions governing the trading of fixed-income securities are discussed. The major focus of this chapter is interest rate risk management. To this end, the notions of modified duration and convexity are introduced and applied. Following that, the relation between short-term and long-term rates, that is, the term structure of spot interest rates, is presented. From the spot rates, forward rates of interest are derived, and the forward rates implied by cash and futures prices are compared. A detailed discussion of the specifics of T-bond futures contract delivery and pricing is provided. The chapter concludes with two interest rate risk management illustrations.

9 CURRENCY FUTURES CONTRACTS

Currency futures contracts were developed in response to the shift from fixed to flexible exchange rates in 1971. At that time, the United States ceased redeeming dollars for gold. By 1973, most countries stopped maintaining the price of their currencies with respect to the dollar and allowed market forces to determine their exchange rates. The increased volatility of exchange rates created a demand for currency futures markets both as speculative and hedging vehicles.[1]

9.1 MARKETS FOR CURRENCIES[2]

Futures Market

The U.S. futures market in currencies operates like futures in any other item. Table 9.1 gives contract terms for the major foreign currency contracts, all of which are traded on the Chicago Mercantile Exchange's International Monetary Market. Prices are quoted in U.S. dollars per unit of foreign currency. An example of currency futures price quotes is contained in Table 9.2. While Table 9.1 indicates that eight maturity months are available, only the nearby months are actively traded. Unlike other futures contracts, delivery of currencies has relatively few complications. Only one "grade" of currency is available, delivery takes place on a specific date during the delivery month, and no transportation costs are incurred.

---

[1] While flexible exchange rate systems have short run variability, they do not have the periodic large price changes and trade dislocations that were typical of fixed exchange rate systems.

[2] See Grabbe (1986) and Solnik (1988) for greater detail on currency markets and international bond and stock markets.

154

TABLE 9.1 Currency futures contracts specifications (most active contracts in U.S. markets).

Security (Exchange)	Trading Hours	Contract Months[a]	Units/ Minimum Price Fluctuation	Last Day of Trading	Delivery
Canadian Dollar (CME)	7:20–2:00 (CST)	1,3,4,6 7,9,10,12 current	100,000Can$/ .0001 ($10)	Two business days prior to third Wednesday	Third Wednesday
Deutsche Mark (CME)	7:20–2:00 (CST)	1,3,4,6 7,9,10,12 current	125,000DM/ .0001 ($12.50)	Two business days prior to third Wednesday	Third Wednesday
French Franc (CME)	7:20–2:00 (CST)	1,3,4,6 7,9,10,12 current	250,000FF/ .00005 ($12.50)	Two business days prior to third Wednesday	Third Wednesday
Japanese Yen (CME)	7:20–2:00 (CST)	1,3,4,6 7,9,10,12 current	12,500,000yen/ .000001 ($12.50)	Two business days prior to third Wednesday	Third Wednesday
British Pounds (CME)	7:20–2:00 (CST)	1,3,4,6 7,9,10,12 current	62,500pounds/ .0002 ($12.50)	Two business days prior to third Wednesday	Third Wednesday
Swiss Franc (CME)	7:20–2:00 (CST)	1,3,4,6 7,9,10,12 current	125,000SFr/ .0001 ($12.50)	Two business days prior to third Wednesday	Third Wednesday

a. The notation used in this column corresponds to the month of the calendar year (e.g., 1 is January, 2 is February, and so on).

Interbank Spot and Forward Market

By far the largest market in currencies is the interbank market. Major banks around the world trade currencies on a 24-hour basis. Banks supply currencies to their business customers and even out their positions by trading with other banks. Table 9.3 contains an example of prices from the interbank market.

The interbank market trades spot and forward currencies. Spot transactions call for delivery and payment within two days. Forward transactions call for delivery and payment at the time specified in the forward contract. Actively traded

TABLE 9.2   Currency futures contract prices.

FUTURES

JAPAN YEN (IMM) – 12.5 million yen; $ per yen (.00)	Open	High	Low	Settle	Change	Lifetime High	Lifetime Low	Open Interest
Dec	.7691	.7699	.7671	.7679	– .0012	.7770	.6997	69,869
Mr92	.7666	.7684	.7659	.7665	– .0011	.7737	.7000	3,572
June	....	....	.7659	– .0010		.7730	.7015	917
Sept	....	....	.7659	– .0010		.7710	.7265	599
Dec	....	....	.7662	– .0009		.7700	.7512	1,290

Est vol 19,740; vol Tues 19,486; open Int 76,247, +756.

DEUTSCHEMARK (IMM) – 125,000 marks; $ per mark
Dec	.6088	.6108	.6060	.6088 +	.0007	.6770	.5365	72,328
Mr92	.6012	.6045	.5998	.6024 +	.0007	.6065	.5353	6,380
June	.5965	.5970	.5960	.5963 +	.0007	.5985	.5322	715

Est vol 56,177; vol Tues 36,905; open Int 79,626, – 1,188.

CANADIAN DOLLAR (IMM) – 100,000 dirs.; $ per Can $
Dec	.8771	.8817	.8763	.8812 +	.0019	.8906	.8175	20,341
Mr92	.8720	.8769	.8713	.8767 +	.0020	.8857	.8253	4,840
June	.8675	.8725	.8675	.8725 +	.0018	.8820	.8330	734
Sept	.8630	.8685	.8630	.8685 +	.0016	.8774	.8348	105

Est vol 13,890; vol Tues 7,534; open Int 26,078, –782.

BRITISH POUND (IMM) – 62,500 pds.; $ per pound
Dec	1.7640	1.7696	1.7560	1.7650 +.0024	1.7900	1.5670	27,784
Mr92	1.7430	1.7490	1.7370	1.7436 +.0024	1.7570	1.5560	2,964

Est vol 13,723; vol Tues 7,681; open Int 30,780, –899.

SWISS FRANC (IMM) – 125,000 francs; $ per franc
Dec	.6877	.6905	.6849	.6869 +	.0002	.8090	.6235	29,074
Mr92	.6829	.6852	.6797	.6819 +	.0004	.6995	.6225	2,196
June	.6766	.6795	.6750	.6771 +	.0004	.6840	.6546	296

Est vol 23,401; vol Tues 16,538; open Int 31,566, –1,353.

AUSTRALIAN DOLLAR (IMM) – 100,000 dirs.; $ per A.$
Dec	.7825	.7839	.7822	.7832 –	.0006	.7960	.7380	1,204

Est vol 113; vol Tues 164; open Int 1,221, –246.

U.S. DOLLAR INDEX (FINEX) – 500 times USDX
Dec	89.04	89.40	88.78	88.99 –	.11	98.96	88.47	5,019
Mr92	90.07	90.30	89.90	90.08 –	.10	98.90	89.60	1,045

Est vol 1,896; vol Tues 2,675; open Int 6,090, –671.
The Index: High 88.86; Low 88.34; Close 88.54 –.08

OTHER FUTURES

Settlement prices of contracts. Volume and open Interest of all contract months.

British Pound (MCE) 12,500 pounds; $ per pound
Dec 1.7650 +.0024; Est. vol. 120; Open Int. 422
Japanese Yen (MCE) 6.25 million yen; $ per yen (.00)
Dec .7679 –.0012; Est. vol. 240; Open Int. 353
Swiss Franc (MCE) 62,500 francs; $ per franc
Dec .6869 +.0002; Est. vol. 1,020; Open Int. 253
Deutschemark (MCE) 62,500 marks; $ per mark
Dec .6088 +.0007; Est. vol. 360; Open Int. 837
BP/DM Cross Rate (IMM) US $50,000 times BP/DM
Dec 2.8990 +.0005; Est. vol. 80; Open Int. 245
DM/JY Cross Rate (IMM) US $125,000 times DM/JY
Dec .7928 +.0022; Est. vol. 6; Open Int. 583
FINEX – Financial Instrument Exchange, a division of the New York Cotton Exchange. IMM – International Monetary Market at the Chicago Mercantile Exchange. MCE – MidAmerica Commodity Exchange.

Source: Reprinted by permission of *Wall Street Journal,* © (November 14, 1991) Dow Jones & Company, Inc. All Rights Reserved Worldwide.

maturities are 30, 90, and 180 days, but other maturities are available. Forward contracts are contracts between two banks without the intervention of a clearing house. To reverse a forward contract, another contract must be entered into that reverses the first contract. For example, suppose a bank purchased British pounds 90 days forward. Ten days later, the bank wishes to offset that position. It could do so by selling British pounds 80 days forward.

Forward contracts are subject to two kinds of default risk—*credit risk* and *country risk*. Credit risk is the risk that the contra bank has poor credit. This risk is low because only the most creditworthy international banks participate in the interbank market. In the futures market, clearing house margin requirements serve to limit credit risk. Country risk is the risk that a country will impose restrictions on the transfer of currencies and thereby make it impossible for two banks to carry out the terms of their forward contract. Such restrictions were quite frequent under fixed exchange rate systems, but are less frequent today.

9.2 CURRENCY QUOTATIONS AND TRIANGULAR ARBITRAGE

We will follow the convention of quoting the price of a foreign currency just as we quote the price of any other commodity, in dollars per unit. Thus the price of the German mark might be 0.57 dollars per mark. Sometimes foreign currency prices are quoted as the number of units of foreign currency per dollar. In the case

TABLE 9.3   Spot and forward currency prices from the interbank market.

EXCHANGE RATES

Wednesday, November 13, 1991

The New York foreign exchange selling rates below apply to trading among banks in amounts of $1 million and more, as quoted at 3 p.m. Eastern time by Bankers Trust Co.and other sources. Retail transactions provide fewer units of foreign currency per dollar.

Country	U.S. $ equiv. Wed.	Tues.	Currency per U.S. $ Wed.	Tues.
Argentina (Austral) ...	.0001008	.0001008	9918.67	9918.67
Australia (Dollar)	.7860	.7870	1.2723	1.2706
Austria (Schilling)	.08681	.08681	11.52	11.52
Bahrain (Dinar)	2.6539	2.6539	.3768	.3768
Belgium (Franc)	.02966	.02966	33.72	33.72
Brazil (Cruzeiro)	.00144	.00146	694.71	685.60
Britain (Pound)	1.7730	1.7725	.5640	.5642
30-Day Forward	1.7648	1.7640	.5666	.5669
90-Day Forward	1.7504	1.7496	.5713	.5716
180-Day Forward	1.7299	1.7291	.5781	.5783
Canada (Dollar)	.8842	.8838	1.1310	1.1315
30-Day Forward	.8815	.8814	1.1344	1.1346
90-Day Forward	.8784	.8779	1.1384	1.1391
180-Day Forward	.8737	.8733	1.1445	1.1451
Chile (Peso)	.002844	.002780	351.56	359.65
China (Renminbi)	.185642	.185642	5.3867	5.3867
Colombia (Peso)	.001753	.001753	570.38	570.38
Denmark (Krone)	.1573	.1573	6.3570	6.3555
Ecuador (Sucre)				
Floating rate	.000966	.000966	1035.00	1035.00
Finland (Markka)	.24984	.24941	4.0025	4.0095
France (Franc)	.17881	.17879	5.5925	5.5930
30-Day Forward	.17813	.17808	5.6140	5.6156
90-Day Forward	.17690	.17685	5.6529	5.6545
180-Day Forward	.17510	.17504	5.7110	5.7130
Germany (Mark)	.6112	.6111	1.6362	1.6365
30-Day Forward	.6090	.6088	1.6421	1.6426
90-Day Forward	.6045	.6044	1.6543	1.6544
180-Day Forward	.5982	.5982	1.6717	1.6718
Greece (Drachma)	.005405	.005405	185.00	185.00
Hong Kong (Dollar) ...	.12884	.12884	7.7615	7.7615
India (Rupee)	.03880	.03880	25.77	25.77
Indonesia (Rupiah)	.0005056	.0005056	1978.00	1978.00
Ireland (Punt)	1.6330	1.6318	.6124	.6128
Israel (Shekel)	.4308	.4321	2.3215	2.3142
Italy (Lira)	.0008121	.0008117	1231.41	1232.01
Japan (Yen)	.007686	.007707	130.10	129.75
30-Day Forward	.007678	.007698	130.24	129.90
90-Day Forward	.007666	.007686	130.45	130.10
180-Day Forward	.007656	.007677	130.62	130.26
Jordan (Dinar)	1.4500	1.4500	.6897	.6897
Kuwait (Dinar)	3.4965	3.4965	.2860	.2860
Lebanon (Pound)	.001134	.001134	881.50	881.50
Malaysia (Ringgit)	.3650	.3647	2.7400	2.7420
Malta (Lira)	3.1250	3.1250	.3200	.3200
Mexico (Peso)				
Floating rate	.0003254	.0003254	3073.01	3073.01
Netherland (Guilder) .	.5423	.5422	1.8440	1.8445
New Zealand (Dollar) .	.5610	.5620	1.7825	1.7794
Norway (Krone)	.1558	.1558	6.4175	6.4185
Pakistan (Rupee)	.0405	.0405	24.72	24.72
Peru (New Sol)	1.0152	1.0051	.99	.99
Philippines (Peso)	.03839	.03839	26.05	26.05
Portugal (Escudo)	.007067	.007063	141.50	141.59
Saudi Arabia (Riyal) ..	.26663	.26663	3.7505	3.7505
Singapore (Dollar)	.5958	.5959	1.6785	1.6780
South Africa (Rand)				
Commercial rate	.3568	.3574	2.8023	2.7981
Financial rate	.3248	.3240	3.0790	3.0860
South Korea (Won)	.0013310	.0013310	751.30	751.30
Spain (Peseta)	.009723	.009699	102.85	103.10
Sweden (Krona)	.1673	.1672	5.9775	5.9815
Switzerland (Franc) ..	.6888	.6892	1.4517	1.4510
30-Day Forward	.6872	.6875	1.4552	1.4546
90-Day Forward	.6835	.6839	1.4631	1.4621
180-Day Forward	.6788	.6792	1.4732	1.4724
Taiwan (Dollar)	.038850	.037908	25.74	26.38
Thailand (Baht)	.03926	.03926	25.47	25.47
Turkey (Lira)	.0002044	.0002020	4892.01	4950.00
United Arab (Dirham) .	.2723	.2723	3.6725	3.6725
Uruguay (New Peso)				
Financial	.000425	.000425	2352.94	2352.94

Source: Reprinted by permission of *Wall Street Journal,* © (November 14, 1991) Dow Jones & Company, Inc. All Rights Reserved Worldwide.

of the German mark, that would be 1/.57 Deutsche marks per dollar.[3] Table 9.4 contains spot currency prices from both perspectives for some key currencies.

The dollar cost of a German mark should be the same if one first purchased francs and then used the francs to buy marks or if one purchased marks directly. In Table 9.4, the dollar price of a German mark is 0.612000 dollars. The French franc price of a German mark is 3.4171 francs. The number of dollars needed to buy 3.4171 francs (which buy one mark) is (.1791)(3.4171) = 0.612003. The two methods of buying one mark are virtually identical and differ only in the sixth decimal. If the two methods gave different answers, an opportunity for triangular arbitrage would exist. For example, suppose the dollar price of a French franc is only .1720 dollars and the franc price of the mark is as shown in the table. Then a mark could be purchased for (.1720)(3.4171) = 0.5877 dollars. An arbitrageur could borrow marks and sell them for 0.6120 dollars per mark and simultaneously take 0.5877 dollars to buy back the marks needed to repay the borrowings. The profit from this triangular arbitrage would be 0.6120 − 0.5877 = 0.0243 dollars per mark. To avoid triangular arbitrage opportunities, the following condition must be met for all trios of currencies:

$$S_{1,2} = S_{1,3}S_{3,2}, \tag{9.1}$$

where $S_{i,j}$ is the number of units of the i-th currency required to purchase one unit of the jth currency.

TABLE 9.4   Key currency cross rates.

Key Currency Cross Rates Late New York Trading Nov. 13, 1991

	Dollar	Pound	SFranc	Guilder	Yen	Lira	D-Mark	FFranc	CdnDlr
Canada	1.1313	2.0098	.78021	.61434	.00870	.00092	.69235	.20261	....
France	5.5835	9.919	3.8507	3.0320	.04292	.00454	3.4171	....	4.9355
Germany	1.6340	2.9028	1.1269	.88732	.01256	.00133	....	.29265	1.4444
Italy	1229.3	2183.8	847.76	667.53	9.449	....	752.29	220.16	1086.6
Japan	130.10	231.12	89.724	70.649	....	.10584	79.621	23.301	115.00
Netherlands	1.8415	3.2714	1.2700	....	.01415	.00150	1.1270	.32981	1.6278
Switzerland	1.4500	2.5759	....	.78740	.01115	.00118	.88739	.25969	1.2817
U.K.	.56290	....	.38821	.30568	.00433	.00046	.34449	.10082	.49757
U.S.	....	1.7765	.68966	.54304	.00769	.00081	.61200	.17910	.88394
Source: Telerate									

---

[3] In principle, the price of wheat could be quoted both as the dollar price of wheat, say four dollars per bushel, or the wheat price of dollars, which would be 1/4 bushels per dollar.

9.3 STRUCTURE OF CURRENCY FUTURES PRICES

Unlike agricultural commodities, which are sometimes in short supply, currencies
are always in large supply. As a result, currency futures obey the cost-of-carry equilibrium developed in Chapter 3: $F_t = S_t e^{b(T-t)}$. In currencies, the cost of carry is
the difference between the interest cost of the dollars invested in a currency and
the interest earned on the foreign currency. The cost-of-carry relation can therefore
be written as

$$F_t = S_t e^{(r_d - r_f)(T-t)}, \tag{9.2}$$

where $r_d(r_f)$ is the continuously compounded, riskless rate of interest in the domestic (foreign) currency and T is the maturity of the futures contract.

   In international finance, the relation (9.2) is called the *interest rate parity
(IRP) relation*. It is instructive to derive IRP in a somewhat different way. Consider
an investor who has one U.S. dollar to invest. If the dollar is invested domestically
at the riskless rate, the value at maturity is

$$e^{r_d(T-t)}.$$

On the other hand, the dollar may also be used to purchase foreign currency that
is then invested at the foreign riskless rate of interest. If the proceeds at maturity
of the foreign investment are sold in the futures market, a dollar return can be
guaranteed at time t. At maturity, the dollar cash proceeds of a hedged foreign
investment are

$$(1/S_t)e^{r_f(T-t)}F_t.$$

For example, consider an investment in Germany. Suppose $S_t = 0.57$, $r_f = 0.05$
per year, $T - t = 0.25$ years, and $F_t = 0.58$. The hedged dollar proceeds on the
investment in Germany are 1.03034 dollars.

   In equilibrium, the two ways of investing the dollar—directly in the U.S. or
indirectly in a foreign country—must have the same value at maturity, assuming
that both investments offer a riskless return and that there is no default risk on the
futures or forward contract. In other words, the absence of costless arbitrage opportunities in the marketplace ensures that

$$e^{r_d(T-t)} = (1/S_t)e^{r_f(T-t)}F_t.$$

This expression is easily manipulated to give (9.2). Dividing by S_t and subtracting
one from each side, equation (9.2) can also be written as

$$\frac{F_t - S_t}{S_t} = e^{(r_d - r_f)(T-t)} - 1. \tag{9.3}$$

The left-hand side of this expression, which in other futures markets we call the percentage basis, is called the *forward premium* or the *swap rate* in the currency markets. The term *swap rate* comes from the fact that investors frequently buy a foreign currency and agree to swap it back for dollars. The swap rate specifies the gain or loss on such a transaction. The right-hand side is the interest differential between the two countries over the time period $T - t$.

The IRP relation can also be derived for the case in which interest is earned discretely over the life of the futures contract. Suppose r_d^* and r_f^* are the U.S. and foreign riskless rates of interest for the time over which funds are invested, $T - t$. Then an investment in the U.S. is worth $\$(1 + r_d^*)$ at maturity, and a hedged investment in the foreign country is worth $\$(1/S)(1 + r_f^*)F$ at maturity. To eliminate riskless arbitrage opportunities, these outcomes must be equal, which implies

$$\frac{F - S}{S} = \frac{r_d^* - r_f^*}{1 + r_f^*}. \tag{9.4}$$

This equilibrium relation is plotted in Figure 9.1 as the 45-degree line. Arbitrage opportunities arise if an observation is not on the line.

For example, consider point A. At A, exchange rates are $S = 0.50$ and $F = 0.51$, yielding a forward premium $(F - S)/S = 0.02$; and three-month interest rates are $r_d^* = 0.03$ and $r_f^* = 0.02$, yielding an interest differential of $(r_d^* - r_f^*)/(1 + r_f^*) = 0.01$. Although the interest differential is in favor of the U.S., it is profitable to borrow in the U.S. and invest in the foreign country because the profit on the foreign exchange transaction exceeds the loss on the interest differential. An arbitrageur could borrow one million dollars in the U.S., thereby incurring an obligation to repay $(1 + r_d^*) = 1.03$ million dollars at maturity; and she would invest in the hedged foreign investment, which pays $(1/S)(1 + r_f^*)F = 1.0404$ million dollars at maturity. The arbitrage profit is 1.0404 million minus 1.03 million or 10,400 dollars. The activity of arbitrageurs results in a capital outflow from the U.S. that raises U.S. interest rates, raises the spot exchange rate, lowers foreign interest rates, and lowers the futures price, until equilibrium is restored. In fact, all points above the line in the figure imply a capital outflow from the U.S.

Points below the line, such as point B, imply a capital inflow into the United States. At point B, the interest differential is in favor of the U.S., but the forward premium is zero. Arbitrage profits could be earned by borrowing in the foreign country at r_f^*, selling the foreign currency at S, investing in the U.S. at r_d^*, and entering into a futures contract to purchase the foreign currency at F to repay the loan. The dollar value of the face amount of the foreign loan is $(1/S)(1 + r_f^*)F$, and the value of the dollar investment is $(1 + r_d^*)$. Assuming that $F = 0.50$, $S = 0.50$, $r_d^* = 0.03$, and $r_f^* = 0.02$, the profit is 0.01 for every dollar borrowed and invested in the United States.

In today's highly efficient international financial markets, arbitrage is instantaneous, and deviations from IRP are rarely observed except for very small devi-

FIGURE 9.1   Interest Rate Parity

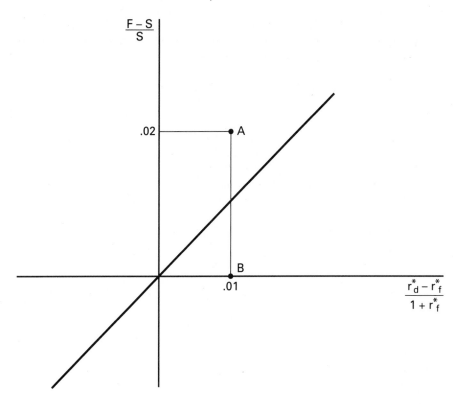

ations caused by transaction costs. Apparent deviations may be observed for certain interest rates. Each country has only one spot rate and one futures rate for any maturity, but each country has many short-term interest rates that reflect different degrees of risk. Thus, it is possible to find two interest rates that cause IRP to be violated. Differences in risk or differences in transaction costs, however, usually explain deviations from IRP.

9.4 FACTORS AFFECTING EXCHANGE RATES

Many factors affect exchange rates. While it is beyond the scope of this book to consider all of these factors in detail, understanding some of the key factors that analysts consider is useful from a practical standpoint.[4]

Purchasing Power Parity
An important factor determining a country's currency value is the rate of inflation in the country. The higher the rate of inflation, the greater the decline in the pur-

---

[4]For detailed discussions of factors determining exchange rates, see Lessard (1985).

chasing power of one unit of the currency, and the lower the price of the currency. The theory of Purchasing Power Parity (*PPP*) is a macroeconomic version of the Law of One Price (*LOP*) discussed in Chapter 6. The *LOP* takes the exchange rate as given and says that the prices of a commodity in two different countries must be the same after adjustment for the exchange rate:

$$G_d = SG_f,$$

where G_d and G_f are the U.S. and foreign prices of the commodity and S is the spot exchange rate (the dollar price of the foreign currency). If commodity arbitrage takes place for every commodity, the *LOP* must hold for bundles of the same commodities in the two countries. Changes in the price of the bundle in one country due to inflation without a corresponding change in the price of the bundle in the other country must imply a change in the exchange rate. In other words, under *PPP*, the exchange rate is the dependent variable, and the prices of commodities in the two countries are independent variables.

The *absolute version of PPP* is written as

$$S_t = \frac{P_{d,t}}{P_{f,t}}. \tag{9.5}$$

The variable $P_{d,t}$ is the dollar price of a bundle of commodities in the U.S. and $P_{f,t}$ is the foreign currency price of the same bundle. For example, at $t = 1991$, $P_{d,t} = 500$ dollars and $P_{f,t} = 2{,}000$ units of foreign currency. That implies an exchange rate of .25 according to *PPP*. The *relative version of PPP* looks at the change in the exchange rate as a function of the relative changes in the prices of the bundle of commodities in each country. We can derive the relative version of *PPP* by writing equation (9.5) for a base period, time 0. Dividing the base period equation into (9.5) yields

$$\frac{S_t}{S_0} = \frac{P_{d,t}/P_{f,t}}{P_{d,0}/P_{f,0}} = \frac{P_{d,t}/P_{d,0}}{P_{f,t}/P_{f,0}}$$

or

$$\frac{S_t}{S_0} = \frac{I_{d,t}}{I_{f,t}}, \tag{9.6}$$

where $I_{d,t}$ and $I_{f,t}$ are the U.S. and foreign country price indexes with a time 0 base year. Equation (9.6) is the relative version of *PPP*. Suppose the base year is 1967 and that in that year the bundle costs $P_{d,0} = 200$ in the U.S. and $P_{f,0} = 400$ in the foreign country. That implies an exchange rate of .50 dollars in 1967. Using the 1991 bundle prices assumed above, the price indexes are $I_{d,t} = 2.50$ in the U.S. and $I_{f,t} = 5.00$ in the foreign country. The ratio of these indexes implies a ratio of exchange rates in 1991 versus 1967 of 0.5, which, according to *PPP*, means the exchange rate is 0.25 in 1991.

In practice, *PPP* does not seem to hold as well as in the example we have just presented. A difficulty arises from measurement problems. Price indexes in different countries do not include the same commodities or have the same weights when the same commodities are included. Difficulties also arise in measuring prices of commodities accurately and at the same time in the different countries. Another difficulty arises from the fact that transportation costs are high for many commodities, so that the law of one price cannot be established. Indeed, transport costs are prohibitive for certain commodities. Moreover, many items such as services are simply not traded. Services (say, haircuts) can only be traded by moving labor, but restrictions on international migration prevent arbitrage of services. Neither of these difficulties is severe if the source of a change in currency values is inflation that affects the prices of all commodities—traded and non-traded—in the same way. In that case, any index will be representative. *PPP* does not hold in practice, however, because the prices of different commodities move in different ways in different countries. It is possible, for example, for a country's traded goods not to increase in price (because of cost cutting measures in the traded goods sector of the economy), while the prices of non-traded goods increase considerably more. The exchange rate of that country will not depreciate as much as would be predicted by the aggregate inflation in the country because it has remained competitive in those goods that are traded internationally.

Despite these difficulties, *PPP* remains an important determinant of exchange rate changes over longer periods of time, particularly when comparing countries with significantly different inflation rates. Table 9.5 presents some data for the exchange rates and inflation of seven industrial nations for the period 1967 to 1983 in which substantial differences in inflation arose. The second column gives the ratio of the dollar price of the foreign currency in 1983 to the dollar price in 1967. During this period, the dollar appreciated relative to every country except West Germany and Japan. For example, the price of the British pound fell by 44.9 percent, whereas the price of the German mark rose by 56.4 percent. The third column shows that much of the change in exchange rates can be explained by differences in inflation rates. Typically, when U.S. inflation is less than foreign inflation, the price of the foreign currency falls, and when U.S. inflation is greater than foreign inflation, the price of the foreign currency rises. Japan is the only exception. According to the consumer price indexes for the U.S. and Japan, inflation was about equal in the two countries, yet the Japanese yen appreciated by 52.6 percent. Part of the explanation for this discrepancy lies in the fact that the consumer price index is not representative of the price of Japanese traded goods. Consumer goods within Japan have risen in price, but goods traded internationally have not risen in price to the extent implied by the Japanese consumer price index.

The Monetarist Approach to Exchange Rate Determination

The monetarist approach is an extension of purchasing power parity. Under the monetarist approach, the price level in each country is determined by monetary

TABLE 9.5   Exchange rates and inflation, 1967–1983.

Country	S_{83}/S_{67}	I_d/I_f	Real Exchange Rate
Canada	0.875	0.929	0.94
France	0.649	0.732	0.89
West Germany	1.564	1.468	1.07
Italy	0.412	0.472	0.87
Japan	1.526	0.963	1.58
United Kingdom	0.551	0.554	0.99

The second column is the ratio of the dollar price of the foreign currency in 1983 to the dollar price of the foreign currency in 1967. The third column is the ratio of the consumer price index in the United States to the consumer price index in the foreign country. The base year for both indexes is 1967. The fourth column is the ratio of the second column to the third column. A number greater than (less than) one indicates that the currency had a real appreciation (depreciation) relative to the dollar.

Source: International Monetary Fund, *International Financial Statistics*, monthly.

factors. The exchange rate then depends on the factors that determine the price level in each country.

The quantity theory of money states that

$$m_t v = I_t y_t, \tag{9.7}$$

where m_t is the money supply at time t divided by the money supply in the base period, v is the velocity of money, I_t is the price index, and y_t is real income at time t divided by real income in the base period. The price index can be written as

$$I_t = (m_t v)/y_t, \tag{9.8}$$

which shows that, under the assumption that the velocity of money is stable, the quantity theory states that inflation occurs if the money supply expands faster than real income.

Under the quantity theory, the price level may be written for both the domestic and foreign countries:

$$I_{d,t} = (m_{d,t}v_d)/y_{d,t}, \qquad \textbf{(9.8a)}$$

$$I_{f,t} = (m_{f,t}v_f)/y_{f,t}. \qquad \textbf{(9.8b)}$$

The base period for the variables is assumed to be the same in the two countries. Substituting (9.8a) and (9.8b) in (9.6) yields

$$\frac{S_t}{S_0} = \frac{I_{d,t}}{I_{f,t}} = \frac{m_{d,t}v_d y_{f,t}}{m_{f,t}v_f y_{d,t}}. \qquad \textbf{(9.9)}$$

Equation (9.9) says that the change in the exchange rate depends on relative money supply growths and relative real income growths in the two countries, assuming constant velocities. Suppose that velocities in two countries are one, that real income grew 100 percent in the foreign country ($y_{f,t} = 2$) and 50 percent in the domestic economy ($y_{d,t} = 1.5$), that the money supply grew 300 percent in the foreign country ($m_{f,t} = 4$) and 100 percent in the domestic economy ($m_{d,t} = 2$). That would imply $S_t/S_0 = 0.67$, a 33 percent decline in the price of the foreign currency. The monetary approach can become a good deal more complicated as other factors that affect the impact of money supply changes on the economy are considered.

Like *PPP*, the monetarist approach is less successful in explaining short-run changes in exchange rates than in explaining long-run changes. Using the monetarist approach to predict exchange rates requires predicting money supply growths in the two countries and other variables that affect inflation, something that is not an easy task over short intervals.

Balance of Payments Approach to Exchange Rate Determination

Another set of factors considered by analysts is the balance of payments, particularly the current account. The current account balance of a country is the exports of goods and services minus imports. A country has a current account *surplus* when its exports exceed its imports, and it has a current account *deficit* when imports exceed exports. The U.S., for example, had a large current account deficit in the 1980s. Analysts who take the balance of payments approach argue that a deficit increases the demand for foreign exchange and raises the price of foreign currencies, whereas a surplus lowers the price of foreign currencies. It has been difficult to show, however, that exchange rates are, in fact, related to the current account deficit in this way. For example, the U.S. dollar appreciated during some periods in the 1980s when the current account deficit was large.

Part of the problem is that the current account is endogenous, that is, it depends on fundamental forces that also affect the exchange rate. For example, the current account depends on monetary and fiscal policy that also have a direct effect on the exchange rate. A country might import more because its real income has grown. A growth in real income could be consistent with a decline in the price of foreign currencies (a strengthening of the domestic exchange rate) as shown above for the monetarist approach.

Analysts often emphasize the current account, but the balance of payments also includes a capital account. Overall, the balance of payments must balance. A current account deficit must be matched by a capital account surplus (assuming government reserves and borrowings do not change), and a current account surplus must be matched by a capital account deficit. If a country imports more than it exports, the cost of the net imports must be financed by borrowing from abroad. If a country exports more than it imports, the foreign currency earnings must be invested abroad (or used to reduce foreign debt). Some analysts argue that capital flows are exogenous and that the current account is endogenous. Under this argument, the U.S. trade deficit results from a large capital inflow to the U.S. in response to higher U.S. interest rates and other factors. The capital account surplus, in turn, made resources available to the U.S., some of which were spent on imports, thereby generating the current account deficit. Under this scenario, the price of foreign currencies declined even though the U.S. ran a current account deficit.

Because of capital flows and other macroeconomic factors, the balance of payments approach, with its focus on the current account, has not proved adequate to explain the behavior of exchange rates.

The Asset Market Approach to Exchange Rate Determination
The asset approach to exchange rate determination argues that investors throughout the world allocate investment according to anticipated real returns and anticipated exchange rate changes. If Japan has a low expected real return relative to the U.S., funds will flow to the U.S., and the U.S. dollar will appreciate. The asset approach thus focuses on capital flows and the factors that determine capital flows. In addition to expected real returns, capital flows respond to risk.

In summary, a variety of complicated forces affect exchange rates. *PPP* is important, but short-run deviations from *PPP* are prevalent. These short-run deviations depend on monetary and fiscal policy, exogenous changes in the demand for imports and exports, and exogenous changes in capital flows.

9.5 RETURNS TO SPECULATORS IN CURRENCIES

As in other financial markets, it is difficult for currency speculators to make abnormal returns because competition among traders causes the currency markets to be efficient. One potential source of inefficiency is the intervention by central banks in the currency markets to "stabilize" their exchange rates. Such stabilization sometimes slows adjustment of exchange rates and makes it possible to predict future exchange rates. Most of the evidence, however, indicates that, like stock prices, exchange rate changes are hard to predict.

Spot Speculation and Futures Speculation
The fact that exchange rate changes are hard to predict does not keep people from trying. Speculation on exchange rate changes can be done in either the spot market

or the futures market. In the futures market, a speculator would buy currency futures if she expects the spot rate at maturity to exceed the current futures price, and she would sell currency futures if she expected the spot rate at maturity to be less than the futures price. Her expected profit is $E(\tilde{S}_T) - F_t(T)$. In equilibrium, competition among speculators would eliminate profits and cause the futures price to equal the expected spot price:

$$F_t(T) = E(\tilde{S}_T).$$ (9.10)

We noted in Chapter 4 that the trading pressures of hedgers might cause speculators to demand a risk premium that brings about a divergence between the futures price and the expected spot price. In currency markets, the risk premium could easily be positive or negative since hedgers could be buying foreign currency or selling foreign currency. In the absence of a reason to assume the risk premium is a particular sign, we shall assume that condition (9.10) is met and that no risk premium exists.

A speculator who expects a foreign currency to appreciate could also borrow dollars and buy the foreign currency. The speculation is profitable if the currency appreciates more than the cost of holding the currency. The mechanics of spot speculation are as follows: borrow a dollar, buy $1/S_t$ units of foreign currency, invest the foreign currency at the foreign interest rate, r_f^*, sell the foreign currency at the future spot rate, $\tilde{S}_T$, and pay back the dollar plus interest of r_d^*. The expected profit is

$$(1/S_t)(1 + r_f^*)E(\tilde{S}_T) - (1 + r_d^*)$$

In the absence of a risk premium, equilibrium requires a zero-expected profit, which implies

$$S_t \left(\frac{1 + r_d^*}{1 + r_f^*} \right) = E(\tilde{S}_T).$$ (9.11)

It is worth noting that the left-hand sides of (9.10) and (9.11), taken together, yield IRP. Under IRP, spot speculation and futures speculation are equivalent.

The International Fisher Effect
Relation (9.11) is often called the *international Fisher effect (IFE)*. The *IFE* is usually written as

$$\frac{E(\tilde{S}_T)}{S_t} = \frac{1 + r_d^*}{1 + r_f^*}.$$

The *IFE* says that the expected change in the exchange rate equals the interest rate differential between the countries. For example, if the one-year interest rate in the U.S. is 8 percent and the one-year interest rate in Brazil is 80 percent, the IFE says the price of the Brazilian cruzeiro is expected to be 60 percent of its current value.

The *IFE* takes its name from Irving Fisher, who argued that the domestic interest rate is approximately equal to the real rate of interest plus the expected rate of inflation. The *IFE* assumes that international differences in interest rates reflect differences in expected inflation rates. According to Fisher,

$$(1 + r_d^*) = (1 + a_d^*)[1 + E(\tilde{\pi}_d^*)]$$

$$(1 + r_f^*) = (1 + a_f^*)[1 + E(\tilde{\pi}_f^*)],$$

where a_d^* and a_f^* are the domestic and foreign real rates of interest, and π_d^* and π_f^* are the U.S. and foreign inflation rates. If $a_d^* = a_f^*$, the *IFE* becomes

$$\frac{E(\tilde{S}_T)}{S_t} = \frac{1 + E(\tilde{\pi}_d^*)}{1 + E(\tilde{\pi}_f^*)}. \qquad \text{(9.12)}$$

In this form, the *IFE* is very much like the relative *PPP* equation (9.6), except that *PPP* is an *ex post* relation between the realized exchange rate change and realized inflation while the *IFE* is an *ex ante* relation between the expected exchange rate change and expected inflation.

Forecasting Exchange Rates

In an efficient market without inside information, it is impossible to make better forecasts of exchange rates than the forecasts available from the financial markets. As we have just seen, financial markets provide two forecasts: the futures price and the difference in interest rates. In the absence of forecasting skill or inside information and an understanding of the actions of world monetary authorities, these readily available forecasts are as useful as more sophisticated forecasting. Careful analysis of fundamental factors such as inflation, monetary policy, balance of payments, and asset flows may result in superior forecasts, but competition among forecasters tends to eliminate abnormal returns.[5] Market-based forecasts are not necessarily accurate since unexpected events have a way of altering outcomes from the outcome that was expected, but they are unbiased and readily available.

9.6 HEDGING CURRENCY RISK

Given the uncertainties about the future value of a currency, companies engaged in international operations frequently want to hedge against the risks of exchange rate changes. Currency risk can arise in regard to a particular import or export transaction or because a company's balance sheet contains assets and liabilities denominated in a foreign currency.[6]

---

[5]Evidence on forecasting ability is provided by Levich, "Evaluating the Performance of the Forecasters," in Lessard (1985).

[6]For greater detail on hedging and on other financial issues in managing international operations see Shapiro (1989) and Eiteman and Stonehill (1986).

Transactions Risk

Transactions risk refers to the foreign currency risk of a particular future transaction denominated in a foreign currency. For example, a U.S. company sells a product to a German importer who agrees to pay for the product in three months, when shipment is received. Payment is specified in German marks. The dollar value of that account receivable for the U.S. company is uncertain. This transaction can be hedged by selling forward the German marks to be received in three months. Such a forward sale is usually done through a bank because the quantity and other terms of the forward contract can be tailored to the specific transaction incurring currency risk. Futures contracts could also be used, but the size and maturity of a futures contract may not match the hedging need exactly.

An example of transactions risk might be a U.S. airplane manufacturer who has committed to deliver a jet to Lufthansa in one year for 40,000,000 marks, with payment to be made in one year. The spot price of the mark is assumed to be $S_t = \$0.6000$ and the one year forward price, $F_t = \$0.61132075$. If left unhedged, the dollar value of the contract is subject to fluctuations in the value of the German mark. At the current forward price, the contract is worth \$24,452,830, but if the spot price should fall two percent below its current value to \$0.5880, the contract would be worth \$23,520,000, a loss of nearly one million dollars. The manufacturer can hedge foreign exchange risk by entering a forward contract today to sell 40,000,000 marks a year from now at the forward price. At maturity, when payment is made, the German mark proceeds from the export of the jet are delivered to the bank in return for dollars. The manufacturer has a problem if there are delays in delivery and payment. In that case, the forward contract has to be rolled over at some cost.

An alternative to the forward market hedge is a money market hedge. Under interest rate parity, a money market hedge is equivalent to a forward market hedge. U.S. and German interest rates consistent with the spot, and forward rates in the example are $r_d^* = .08$ and $r_f^* = .06$. Under a money market hedge, the U.S. jet manufacturer borrows German marks against the proceeds of the sale of the jet, which amounts to $40,000,000/(1.06) = 37,735,849$ marks, and converts the marks to dollars at the current spot rate to get $(0.60)(37,735,849) = 22,641,509$. If this amount is invested at 8 percent, the proceeds at maturity are $(22,641,509)(1.08) = 24,452,830$, the same as under the forward contract. In practice, the two approaches may not be the same since the short-term interest rates that cause interest rate parity to hold may not be the rates at which the manufacturer can borrow and lend. If the manufacturer is in need of funds, the money market hedge is preferable to the forward market hedge.

Balance Sheet Risk

In many cases, a company faces foreign exchange risk that is less specifically tied to a particular transaction. For example, a company exporting to Germany may build up accounts receivable with many different maturity dates, or it may hold inventory in Germany which is exposed to currency risk. Indeed, a company's balance sheet may have both assets and liabilities denominated in various foreign currencies. Appropriate hedging procedures for this more general case are quite complex. They depend on whether the foreign currency obligation is contractual or not. A *contractual* obligation denominated in a foreign currency is subject to foreign exchange risk because the contract price is set and cannot be changed, as in the case of the U.S. exporter of jets. If the value of the currency falls, the foreign currency price cannot be adjusted. On the other hand, a *non-contractual* business operation is less subject to exchange risk because changes in exchange rates can, perhaps, be offset by price changes in the foreign currency. A U.S. toothpaste manufacturer with an Italian subsidiary, for example, may find it possible to offset declines in the value of the Italian lira with increases in the price of toothpaste sold in Italy.

A simple example of a balance sheet hedge of a contractual asset is that of a British subsidiary with a cash balance of 5,000 pounds. The U.S. parent, worried about a possible decline in the British pound, decides to hedge that position by selling futures in the amount of 5,000 pounds. If the value of the pound falls, the decline in the dollar value of the cash is offset by the profit on the short futures position. This hedge is equivalent to a hedge of a particular transaction, in the sense that both are contractual. It is different in that the cash balance has no maturity and is changed daily as a result of business operations.

An example of a balance sheet hedge of a non-contractual item is hedging a finished goods inventory position valued at 5,000 pounds at the current price of the product in Britain. This hedge is more complicated because a decline in the value of the British pound that would reduce the dollar value of the inventory might be offset by an increase in the price of the finished good in the United Kingdom. Indeed, under *PPP*, that is exactly what would be expected. Suppose declines in the dollar price of the British pound can be partially offset by increasing product prices by 50 percent of the amount they would increase under *PPP*. If repricing offsets half the decline in the price of the pound, the optimal hedge is to sell short about 2,500 pounds. In effect, the ability to reprice inventory in the U.K. provides a partial natural hedge (for 50 percent of the decline). The futures market hedge hedges the other half of the exchange rate decline. Table 9.6 details this example.

9.7 SUMMARY

This chapter begins by describing currency markets and currency quotations. The cost-of-carry model for currency futures is then derived and shown to be the same as the well-known interest rate parity condition. Theories of the determinants of exchange rates—the purchasing power parity approach, the monetarist approach, the balance of payments approach, and the asset approach—are described.

We distinguish futures speculation and spot speculation. Competition among speculators in the futures market implies that the futures price is a good estimate of the expected spot price. Similarly, competition in spot speculation leads to the international Fisher effect—that the expected change in the exchange rate equals the interest differential between two countries.

Currency futures may be used to hedge against fluctuations in exchange rates. The chapter concludes with descriptions of hedging transaction risk and balance sheet risk.

TABLE 9.6   Hedging foreign exchange risk of 1000 units of finished goods inventory when 50 percent of the exchange rate change can be offset by raising the sale price.

| | Inventory | | | Futures Market | | |
Date	Value[a] (pounds)	Exch. Rate	Value (dollars)	Futures Position (pounds)	Futures Price	Value (dollars)
Sept. 1	5,000	1.60	8,000	−2,500	1.60	−4,000
Dec. 1	5,833	1.20	7,000	−2,500	1.20	−3,000
Gain			−1,000			1,000

a. The initial price of inventory is assumed to be 5 pounds per unit. The old exchange rate is 1/3 greater than the new exchange rate. The table assumes the selling price can be raised by half the amount that would offset the change in the exchange rate, or by .5(1/3)(5).

3

OPTIONS

10 STRUCTURE OF OPTION PRICES: ARBITRAGE RELATIONS

Option contracts confer the right, but not the obligation to consummate a transaction in a particular commodity, at a particular price, at some future date. Like futures contracts, option contracts intermediate between the present and the future. Unlike futures, however, the option holder can choose whether or not he wants to exercise his right to buy or sell the underlying commodity.

This chapter is the option pricing counterpart to Chapter 3 in which the structure of futures prices was examined. We derive and explain the arbitrage links among commodity options, futures options, commodity futures, and commodities, as depicted in the horizontal and vertical lines of Figure 10.1. In this chapter, we explain how the prices of these instruments are related to each other, and we set bounds on the prices of options relative to the prices of the underlying commodity. We do not specify the factors determining the level of option prices. The determinants of the level of option prices are discussed in Chapter 11.

As a reminder, the assumptions that underlie the arbitrage arguments to follow are (a) individuals are rational; (b) markets are frictionless (i.e., there are no transaction costs, etc.); (c) individuals can borrow or lend risklessly at a continuously compounded interest rate, r; and (d) the cost of carrying the commodity underlying the futures and commodity option contracts is a continuous known rate, b. In addition, for the sake of convenience, we assume that (e) futures, commodity option, and futures option contracts have the same time remaining to expiration, T.

10.1 OPTION NOMENCLATURE, NOTATION, AND DEFINITIONS

An *option* is a contract that provides its holder with the right to buy or sell a commodity at a specified price within a specified period of time. Options are usually

174

FIGURE 10.1   Interrelations Between Commodity Market and Markets for the Commodity's Derivative Instruments

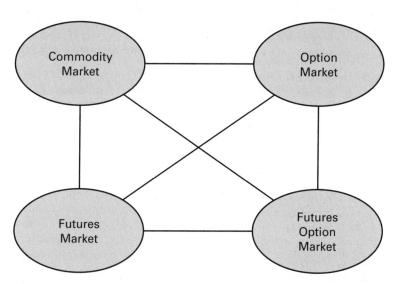

prefixed by the nature of the commodity underlying the option contract, that is, a *stock option* is the right to buy or sell a common stock, a *foreign currency option* is the right to buy or sell a currency, a *bond option* is the right to buy or sell a bond, a *futures option* is the right to buy or sell a futures contract, and so on.

A contract that provides its holder with the right to buy the underlying commodity is called a *call option*; a contract that provides the right to sell is called a *put option*. In the option contract, the specified price at which the commodity may be bought or sold is called the *exercise price* or the *striking price* of the option. If the current commodity price exceeds the exercise price of the option, the call is *in-the-money* and the put is *out-of-the-money*. If the current commodity price is below the exercise price of the option, the call is *out-of-the-money* and the put is *in-the-money*. When the current commodity price is approximately equal to the exercise price of the options, both the call and the put are *at-the-money*.

Two different styles of option contracts trade in the U.S., *European* and *American* options. These option contracts are alike in all respects, except that European options may be exercised only at expiration, while American options may be exercised at any time up to and including the expiration day.

The notation that is most commonly used to represent parameters related to option pricing is as follows:

$S(\tilde{S}_T) \equiv$ current (random terminal) commodity price.

$F(\tilde{F}_T) \equiv$ current (random terminal) futures price.

$X \equiv$ exercise price or striking price.

$T \equiv$ time to expiration of the option.

$c(S, T; X)$ ≡ European call option with exercise price X and time to expiration T.

$p(S, T; X)$ ≡ European put option with exercise price X and time to expiration T.

$C(S, T; X)$ ≡ American call option with exercise price X and time to expiration T.

$P(S, T; X)$ ≡ American put option with exercise price X and time to expiration T.

Where the first argument in the parentheses of the option notation is S [e.g., $c(S, T; X)$], the option is a commodity option and the current commodity price is S. Where the first argument in the parentheses of the option notation is F [e.g., $c(F, T; X)$], the option is a futures option and the current futures price is F.

10.2. PROFIT DIAGRAMS AND VECTOR NOTATION

In Chapter 1, we illustrated the profits at expiration for different option positions. In this section, we introduce a simple vector notation that promotes understanding of the profit contingencies of complex option/commodity positions.

Figure 10.2 plots the profit at maturity, T, of different positions as a function of the price of the underlying commodity at maturity, S_T. (Option premiums are ignored in the current discussion.) We assume that all options have the same exercise price, X. Buying a call is profitable if $S_T > X$ and is not profitable if the commodity price fails to exceed the exercise price at maturity. The vector representation of this outcome is $\binom{1}{0}$. The first position in the vector indicates the dollar profit for every dollar that the commodity price at maturity exceeds the exercise price, and the second position indicates the dollar profit for every dollar that the commodity price at maturity falls below the exercise price. The vector notation for the seller of the call is $\binom{-1}{0}$. The seller of a call loses if $S_T > X$. The outcomes for the buyer and the seller of a put are also plotted in Figure 10.2. The vector notation for the buyer of a put is $\binom{0}{1}$ since the buyer makes money if the commodity price at maturity is below the exercise price. The vector notation for the seller of the put is $\binom{0}{-1}$ since the seller of the put loses if the commodity price at maturity falls below the exercise price.

Finally, the figure plots the profits to a long position and to a short position in the commodity, each initially established at the price, S, where $S = X$. We assume that no costs are incurred to store the commodity and that no dividends or other payments are made to the owners of the commodity. The vector notation for the long position is $\binom{1}{-1}$ and for the short position is $\binom{-1}{1}$.

The vector notation is useful for determining the profit to combinations of positions established at a single exercise price because corresponding positions in vectors may be added. For example, the equivalent of a long position in the commodity can be established by buying a call and selling a put: $\binom{1}{0} + \binom{0}{-1} = \binom{1}{-1}$. This is a *synthetic long*. Another way to see this is to add vertically the profits from the buy call and sell put positions in Figure 10.2. The equivalent of a short position, a *synthetic short*, can be established by selling a call and buying a put: $\binom{-1}{0} + \binom{0}{1} = \binom{-1}{1}$.

FIGURE 10.2   Profit at Maturity of Different Options Positions Ignoring the Initial Option Premiums

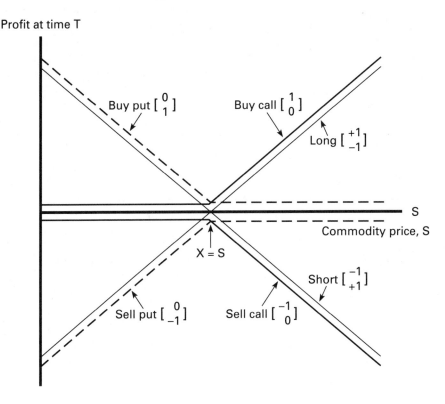

Just as options can be used to replicate positions in the underlying commodity, a position in the underlying commodity combined with one option can be used to replicate a position in the other option. A long position in a call, $\binom{1}{0}$, for example, can be replicated by buying the commodity and buying a put: $\binom{1}{-1} + \binom{0}{1} = \binom{1}{0}$. Similarly, a long position in a put, $\binom{0}{1}$, can be replicated by selling short the commodity and buying a call: $\binom{-1}{1} + \binom{1}{0} = \binom{0}{1}$. A frequent investment strategy is to sell a call against a long position in an underlying commodity, $\binom{-1}{0} + \binom{1}{-1}$, which yields the same profits as selling a put, $\binom{0}{-1}$.

A position that makes money whichever way the commodity price changes is a straddle. A straddle consists of buying a call and buying a put: $\binom{1}{0} + \binom{0}{1} = \binom{1}{1}$. Of course, such a position has a high price because the seller of the straddle must be compensated for the expected losses from selling the straddle. Someone who thinks the price of the underlying commodity is likely to rise might buy two calls. The vector notation for that is $\binom{2}{0}$ because the value of the options goes up two dollars for every dollar increase in the commodity price above the exercise price.

10.3 GENERAL DISCUSSION OF LOWER PRICE BOUNDS FOR OPTIONS

The lower price bound of an option is the lowest price at which the option could sell corresponding to each price of the underlying commodity. Before maturity, an option will usually sell for more than the lower bound because the option has a potential for profit that exceeds the potential for loss. In this section, we develop the intuition that underlies the structure of the lower price bounds for European and American call and put options. In the next section, we show the arbitrage portfolio transactions that ensure that each bound holds.

European Options

At maturity, the lower bounds of European options are given by the profit diagram of Figure 10.2. The call sells for its exercise value, that is, $c = \max[0, S_T - X]$ and the put sells for its exercise value, $p = \max[0, X - S_T]$. Before maturity, a European option sells for at least as much as the present value of its exercise value plus an allowance for the present value of the cost of storing the commodity. The price of the call option must satisfy the following condition for an in-the-money option:

$$c(S, T; X) \geq \frac{S(e^{bT} - 1)}{e^{rT}} + \frac{S - X}{e^{rT}}, \qquad (10.1)$$

where S is the price of the underlying asset at some time before maturity and T is the time until maturity.[1] If the commodity price at maturity were S, the exercise value of the call would be $S - X$. The value before maturity is the discounted value, the second term in (10.1). The call option must also reflect the storage costs associated with a long commodity position because in purchasing an option those storage costs are avoided. The present value of the storage costs, including the interest cost of the funds tied up at S, is the first term of (10.1).

Since the option could be out-of-the-money, the full lower bound condition, which is plotted in Figure 10.3, is

$$c(S, T; X) \geq \max[0, \frac{S(e^{bT} - 1)}{e^{rT}} + \frac{S - X}{e^{rT}}]. \qquad (10.2a)$$

The condition states that a European call option can never sell for less than the amount given in the right-hand side of (10.2a). Correspondingly, the lower bound for a European put is

$$p(S, T; X) \geq \max[0, \frac{-S(e^{bT} - 1)}{e^{rT}} + \frac{X - S}{e^{rT}}]. \qquad (10.2b)$$

---

[1] The right-hand side of (10.1) can be simplified to $Se^{(b-r)T} - Xe^{-rT}$, which will be done later in the chapter.

FIGURE 10.3   Lower Price Bound of European Call Option

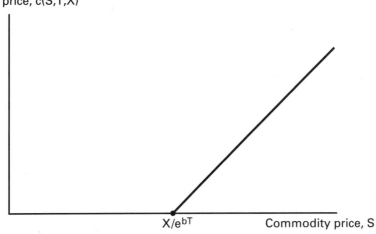

Call option price, c(S,T;X)

X/e^{bT} Commodity price, S

For $S > X/e^{bT}$, $c(S,T;X) = \dfrac{S(e^{bT} - 1)}{e^{rT}} + \dfrac{S - X}{e^{rT}}$.

For non-zero put values, the lower bound is the present value of the exercise value of the put plus an adjustment for storage costs.

American Options

The distinguishing feature of American options, in contrast to European options, is that they can be exercised early. Because the right to early exercise cannot have a negative value (i.e., you do not have to be paid to be induced to take on a privilege), the following two conditions apply:

$$C(S,T;X) \geq c(S,T;X) \tag{10.3a}$$

and

$$P(S,T;X) \geq p(S,T;X). \tag{10.3b}$$

These conditions do not say that the American options *will* have greater values than their European counterparts—only that they *will not* have lower values. The right to early exercise may not have positive value, but it will never have negative value.

Since American options cannot sell for less than European options, a lower bound of American options is the lower bound of the corresponding European option with the same exercise price and maturity. An American option has the additional benefit that it may be exercised immediately to receive the exercise value—$S - X$ for the American call and $X - S$ for the American put. This means the lower bound for the American option is the lower bound of the European option or the current exercise value, whichever is higher. The lower bounds are

$$C(S,T;X) \geq \max[0, \frac{S(e^{bT}-1)}{e^{rT}} + \frac{S-X}{e^{rT}}, S-X], \qquad \textbf{(10.4a)}$$

and

$$P(S,T;X) \geq \max[0, \frac{-S(e^{bT}-1)}{e^{rT}} + \frac{X-S}{e^{rT}}, X-S]. \qquad \textbf{(10.4b)}$$

10.4 ARBITRAGE PROOFS OF LOWER PRICE BOUNDS

Before proceeding with developments of rational price bounds on commodity options, it is worthwhile to reintroduce the concept of a rollover position. Recall that in Chapter 3 we introduced a storage fund that was invested in the commodity. The sum of the storage fund and the position in one unit of the commodity is called a rollover position in the commodity. In Chapter 3, we used a portfolio consisting of a short futures position and a long rollover position in the underlying commodity to demonstrate basis arbitrage. In this chapter, we use the rollover commodity position to demonstrate the links between the price of an option and the commodity underlying the option. A long rollover position in the underlying commodity begins with an investment of $e^{(b-r)T}$ in the underlying commodity at the end of day 0. At the end of each subsequent day, the position is reduced (increased) by the factor $e^{-(b-r)}$ if $b > r$ ($b < r$). At the end of day T, exactly one unit of the commodity is on hand. It is also worthwhile to point out that a futures contract is a commodity that costs nothing to carry, that is, the cost-of-carry rate, b, equals zero. A rollover futures position, therefore, begins with e^{-rT} futures contracts at the end of day 0 and increases by the factor e^r each day.

European Call Option

The lower price bound of a European call option can be determined by considering the initial and terminal values of a portfolio that consists of a long position in the European call option $c(S, T; X)$, a long position of Xe^{-rT} riskless bonds, and a short rollover position in the commodity at price $Se^{(b-r)T}$, as illustrated in Table 10.1.[2] The amount of riskless lending is determined by the fact that we need X on hand at time T in order to exercise the call. If, at the option's expiration, the commodity price exceeds the exercise price, the call is exercised and the one unit of the underlying commodity received is used to cover the short commodity position. To pay for exercising the call, the riskless bonds are used exactly. The net terminal value of the portfolio is therefore 0. On the other hand, if the commodity price is below the exercise price at expiration, the call expires worthless and the value of the riskless bonds exceeds the value necessary to cover the short commodity position. In

---

[2]Note that the arguments of the option price notation in the table have been suppressed for convenience.

TABLE 10.1   Arbitrage transactions for establishing lower price bound of European call option.

$$c(S,T;X) \geq Se^{(b-r)T} - Xe^{-rT}$$

		Terminal Value	
Position	Initial Value	$\tilde{S}_T \leq X$	$\tilde{S}_T > X$
Buy European call	$-c$	0	$\tilde{S}_T - X$
Buy riskless bonds	$-Xe^{-rT}$	X	X
Sell rollover position in commodity	$Se^{(b-r)T}$	$-\tilde{S}_T$	$-\tilde{S}_T$
Net portfolio value	$-c + Se^{(b-r)T} - Xe^{-rT}$	$X - \tilde{S}_T$	0

this case, the net terminal portfolio value is positive. Since the portfolio holder is assured to have a nonnegative terminal value to his portfolio, the initial value must be nonpositive, that is,

$$-c(S,T;X) + Se^{(b-r)T} - Xe^{-rT} \leq 0$$

or

$$c(S,T;X) \geq Se^{(b-r)T} - Xe^{-rT}, \tag{10.5a}$$

otherwise, costless arbitrage profits are possible. This condition is the same as (10.1), which can be seen by adding and subtracting Se^{-rT} on the right hand side of (10.5a).

Condition (10.5a) shows only one of the lower price bounds of the European call. In a rational market, the option price will never be negative since it is a right rather than an obligation. The complete lower price bound condition for the European call is, therefore,

$$c(S,T;X) \geq \max[0, Se^{(b-r)T} - Xe^{-rT}], \tag{10.6a}$$

which can be shown to be the same as (10.2a).

American Call Option

Since the American option always sells for more than the corresponding European option, the American call option is bounded from below by (10.6a). It is also bounded from below by the proceeds from exercising the call immediately, $S - X$. Otherwise, costless arbitrage profits could be earned by buying the call and exercising it immediately. The complete lower price bound condition for the American call option is, therefore,

$$C(S, T; X) \geq \max[0, Se^{(b-r)T} - Xe^{-rT}, S - X], \qquad \textbf{(10.7a)}$$

which can be shown to be the same as (10.4a).

If $b \geq r$, the second term in the brackets of (10.7a) exceeds the third, which means that the lower bound of the American call is $Se^{(b-r)T} - Xe^{-rT}$, the European lower bound. In other words, when $b \geq r$, an American call behaves like a European call; it will not be exercised before maturity. One can write the condition that the second term in the brackets of (10.7a) exceeds the third term in the brackets as follows:

$$S < X \left[\frac{1 - e^{-rT}}{1 - e^{(b-r)T}} \right]. \qquad \textbf{(10.8)}$$

If this condition is met, the American call will have the same lower bound as the European call. The condition, (10.8) will be met if $b \geq r$ (keeping in mind that we are looking at values of S for which the lower bound of the call option exceeds zero). On the other hand, for values of $b < r$, the second term in the brackets of (10.7a) can be less than the third term with the result that (10.8) is not satisfied. This implies that the lower bound of the American call is $S - X$. Options that do not satisfy (10.8) may be exercised early and will have a value greater than the corresponding European option.

European Put Option

The lower price bound for a European put option can be derived by considering the initial and terminal values of a portfolio that consists of a long position in the European put option, $p(S, T; X)$, a long rollover position in the underlying commodity, $Se^{(b-r)T}$, and a short position of Xe^{-rT} of riskless bonds, as is done in Table 10.2. The amount of the riskless borrowing is determined by the fact that exercising the put at expiration will provide X. Here, if the commodity price is below the exercise price at the put option's expiration, the commodity on hand is sold for the exercise price of the put by exercising the put option. The exercise proceeds are then used to repay the riskless borrowing. The net effect is that the terminal value of the portfolio will be equal to 0. On the other hand, if the commodity price exceeds the exercise price at expiration, the net portfolio value will be positive because the put option expires worthless and the commodity price exceeds the amount necessary to repay the riskless borrowing. Since this portfolio provides a nonnegative terminal value, it must be the case that the initial value is nonpositive. If the net initial value of the portfolio is nonpositive, that is, if

$$-p(S, T; X) - Se^{(b-r)T} + Xe^{-rT} \leq 0,$$

TABLE 10.2   Arbitrage transactions for establishing lower price bound of European put option.

$$p(S,T;X) \geq Xe^{-rT} - Se^{(b-r)T}$$

Position	Initial Value	Terminal Value $\tilde{S}_T \leq X$	$\tilde{S}_T > X$
Buy European put	$-p$	$X - \tilde{S}_T$	0
Buy rollover position in commodity	$-Se^{(b-r)T}$	$\tilde{S}_T$	$\tilde{S}_T$
Borrow Xe^{-rT}	Xe^{-rT}	$-X$	$-X$
Net portfolio value	$-p - Se^{(b-r)T} + Xe^{-rT}$	0	$\tilde{S}_T - X$

then

$$p(S,T;X) \geq Xe^{-rT} - Se^{(b-r)T}. \tag{10.5b}$$

Adding the nonnegativity constraint of the European put option value,

$$p(S,T;X) \geq \max[0, Xe^{-rT} - Se^{(b-r)T}], \tag{10.6b}$$

which can be shown to be the same as (10.2b).

American Put Option

Naturally, the lower price bound condition for the European put also applies to the American put. But, the exercisable proceeds of the American put, $X - S$, may be greater than $Xe^{-rT} - Se^{(b-r)T}$, and we know that in a rationally functioning market the American put is bounded from below by $X - S$. Otherwise, costless arbitrage profits could be earned by buying the put option and immediately exercising it. So, the complete lower bound condition for the American put is

$$P(S,T;X) \geq \max[0, Xe^{-rT} - Se^{(b-r)T}, X - S], \tag{10.7b}$$

which is the same as (10.4b).

It is worthwhile to note that at least part of the lower price bound of the European put lies to the left of the exercisable proceeds of the American put, independent of whether or not the cost-of-carry rate is greater than or less than the riskless rate of interest. (This is shown in Figure 10.5 on page 189.) The implication is that, for commodity options, it cannot be said that the American put option will never be exercised early.

TABLE 10.3   Summary of lower price bounds for European and American commodity and futures options.

Option Type	Commodity Option	Futures Option
European call	$\max[0, Se^{(b-r)T} - Xe^{-rT}]$	$\max[0, (F - X)e^{-rT}]$
American call	$\max[0, Se^{(b-r)T} - Xe^{-rT}, S - X]$	$\max[0, F - X]$
European put	$\max[0, Xe^{-rT} - Se^{(b-r)T}]$	$\max[0, (X - F)e^{-rT}]$
American put	$\max[0, Xe^{-rT} - Se^{(b-r)T}, X - S]$	$\max[0, X - F]$

Futures Options

Table 10.3 contains a summary of the lower price bound conditions for commodity and futures options. Recall that earlier in this chapter we noted that a futures contract is a commodity with a zero cost-of-carry rate. The price bounds in the last column of the table make this substitution.

10.5 EARLY EXERCISE

Earlier, we noted that the right to early exercise of American options is a privilege and must have a nonnegative value. If we consider the value of American options to be the sum of their European counterparts plus their respective early exercise premiums, ϵ_C and ϵ_P, that is,

$$C(S, T; X) = c(S, T; X) + \epsilon_C(S, T; X) \qquad \textbf{(10.9a)}$$

and

$$P(S, T; X) = p(S, T; X) + \epsilon_P(S, T; X), \qquad \textbf{(10.9b)}$$

it is obvious that the American options sell for at least as much as their European counterparts.

That is not to say, however, that the American options will always be exercised early, or even that they may be. In the case of options on non-dividend-paying stocks, for example, the American call will never be exercised early.

American Call Option

Whether an American call option written on a commodity may be exercised early or not is contingent on the cost-of-carry rate, b. If $b \geq r$, the American call will not be exercised early. To see this, consider the lower price bound condition (10.7a) or, alternatively, Figure 10.4a. If $b \geq r$, the exercisable proceeds of the call, $S -$

FIGURE 10.4a   European and American call option prices as a function of the underlying commodity price when the cost-of-carry rate (*b*) exceeds the riskless rate of interest (*r*) so the American call will not be optimally exercised early.

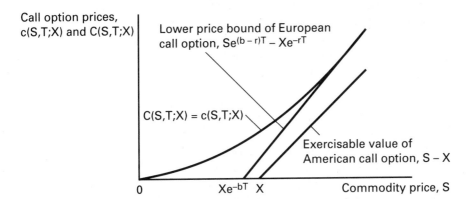

X, are always less than the minimum value for which the call will trade in the marketplace, $Se^{(b-r)T} - Xe^{-rT}$. Since the American call is worth more unexercised or "alive" than exercised or "dead," it will never be exercised prior to expiration. Thus, if $b \geq r$, the early exercise premium of the American call is worth nothing, that is,

$$\epsilon_C(S, T; X) = 0; \tag{10.10}$$

and, from equation (10.9a), the American call option has a value equal to the European call option,

$$C(S, T; X) = c(S, T; X). \tag{10.11}$$

The intuition underlying the fact that the American call will not be exercised early when $b \geq r$ can be developed most easily by considering the minimum amount lost by early exercise, that is,

$$S - X - [Se^{(b-r)T} - Xe^{-rT}]. \tag{10.12}$$

Rearranging (10.12) to isolate terms on S and X, we get

$$S[1 - e^{(b-r)T}] - X(1 - e^{-rT}). \tag{10.13}$$

Expression (10.13) says the following: If the American call option is exercised now instead of at expiration, the American call holder loses in two ways. First, he incurs the present value of the storage costs that he will pay as a result of taking delivery of the underlying commodity, $S[1 - e^{(b-r)T}]$.[3] By holding the option, the option holder does not have direct investment in the underlying commodity—only the right to buy the commodity in the future. If he takes delivery now he faces the prospect of storing the commodity, insuring it, etc. Second, he incurs the present value of the interest foregone on the exercise price of the option, $X(1 - e^{-rT})$. If the option is exercised now, the option holder is obliged to make payment in the amount X now instead of later, thereby foregoing the interest income that he could earn on the exercise price of the option. Figure 10.4a conveniently summarizes these effects by showing that the lower price bound of the European call option exceeds the exercisable proceeds of the American call option for all plausible values of the option price.

In the case where the cost-of-carry rate, b, is less than the riskless rate of interest, r, it may be optimal to exercise the American call early, as is seen by examining expression (10.13). When $b < r$, there are offsetting influences affecting the decision about early exercise. On one hand, deferring early exercise allows the call option holder to implicitly earn interest on the exercise price of the option, as was noted above. On the other hand, $b < r$ means that some form of yield accrues to the holder of the underlying commodity. For example, suppose that the call is written on a stock index and that the stock index portfolio accrues dividends at a known rate.[4] Deferring exercise means interest income is being earned, but dividend yield is being foregone. Note that the larger the value of the current commodity price S, the larger the value of expression (10.13), and the higher the profitability of early exercise. This fact is reflected in Figure 10.4b, through the increasing distance between the exercisable value of the American call and the lower price bound of the European call as the underlying commodity price grows larger. At any level of commodity price, however, there is a non-zero benefit to early exercise if $b < r$, so the early exercise premium has positive value,

$$\epsilon_C(S, T; X) > 0, \qquad\qquad\qquad \textbf{(10.14)}$$

and the American call option has a value greater than the European call option,

$$C(S, T; X) > c(S, T; X). \qquad\qquad\qquad \textbf{(10.15)}$$

---

[3] Because $b \geq r$, this term is nonpositive.

[4] Recall that the cost-of-carry rate, b, consists of the interest rate, r, plus the cost of storage, insurance, etc. Because the only "cost" other than interest involved in carrying a stock portfolio is the dividend yield (i.e., a negative cost), $b < r$.

FIGURE 10.4b   European and American call option prices as a function of the underlying commodity price when the cost-of-carry rate (*b*) is less than the riskless rate of interest (*r*) so the American call may be optimally exercised early.

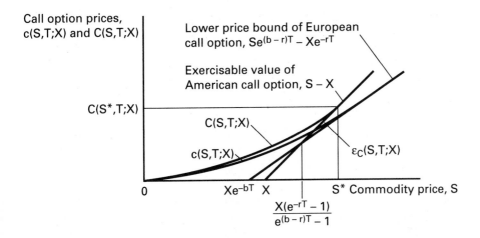

Table 10.4 contains an example of a call option for which early exercise can be optimal. The underlying commodity in this example is a foreign currency. The U.S interest rate is assumed to be 8 percent annually and the foreign interest rate is assumed to be 12 percent annually. As a result, the cost of carry is negative, that is, −4 percent annually. The exercise price of the call option is 150 cents and the maturity is 30 days. In this example, early exercise occurs if the price of the currency reaches 165 cents. At this point, the American option price equals the American lower bound because the option is being priced on the assumption that it will be exercised. Early exercise is desirable because taking possession of the currency and investing the currency in the foreign country provides a relatively higher rate of interest income (12 percent versus 8 percent domestically). If the option were held to maturity, its value is only 14.5692 (i.e., the European option value). It is worth noting that, for currency prices from 161 to 164, the American lower bound *exceeds* the price of the European option but early exercise is not optimal. In this range, the market price of the American option exceeds the American option lower bound, hence early exercise is not optimal.

American Put Option

Condition (10.7b), as well as Figure 10.5, show that there always exists an opportunity that any American put can be optimally exercised early. There is always some region of commodity prices over which the exercisable proceeds of the put will be higher than the lower price bound condition of the European put option. To gain intuition about the nature of the tradeoff involved here, difference the exercisable proceeds of the American put and the lower price bound of the European put, as we did for the American call in expression (10.13). The difference is

TABLE 10.4   Lower bounds and prices for European and American foreign currency call options. The option exercise price (X) is 150, and time to expiration (T) is 30 days (.08219 years). The domestic riskless rate of interest (r_d) is 8 percent, and the foreign riskless rate of interest (r_f) is 12 percent. The cost-of-carry rate (b) is therefore -4 percent. (The underlying currency has an annual volatility rate of 20 percent.)

Currency Price	European Lower Bound	American Lower Bound	European Option Price	American Option Price
150	0.0000	0.0000	3.1637	3.1991
151	0.5011	1.0000	3.6704	3.7125
152	1.4913	2.0000	4.2224	4.2726
153	2.4814	3.0000	4.8189	4.8784
154	3.4716	4.0000	5.4581	5.5288
155	4.4618	5.0000	6.1381	6.2219
156	5.4520	6.0000	6.8564	6.9556
157	6.4422	7.0000	7.6103	7.7276
158	7.4324	8.0000	8.3969	8.5355
159	8.4226	9.0000	9.2132	9.3767
160	9.4127	10.0000	10.0560	10.2489
161	10.4029	11.0000	10.9225	11.1496
162	11.3931	12.0000	11.8097	12.0769
163	12.3833	13.0000	12.7149	13.0289
164	13.3735	14.0000	13.6355	14.0041
165	14.3637	15.0000	14.5692	15.0000
166	15.3538	16.0000	15.5138	16.0000
167	16.3440	17.0000	16.4677	17.0000
168	17.3342	18.0000	17.4291	18.0000
169	18.3244	19.0000	18.3967	19.0000
170	19.3146	20.0000	19.3693	20.0000

$$X - S - [Xe^{-rT} - Se^{(b-r)T}] \qquad \textbf{(10.16)}$$

or, more simply,

$$X(1 - e^{-rT}) - S[1 - e^{(b-r)T}]. \qquad \textbf{(10.17)}$$

The first term of (10.17) is the present value of the interest that can be earned if the option is exercised immediately. If the option holder exercises his put, he receives X and delivers the underlying commodity worth S.

FIGURE 10.5   European and American Put Option Prices as a Function of the Underlying Commodity Price

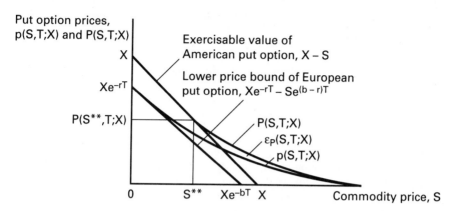

The proceeds from exercise can be invested immediately to earn interest. The net effect of the second term may be positive or negative, depending on whether $b > r$ or $b < r$. In the former case, exercising the put means the option holder can deliver the underlying commodity and forego the storage costs involved with deferring exercise. In the latter case, exercising the put means the option holder will be delivering a commodity that is currently providing her with some form of yield. She may be reluctant to do so, but expression (10.17) will be unambiguously positive for cases where the yield on the commodity is less than the riskless rate of interest.

The prospect of early exercise of the American put may also be seen geometrically in Figure 10.5. Independent of the value of b, there is always some range of commodity prices over which the exercisable proceeds of the American put, $X - S$, are greater than those of the European put option; therefore, there is always some possibility that the American put will be exercised early. To see that this is the case, consider what happens if the commodity price falls to zero. The value of the American put equals the exercise price of the put since the American put option holder has the right to sell a commodity with price zero for X at any time. In fact, in the event that the commodity price falls to zero, the American put option holder exercises his option immediately because (a) he can start earning interest on the proceeds from exercise, and (b) the commodity price may rise in which case the put price will fall. At $S = 0$, however, the European put option has a value of Xe^{-rT}. To recognize this, consider the boundary conditions on the put's price. The lower price bound is given by condition (10.2b). At $S = 0$, the minimum value for the put option is Xe^{-rT}. On the other hand, because the commodity price cannot be less than zero at the option's expiration, the present value of the maximum exercise proceeds is Xe^{-rT}. If the European put option's price is bounded from above and below by Xe^{-rT}, it follows that its price is Xe^{-rT}. Because the American put can be exercised immediately for proceeds equal to X while the European put has a lesser value, the early exercise premium must be positive for $S = 0$. In general, as long as there is some chance of early exercise, the early exercise premium has positive value,

$$\epsilon_P(S,T;X) > 0 \qquad \textbf{(10.18)}$$

and the American put is worth more than the European put,

$$P(S,T;X) > p(S,T;X). \qquad \textbf{(10.19)}$$

American Futures Options

Unlike the American option on the underlying commodity, there are no conditions under which it can be said that the American call or put option on a futures contract will not be exercised early. One can think of a futures contract as a commodity with a zero carrying cost ($b = 0$) and analyze the minimum loss from early exercise for calls, (10.13), and for puts, (10.17). When $b = 0$, both these expressions are positive, which means that early exercise of an in-the-money American futures option might be profitable.

The intuition for the possible early exercise of American futures options is straightforward. Consider a call option on a futures contract. If the call is exercised, a long futures position is established for the call buyer at the exercise price of the call. But payment of the exercise price is not required just as payment of the futures price is not required when a futures contract is entered into; only profits and losses are paid. If the option is in the money, profits are paid to the call buyer upon exercise. By way of example, consider a call on wheat futures at $X = \$3.00$ per bushel, and assume the current futures price is \$3.50 per bushel. If a call option on one futures contract is exercised, the call buyer assumes a futures position at a futures price of \$3.00. Since the current price is \$3.50, he is paid the profit of 50 cents per bushel, or \$2,500 on a contract of 5,000 bushels. These profits can be invested immediately to earn interest. At the same time, ownership of the futures contract does not impose the carrying cost that would be incurred if the underlying commodity were owned. Early exercise might be desirable because it allows profits to be invested sooner. Of course, the desirability of early exercise is offset, as usual, by the loss of the downside protection provided by the option. The intuition is the same for a futures put option. By exercising a put option on a commodity contract that has fallen in price, profits can be received early and interest earned.

10.6 GENERAL DISCUSSION OF PUT-CALL PARITY

Put-call parity refers to the relation between the price of a put and the price of a call with the same exercise price, expiration date, and underlying commodity price. We showed earlier that the outcome at maturity from the purchase of a call option could be replicated by a long position in the commodity plus the purchase of a put. Since one can buy a call directly or indirectly by purchasing a put and taking a long position, the prices of puts and calls must clearly be related. We restrict our discussion here to European options that are held to maturity.

Option *converters* take advantage of discrepancies in the prices of puts and calls. If call prices are too high, they sell calls, buy puts, and go long the underlying commodity. The vector notation for the resulting position is

$$\begin{pmatrix} -1 \\ 0 \end{pmatrix} + \begin{pmatrix} 0 \\ 1 \end{pmatrix} + \begin{pmatrix} 1 \\ -1 \end{pmatrix} = \begin{pmatrix} 0 \\ 0 \end{pmatrix}.$$

Selling a call and buying a put is a synthetic short position. By going long the underlying commodity, a perfect hedge is established, with the result that however the commodity price changes, no losses or gains result. Since the ending position is riskless, the profits to converters must be zero in equilibrium. We assume first that the exercise price of the options, X, is equal to the current price of the commodity, S. In that case, the present value of the cash flows associated with the hedged position is the revenue from selling the call, $c(S, T; X)$, the cost of the put, $-p(S, T; X)$, and the present value of the cost of going long the commodity, $-S(e^{bT} - 1)/e^{rT}$. The cost of going long includes the interest cost of funds tied up plus any storage costs less any income payments. Equilibrium requires the sum of these cash flows to be zero:

$$c(S, T; X) - p(S, T; X) - \frac{S(e^{bT} - 1)}{e^{rT}} = 0,$$

or

$$c(S, T; X) - p(S, T; X) = \frac{S(e^{bT} - 1)}{e^{rT}}. \tag{10.20}$$

If put prices were high relative to call prices, converters would sell puts, $\begin{pmatrix} 0 \\ -1 \end{pmatrix}$, buy calls, $\begin{pmatrix} 1 \\ 0 \end{pmatrix}$, and take a short position in the underlying commodity, $\begin{pmatrix} -1 \\ 1 \end{pmatrix}$, to establish a perfect hedge. Under the assumption that the short can earn the storage fees that the long pays, the same equilibrium relation results.

A slight adjustment to the put-call parity relation is required if the price at which the position in the underlying commodity is established differs from the exercise price of the options. If $S \neq X$, the put-call parity relation for European options is

$$c(S, T; X) - p(S, T; X) = \frac{S(e^{bT} - 1)}{e^{rT}} + \frac{S - X}{e^{rT}}, \tag{10.21}$$

where the last term accounts for the call or the put being in the money. While the put-call parity equation, (10.21), looks formidable, the basic idea is very simple. The put-call parity relation simply says that the call price minus the put price is the present value of the cost of holding the underlying commodity until maturity of the options plus the present value of the amount by which the commodity price exceeds the exercise price. We assume that storage costs are incurred at a continuous rate, b, but other assumptions could be made. For example, holding costs might be paid at the beginning as a lump sum, B. In that case, the first term on the right-hand side of (10.21) would be B.

To illustrate put-call parity for European options, consider the example in Table 10.4. Specifically, when the underlying currency price is 155, the European call price is 6.1381. On the basis of this price, the European put price can be computed as

$$6.1381 - p(S, T; X) = \frac{155(e^{(-.04)(.08219)} - 1) + 155 - 150}{e^{(.08)(.08219)}} = 4.4618.$$

Therefore, the value of the European put implied by put-call parity is 1.6763.

The put-call parity relation established above may not hold exactly for American options because early exercise of an American option can break up the riskless hedge. For example, the converter who sells puts, buys calls, and goes short the underlying commodity, may have the put exercised. The commodity delivered to the converter at the exercise price can be used to pay back the commodity borrowed for the short sale, but the converter must also liquidate the investment of the proceeds of the short sale (which are needed to pay for the commodity delivered) and that might be done at a loss. As a result, for American options, one can only establish bounds on the difference between call and put prices, something that is done in the next section.

10.7 ARBITRAGE PROOFS OF PUT-CALL PARITY RELATIONS

European Options

The put-call parity relation, (10.21), established above for European commodity options, can also be written as

$$c(S, T; X) - p(S, T; X) = Se^{(b-r)T} - Xe^{-rT}. \tag{10.22}$$

To understand how this relation is derived, consider an investment portfolio that consists of selling a European call, buying a European put at the same exercise price, buying a rollover position in the underlying commodity beginning with $e^{(b-r)T}$ units, and borrowing Xe^{-rT} at the riskless rate of interest. The initial and terminal values of this portfolio are presented in Table 10.5. Note that the terminal values are equal to zero, independent of whether or not the terminal commodity price is above or below the exercise price of the options. If the call is in-the-money at expiration, we are required to deliver one unit of the commodity and receive X. By virtue of the rollover position, we have one unit of the commodity on hand to make the delivery. The exercise proceeds are used to cover the riskless borrowings, and the put option expires worthless. If the put is in-the-money at expiration, we exercise the put, delivering the commodity and receiving X. The remaining transactions

TABLE 10.5 Arbitrage transactions for establishing put-call parity for European options.

$$c(S, T; X) - p(S, T; X) = Se^{(b-r)T} - Xe^{-rT}$$

Position	Initial Value	Terminal Value $\tilde{S}_T \leq X$	$\tilde{S}_T > X$
Sell European call	c	0	$-(\tilde{S}_T - X)$
Buy European put	$-p$	$X - \tilde{S}_T$	0
Buy rollover position in commodity	$-Se^{(b-r)T}$	$\tilde{S}_T$	$\tilde{S}_T$
Borrow Xe^{-rT}	Xe^{-rT}	$-X$	$-X$
Net portfolio value	$c - p - Se^{(b-r)T} + Xe^{-rT}$	0	0

are as described above. Since the terminal values are certain to be equal to zero, it must be the case that no one would pay a price other than zero to take on the portfolio. Setting the net initial portfolio value equal to zero produces equation (10.22).

The put-call parity relation for European futures options is a special case of (10.22), where the cost-of-carry rate, b, equals zero. (Recall that futures positions require no initial investment outlay.) The relation is

$$c(F, T; X) - p(F, T; X) = e^{-rT}(F - X). \tag{10.23}$$

This relation first appeared in Black (1976).

American Options
The early exercise feature of American options causes the specification of the put-call parity relation to be different from that for European options. The relations linking the commodity price and the American commodity options prices,

$$S - X \leq C(S, T; X) - P(S, T; X) \leq Se^{(b-r)T} - Xe^{-rT}, \text{ if } b \geq r, \tag{10.24a}$$

and

$$Se^{(b-r)T} - X \leq C(S, T; X) - P(S, T; X) \leq S - Xe^{-rT}, \text{ if } b < r, \tag{10.24b}$$

must be developed through two separate sets of arbitrage transactions. We consider each inequality in turn.

The left-hand side condition of (10.24a) can be derived by considering the values of a portfolio that consists of buying a call, selling a put, lending X risklessly, and selling a rollover position in the commodity starting with one unit and decreasing the position by the factor $e^{-(b-r)}$ each day, and lending X risklessly. Table 10.6 contains these portfolio values. Note that there is now an additional column in the table with the heading "Intermediate Value." Because the portfolio holder is short an option, she runs the risk of being assigned delivery on the option prior to expiration. We must account for this possibility in deriving rational price bounds for American options.

In Table 10.6, it can be seen that, if all of the security positions stay open until expiration, the terminal value of the portfolio will be positive, independent of whether the terminal commodity price is above or below the exercise price of the options. If the terminal commodity price is above the exercise price, the call option is exercised, and the commodity acquired at exercise price X is used to deliver, in part, against the short commodity position. If the terminal commodity price is below the exercise price, the put option holder exercises her option by selling us the underlying commodity at exercise price X. In turn, we use the commodity to deliver against our short commodity position established at the outset. Therefore, if the option positions are held to expiration, the portfolio terminal value is certain to be positive.

In the event the put option holder decides to exercise her option early at time t, the investment in the riskless bonds is more than sufficient to cover the payment

TABLE 10.6   Arbitrage transactions for establishing put-call parity for American options, where $b \geq r$.

$$S - X \leq C(S,T;X) - P(S,T;X)$$

Position	Initial Value	Put Exercised Early — Intermediate Value	Put Exercised at Expiration — Terminal Value $\tilde{S}_T \leq X$	$\tilde{S}_T > X$
Buy American call	$-C$	$\tilde{C}_t$	0	$\tilde{S}_T - X$
Sell American put	P	$-(X - \tilde{S}_t)$	$-(X - \tilde{S}_T)$	0
Sell rollover position in commodity	S	$-\tilde{S}_t e^{-(b-r)t}$	$-\tilde{S}_T e^{-(b-r)T}$	$-\tilde{S}_T e^{-(b-r)T}$
Lend X	$-X$	$X e^{rt}$	$X e^{rT}$	$X e^{rT}$
Net portfolio value	$-C + P$ $+S - X$	$\tilde{C}_t + X(e^{rt} - 1)$ $+\tilde{S}_t[1 - e^{-(b-r)t}]$	$X(e^{rT} - 1)+$ $\tilde{S}_T[1 - e^{-(b-r)T}]$	$X(e^{rT} - 1)+$ $\tilde{S}_T[1 - e^{-(b-r)T}]$

of the exercise price to the put option holder, and the commodity received from the exercise of the put is used to cover the commodity sold when the portfolio was formed. In addition, we still hold a call option, which may have significant value. In other words, by forming the portfolio of securities in the proportions noted above, we have formed a portfolio that will never have a negative future value. If the future value is assured to be nonnegative, the initial value is assured to be non-positive, or

$$-C(S, T; X) + P(S, T; X) + S - X \leq 0.$$

Rearranging provides the left-hand side of equation (10.24a). The left-hand side of (10.24b) can be established using arbitrage transactions and arguments similar to those in Table 10.6, except that the rollover commodity position begins with an investment of $e^{(b-r)T}$ units.

The right-hand side of (10.24a) may be derived by considering the portfolio used to prove European put-call parity. Changing the notation to reflect the fact that we are discussing American options and introducing the "Intermediate Value" column to reflect the prospect of early exercise, the portfolio value table becomes Table 10.7. Here, the terminal value of the portfolio is certain to be equal to zero, if the option positions stay open until that time. The option positions are offset by the commodity position and the riskless borrowings are offset by the exercise prices of the options. In the event the American call option holder decides to exercise his call option early, the portfolio holder uses her long commodity position to cover her commodity obligation on the exercised call and uses the exercise proceeds to retire her outstanding debt. After these actions are taken, she still has an open long put position, cash in the amount of $X[1 - e^{-r(T-t)}]$, and a commodity position worth $S[e^{(b-r)(T-t)} - 1]$. Since the portfolio is certain to have nonnegative outcomes, the initial value must be nonpositive or

$$C(S, T; X) - P(S, T; X) - Se^{(b-r)T} + Xe^{-rT} \leq 0. \qquad \textbf{(10.25)}$$

Rearranging provides the right-hand side of the American put-call parity condition (10.24a). The right-hand side of (10.24b) can be established by considering the portfolio in Table 10.7, with the exception that the rollover commodity position begins with one unit instead of $e^{(b-r)T}$.

The put-call parity relation for American futures options is a special case of (10.24b). Since the cost-of-carry rate, b, equals zero, the relation becomes

$$Fe^{-rT} - X \leq C(F, T; X) - P(F, T; X) \leq F - Xe^{-rT}. \qquad \textbf{(10.26)}$$

Table 10.8 contains a summary of the put-call parity relations developed in this section.

TABLE 10.7   Arbitrage transactions for establishing put-call parity for American options, where $b \geq r$.

$$C(S,T;X) - P(S,T;X) \leq Se^{(b-r)T} - Xe^{-rT}$$

Position	Initial Value	Call Exercised Early	Call Exercised at Expiration	
		Intermediate Value	Terminal Value	
			$\tilde{S}_T \leq X$	$\tilde{S}_T > X$
Sell American call	C	$-(\tilde{S}_t - X)$	0	$-(\tilde{S}_T - X)$
Buy American put	$-P$	$\tilde{P}_t$	$X - \tilde{S}_T$	0
Buy rollover position in commodity	$-Se^{(b-r)T}$	$\tilde{S}_t e^{(b-r)(T-t)}$	$\tilde{S}_T$	$\tilde{S}_T$
Borrow Xe^{-rT}	Xe^{-rT}	$-Xe^{-r(T-t)}$	$-X$	$-X$
Net portfolio value	$C - P - Se^{(b-r)T}$ $+ Xe^{-rT}$	$\tilde{P}_t + X[1 - e^{-r(T-t)}]$ $+S[e^{(b-r)(T-t)} - 1]$	0	0

TABLE 10.8   Summary of put-call parity relations for commodity and futures options.

Option Type	Commodity Options
European	$c(S,T;X) - p(S,T;X) = Se^{(b-r)T} - Xe^{-rT}$
American	$S - X \leq C(S,T;X) - P(S,T;X) \leq Se^{(b-r)T} - Xe^{-rT}$, if $b \geq r$
	$Se^{(b-r)T} - X \leq C(S,T;X) - P(S,T;X) \leq S - Xe^{-rT}$, if $b < r$

Option Type	Futures Options
European	$c(F,T;X) - p(F,T;X) = e^{-rT}(F - X)$
American	$Fe^{-rT} - X \leq C(F,T;X) - P(F,T;X) \leq F - Xe^{-rT}$

10.8 COMMODITY OPTIONS VERSUS FUTURES OPTIONS

Thus far in the chapter, we have discussed the arbitrage linkages between options and their underlying instruments, as depicted by the horizontal line segments in Figure 10.1. In this section, we complete the discussion by focusing on the arbitrage price relations that exist between commodity options and futures options, should both markets exist for a particular underlying commodity.[5]

European Options

The relation between commodity option and futures option prices is straightforward for European options. Since the futures contract has the same time to expiration as the option contracts (by assumption (e) at the beginning of the chapter), and since the price of the futures contract equals the underlying commodity price at expiration, the European call (put) option on a futures contract will have exactly the same value as the European call (put) option written on the underlying commodity itself. That is,

$$c(S, T; X) = c(F, T; X) \qquad \textbf{(10.27a)}$$

and

$$p(S, T; X) = p(F, T; X). \qquad \textbf{(10.27b)}$$

In the case of European options, commodity options and futures options are perfect substitutes for one another.

American Options

The equality of the European option prices arises because the options cannot be exercised early and at the options' expiration the futures price equals the commodity price. American options, however, have an early exercise privilege and must reflect the fact that, prior to expiration, the futures price may differ from the commodity price. When the futures price is at least as great as the price of the underlying commodity (i.e., in the cost-of-carry model, $F = Se^{bT}$, $F \geqslant S$ if $b \geqslant 0$), the American call option written on the futures is worth at least as much as the American call written on the commodity,

$$C(F, T; X) \geq C(S, T; X). \qquad \textbf{(10.28a)}$$

---

[5] Recall that in Chapter 1 we noted that commodity options and futures options markets exist for many foreign currencies such as the German Deutsche mark and for stock indexes such as the S&P 500.

To see this, consider the initial, intermediate and terminal values of a portfolio that consists of a long position in the futures option and a short position in the commodity option, as illustrated in Table 10.9. If both options are held to expiration, the net terminal value of the portfolio equals zero. If the options are out-of-the-money they expire worthless, and if they are in-the-money the options' payoffs negate each other. In the event the American commodity option is exercised early against the portfolio holder, the value of the portfolio is $\tilde{C}_t - \tilde{S}_t + X$. But, the lower price bound of the call is $\tilde{F}_t - X$. Since we have assumed $F_t \geq S_t$, the intermediate value of the portfolio is nonnegative. In the absence of costless arbitrage opportunities, the initial value of the portfolio must be nonpositive, so condition (10.28a) must hold.

A similar arbitrage argument can be developed for American put options. Since a put option represents the right to sell the underlying instrument, the instrument with the lowest price provides the highest option value. Thus, if $F \geq S$,

$$P(S, T; X) \geq P(F, T; X). \tag{10.28b}$$

Conditions (10.28a) and (10.28b) present the price relations between American options written on commodities and futures in the usual case where the cost-of-carry rate, b, is positive or equal to zero. In a few markets, however, b may be less than zero. For example, with foreign currencies, $b < 0$ when the foreign riskless rate of interest is greater than the domestic riskless rate (as shown in Chapter 9). When this happens, it can be easily shown, using arguments similar to those above, that the conditions (10.28a) and (10.28b) will be reversed. Table 10.10 provides a summary of the price relations developed in this section.

TABLE 10.9   Arbitrage transactions for establishing price relation between commodity and futures options, where $b \geq 0$.

$$C(F, T; X) \geq C(S, T; X)$$

		Call Exercised Early	Call Exercised at Expiration	
Position	Initial Value	Intermediate Value	Terminal Value $\tilde{S}_T \leq X$	$\tilde{S}_T > X$
Buy futures option	$-C(F, T; X)$	$C(\tilde{F}_t, T-t; X)$	0	$\tilde{S}_T - X$
Sell commodity option	$C(S, T; X)$	$-(\tilde{S}_t - X)$	0	$-(\tilde{S}_T - X)$
Net portfolio value	$C(S, T; X)$ $-C(F, T; X)$	$C(\tilde{F}_t, T-t; X)$ $-\tilde{S}_t + X$	0 0	0 0

TABLE 10.10   Summary of price relations between commodity and futures options.

Option Type	Call Option	Put Option
European	$c(S,T;X) = c(F,T;X)$	$p(S,T;X) = p(F,T;X)$
American	$C(S,T;X) \leq C(F,T;X)$ if $b \geq 0$ $C(S,T;X) > C(F,T;X)$ if $b < 0$	$P(S,T;X) \geq P(F,T;X)$ if $b \geq 0$ $P(S,T;X) < P(F,T;X)$ if $b < 0$

10.9 SUMMARY

We show first how option positions can be characterized using vector notation. Lower bounds on the prices of European and American options are derived and explained.

The distinction between European and American options is the early exercise privilege of American options. We discuss the conditions under which the early exercise privilege has value. First, early exercise will only occur if the option is substantially in the money. Second, for call options, early exercise requires that the cost of carrying the commodity is "small" relative to the interest rate; and, for put options, early exercise requires that the cost of carrying the commodity is "high" relative to the interest rate.

The put-call parity relation, linking the prices of options and the underlying commodity, is derived for European and American options and for commodity options and futures options. Finally, the relation between the price of a commodity option and a futures option is derived.

11 VALUATION OF OPTIONS

In the last chapter, we examined the structure of option prices implied by the absence of arbitrage opportunities. The approach in that chapter provided many interesting pricing relations, but the results took the form of option pricing bounds rather than valuation equations. In this chapter, we develop valuation equations for European commodity options by invoking an assumption that commodity prices are lognormally distributed at the option's expiration.

The approach used here also assumes that options are valued as though all individuals in the economy are risk-neutral. This assumption is reasonable because the value of the option does not depend on the expected rate of return of the underlying commodity. The concept of risk-neutral valuation of options and its equivalence to risk-averse valuation are explained in section 1. Section 2 examines the implications of the assumption that commodity prices are lognormally distributed. The assumptions of lognormality and risk-neutrality are then used to price a European call option in the third section and a European put option in the fourth section. Section 5 describes the sensitivity of option price to changes in the option's underlying determinants. Section 6 presents the valuation equation for an option that permits its holder to exchange one risky commodity for another. This option, called an exchange option, is embedded in many types of futures contracts. Valuation approximation methods for American options are briefly described in section 7. Section 8 describes how the parameters of the valuation equations can be estimated, and section 9 concludes with a brief summary.

11.1 RISK-NEUTRAL VALUATION

The value of an option at maturity depends on the value of the underlying commodity. Before maturity, one can calculate the expected value of an option based on the probability distribution of the terminal value of the commodity underlying the option. A probability distribution is given in Figure 11.1, and an option exercise value, X, is shown. The expected value of a call option at maturity is the profit from the call times its probability, summed over all possible values of the underlying commodity. Since the value of the call is zero to the left of X, the expected value of the call is the partial expectation to the right of X. To illustrate this pricing principle, suppose, instead of the smooth probability distribution shown in Figure 11.1, the underlying commodity can only take on the values, 80, 90, 100, 110, and 120, with corresponding probabilities of 0.15, 0.20, 0.30, 0.20, and 0.15. Also, suppose that the exercise price of the call is 100. The expected value of a call is, therefore, $(110 - 100).20 + (120 - 100).15 = 5.0$.

The current value of the call is the discounted value of its expected value at maturity. Determining this present value is a perplexing problem. Under the traditional approach of risk-averse individuals in the economy, the current value of the call is computed by discounting the expected value of the call at expiration at the risk-adjusted rate of return of the call. This is the approach derived by Samuelson in 1965. Unfortunately, his approach requires the estimation of both the expected rate of return on the commodity and the expected rate of return on the call. In practice, reliable estimation of these parameters is extremely difficult.

For many years, option valuation could not overcome this difficulty. A breakthrough came in 1973 with a paper by Black and Scholes. They showed that one could establish a riskless hedge between a stock option and the underlying stock,

FIGURE 11.1 Commodity Price Distribution at Time T

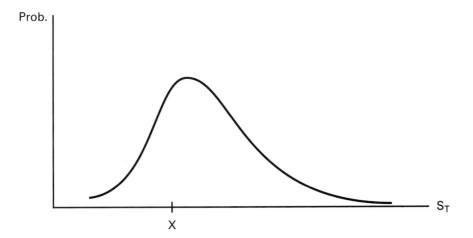

FIGURE 11.2   Commodity Price Distributions for Risk-Neutral and Risk-Averse Individuals

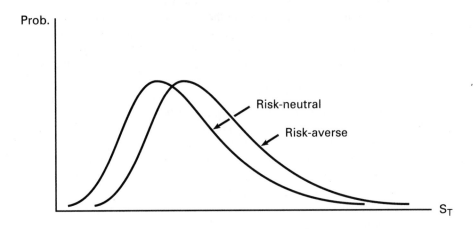

so the option is riskless relative to the stock.[1] Cox and Ross (1976) further showed that they would get the correct option value if they assumed the expected return on the stock and the expected rate of return on the call are the riskless rate, as long as the probability distribution of the ending stock value is otherwise maintained. To illustrate, consider the two probability distributions plotted in Figure 11.2. The probability distribution on the right is the distribution implied if individuals are risk-averse, and the probability distribution on the left is the distribution implied if individuals are risk-neutral. The variances of the two distributions are the same, but the expected value of the risk-neutral distribution is less than the expected value of the risk-averse distribution. Under the Cox-Ross approach, the expected value of the risk-neutral distribution is discounted at the riskless rate of interest, and under the Samuelson approach, the expected value of risk-averse distribution is discounted at a risk-adjusted rate of return. In the end, both approaches provide the same current value for the call.

In this chapter, we use the risk-neutral valuation approach because of its mathematical tractability. Prior to doing so, however, we will demonstrate through an illustration using a simple binomial model that the two approaches produce the same result. First, we demonstrate the concept of a riskless hedge. Second, we show risk-neutral valuation. Finally, we show the equivalence of risk-averse valuation to risk-neutral valuation.

Riskless Hedge Portfolio Using a Simple Binomial Model

The key insight in the derivation of the option pricing formulas presented in this chapter is that a riskless hedge may be formed between the option and the underlying commodity. To understand the riskless hedge concept, consider the following simple numerical problem. Suppose that the current commodity price is $40 and

---

[1] For an historical recount of the development of the Black–Scholes option pricing model, see Black (1989).

that at the end of three months the commodity price will be $45 or $35. The figure below illustrates the possible commodity price movements.

Now, consider a European call option written on this commodity. This call has an exercise price of $40 and expires in exactly three months. At expiration, this call will have a value of $5 or $0, depending on whether the commodity price is $45 or $35, as is seen in the figure below.

Now, suppose we were to buy one unit of the commodity and sell n_c call options. The terminal value of this portfolio is $45 - 5n_c$ if the commodity price rises and $35 if the commodity price falls. The uncertainty of the portfolio's terminal value can be completely eliminated by setting n_c such that

$$45 - 5n_c = 35 \quad \text{or} \quad n_c = 2.$$

In other words, if we buy one unit of the commodity and sell two calls, the terminal value of the portfolio is certain to be $35. This is the concept of a *riskless hedge portfolio.*

Due to the existence of this riskless hedge portfolio, we can price the European call option in the above example. The cost of forming this riskless hedge portfolio at time 0 is $40 - $2c. Since the investment of $40 - $2c provides a certain terminal value of $35, it must be the case that if we would alternatively invest the $40 - $2c in riskless securities we would also realize a terminal value of $35. If the riskless rate of interest over the three-month interval is 2 percent, then the absence of costless arbitrage opportunities in the marketplace requires that

$$\$(40 - 2c)(1.02) = \$35.$$

In other words, the price of the European call is $2.84.

The fact that a riskless hedge may be formed between the option and the underlying commodity has an important implication—the price of the risky call option can be derived without knowing the expected rate of return on the commodity. Even though the probabilities of the commodity price moving up to $45 or down to $35 were not known in the above example, we were still able to price the option. In other words, the value of the call relative to the commodity is not influenced by investor preferences. It does not matter whether an individual is risk-averse or risk-neutral, both are willing to pay $2.84 for the call option in the above example.

Risk-Neutral Valuation Using the Binomial Model

Cox and Ross (1976) carry this argument one step further. They recognize that, since the price of the call is invariant to investor preferences, nothing is lost if we assume that everyone is risk-neutral. Under an assumption of risk-neutrality, we can find the "risk-neutral" probabilities of an upstate or a downstate in the above example. In a risk-neutral world, the expected terminal value of the commodity is simply its current price times one plus the riskless rate of interest. Hence,

$$\$40(1.02) = \$45p + \$35(1 - p),$$

or p equals 58 percent. We then use this probability to compute the expected terminal value of the call option, that is,

$$E(c_T) = \$5(.58) + \$0(.42) = \$2.90.$$

Finally, the current value of the call is simply the present value of the expected terminal value. Under the assumption of risk-neutrality, the discount rate is the riskless rate of interest, so the current call price is

$$c = \frac{\$2.90}{1.02} = \$2.84,$$

exactly the result that we obtained using the riskless hedge portfolio. It is important to remember that this approach prices the option relative to the current commodity price, which is assumed to be "correct."

Risk-Averse Valuation Using the Binomial Model

The price of the option computed using the risk-neutral valuation approach is the same as the price computed using an economy where individuals are assumed to be risk-averse. To see this, consider a binomial framework where the commodity price is currently at $40 and has "risk-averse" probabilities, p', of rising to $45 and $1 - p'$ of falling to $35. Suppose that the expected rate of return on the commodity is 4 percent over the next three months, where the riskless rate of interest is 2 percent. The difference between the two rates reflects the risk premium demanded by individuals for holding the risky commodity. If the expected rate of return on the commodity is 4 percent, then the risk-averse probabilities are determined by

$$\$40(1.04) = \$45p' + \$35(1 - p'),$$

that is, p' is 66 percent. The higher probability of an upstate reflects the fact that the risk-averse individual demands a greater reward for bearing risk than the risk-neutral individual. The expected option price at expiration is, therefore,

$$E(c_T) = \$5(.66) + \$0(.34) = \$3.30.$$

The next step in valuation is to determine the appropriate risk-adjusted discount rate for the call option. In a risk-neutral economy, the rate is simply the riskless rate of interest since individuals are indifferent about risk. Risk-averse individuals, however, care about risk and demand higher rates of return for risky assets or commodities. For example, under the capital asset pricing model, the expected rate of return on the commodity is

$$E_S = r + (E_M - r)\beta_S,$$

where E_s and E_M are the expected returns for the commodity and the market portfolio, respectively, r is the riskless rate of return, and β_s is the commodity's relative systematic risk coefficient. Substituting in the example values, we find

$$.04 = .02 + (E_M - .02)\beta_S$$

or

$$(E_M - .02)\beta_S = .02.$$

Since β_s represents the percentage change in the commodity price with respect to a percentage change in the market portfolio, we can multiply β_s by the percentage change in the call price with respect to a percentage change in the commodity price to obtain the call option's beta and, hence, expected rate of return. That is,

$$E_c = r + (E_M - r)\beta_c$$
$$= r + (E_M - r)\beta_S \left(\frac{dc/c}{dS/S} \right).$$

But, in the case of our illustration, the percentage change in the option price is

$$\frac{dc/c}{dS/S} = \frac{dc}{dS} \times \frac{S}{c} = \frac{5 - 0}{45 - 35} \times \frac{40}{c} = \frac{20}{c}.$$

Thus, substituting for $(E_M - .02)\beta_S$, we find

$$E_c = .02 + .02 \left(\frac{20}{c} \right).$$

The present value of the call is, therefore,

$$c = \frac{E(c_t)}{1 + E_c} = \frac{3.30}{1 + .02 + \frac{.40}{c}},$$

so the call price is

$$c = \frac{3.30 - .40}{1.02} = 2.84,$$

exactly the same result as obtained for the risk-neutral economy.

11.2 COMMODITY PRICE AND RETURN DISTRIBUTIONS

The valuation of European call options is nearly as simple as the illustration shows. The only additional feature that must be incorporated in the valuation of the European call option is a more realistic assumption about the distribution of the commodity price at the time the option expires. This section deals with the distributional characteristics of the commodity prices and returns.

Before discussing specific distributional properties, a few basic definitions are required. First, consider a sequence of periodic commodity prices beginning today and continuing through time T,[2]

$$S_0, \tilde{S}_1, \tilde{S}_2, \cdots, \tilde{S}_T.$$

The random *rate of return* on the commodity over the T periods is defined as being the price relative less one, that is,

$$\tilde{S}_T/S_0 - 1. \tag{11.1}$$

The random *continuously compounded rate of return* over the T periods is

$$\tilde{x} = \ln(\tilde{S}_T/S_0), \tag{11.2}$$

or, alternatively, the random *terminal commodity price* is

$$\tilde{S}_T = S_0 e^{\tilde{x}}. \tag{11.3}$$

Note that the continuously compounded T-period return is the sum of the T continuously compounded periodic returns, that is,

---

[2] These commodity prices are observed at intervals equally spaced through time.

$$\ln(\tilde{S}_T/S_0) = \sum_{t=1}^{T} \ln(\tilde{S}_t/\tilde{S}_{t-1}). \qquad (11.4)$$

An assumption that is commonly used in the development of finance models is that security returns are independently and identically distributed each period. Thus, the expected continuously compounded periodic return is

$$E[\ln(\tilde{S}_t/\tilde{S}_{t-1})] = \mu, \qquad (11.5)$$

and, by equation (11.4), the expected continuously compounded return from 0 to T is

$$E[\ln(\tilde{S}_T/S_0)] = \sum_{t=1}^{T} E[\ln(\tilde{S}_t/\tilde{S}_{t-1})] = \mu T. \qquad (11.6)$$

Similarly, the variance of the continuously compounded periodic return is

$$\mathrm{Var}[\ln(\tilde{S}_t/\tilde{S}_{t-1})] = \sigma^2, \qquad (11.7)$$

so the variance of the continuously compounded return from 0 to T is

$$\mathrm{Var}[\ln(\tilde{S}_T/S_0)] = \sum_{t=1}^{T} \mathrm{Var}[\ln(\tilde{S}_t/\tilde{S}_{t-1})] = \sigma^2 T. \qquad (11.8)$$

The first and the second terms in (11.8) are equal by virtue of the assumption of independence between returns in different periods. The standard deviation of the continuously compounded return from 0 to T is $\sigma\sqrt{T}$.

The second assumption that we invoke is that the continuously compounded periodic rates of return are normally distributed with mean μ and variance σ^2. In this case, the continuously compounded return from 0 to T is also normally distributed with mean μT and variance $\sigma^2 T$. It also implies that the distribution of stock prices is lognormal with mean

$$E(\tilde{S}_T) = S_0 e^{\alpha T}, \qquad (11.9)$$

where

$$\alpha = \mu + \sigma^2/2. \qquad (11.9a)$$

(A proof of this is contained in Appendix 11.1.)

Figures 11.3a and 11.3b contain illustrations of the two distributions that we are implicitly using. The first is the normal distribution for $\tilde{x}$, which has mean μT

FIGURE 11.3(a) Normal Distribution

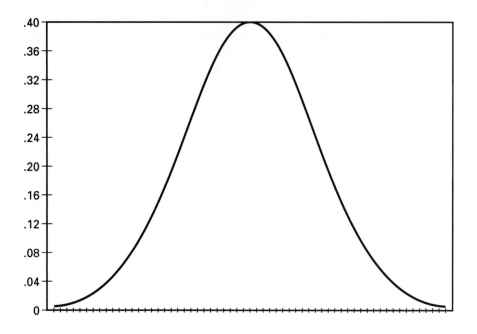

FIGURE 11.3(b) Lognormal Distribution

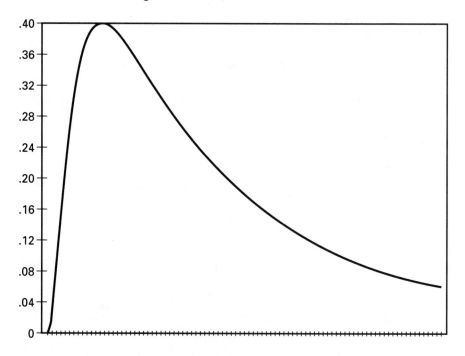

and variance $\sigma^2 T$. The second is the lognormal distribution of $\tilde{S}_T$, which has mean $S_0 e^{\alpha T}$. Note that the price distribution has the intuitively appealing characteristic that the terminal commodity price cannot fall below zero. If terminal prices were assumed to be normally distributed, there would be some chance that the commodity price would go below zero.

Our use of the normal distribution is further facilitated by transforming the continuously compounded return, $\tilde{x}$ or $\ln(\tilde{S}_T/S_0)$, into a standard normally distributed variable, $\tilde{z}$, which has mean zero and variance one, that is,

$$\tilde{z} = \frac{\tilde{x} - \mu T}{\sigma \sqrt{T}} = \frac{\ln(\tilde{S}_T/S_0) - \mu T}{\sigma \sqrt{T}}, \tag{11.10}$$

which may also be written in terms of the terminal commodity price

$$\tilde{S}_T = S_0 e^{\mu T + \sigma \sqrt{T} \tilde{z}}. \tag{11.11}$$

The variable $\tilde{z}$ has the density function

$$n(z) = \frac{1}{\sqrt{2\pi}} e^{-z^2/2}. \tag{11.12}$$

The probability that a drawing from this unit normal distribution will produce a value less than the constant, d, is

$$\text{Prob}(\tilde{z} < d) = \int_{-\infty}^{d} \frac{1}{\sqrt{2\pi}} e^{-z^2/2} dz$$
$$= N(d). \tag{11.13}$$

To evaluate the probability $N(d)$ in (11.13), a variety of methods can be used. Polynomial approximations are popular because they are simple to program. Appendix 11.2 contains two such approximations and their levels of accuracy. Another option is to use the values of the normal probabilities tabulated in statistics textbooks and other publications. Appendix 11.3 contains normal probabilities tabulated over the range of d from -4.99 to $+4.99$.

Two properties of the cumulative unit normal density function will prove useful later in this chapter. First, the probability of drawing a value greater than d from a unit normal distribution equals one minus the probability of drawing a value less than d,[3] that is,

$$\text{Prob}(\tilde{z} \geq d) = 1 - N(d). \tag{11.14}$$

---

[3] This result follows simply from $\text{Prob}(\tilde{z} < d) + \text{Prob}(\tilde{z} \geq d) = 1$ and (11.13).

Second, since the unit normal distribution is symmetric around 0, the probability of drawing a value less than d equals one minus the probability of drawing a value less than $-d$,[4] that is,

$$N(d) = 1 - N(-d). \tag{11.15}$$

EXAMPLE 11.1

Compute the probabilities that a drawing from a normal distribution will provide a value that is (a) within one standard deviation of the mean, (b) within two standard deviations of the mean, and (c) within three standard deviations of the mean.

First, it should be noted that any normally distributed variable, $\tilde{x}$, can be transformed into a unit normally distributed variable (i.e., a variable with mean zero and variance one) by applying the transformation (11.10). Second, we assess the probabilities using the tabulated values for the cumulative unit normal distribution. (See Appendix 11.3)

$$\text{Prob}(-1 \leq \tilde{z} \leq 1) = \text{Prob}(\tilde{z} \leq 1) - \text{Prob}(\tilde{z} \leq -1)$$
$$= .84134 - .15866 = .68268$$

$$\text{Prob}(-2 \leq \tilde{z} \leq 2) = \text{Prob}(\tilde{z} \leq 2) - \text{Prob}(\tilde{z} \leq -2)$$
$$= .97725 - .02275 = .95450$$

$$\text{Prob}(-3 \leq \tilde{z} \leq 3) = \text{Prob}(\tilde{z} \leq 3) - \text{Prob}(\tilde{z} \leq -3)$$
$$= .99865 - .00135 = .99730$$

EXAMPLE 11.2

Assume that the current commodity price is $50 and that the continuously compounded rate of return has an annualized mean of 16 percent and a standard devi-

---

[4]This result is derived as follows:

$$N(d) = \int_{-\infty}^{d} \frac{1}{\sqrt{2\pi}} e^{-z^2/2} dz,$$

$$= \int_{-d}^{+\infty} \frac{1}{\sqrt{2\pi}} e^{-z^2/2} dz$$

$$= \int_{-\infty}^{+\infty} \frac{1}{\sqrt{2\pi}} e^{-z^2/2} dz - \int_{-\infty}^{-d} \frac{1}{\sqrt{2\pi}} e^{-z^2/2} dz,$$

$$= 1 - N(-d).$$

ation of 32 percent. Compute the probability that the commodity price will exceed 75 at the end of three months.

First, we use equation (11.10) to transform the lognormal terminal price to a unit normal variable value. Specifically,

$$d = \frac{\ln(75/50) - .16(.25)}{.32\sqrt{.25}} = 2.28416.$$

Second, we round d to the nearest one-hundredth and use the probability tables:

$$\text{Prob}(\tilde{S}_T < 75) = \text{Prob}(\tilde{z} < 2.28) = .98870.$$

Note that we are evaluating the probability of the terminal commodity price being less than 75 because the tables find the area under the unit normal density function from minus infinity up to the limit d. To compute the probability that the terminal commodity price will be greater than 75, we simply take the complement or

$$\begin{aligned}
\text{Prob}(\tilde{S}_T \geq 75) &= 1 - \text{Prob}(\tilde{S}_T < 75) \\
&= 1 - \text{Prob}(\tilde{z} < 2.28) \\
&= 1 - .98870 = .01130.
\end{aligned}$$

Note that we are introducing some error as a result of rounding the upper integral limit d to the nearest hundredth when using the tables. We could interpolate between table values to achieve greater accuracy, or we could use one of the polynomial approximations in Appendix 11.2. Using the second polynomial approximation in the appendix provides

$$N(2.28416) = .98882.$$

EXAMPLE 11.3

Using the parameters from Example 11.2, compute the probability that the commodity price will fall between 40 and 60 at the end of six months.

Again, we use equation (11.10) to transform the terminal commodity price to a unit normally distributed variable. The limits of integration are

$$d_1 = \frac{\ln(60/50) - .16(.5)}{.32\sqrt{.5}} = .45220$$

$$d_2 = \frac{\ln(40/50) - .16(.5)}{.32\sqrt{.5}} = -1.33972$$

The probabilities are

$$\text{Prob}(\tilde{z} < .45220) = N(.45220) = .67444$$
$$\text{Prob}(\tilde{z} < -1.33972) = N(-1.33972) = .09017,$$

where the probabilities were again computed using the second polynomial approximation in Appendix 11.2.

The final step involves differencing the probabilities, that is,

$$
\begin{aligned}
\text{Prob}(40 \leq \tilde{S}_T \leq 60) &= \text{Prob}(-1.33972 \leq \tilde{z} \leq .45220) \\
&= \text{Prob}(\tilde{z} \leq .45220) - \text{Prob}(\tilde{z} \leq -1.33972) \\
&= .67444 - .09017 = .58427.
\end{aligned}
$$

EXAMPLE 11.4

Using the parameters from Example 11.2, compute the range of the commodity price in three months assuming that it will be within two standard deviations of its current level.

Use equation (11.11) and set $\tilde{z}$ equal to ± 2. The two terminal commodity prices are

$$S_{T1} = 50e^{.16(.25)+.32\sqrt{.25}(-2)} = 37.78919$$
$$S_{T2} = 50e^{.16(.25)+.32\sqrt{.25}(2)} = 71.66647.$$

EXAMPLE 11.5

Suppose that there is a three-month European call option written on the commodity in Example 11.2 and its exercise price is 50. Compute the probability that the call option will be in-the-money at expiration. The upper integral limit d is

$$d = \frac{\ln(50/50) - .16(.25)}{.32\sqrt{.25}} = -.25000.$$

The probability that the terminal commodity price will be less than the exercise price is

$$\text{Prob}(\tilde{S}_T < 50) = N(-.25000) = .40129,$$

so the probability that the commodity price will exceed the exercise price is

$$\text{Prob}(\tilde{S}_T \geq 50) = 1 - N(-.25000) = .59871.$$

EXAMPLE 11.6

Compute the expected rate of return on the commodity over a three-month interval and the expected commodity price at that point in time.

By equation (11.9a), we know that the expected rate of return on the commodity is equal to the mean plus one-half of the variance of the distribution of the logarithm of the commodity price ratio, $\ln(\tilde{S}_T/S)$, that is,

$$\alpha = \mu + \sigma^2/2$$
$$= .16 + .32^2/2$$
$$= .2112.$$

The expected terminal commodity price is, therefore,

$$E(\tilde{S}_T) = Se^{\alpha T} = 50e^{.2112(.25)} = 52.71094.$$

11.3 RISK-NEUTRAL VALUATION OF EUROPEAN CALL OPTION

The European call option valuation equation is now derived under the distributional assumptions discussed in the previous section. The valuation approach is consistent with the numerical illustration used in Section 11.1—first, we estimate the expected terminal value of the call, and then we discount the expected terminal value to the present. The theoretical call price is simply

$$c = e^{-rT}E(\tilde{c}_T). \qquad\qquad (11.16)$$

To evaluate the expected terminal call price, we assume that the expected rate of return on the commodity equals the riskless rate of interest (risk-neutrality) and that the commodity prices are lognormally distributed at the option's expiration. To discount the expected terminal call price to the present, we assume that the expected rate of return on the call equals the riskless rate of interest (risk-neutrality).

In order to make equation (11.16) operational, we need to evaluate the term $E(\tilde{c}_T)$, the expected terminal value of the call option. If $\tilde{S}_T$ is assumed to be lognormally distributed, the distribution of the terminal call price, $\tilde{c}_T$, is known since $\tilde{c}_T$ is simply

$$\tilde{c}_T = \begin{cases} \tilde{S}_T - X & \text{for } S_T \geq X \\ 0 & \text{for } S_T < X. \end{cases} \tag{11.17}$$

With the terminal commodity price having a lognormal distribution, condition (11.17) implies that the terminal call price has a truncated lognormal distribution and that the mean of the call price distribution is:

$$\begin{aligned} E(\tilde{c}_T) &= E(\tilde{S}_T - X | S_T \geq X) + E(0 | S_T < X) \\ &= E(\tilde{S}_T - X | S_T \geq X) \\ &= E(\tilde{S}_T | S_T \geq X) - E(X | S_T \geq X) \\ &= E(\tilde{S}_T | S_T \geq X) - X\mathrm{Prob}(S_T \geq X), \end{aligned} \tag{11.18}$$

where $\mathrm{Prob}(S_T \geq X)$ is the probability that the commodity price exceeds the option's exercise price at expiration. To evaluate $E(\tilde{c}_T)$, we must evaluate each of the two terms on the right-hand side of (11.18). We will begin with the second term.

Evaluation of $X\mathrm{Prob}(S_T \geq X)$

Letting $L(S_T)$ be the lognormal density function of S_T, the term $X\mathrm{Prob}(S_T \geq X)$, is

$$X\mathrm{Prob}(S_T \geq X) = X \int_X^{+\infty} L(S_T)dS_T.$$

The easiest way to evaluate the integral is to perform a change of variables on S_T. Equation (11.10) shows us the transformation that we apply to S_T. The upper and lower limits of integration for the new variable z are obtained by substituting $+\infty$ and X for S_T in (11.10). The limits are therefore $+\infty$ and $[\ln(X/S) - \mu T]/\sigma\sqrt{T}$, respectively. Thus,

$$\begin{aligned} X\mathrm{Prob}(S_T \geq X) &= X \int_{\frac{\ln(X/S)-\mu T}{\sigma\sqrt{T}}}^{+\infty} n(z)dz \\ &= X \int_{-\infty}^{\frac{\ln(S/X)+\mu T}{\sigma\sqrt{T}}} n(z)dz \\ &= XN(d_2), \end{aligned} \tag{11.19}$$

where $d_2 = [\ln(S/X) + \mu T]/(\sigma\sqrt{T})$. In other words, the value $N(d_2)$ is the probability that the commodity price will exceed the exercise price at the option's expiration.

Evaluation of $E(\tilde{S}_T | S_T \geq X)$

The evaluation of the first term of equation (11.18), $E(\tilde{S}_T | S_T \geq X)$, is slightly more difficult. The initial steps are as follows:

$$
\begin{aligned}
E(\tilde{S}_T | S_T \geq X) &= \int_X^{+\infty} S_T L(S_T) dS_T \\
&= \int_{\frac{\ln(X/S)-\mu T}{\sigma\sqrt{T}}}^{+\infty} S e^{\mu T + \sigma\sqrt{T}z} e^{-z^2/2} \frac{1}{\sqrt{2\pi}} dz \\
&= S e^{\mu T} \int_{\frac{\ln(X/S)-\mu T}{\sigma\sqrt{T}}}^{+\infty} e^{\sigma^2 T/2 - \sigma^2 T/2 + \sigma\sqrt{T}z - z^2/2} \frac{1}{\sqrt{2\pi}} dz \\
&= S e^{\mu T + \sigma^2 T/2} \int_{\frac{\ln(X/S)-\mu T}{\sigma\sqrt{T}}}^{+\infty} e^{-(\sigma\sqrt{T}-z)^2/2} \frac{1}{\sqrt{2\pi}} dz \\
&= S e^{\mu T + \sigma^2 T/2} \int_{-\infty}^{\frac{\ln(S/X)+\mu T}{\sigma\sqrt{T}} + \sigma\sqrt{T}} e^{-y^2/2} \frac{1}{\sqrt{2\pi}} dy \\
&= S e^{\mu T + \sigma^2 T/2} N(d_1),
\end{aligned}
\tag{11.20}
$$

where $d_1 = [\ln(S/X) + \mu T]/(\sigma\sqrt{T}) + \sigma\sqrt{T}$. The steps in (11.20) are as follows: (a) the conditional expected value is expressed in integral form where $L(S_T)$ is the lognormal density function for S_T; (b) a change of variables is performed on S_T, and the density function of the standardized normal variable, z, is written out; (c) $S e^{\mu T}$ is factored out of the integral and the square in the exponent within the integral is completed; (d) $e^{\sigma^2 m}$ is factored out of the intergral and the remaining expression in the exponent within the integral is simplified; (e) a change of variables $y = \sigma\sqrt{T} - z$ is performed and the limits of the integration are redefined;[5] and (f) the expression is simplified.

Evaluation of $E(\tilde{c}_T)$

To summarize, under the assumption that commodity prices are lognormally distributed and that individuals are risk-neutral, we are attempting to value a European call option. We are in the process of valuing the expected terminal value of the call option, $E(\tilde{c}_T)$. Substituting equations (11.20) and (11.19) into equation (11.18), we now have

$$
E(\tilde{c}_T) = S e^{\mu T + \sigma^2 T} N(d_1) - X N(d_2)
\tag{11.21}
$$

---

[5]Where $y = -z$, the following property holds:

$$
\int_{-d}^{\infty} e^{-z^2/2} \frac{1}{\sqrt{2\pi}} dz = \int_{-\infty}^{d} e^{-y^2/2} \frac{1}{\sqrt{2\pi}} dy.
$$

This property is used in simplifying (11.20).

where

$$d_1 = \frac{\ln(S/X) + \mu T}{\sigma\sqrt{T}} + \sigma\sqrt{T}, \qquad \textbf{(11.21a)}$$

$$d_2 = \frac{\ln(S/X) + \mu T}{\sigma\sqrt{T}}. \qquad \textbf{(11.21b)}$$

We will not stop here, however. The expected rate of return of the commodity in the integral limits d_1 and d_2 is the mean of the logarithm of the commodity price ratios—$E[\ln(\tilde{S}_t/\tilde{S}_{t-1})]$. We would like to express the expected rate of return of the commodity in terms of the raw price relatives—$E(\tilde{S}_T/S)$. We know that

$$E(\tilde{S}_T/S) = e^{\alpha T} = e^{(\mu+\sigma^2/2)T}. \qquad \textbf{(11.22)}$$

Now, recall that we have invoked an assumption of risk-neutrality. The value of α in (11.22) is the expected rate of return on the commodity, and, in a risk-neutral world, the expected rate of return on the commodity equals the cost-of-carry rate, b (i.e., the cost of interest plus any additional costs). Substituting b for α in (11.9a) and isolating μ, we get

$$\mu = b - \sigma^2/2. \qquad \textbf{(11.23)}$$

Substituting this into (11.21), we get

$$E(\tilde{c}_T) = Se^{bT}N(d_1) - XN(d_2), \qquad \textbf{(11.24)}$$

where

$$d_1 = \frac{\ln(S/X) + (b + .5\sigma^2)T}{\sigma\sqrt{T}}, \qquad \textbf{(11.24a)}$$

$$d_2 = \frac{\ln(S/X) + (b - .5\sigma^2)T}{\sigma\sqrt{T}},$$

$$= d_1 - \sigma\sqrt{T}. \qquad \textbf{(11.24b)}$$

Current Value of Call

With an explicit valuation of $E(\tilde{c}_T)$ in hand, we can substitute into equation (11.16) to find the *valuation formula for the European call option on a commodity with cost-of-carry rate b,* that is,

$$c(S, T; X) = Se^{(b-r)T}N(d_1) - Xe^{-rT}N(d_2), \qquad \textbf{(11.25)}$$

where

$$d_1 = \frac{\ln(S/X) + (b + .5\sigma^2)T}{\sigma\sqrt{T}},$$

(11.25a)

$$d_2 = d_1 - \sigma\sqrt{T}.$$

(11.25b)

The interpretation of the terms in (11.25) is fairly straightforward given our risk-neutral valuation approach. The term $Se^{(b-r)T}N(d_1)$ is the present value of the expected benefit of exercising the call option at expiration, conditional on the terminal commodity price being greater than the exercise price at the option's expiration. The term $N(d_2)$ is the probability that the commodity price will be greater than the exercise price at expiration. The present value of the expected cost of exercising the call option conditional upon the call being in-the-money at expiration is $Xe^{-rT}N(d_2)$.

EXAMPLE 11.7

Compute the price of a three-month European foreign currency call option with an exercise price of 40. The spot exchange rate is currently 40, the domestic interest rate is 8 percent annually, the foreign interest rate is 12 percent annually, and the standard deviation of the continuously compounded return is 30 percent on an annualized basis. Note that the cost-of-carry rate, b, is, therefore, -4 percent.

$$c = 40e^{(-.04-.08).25}N(d_1) - 40e^{-.08(.25)}N(d_2),$$

where

$$d_1 = \frac{\ln(40/40) + [-.04 + .5(.30)^2](.25)}{.30\sqrt{.25}} = .0083,$$

$$d_2 = d_1 - .30\sqrt{.25} = -.1417.$$

The values of $N(d_1)$ and $N(d_2)$ are .5033 and .4437, respectively, so the European call option price is

$$c = 38.818(.5033) - 39.208(.4437) = 2.14.$$

11.4 RISK-NEUTRAL VALUATION OF EUROPEAN PUT OPTION

The risk-neutral valuation approach can be applied to the European put option pricing problem to find the put's valuation equation. A simpler way, however, is to combine the European put-call parity relation from the last chapter with the European call option valuation equation (11.25). In the absence of costless arbitrage opportunities in the marketplace, the European put-call parity relation,

$$c(S,T;X) - p(S,T;X) = Se^{(b-r)T} - Xe^{-rT},$$ **(11.26)**

holds at all points in time. Isolating $p(S,T;X)$ in (11.26), we get

$$p(S,T;X) = c(S,T;X) - Se^{(b-r)T} + Xe^{-rT}.$$ **(11.27)**

Substituting the European call option valuation equation (11.25) for the term $c(S,T;X)$, we find that the *valuation equation for a European put option on a commodity* is

$$\begin{aligned}
p(S,T;X) &= Se^{(b-r)T}N(d_1) - Xe^{-rT}N(d_2) - Se^{(b-r)T} + Xe^{-rT} \\
&= Xe^{-rT}[1 - N(d_2)] - Se^{(b-r)T}[1 - N(d_1)] \\
&= Xe^{-rT}N(-d_2) - Se^{(b-r)T}N(-d_1),
\end{aligned}$$ **(11.28)**

where

$$d_1 = \frac{\ln(S/X) + (b + .5\sigma^2)T}{\sigma\sqrt{T}},$$ **(11.28a)**

$$d_2 = d_1 - \sigma\sqrt{T}.$$ **(11.28b)**

Thus, the valuation of the European put option follows straightforwardly from European put-call parity and the valuation of the European call option.

The interpretation of the terms in (11.28) parallels the risk-neutral interpretation for the call. The term $Xe^{-rT}N(-d_2)$ is the present value of the expected benefit of exercising the put option at expiration conditional upon the terminal commodity price being less than the exercise price at the option's expiration. Recall the put option provides the right to sell the commodity so the benefit from holding the option is the cash we receive when we exercise the option, that is, X. $N(-d_2)$ is the probability that the commodity price will be less than the exercise price at expiration. Note that it is the complement of $N(d_2)$, the probability that the terminal commodity price will exceed the exercise price. The present value of the expected cost of exercising the put option conditional upon the put option being in-the-money at expiration is $Se^{(b-r)T}N(-d_1)$. If we exercise the put, we must forfeit the commodity as fulfillment of our obligation so the present value of the expected terminal commodity price conditional upon exercise is our cost today.

EXAMPLE 11.8

Compute the price of a three-month European foreign currency put option with an exercise price of 40. The spot exchange rate is currently 40, the domestic interest rate is 8 percent annually, the foreign interest rate is 12 percent annually, and the standard deviation of the continuously compounded return is 30 percent on an annualized basis. Note that the cost-of-carry rate, b, is, therefore, -4 percent.

$$p = 40e^{-.08(.25)}N(-d_2) - 40e^{(-.04-.08).25}N(-d_1),$$

where

$$d_1 = \frac{\ln(40/40) + [-.04 + .5(.30)^2](.25)}{.30\sqrt{.25}} = .0083,$$

$$d_2 = d_1 - .30\sqrt{.25} = -.1417.$$

The values of $N(-d_2)$ and $N(-d_1)$ are .5563 and .4967, respectively, so the European put option price is

$$p = 39.208(.5563) - 38.818(.4967) = 2.53.$$

Note that this result, together with the result of Exercise 11.7 verifies the put-call parity relation (11.26), that is,

$$2.14 - 2.53 = 38.818 - 39.208.$$

11.5 PROPERTIES OF THE EUROPEAN CALL AND PUT OPTION PRICING FORMULAS

The valuation equations for the European call and put options are

$$c(S, T; X) = Se^{(b-r)T}N(d_1) - Xe^{-rT}N(d_2) \qquad \textbf{(11.25)}$$

and

$$p(S, T; X) = Xe^{-rT}N(-d_2) - Se^{(b-r)T}N(-d_1), \qquad \textbf{(11.28)}$$

respectively, where

$$d_1 = \frac{\ln(S/X) + (b + .5\sigma^2)T}{\sigma\sqrt{T}}$$

and

$$d_2 = d_1 - \sigma\sqrt{T}.$$

The option price depends on six variables—S, X, b, r, σ, T. In this section, we analyze how the European call and put option prices respond to changes in the underlying option variables. Each of the variables will be discussed in turn beginning with the commodity price. The derivations of each of the expressions below are contained in Appendix 11.4.

Change in Commodity Price

The change in the option price with respect to a change in the commodity price is called the option's *delta*. The delta of a European call option is

$$\Delta_c = \frac{\partial c}{\partial S} = e^{(b-r)T}N(d_1) > 0. \qquad\qquad \textbf{(11.29a)}$$

The call option's delta is unambiguously positive in sign, implying that an increase in commodity price causes the call price to increase. The result is intuitive since the call option conveys the right to buy the underlying commodity at a fixed price and the underlying commodity has just become more valuable.

Figure 11.4 shows the how the value of a European call option changes as the underlying commodity price changes. The option has three months to expiration. Notice that when the call option is out-of-the-money, its slope is fairly flat. Out-of-the-money call options have very low delta values; that is, they do not respond very quickly to changes in the commodity price. As the commodity price increases and the call becomes at-the-money and then in-the-money, the slope becomes steeper and steeper. Where the option is very deep in-the-money, the delta value is nearly one, and the call price changes in a one-to-one correspondence with the commodity price. Figure 11.5 shows the option's delta value as a function of the commodity price.

The put option's delta is

$$\Delta_p = \frac{\partial p}{\partial S} = -e^{(b-r)T}N(-d_1) < 0. \qquad\qquad \textbf{(11.29b)}$$

This derivative is negative because an increase in the commodity price makes the put option less valuable. Again, it can be shown that the sensitivity of the put price

FIGURE 11.4   European call option price (*c*) as a function of the underlying commodity price (*S*). The commodity price range
is from 50 through 150. The option has an exercise price
(*X*) of 100 and a time to expiration (*T*) of three months.
The cost-of-carry rate (*b*) is 8 percent, and the riskless
rate of interest (*r*) is 8 percent. The standard deviation
of the logarithm of the commodity price ratios (*σ*) is 30
percent.

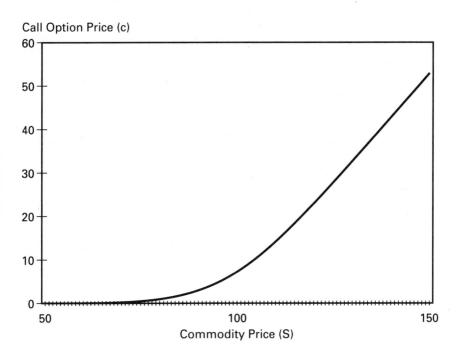

to changes in the underlying commodity price is itself sensitive to the "moneyness"
of the option. Figure 11.6 shows this sensitivity for a European put option with
three months to expiration. The in-the-money option has a steeper slope than the
at-the-money option, which, in turn, has a steeper slope than the out-of-the-money
option. Figure 11.7 shows the put's delta value as a function of the underlying
commodity price.

Percentage Change in the Commodity Price
It is often the case that, instead of the dollar change in the option price with respect
to a dollar change in the underlying commodity price, one is interested in the elasticity of the option price with respect to the commodity price. This elasticity, called
the option's *eta*, is the percentage change in the option price with respect to the

FIGURE 11.5 European call option delta (Δ_c) as a function of the underlying commodity price (S). The commodity price range is from 50 through 150. The option has an exercise price (X) of 100 and a time to expiration (T) of three months. The cost-of-carry rate (b) is 8 percent, and the riskless rate of interest (r) is 8 percent. The standard deviation of the logarithm of the commodity price ratios (σ) is 30 percent.

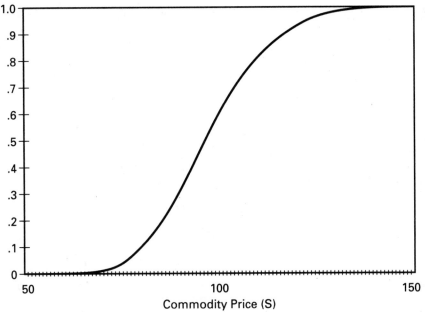

Delta Value of Call Option

Commodity Price (S)

percentage change in the commodity price. The elasticity of the call price with respect to the commodity price is greater than one,[6] that is,

$$\eta_c = \Delta_c \frac{S}{c} = e^{(b-r)T} N(d_1) \frac{S}{c} > 1, \qquad \textbf{(11.30a)}$$

---

[6] The elasticity of the call price with respect to the commodity price can be shown to be greater than one by rewriting (11.30a) as

$$\eta_c = \frac{1}{1 - \dfrac{Xe^{-rT} N(d_2)}{Se^{(b-r)T} N(d_1)}}.$$

The last term in the denominator is less than one because the European call price cannot be less than zero, therefore, the value of η_c must be greater than one.

FIGURE 11.6   European put option price (p) as a function of the under-lying commodity price (S). The commodity price range is from 50 through 150. The option has an exercise price (X) of 100 and a time to expiration (T) of three months. The cost-of-carry rate (b) is 8 percent, and the riskless rate of interest (r) is 8 percent. The standard deviation of the logarithm of the commodity price ratios (σ) is 30 percent.

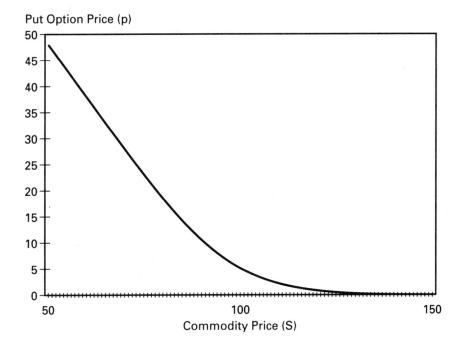

Put Option Price (p)

Commodity Price (S)

and the elasticity of the put price with respect to the commodity price is less than minus one,[7] that is,

$$\eta_p = \Delta_p \frac{S}{p} = -e^{(b-r)T} N(-d_1) \frac{S}{p} < -1. \qquad \textbf{(11.30b)}$$

Table 11.1 contains option prices, delta values and elasticities for alternative prices of the underlying commodity. It is interesting to note that (i) the elasticities have very large magnitudes and (ii) the magnitudes are larger for farther out-of-the-money options. If someone has a strong belief that the price of an individual commodity will rise, an investment in a call option will provide a larger rate of

---

[7] The proof that η_p is less than -1 follows along the same lines as the proof that $\eta_c > 1$ in the previous footnote.

FIGURE 11.7 European put option delta (Δ_p) as a function of the underlying commodity price (S). The commodity price range is from 50 through 150. The option has an exercise price (X) of 100 and a time to expiration (T) of three months. The cost-of-carry rate (b) is 8 percent, and the riskless rate of interest (r) is 8 percent. The standard deviation of the logarithm of the commodity price ratios (σ) is 30 percent.

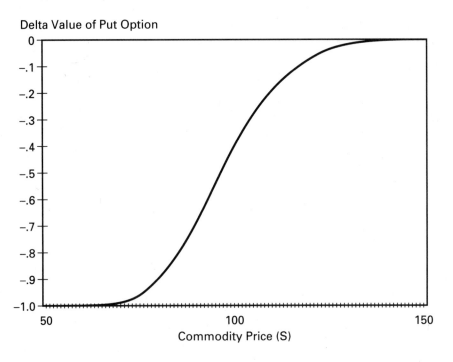

TABLE 11.1 Simulated stock index call and put option prices, deltas, etas, and gammas for option parameters: $X = 100$, $b = .08$, $r = .08$, $T = .25$, and $\sigma = .30$.

Commodity Price S	Call Price c	Delta Δ_c	Eta η_c	Gamma γ_c	Put Price p	Delta Δ_p	Eta η_p	Gamma γ_p
80	.537	.100	14.952	.014	18.557	−.899	−3.878	.014
90	2.494	.310	11.207	.026	10.514	−.689	−5.900	.026
100	6.961	.582	8.367	.026	4.981	−.417	−8.380	.026
110	13.954	.800	6.310	.016	1.974	−.199	−11.109	.016
120	22.645	.922	4.889	.008	.665	−.077	−13.924	.008

return than an investment directly in the commodity and, moreover, an investment in an out-of-the-money call will provide a greater rate of return than an in-the-money call.

These greater rates of return are not without a corresponding increase in risk, however. In fact, just as the rates of return on the options are proportionally related to the rate of return on the commodity, the risk or "beta" of an option is proportionally related to the beta of the commodity, that is, $\beta_c = \eta_c \beta_S$ and $\beta_p = \eta_p \beta_S$. The increase in the expected rate of return as a result of holding a call option is exactly what is justified on the basis of the capital asset pricing model.

Change in Delta

Earlier we described the option's delta, how the option price changes as the commodity price changes. Related to this concept is the option's *gamma*—the change in delta as the commodity price changes. The expression for the gamma of a call option is

$$\gamma_c = \frac{\partial \Delta_c}{\partial S} = \frac{e^{(b-r)T} n(d_1)}{S \sigma \sqrt{T}} > 0, \qquad (11.31a)$$

and the gamma for a put is

$$\gamma_p = \frac{\partial \Delta_p}{\partial S} = \frac{e^{(b-r)T} n(d_1)}{S \sigma \sqrt{T}} = \gamma_c > 0, \qquad (11.31b)$$

where $n(d_1)$ is the density at d_1. In short, this value tells you how quickly the delta changes as the commodity price changes. Because an option's gamma is largest when the options are approximately at-the-money, these options are the hardest to hedge. In addition, if you believe that the commodity price is about to move in one direction or another (recall the motivation for placing a volatility spread), the at-the-money spread will maximize the portfolio's dollar response to underlying commodity price movements. Figure 11.8 shows the option gamma as a function of the underlying commodity price.

Change in the Exercise Price

The partial derivatives of the call and put option prices with respect to the exercise price of the option are

$$\frac{\partial c}{\partial X} = -e^{-rT} N(d_2) < 0 \qquad (11.32a)$$

and

$$\frac{\partial p}{\partial X} = e^{-rT} N(-d_2) > 0, \qquad (11.32b)$$

FIGURE 11.8   European option gamma ($\gamma_c = \gamma_p$) as a function of the underlying commodity price (S). The commodity price range is from 50 through 150. The options have exercise price (X) of 100 and time to expiration (T) of three months. The cost-of-carry rate (b) is 8 percent, and the riskless rate of interest (r) is 8 percent. The standard deviation of the logarithm of the commodity price ratios (σ) is 30 percent.

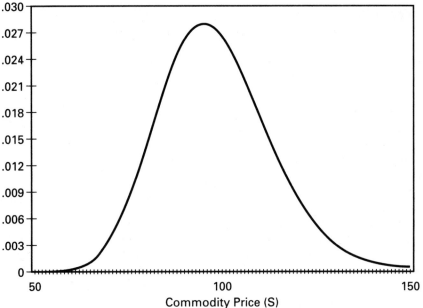

Gamma Value of Call and Put Options

respectively. Note that, if the exercise price of the options increases, the value of the call option diminishes and the value of the put option increases. This follows from the fact that the call would become more out-of-the-money and the put more in-the-money.

The partial derivatives of the option prices, with respect to the exercise price, are of little practical value in the sense that once the option is created, the exercise price does not change. They are expressed here only in the interest of completeness.

Change in the Cost-of-Carry Rate

The change in the call option price with respect to a change in the cost-of-carry rate is

$$\frac{\partial c}{\partial b} = TSe^{(b-r)T}N(d_1) > 0. \tag{11.33a}$$

As the cost-of-carry rate increases, the call option value increases, holding constant the spot price and the other variables. The higher the cost of carrying the underlying commodity, the greater the rate of appreciation in the commodity price and hence the greater the call option value. The magnitude of the derivative is small, however. For the foreign currency call option valued in Example 11.7, the partial derivative with respect to the cost-of-carry rate is 4.884. In other words, if the cost-of-carry rate on the underlying commodity increases by 100 basis points, the call price will increase by approximately five cents.

The partial derivative of the put option price with respect to the cost-of-carry rate is

$$\frac{\partial p}{\partial b} = -TSe^{(b-r)T}N(-d_1) < 0. \tag{11.33b}$$

As the cost-of-carry rate increases, the expected rate of appreciation in the commodity price increases and hence the value of the put option declines. The numerical value of this partial derivative for the put option in Example 11.8 is -4.8200.

Change in the Interest Rate

The change in the call option price with respect to a change in the riskless rate of interest is

$$\frac{\partial c}{\partial r} = TXe^{-rT}N(d_2) > 0. \tag{11.34a}$$

The call price increases with an increase in the interest rate because the present value of the exercise price decreases. The value of this derivative is 4.3489 for the call option in Example 11.7.

The partial derivative of the put option price with respect to the riskless rate of interest is

$$\frac{\partial p}{\partial r} = -TXe^{-rT}N(-d_2) < 0. \tag{11.34b}$$

Here the sign is negative because, as the riskless rate of interest increases, the present value of the exercise price received upon exercising the option decreases. The value of the derivative for the put option in Example 11.8 is -5.4531, implying that an increase in the interest rate of 100 basis points reduces the option value by about five cents.

Change in the Volatility

The change in the option price with respect to a change in the volatility[8] of the underlying commodity return is called the option's *vega*. The vega of a European call option is

---

[8] Up to this point, we have used the term "standard deviation" to describe the dispersion of commodity returns, σ. In the industry, σ is more typically referred to as the *volatility* or the *volatility rate* of the underlying commodity returns, and we adopt that convention for the remainder of the chapter.

$$\text{Vega}_c = \frac{\partial c}{\partial \sigma} = Se^{(b-r)T} n(d_1)\sqrt{T} > 0. \qquad \textbf{(11.35a)}$$

The sign of the derivative is positive, indicating that as the volatility of the underlying commodity return increases, the call option value increases. The intuition for this result is that an increase in the volatility rate increases the probability of large upward movements in the underlying commodity price. The probability of large downward commodity price movements also increases, however, it is of no consequence since the call option holder has limited liability.

The numerical value of the call option vega implies that the options price is more sensitive to volatility than it is to either the cost-of-carry rate or the interest rate. The option in Example 11.7 has a vega of 7.7428. An increase in volatility of 100 basis points increases the call's price by nearly eight cents.

The put option's vega is the same as that of the call, that is,

$$\text{Vega}_p = \frac{\partial p}{\partial \sigma} = Se^{(b-r)T} n(d_1)\sqrt{T} = \text{Vega}_c > 0. \qquad \textbf{(11.35b)}$$

The put option value also increases with an increase in volatility since the probability increases of a large commodity price decrease. The numerical value of the vega for the put option in Example 11.8 is, therefore, also 7.7428.

Figure 11.9 shows the option's vega as a function of the commodity price. Note that the vega has its highest value where the option is approximately at-the-money.

Change in the Time to Expiration

The partial derivative of the option price with respect to the time to expiration parameter is called the option's *theta*. The theta of the call is

$$\Theta_c = \frac{\partial c}{\partial T} = Se^{(b-r)T} n(d_1)\frac{\sigma}{2\sqrt{T}} + (b-r)Se^{(b-r)T} N(d_1)$$
$$+ rXe^{-rT} N(d_2) \lessgtr 0. \qquad \textbf{(11.36a)}$$

The expression shows that the sensitivity of call option price to changes in the time to expiration of the option is the sum of three components. The first term on the right-hand side is positive and reflects the increase in option price due to the fact that an increase in the time to expiration increases the probability of upward price movements in the commodity price and, hence, increases the value of the option. The second term may be positive or negative depending on whether the cost-of-carry rate, b, is greater than or less than the interest rate, r. If $b > r$, the term is positive since as the time to expiration increases the present value of the expected terminal commodity price grows large (recall that the underlying commodity price grows at rate b while the discount rate of the terminal value of the option is r). Finally, the third term is positive. As time to expiration increases, the present value

FIGURE 11.9   European option vega as a function of the underlying commodity price (S). The commodity price range is from 50 through 150. The options have exercise price (X) of 100 and time to expiration (T) of three months. The cost-of-carry rate (b) is 8 percent, and the riskless rate of interest (r) is 8 percent. The standard deviation of the logarithm of the commodity price ratios (σ) is 30 percent.

Vega of Call and Put Options

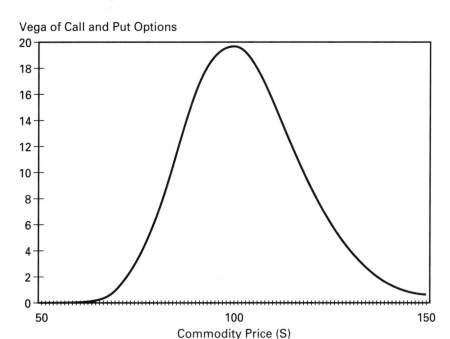

Commodity Price (S)

of the exercise price grows small. Note that the only case where the overall value of theta is unambiguously positive is when $b \geq r$.

For the call option in Example 11.7, $b < r$, so we know that theta need not be positive. The value of theta is, nonetheless, positive at 3.6927. In other words, the option price increases as the time to expiration increases. To see the origin of this result, we examine the values of each of the three terms in the derivative: 4.6457, -2.3446 and 1.3916. The largest component of the call option's theta in this illustration, 4.6457, comes from the increased probability of large commodity price movements. Because $b < r$, the second term is negative. As the time to expiration increases, the value of the call option falls because the commodity price is expected to increase at a lower rate than the riskless rate of interest. The value of this component is -2.3466. Finally, the value of the third term is 1.3916, indicating that the call option value increases because the present value of the exercise price is reduced as the time to expiration is increased.

Theta provides information on the decay in option value as the time to expiration elapses. The theta of the call option in Example 11.7 is 3.6927. This implies that the *time decay* of this option is $3.6927 \times 1/365$ or slightly over one cent over the next day and $3.6927 \times 7/365$ or about seven cents over the next week, holding other factors constant.

The theta of the European put option is

$$\Theta_p = \frac{\partial p}{\partial T} = Se^{(b-r)T}n(d_1)\frac{\sigma}{2\sqrt{T}} - (b-r)Se^{(b-r)T}N(-d_1)$$
$$- rXe^{-rT}N(-d_2) \lessgtr 0. \tag{11.36b}$$

The interpretation of the terms in the expression of the put option's theta parallel those of the call option. The first term is the increase in put value resulting from the prospect of larger commodity price movements when the time to expiration is longer. The second term is negative if $b > r$. In the case of the put, option value increases when the cost-of-carry rate is below the interest rate. The third term is positive. It reflects the fact that an increase in the time to expiration delays the receipt of the exercise price and hence reduces the put option value. The value of the theta for the put option in Exercise 11.8 is 5.2143, with the individual components of the sum being 4.6457, 2.3136, and -1.7450.

11.6 EUROPEAN EXCHANGE OPTION

Closely related to the European commodity options with a fixed exercise price are European options that entitle the holder to exchange one commodity for another. Such options are commonplace, although they are usually embedded within some other contract. In Chapter 8, for example, we discussed the fact that the T-bond futures contract permits delivery of any of a number of eligible T-bond issues and that the short will deliver the cheapest. The short, in this instance, has a exchange option that permits him to exchange the T-bond bond he presently holds for a cheaper issue, should a cheaper issue become available. Many agricultural futures contracts also have such an *exchange option* or *quality option* embedded in their contract design.

The derivation of the exchange option formula can follow the same risk-neutral valuation approach that was used earlier in the chapter, so the approach will not be repeated here. The *valuation equation of a European exchange option* that permits its holder to exchange commodity 2 for commodity 1, that is, to "buy" commodity 1 with commodity 2, is

$$c(S_1, T; S_2) = S_1 e^{(b_1 - r)T}N(d_1) - S_2 e^{(b_2 - r)T}N(d_2), \tag{11.37}$$

where

$$d_1 = \frac{\ln(S_1/S_2) + (b_1 - b_2 + .5\sigma^2)T}{\sigma\sqrt{T}}, \tag{11.37a}$$

$$d_2 = d_1 - \sigma\sqrt{T}, \tag{11.37b}$$

and

$$\sigma^2 = \sigma_1^2 + \sigma_2^2 - 2\rho_{12}\sigma_1\sigma_2. \tag{11.37c}$$

Variables subscripted with 1 apply to commodity 1, and variables subscripted with 2 apply to commodity 2. The meaning of each variable is described earlier in the chapter.

An important observation regarding (11.37) is that the call option formula described earlier in this chapter is simply a special case of this valuation equation. Suppose we allow commodity 2 to be the riskless asset. The current price of commodity 2, S_2, is, therefore, Xe^{-rT}, the cost-of-carry rate, b_2, is the riskless rate of interest, r, and the standard deviation of return, σ_2, equals zero. With these substitutions, equation (11.37) becomes the European call option formula (11.25).

Another important observation regarding (11.39) is that the value of a call option to "buy" commodity 1 with commodity 2, $c(S_1, T; S_2)$, equals the value of a put option to "sell" commodity 2 for commodity 1, $p(S_2, T; S_1)$. In the case of the call, the option is exercised at expiration if the proceeds $S_{1,T} - S_{2,T} > 0$, that is, if the terminal price of commodity 1 exceeds the terminal price of commodity 2; otherwise, it is not exercised. In the case of the put, the option is exercised at expiration if the proceeds $S_{1,T} - S_{2,T} > 0$; that is, if commodity 2 is cheaper than commodity 1; otherwise, it is not exercised. But the structure of these two valuation problems is identical, so

$$c(S_1, T; S_2) = p(S_2, T; S_1). \tag{11.38}$$

Returning to the T-bond futures contract specification, recall that at the end of Chapter 8, we argued that the futures price equals the price of the cheapest-to-deliver bond less the value of the quality option. If the T-bond futures contract has only two T-bond issues eligible for delivery, the valuation formula (11.38) can be used to value the quality option. With more eligible issues, the model must be generalized.[9]

EXAMPLE 11.9

Suppose that there are two bonds eligible for delivery on the T-bond futures contract. The time to expiration of the futures is three months. Bond 1 is currently the cheapest to deliver. Its price is 99 and its coupon is 6 percent. Bond 2 is priced at

---

[9]The exchange option formula for the two-asset case where both assets have a cost-of-carry rate equal to the riskless rate of interest was derived by Margrabe (1978). The formula presented here generalizes the Margrabe result to allow the assets to have different carry rates. The n-asset exchange option was later developed by Margrabe (1982).

102, and its coupon is 9 percent. The standard deviation of the continuously compounded return is 15 percent for bond 1 and 12 percent for bond 2. The correlation between their rates of return is .9. The riskless rate of interest is 7 percent. Compute the value of the exchange option. For the sake of simplicity, assume that both bonds have conversion factors equal to one and that coupon interest is paid continuously over the futures contract's remaining life.

$$p(B_2, T; B_1) = 99e^{(.07-.06-.07).25} N(d_1) - 102e^{(.07-.09-.07).25} N(d_2),$$

where

$$d_1 = \frac{\ln(99/102) + (.07 - .06 - .07 + .09 + .5\sigma^2).25}{\sigma\sqrt{.25}},$$

$$d_2 = d_1 - \sigma\sqrt{.25},$$

and

$$\sigma^2 = .15^2 + .12^2 - 2 \times .9 \times .15 \times .12 = .0045.$$

Substituting $\sigma = .0671$ into the expressions for d_1 and d_2, and then the values $d_1 = -.6495$ and $d_2 = -.6830$ into the option formula shows that the value of the exchange option is .50.

11.7 VALUATION OF AMERICAN OPTIONS

We noted in Chapter 10 that the American option is worth at least as much as the European option because of the fact the American option may be exercised early. The value of the American call and put can, therefore, be written as

$$C(S, T; X) = c(S, T; X) + \epsilon_C(S, T; X), \qquad \text{(10.9a)}$$

and

$$P(S, T; X) = p(S, T; X) + \epsilon_P(S, T; X). \qquad \text{(10.9b)}$$

The value of the early exercise privilege, $\epsilon_C(S,T;X)$, depends on the relation between the cost-of-carry rate, b, and the riskless rate, r.

In the case of the call option, the early exercise privilege has value only if $b < r$. In this case, the cost of carrying the underlying commodity is less than the cost of funds tied up in the commodity. As a result, it may be beneficial to exercise a call option and take possession of the commodity because the earnings on the commodity exceed the cost of funds tied up in the commodity. For example, it may be desirable to exercise a call option on a foreign currency to earn the interest on the foreign currency if the foreign interest rate exceeds the U.S. rate. If $b \geq r$, early exercise of a call is not optimal because there is a cost to holding the commodity. By continuing to hold the call option, all the potential price gains achievable from holding the commodity are also achievable, and the cost of holding the commodity is avoided. For example, it is never optimal to exercise early an option on a stock that does not pay dividends (i.e., $b = r$).

In the case of the put option, early exercise is always a possibility. Intuitively, early exercise is desirable if the profit from the put option is sufficiently large so that the interest that could be earned by investing the profit now exceeds the possibility of an even greater profit from continuing to hold the put.

Explicit analytical solutions for the price of American options are unknown. If the American option will not be exercised early, the European option formula holds. But if early exercise could be desirable, the American option value exceeds the European value by an amount (frequently quite small) that can only be approximated by numerical techniques. Two approximation techniques that are commonly applied in practice are the binomial method of Cox, Ross, and Rubinstein (1979), and the quadratic approximation method of Barone–Adesi and Whaley (1987). The binomial method is used in Chapter 13 to value a put on a dividend-paying stock, and the quadratic approximation is used in Chapter 14 to value stock index and stock index futures options.

11.8 ESTIMATION OF THE OPTION PRICING PARAMETERS

The European option pricing models (11.25) and (11.28) and the American option approximation methods to be discussed in Chapters 13 and 14 are, in general, very easy to use. The exercise price, X, and the time to expiration, T, are terms of the option contract. The commodity price, S, the riskless rate of interest, r, and the cost-of-carry rate, b, are easily accessible, market-determined values.[10] The most difficult parameter to estimate (and, for that matter, the parameter estimate about which investors most commonly disagree) is the standard deviation of the rate of return of the underlying commodity. In general, two methods are used—historical volatility estimation and implied volatility estimation.

---

[10] As a proxy for the riskless interest rate, T-bill rates are typically used. Recall from footnote 2 in Chapter 8 that the continuously compounded, effective annual interest rate, r, is obtained by computing

$$r = \frac{\ln(100/B_d)}{T},$$

where B_d is the price of the T-bill (e.g., 100 less the average of the T-bill's bid and ask discounts) and T is the time to maturity of the T-bill expressed in years.

Historical Volatility Estimation

Earlier in this chapter, we assumed that the mean and the standard deviation of the continuously compounded rates of return, $R_t = \ln(S_t/S_{t-1})$, are constant through time. The volatility parameter in the option pricing formula is the future volatility rate of the commodity. If the volatility parameter is stationary through time, however, we can use past returns to estimate historical volatility and then use historical volatility as the estimate of future volatility.

The estimator most commonly used for calculating the variance of the rate of return on the commodity, σ_h^2, is

$$\hat{\sigma}_h^2 = \frac{1}{T-1} \sum_{t=1}^{T} (R_t - \hat{\mu})^2, \tag{11.39}$$

where T is the number of time series return observations used in the estimation,[11] R_t is the continuously compounded rate of return on the commodity in month t [i.e., $\ln(S_t/S_{t-1})$], and $\hat{\mu}$ is the estimate of the mean rate of return,

$$\hat{\mu} = \frac{1}{T} \sum_{t=1}^{T} R_t. \tag{11.40}$$

An estimate of the standard deviation of the rate of return on the commodity can be obtained by taking the square root of the variance estimate, that is, $\hat{\sigma}_h = \sqrt{\hat{\sigma}_h^2}$.

The rates of return used in equations (11.39) and (11.40) may be for any length period—a day, a week, or a month. In general, the shorter the distancing interval between price observations, the better since more information goes into the estimate. So weekly returns are certainly superior to monthly returns in the estimation of volatility, holding the overall length of the estimation period constant.

Following the same logic, it would seem daily returns are a better source of information than weekly returns. This is generally not the case, however. Stock returns, for example, demonstrate seasonality by day of week.[12] In general, stock returns on Fridays are significantly higher than average, and those on Mondays are significantly lower than average. Other commodities also have day-of-the-week seasonality, but the seasonality has a different structure. Furthermore, independent of the underlying commodity, using daily data forces the investigator to decide how weekend returns should be accounted for. Should the rate of return from Friday close to Monday close be counted as a 3-day rate of return (calendar days) or a 1-day rate of return (trading days)? Because of the empirical anomalies associated with daily returns and because the issue of how to handle weekend returns has not been satisfactorily resolved, weekly returns are probably the best bet when it comes to estimating the historical volatility of commodity returns.

Another issue that arises when using the historical estimator has to do with

---

[11] Note that $T + 1$ price observations are needed to generate T rates of return.
[12] See, for example, French (1980) and Gibbons and Hess (1981).

how many return observations to use in the computation of the volatility. On one hand, the more information that is used in the estimation process, the more precise that estimate becomes. On the other hand, the longer the time period over which volatility is estimated, the greater the likelihood that the stationarity assumption will be violated, in which case, formula (11.39) is no longer an unbiased estimate of the commodity's rate-of-return variance. In the absence of information indicating that the stationarity assumption has been violated, twenty-six weeks of return observations are probably enough to ensure reasonably accurate volatility estimation.

The volatility estimate computed using equation (11.39) computes the variance of the rate of return for the length of time between the price observations used to compute the rates of return. Thus, if weekly returns are used, the variance estimate from (11.39) is the variance of the rate of return over a week. To annualize this value, we have to multiply the variance by the number of weeks in the year, that is, $\sigma_{ha}^2 = 52\sigma_{hw}^2$, where the subscripts a and w denote annual and weekly, respectively. The transformation for annualizing the weekly standard deviation is therefore $\sigma_{ha} = \sqrt{52}\sigma_{hw}$.[13]

One final issue with respect to historical volatility estimation is worth noting. The estimators shown above generally use close-to-close price information when generating the rates of return. This has been accepted as common practice since, traditionally, the recorded histories of commodity prices are prices reported for the last transaction of the day. With the advent of sophisticated computer and database technologies, it has now become easier to record and maintain larger information sets, with most commodity and option exchanges now recording and maintaining transaction price files. This more refined information allows more precise estimation of volatility. For example, Parkinson (1980) and Garman and Klass (1980) develop alternative estimators of variance that use open, high, low, and close commodity prices and show that these estimators are eight times "better" than the traditional estimator (11.39).

Implied Volatility Estimation

An alternative volatility estimation procedure arises from the option pricing model itself. Since all of the parameters of the option pricing model, except σ, are known or can be estimated with little uncertainty, one needs only to equate the observed market price of the option with its formula value, that is,

$$V_j = \hat{V}_j(\sigma_j), \qquad \qquad \textbf{(11.41)}$$

---

[13] To transform a volatility estimate computed using daily returns to an annual volatility, the daily estimate is usually multiplied by the square root of the number of trading days in the year (typically, $\sqrt{253}$), rather than the number of calendar days in the year ($\sqrt{365}$). The motivation for this adjustment is that studies of daily stock returns indicate that the volatility of return from Friday close to Monday close (three days) is about the same as the volatility from close-to-close during any other pair of adjacent trading days (one day). See, for example, Stoll and Whaley (1990a). Thus, treating weekends like a single trading day provides the most appropriate adjustment for daily stock return volatilities. The empirical evidence regarding weekend volatility in non-stock markets, however, is scant, so the generality of this result to other commodities is not known. For non-stock markets, a safer procedure may be to use weekly returns, as was noted earlier in this section.

where V is the observed price of the option, $\hat{V}$ is the model price of the option, and solve for σ. An analytical expression for the variance parameter cannot be derived; however, accurate approximation is possible through "trial-and-error," in much the same manner as one solves for a yield to maturity on a bond.

Volatilities computed in this manner are called "implied volatilities" or "implied standard deviations." They may be interpreted as the market consensus volatility in the sense that the market price of the option is used to impute the volatility estimate.

If one considers all of the options written on a given commodity, it would seem reasonable to believe that they will all yield the same estimate of volatility on the underlying commodity. This is not the case, however. There are a variety of reasons to cause the estimates to be different.

Non-Simultaneity of Prices. Estimating the implied volatility using (11.41) assumes that the option price and the commodity price are observed at the same instant in time. Frequently, it is the case that the only information that is available is the option and commodity prices at the times at which they were last traded. It is unlikely that these trades, one in the option market and one in the commodity market, occurred at the same instant, and, to the extent that they are not contemporaneous, there will be error in the estimate of volatility.

Bid-Ask Prices. Even if the option and commodity price observations used in (11.41) are simultaneous, there is a problem with what the prices represent. If markets were perfectly liquid and frictionless, trades would clear at the equilibrium price of the security. Neither descriptor is true, however. Market makers provide market liquidity by standing ready to immediately buy or sell securities. Since market makers have capital (both investment and human) tied up in their operations, they demand a rate of return on their capital, which they extract by setting the bid price of a security below the ask price. When market orders are executed, therefore, they are at the bid or the ask, depending upon whether the individual entering the market to trade wanted to sell or buy. Since there is no way of discerning the motivation of the trader who was involved in the last observed transaction, implied volatility estimates have error when the bid price of the option is matched with the ask price of the commodity and vice versa.

Model Mis-Specification. Using (11.41) to estimate volatility is also subject to model mis-specification. The technique assumes that the option pricing model used for $\hat{V}_j(\sigma_j)$ is correctly specified. If it is not, then there is obviously going to be error in the estimate of the standard deviation of the rate of return on the commodity. Model assumptions that could be violated, for example, are the assumption of log normality of stock prices or independence of returns.

To mitigate the problems associated with using a single implied volatility estimate to represent the volatility of the underlying commodity, the implied volatilities for several options on the same commodity are averaged to form an overall estimate. The nature of the averaging schemes vary, so it is best to begin with a general statement of the average implied volatility, that is,

$$\hat{\sigma} = \sum_{j=1}^{n} \omega_j \hat{\sigma}_j \bigg/ \sum_{j=1}^{n} \omega_j, \tag{11.42}$$

where ω_j is the weight applied to the jth estimate of volatility and n is the number of options for which volatility estimates were obtained.

The particular weighting schemes used in the literature have been many and varied. Schmalensee and Trippi (1978) and Patell and Wolfson (1979), for example, use an equal weighted average, $\omega_j = 1/n$, $j = 1,...,n$. Their motivation for doing so is that each volatility estimate is equally valuable in the determination of the overall volatility for the commodity. Latane and Rendleman (1976), on the other hand, weight according to the partial derivative of the call price with respect to the standard deviation of the commodity return, that is, $\partial V_j/\partial \hat{\sigma}_j$, $j = 1,...,n$. In doing so, the standard deviation estimates of options that are theoretically more sensitive to the value of σ are weighted more heavily than those that are not. Chiras and Manaster (1978) follow a similar logic in using the elasticity of the call price with respect to standard deviation, $\partial V_j \hat{\sigma}_j / \partial \hat{\sigma}_j V_j$, $j = 1,...,n$. Unfortunately, their scheme is seriously flawed. Using elasticity as the basis of the weighting scheme implies that volatility estimates for out-of-the-money options receive the highest weight. Out-of-the-money options generally do not produce very accurate volatility estimates because the markets for these options are relatively illiquid (inducing serious nonsimultaneity problems) and the options themselves have high bid-ask spreads (inducing bid-ask errors). Finally, Whaley (1982) uses nonlinear regression to estimate one value of σ using all of the option pricing information simultaneously, that is,

$$V_j = \hat{V}_j(\sigma) + \epsilon_j. \tag{11.43}$$

The properties of the maximum likelihood estimator from (11.43) are, perhaps, the best understood of the available alternatives.

Regardless of the weighting scheme, however, there appears to be strong empirical support in favor of an implied volatility measure. Latane and Rendleman and Chiras and Manaster correlate the historical and implied measures on the actual standard deviation of return and conclude that the implied estimate is a markedly superior predictor. The market apparently uses more information than merely an historical estimate in assessing the commodity's expected volatility.

11.9 SUMMARY

In this chapter, option pricing equations have been derived in detail for European options on different types of underlying assets. The chapter begins with an intuitive discussion of the risk-neutral valuation approach used in deriving option pricing formulas. Next the price and return distributions assumed for commodities are described. In section 3, risk-neutral valuation of a European option is carried out in detail, and variations of the basic valuation equation for different types of underlying commodities are shown. Using put-call parity, put valuation equations are then derived.

The price of an option on a commodity depends on the spot price of the commodity, the exercise price of the option, the cost of carry of the commodity, the riskless rate, the standard deviation of the return of the commodity, and the time to maturity of the option. In section 5, the effect of changes in each of these variables on the option price is analyzed.

Section 6 presents the valuation equation for an option that permits its holder to exchange one risky commodity for another. This option, called an exchange option, is embedded in many types of futures contracts and was introduced in earlier chapters. Valuing the delivery option embedded in the T-bond futures contract is used as an illustration.

The factors underlying the value of an American option are the same as those underlying a European option except that the American option has the additional benefit of early exercise. Section 7 names two popular approaches for valuing American options. The methods are described in detail in Chapters 13 and 14.

In practice, the most important variable affecting the price of an option is the volatility of the underlying commodity. Section 8 explains the two approaches for estimating volatility—historical volatility and implied volatility.

APPENDIX 11.1

Proof that $E(\tilde{S}_T) = S_0 e^{\alpha T} = S_0 e^{(\mu + \sigma^2/2)T}$,
where μ and σ^2 are the mean and the variance
of the normally distributed continuously compounded rate of return

Begin by rewriting the expected terminal price as the expected price relative,

$$E(\tilde{S}_T/S_0) = e^{\alpha T} = E(e^{\tilde{x}}), \tag{A1.1}$$

where $\tilde{x}$ is the normally distributed, continuously compounded rate of return from 0 through T. $\tilde{x}$ can be reexpressed in terms of μ, σ, and the unit normally distributed variable z. Using (11.10),

$$\tilde{S}_T/S_0 = e^{\tilde{x}} = e^{\mu T + \sigma\sqrt{T} z}.$$

Substituting this result into (A1.1),

$$e^{\alpha T} = E(e^{\mu T + \sigma\sqrt{T} z}) \tag{A1.2}$$
$$= e^{\mu T} E(e^{\sigma\sqrt{T} z}).$$

The term $E(e^{\sigma\sqrt{T} z})$ in (A1.2) may be simplified as follows:

$$\begin{aligned}
E(e^{\sigma\sqrt{T} z}) &= \int_{-\infty}^{+\infty} e^{\sigma\sqrt{T} z} e^{-z^2/2} \frac{1}{\sqrt{2\pi}} dz \\
&= \int_{-\infty}^{+\infty} e^{\sigma\sqrt{T} z - z^2/2} \frac{1}{\sqrt{2\pi}} dz \\
&= \int_{-\infty}^{+\infty} e^{\sigma^2 T/2 - \sigma^2 T/2 + \sigma\sqrt{T} z - z^2/2} \frac{1}{\sqrt{2\pi}} dz \\
&= e^{\sigma^2 T/2} \int_{-\infty}^{+\infty} e^{-\sigma^2 T/2 + \sigma\sqrt{T} z - z^2/2} \frac{1}{\sqrt{2\pi}} dz \\
&= e^{\sigma^2 T/2} \int_{-\infty}^{+\infty} e^{-(\sigma\sqrt{T} - z)^2/2} \frac{1}{\sqrt{2\pi}} dz \\
&= e^{\sigma^2 T/2}. \tag{A1.3}
\end{aligned}$$

Substituting (A1.3) into (A1.2), taking the logarithm of both sides, and then factoring T gives

$$\alpha = \mu + \sigma^2/2. \tag{A1.4}$$

APPENDIX 11.2

APPROXIMATIONS FOR THE CUMULATIVE NORMAL DENSITY FUNCTION

The probability that a drawing from a unit normal distribution will produce a value less than the constant d is

$$\text{Prob}(\tilde{z} < d) = \int_{-\infty}^{d} \frac{1}{\sqrt{2\pi}} e^{-z^2/2} dz = N(d).$$

Below are two polynomials that provide reasonably accurate approximations for the above integral.

Approximation 1

$$N(d) \approx 1 - a_0 e^{-d^2/2}(a_1 t + a_2 t^2 + a_3 t^3),$$

where

$$t = 1/(1 + 0.33267d)$$

$a_0 = 0.3989423$	$a_1 = 0.4361836$
$a_2 = -0.1201676$	$a_3 = 0.9372980$

With this approximation method, the value of d must be greater than or equal to 0. The maximum absolute error of this approximation method is 0.00001.

Approximation 2

$$N(d) \approx 1 - a_0 e^{-d^2/2}(a_1 t + a_2 t^2 + a_3 t^3 + a_4 t^4 + a_5 t^5),$$

where

$$t = 1/(1 + 0.2316419d)$$

$a_0 = 0.3989423$	$a_1 = 0.319381530$
$a_2 = -0.356563782$	$a_3 = 1.781477937$
$a_4 = -1.821255978$	$a_5 = 1.330274429$

With this approximation method, the value of d must be greater than or equal to 0. The maximum absolute error of this approximation method is 0.000000075.

APPENDIX 11.3

CUMULATIVE NORMAL PROBABILITY TABLES

The probability that a drawing from a unit normal distribution will produce a value less than the constant d is

$$\text{Prob}(\tilde{z} < d) = \int_{-\infty}^{d} \frac{1}{\sqrt{2\pi}} e^{-z^2/2} dz = N(d).$$

Range of d: $-4.99 \leq d \leq -2.50$

d	-0.00	-0.01	-0.02	-0.03	-0.04	-0.05	-0.06	-0.07	-0.08	-0.09
-4.90	0.00000	0.00000	0.00000	0.00000	0.00000	0.00000	0.00000	0.00000	0.00000	0.00000
-4.80	0.00000	0.00000	0.00000	0.00000	0.00000	0.00000	0.00000	0.00000	0.00000	0.00000
-4.70	0.00000	0.00000	0.00000	0.00000	0.00000	0.00000	0.00000	0.00000	0.00000	0.00000
-4.60	0.00000	0.00000	0.00000	0.00000	0.00000	0.00000	0.00000	0.00000	0.00000	0.00000
-4.50	0.00000	0.00000	0.00000	0.00000	0.00000	0.00000	0.00000	0.00000	0.00000	0.00000
-4.40	0.00001	0.00001	0.00000	0.00000	0.00000	0.00000	0.00000	0.00000	0.00000	0.00000
-4.30	0.00001	0.00001	0.00001	0.00001	0.00001	0.00001	0.00001	0.00001	0.00001	0.00001
-4.20	0.00001	0.00001	0.00001	0.00001	0.00001	0.00001	0.00001	0.00001	0.00001	0.00001
-4.10	0.00002	0.00002	0.00002	0.00002	0.00002	0.00002	0.00002	0.00002	0.00001	0.00001
-4.00	0.00003	0.00003	0.00003	0.00003	0.00003	0.00003	0.00002	0.00002	0.00002	0.00002
-3.90	0.00005	0.00005	0.00004	0.00004	0.00004	0.00004	0.00004	0.00004	0.00003	0.00003
-3.80	0.00007	0.00007	0.00007	0.00006	0.00006	0.00006	0.00006	0.00005	0.00005	0.00005
-3.70	0.00011	0.00010	0.00010	0.00010	0.00009	0.00009	0.00008	0.00008	0.00008	0.00008
-3.60	0.00016	0.00015	0.00015	0.00014	0.00014	0.00013	0.00013	0.00012	0.00012	0.00011
-3.50	0.00023	0.00022	0.00022	0.00021	0.00020	0.00019	0.00019	0.00018	0.00017	0.00017
-3.40	0.00034	0.00032	0.00031	0.00030	0.00029	0.00028	0.00027	0.00026	0.00025	0.00024
-3.30	0.00048	0.00047	0.00045	0.00043	0.00042	0.00040	0.00039	0.00038	0.00036	0.00035
-3.20	0.00069	0.00066	0.00064	0.00062	0.00060	0.00058	0.00056	0.00054	0.00052	0.00050
-3.10	0.00097	0.00094	0.00090	0.00087	0.00084	0.00082	0.00079	0.00076	0.00074	0.00071
-3.00	0.00135	0.00131	0.00126	0.00122	0.00118	0.00114	0.00111	0.00107	0.00104	0.00100
-2.90	0.00187	0.00181	0.00175	0.00169	0.00164	0.00159	0.00154	0.00149	0.00144	0.00139
-2.80	0.00256	0.00248	0.00240	0.00233	0.00226	0.00219	0.00212	0.00205	0.00199	0.00193
-2.70	0.00347	0.00336	0.00326	0.00317	0.00307	0.00298	0.00289	0.00280	0.00272	0.00264
-2.60	0.00466	0.00453	0.00440	0.00427	0.00415	0.00402	0.00391	0.00379	0.00368	0.00357
-2.50	0.00621	0.00604	0.00587	0.00570	0.00554	0.00539	0.00523	0.00508	0.00494	0.00480

CUMULATIVE NORMAL PROBABILITY TABLES

The probability that a drawing from a unit normal distribution will produce a value less than the constant d is

$$\text{Prob}(\tilde{z} < d) = \int_{-\infty}^{d} \frac{1}{\sqrt{2\pi}} e^{-z^2/2} dz = N(d).$$

Range of d: $-2.49 \leq d \leq 0.00$

d	-0.00	-0.01	-0.02	-0.03	-0.04	-0.05	-0.06	-0.07	-0.08	-0.09
-2.40	0.00820	0.00798	0.00776	0.00755	0.00734	0.00714	0.00695	0.00676	0.00657	0.00639
-2.30	0.01072	0.01044	0.01017	0.00990	0.00964	0.00939	0.00914	0.00889	0.00866	0.00842
-2.20	0.01390	0.01355	0.01321	0.01287	0.01255	0.01222	0.01191	0.01160	0.01130	0.01101
-2.10	0.01786	0.01743	0.01700	0.01659	0.01618	0.01578	0.01539	0.01500	0.01463	0.01426
-2.00	0.02275	0.02222	0.02169	0.02118	0.02068	0.02018	0.01970	0.01923	0.01876	0.01831
-1.90	0.02872	0.02807	0.02743	0.02680	0.02619	0.02559	0.02500	0.02442	0.02385	0.02330
-1.80	0.03593	0.03515	0.03438	0.03362	0.03288	0.03216	0.03144	0.03074	0.03005	0.02938
-1.70	0.04457	0.04363	0.04272	0.04182	0.04093	0.04006	0.03920	0.03836	0.03754	0.03673
-1.60	0.05480	0.05370	0.05262	0.05155	0.05050	0.04947	0.04846	0.04746	0.04648	0.04551
-1.50	0.06681	0.06552	0.06426	0.06301	0.06178	0.06057	0.05938	0.05821	0.05705	0.05592
-1.40	0.08076	0.07927	0.07780	0.07636	0.07493	0.07353	0.07215	0.07078	0.06944	0.06811
-1.30	0.09680	0.09510	0.09342	0.09176	0.09012	0.08851	0.08691	0.08534	0.08379	0.08226
-1.20	0.11507	0.11314	0.11123	0.10935	0.10749	0.10565	0.10383	0.10204	0.10027	0.09853
-1.10	0.13567	0.13350	0.13136	0.12924	0.12714	0.12507	0.12302	0.12100	0.11900	0.11702
-1.00	0.15866	0.15625	0.15386	0.15150	0.14917	0.14686	0.14457	0.14231	0.14007	0.13786
-0.90	0.18406	0.18141	0.17879	0.17619	0.17361	0.17106	0.16853	0.16602	0.16354	0.16109
-0.80	0.21186	0.20897	0.20611	0.20327	0.20045	0.19766	0.19489	0.19215	0.18943	0.18673
-0.70	0.24196	0.23885	0.23576	0.23270	0.22965	0.22663	0.22363	0.22065	0.21770	0.21476
-0.60	0.27425	0.27093	0.26763	0.26435	0.26109	0.25785	0.25463	0.25143	0.24825	0.24510
-0.50	0.30854	0.30503	0.30153	0.29806	0.29460	0.29116	0.28774	0.28434	0.28096	0.27760
-0.40	0.34458	0.34090	0.33724	0.33360	0.32997	0.32636	0.32276	0.31918	0.31561	0.31207
-0.30	0.38209	0.37828	0.37448	0.37070	0.36693	0.36317	0.35942	0.35569	0.35197	0.34827
-0.20	0.42074	0.41683	0.41294	0.40905	0.40517	0.40129	0.39743	0.39358	0.38974	0.38591
-0.10	0.46017	0.45620	0.45224	0.44828	0.44433	0.44038	0.43644	0.43251	0.42858	0.42465
0.00	0.50000	0.49601	0.49202	0.48803	0.48405	0.48006	0.47608	0.47210	0.46812	0.46414

CUMULATIVE NORMAL PROBABILITY TABLES

The probability that a drawing from a unit normal distribution will produce a value less than the constant d is

$$\text{Prob}(\tilde{z} < d) = \int_{-\infty}^{d} \frac{1}{\sqrt{2\pi}} e^{-z^2/2} dz = N(d).$$

Range of d: $0.00 \le d \le 2.49$

d	0.00	0.01	0.02	0.03	0.04	0.05	0.06	0.07	0.08	0.09
0.00	0.50000	0.50399	0.50798	0.51197	0.51595	0.51994	0.52392	0.52790	0.53188	0.53586
0.10	0.53983	0.54380	0.54776	0.55172	0.55567	0.55962	0.56356	0.56749	0.57142	0.57535
0.20	0.57926	0.58317	0.58706	0.59095	0.59483	0.59871	0.60257	0.60642	0.61026	0.61409
0.30	0.61791	0.62172	0.62552	0.62930	0.63307	0.63683	0.64058	0.64431	0.64803	0.65173
0.40	0.65542	0.65910	0.66276	0.66640	0.67003	0.67364	0.67724	0.68082	0.68439	0.68793
0.50	0.69146	0.69497	0.69847	0.70194	0.70540	0.70884	0.71226	0.71566	0.71904	0.72240
0.60	0.72575	0.72907	0.73237	0.73565	0.73891	0.74215	0.74537	0.74857	0.75175	0.75490
0.70	0.75804	0.76115	0.76424	0.76730	0.77035	0.77337	0.77637	0.77935	0.78230	0.78524
0.80	0.78814	0.79103	0.79389	0.79673	0.79955	0.80234	0.80511	0.80785	0.81057	0.81327
0.90	0.81594	0.81859	0.82121	0.82381	0.82639	0.82894	0.83147	0.83398	0.83646	0.83891
1.00	0.84134	0.84375	0.84614	0.84850	0.85083	0.85314	0.85543	0.85769	0.85993	0.86214
1.10	0.86433	0.86650	0.86864	0.87076	0.87286	0.87493	0.87698	0.87900	0.88100	0.88298
1.20	0.88493	0.88686	0.88877	0.89065	0.89251	0.89435	0.89617	0.89796	0.89973	0.90147
1.30	0.90320	0.90490	0.90658	0.90824	0.90988	0.91149	0.91309	0.91466	0.91621	0.91774
1.40	0.91924	0.92073	0.92220	0.92364	0.92507	0.92647	0.92785	0.92922	0.93056	0.93189
1.50	0.93319	0.93448	0.93574	0.93699	0.93822	0.93943	0.94062	0.94179	0.94295	0.94408
1.60	0.94520	0.94630	0.94738	0.94845	0.94950	0.95053	0.95154	0.95254	0.95352	0.95449
1.70	0.95543	0.95637	0.95728	0.95818	0.95907	0.95994	0.96080	0.96164	0.96246	0.96327
1.80	0.96407	0.96485	0.96562	0.96637	0.96712	0.96784	0.96856	0.96926	0.96995	0.97062
1.90	0.97128	0.97193	0.97257	0.97320	0.97381	0.97441	0.97500	0.97558	0.97615	0.97670
2.00	0.97725	0.97778	0.97831	0.97882	0.97932	0.97982	0.98030	0.98077	0.98124	0.98169
2.10	0.98214	0.98257	0.98300	0.98341	0.98382	0.98422	0.98461	0.98500	0.98537	0.98574
2.20	0.98610	0.98645	0.98679	0.98713	0.98745	0.98778	0.98809	0.98840	0.98870	0.98899
2.30	0.98928	0.98956	0.98983	0.99010	0.99036	0.99061	0.99086	0.99111	0.99134	0.99158
2.40	0.99180	0.99202	0.99224	0.99245	0.99266	0.99286	0.99305	0.99324	0.99343	0.99361

CUMULATIVE NORMAL PROBABILITY TABLES

The probability that a drawing from a unit normal distribution will produce a value less than the constant d is

$$\text{Prob}(\tilde{z} < d) = \int_{-\infty}^{d} \frac{1}{\sqrt{2\pi}} e^{-z^2/2} dz = N(d).$$

Range of d: $2.50 \leq d \leq 4.99$

d	0.00	0.01	0.02	0.03	0.04	0.05	0.06	0.07	0.08	0.09
2.50	0.99379	0.99396	0.99413	0.99430	0.99446	0.99461	0.99477	0.99492	0.99506	0.99520
2.60	0.99534	0.99547	0.99560	0.99573	0.99585	0.99598	0.99609	0.99621	0.99632	0.99643
2.70	0.99653	0.99664	0.99674	0.99683	0.99693	0.99702	0.99711	0.99720	0.99728	0.99736
2.80	0.99744	0.99752	0.99760	0.99767	0.99774	0.99781	0.99788	0.99795	0.99801	0.99807
2.90	0.99813	0.99819	0.99825	0.99831	0.99836	0.99841	0.99846	0.99851	0.99856	0.99861
3.00	0.99865	0.99869	0.99874	0.99878	0.99882	0.99886	0.99889	0.99893	0.99897	0.99900
3.10	0.99903	0.99906	0.99910	0.99913	0.99916	0.99918	0.99921	0.99924	0.99926	0.99929
3.20	0.99931	0.99934	0.99936	0.99938	0.99940	0.99942	0.99944	0.99946	0.99948	0.99950
3.30	0.99952	0.99953	0.99955	0.99957	0.99958	0.99960	0.99961	0.99962	0.99964	0.99965
3.40	0.99966	0.99968	0.99969	0.99970	0.99971	0.99972	0.99973	0.99974	0.99975	0.99976
3.50	0.99977	0.99978	0.99978	0.99979	0.99980	0.99981	0.99981	0.99982	0.99983	0.99983
3.60	0.99984	0.99985	0.99985	0.99986	0.99986	0.99987	0.99987	0.99988	0.99988	0.99989
3.70	0.99989	0.99990	0.99990	0.99990	0.99991	0.99991	0.99992	0.99992	0.99992	0.99992
3.80	0.99993	0.99993	0.99993	0.99994	0.99994	0.99994	0.99994	0.99995	0.99995	0.99995
3.90	0.99995	0.99995	0.99996	0.99996	0.99996	0.99996	0.99996	0.99996	0.99997	0.99997
4.00	0.99997	0.99997	0.99997	0.99997	0.99997	0.99997	0.99998	0.99998	0.99998	0.99998
4.10	0.99998	0.99998	0.99998	0.99998	0.99998	0.99998	0.99998	0.99998	0.99999	0.99999
4.20	0.99999	0.99999	0.99999	0.99999	0.99999	0.99999	0.99999	0.99999	0.99999	0.99999
4.30	0.99999	0.99999	0.99999	0.99999	0.99999	0.99999	0.99999	0.99999	0.99999	0.99999
4.40	0.99999	0.99999	1.00000	1.00000	1.00000	1.00000	1.00000	1.00000	1.00000	1.00000
4.50	1.00000	1.00000	1.00000	1.00000	1.00000	1.00000	1.00000	1.00000	1.00000	1.00000
4.60	1.00000	1.00000	1.00000	1.00000	1.00000	1.00000	1.00000	1.00000	1.00000	1.00000
4.70	1.00000	1.00000	1.00000	1.00000	1.00000	1.00000	1.00000	1.00000	1.00000	1.00000
4.80	1.00000	1.00000	1.00000	1.00000	1.00000	1.00000	1.00000	1.00000	1.00000	1.00000
4.90	1.00000	1.00000	1.00000	1.00000	1.00000	1.00000	1.00000	1.00000	1.00000	1.00000

APPENDIX 11.4

PARTIAL DERIVATIVES OF EUROPEAN COMMODITY OPTION VALUATION EQUATIONS

The valuation equations for the European call and put options are

$$c(S, T; X) = Se^{(b-r)T}N(d_1) - Xe^{-rT}N(d_2) \qquad \text{(A4.1)}$$

and

$$p(S, T; X) = Xe^{-rT}N(-d_2) - Se^{(b-r)T}N(-d_1), \qquad \text{(A4.2)}$$

respectively, where

$$d_1 = \frac{\ln(S/X) + (b + .5\sigma^2)T}{\sigma\sqrt{T}} \quad \text{and} \quad d_2 = d_1 - \sigma\sqrt{T}.$$

$$d_2 = d_1 - \sigma\sqrt{T} \qquad \text{(A4.3)}$$

$$d_2^2 = d_1^2 - 2d_1\sigma\sqrt{T} + \sigma^2 T \qquad \text{(A4.4)}$$

$$
\begin{aligned}
d_2^2 &= d_1^2 - 2[\ln(S/X) + bT + .5\sigma^2 T] + \sigma^2 T \\
&= d_1^2 - 2\ln(Se^{bT}/X)
\end{aligned}
\qquad \text{(A4.5)}
$$

$$n(d_2) = \frac{1}{\sqrt{2\pi}}e^{-d_2^2/2} \qquad \text{(A4.6)}$$

$$
\begin{aligned}
n(d_2) &= \frac{1}{\sqrt{2\pi}}e^{-d_1^2/2 + 2\ln(Se^{bT}/X)} \\
&= \frac{1}{\sqrt{2\pi}}e^{-d_1^2}e^{\ln(Se^{bT}/X)} \\
&= n(d_1)Se^{bT}/X
\end{aligned}
\qquad \text{(A4.7)}
$$

$$n(d_1) = n(d_2)X/Se^{bT} \qquad \text{(A4.8)}$$

$$\Delta_c = \frac{\partial c}{\partial S} = e^{(b-r)T} N(d_1) + Se^{(b-r)T}\frac{\partial N(d_1)}{\partial S} - Xe^{-rT}\frac{\partial N(d_2)}{\partial S}$$

$$= e^{(b-r)T} N(d_1) + Se^{(b-r)T}\frac{\partial N(d_1)}{\partial d_1}\frac{\partial d_1}{\partial S} - Xe^{-rT}\frac{\partial N(d_2)}{\partial d_2}\frac{\partial d_2}{\partial S}$$

$$= e^{(b-r)T} N(d_1) + Se^{(b-r)T} n(d_1)\frac{\partial d_1}{\partial S} - Xe^{-rT} n(d_2)\frac{\partial d_2}{\partial S}$$

$$= e^{(b-r)T} N(d_1) + Se^{(b-r)T} n(d_1)\frac{\partial d_1}{\partial S} - Xe^{-rT} n(d_1)Se^{bT}/X\frac{\partial d_1}{\partial S}$$

$$= e^{(b-r)T} N(d_1) > 0 \qquad\qquad\text{(A4.9a)}$$

$$\Delta_p = \frac{\partial p}{\partial S} = Xe^{-rT}\frac{\partial N(-d_2)}{\partial S} - e^{(b-r)T} N(-d_1) - Se^{(b-r)T}\frac{\partial N(-d_1)}{\partial S}$$

$$= -e^{(b-r)T} N(-d_1) - Xe^{-rT} n(-d_1)Se^{bT}/X\frac{\partial d_1}{\partial S} + Se^{(b-r)T} n(-d_1)\frac{\partial d_1}{\partial S}$$

$$= -e^{(b-r)T} N(-d_1) < 0 \qquad\qquad\text{(A4.9b)}$$

$$\eta_c = \frac{\partial c/c}{\partial S/S} = \Delta_c\frac{S}{c} = e^{(b-r)T} N(d_1)\frac{S}{c} > 1 \qquad\qquad\text{(A4.10a)}$$

$$\eta_p = \frac{\partial p/p}{\partial S/S} = \Delta_p\frac{S}{p} = -e^{(b-r)T} N(-d_1)\frac{S}{p} < -1 \qquad\qquad\text{(A4.10b)}$$

$$\gamma_c = \frac{\partial\Delta_c}{\partial S} = \frac{\partial e^{(b-r)T} N(d_1)}{\partial S} = e^{(b-r)T} n(d_1)\frac{\partial d_1}{\partial S} = \frac{e^{(b-r)T} n(d_1)}{S\sigma\sqrt{T}} > 0 \quad\text{(A4.11a)}$$

$$\gamma_p = \frac{\partial\Delta_p}{\partial S} = \frac{-\partial e^{(b-r)T} N(-d_1)}{\partial S} = \frac{e^{(b-r)T} n(d_1)}{S\sigma\sqrt{T}} = \gamma_c > 0 \qquad\text{(A4.11b)}$$

$$\frac{\partial c}{\partial X} = -e^{-rT} N(d_2) < 0 \qquad\qquad\text{(A4.12a)}$$

$$\frac{\partial p}{\partial X} = e^{-rT} N(-d_2) > 0 \qquad\qquad\text{(A4.12b)}$$

$$\frac{\partial c}{\partial b} = TSe^{(b-r)T} N(d_1) + Se^{(b-r)T}\frac{\partial N(d_1)}{\partial b} - Xe^{-rT}\frac{\partial N(d_2)}{\partial b} \qquad\text{(A4.13a)}$$

$$= TSe^{(b-r)T} N(d_1) > 0$$

$$\frac{\partial p}{\partial b} = Xe^{-rT}\frac{\partial N(-d_2)}{\partial b} - TSe^{(b-r)T} N(-d_1) - Se^{(b-r)T}\frac{\partial N(-d_1)}{\partial b} \qquad\text{(A4.13b)}$$

$$= -TSe^{(b-r)T} N(-d_1) < 0$$

$$\frac{\partial c}{\partial r} = TSe^{(b-r)T}N(d_1) - TSe^{(b-r)T}N(d_1) + Se^{(b-r)T}\frac{\partial N(d_1)}{\partial r}$$

$$+ TXe^{-rT}N(d_2) - Xe^{-rT}\frac{\partial N(d_2)}{\partial r}$$

$$= TXe^{-rT}N(d_2) > 0 \qquad\qquad \textbf{(A4.14a)}$$

$$\frac{\partial p}{\partial r} = -TXe^{-rT}N(-d_2) + Xe^{-rT}\frac{\partial N(-d_2)}{\partial r}$$

$$- TSe^{(b-r)T}N(-d_1) + TSe^{(b-r)T}N(-d_1) - Se^{(b-r)T}\frac{\partial N(-d_1)}{\partial r}$$

$$= -TXe^{-rT}N(-d_2) < 0 \qquad\qquad \textbf{(A4.14b)}$$

$$\text{Vega}_c = \frac{\partial c}{\partial \sigma} = Se^{(b-r)T}\frac{\partial N(d_1)}{\partial \sigma} - Xe^{-rT}\frac{\partial N(d_2)}{\partial \sigma}$$

$$= Se^{(b-r)T}n(d_1)\frac{\partial d_1}{\partial \sigma} - Xe^{-rT}n(d_2)\frac{\partial d_2}{\partial \sigma}$$

$$= Se^{(b-r)T}n(d_1)\frac{\partial d_1}{\partial \sigma} - Xe^{-rT}n(d_1)Se^{rT}/X\frac{\partial d_2}{\partial \sigma}$$

$$= Se^{(b-r)T}n(d_1)\left[\frac{\partial d_1}{\partial \sigma} - \frac{\partial d_2}{\partial \sigma}\right]$$

$$= Se^{(b-r)T}n(d_1)\sqrt{T} > 0 \qquad\qquad \textbf{(A4.15a)}$$

$$\text{Vega}_p = \frac{\partial p}{\partial \sigma} = Xe^{-rT}\frac{\partial N(-d_2)}{\partial \sigma} - Se^{(b-r)T}\frac{\partial N(-d_1)}{\partial \sigma}$$

$$= Xe^{-rT}n(-d_2)\left[-\frac{\partial d_2}{\partial \sigma}\right] - Se^{(b-r)T}n(-d_1)\left[-\frac{\partial d_1}{\partial \sigma}\right]$$

$$= Se^{(b-r)T}n(d_1)\left[\frac{\partial d_1}{\partial \sigma} - \frac{\partial d_2}{\partial \sigma}\right]$$

$$= Se^{(b-r)T}n(d_1)\sqrt{T} > 0 \qquad\qquad \textbf{(A4.15b)}$$

$$\frac{\partial d_1}{\partial \sigma} - \frac{\partial d_2}{\partial \sigma} = \left[-\frac{\ln(Se^{bT}/X)}{\sigma^2\sqrt{T}} + .5\sqrt{T}\right] - \left[-\frac{\ln(Se^{bT}/X)}{\sigma^2\sqrt{T}} - .5\sqrt{T}\right] = \sqrt{T}$$

$$\Theta_c = \frac{\partial c}{\partial T} = (b-r)Se^{(b-r)T}N(d_1)Se^{(b-r)T}\frac{\partial N(d_1)}{\partial T}$$

$$+ rXe^{-rT}N(d_2) - Xe^{-rT}\frac{\partial N(d_2)}{\partial T}$$

$$= Se^{(b-r)T}n(d_1)\left[\frac{\partial d_1}{\partial T} - \frac{\partial d_2}{\partial T}\right] + (b-r)Se^{(b-r)T}N(d_1) + rXe^{-rT}N(d_2)$$

$$= Se^{(b-r)T}n(d_1)\frac{\sigma}{2\sqrt{T}} + (b-r)Se^{(b-r)T}N(d_1) + rXe^{-rT}N(d_2) \lessgtr 0 \qquad \textbf{(A4.16a)}$$

$$\Theta_p = \frac{\partial p}{\partial T} = -rXe^{-rT}N(-d_2) + Xe^{-rT}\frac{\partial N(-d_2)}{\partial T}$$

$$- (b-r)Se^{(b-r)T}N(-d_1) - Se^{(b-r)T}\frac{\partial N(-d_1)}{\partial T}$$

$$= -rXe^{-rT}N(-d_2) - (b-r)Se^{(b-r)T}N(-d_1) + Se^{(b-r)T}n(d_1)\left[\frac{\partial d_1}{\partial T} - \frac{\partial d_2}{\partial T}\right]$$

$$= Se^{(b-r)T}n(d_1)\frac{\sigma}{2\sqrt{T}} - (b-r)Se^{(b-r)T}N(-d_1) - rXe^{-rT}N(-d_2) \leq\geq 0 \qquad \textbf{(A4.16b)}$$

$$\frac{\partial d_1}{\partial T} - \frac{\partial d_2}{\partial T} = \left[-\frac{\ln(S/X)}{2\sigma T^{3/2}} + \frac{b}{2\sigma\sqrt{T}} + \frac{\sigma}{4\sqrt{T}}\right] - \left[-\frac{\ln(S/X)}{2\sigma T^{3/2}} + \frac{b}{2\sigma\sqrt{T}} - \frac{\sigma}{4\sqrt{T}}\right] = \frac{\sigma}{2\sqrt{T}}$$

12 OPTION TRADING STRATEGIES

In Chapter 10, we developed no-arbitrage pricing relations between options and the underlying commodity. In Chapter 11, we developed option valuation equations. In this chapter, essential elements of the last two chapters are used to describe and analyze option/commodity portfolio positions. We begin by using arbitrage principles to examine in detail the six basic option/commodity terminal profit diagrams. Long and short positions in the call, the put, and the underlying commodity are considered. Combinations of these positions are then used to create a wide array of portfolios with different breakeven commodity prices, maximum losses, and maximum gains. Synthetic positions, spread strategies, write strategies, and speculative strategies are considered. In the second section, the assumption of a lognormal price distribution is used to extend the profit diagram analysis. Probabilities of maximum losses and maximum gains are computed, as are expected profits for the various strategies. The third section discusses a methodology for simulating long-term option positions using short-term options. This methodology is particularly useful in markets where long-term options are not actively traded. In the fourth section, we discuss dynamic return/risk management. First, we discuss the expected return/risk tradeoffs created using naked options and options in combination with investment in the underlying commodity. We then focus on portfolio risk management over short intervals of time and show how the risk exposures of individual option positions can be aggregated across options to find portfolio risk exposures. We show that judicious selection of investments in options, futures, and the underlying commodity can effectively manage these risks.

12.1 TRADING STRATEGIES AND PROFIT DIAGRAMS

This section focuses on strategies where the option/commodity positions are held until option expiration. After stating the assumptions underlying our analysis, we present the six basic profit diagrams upon which the trading strategies are built. The diagrams are first used to reconfirm the put-call parity relation using conversion and reverse conversion arbitrage. We then focus on spread strategies, where offsetting positions are taken to reduce commodity price risk. Following that, option writing strategies, together with certain speculative strategies, are presented. The specific trading strategies provided here are intended only to be illustrative, as the number of possible trading strategies is limitless. The framework of analysis is sufficiently general, however, that the reader can analyze more complex portfolios with the tools presented.

Assumptions

The only new assumption made in this section is that all positions, including any position in the underlying commodity, are held until the options' expiration, T. As in the previous chapters, the cost of carrying the underlying commodity occurs at the rate b. A long position implies that the holder pays the carry cost, and a short position implies that the holder receives the carry cost. Also, as in previous chapters, the carry cost includes not only interest but also additional charges (receipts) from holding the commodity. The cost of carrying an option contract is only the riskless rate of interest, r. The initial price of the commodity is denoted by S and the terminal price is denoted by S_T. The initial call and put option prices are denoted as c and p, respectively. If the option is purchased, the purchase price is financed at rate r, and, if the option is sold, the sales proceeds are invested at rate r until the option's expiration. Unless otherwise noted, the call and the put are assumed to have the same exercise price. A profit occurs when a position earns more than the interest cost of the funds tied up in the position.

The analysis of each strategy proceeds in a stepwise fashion. First, we present the profit function at maturity, π_T, and then show the profit function in diagram form. We then summarize the strategy by describing the breakeven terminal commodity prices (i.e., where the strategy has zero profit at the option expiration), the maximum loss, and the maximum gain. The diagrams plot the zero profit position as a solid horizontal line and plot the profit function as another solid line. The intersection of the solid lines represents the zero profit position.

Six Basic Positions

The terminal profit functions of the six basic option/commodity positions are

1. *Long commodity:* Commodity is purchased and is carried at rate b until option expiration at time T.

$$\pi_T = S_T - Se^{bT} \qquad\qquad \textbf{(12.1a)}$$

FIGURE 12.1a   Trading Strategy: Long Commodity

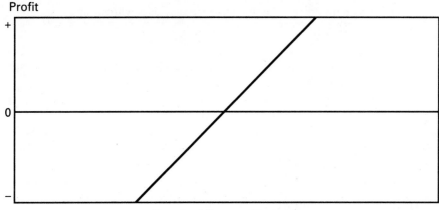

Profit

Terminal Commodity Price

Breakeven point:	$S_T = Se^{bT}$
Maximum loss:	Se^{bT}, where S_T falls to zero
Maximum gain:	unlimited, where S_T rises without limit

2. *Short commodity:* Commodity is sold, and proceeds from sale earn rate b until option expiration at time T.

$$\pi_T = -S_T + Se^{bT} \tag{12.1b}$$

FIGURE 12.1b   Trading Strategy: Short Commodity

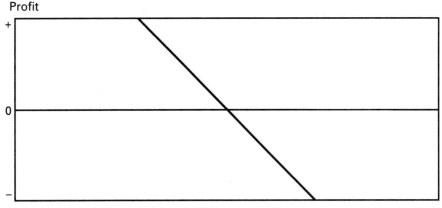

Profit

Terminal Commodity Price

> Breakeven point: $S_T = Se^{bT}$
> Maximum gain: Se^{bT}, where S_T falls to zero
> Maximum loss: unlimited, where S_T rises without limit

3. *Long call:* Call option is purchased and carried at rate r until option expiration at time T.

$$\pi_T = \begin{cases} S_T - X - ce^{rT} & \text{if} \quad S_T > X \\ -ce^{rT} & \text{if} \quad S_T \leq X \end{cases} \qquad \text{(12.2a)}$$

FIGURE 12.2a   Trading Strategy: Long Call

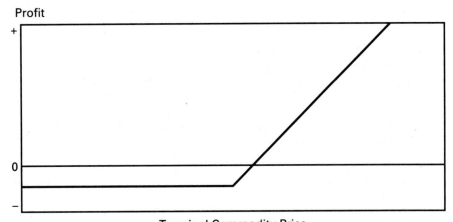

Terminal Commodity Price

> Breakeven point: $S_T = X + ce^{rT}$
> Maximum loss: ce^{rT}, where $S_T < X$
> Maximum gain: unlimited, where S_T rises without limit

4. *Short call:* Call is sold, and proceeds from sale earn rate r until option expiration at time T.

$$\pi_T = \begin{cases} -S_T + X + ce^{rT} & \text{if} \quad S_T > X \\ ce^{rT} & \text{if} \quad S_T \leq X \end{cases} \qquad \text{(12.2b)}$$

FIGURE 12.2b   Trading Strategy: Short Call

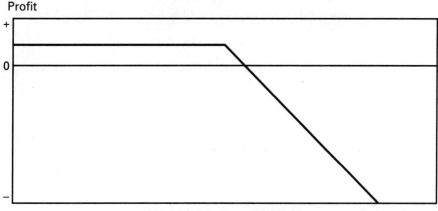

Breakeven point:	$S_T = X + ce^{rT}$
Maximum gain:	ce^{rT}, where $S_T < X$
Maximum loss:	unlimited, where S_T rises without limit

5. *Long put:* Put option is purchased and is carried at rate r to the option expiration at time T.

$$\pi_T = \begin{cases} -pe^{rT} & \text{if } S_T > X \\ X - S_T - pe^{rT} & \text{if } S_T \le X \end{cases}$$ **(12.3a)**

FIGURE 12.3a   Trading Strategy: Long Put

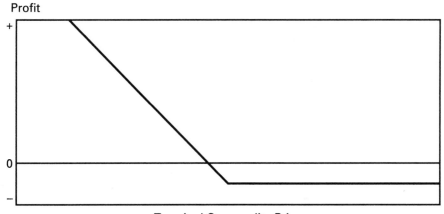

Breakeven point: $S_T = X + pe^{rT}$
Maximum loss: pe^{rT}, where $S_T > X$
Maximum gain: $X - pe^{rT}$, where S_T falls to zero

6. *Short put:* Put is sold, and proceeds from sale earn rate r until option expiration at time T.

$$\pi_T = \begin{cases} pe^{rT} & \text{if } S_T > X \\ -X + S_T + pe^{rT} & \text{if } S_T \leq X \end{cases} \qquad \text{(12.3b)}$$

FIGURE 12.3b   Trading Strategy: Short Put

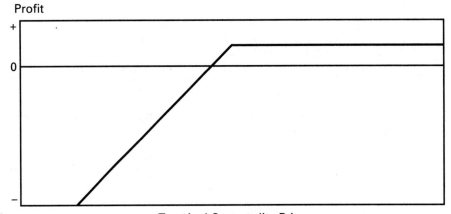

Profit

Terminal Commodity Price

Breakeven point: $S_T = X + pe^{rT}$
Maximum gain: pe^{rT}, where $S_T > X$
Maximum loss: $X - pe^{rT}$, where S_T falls to zero

    In the option positions described above and later in the chapter, the premium paid by the buyer or received by the seller depends on the commodity price at the time the option contract was written. In plotting the profit diagrams, we make reasonable assumptions about the initial put or call premiums, but the shape of the profit diagrams is not affected by particular initial premiums paid. For positions involving a single exercise price, we generally assume options were at-the-money when first traded. For positions involving different exercise prices, we generally assume one option was at-the-money, while the other was not.

Riskless Arbitrage Strategies

The first two strategies, called *conversion* and *reverse conversion arbitrage*, were discussed in Chapter 10 in the put-call parity sections. These are riskless trading strategies designed to take advantage of temporary mispricings between the call, put, and underlying commodity. To determine the profit functions of these, as well as all subsequent trading strategies discussed in this section, we simply sum the corresponding profit functions of the component securities presented in equations (12.1) through (12.3).

7. *Conversion:* Buy commodity, buy put, and sell call.

$$\pi_T = -Se^{bT} + X + ce^{rT} - pe^{rT} \qquad \textbf{(12.4)}$$

FIGURE 12.4   Trading Strategy: Conversion

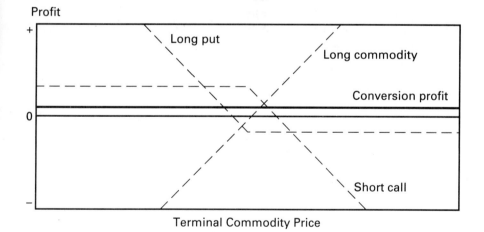

Terminal Commodity Price

Breakeven point:	none
Maximum loss:	$\pi_T = -Se^{bT} + X + ce^{rT} - pe^{rT}$
Maximum gain:	$\pi_T = -Se^{bT} + X + ce^{rT} - pe^{rT}$

The profit function (12.4) shows that the portfolio profit at option expiration is certain since the terminal commodity price, S_T, does not appear in the expression (i.e., the portfolio profit is insensitive to the future commodity price). This fact can also been seen in Figure 12.4, where the portfolio profit is depicted as the upper horizontal line. Since this line never crosses the zero profit line below it, the profit is certain for all values of the terminal commodity price.

The economic meaning of this certain-profit result is important. Recall that all positions in the commodity/options are entirely financed. It, therefore, stands to reason that if the options and commodity are properly priced in the marketplace, the terminal profit from this strategy is zero. And, if the terminal profit is zero, then the put-call parity relation,

$$c - p = Se^{(b-r)T} - Xe^{-rT}, \tag{10.22}$$

which was derived in Chapter 10, must hold. When put-call parity holds, the two solid lines in Figure 12.4 are coincident.

Conversion arbitrage comes into play when there are temporary mispricings. For example, an institutional trader might buy a large number of index call options in reaction to new information about the stock market. As a result of the excess buying pressure on calls, the call price might increase by more than is warranted relative to the prices of the put and the underlying stock index. As the market maker sells the calls to the institutional trader, she may simultaneously buy the puts and the index portfolio to lay off the commodity price risk of the short call position, thereby capturing the temporary violation of put-call parity. Such trading activity locks in a certain, positive profit.

8. *Reverse conversion or reversal:* Sell commodity, sell put, and buy call.

This strategy is simply the reverse of Trading Strategy 7 and is used when put-call parity is violated in the opposite direction.

Synthetic Positions

Conversions and reversals exploit arbitrage opportunities by creating a synthetic position in any one security from judiciously selected positions in the other two securities. In a conversion, for example, a long position in a commodity, combined with a long put position, is equivalent to a long call position. When this long call position is combined with a short call position, a riskless portfolio results. To demonstrate this idea in greater detail, we now show how synthetic long and short positions in the underlying commodity can be created by using call and put options.

9. *Synthetic long commodity:* Buy call and sell put.

$$\pi_T = S_T - X - ce^{rT} + pe^{rT} \qquad\qquad \textbf{(12.5a)}$$

FIGURE 12.5a Trading Strategy: Synthetic Long Commodity

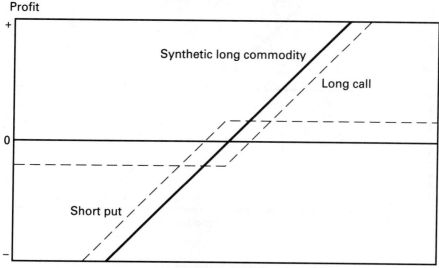

Profit

Terminal Commodity Price

Breakeven point:	$S_T = X + ce^{rT} - pe^{rT}$
Maximum loss:	$X + ce^{rT} - pe^{rT}$, where S_T falls to zero
Maximum gain:	unlimited, where S_T rises without limit

Figure 12.5a shows that the profit function of the long call/short put position is virtually identical to the long commodity position shown in Figure 12.1a. The only difference between the profit functions (12.1a) and (12.5a) is that (12.1a) has the term Se^{bT}, where (12.5a) has the term $X + ce^{rT} - pe^{rT}$. But this is expected. If put-call parity (10.22) holds, these two values are equal. If, for whatever reason, $Se^{bT} > X + ce^{rT} - pe^{rT}$, it is cheaper to create a long commodity position synthetically than it is to buy the commodity itself.

10. *Synthetic short commodity:* Sell call and buy put.

$$\pi_T = -S_T + X + ce^{rT} - pe^{rT} \qquad\qquad \textbf{(12.5b)}$$

FIGURE 12.5b   Trading Strategy: Synthetic Short Commodity

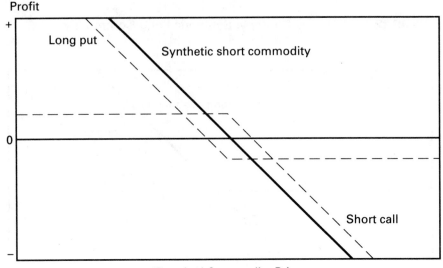

Profit

Terminal Commodity Price

Breakeven point:	$S_T = X + ce^{rT} - pe^{rT}$
Maximum gain:	$-X - ce^{rT} + pe^{rT}$, where S_T falls to zero
Maximum loss:	unlimited, where S_T rises without limit

The synthetic short commodity position is completely analogous to the short commodity position discussed earlier. This strategy is particularly well suited if short sale of the underlying commodity is difficult or expensive (e.g., short selling the S&P 500 index). In such cases, the short call/long put portfolio becomes a viable alternative.

Synthetic long and short option positions are also possible. Since the analyses of these positions are fairly straightforward, we only describe the portfolio compositions below:

11. *Synthetic long call:* Long commodity and long put.
12. *Synthetic short call:* Short commodity and short put.
13. *Synthetic long put:* Short commodity and long call.
14. *Synthetic short put:* Long commodity and short call.

Multiple Option/Commodity Positions

One last basic idea is needed before proceeding with the analyses of more complex option strategies. What happens when several options are purchased or sold? To understand this, recall the profit function for the long position. To generalize it for the purchase of n calls, we simply multiply (12.2a) by n, that is,

$$n\pi_T = \begin{cases} n(S_T - X - ce^{rT}) & \text{if} \quad S_T > X \\ -nce^{rT} & \text{if} \quad S_T \leq X \end{cases} \qquad \textbf{(12.6)}$$

FIGURE 12.6   Trading Strategy: Long Multiple Calls

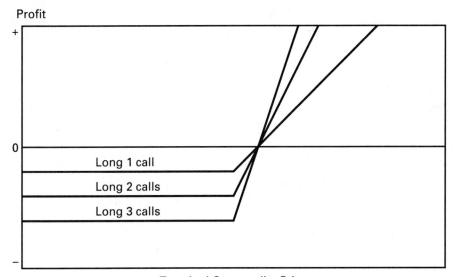

Figure 12.6 shows the profit diagrams for the purchase of one, two, and three calls. Note that the breakeven point is independent of the number of calls purchased. The important change is that more option premium is lost should the option expire out-of-the-money, and the rate of profit per dollar of commodity price is increased should the option expire in-the-money. This concept is used later in the chapter when various ratio spreading and ratio writing strategies are discussed.

Spread Strategies

Spread strategies are strategies in which the risk of one security position is offset, at least in some degree, by another security position; that is, one position benefits from a commodity price increase and the other loses. A strategy will usually wind up being *neutral, bullish,* or *bearish.* A neutral strategy is one in which the strategy is profitable when the commodity price does not move by very much after the position is taken. A bullish strategy is one that profits in the event that the underlying commodity price rises, and a bearish strategy profits when the commodity price falls.

Spread strategies typically involve offsetting positions in options with different exercise prices or different maturities. One might buy a call option with one exercise price or one maturity and sell another call option with another exercise price or maturity. Some of the possible spread positions are now described under four categories: *volatility spreads, spreads based on differences in exercise prices, calendar spreads,* and *diagonal spreads.*

      Volatility Spreads. Volatility spreads involve the purchase of a put and a call or the sale of a put and a call.

      15. *Long straddle or long volatility spread:* Buy call and buy put.

$$\pi_T = \begin{cases} S_T - X - (ce^{rT} + pe^{rT}) & \text{if} \quad S_T > X \\ X - S_T - (pe^{rT} + ce^{rT}) & \text{if} \quad S_T \le X \end{cases} \qquad \textbf{(12.7)}$$

FIGURE 12.7   Trading Strategy: Long Straddle

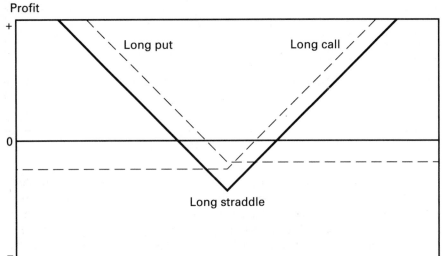

Breakeven points:
Breakeven points:	(a) $S_T = X - (ce^{rT} + pe^{rT})$
	(b) $S_T = X + (ce^{rT} + pe^{rT})$
Maximum loss:	$ce^{rT} + pe^{rT}$, where $S_T = X$
Maximum gain:	(a) $X - (ce^{rT} + pe^{rT})$, where S_T falls to zero
	(b) unlimited, where S_T rises without limit

      As the profit function (12.7) and Figure 12.7 show, the straddle produces positive profits where the underlying commodity price moves up *or* down by a sufficient amount. For this reason, buying a straddle is often referred to as *buying volatility.* The strategy loses money where the terminal commodity price, S_T, is within the band $X \pm (ce^{rT} + pe^{rT})$ at the options' expiration.

16. *Short straddle or short volatility spread:* Sell call and sell put.

This strategy is the reverse of a long straddle. Investors short straddles or *sell volatility* when they believe that the commodity price will not move by much before the options' expiration.

17. *Long strangle:* Buy call and buy put, where the exercise price of the put, X_p, is less than the exercise price of the call, X_c (i.e., $X_p < X_c$).

$$\pi_T = \begin{cases} S_T - X_c - (ce^{rT} + pe^{rT}) & \text{if } S_T > X_c \\ -(ce^{rT} + pe^{rT}) & \text{if } X_p < S_T \leq X_c \\ X_p - S_T - (pe^{rT} + ce^{rT}) & \text{if } S_T \leq X_p \end{cases} \tag{12.8}$$

FIGURE 12.8 Trading Strategy: Long Strangle

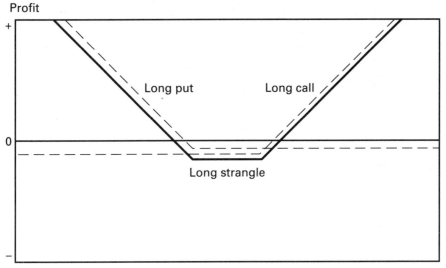

Breakeven points:	(a) $S_T = X_p - (ce^{rT} + pe^{rT})$
	(b) $S_T = X_c + (ce^{rT} + pe^{rT})$
Maximum loss:	$ce^{rT} + pe^{rT}$, where $X_p < S_T \leq X_c$
Maximum gain:	(a) $X_p - (ce^{rT} + pe^{rT})$, where S_T falls to zero
	(b) unlimited, where S_T rises without limit

A long strangle has the same investment objective as a long straddle. The difference is that the strangle requires a lower investment since the call or the put is more out-of-the-money than with the straddle. With the lower investment cost, however, comes a wider region over which the strategy will be unprofitable, as Figure 12.8 shows. In other words, the commodity price must move by a greater amount than with the straddle in order for the strangle to be profitable at expiration. A variation on the long strangle is for the exercise price of the call to be below the exercise price of the put. Since both the put and call can be in the money under this strategy, the cost is greater and the profitability is greater.

18. *Short strangle:* Sell call and sell put, where the exercise price of the put, X_p, is less than the exercise price of the call, X_c (i.e., $X_p < X_c$).

Spreading Options with Different Exercise Prices. Call or put options with different exercise prices can be combined to create bull or bear spreads, ratio or reverse ratio spreads, and long or short butterfly spreads.

19. *Bull spread − Call:* Buy call with a lower exercise price, X_l, and sell an otherwise identical call with a higher exercise price, X_h (i.e., $X_l < X_h$).

$$\pi_T = \begin{cases} X_h - X_l - (c_l - c_h)e^{rT} & \text{if} \quad S_T > X_h \\ S_T - X_l - (c_l - c_h)e^{rT} & \text{if} \quad X_l < S_T \leq X_h \\ -(c_l - c_h)e^{rT} & \text{if} \quad S_T \leq X_l \end{cases} \qquad \textbf{(12.9a)}$$

FIGURE 12.9a   Trading Strategy: Bull Spread − Call   6. C.

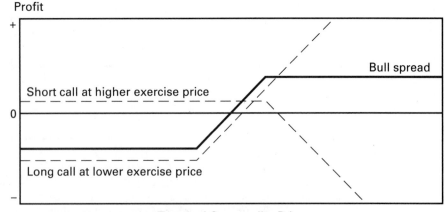

Profit

Short call at higher exercise price

Bull spread

Long call at lower exercise price

Terminal Commodity Price

> Breakeven point: $S_T = X_l + (c_l - c_h)e^{rT}$
> Maximum loss: $(c_l - c_h)e^{rT}$, where $S_T \le X_l$
> Maximum gain: $X_h - X_l - (c_l - c_h)e^{rT}$, where $S_T > X_h$

The term *bull* is used to describe the fact that this strategy profits when the underlying commodity price increases. The strategy is fairly conservative in the sense that if the investor were confident of a commodity price increase, a naked long call position would be more profitable. The benefit of buying the bull spread is that selling the out-of-the-money call provides income that offsets the cost of buying the other call. The cost is the loss of upside profit potential should the commodity price rise dramatically.

Prior to maturity, a bull spread takes advantage of the fact that the delta is higher for the in-the-money call option than it is for the out-of-the-money call option. As the commodity price increases, the gain on the long in-the-money call outstrips the loss on the short out-of-the-money call. As the commodity price rises further and both calls become deep in-the-money or as maturity is approached, the gain and the loss on the two positions become completely offsetting.

20. *Bear spread − Call:* Sell call with a lower exercise price, X_l, and buy an otherwise identical call with a higher exercise price, X_h (i.e., $X_l < X_h$).

$$
\pi_T = \begin{cases} X_l - X_h + (c_l - c_h)e^{rT} & \text{if} \quad S_T > X_h \\ X_l - S_T + (c_l - c_h)e^{rT} & \text{if} \quad X_l < S_T \le X_h \\ (c_l - c_h)e^{rT} & \text{if} \quad S_T \le X_l \end{cases} \tag{12.9b}
$$

FIGURE 12.9b   Trading Strategy: Bear Spread − Call $6, \mathcal{Q}.$

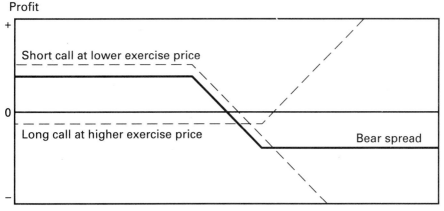

> Breakeven point: $S_T = X_l + (c_l - c_h)e^{rT}$
> Maximum gain: $(c_l - c_h)e^{rT}$, where $S_T \leq X_l$
> Maximum loss: $X_h - X_l - (c_l - c_h)e^{rT}$, where $S_T > X_h$

21. *Bull spread − Put:* Buy put with a lower exercise price, X_l, and sell an otherwise identical put with a higher exercise price, X_h (i.e., $X_l < X_h$).

$$\pi_T = \begin{cases} (p_h - p_l)e^{rT} & \text{if} \quad S_T > X_h \\ S_T - X_h + (p_h - p_l)e^{rT} & \text{if} \quad X_l < S_T \leq X_h \\ X_l - X_h + (p_h - p_l)e^{rT} & \text{if} \quad S_T \leq X_l \end{cases} \qquad \textbf{(12.10a)}$$

FIGURE 12.10a   Trading Strategy: Bull Spread − Put

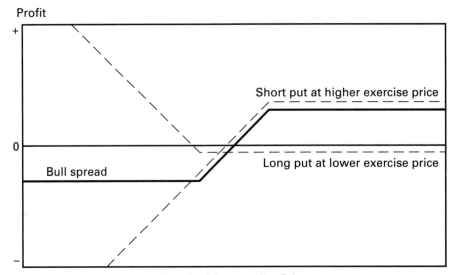

Terminal Commodity Price

> Breakeven point: $S_T = X_h - (p_h - p_l)e^{rT}$
> Maximum loss: $X_l - X_h + (p_h - p_l)e^{rT}$, where $S_T \leq X_l$
> Maximum gain: $(p_h - p_l)e^{rT}$, where $S_T > X_h$

The bull spread using puts is equivalent to the bull spread using calls, although the sources of the outcomes are different. For the put bull spread, the profit, if the commodity price increases, comes from the premium on the put sold at the higher exercise price. For the call bull spread, the profit, if the commodity price increases, comes from the fact that the gain on the long call at the lower exercise price exceeds the loss on the short call at the higher exercise price.

22. *Bear spread – Put:* Sell put with a lower exercise price, X_l, and buy an otherwise identical put with a higher exercise price, X_h (i.e., $X_l < X_h$).

$$\pi_T = \begin{cases} -(p_h - p_l)e^{rT} & \text{if} \quad S_T > X_h \\ X_h - S_T - (p_h - p_l)e^{rT} & \text{if} \quad X_l < S_T \leq X_h \\ X_h - X_l - (p_h - p_l)e^{rT} & \text{if} \quad S_T \leq X_l \end{cases} \qquad \textbf{(12.10b)}$$

FIGURE 12.10b   Trading Strategy: Bear Spread – Put

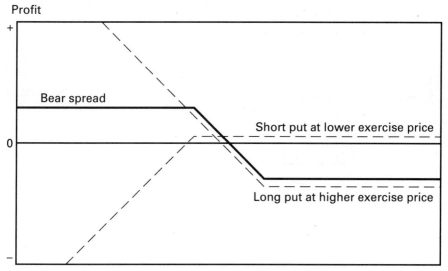

Breakeven point:	$S_T = X_h - (p_h - p_l)e^{rT}$
Maximum gain:	$X_l - X_h + (p_h - p_l)e^{rT}$, where $S_T \leq X_l$
Maximum loss:	$-(p_h - p_l)e^{rT}$, where $S_T > X_h$

23. *Ratio spread – Call:* Buy call with a lower exercise price, X_l, and sell n otherwise identical calls with higher exercise price, X_h (i.e., $X_l < X_h$).

$$\pi_T = \begin{cases} nX_h - X_l - (n-1)S_T + (nc_h - c_l)e^{rT} & \text{if} \quad S_T > X_h \\ S_T - X_l + (nc_h - c_l)e^{rT} & \text{if} \quad X_l < S_T \leq X_h \\ (nc_h - c_l)e^{rT} & \text{if} \quad S_T \leq X_l \end{cases}$$

$$\textbf{(12.11a)}$$

FIGURE 12.11a   Trading Strategy: Ratio Spread − Call

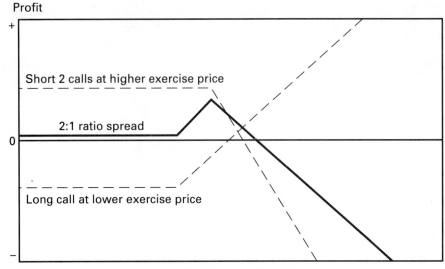

Terminal Commodity Price

Breakeven points:	(a)	$S_T = \dfrac{nX_h - X_l + (nc_h - c_l)e^{rT}}{n - 1}$
	(b)	$S_T = X_l - (nc_h - c_l)e^{rT}$, where $nc_h < c_l$
Maximum loss:	(a)	unlimited, where S_T rises without limit
	(b)	$(nc_h - c_l)e^{rT}$, where $nc_h < c_l$ and $S_T \le X_l$
Maximum gain:		$X_h - X_l + (nc_h - c_l)e^{rT}$, where $S_T = X_h$

A call ratio spread is like a call bull spread except that several identical options are sold at the higher exercise price.

The "ratio" of the ratio spread is defined in terms of the quantity of calls sold, n, per call purchased, that is, an n:1 ratio spread. The ratio spread depicted in Figure 12.11a is a 2:1 ratio spread, which involves selling two calls with a higher exercise price against the purchase of one call with a lower exercise price.

The ratio spread is most profitable when the commodity price does not move by much. Its maximum profit is when the commodity price equals the exercise price of the shorted option. If the commodity price falls, the downside risk is fixed. If the commodity price falls below the lower exercise price, both options expire worthless. The initial investment can be either a net debit or net credit, depending upon the relative magnitudes of the premiums and the ratio of the spread. Figure 12.11a indicates that the 2:1 ratio spread shown has an initial net credit. If the commodity price rises without limit, the strategy loses money without limit.

24. *Backspread or reverse ratio spread – Call:* Sell call with a lower exercise price, X_l, and buy n otherwise identical calls with a higher exercise price, X_h (i.e., $X_l < X_h$).

$$\pi_T = \begin{cases} (n-1)S_T - nX_h + X_l - (nc_h - c_l)e^{rT} & \text{if } S_T > X_h \\ X_l - S_T - (nc_h - c_l)e^{rT} & \text{if } X_l < S_T \leq X_h \\ -(nc_h - c_l)e^{rT} & \text{if } S_T \leq X_l \end{cases}$$

$$\text{(12.11b)}$$

FIGURE 12.11b   Trading Strategy: Reverse Ratio Spread – Call

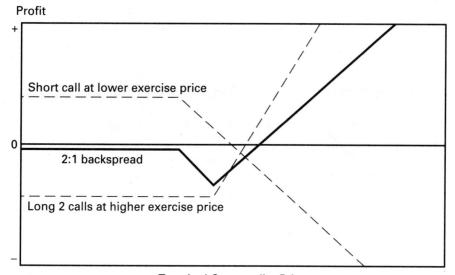

Profit

Short call at lower exercise price

2:1 backspread

Long 2 calls at higher exercise price

Terminal Commodity Price

Breakeven points:	(a) $S_T = \dfrac{nX_h - X_l + (nc_h - c_l)e^{rT}}{n-1}$	
	(b) $S_T = X_l - (nc_h - c_l)e^{rT}$, where $nc_h < c_l$	
Maximum gain:	(a) unlimited, where S_T rises without limit	
	(b) $(nc_h - c_l)e^{rT}$, where $nc_h < c_l$ and $S_T \leq X_l$	
Maximum loss:	$X_h - X_l + (nc_h - c_l)e^{rT}$, where $S_T = X_h$	

25. *Ratio spread – Put:* Buy put with a higher exercise price, X_h, and sell n otherwise identical puts with a lower exercise price, X_l (i.e., $X_l < X_h$).

$$\pi_T = \begin{cases} (np_l - p_h)e^{rT} & \text{if } S_T > X_h \\ X_h - S_T + (np_l - p_h)e^{rT} & \text{if } X_l < S_T \le X_h \\ X_h - nX_l + (n-1)S_T + (np_l - p_h)e^{rT} & \text{if } S_T \le X_l \end{cases}$$

$$\text{(12.12a)}$$

FIGURE 12.12a   Trading Strategy: Ratio Spread − Put

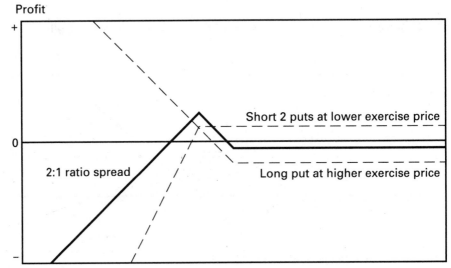

Breakeven points:	(a) $S_T = \dfrac{nX_l - X_h - (np_l - p_h)e^{rT}}{n-1}$
	(b) $S_T = X_h - (np_l - p_h)e^{rT}$, where $np_l < p_h$
Maximum loss:	(a) $X_h - nX_l + (np_l - p_h)e^{rT}$, where S_T falls to zero
	(b) $(np_l - p_h)e^{rT}$, where $np_l < p_h$ and $S_T \le X_h$
Maximum gain:	$X_h - X_l + (np_l - p_h)e^{rT}$, where $S_T = X_l$

26. *Backspread or reverse ratio spread − Put:* Sell put with a higher exercise price, X_h, and buy n otherwise identical puts with a lower exercise price, X_l (i.e., $X_l < X_h$).

$$\pi_T = \begin{cases} -(np_l - p_h)e^{rT} & \text{if } S_T > X_h \\ S_T - X_h - (np_l - p_h)e^{rT} & \text{if } X_l < S_T \le X_h \\ nX_l - X_h - (n-1)S_T - (np_l - p_h)e^{rT} & \text{if } S_T \le X_l \end{cases}$$

(12.12b)

FIGURE 12.12b   Trading Strategy: Reverse Ratio Spread — Put

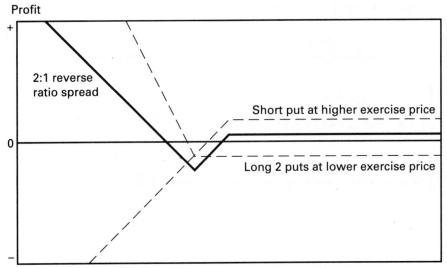

Breakeven points:	(a) $S_T = \dfrac{nX_l - X_h - (np_l - p_h)e^{rT}}{n-1}$
	(b) $S_T = X_h - (np_l - p_h)e^{rT}$, where $np_l < p_h$
Maximum gain:	(a) $X_h - nX_l + (np_l - p_h)e^{rT}$, where S_T falls to zero
	(b) $(np_l - p_h)e^{rT}$, where $np_l < p_h$ and $S_T \le X_h$
Maximum loss:	$X_h - X_l + (np_l - p_h)e^{rT}$, where $S_T = X_l$

27. *Long butterfly spread—Call:* Sell call with a lower exercise price, X_l, buy two calls with a middle exercise price, X_m, and sell call with a higher exercise price, X_h.

$$\pi_T = \begin{cases} X_l - 2X_m + X_h + (c_l - 2c_m + c_h)e^{rT} & \text{if } S_T > X_h \\ S_T - (2X_m - X_l) + (c_l - 2c_m + c_h)e^{rT} & \text{if } X_m < S_T \le X_h \\ X_l - S_T + (c_l - 2c_m + c_h)e^{rT} & \text{if } X_l < S_T \le X_m \\ (c_l - 2c_m + c_h)e^{rT} & \text{if } S_T \le X_l \end{cases}$$

(12.13)

FIGURE 12.13   Trading Strategy: Long Butterfly Spread − Call

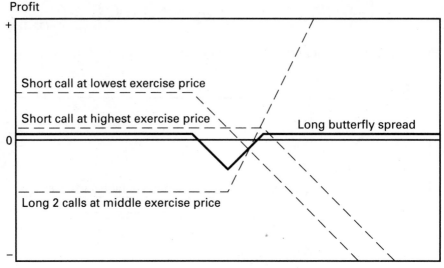

Breakeven points: (a) $S_T = 2X_m - X_l - (c_l - 2c_m + c_h)e^{rT}$
                   (b) $S_T = X_l + (c_l - 2c_m + c_h)e^{rT}$
Maximum loss: $X_l - X_m + (c_l - 2c_m + c_h)e^{rT}$, where $S_T = X_m$
Maximum gain: (a) $X_l - 2X_m + X_h + (c_l - 2c_m + c_h)e^{rT}$,
                   where $S_T > X_h$
                   (b) $(c_l - 2c_m + c_h)e^{rT}$, where $S_T \leq X_l$

A long butterfly spread combines a bear spread and a bull spread. Profits are similar to those of a bull spread if the commodity price increases and to those of a bear spread if the commodity price falls. The investor loses money when the commodity price remains neutral. The resulting profit diagram (Figure 12.13) resembles a butterfly − hence, its name.

28. *Short butterfly spread − Call:* Buy call with a lower exercise price, X_l, sell two calls with a middle exercise price, X_m, and buy call with a higher exercise price, X_h.

29. *Long butterfly spread − Put:* Sell put with a lower exercise price, X_l, buy two puts with a middle exercise price, X_m, and sell put with a higher exercise price, X_h.

30. *Short butterfly spread − Put:* Buy put with a lower exercise price, X_l, sell two puts with a middle exercise price, X_m, and buy put with a higher exercise price, X_h.

Calendar Spreads. A calendar spread requires the purchase of a call or put of one maturity and the sale of an identical option with a different maturity. Presenting a profit function for a calendar spread is cumbersome since a pricing equation is required to show the value of the distant option at the nearby option expiration.[1] For this reason, we go immediately to the profit diagram.

   31. *Long calendar spread − Call:* Buy call with a distant maturity, and sell
        identical call with a nearby maturity.

FIGURE 12.14   Trading Strategy: Long Calendar Spread − Call

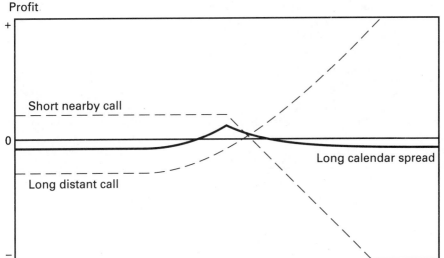

Terminal Commodity Price

   At-the-money call options are used to generate the calendar spread in Figure 12.14, and the outcomes are plotted at the maturity of the nearby call. This spread is neutral since positive profits are earned as long as the commodity price does not move very much by the nearby option expiration.[2] Because the longer-term option has a higher price, this strategy has a net debit position (i.e., we *pay* the difference between the option prices when the position is formed). The maximum loss, however, is limited to the net debit amount. The maximum gain occurs where the commodity price equals the exercise price of the nearby option, but the amount is

---

[1] The European call and put option valuation equations (11.25) and (11.28) are used to price the distant option at the nearby option's expiration.
   [2] If out-of-the-money calls are used to form the calendar spread, the position is slightly bullish.

unclear since it depends on the remaining life of the distant option and the commodity's return volatility. The width of the profit range and the breakeven points are also functions of volatility and time to expiration.

Holding other factors constant, the profitability of a calendar spread is driven by the time decay of the option premiums. As we will show later in the chapter, the rate of time decay (i.e., the option's theta) is greater the shorter the option's time to expiration. In a long calendar spread, a short position is established in the nearby option in order to capture its time decay at the expense of the time decay in the distant option.

32. *Short calendar spread − Call:* Sell call with a distant maturity, and buy identical call with a nearby maturity.
33. *Long calendar spread − Put:* Buy put with a distant maturity, and sell identical put with a nearby maturity.
34. *Short calendar spread − Put:* Sell put with a distant maturity, and buy identical put with a nearby maturity.
35. *Long ratio calendar spread − Call:* Buy call with a distant maturity, and sell more than one identical calls with a nearby maturity.

FIGURE 12.15   Trading Strategy: Long Ratio Calendar Spread

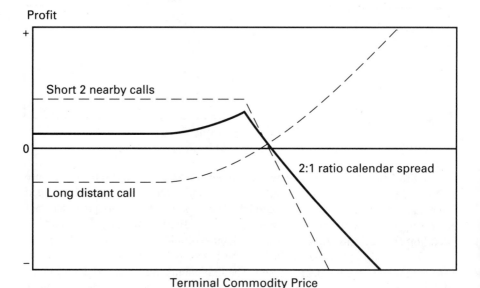

By writing more than one of the nearby calls, the calendar spreader usually receives an initial credit (i.e., he *receives* money when the position is formed). The net credit increases the profit if the commodity price falls below the exercise price prior to the expiration of the nearby option. Increases in the commodity price beyond the exercise price of the nearby option reduce the amount of the profit since, when both options are deep in-the-money, the spreader is synthetically short the commodity. Overall, the position is bearish. Figure 12.15 shows the profit diagram of a 2:1 ratio calendar spread.

36. *Short ratio calendar spread — Call:* Sell call with a distant maturity, and buy more than one identical calls with a nearby maturity.
37. *Long ratio calendar spread — Put:* Buy put with a distant maturity, and sell more than one identical puts with a nearby maturity.
38. *Short ratio calendar spread — Put:* Sell put with a distant maturity, and buy more than one identical puts with a nearby maturity.

Diagonal Spreads. In general, diagonal spreads are any spread positions consisting of different exercise prices and different expirations. A long diagonal spread requires that the distant option is purchased and the nearby option is shorted. If the ratio of the spread is 1:1, a diagonal bull (bear) spread results, depending upon whether the distant option has the lower (higher) exercise price. Long and short diagonalized spreads using other ratios produce a wide array of bullish and bearish positions. One possible diagonalized spread is described below.

39. *Diagonal bull spread — Call:* Buy call with a lower exercise price and distant maturity, and sell identical call with a higher exercise price and nearby maturity.

FIGURE 12.16   Trading Strategy: Long Diagonal Bull Spread

Profit

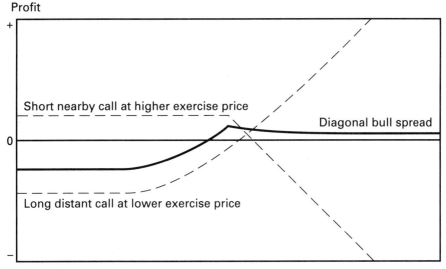

Terminal Commodity Price

As Figure 12.6 shows, a diagonal bull spread is very similar to the bull spread described earlier in this section. The maximum loss is limited to the difference between the distant and nearby option prices (i.e., the net debit amount). The maximum gain occurs when the commodity price equals the nearby option exercise price at the nearby option's expiration. Beyond that level, increases in the commodity price reduce the profit level to the difference between the exercise prices and the net debit amount.

Writing/Speculative Strategies

In this section, we examine the effects of buying and selling options against a position in the underlying commodity. In general, we discuss strategies that reduce the risk of a long position in the commodity by writing calls or buying puts. But we also consider the effects of buying calls and writing puts in order to increase leverage.

40. *Covered call option writing:* Sell call against a long position in the underlying commodity.

$$\pi_T = \begin{cases} X - Se^{bT} + ce^{rT} & \text{if} \quad S_T > X \\ S_T - Se^{bT} + ce^{rT} & \text{if} \quad S_T \le X \end{cases} \qquad \textbf{(12.14)}$$

FIGURE 12.17   Trading Strategy: Covered Call Writing

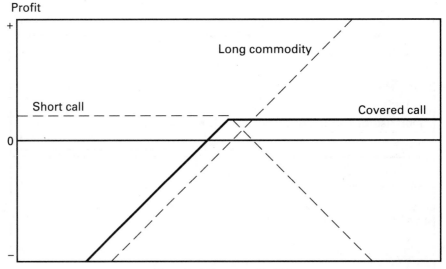

Breakeven point:	$S_T = Se^{bT} - ce^{rT}$
Maximum loss:	$Se^{bT} - ce^{rT}$, where S_T falls to zero
Maximum gain:	$X - Se^{bT} + ce^{rT}$, where $S_T > X$

Figure 12.17 shows that the covered call writer receives the option premium in exchange for the upside potential of the long commodity position. The position is equivalent to selling a naked put. Such a strategy makes sense only if an investor believes that the commodity price will not move much during the option's life. She does not benefit if the commodity price rises, and the option premium is little consolation if the commodity price falls dramatically.

Large stock funds often engage in a special form of covered call writing called *option overwriting*. In the usual case, the fund has separate stock and option portfolio managers. The stock portfolio manager handles the investment in stocks and advises the option overwriter on the current composition of the stock portfolio. The option overwriter then writes calls against the stocks. In the event that a call is exercised against the option overwriter, the overwriter must buy the stock for delivery on the option because she has no authority to deliver an existing stock position. The fund owner, however, should expect that some of her stocks will have to be liquidated, since writing call options against stocks is a risk-reducing strategy.

41. *Combination covered call option writing:* Sell in-the-money calls on half the commodity position, and sell out-of-the-money calls against the other half.

FIGURE 12.18   Trading Strategy: Combination Covered Call

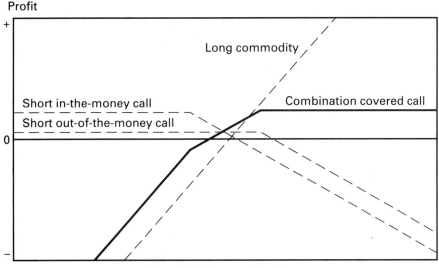

Terminal Commodity Price

This strategy is, generally, the same as the covered call strategy. Figure 12.18 shows that the profit structure is just slightly different. Over the commodity price range between the exercise prices, the option writer shares in half of any gains made in the share price. However, like the previous covered call strategy, the upside potential of the long commodity position is completely negated once the commodity price exceeds a certain level, in this case the exercise price of the out-of-the-money option.

42. *Ratio call writing:* Sell more than one call against a long position in the underlying commodity.

$$\pi_T = \begin{cases} nX - (n-1)S_T + nce^{rT} & \text{if} \quad S_T > X \\ S_T - Se^{bT} + nce^{rT} & \text{if} \quad S_T \le X \end{cases} \qquad \textbf{(12.15)}$$

FIGURE 12.19   Trading Strategy: Ratio Call Writing

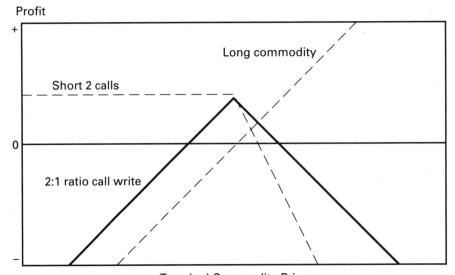

Breakeven point:	$S_T = Se^{bT} - nce^{rT}$
Maximum loss:	unlimited, where S_T rises without limit
Maximum gain:	nce^{rT}, where $S_T = X$ at expiration

Like ratio spreads, ratio writes are expressed in terms of the number of options sold, n, per unit of the underlying commodity. A 2:1 ratio write, therefore, refers to writing two call options against one unit of the commodity. In a 2:1 ratio write, half of the calls are covered while the other half are not. A 2:1 ratio write, such as that shown in Figure 12.19 creates a payoff diagram that looks exactly as if we have written a straddle. The maximum gain occurs when the commodity price equals the exercise price at the option expiration. Large commodity price swings in either direction, however, produce losses.

Ratio writing is usually pursued to earn premium income by those who expect that the commodity price will not move during the option life. The calls are written at the exercise price closest to the current commodity price. Profits are earned if the commodity price remains relatively unchanged. However, losses can be significant if the underlying commodity price changes significantly.

43. *Variable ratio writing:* Sell in-the-money calls and out-of-the-money calls against a long position in the commodity, such that the long position in the commodity is less than sufficient to cover delivery should the options be exercised.

FIGURE 12.20   Trading Strategy: Variable Ratio Writing

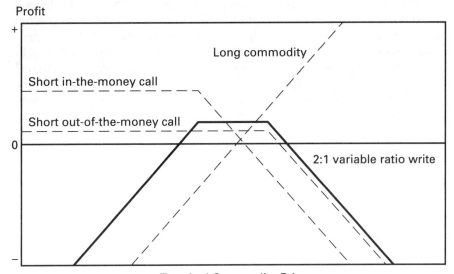

A 2:1 variable ratio writing strategy is shown in Figure 12.20. As the illustration shows, variable ratio writing can produce a profit diagram that looks exactly like a short strangle position. Maximum profit is realized when the commodity price falls between the two exercise prices at the options' expiration. Large commodity price moves in either direction will produce losses.

44. *Protected short sale:* Buy call option against a short position in the underlying commodity.

FIGURE 12.21   Trading Strategy: Protected Short Sale

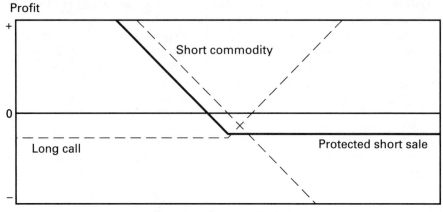

Terminal Commodity Price

Occasionally, an investor is short the commodity and wants to insure himself against possible large increases in the underlying commodity price. Buying a call option provides such insurance. As Figure 12.21 shows, buying a call option against a short position in the commodity produces a portfolio profit structure that looks exactly like a long put position. The position is also the opposite of the covered call. The maximum gain equals $Se^{bT} - ce^{rT}$, where the commodity price falls to zero. The maximum loss is $Se^{bT} - X - ce^{rT}$, which should be approximately equal to the value of a put with an exercise price of X and a time to expiration of T.

45. *Reverse hedge or simulated straddle:* Buy more than one call option against a short position in the underlying commodity.

FIGURE 12.22   Trading Strategy: Reverse Hedge

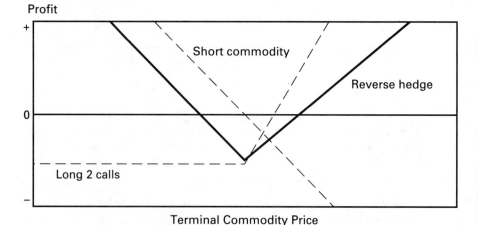

Terminal Commodity Price

Buying two call options against a short position in the underlying commodity creates a profit diagram that looks exactly like a long straddle. For this reason, this strategy is sometimes referred to as a *simulated straddle*. The position is also the opposite of the ratio call writing position described earlier. The maximum loss is sustained when the commodity price equals the exercise price of the options at their expiration. The gain on the upside is unlimited, should the commodity price rise without limit. Downside commodity price movements are also beneficial, since the options expire worthless and the investor has a short commodity position.

46. *Protected commodity position:* Buy a put option against a long commodity position.

$$\pi_T = \begin{cases} S_T - Se^{bT} - pe^{rT} & \text{if} \quad S_T > X \\ X - Se^{bT} - pe^{rT} & \text{if} \quad S_T \leq X \end{cases} \qquad \textbf{(12.16)}$$

FIGURE 12.23   Trading Strategy: Protected Commodity Position

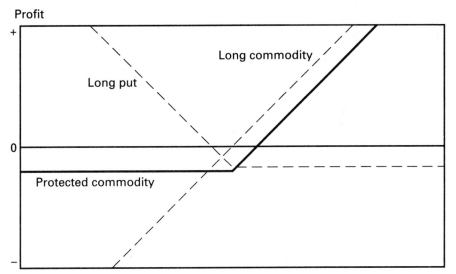

Breakeven point: $S_T = Se^{bT} + pe^{rT}$
Maximum loss: $X - Se^{bT} - pe^{rT}$, where $S_T \leq X$
Maximum gain: unlimited, where S_T rises without limit

Buying protective puts is a favored form of commodity insurance. As Figure 12.23 indicates, an investor with a long commodity position is well protected in the event that the commodity price falls dramatically. The cost of such insurance is the put option premium. The resulting position is the same as buying a call.

47. *Protected covered call write:* Buy a put against a covered call write.

FIGURE 12.24 Trading Strategy: Protected Covered Call Write

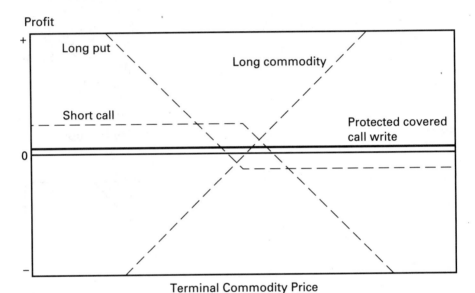

A covered call write means that the investor holds a long commodity/short call position. In the event that some time has elapsed since the covered call write was formed and the commodity price has not moved, the investor may want to lock in her profit from the time decay of the call by buying a put. When she does, she has, in effect, created a conversion arbitrage. Independent of which direction the commodity price moves subsequently, the portfolio profit is unchanged. Figure 12.24 demonstrates this clearly.

48. *Covered straddle write:* Buy commodity, sell call, and sell put.

$$\pi_T = \begin{cases} X - Se^{bT} + (c+p)e^{rT} & \text{if} \quad S_T > X \\ 2S_T - Se^{bT} - X + (c+p)e^{rT} & \text{if} \quad S_T \leq X \end{cases} \qquad \textbf{(12.17)}$$

FIGURE 12.25   Trading Strategy: Covered Straddle Write

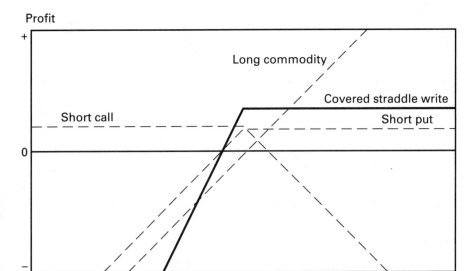

Breakeven point:	$S_T = \dfrac{Se^{bT} + X - (c+p)e^{rT}}{2}$
Maximum loss:	$-Se^{bT} - X + (c+p)e^{rT}$, where S_T falls to zero.
Maximum gain:	$X - Se^{bT} + (c+p)e^{rT}$, where $S_T > X$

In this case, the investor has written both a call and a put against a position in the underlying commodity. He has collected two option premiums, which equal the amount of the portfolio profit if the commodity price is above the option's exercise price at the option expiration. Should the commodity price fall, however, the portfolio profit drops by twice the amount, since the investor not only loses on the long commodity position, but also on the short put position.

49. *Buy call against commodity:* Buy call against a long position in the commodity.

FIGURE 12.26a   Trading Strategy: Long Commodity/Long Call Position

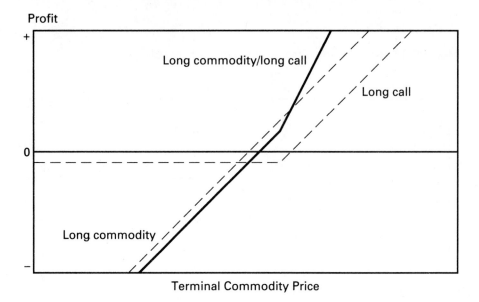

Terminal Commodity Price

50. *Sell put against commodity:* Sell put against a long position in the commodity.

FIGURE 12.26b   Trading Strategy: Long Commodity/Short Put Position

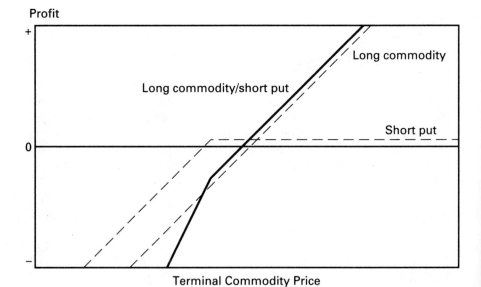

Terminal Commodity Price

Buying a call against a long commodity position and selling a put against a long commodity position serve to leverage the rate at which portfolio profits are earned. The long commodity/long call position in Figure 12.26a, for example, shows that below a certain level of commodity price, the portfolio profit is less than the long commodity position, since the call option had to be purchased. Above a certain level of commodity price, however, portfolio profit increases at twice the rate that the commodity price does by itself. Hence, we have increased the leverage of the strategy.

Writing a put against a long position in the commodity has a similar effect. The proceeds from the sale of the option enhance portfolio profit on the upside. On the downside, if the commodity price drops, the investor loses both on the long commodity position and the short put position.

12.2 COMPUTING BREAKEVEN PROBABILITIES AND EXPECTED PROFITS

Two useful concepts for analyzing the commodity/option strategies just discussed are the probability that the portfolio will be profitable at the options' expiration and the expected profit from the trading strategy. Both of these concepts rely on the option pricing mechanics presented in Chapter 11. Since the expected profit concept itself relies on probability computations, the probability computations are reviewed first.[3]

Breakeven Probabilities

To compute the probability that a particular strategy will be profitable at expiration, we need to first establish the full set of breakeven points associated with the strategy. For example, for the long straddle position, Trading Strategy 15, two breakeven points exist. One breakeven point is where the terminal commodity price, S_T, equals the value $BE_a = X - (c + p)e^{rT}$, and the other is where S_T equals the value $BE_b = X + (c + p)e^{rT}$. Figure 12.7 shows that a long straddle has positive profit, where $S_T < BE_a$ or where $S_T > BE_b$. If we assume that the commodity price is lognormally distributed, as we did in Chapter 11, the risk-neutral probability that the straddle will be profitable at expiration, $\text{Prob}(\tilde{S}_T < BE_a \text{ or } \tilde{S}_T > BE_b)$, can be found by using the cumulative standard normal distribution function, that is,

$$\text{Prob}(\tilde{S}_T < BE_a \text{ or } \tilde{S}_T > BE_b) = N(-d_a) + N(d_b),$$

where $d_a = \dfrac{\ln(S/BE_a) + (b - .5\sigma^2)T}{\sigma\sqrt{T}}$ and $d_b = \dfrac{\ln(S/BE_b) + (b - .5\sigma^2)T}{\sigma\sqrt{T}}$. Recall that a minus sign on the argument d implies that the probability computation is for the region below a critical terminal commodity price, while a positive value implies that the probability is for the region above a critical terminal price. Recall also that

---

[3] In this section, we assume that we are in a risk-neutral world in which possible future commodity prices are brought forward at the riskless rate.

the expression for d transforms the lognormally distributed commodity price to a unit normal distribution.

EXAMPLE 12.1

Assume that the current commodity price is $50 and that the prices of at-the-money, three-month options are $3.35 for the call and $2.90 for the put. Compute the probability that a long straddle position using these options will be profitable at the end of three months. Assume that the cost-of-carry rate for the underlying commodity is 4 percent, the volatility rate of the underlying commodity is 32 percent, and the riskless rate of interest is 6 percent.

The first step is to compute the breakeven points:

$$BE_a = 50 - (3.35 + 2.90)e^{.06(.25)} = 43.656$$

and

$$BE_b = 50 + (3.35 + 2.90)e^{.06(.25)} = 56.344.$$

The second step is to transform the commodity price breakeven points to the breakeven points in terms of the unit normal distribution, that is,

$$d_a = \frac{\ln(50/43.656) + [.04 - .5(.32)^2](.25)}{.32\sqrt{.25}} = .8305$$

and

$$d_b = \frac{\ln(50/56.344) + [.04 - .5(.32)^2](.25)}{.32\sqrt{.25}} = -.7641.$$

Finally, the probability that the straddle will be profitable at the end of three months is

$$\text{Prob}(\tilde{S}_T < BE_a \text{ or } \tilde{S}_T > BE_b) = N(-.8305) + N(-.7641) = .4255$$

or 42.55 percent.

Expected Terminal Profit

The expected terminal profit from a commodity/option portfolio position is our best guess of what the portfolio profit will be at expiration. It can be computed by multiplying portfolio profit at each conceivable terminal commodity price by the probability of that commodity price occurring and then summing across all of these products. Conceptually, while the above procedure is straightforward, two important practical suggestions will make the procedure easier to implement.

First, given the assumption of lognormally distributed commodity prices, the range of future commodity prices is infinite. Computationally, however, we cannot use an infinite number of option profit positions. A practical alternative is to define the range of possible future commodity prices as ± 4 standard deviations from the expected commodity price, Se^{bT}, which, according to Appendix 11.3, should account for 99.994 percent of the commodity price distribution. The range of future commodity prices implied by ± 4 standard deviations around the expected price is defined by

$$+4 = \frac{\ln(S/S_{\min}) + (b - .5\sigma^2)T}{\sigma\sqrt{T}}$$

and

$$-4 = \frac{\ln(S/S_{\max}) + (b - .5\sigma^2)T}{\sigma\sqrt{T}}.$$

Rearranging, the expressions for the minimum and maximum of the commodity price range are

$$S_{\min} = Se^{(b-.5\sigma^2)T - 4\sigma\sqrt{T}} \qquad \qquad \textbf{(12.18a)}$$

and

$$S_{\max} = Se^{(b-.5\sigma^2)T + 4\sigma\sqrt{T}}. \qquad \qquad \textbf{(12.18b)}$$

A second consideration has to do with the computation of profit for a given probability. Even with a prespecified range of terminal commodity prices, S_T, there are an infinite number of commodity prices and, hence, an infinite number of portfolio profits and probabilities to evaluate. The computation is practical if we approximate the continuous distribution of terminal commodity prices with a discrete distribution. To do so, we partition the terminal commodity price distribution into n equal increments of S_{inc}, where

$$S_{\text{inc}} = \frac{S_{\max} - S_{\min}}{n - 1}. \qquad \qquad \textbf{(12.19)}$$

We then begin at the lowest commodity price and assume that, over the first interval $S_{\min} - .5S_{\text{inc}}$ to $S_{\min} + .5S_{\text{inc}}$, the commodity price is $S_{\min}$. More generally, the commodity price is assumed to be S_i over the i-th interval, which has range $S_{i,T} \pm .5S_{\text{inc}}$,

where

$$S_{i,T} = S_{\min} + (i-1)(S_{\text{inc}}). \qquad \text{(12.20)}$$

The probability that the terminal commodity price will fall in this range is

$$\text{Prob}(S_{i,T} - .5S_{\text{inc}} < \tilde{S}_T < S_{i,T} + .5S_{\text{inc}}) = N(d_{l,i}) - N(d_{u,i}), \qquad \text{(12.21)}$$

where

$$d_{l,i} = \frac{\ln[S/(S_i - .5S_{\text{inc}})] + (b - .5\sigma^2)T}{\sigma\sqrt{T}} \text{ and } d_{u,i} = \frac{\ln[S/(S_i + .5S_{\text{inc}})] + (b - .5\sigma^2)T}{\sigma\sqrt{T}}.$$

The expected terminal commodity price may, therefore, be computed as

$$E(\tilde{S}_T) = \sum_{i=1}^{n}[N(d_{l,i}) - N(d_{u,i})]S_{i,T}. \qquad \text{(12.22)}$$

EXAMPLE 12.2

Compute the expected commodity price in three months, assuming the current commodity price is $50, the cost-of-carry rate is 4 percent, and the volatility rate is 32 percent.

The first step is to compute the minimum and maximum of the commodity price range using (12.18):

$$S_{\min} = 50e^{[.04-.5(.32)^2].25-4(.32)\sqrt{.25}} = 26.2909$$

$$S_{\max} = 50e^{[.04-.5(.32)^2].25+4(.32)\sqrt{.25}} = 94.5589.$$

The next step is to divide the range of commodity prices into equal-spaced intervals. Choosing $n = 11$, the size of each interval is

$$S_{\text{inc}} = \frac{94.5589 - 26.2909}{11 - 1} = 6.8268.$$

The midpoint of each interval is assumed to be

$$S_{i,T} = 26.2909 + 6.8268(i - 1),$$

the values of which are reported in the second column of Table 12.1.
The endpoints of each interval are then defined as

$$S_{l,i} = S_i - .5S_{\text{inc}}$$

TABLE 12.1   Estimation of expected terminal commodity price, using an equally spaced, discrete commodity price distribution approach: $S = 50$, $b = .04$, $T = .25$, and $\sigma = .32$.

Interval No.	(1) Commodity Price $S_{i,T}{}^a$	Lower Integral Limit $d_{l,i}$	Upper Integral Limit $d_{u,i}$	(2) $N(d_{l,i}) - N(d_{u,i})^b$	(1) Times (2)
1	26.2909	4.8692	3.2371	0.0006	0.0159
2	33.1177	3.2371	1.9441	0.0253	0.8391
3	39.9445	1.9441	0.8733	0.1653	6.6028
4	46.7713	0.8733	−0.0405	0.3249	15.1975
5	53.5981	−0.0406	−0.8377	0.2827	15.1536
6	60.4249	−0.8377	−1.5446	0.1399	8.4521
7	67.2517	−1.5446	−2.1796	0.0466	3.1326
8	74.0785	−2.1796	−2.7559	0.0117	0.8681
9	80.9053	−2.7559	−3.2836	0.0024	0.1953
10	87.7321	−3.2836	−3.7702	0.0004	0.0378
11	94.5589	−3.7702	−4.2216	0.0001	0.0066
				$E(\tilde{S}_T) =$	50.5013

a. $S_{i,T}$ is the terminal commodity price at the midpoint of the i-th interval.
b. $N(d_{l,i}) - N(d_{u,i})$ is the probability that the terminal commodity price will fall in the i-th interval.

and

$$S_{u,i} = S_i + .5S_{\text{inc}},$$

for $i = 1,\cdots,n$. Based on the interval endpoint values, the unit normal integral limits are computed and reported as the third and fourth columns of Table 12.1. Based on these limits, the probability that the terminal commodity price will fall in the i-th interval is computed using (12.21) and is reported in the fifth column.

The last column contains the product of the terminal commodity price and its respective probability. Summing across the values reported in the last column, we find that the expected terminal commodity price is

$$E(\tilde{S}_T) = \sum_{i=1}^{11} [N(d_{l,i}) - N(d_{u,i})]S_{i,T} = \$50.5013.$$

Note that this value corresponds closely to the true expected terminal commodity price, which we know from Chapter 11 to be

$$S = \$50e^{.04(.25)} = \$50.5025.$$

The slight discrepancy is due to the fact that this numerical method for computing the expected terminal commodity price is only an approximation, albeit a fairly accurate one in this illustration. Greater accuracy can be obtained by setting n to a higher value or by expanding the possible range of terminal commodity prices considered.

Extending this approach to compute expected terminal profit of an option portfolio is straightforward: simply replace the terminal commodity price $S_{i,T}$ in (12.22) with the option portfolio profit, given a commodity price of $S_{i,T}$, that is,

$$E(\tilde{\pi}_T) = \sum_{i=1}^{n}[N(d_{l,i}) - N(d_{u,i})]\pi(S_{i,T}). \qquad \textbf{(12.23)}$$

The profit functions $\pi(\cdot)$ for a wide array of strategies were presented in the last section.

EXAMPLE 12.3

Compute the expected terminal profit of an at-the-money call option, assuming the current commodity price is $50, the cost-of-carry rate is 4 percent, and the volatility rate is 32 percent. The riskless rate is assumed to be 6 percent, and the current call price is $3.410.

All steps in this example are the same as those in Example 12.2, except that in place of multiplying the probability by the terminal commodity price in the interval, we multiply the probability by the call option profit conditional on the terminal commodity price, as shown in Table 12.2. The profit is the difference between the exercise value of the call and the initial price of the call adjusted for interest. Note that the expected terminal profit of the call option portfolio is approximately $0.1937, which appears to indicate mispricing.

The theoretical value of this call using valuation (11.25) is $3.410, the same as the initial value of the call, which means that there is no mispricing. The positive profit arises from the approximation implicit in Table 12.2 and the fact that the call option profit is a nonlinear function of the terminal commodity price. To rectify this problem, we should be careful to set n to a large value. With a larger number of steps, the discrepancy will be reduced. For example, where $n = 500$, the expected terminal profit is 0.0010—an approximation error of about one-tenth of one cent.

12.3 REPLICATING LONG-TERM OPTIONS

Portfolio managers occasionally want to buy or sell long-term options, but no such options are listed or the markets for the options are very inactive. In these cases, it is possible to replicate a long-term option with a portfolio that consists of short-

TABLE 12.2   Estimation of expected terminal profit of a long call position, whose current price is $c = 3.410$. The pricing parameters are: $S = 50$, $X = 50$, $b = .04$, $r = .06$, $T = .25$, and $\sigma = .32$.

Interval No.	Commodity Price $S_{i,T}{}^a$	(1) $N(d_{l,i}) - N(d_{u,i})^b$	(2) Profit $\pi_{i,T}{}^c$	(1) Times (2)
1	26.2909	0.0006	−3.4615	−0.0021
2	33.1177	0.0253	−3.4615	−0.0877
3	39.9445	0.1653	−3.4615	−0.5722
4	46.7713	0.3249	−3.4615	−1.1248
5	53.5981	0.2827	0.1366	0.0386
6	60.4249	0.1399	6.9634	0.9740
7	67.2517	0.0466	13.7902	0.6424
8	74.0785	0.0117	20.6170	0.2416
9	80.9053	0.0024	27.4438	0.0662
10	87.7321	0.0004	34.2706	0.0148
11	94.5589	0.0001	41.0974	0.0028
			$E(\tilde\pi_T) =$	0.1937

a. $S_{i,T}$ is the terminal commodity price at the midpoint of the i-th interval.
b. $N(d_{l,i}) - N(d_{u,i})$ is the probability that the terminal commodity price will fall in the i-th interval.
c. $\pi_{i,T} = \max(0, S_{i,T} - X) - ce^{rT}$.

term options and a short-term riskless asset, such as T-bills.[4] The tools necessary to carry out this replication are the expected profit mechanics of the last section, together with multiple linear regression.

The approach is simple. First, as in the last section, find a range of plausible commodity prices at the end of the short-term options' life, t. Using expressions (12.18a) and (12.18b), identify a range that encompasses 99.994 percent of the probability distribution at t. Second, partition the range into n equal increments using (12.19), and identify the commodity prices, $S_{i,t}$, at the midpoint of each interval, using (12.20). Third, find the probability of the terminal commodity price falling within the i-th interval, using (12.21). So far, everything is as it was in the previous section.

On the basis of the commodity prices created in the second step of the last paragraph, $S_{i,t}$, $i = 1, \cdots, n$, compute the values of the long-term option value, $V_{LT}(S_{i,t})$, as well as the terminal values of all m short-term options, $V_{ST,j}(S_{i,t})$, that are assumed to be available, $j = 1, \cdots, m$. Use the values of the long-term option as

---

[4]Dynamic rebalancing of a portfolio that consists of the commodity and T-bills is another way of replicating a long-term option. We discuss this possibility in Chapter 14 under the heading "Dynamic Portfolio Insurance."

the dependent variable and the values of the short-term option as the independent variables, and perform a regression that minimizes the sum of squared errors,

$$\text{Min} \sum_{i=1}^{n} p_i [V_{LT}(S_{i,t}) - b_0 - \sum_{j=1}^{m} b_j V_{ST,j}(S_{i,t})]^2. \qquad \textbf{(12.24)}$$

The estimated regression coefficients, $\hat{b}_j, j = 1, \cdots, m$, are the amounts of the investments in the short-term options. The estimated intercept term, b_0 is the amount invested in the riskless asset. A check of how well the technique has performed can be made by comparing the current short-term option portfolio value to the theoretical value of the long-term option.[5]

EXAMPLE 12.4

Assume an investor owns a commodity portfolio and wants to buy a European put option with an exercise price of 100 and a maturity of one year. The current commodity price is 100, the cost-of-carry rate is 4 percent, and the volatility is 32 percent. The riskless rate of interest is 6 percent. The theoretical price of this option is $10.3887 on the basis of the European option valuation equation (11.28). However, no such long-term option exists.

Instead, the investor is considering buying a portfolio of three-month put options that can be used to replicate the performance of the one year option over the next three months. In three months, a new short-term position can be established to replicate the then nine-month option.[6] Seven three-month options are available:

Exercise Price	Option Price
85	1.0438
90	2.0681
95	3.6432
100	5.8302
105	8.6265
110	11.9752
115	15.7855

Setting the number of increments, n, to 300, the replication procedure described above is applied. First the values of the long-term option in three months for the possible values of the underlying commodity in three months are calculated. These

---

[5] Choie and Novomestky (1989) point out that if the terminal value of the short-term option portfolio corresponds to the long-term option value for all levels of commodity price at time t, then, in the absence of costless arbitrage opportunities in the marketplace, the current value of the short-term option portfolio should equal the current value of the long-term option.

[6] In practice, using short-term options with more than one expiration date (e.g., three-month and six-month options) and/or rolling out of the short-term option positions prior to their expiration may provide a more effective replication of the long-term option position.

values are regressed against the possible values of the short-term options at maturity. Using the estimated regression coefficients, the portfolio composition is

Exercise Price	(1) Option Price	(2) Estimated Coefficient	(1) Times (2)
85	1.0438	.2286	.2386
90	2.0681	.0018	.0036
95	3.6432	.1004	.3657
100	5.8302	.0362	.2109
105	8.6265	.1730	1.4924
110	11.9752	−.4009	−4.8009
115	15.7855	.6136	9.6860
T-bill	.9851	3.2406	3.1923
Total			10.3887

With the exception of shorting the 110 put, all other puts are purchased. The sum of the portfolio weights times the security prices, 10.3887 equals exactly the long-term put option price. (The price of the T-bill is assumed to be $e^{-.06(.25)} = .9851$.) A comparison of the actual long-term put option with the simulated put option value is provided in Figure 12.27. Note how closely the values match until the commodity price becomes very high.

FIGURE 12.27 Simulated versus Long-Term Option Price

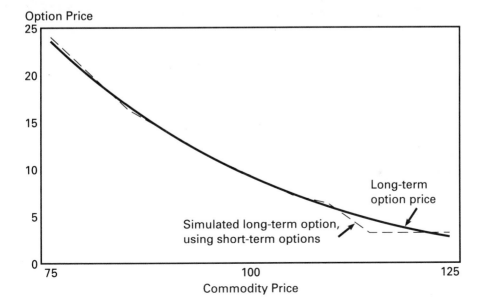

Option Price

   This procedure may be refined to account for non-negativity constraints, market liquidity, and observed option mispricings of short-term options. Changes in volatility through the life of the long-term option are also possible.[7] Our approach assumes that purchases and sales of short-term options are freely allowed in whatever quantity is demanded. We also assume that option prices conform with the European option valuation equations (11.25) and (11.28) and that the volatility rate is constant over the life of the long-term option.

   Portfolio managers interested in long-dated options can either create them as indicated above or, as is more often the case, buy them from investment bankers in an over-the-counter transaction. The investment banker sells the option for her own account and hedges her position by taking an offsetting position in the replicating short-term option portfolio.

12.4 DYNAMIC PORTFOLIO RISK MANAGEMENT

Up to this point in the chapter, option positions have been held to maturity. In this section, we address the issue of dynamic risk management, that is, portfolio risk management that attempts to account for short-term price movements in the underlying commodity, short-term shifts in volatility, and the natural erosion of option premium as the time to option expiration is decreased. In this context, we rely particularly on the partial derivatives of the European option pricing formulas that we derived in Chapter 11. We will show that option deltas, gammas, etas, thetas, and vegas are invaluable aids in managing expected return and risk of a portfolio of options and the underlying commodity.

Expected Return and Risk

To begin, it is useful to have a clear understanding of the expected return/risk characteristics of option positions. In Chapter 11, we showed that the beta of an option equals the elasticity of the option price with respect to the commodity price times the beta of the underlying commodity, that is, $\beta_c = \eta_c \beta_S$ and $\beta_p = \eta_p \beta_S$. We also showed that the volatility of an option equals the absolute value of the elasticity of the option price with respect to the commodity price times the volatility of the underlying commodity, that is, $\sigma_c = |\eta_c| \sigma_S$ and $\sigma_p = |\eta_p| \sigma_S$. Recall that the elasticity depends on the commodity and option prices and on the other variables in the option pricing formula, such as volatility, time to expiration, and so on. As a result, the risk and return characteristics of option/commodity positions change through time as these variables change. If the risk of a position is to remain unchanged through time, the position must be appropriately rebalanced.

---

[7] See, for example, Jamshidian, and Zhu (1990).

We now examine the risk/return characteristics of a portfolio of options and the underlying commodity with the help of a simple numerical illustration. We assume that the commodity price is 50, the expected rate of return on the commodity is 16 percent, the commodity beta is 1.20, and the volatility of the commodity return is 40 percent. We assume a cost-of-carry rate of 4 percent and a riskless rate of 6 percent. Three-month European call and put options with exercise prices of 45, 50, and 55 are available, and all of these options have prices equal to their theoretical values, as determined by the pricing equations in the last chapter.

Focusing on the beta risk measure first, we can find the expected return/risk attributes of the options by first finding their respective betas, and then finding their equilibrium expected returns based on their betas. For example, the beta for the in-the-money call, which has an elasticity of $\eta_c = 5.289$, may be computed as

$$\beta_c = \eta_c \beta_S$$
$$= 5.289(1.20) = 6.35.$$

Assuming the capital market is in equilibrium, the expected return on the commodity is

$$E(R_S) = r + [E(R_M) - r]\beta_S.$$

Substituting for $E(R_S)$ the expected return of the commodity and for r, the riskless rate of interest, we find the term $[E(R_M) - r]\beta_S$ equals .10. To find the expected return for the in-the-money call, we again use the security market line from the capital asset pricing model:

$$E(R_c) = r + [E(R_M) - r]\beta_c$$
$$= r + [E(R_M) - r]\beta_S \eta_c$$
$$= .06 + .10\eta_c$$
$$= .06 + .10(5.289) = 58.89\%.$$

Using a similar procedure for the remaining options, we find the following expected returns and betas:

Option	Price	Delta	Elasticity	Expected Return	Beta
45 call	7.061	.747	5.289	58.89	6.35
50 call	4.196	.557	6.636	72.36	7.96
55 call	2.294	.370	8.069	86.69	9.68
45 put	1.640	−.248	−7.559	−69.59	−9.07
50 put	3.701	−.438	−5.920	−53.20	−7.10
55 put	6.724	−.625	−4.645	−40.45	−5.57
Commodity		1	1	16.00	1.20
Riskless Asset		0	0	6.00	0.00

Figure 12.28a illustrates these results.

FIGURE 12.28a   Relation Between Expected Return and Beta

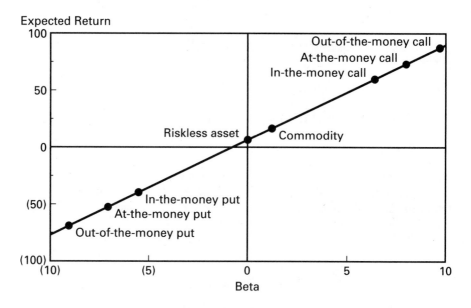

The expected return/beta relation depicted in Figure 12.28a is startling. The expected returns and betas of options are drastically different from the expected return and beta of the underlying commodity. Long call option positions, for example, have very high expected returns and betas—in fact, several times higher than the underlying commodity. The illustration also shows that the expected return and beta of the long call increase as the call goes deeper and deeper out-of-the-money. On the other hand, we see that put options generally have negative expected returns and negative betas, and the deeper the put is out-of-the-money, the lower (more negative) its expected return and its beta are.

Portfolio managers are also interested in knowing the level of return volatility. As noted above, option return volatility is simply the elasticity of the option price with respect to commodity price times the volatility of the underlying commodity return. In the illustration, the volatility of the commodity return is 40 percent. The option volatilities are, therefore,

Option	Elasticity	Return Volatility
45 call	5.289	211.56
50 call	6.636	265.44
55 call	8.069	322.76
45 put	−7.559	302.36
50 put	−5.920	236.80
55 put	−4.645	185.80
Commodity	1	40.00
Riskless Asset	0	0

Figure 12.28b illustrates these results.

FIGURE 12.28b   Relation Between Expected Return and Volatility

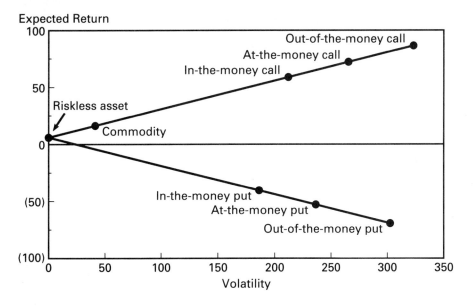

The extreme riskiness of options is further confirmed by these values. Where the return volatility of the underlying commodity is 40 percent, the option return volatilities exceed, in some cases, several hundred percent.

Combining options with a position in the underlying commodity, however, can be risk-reducing. For example, a covered call strategy (i.e., writing a call against the underlying commodity) or a protective put strategy (i.e., buying a put against the underlying commodity) reduces the risk of the overall position. The expected return, beta, and return volatility of a portfolio that consists of an option and the underlying commodity may be computed using the following equations:

$$E(R_P) = X_S E(R_S) + (1 - X_S)E(R_o), \tag{12.25}$$

$$\beta_P = X_S \beta_S + (1 - X_S)\beta_o, \tag{12.26}$$

and

$$\sigma_P = \sqrt{X_S^2 \sigma_S^2 + (1 - X_S)^2 \sigma_o^2 + 2d_o X_S(1 - X_S)\sigma_S \sigma_o}, \tag{12.27}$$

where the subscript o indicates option and the indicator variable d_o is $+1$ for calls and -1 for puts (i.e., call [put] option returns are perfectly positively [negatively] correlated with commodity returns). The weight X_S is the proportion of the S dollars invested directly in the commodity, that is,

$$X_S = \frac{S - n_o O_o}{S}, \tag{12.28}$$

where n_o is the number of options purchased (i.e., a positive value of n_o indicates the options are purchased, and a negative value indicates that the options are sold) and O_o is the market value of each option. Note that where n_o equals zero, all portfolio wealth is invested in the commodity. The value $1 - X_S$ is the proportion of the original investment in options.

To reinforce these mechanics, reconsider the above illustration and assume that a covered call write is created by selling the in-the-money call against a long position in the commodity. The proceeds from selling the call are invested in the commodity so the total investment in the commodity is

$$50 - (-1)(7.061) = 57.061.$$

The proportion of the original investment in the underlying commodity is therefore $X_S = 57.061/50 = 1.141$. The proportion of portfolio value invested in the call is $1 - X_S = -.141$.

With the weights known, we can compute the expected return, beta, and volatility of the covered call position using expressions (12.25), (12.26), and (12.27):

$$E(R_P) = 1.141(16.00) - .141(58.89) = 9.94\%;$$

$$\beta_P = 1.141(1.20) - .141(6.35) = .47,$$

and

$$\sigma_P = \sqrt{1.141^2(.40^2) + (-.141)^2(2.1156^2) + 2(1.141)(-.141)(.40)(2.1156)}$$
$$= 15.81\%.$$

In other words, writing the in-the-money call against the underlying commodity reduces the expected return and the risk of the underlying portfolio. In fact, all one-to-one covered call writes and all one-to-one protective put buys will share these attributes. For the illustration at hand, the characteristics of the commodity and the six different commodity/option portfolios are

Option	Commodity Investment	X_S	Expected Return	Beta	Return Volatility
no option	50.000	1.000	16.00	1.20	40.00
45 call write	57.061	1.141	9.94	.47	15.81
50 call write	54.196	1.084	11.27	.63	21.06
55 call write	52.294	1.046	12.75	.81	26.99
45 put buy	48.360	.967	13.18	.86	28.69
50 put buy	46.299	.926	10.88	.59	19.52
55 put buy	43.276	.866	8.44	.29	9.74

The above results are plotted in Figures 12.29a and 12.29b.

FIGURE 12.29a Relation Between Expected Return and Beta

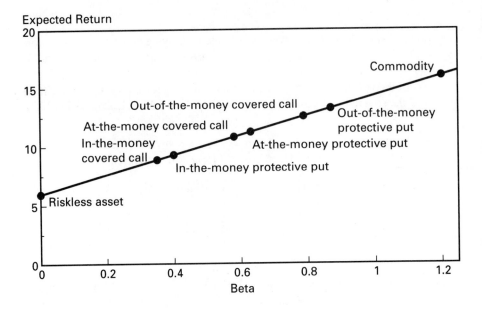

FIGURE 12.29b Relation Between Expected Return and Volatility

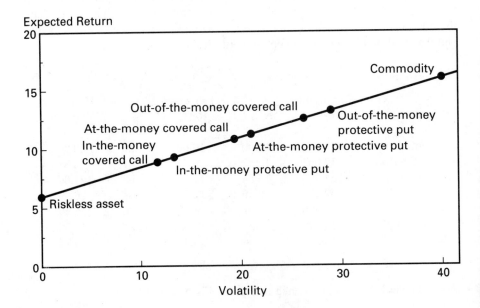

These figures show clearly that covered call writes and protective put buys serve to reduce portfolio expected return and risk.[8] For the covered calls, the return/risk reduction becomes larger the deeper in-the-money the call option is. This is simply because the option writer is willing to accept more cash (i.e., option premium) in exchange for the upside potential of commodity price movements. This activity is completely analogous to withdrawing investment from the commodity and investing in the riskless asset. In fact, given that the 45 call option has a delta of .747, the 45 covered call portfolio has a net delta value of $1.141 - .747 = .394$. If we create a portfolio that consists of .394 in the commodity and .606 in the riskless asset, the expected return, beta, and volatility of return are

$$E(R_P) = .394(16.00) + .606(6.00) = 9.94\%,$$

$$\beta_P = .394(1.20) + .606(0.00) = .47,$$

and

$$\sigma_P = \sqrt{.394^2(.40^2)} = 15.76\%,$$

the same return/risk attributes as the 45 covered call write.

That is not to say that writing call options against the underlying commodity is always risk-reducing. If too many calls are sold, portfolio risk may increase. Consider a 4:1 ratio call write. The total investment in the commodity is

$$50 + 4(7.061) = 78.244.$$

The proportion of the original investment in the underlying commodity is, therefore, $X_S = 78.244/50 = 1.565$. The proportion of portfolio value invested in the call is $1 - X_S = -.565$. The expected return on this portfolio is

$$E(R_P) = 1.565(16.00) - .565(58.90) = -8.24\%,$$

and the volatility is

$$\sigma_P = \sqrt{1.565^2(.40^2) + .565^2(2.1156^2) - 2(1.565)(.565)(.40)(2.1156)} = 56.93\%.$$

---

[8]Recall that the expected return and beta of the option positions hold for the next instance over which the underlying variables don't change much.

Where the volatility of a portfolio that consists exclusively of the commodity is 40 percent, the volatility of a 4:1 ratio write is 56.93 percent. In this situation, we are overhedged.

Figure 12.30 helps clarify this point.

FIGURE 12.30   Relation Between Expected Return and Volatility

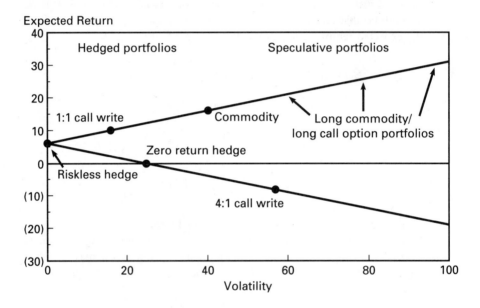

In the figure, we see the commodity plotted with an expected return of 16 percent and a volatility of 40 percent. The point labelled "1:1 call write" shows that the expected return and the volatility of the portfolio is reduced when a single 45 call is written against the commodity. As more calls are written, the expected return and volatility continue to decrease, until, finally, where 1.65 calls are written against the commodity, the portfolio is riskless.[9] Beyond this number, if more calls are written, expected return continues to decrease, but volatility increases. Eventually, the expected portfolio return becomes negative, and, if the number of calls written continues to grow, volatility begins to exceed 40 percent. The 4:1 call write portfolio, for example, has greater volatility than the commodity held in isolation. The critical number of calls written against the commodity to generate a 40 percent

---

[9]Earlier we illustrated that a covered call position is analogous to a portfolio that consists of somewealth in the commodity and some wealth in the riskless asset. The wealth invested in the commodity is $(S + n_c c - n_c S \Delta_c)$. If we set this value equal to zero (i.e., all wealth is invested in the riskless asset) and solve for n_c, we get $n_c = 1/(\Delta_c - c/S)$. Substituting the example values, $n_c = 1/(.747 - 7.061/50) = 1.65$.

volatility is 3.30, exactly double the number of calls that generated the riskless hedge.[10]

Managing Unexpected Changes in the Commodity Price

The risk of an option portfolio is subject to change as the price of the underlying commodity changes. Consequently, a portfolio manager needs not only to identify the current risk of the portfolio, as shown in the preceding section, but also to manage the portfolio to minimize the effects of unexpected changes in the commodity price. As a practical matter, knowledge of option deltas and gammas provide the tools necessary to immunize portfolios against adverse price movements in the underlying commodity.

In Chapter 11, we developed expressions for the partial derivatives of individual European options based on the valuation equations (11.25) and (11.28). The delta, for example, is the partial derivative of the option price with respect to a change in the underlying commodity price. The question that arises in option portfolio management is how the option portfolio value changes as a result of a change in the commodity price.

To understand the answer to this question, we first develop a simple, intuitive answer to the question that applies to all of the partial derivatives of the option price. First, write the expression for the value of the portfolio. Assume the portfolio consists of N different option positions, an underlying commodity position, and an investment in the riskless asset. Each option position has n_i contracts at current price O_i. Summing across positions and adding n_S units of the commodity at price S and the riskless asset, B, the value of the portfolio is

$$V = \sum_{i=1}^{N} n_i O_i + n_S S + B. \qquad \textbf{(12.29)}$$

The partial derivative of the portfolio value with respect to a change in one of the option's determinants, k, is

$$\frac{\partial V}{\partial k} = \sum_{i=1}^{N} n_i \frac{\partial O_i}{\partial k} + n_S \frac{\partial S}{\partial k} + \frac{\partial B}{\partial k}. \qquad \textbf{(12.30)}$$

---

[10] In the last footnote, we used the fact that a covered call is like a portfolio that consists of some wealth in the commodity and some wealth in the riskless asset in order to deduce the composition of the riskless hedge. The wealth invested in the commodity is $(S + n_c c - n_c S \Delta_c)$. If we set this value equal to $-S$ (i.e., a short sale of the underlying commodity) and solve for n_c, we get $n_c = 2/(\Delta_c - c/S)$. Substituting the example values, $n_c = 2/(.747 - 7.061/50) = 3.30$.

In other words, to find the change in the value of the portfolio resulting from a change in k, we simply compute how each option value changes from a change in k, multiply by the number of contracts of that option, and then sum across all option positions. The commodity and riskless asset positions may also affect the portfolio value. The same result holds when we examine the second partial derivative:

$$\frac{\partial^2 V}{\partial k^2} = \sum_{i=1}^{N} n_i \frac{\partial^2 O_i}{\partial k^2} + n_S \frac{\partial^2 S}{\partial k^2} + \frac{\partial^2 B}{\partial k^2}. \qquad \textbf{(12.31)}$$

Now, let us return to the problem of managing changes in commodity price. The change in portfolio value with respect to a change in commodity price (i.e., the portfolio's delta) is

$$\Delta_V = \sum_{i=1}^{N} n_i \Delta_o + n_S. \qquad \textbf{(12.32)}$$

Note that by assumption, the value of the riskless asset does not change as the commodity price changes. To immunize this portfolio from changes in the commodity price, we simply compute Δ_V and then take a position in options or the underlying commodity that makes the portfolio delta value zero.

EXAMPLE 12.5

Assume a futures option market maker has long positions of 150 calls with an exercise price of 45 and a time to expiration of two months, 200 puts with an exercise price of 50 and a time to expiration of three months, and 225 calls with an exercise price of 55 and a time to expiration of three months. Rather than face the risk that the underlying futures price may move significantly overnight, he decides to hedge the position using either the futures or calls with an exercise price of 50 and a time to expiration of three months. Compare the effectiveness of using the futures and the 50 call in creating a delta-neutral hedge. Assume the current futures price is $50, the 50 call is priced at $2.455 and has a delta of .5171, the riskless rate of interest is 6 percent, and the volatility rate is 25 percent.

Quantity	Option Type	Exercise Price	Time to Expiration	Option Price	Delta
150	Call	45	.16667	5.325	0.852
200	Put	50	.25	2.455	−0.468
225	Call	55	.25	0.828	0.238

Thus, the portfolio value is

$$V = 150(5.325) + 200(2.455) + 225(.828) = 1,476.05,$$

and the portfolio delta is

$$\Delta_V = 150(.852) + 200(-.468) + 225(.238) = 87.75.$$

The portfolio delta of 87.75 says that holding this portfolio is like holding a long position in 87.75 futures contracts. To create a delta neutral portfolio, we can either (a) sell 87.75 futures contracts or (b) sell $87.75/.5171 = 169.70$ calls. Figure 12.31 shows the effectiveness of each hedge.

Figure 12.31 demonstrates that both the delta-neutral futures hedge and the delta-neutral option hedge reduce the range of possible portfolio values. The unhedged portfolio has a range of value from about 1400 to 3600 over the range of commodity prices—the futures hedge from about 1475 to 3000 and the options hedge from about 1475 to 2500. Clearly, the option hedge is the most effective.

FIGURE 12.31   Portfolio Value as a Function of Commodity Price

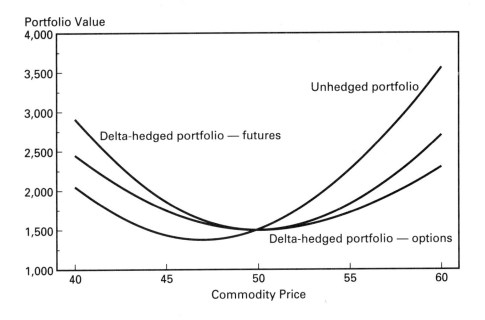

The reason that the option hedge winds up being the most effective has to do with gamma—the change in delta as the commodity price changes. As the commodity price changes, the option portfolio delta value changes. In fact, the option portfolio gamma is 30.08, as shown below. The futures contract has zero gamma, so the delta-neutral futures hedge still has a gamma of 30.08. On the other hand, the 169.70 calls that we sold have a gamma of $-169.70(.062758) = -10.65$, so the gamma of the delta-neutral option hedge is 19.43. Nonetheless, the gamma reduction with the option hedge is incidental in this case, so we will now illustrate how to account for both delta and gamma in hedging the portfolio against commodity price moves.

EXAMPLE 12.6

Again, we are considering the market maker described in Example 12.5. His portfolio position is

Quantity	Option Type	Exercise Price	Time to Expiration	Option Price	Delta	Gamma
150	Call	45	.16667	5.325	0.852	.04304
200	Put	50	.25	2.455	-0.468	.06276
225	Call	55	.25	0.828	0.238	.04922

As in the last example, the portfolio value is 1476.05, and the portfolio delta is 87.75. The portfolio gamma is

$$\gamma_V = 150(.04304) + 200(.06276) + 225(.04922) = 30.08.$$

To hedge both delta and gamma risk, two options are needed (i.e., the futures has zero gamma, so it is not effective at tailoring the gamma risk of the portfolio). In addition to the 50 call, which was available in Example 12.5, we will also assume that a three-month 55 put is available. Its price is $7.754, its delta is $-.7468$, and its gamma is .04922. The 50 call has a gamma of .06276.

To compute the optimal delta-neutral/gamma-neutral hedge from these two options, we solve the following system of equations. We want the portfolio to be delta-neutral, so

$$n_c(.5171) + n_p(-.7468) = -87.75.$$

We also want the portfolio to be gamma-neutral, so

$$n_c(.06276) + n_p(.04922) = -30.08.$$

To solve, we can isolate n_c in the first equation, substitute into the second, and solve for n_p. The value of n_p is -138.93. We then substitute for n_p in the first equation and find that n_c is -370.34.

The value of the delta-neutral/gamma-neutral hedge portfolio is plotted in Figure 12.32, along with the unhedged portfolio value. Clearly, the hedge is effective. Where the unhedged portfolio varies by more than 2000 over the commodity price range shown, the hedged portfolio appears to vary by less than 200.

FIGURE 12.32   Portfolio Value as a Function of Commodity Price

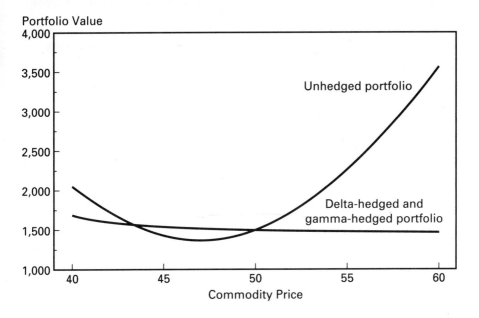

Note that in Example 12.6, only two options are assumed to be available for setting the delta-neutral/gamma-neutral hedge. In practice, many options are available with which to set this hedge. At least two options are needed to execute the hedge, but more options can be used. Linear programming is sometimes used to find the minimum-cost set of options that will eliminate delta and gamma risk.

Managing Unexpected Changes in Volatility

Along with commodity price risk, traders also find themselves in a position where their option portfolios may suffer large losses if the volatility underlying the options shifts. For example, a market maker may be short calls and puts, and, while the position may be delta-neutral, a sudden increase in volatility will cause the market maker to incur significant losses. Like the delta-hedge shown above, the market maker can hedge volatility through vega-hedging.

EXAMPLE 12.7

Again, we are considering a market maker in the futures option contracts described in Example 12.5. This market maker's portfolio, however, is distinctly different. He is short 180 three-month 50 calls and 200 three-month 50 puts.

Quantity	Option Type	Exercise Price	Time to Expiration	Option Price	Delta	Vega
−180	Call	50	.25	2.455	0.517	9.806
−200	Put	50	.25	2.455	−0.468	9.806

Note that at-the-money futures options have the same price.

The portfolio is nearly delta-neutral, as is shown below:

$$\Delta_V = -180(.517) + -200(-.468) = .54.$$

Unfortunately, the vega-exposure is substantial:

$$\text{Vega}_V = -180(9.806) + -200(9.806) = -3726.28.$$

This means that if volatility increases from its current level of 25 percent to, say, 26 percent, the portfolio value will drop by 37.26 dollars.

To hedge this risk, assume that the three-month 55 put from Example 12.6 is available. The 55 put has a vega of 7.69. In order to eliminate the vega risk of the portfolio, we should buy

$$n_p = \frac{3726.28}{7.69} = 484.56$$

puts. Figure 12.33 illustrates the effectiveness of this procedure.

Clearly, the vega-hedge is shown to be effective at eliminating the effects of shifts in volatility. Note, however, that the purchase of the 55 puts dramatically affected the portfolio's delta. It is now at a level of $484.56(-.7468) + .54 = -361.33$. This example is intended only to show how vega risk can be managed. Obviously, simultaneously considering delta, gamma, and vega may be sensible; this can be done with three or more available options.

FIGURE 12.33   Portfolio Value as a Function of Volatility

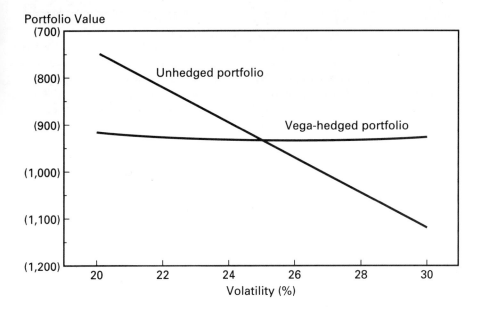

Managing Time Decay

Our final discussion has to do with time decay. Long positions in options deteriorate in value through time as the prospect of a large commodity price move diminishes. Figure 12.34 illustrates how an at-the-money call option drops in value as its expiration date approaches.

FIGURE 12.34   Time Decay of an At-the-Money Call Option

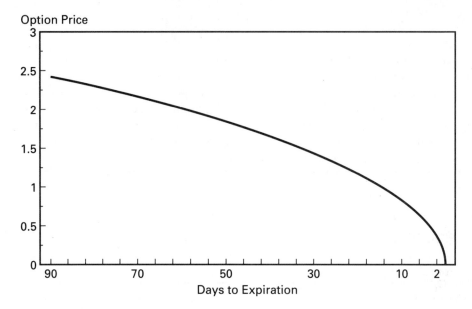

Option Price

Days to Expiration

The slope of the curve shown is the option's theta, that is, the change in option value as the time to expiration changes. At first the rate of decay is slow. In the final days before expiration, the rate is considerably faster. An implication of this figure is that managing time decay is more difficult as the time to option expiration is shortened.

To manage time decay, we use the same mechanics as we used for the other partial derivatives. In place of using delta, gamma, or vega, we find an option or options to negate the portfolio theta.

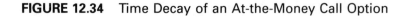

EXAMPLE 12.8

Consider the portfolio of the futures option market maker in Example 12.7. How can this person eliminate the time decay in his portfolio by using the 50 call option?

The portfolio position is

Quantity	Option Type	Exercise Price	Time to Expiration	Option Price	Theta
150	Call	45	.16667	5.325	3.043
200	Put	50	.25	2.455	4.756
225	Call	55	.25	0.828	7.690

The portfolio theta is, therefore,

$$\Theta = 150(3.043) + 200(4.756) + 225(7.690) = 3,137.90,$$

which means that, over the next day, the portfolio value will erode by 3,137.90 (1/365) = 8.597.

A theta-hedge can be created using the 50 call. Its theta is 4.756. To eliminate the time decay, we should sell 3,137.90/4.756 = 659.78 contracts.

In this section, we showed how portfolio delta, gamma, vega, and theta values may be used to effectively manage the value of an option portfolio. While the illustrations typically focused on one dimension at a time, it is clear that the daily man-

12.5 SUMMARY

In this chapter, we accomplished four things. First, we developed and analyzed more than fifty option trading strategies. Each strategy was put together from its basic security components and illustrated with a profit diagram. Breakeven commodity prices, maximum losses, and maximum gains were provided. Second, we showed that by using the lognormal commodity price distribution assumption from Chapter 11, we can compute probabilities of losses and gains, as well as the expected profit for each trading strategy. In the third section, we showed that a regression approach can be used to create long-term options from short-term options. Finally, we discussed the daily risk management of option portfolios.

13 COMMON STOCK OPTION CONTRACTS

Common stock option contracts have been traded in the U.S. for many decades. Trading began in the over-the-counter market more than fifty years ago. In April 1973, the Chicago Board Options Exchange (CBOE) became the first organized secondary market in call options on sixteen NYSE common stocks. In 1977, the CBOE introduced put options on stocks. Today, both call and put options are traded on over five hundred different stocks and on five exchanges. In addition to the CBOE, active secondary stock option markets exist on the American Stock Exchange, the Pacific Coast Exchange, the Philadelphia Stock Exchange, and the New York Stock Exchange.

This chapter focuses on stock options. In the first section, the stock option market is described. In the second section, we adapt the arbitrage pricing relations of Chapter 10 to stock option contracts. The principles are modified somewhat to account for the fact that common stocks typically pay discrete dividends during the option's life. In section 3, we value European and American call options on dividend-paying stocks. Even though an American call option may be exercised early, a valuation equation for this option exists. For American put options on stocks, no valuation equation exists. In section 4, the binomial method is used to approximate the value of American put options on dividend-paying stocks. Although the application is specific, the binomial method can be applied to the valuation of virtually any type of option. This method is used again in Chapter 15, for example, to value interest rate options. Finally, in section 5, warrants used to raise new capital are studied. Warrants are like options except that they are issued by a company. If the warrants are exercised, the company's equity may be diluted, something that must be incorporated into warrant valuation.

13.1 COMMON STOCK OPTION MARKETS

In the U.S., stock option contracts are written in denominations of one hundred shares, expire on the Saturday after the third Friday of the contract month, and are American-style. A call option on a stock represents the right to buy one hundred shares of the underlying stock, and a put option represents the right to sell one hundred shares. Although the contract denomination is one hundred shares, the option prices are quoted on a per-share basis. The exercise prices of stock options are in $5 increments above $25 and in $2.50 increments below.

To illustrate these conventions, consider the option prices reported in Table 13.1. The IBM call option with an exercise price of 100 and a January maturity has a price of $3.625. To buy this contract, it would cost $3.625 × 100 = $362.50. The implied terms of this contract are that the buyer has the right to buy one hundred shares of IBM for a total amount of $10,000 at any time between November 13, 1991, and January 17, 1992 (i.e., the third Friday of January).[1]

In reporting stock option prices, a number of conventions are used. In Table 13.1, a number of cells of the table have the entry "r." This means that the particular option did not trade on that day. Other cells have the entry "s," implying that the particular option contract does not exist. Also, beneath the firm's ticker symbol, the closing stock price is reported. This is done for convenience, so the reader does have to turn to the stock market page to find the closing price of the underlying stock.

One final note about Table 13.1 is that the most actively traded stock options on the various exchanges are listed. These are simply the option contracts with the greatest number of transactions on that day. Interspersed among the stock options are usually some stock index options, the subject of the next chapter. In the CBOE active option list, for example, nine of the ten most active options are written on the S&P 100 index.

13.2 PRICE BOUNDS AND ARBITRAGE RELATIONS

The lower price bounds and the put-call parity relations for stock options are presented for non-dividend- and dividend-paying stocks. Without dividends, the arbitrage relations are straightforward since a common stock is a commodity for which the cost-of-carry-rate, b, equals the riskless rate of interest, r. With dividends, the relations are modified slightly to account for the fact that the underlying stock drops in price at the ex-dividend instant, while the exercise price does not.[2] As a result, an anticipated cash dividend generally reduces the value of calls and increases the value of puts.

---

[1] For practical purposes, assuming the option expires Friday seems prudent since both the stock market and the option market are closed on Saturday.

[2] The exercise price is, however, adjusted for stock splits and stock dividends. Where the stock split/dividend produces a fractional result, the exercise price is rounded to the nearest eighth.

TABLE 13.1 Stock option contract prices.

LISTED OPTIONS QUOTATIONS

Wednesday, November 13, 1991

Options closing prices. Sales unit usually is 100 shares.
Stock close is New York or American exchange final price.

CHICAGO BOARD

Option & NY Close	Strike Price	Calls-Last Nov	Calls-Last Dec	Calls-Last Jan	Puts-Last Nov	Puts-Last Dec	Puts-Last Jan
Alcoa	55	r	s	8¼	r	s	r
61⅞	60	r	3	4	1/16	1 1/16	1 13/16
61⅞	65	r	⅞	1¾	3¼	3½	4½
61⅞	70	r	r	½	r	r	8¼
61⅞	75	s	s	⅛	s	s	r
AmGenl	40	r	r	3⅞	r	r	½
43½	45	1/16	r	⅞	r	r	r
Chryslr	10	r	r	3⅛	r	1/16	⅛
13	12½	9/16	¾	1 1/16	1/16	½	¾
13	15	r	⅛	5/16	r	2⅜	2⅜
Cisco	45	7⅞	8¾	r	r	r	⅞
54¾	50	4½	6	6⅝	r	r	r
54¾	55	r	3¼	4	r	3	r
Citicp	10	s	1¾	1⅞	s	r	5/16
11½	12½	1/16	7/16	½	1 1/16	r	1 5/16
11½	15	r	s	⅛	3¾	s	3⅝
Homstk	12½	r	r	2⅞	r	r	r
15⅜	15	7/16	15/16	1⅛	1/16	5/16	11/16
15⅜	17½	r	1/16	⅜	r	r	r
I B M	90	r	s	10¼	r	s	11/16
98⅞	95	4	5⅜	6⅝	1/16	15/16	1 11/16
98⅞	100	⅜	2½	3⅝	1⅜	2 15/16	3¾
98⅞	105	1/16	⅞	1 13/16	6⅜	6¼	r
98⅞	110	r	s	13/16	r	s	11⅜
98⅞	115	r	s	⅜	r	s	r
In Pap	65	8	s	r	r	s	r
74⅜	70	3¼	3¾	r	r	¾	1⅞

Option & NY Close	Strike Price	Calls-Last Nov	Calls-Last Dec	Calls-Last Feb	Puts-Last Nov	Puts-Last Dec	Puts-Last Feb
17⅝	20	r	r	r	3	r	r
Boeing	40	9	s	r	r	s	r
49¼	45	4¼	4½	5½	r	¼	⅞
49¼	50	⅛	1⅛	2 3/16	1	1⅝	2½
49¼	55	1/16	3/16	⅝	6	5⅞	6½
Bois C	22½	r	r	r	r	r	½
25½	25	9/16	r	1⅝	1/16	r	r
C B S	150	5	r	r	r	1⅞	r
155½	155	1 9/16	4⅜	10	1⅛	r	7⅜
155½	160	¼	2⅞	7	4½	7	r
Honwll	55	5¼	r	6½	r	r	1⅝
60	60	¾	2¼	3¾	⅝	r	r
60	65	r	r	1½	r	r	r
Humana	25	2⅝	r	3¼	r	½	r
27⅜	30	r	9/16	r	2 15/16	3	r
27⅜	35	r	r	r	7⅝	r	r
ImunRs	35	r	r	r	3/16	2	3⅝
46	40	9	9⅛	14⅜	½	3¼	5¼
46	45	3⅛	7	9½	1⅜	5⅜	7
TelMex	35	r	r	11	r	r	5/16
45¼	40	5¼	5¾	7	r	⅜	r
45¼	45	11/16	2¼	3⅞	r	1 13/16	2 15/16
45¼	50	r	⅝	1 13/16	r	5¼	6⅛
Tribune	40	r	⅜	1⅜	r	r	r
TritEn	40	8½	8¾	11⅛	r	⅞	r
48	45	3½	5½	7⅜	¼	2½	r
48	50	9/16	3½	5¾	2 3/16	r	r
48	55	r	1⅝	4¼	r	r	r
UAL	20	r	s	r	1/16	s	r
131⅞	25	6¾	s	r	r	s	5¼

Option & NY Close	Strike Price	Calls-Last Nov	Calls-Last Dec	Calls-Last Mar	Puts-Last Nov	Puts-Last Dec	Puts-Last Mar
Oracle	7½	s	r	7½	s	r	r
15½	12½	2⅝	3	r	r	r	r
15½	15	½	1 5/16	2⅜	r	⅝	r
15½	17½	r	r	1⅛	r	r	3
Pall	30	r	r	r	r	r	⅜
38⅛	35	r	r	r	r	r	1
38⅛	40	r	r	2	r	r	r
38⅛	45	s	r	9/16	s	r	r
ParaCm	35	6⅜	6½	r	r	r	½
41¼	40	1 5/16	2⅜	4	1/16	⅞	2¼

AMERICAN

Option & NY Close	Strike Price	Calls-Last Nov	Calls-Last Dec	Calls-Last Jan	Puts-Last Nov	Puts-Last Dec	Puts-Last Jan
Aetna	30	r	r	r	r	r	⅛
41⅜	35	r	r	6⅞	r	r	⅜
41⅜	40	1½	2¼	3	⅛	⅞	1¼
34⅞	40	r	r	r	r	r	5⅜
Cabltr	40	4⅜	5¼	r	1/16	r	r
43½	45	⅜	3¼	3¾	r	r	r
43½	50	r	1 1/16	r	r	r	r
Cetus	12½	s	s	6½	s	s	r
19	15	3⅞	r	4½	r	r	r
19	17½	1½	2 1/16	2⅝	r	⅜	¾
19	20	1/16	½	1 3/16	r	r	r
Chips	7½	r	r	1⅛	r	r	r
8⅜	10	r	r	5/16	r	r	r
Chiron	60	r	s	13½	r	s	r

MOST ACTIVE OPTIONS

CHICAGO BOARD

	Sales	Last	Chg	N.Y. Close
CALLS				
SP100 Nov 370	50767	2 5/16	+ 3/16	371.20
SP100 Nov 365	30573	6⅜	+ ½	371.20
SP100 Nov 375	9832	⅜	− 1/16	371.20
SP100 Nov 360	9570	11¼	+ ¾	371.20
SP100 Dec 370	8047	7⅜	+ ¾	371.20
SP100 Dec 375	7012	4⅜	+ ½	371.20
SP100 Nov 380	5476	1/16	− 1/16	371.20
I B M Nov 100	4699	⅜	− 3/16	98⅞
SP100 Dec 365	4243	10⅝	+ ⅛	371.20
TelMex Feb 50	3172	1 13/16	− 1/16	45¼
PUTS				
SP100 Nov 370	33791	1 1/16	− 1 1/16	371.20
SP100 Nov 365	28524	5/16	− ⅜	371.20
SP100 Nov 360	13976	⅛	− ⅛	371.20
SP100 Dec 365	10083	3⅝	− ½	371.20
SP100 Dec 360	7759	2½	− 5/16	371.20
SP100 Nov 355	5404	1/16	− 1/16	371.20
SP100 Nov 375	5266	4⅛	− 1¼	371.20
SP100 Dec 370	4556	5¼	− ½	371.20
SP100 Dec 340	3482	⅝	− 1/16	371.20
SP500 Nov 390	3445	¼	− 3/16	397.41

AMERICAN

	Sales	Last	Chg	N.Y. Close
CALLS				
Glaxo Dec 30	3534	1 11/16	+ 1 11/16	30⅜
RJR Nb Nov 7½	2964	2⅝	− 1/16	10⅛
MMIdx Nov 325	2496	3⅛	+ 1	327.25
Dig Eq Nov 60	2214	2⅞	+ ⅝	62¾
Ph Mor Nov 70	1946	¾	− ⅛	70⅝
RJR Nb Dec 7½	1900	2⅝	− 1/16	10⅛
TelMex Feb 50	1821	1⅞	+ 3/16	45¼
MMIdx Nov 320	1632	7½	+ 1¼	327.25
Gillet Dec 45	1599	1⅜	+ ⅛	44¾
TritEn Nov 50	1549	¾	+ 9/16	48
PUTS				
Disney Nov 110	2089	1	+ ⅝	110⅜
RJR Nb Dec 10	2010	¼	...	10⅛
RJR Nb Dec 7½	1900	1/16	...	10⅛
RJR Nb Nov 7½	1900	1/16	...	10⅛
MMIdx Nov 325	1627	11/16	− 13/16	327.25
Disney Dec 110	1054	3¼	+ 1	110⅜
MMIdx Nov 320	1035	⅛	− ¼	327.25
Chase Nov 15	1000	⅛	...	18¼
Ph Mor Nov 70	925	3/16	...	70⅝
Pfizer Nov 70	779	11/16	+ 5/16	70⅛

PHILADELPHIA

	Sales	Last	Chg	N.Y. Close
CALLS				
NCNB Dec 35	2225	4⅛	+ ¼	39
NCNB Nov 35	2130	4	+ ⅛	39
RJR Nb Nov 10	1800	3/16	− 1/16	10⅛
RJR Nb Dec 10	1750	7/16	...	10⅛
RJR Nb Nov 7½	1049	2⅝	+ 1/16	10⅛
Synrgn Nov 65	965	⅜	− 2½	59⅞
HomeD Nov 60	805	1	− ⅜	60¾
HomeD Dec 60	775	3⅛	− ⅛	60¾
Synrgn Nov 60	619	1 13/16	− 4 5/16	59⅞
Abbt L Dec 55	571	6⅜	− ⅜	61⅛
PUTS				
HomeD Dec 55	2187	¾	+ ¼	60¾
Comeric Jan 50	2000	1	− 1⅜	52¼
Synrgn Nov 65	1074	5½	+ 3⅝	59⅞
BkBost Nov 12½	1020	¼	...	12½
SecPac Dec 35	578	4⅜	+ ⅛	31⅜
RJR Nb Nov 12½	515	2⅜	...	10⅛
HomeD Dec 50	505	¼	+ 1/16	60¾
RJR Nb Dec 10	500	¼	...	10⅛
Abbt L Feb 60	434	2	− 3/16	61⅛
HomeD Nov 60	426	¼	...	60¾

Source: Reprinted by permission of *Wall Street Journal*, © (November 14, 1991) Dow Jones & Company, Inc. All Rights Reserved Worldwide.

Non-Dividend-Paying Stocks

To derive the lower price bounds and the put-call parity relations for options on non-dividend-paying stocks, simply set the cost-of-carry rate, b, equal to the riskless rate of interest, r, in the relations presented in Chapter 10. The only cost of carrying the stock is interest.

The lower price bounds for the European call and put options are

$$c(S, T; X) \geq \max[0, S - Xe^{-rT}] \tag{13.1a}$$

and

$$p(S, T; X) \geq \max[0, Xe^{-rT} - S], \tag{13.1b}$$

respectively, and the lower price bounds for the American call and put options are

$$C(S, T; X) \geq \max[0, S - Xe^{-rT}] \tag{13.2a}$$

and

$$P(S, T; X) \geq \max[0, X - S], \tag{13.2b}$$

respectively. The put-call parity relation for non-dividend-paying European stock options[3] is

$$c(S, T; X) - p(S, T; X) = S - Xe^{-rT}, \tag{13.3a}$$

and the put-call parity relation for American options on non-dividend-paying stocks is

$$S - X \leq C(S, T; X) - P(S, T; X) \leq S - Xe^{-rT}. \tag{13.3b}$$

For non-dividend-paying stock options, the American call option will not rationally be exercised early, while the American put option may be.[4]

Dividend-Paying Stocks

If dividends are paid during the option's life, the above relations must reflect the stock's drop in value when the dividends are paid. To manage this modification, we assume that the underlying stock pays a single dividend during the option's life

---

[3]The original formulation of put-call parity for European stock options is contained in Stoll (1969).
[4]For proofs of any of the relations (13.1a) through (13.3b), see Chapter 10.

at a time that is known with certainty. The dividend amount is D and the time to ex-dividend is t.[5]

If the amount and the timing of the dividend payment is known, the lower price bound for the European call option on a stock is

$$c(S, T; X) \geq \max[0, S - De^{-rt} - Xe^{-rT}]. \qquad \textbf{(13.4a)}$$

In this relation, the current stock price is reduced by the present value of the promised dividend. Because a European-style option cannot be exercised before maturity, the call option holder has no opportunity to exercise the option while the stock is selling cum dividend. In other words, to the call option holder, the current value of the underlying stock is its observed market price less the amount that the promised dividend contributes to the current stock value, that is, $S - De^{-rt}$. To prove this pricing relation, we use the same arbitrage transactions as in Chapter 10, except we use the reduced stock price $S - De^{-rt}$ in place of S.

The lower price bound for the European put option on a stock is

$$p(S, T; X) \geq \max[0, Xe^{-rT} - S + De^{-rt}]. \qquad \textbf{(13.4b)}$$

Again, the stock price is reduced by the present value of the promised dividend. Unlike the call option case, however, this serves to increase the lower price bound of the European put option. Because the put option is the right to sell the underlying stock at a fixed price, a discrete drop in the stock price such as that induced by the payment of a dividend serves to increase the value of the option. An arbitrage proof of this relation is straightforward when the stock price, net of the present value of the dividend is used in place of the commodity price.

The lower price bounds for American stock options are slightly more complex. In the case of the American call option, for example, it may be optimal to exercise just prior to the dividend payment because the stock price falls by an amount D when the dividend is paid. The lower price bound of an American call option expiring at the ex-dividend instant would be 0 or $S - Xe^{-rt}$, whichever is greater. On the other hand, it may be optimal to wait until the call option's expiration to exercise. The lower price bound for a call option expiring normally is (13.4a).[6] Combining the two results, we get

$$C(S, T; X) \geq \max[0, S - Xe^{-rt}, S - De^{-rt} - Xe^{-rT}]. \qquad \textbf{(13.5a)}$$

---

[5] Generalizations of the results to cases where there are more than one known dividend are derived in the same manner as the single dividend results shown here.

[6] Recall that in Chapter 10 we showed that an American call is never optimally exercised early if $b \geq r$. Between dividends, the cost-of-carry rate is r, so exercise is not optimal. At the ex-dividend instant, however, the call option holder may wish to exercise to capture the dividend.

The last two terms on the right-hand side of (13.5a) provide important guidance in deciding whether to exercise the American call option early, just prior to the ex-dividend instant. The second term in the squared brackets is the present value of the early exercise proceeds of the call. If the amount is less than the lower price bound of the call that expires normally, that is, if

$$S - Xe^{-rt} < S - De^{-rt} - Xe^{-rT}, \tag{13.6}$$

the American call option will not be exercised just prior to the ex-dividend instant. To see why, simply rewrite (13.6) so it reads

$$D < X[1 - e^{-r(T-t)}]. \tag{13.7}$$

In other words, the American call will not be exercised early if the dividend captured by exercising prior to the ex-dividend date is less than the interest implicitly earned by deferring exercise until expiration.

Figure 13.1 depicts a case in which early exercise could occur at the ex-dividend instant, t. Just prior to ex-dividend, the call option may be exercised yielding proceeds $S_t + D - X$, where S_t is the ex-dividend stock price. An instant later, the option is left unexercised with value $c(S_t, T - t; X)$, where $c(\cdot)$ is the European call option formula. Thus, if the ex-dividend stock price, S_t, is above the critical ex-dividend stock price where the two functions intersect, S_t^*, the option holder will choose to exercise her option early just prior to the ex-dividend instant. On the other hand, if $S_t \le S_t^*$, the option holder will choose to leave her position open until the option's expiration.

FIGURE 13.1   American call option price as a function of the ex-dividend stock price immediately prior to the ex-dividend instant. Early exercise may be optimal.

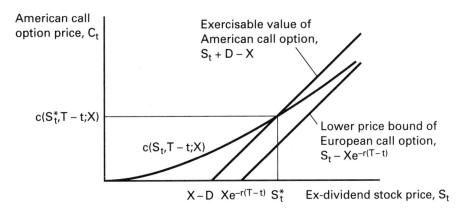

FIGURE 13.2   American call option price as a function of the ex-dividend stock price immediately prior to the ex-dividend instant. Early exercise will not be optimal.

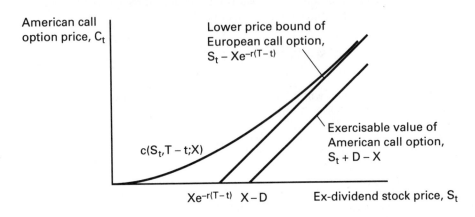

Figure 13.2 depicts a case in which early exercise will not occur at the ex-dividend instant, t. Early exercise will not occur if the functions, $S_t + D - X$ and $c(S_t, T - t; X)$ do not intersect, as is depicted in Figure 13.2. In this case, the lower boundary condition of the European call, $S_t - Xe^{-r(T-t)}$, lies above the early exercise proceeds, $S_t + D - X$, and hence the call option will not be exercised early. Stated explicitly, early exercise is not rational if

$$S_t + D - X < S_t - Xe^{-r(T-t)}.$$

This condition for no early exercise is the same as (13.6), where S_t is the ex-dividend stock price and where the investor is standing at the ex-dividend instant, t. The condition can also be written as

$$D < X[1 - e^{-r(T-t)}]. \tag{13.7}$$

In words, if the ex-dividend stock price decline—the dividend—is less than the present value of the interest income that would be earned by deferring exercise until expiration, early exercise will not occur. When condition (13.7) is met, the value of the American call is simply the value of the corresponding European call.

The lower price bound of an American put option is somewhat different. In the absence of a dividend, an American put may be exercised early. In the presence of a dividend payment, however, there is a period just prior to the ex-dividend date when early exercise is suboptimal. In that period, the interest earned on the exercise proceeds of the option is less than the drop in the stock price from the payment of the dividend. If t_n represents a time prior to the dividend payment at time t, early exercise is suboptimal, where $(X - S)e^{r(t - t_n)}$ is less than $(X - S + D)$. Rearranging, early exercise will not occur between t_n and t if [7]

$$t_n > t - \frac{\ln(1 + \frac{D}{X - S})}{r}.$$ (13.8)

Early exercise will become a possibility again immediately after the dividend is paid. Overall, the lower price bound of the American put option is

$$P(S, T; X) \geq \max[0, X - (S - De^{-rt})].$$ (13.5b)

Put-call parity for European options on dividend-paying stocks also reflects the fact that the current stock price is deflated by the present value of the promised dividend, that is,

$$c(S, T; X) - p(S, T; X) = S - De^{-rt} - Xe^{-rT}.$$ (13.9)

That the presence of the dividend reduces the value of the call and increases the value of the put is again reflected here by the fact that the term on the right-hand side of (13.9) is smaller than it would be if the stock paid no dividend.

Put-call parity for American options on dividend-paying stocks is represented by a pair of inequalities, that is,

$$S - De^{-rt} - X \leq C(S, T; X) - P(S, T; X) \leq S - De^{-rt} - Xe^{-rT}.$$ (13.10)

To prove the put-call parity relation (13.10), we consider each inequality in turn. The left-hand side condition of (13.10) can be derived by considering the values of a portfolio that consists of buying a call, selling a put, selling the stock, and lending $X + De^{-rt}$ risklessly. Table 13.2 contains these portfolio values.

In Table 13.2, it can be seen that, if all of the security positions stay open until expiration, the terminal value of the portfolio will be positive, independent of whether the terminal stock price is above or below the exercise price of the options. If the terminal stock price is above the exercise price, the call option is exercised, and the stock acquired at exercise price X is used to deliver, in part, against the short stock position. If the terminal stock price is below the exercise price, the put

---

[7] It is possible that the dividend payment is so large that early exercise prior to the dividend payment is completely precluded. For example, consider the case where $X = 50$, $S = 40$, $D = 1$, $t = .25$ and $r = .10$. Early exercise is precluded if $t_n = .25 - \ln[1 - 1/(50 - 40)]/.10 = -.7031$. Because the value is negative, the implication is that there is no time during the current dividend period (i.e., from 0 to t) where it will not pay the American put option holder to wait until the dividend is paid to exercise his option.

TABLE 13.2   Arbitrage transactions for establishing put-call parity for American stock options. $S - De^{-rt} - X \le C(S,T;X) - P(S,T;X)$

Position	Initial Value	Ex-Dividend Day (t)	Put Exercised Early (τ) Intermediate Value	Put Exercised Normally (T) Terminal Value $\tilde{S}_T \le X$	$\tilde{S}_T > X$
Buy American Call	$-C$		$\tilde{C}_\tau$	0	$\tilde{S}_T - X$
Sell American Put	P		$-(X - \tilde{S}_\tau)$	$-(X - \tilde{S}_T)$	0
Sell Stock	S	$-D$	$-\tilde{S}_\tau$	$-\tilde{S}_T$	$-\tilde{S}_T$
Lend De^{-rt}	$-De^{-rt}$	D			
Lend X	$-X$		$Xe^{r\tau}$	Xe^{rT}	Xe^{rT}
Net Portfolio Value	$-C + P$ $+S - De^{-rt}$ $-X$	0	$\tilde{C}_\tau +$ $X(e^{r\tau} - 1)$	$X(e^{rT} - 1)$	$X(e^{rT} - 1)$

is exercised. The stock received in the exercise of the put is used to cover the short stock position established at the outset. In the event the put is exercised early at time τ, the investment in the riskless bonds is more than sufficient to cover the payment of the exercise price to the put option holder, and the stock received from the exercise of the put is used to cover the stock sold when the portfolio was formed. In addition, an open call option position that may still have value remains. In other words, by forming the portfolio of securities in the proportions noted above, we have formed a portfolio that will never have a negative future value. If the future value is certain to be nonnegative, the initial value must be nonpositive, or the left-hand inequality of (13.10) holds.

The right-hand side of (13.10) may be derived by considering the portfolio used to prove European put-call parity. Table 13.3 contains the arbitrage portfolio transactions. In this case, the terminal value of the portfolio is certain to equal zero, should the option positions stay open until that time. In the event the American call option holder decides to exercise the call option early, the portfolio holder uses his long stock position to cover his stock obligation on the exercised call and uses the exercise proceeds to retire his outstanding debt. After these actions are taken, the portfolio holder still has an open long put position and cash in the amount of $X[1 - e^{-r(T-t)}]$. Since the portfolio is certain to have nonnegative outcomes, the initial value must be nonpositive or the right-hand inequality of (13.10) must hold.

13.3 VALUATION OF CALL OPTIONS ON STOCKS

European Call Option on Non-Dividend-Paying Stocks

A non-dividend-paying stock has a cost-of-carry rate, b, equal to the riskless rate of interest, r, so, using equation (11.25) from Chapter 11, the *valuation equation*

TABLE 13.3   Arbitrage transactions for establishing put-call parity for American stock options. $C(S,T;X) - P(S,T;X) \le S - De^{-rt} - Xe^{-rT}$

Position	Initial Ex-Dividend	Ex-Dividend Day (t) Value	Call Exercised Early (τ) Intermediate Value	Call Exercised Normally (T) Terminal Value $\tilde{S}_T \le X$	$\tilde{S}_T > X$
Sell American Call	C		$-(\tilde{S}_\tau - X)$	0	$-(\tilde{S}_T - X)$
Buy American Put	$-P$		$\tilde{P}_\tau$	$X - \tilde{S}_T$	0
Buy Stock	$-S$	D	$\tilde{S}_\tau$	$\tilde{S}_T$	$\tilde{S}_T$
Borrow De^{-rt}	De^{-rt}	$-D$			
Borrow Xe^{-rT}	Xe^{-rT}		$-Xe^{-r(T-\tau)}$	$-X$	$-X$
Net Portfolio Value	$C - P - S$ $+De^{-rt} + Xe^{-rT}$	0	$\tilde{P}_\tau$ $+X[1 - e^{-r(T-t)}]$	0	0

of a European call option on a non-dividend-paying stock[8] is

$$c(S,T;X) = SN(d_1) - Xe^{-rT}N(d_2), \qquad \textbf{(13.11)}$$

where

$$d_1 = \frac{\ln(S/X) + (r + .5\sigma^2)T}{\sigma\sqrt{T}}, \quad \text{and} \quad d_2 = d_1 - \sigma\sqrt{T}.$$

European Call Option on Dividend-Paying Stocks

In the presence of a known discrete dividend, option valuation remains relatively straightforward. In place of assuming that future stock prices are lognormally distributed, we now assume that stock prices, net of the present value of the escrowed dividend, are lognormally distributed. The dividend to be paid during the option's life is a known amount on a known date. At the ex-dividend instant, the stock price drops by the amount of the dividend. The stock price net of the present value of the dividend, however, remains unchanged.

Under this modified assumption, the valuation equations for European options maintain the same structure as in Chapter 11. The only change is that the current stock price net of the present value of the promised dividend,

$$S^x = S - De^{-rt}, \qquad \textbf{(13.12)}$$

---

[8] This equation is often referred to as simply the *Black–Scholes formula*, given the important impact that the Black–Scholes (1973) paper has had on the theory of option pricing and, more generally, the practice of finance.

is substituted for the stock price parameter in the European call option pricing formula (13.11). The *valuation equation of a European call option on a dividend-paying stock* is

$$c(S, T; X) = S^x N(d_1) - Xe^{-rT} N(d_2), \qquad \textbf{(13.13)}$$

where

$$d_1 = \frac{\ln(S^x/X) + (r + .5\sigma^2)T}{\sigma\sqrt{T}}, \quad \text{and} \quad d_2 = d_1 - \sigma\sqrt{T}.$$

Naturally, the value of the call decreases as a result of the cash disbursement on the stock.

American Call Option on Non-Dividend-Paying Stocks

In Chapter 11, we showed that if the cost-of-carry rate of the underlying commodity is greater than or equal to the riskless rate of interest (i.e., $b \geq r$), the American call option on the commodity will never be optimally exercised early and its value equals the value of a European call option. In the case of a non-dividend-paying stock, the cost-of-carry rate equals the riskless rate of interest. Hence, the *valuation equation of a American call option on a non-dividend-paying stock* is (13.11).

American Call Option on Dividend-Paying Stocks

When a stock pays a dividend, the problem of valuing an American call is more complex. Whereas an American call option on a non-dividend-paying stock will never optimally be exercised prior to expiration, an American call option on a dividend-paying stock *may* be. This situation arises because the stock price falls at the ex-dividend instant, which causes the call to drop in value. It may be optimal for the American call option holder to exercise his option just prior to this ex-dividend stock price drop.

The easiest way to derive the valuation equation for the American call option on a dividend-paying stock is to use the risk-neutral option valuation. Consider the American call option holder's dilemma as depicted in Figure 13.1. At time t, the American option holder will exercise his option if $S_t > S_t^*$ and will leave his position open if $S_t \leq S_t^*$. And, if he leaves his position open at t, his option will have terminal values $\tilde{S}_T - X$ if $S_T > X$ and 0 if $S_T \leq X$. Recognizing that the option's payoffs will occur at one of two points in time (i.e., just prior to the early exercise instant or at expiration) allows us to write the current value of the call as the present value of the expected future payoffs, that is,

$$
\begin{aligned}
C(S, T; X) &= e^{-rt} E(\tilde{C}_t | S_t > S_t^*) + e^{-rT} E(\tilde{C}_T | S_t \leq S_t^*) \\
&= e^{-rt} E(\tilde{S}_t + D - X | S_t > S_t^*) \\
&\quad + e^{-rT} E(\tilde{S}_T - X | S_t \leq S_t^* \text{ and } S_T > X)
\end{aligned}
$$

$$= e^{-rt}[E(\tilde{S}_t|S_t > S_t^*) - (X - D)\text{Prob}(S_t > S_t^*)]$$
$$+ e^{-rT}[E(\tilde{S}_T|S_t \leq S_t^* \text{ and } S_T > X)$$
$$- X\text{Prob}(S_t \leq S_t^* \text{ and } S_T > X)]. \qquad \textbf{(13.14)}$$

Assuming that the future stock price net of the present value of the promised dividend is lognormally distributed, the expected values on the right-hand side of (13.14) become the *valuation equation of an American call option on a dividend-paying stock*:

$$C(S, T; X) = e^{-rt}[S^x e^{rt} N_1(b_1) - (X - D)N_1(b_2)]$$
$$+ e^{-rT}[S^x e^{rT} N_2(a_1, -b_1; -\sqrt{t/T})$$
$$- X N_2(a_2, -b_2; -\sqrt{t/T})] \qquad \textbf{(13.15a)}$$

$$= S^x[N_1(b_1) + N_2(a_1, -b_1; -\sqrt{t/T})]$$
$$- X e^{-rT}[N_1(b_2)e^{r(T-t)} + N_2(a_2, -b_2; -\sqrt{t/T})]$$
$$+ D e^{-rt} N_1(b_2), \qquad \textbf{(13.15b)}$$

where

$$a_1 = \frac{\ln(S^x/X) + (r + .5\sigma^2)T}{\sigma\sqrt{T}}, \quad a_2 = a_1 - \sigma\sqrt{T},$$

$$b_1 = \frac{\ln(S^x/S_t^*) + (r + .5\sigma^2)t}{\sigma\sqrt{t}}, \quad b_2 = b_1 - \sigma\sqrt{t},$$

$N_1(b)$ is the cumulative univariate normal density function with upper integral limit b[9] and $N_2(a, b; \rho)$ is the cumulative bivariate normal density function with upper integral limits, a and b, and correlation coefficient, ρ.[10] S_t^* is the ex-dividend stock price for which

$$c(S_t^*, T - t; X) = S_t^* + D - X, \qquad \textbf{(13.15c)}$$

as noted earlier in the discussion of Figure 13.1.[11]

---

[9] Recall that the function $N(b)$ was used for the first time in Chapter 11. The subscript 1 is used here only to contrast the univariate integral from the bivariate integral.

[10] More details about the bivariate normal probability, as well as a method of computation and a numerical example, are contained in Appendix 13.1.

[11] Roll (1977) provides a framework for analytically valuing the American call option. The valuation formula (13.15b) is from Whaley (1981).

In equation (13.15a), the American call formula is the sum of the present values of two conditional expected values—the present value of the expected early exercise value of the option conditional on early exercise, $S^x N_1(b_1) - (X - D)e^{-rt}N_1(b_2)$, and the present value of the expected terminal exercise value of the call conditional on no early exercise, $S^x N_1(a_1, -b_1; -\sqrt{t/T}) - Xe^{-rT}N_2(a_2, -b_2; -\sqrt{t/T})$. The term $N_1(b_2)$ is the probability that the call option will be exercised early, and the term $N_2(a_2, -b_2; -\sqrt{t/T})$ is the joint probability that the call option will not be exercised early and will be in-the-money at expiration.

Note that as the amount of the dividend approaches the present value of the interest income that would be earned by deferring exercise until expiration, that is, $D \to X[1 - e^{-r(T-t)}]$, the value of S_t^* approaches $+\infty$, the values of $N_1(b_1)$ and $N_1(b_2)$ approach 0, the values of $N_2(a_1, -b_1; -\sqrt{t/T})$ and $N_2(a_2, -b_2; -\sqrt{t/T})$ approach $N_1(a_1)$ and $N_1(a_2)$, respectively, and the American call option formula (13.15b) becomes the dividend-adjusted Black–Scholes European call option formula (13.13).

EXAMPLE 13.1

Compute the value of an American-style call option whose exercise price is $50 and whose time to expiration is 90 days. Assume the riskless rate of interest is 10 percent annually, the underlying stock price is $50, the standard deviation of the rate of return of the stock is 30 percent, and the stock pays a dividend of $2 in exactly 60 days.

We compute the value of this call first using the European formula (13.13) and then using the American formula (13.15b). In this way, we can identify the value of the early exercise premium on the call.

The current stock price net of the present value of the promised dividend is

$$S^x = 50 - 2e^{-.10(60/365)} = 48.033,$$

so the European call value can be computed as

$$c = 48.033 N_1(d_1) - 50e^{-.10(90/365)} N_1(d_2),$$

where

$$d_1 = \frac{[\ln(48.033/50) + (.10 + .5(.30)^2)(90/365)]}{.30\sqrt{90/365}} = -.029$$

and $d_2 = -.029 - .149 = -.178$. The probabilities $N_1(-.029)$ and $N_1(-.178)$ are .488 and .429, so the European call value is

$$c = 48.033(.488) - 48.782(.429) = 2.51.$$

Prior to applying the valuation equation for the American call option on a dividend-paying stock (13.15b), we must determine if there is a chance of early exercise. Recall that if condition (13.7) holds, the call will not be exercised early. Substituting the exercise values into (13.7), we find

$$2 > 50[1 - e^{-.10(90-60)/365}] = .409,$$

showing that early exercise is not precluded and that formula (13.15b) should be used.

The value of the American call is now computed as

$$
\begin{aligned}
C = {} & 48.033[N_1(b_1) + N_2(a_1, -b_1; -\sqrt{t/T})] \\
& - 50e^{-.10(90/365)}[N_1(b_2)e^{.10(30/365)} + N_2(a_2, -b_2; -\sqrt{t/T})] \\
& + 2e^{-.10(60/365)}N_1(b_2),
\end{aligned}
$$

where $t/T = (60/365)/(90/365) = 60/90 = .667$,

$$a_1 = \frac{\ln(48.033/50) + (.10 + .5(.30)^2)(90/365)}{.30\sqrt{90/365}} = -.029$$

$$a_2 = -.029 - .30\sqrt{90/365} = -.178$$

$$b_1 = \frac{\ln(48.033/49.824) + (.10 + .5(.30)^2)(60/365)]}{.30\sqrt{60/365}} = -.105$$

and

$$b_2 = -.105 - .30\sqrt{60/365} = -.227.$$

The values b_1 and b_2 depend on the critical ex-dividend stock price S_t^*, which is determined by

$$c(S_t^*, 30/365; 50) = S_t^* + 2 - 50$$

and, in this example, equals 49.824. The bivariate normal probabilities are $N_2(a_1, -b_1; -\rho) = .1135$ and $N_2(a_2, -b_2; -\rho) = .1056$, and the univariate normal probabilities are $N_1(b_1) = .4581$ and $N_1(b_2) = .4103$. The value of the American call is 2.931; hence, the early exercise premium on the American option is $2.931 - 2.513 = .418$.

TABLE 13.4   Simulated American and European call option values on a stock with a known discrete dividend. The call option has an exercise price of $50 and a time to expiration of 90 days. The riskless rate of interest is 10 percent, and the standard deviation of the stock return is 30 percent. The stock pays a dividend of $2 in 60 days.

Stock Price S	European Call Price $c(S,T;X)$	American Call Price $C(S,T;X)$	Early Exercise Premium ϵ_C
40	.126	.136	.011
45	.760	.867	.107
50	2.515	2.931	.418
55	5.610	6.481	.871
60	9.726	10.974	1.248

The size of the early exercise premium of an American call option on a dividend-paying stock becomes larger as the option goes deeper in the money. In Table 13.4, we extend the results of Example 13.1 by allowing the stock price to vary from $40 to $60. It is interesting to note that the dividend payment induces a fairly large early exercise premium on the call option, particularly when the call is deep in-the-money. At a $60 stock price, for example, the value of the early exercise premium is about $1.25, more than 11 percent of the call's overall value.

Dividend Spreads

In practice, not all call options are exercised when they should be. And, when they are not, there are ways to profit risklessly. Consider, for example, two in-the-money call options written on a stock that is about to pay a dividend. Assume the deeper in-the-money call is sold and the other is purchased. Now, on the day before ex-dividend, exercise the purchased option and wait. If the holder of the deeper in-the-money call exercises her option before ex-dividend, deliver the stock received from the exercise of the purchased option and pay the net difference between the exercise prices of the options. On the other hand, suppose the holder of the deeper in-the-money call option forgets to exercise her option. In this case, sell the stock the next morning and buy back the remaining option. In the first case, profit equals zero, and, in the second, a profit in the amount of the dividend would be received. A numerical example may serve to clarify this strategy.

Assume that a stock is currently priced at $60 and will pay a $2.00 dividend tomorrow. Call options with exercise prices of 50 and 55 and time to expiration of 30 days are priced at $10.01 and $5.01, respectively. (The riskless rate of interest is assumed to be 10 percent, and the standard deviation of stock returns is 30 percent.) Now, assume the 50 call is sold, and the 55 call is purchased, yielding net proceeds at the outset of $5.00. At the end of the day, the investor exercises the 55 call, receiving proceeds $S_{t-1} + 2.00 - 55$. (Day $t - 1$ is the day before ex-dividend, and the notation S_{t-1} is the stock price net of the value of the escrowed dividend.) If the 50 call option is exercised against the investor before ex-dividend (which will not be known until the next day before market opening), the investor's obligation is $-(S_t + 2.00 - 50)$, and the net terminal value is $S_t + 2.00 - 55 - S_t - 2.00 + 50$ or $-\$5$, exactly a wash, considering $5 was collected up front. However, if the 50 call option is not exercised, the investor goes into the next morning with a long position in the stock (acquired from exercising the 55 call) and a short position in the 50 call, which has a value $S_t + 2.00 - 55 - C_t$. For all intents and purposes, this position is riskless because the uncertainty in the value of the long stock position is offset by that of the short in-the-money call. The outstanding call, being deep in-the-money, is selling for about its floor value of $S_t - 50$, so the net value of the position is $2.00 - 55 + 50$ or $-\$3$. Net of the initial cash receipt of $5, the profit is $2.00, exactly the amount of the dividend. This strategy is usually called a *dividend capture* or a *dividend spread*.

13.4 VALUATION OF PUT OPTIONS ON STOCKS

European Put Option on Non-Dividend-Paying Stocks

The *valuation equation of a European put option on a non-dividend-paying stock* is

$$p(S, T; X) = Xe^{-rT}N(-d_2) - SN(d_1),\qquad\text{(13.16)}$$

where

$$d_1 = \frac{\ln(S/X) + (r + .5\sigma^2)T}{\sigma\sqrt{T}}, \quad \text{and} \quad d_2 = d_1 - \sigma\sqrt{T}.$$

This result follows straightforwardly from substituting the riskless rate of interest, r, for the cost-of-carry rate, b, in equation (11.28) from Chapter 11.

European Put Option on Dividend-Paying Stocks

Like the European call option on a dividend-paying stock, the European put option on a dividend-paying stock is obtained by substituting the stock price net of the present value of the dividend, $S^x = S - De^{-rt}$, for the stock price parameter in the European option pricing formula. The *valuation equation of a European put option on a dividend-paying stock* is

$$p(S, T; X) = Xe^{-rT}N(-d_2) - S^x N(-d_1),\qquad\text{(13.17)}$$

where

$$d_1 = \frac{\ln(S^x/X) + (r + .5\sigma^2)T}{\sigma\sqrt{T}}, \quad \text{and} \quad d_2 = d_1 - \sigma\sqrt{T}.$$

Note that the put value increases as a result of the cash disbursement on the stock.

American Put Option on Non-Dividend-Paying Stocks

The American put option on a non-dividend-paying stock is not a tractable problem from a mathematical standpoint, as was noted in Chapter 11. For this reason, numerical methods must be used to approximate the value of the put. The approach used here is the binomial method.[12] The binomial method assumes the stock price moves in discrete jumps over discrete intervals of time. The up-and-down steps in stock price are defined as a proportion of the stock price at the previous interval. If the current stock price is S_0, the stock price at the end of the first interval is either uS_0 or dS_0. If the total number of time steps is defined as n, where $\Delta t = T/n$ and T is the time to expiration of the option, there are $n + 1$ possible stock prices at the option's expiration. This binomial lattice is illustrated in Figure 13.3. The length of each interval or time step in the figure is Δt. The factors u and d are defined as[13]

$$u = e^{\sigma\sqrt{\Delta t}} \tag{13.18a}$$

and

$$d = \frac{1}{u}. \tag{13.18b}$$

The risk-neutral probabilities of up and down movements are

$$p = \frac{r^* - d}{u - d} \tag{13.18c}$$

and $1 - p$, respectively, where $r^* = e^{r\Delta t}$.

Figure 13.4 provides a numerical illustration of the binomial lattice for the stock price. The current stock price, S_0, is 50, the riskless rate of interest, r, is 10 percent, and the standard deviation of stock returns, σ, is 30 percent. The time to expiration of the option, T, is 90 days, and the number of time steps, n, is 90. The

---

[12] See Cox, Ross, and Rubinstein (1979).
[13] The factors are consistent with the Black–Scholes model. See Cox, Ross, and Rubinstein (1979) for details.

FIGURE 13.3   Possible paths that the stock price may follow under the binomial model.

Stock price at end of time interval:

0	1	2	3	4	$\cdots$	n (even)	or	n (odd)
						$u^n S_0$		$u^n S_0$
			$u^4 S_0$	$\cdots$				
		$u^3 S_0$				$\vdots$		$\vdots$
	$u^2 S_0$		$u^2 S_0$	$\cdots$				
$u S_0$		$u S_0$						$u S_0$
S_0	S_0		S_0	$\cdots$		S_0		
$d S_0$		$d S_0$						$d S_0$
	$d^2 S_0$		$d^2 S_0$	$\cdots$		$\vdots$		
		$d^3 S_0$						$\vdots$
			$d^4 S_0$	$\cdots$				
						$d^n S_0$		$d^n S_0$

FIGURE 13.4   Possible paths that the stock price may follow under the binomial model, where the current stock price is 50, the riskless rate of interest is 10 percent annually, and the standard deviation of stock returns is 30 percent annually. The time to expiration of the option is 90 days, and the number of time steps is also 90. The time increment Δt is, therefore, 1 day or .00274 years.

Stock price at end of time interval:

0	1	2	3	4	$\cdots$	90 days
						205.46
				53.24	$\cdots$	
			52.41			$\vdots$
		51.60		51.60	$\cdots$	
	50.79		50.79			
50		50		50	$\cdots$	50
	49.22		49.22			
		48.45		48.45	$\cdots$	$\vdots$
			47.70			
				46.96	$\cdots$	
						12.17

size of the time increment Δt is, therefore, one day or .00274 years. Based on this information, the factors u and d are

$$u = e^{.30\sqrt{.00274}} = 1.01583$$

and

$$d = \frac{1}{1.01583} = .98442.$$

Also, the probabilities of up-and-down movements are

$$p = \frac{e^{.10(.00274)} - .98442}{1.01583 - .98442} = .5048$$

and $1 - p = .4952$. Note that, in Figure 13.4, possible stock prices range from $S_0 d^n = 50(.98442)^{90} = 12.17$ to $S_0 u^n = 50(1.0158267)^{90} = 205.46$ at the option's expiration.

With the stock price lattice computed, the approximation method starts at the end of the option's life and works back to the present, one increment, Δt, at a time. At the end of the option's life (column n in the figure), the option value at each stock price node is given by the intrinsic value of the put option, that is,

$$P_{n,j}(S_{n,j}) = \begin{cases} 0 & \text{where} \quad S_{n,j} > X \\ X - S_{n,j} & \text{where} \quad S_{n,j} \leq X. \end{cases} \tag{13.19}$$

The option values one step back in time (in column $n - 1$) are computed by taking the present value of the expected future value of the option. At any point j in column $n - 1$, the stock price can move up with probability p or down with probability $1 - p$. The value of the option at time n if the stock price moves up is $P_{n,j+1}$ and if the stock price moves down is $P_{n,j}$. The present value of the expected future value of the option is, therefore,

$$P_{n-1,j} = \frac{pP_{n,j+1} + (1-p)P_{n,j}}{r^*}, \tag{13.20}$$

where $r^* = e^{r\Delta t}$. Using this present value formulation, all of the option values in column $n - 1$ may be identified.

Before proceeding back another time increment, Δt, in the valuation, it is necessary to see if any of the computed option values are below their early exercise proceeds at the respective nodes, $X - S_{n-1,j}$. If the exercise proceeds are greater than the computed option value, the computed value is replaced with the early exercise proceeds. If they are not, the value is left undisturbed. If this step is not performed, the procedure will produce the value of a European put option.

Once the checks are performed, we go to column $n - 2$, repeat the steps and so on back through time. Eventually, we will work our way back to time 0, and the current value of the American put option (in column 0) will be identified.

To complete the binomial method illustration, suppose that the stock price lattice shown in Figure 13.4 underlies a 90-day American put option with an exercise price of 50. Applying the binomial method, the value of the American put is $2.475. The value of this put using the European formula (13.16) is $2.364, which means that the early exercise premium of the American put is worth about 11.1¢. Note that the value produced by the binomial method for the European put (by not checking for the early exercise constraints) is $2.355, which is different from the $2.364 obtained using the European formula. This is error due to the fact that the binomial method is only an approximation. In general, the accuracy of the binomial method increases with the number of time steps, holding other factors constant.

American Put Option on Dividend-Paying Stocks

The binomial method is also well suited to handle the case of valuing an American put option on a dividend-paying stock. If the dividends paid during the put's life are known with certainty, we first subtract the present value of the dividends from the current stock price, that is,

$$S_0^x = S_0 - \sum_{i=1}^{n} D_i e^{-rt_i}, \tag{13.21}$$

where D_i (t_i) is the amount of (time to) the i-th dividend paid during the option's life and S_0 is the current stock price. Next, we set up the binomial lattice, beginning with S_0^x rather than S_0. That is, if the current stock price net of dividends is S_0^x, the stock price at the end of the first time interval is either $u S_0^x$ or $d S_0^x$. The values of u, d, and p are computed as (13.18a), (13.18b), and (13.18c).

With the stock price lattice (net of dividends) computed, the approximation method starts at the end of the option's life and works back to the present. At the end of the option's life, the option value at each stock price node is given by the intrinsic value of the put (13.19), where S^x replaces S. The option values one step back in time (at time $n - 1$) are computed by taking the present value of the expected future value of the option (13.20). Before stepping back another time increment, it is again necessary to see if any of the option values are below their early exercise value. Here is where dividends may enter the picture again. If no dividends are paid at time $n - 1$, then the early exercise value is simply the exercise price less the lattice stock price. If a dividend is paid at time $n - 1$, however, the early exercise proceeds equal the exercise price less the lattice stock price less the dividend. If any of the computed option values are below the exercise proceeds, they are replaced with the value of the exercise proceeds.

As we repeat the process and step back further in time, we must keep track of the sum of the present values of the dividends paid during the option's remaining life. At time $n - 1$, there was only one dividend and it was paid at time $n - 1$, so the sum equals the value of the single dividend paid at time $n - 1$. If we are at time $n - 2$ and there is a dividend paid at time $n - 2$ as well as a dividend paid at time $n - 1$, the sum of the present values of the promised dividends that should be included in the early exercise boundary check at time $n - 2$ is

$$PVD_{n-2} = D_{n-2} + \frac{D_{n-1}}{r^*}. \tag{13.22}$$

In other words, the early exercise boundary at time $n - 2$ is $X - S^x_{n-2,j} - PVD_{n-2}$. By the time the iterative procedure is complete, the early exercise boundary used to check the option price corresponding to the time 0 stock index level node will include the present value of all promised dividends as in equation (13.21).

EXAMPLE 13.2

Compute the value of an American-style put option that has an exercise price of $50 and a time to expiration of 90 days. Assume the riskless rate of interest is 10 percent annually, the stock price is $50, the standard deviation of the rate of return of the stock is 30 percent per year, and the stock pays a dividend of $2 in exactly 60 days.

We proceed in two distinct steps. First we compute the European put option value using the formula (13.17), and then we compute the American put option value using the binomial method. In this way, we can identify the value of the early exercise premium on the put.

The current stock price net of the present value of the promised dividend is

$$S^x = 50 - 2e^{-.10(60/365)} = 48.033,$$

so the European put value can be computed as

$$p = 50e^{-.10(90/365)} N_1(-d_2) - 48.033 N_1(-d_1),$$

where

$$d_1 = \frac{[\ln(48.033/50) + (.10 + .5(.30)^2)(90/365)]}{.30\sqrt{90/365}} = -.029$$

and $d_2 = -.029 - .149 = -.178$. The probabilities $N_1(.029)$ and $N_1(.178)$ are .512 and .571, so the European call value is

$$p = 48.782(.571) - 48.033(.512) = 3.26.$$

The value of the American put is computed using the binomial method. The number of time steps is set equal to 90, so the time increment Δt is one day or

.00274 years. The values of the factors u and d are $u = e^{.30\sqrt{.00274}} = 1.01583$, and $d = 1/.01583 = .98442$, with probabilities $p = (e^{.10(.00274)} - .98442)/(1.01583 - .98442) = .5048$ and $1 - p = .4952$, respectively. The possible values of the stock price (net of dividends) at the option's expiration range from 11.69 to 197.38. The value of the American put is 3.393, hence the early exercise premium on the American option is $3.393 - 3.262 = .131$.

Table 13.5 demonstrates how the value of the early exercise premium increases as the put option goes deeper in-the-money. At a stock price of $40, for example, the early exercise premium is about 35¢, about 3 percent of the overall option value.

Finally, it is worthwhile to note that the dividend-adjusted binomial procedure outlined above not only handles an American put option on a dividend-paying stock but also handles American call options. Where the stock pays only a single dividend during the option's life, the American call option valuation equation (13.15b) is the most computationally efficient. Where the stock pays multiple dividends, however, the dividend-adjusted binomial method is much faster. We address this issue again when we value the American-style S&P 100 index options in the next chapter.

13.5 RIGHTS AND WARRANTS

Rights and warrants are securities issued by the firm. Usually, they are attached to debt offerings by the firm in order to reduce the coupon interest cost. Like call options, rights and warrants provide holders with the right to buy the underlying stock at a predetermined price within a specified period of time. Unlike call options, however, warrants are issued by the firm. Since the firm has a fixed amount of assets, the exercise of rights or warrants means that there will be more stockholders

TABLE 13.5   Simulated American and European put option values on a stock with a known discrete dividend. The put option has an exercise price of $50 and a time to expiration of 90 days. The riskless rate of interest is 10 percent, and the standard deviation of the stock return is 30 percent. The stock pays a dividend of $2 in 60 days.

Stock Price S	European Put Price $p(S, T; X)$	American Put Price $P(S, T; X)$	Early Exercise Premium ϵ_P
40	10.875	11.230	.355
45	6.510	6.757	.247
50	3.264	3.393	.129
55	1.360	1.406	.046
60	.476	.492	.016

sharing the same "pie," hence the value of existing shares will be diluted. Warrant valuation must account for this dilutionary effect.

In this section, we value rights and warrants explicitly recognizing the effects of dilution.[14] Effectively, there is little distinction between rights and warrants from a valuation standpoint. Rights tend to be short-term and at-the-money when they are issued; warrants tend to be long-term and out-of-the-money. For convenience, we use only the term "warrants" in the remaining part of this section.[15] The valuation approach is like that used in Chapter 11. Because a riskless hedge can be formed between the warrant and the value of the firm, we suffer no loss of generality and gain considerable mathematical tractability if we invoke an assumption of risk-neutrality.

Let S be the aggregate market value of the shares of the common stock currently outstanding; W, the aggregate market value of all warrants; r, the riskless rate of interest; and, V, the total market value of the firm. The firm is assumed to have only two sources of financing—stock and warrants—so the total market value of the firm may be defined as $V \equiv S + W$. The number of shares of stock outstanding is n_S, and n_w is the number of shares of stock sold if warrants are exercised. One warrant is assumed to provide the right to buy one share. The dilution factor possible due to the presence of the warrants is $\gamma \equiv n_w/(n_S + n_w)$. The stock is assumed to pay no dividends during the warrant's life. The standard deviation of the overall rate of return on the firm is σ. Finally, the warrant contract parameters are T, the time to expiration of warrants, and X, the aggregate amount paid by warrant holders to acquire the stock (i.e., the aggregate exercise price).

The assumptions used in the development of the warrant valuation equation are the same as those underlying the European call option except it is assumed the total market value of the firm is lognormally distributed at the warrants' expiration, *not* the firm's share price (i.e., $\ln(\tilde{V}_T/V)$ is normally distributed with variance σ^2).

Using risk-neutral valuation, the value of the firm's warrants today is the present value of the expected future terminal value, that is,

$$W = e^{-rT} E(\tilde{W}_T). \qquad \textbf{(13.23)}$$

The terminal value of the warrants, in turn, is the proportion of the firm that the warrant holders will own if the warrants are exercised, γ, times the terminal value of the firm after the warrant holders pay the cash exercise amount, $\tilde{V}_T + X$, less the cash exercise amount, X, that is,

$$\tilde{W}_T = \begin{cases} \gamma(\tilde{V}_T + X) - X & \text{if} \quad \gamma(V_T + X) \geq X \\ 0 & \text{if} \quad \gamma(V_T + X) < X, \end{cases} \qquad \textbf{(13.24)}$$

---

[14] The approach used here is based on Smith (1976).

[15] *Executive stock options*, a popular form of management incentive compensation, can be considered warrants from a valuation standpoint.

which can be rewritten

$$\tilde{W}_T = \begin{cases} \gamma \tilde{V}_T - (1-\gamma)X & \text{if } \gamma V_T \geq (1-\gamma)X \\ 0 & \text{if } \gamma V_T < (1-\gamma)X. \end{cases} \tag{13.25}$$

Note the similarity between the structure of the warrants payoffs in (13.25) and the European call option payoffs discussed in Chapter 11, that is,

$$\tilde{c}_T = \begin{cases} \tilde{S}_T - X & \text{if } S_T \geq X \\ 0 & \text{if } S_T < X. \end{cases} \tag{13.26}$$

In Chapter 11, we showed that the expected terminal value of the European call option for a non-dividend-paying common stock is

$$E(\tilde{c}_T) = e^{rT} SN(d_1) - XN(d_2), \tag{13.27}$$

where

$$d_1 = \frac{\ln(S/X) + (r + .5\sigma^2)T}{\sigma\sqrt{T}} \quad \text{and} \quad d_2 = d_1 - \sigma\sqrt{T},$$

where S_T is lognormally distributed. In the warrant valuation problem, γV_T corresponds to the terminal stock price S_T and is assumed to be lognormally distributed. The term $(1 - \gamma)X$ is certain and corresponds to the exercise price of the stock option. It therefore follows that

$$E(\tilde{W}_T) = e^{rT} \gamma V N(d_1) - (1-\gamma)XN(d_2), \tag{13.28}$$

where

$$d_1 = \frac{\ln[\gamma V/((1-\gamma)X)] + (r + .5\sigma^2)T}{\sigma\sqrt{T}} \quad \text{and} \quad d_2 = d_1 - \sigma\sqrt{T}.$$

Substituting (13.28) into (13.23), we find that the aggregate market value of the warrants of the firm is

$$W = \gamma V N(d_1) - e^{-rT}(1-\gamma)XN(d_2), \tag{13.29}$$

where

$$d_1 = \frac{\ln[\gamma V/((1-\gamma)X)] + (r + .5\sigma^2)T}{\sigma\sqrt{T}} \quad \text{and} \quad d_2 = d_1 - \sigma\sqrt{T}.$$

The *market value per warrant* is simply W from (13.29) divided by n_w.

One problem with applying (13.29) to value warrants is that it is difficult to estimate the volatility rate of the firm, σ. To estimate this parameter using historical data requires a time series of prices for both the stock and the warrant. Since the warrants may not actively trade, acquiring the historical price series for the warrant may be difficult. On the other hand, estimating the volatility rate of the stock, σ_S, is much easier since stocks are more actively traded and historical daily prices are available from a variety of sources. In addition, if the stock has listed options, the stock option pricing model can be used to compute the implied volatility rate of the stock.

Fortunately, the warrant valuation equation can be reformulated in terms of the stock's volatility rate rather than the volatility rate of the firm.[16] Since the rate of return on the stock is perfectly correlated with the rate of return on the overall firm,

$$\sigma_S = \eta_{SV}\sigma, \tag{13.30}$$

where η_{sv} is the elasticity of the stock price with respect to the value of the firm, that is, the percentage change in stock price for a given percentage change in the value of the firm. To estimate η_{sv}, first recall that by assumption the firm's value is the sum of the market value of the stock and the market value of warrants. Thus,

$$S = V - W.$$

The change in the market value of the stock for a given change in the value of the firm is, therefore,

$$\frac{\partial S}{\partial V} = 1 - \frac{\partial W}{\partial V}.$$

Second, from the valuation equation (13.29), we know that

$$\frac{\partial W}{\partial V} = \gamma N(d_1),$$

so

$$\frac{\partial S}{\partial V} = 1 - \gamma N(d_1). \tag{13.31}$$

---

[16]This idea was first suggested by Schulz and Trautmann (1991).

Finally, multiplying this term by V/S, we find that the elasticity of the stock price with respect to the value of the firm is

$$\eta_{SV} = \frac{\partial S/S}{\partial V/V} = [1 - \gamma N(d_1)]\frac{V}{S}. \tag{13.32}$$

Hence, to value the warrant as a function of the stock's volatility rate, we simply substitute the following term for the σ in (13.29):

$$\sigma = \frac{1}{\eta_{SV}}\sigma_S$$

$$= \frac{S}{[1 - \gamma N(d_1)]V}\sigma_S. \tag{13.33}$$

Another somewhat perplexing consideration in applying (13.29) to value warrants is that the warrant value appears on both sides of the equation, directly on the left-hand side and indirectly through V (i.e., W is embedded in V) on the right-hand side. This poses no great difficulty. We simply find the value of W that satisfies the equation through some sort of numerical search procedure, just as we do when finding the yield to maturity of a coupon-bearing bond.

EXAMPLE 13.3

Compute the value of a one-year warrant whose exercise price is $50. The current stock price is $50, and the stock pays no dividends. The firm has only two sources of financing: 2,000 shares of stock and 500 warrants. One warrant entitles its holder to one share of common stock. Assume that the riskless rate of interest is 6 percent, and that the standard deviation of the rate of return on the firm is 30 percent.

The dilution factor posed by the warrants is

$$\gamma = \frac{500}{2,000 + 500} = .2,$$

the aggregate exercise proceeds to the firm are

$$X = 500 \times 50 = 25,000,$$

and the market value of the firm is

$$V = 2,000 \times 50 + W = 100,000 + W.$$

The *aggregate market value of the warrants* is computed by solving

$$W = .2(100,000 + W)N(d_1) - e^{-.06(1)}.8(25,000)N(d_2),$$

where

$$d_1 = \frac{\ln[.2(100,000 + W)/(.8(25,000))] + (.06 + .5(.30)^2)1}{.30\sqrt{1}}$$

and

$$d_2 = d_1 - .30\sqrt{1}.$$

The solution to this problem is obtained iteratively. The values of d_1 and d_2 on the final iteration are .4611 and .1611, respectively. The probabilities are $N(.4611) = .6776$ and $N(.1611) = .5640$. The aggregate market value of the warrants is $3,389.46, so the price per warrant is $6.78.

In the interest of completeness, it is worthwhile to note that the volatility rate of the stock in this exercise equals

$$\sigma_S = \sigma\frac{[1 - \gamma N(d_1)]V}{S}$$
$$= .30\frac{[1 - .2(.6776)]103,389.46}{100,000}$$
$$= .2681.$$

The volatility rate of the stock is lower than the volatility rate of the overall firm so the volatility rate of the warrants must be higher. Since the returns of the stock and the warrant are perfectly correlated,

$$\sigma = \sigma_S\left(\frac{S}{V}\right) + \sigma_W\left(\frac{W}{V}\right).$$

Therefore, the warrant volatility rate is

$$\sigma_W = \left[.3000 - .2661\left(\frac{100,000}{103,389.46}\right)\right]\left(\frac{103,389.46}{3,389.46}\right) = 1.3002.$$

13.6 SUMMARY

The focus of this chapter is stock options. Following a description of exchange-traded stock options in the first section, we adapt the general pricing principles of Chapters 10 and 11 to value call and put options on non-dividend-paying stocks. The principles are modified somewhat to account for the fact that common stocks typically pay discrete dividends during the option's life. We assume that the amount and the timing of the dividends paid during the option's life are known with certainty.

In this chapter, we also introduce the use of the binomial method to price American options. Although the specific application in this chapter is American-style options on stocks, the binomial method can be applied to the valuation of virtually any type of option. We use it again in Chapter 15, for example, to value interest rate options.

Finally, a special type of call option on common stock is considered. Specifically, firms often issue rights or warrants to raise new capital. Like call options, these contracts provide the holder with the right to buy the common shares of the firm at a fixed price within a specified period of time. Unlike call options, however, the firm sells (or gives away) the options, so, if the rights/warrants are exercised, the firm faces the prospect of having the equity of the firm diluted. The prospect of dilution has an important effect on warrant price.

APPROXIMATION FOR THE CUMULATIVE BIVARIATE NORMAL DENSITY FUNCTION

In Appendix 11.2, a cumulative univariate normal density function approximation was provided to help compute the value of options on commodities with a constant, proportional cost-of-carry rate. In this chapter, we found that if a common stock pays a discrete dividend during the option's life, the American call option valuation equation requires the evaluation of a cumulative bivariate normal density function. While there are many available approximations for the cumulative bivariate normal distribution, the approximation provided here relies on Gaussian quadratures.[1] The approach is straightforward and efficient, and its maximum absolute error is .00000055.

The probability that x is less than a and that y is less than b for a standardized bivariate normal distribution is

$$\text{Prob}(x < a \text{ and } y < b) = \frac{1}{2\pi\sqrt{1-\rho^2}} \int_{-\infty}^{a} \int_{-\infty}^{b} exp\left[-\frac{x^2 - 2\rho xy + y^2}{2(1-\rho^2)}\right] dx \ dy$$

$$= N_2(a, b; \rho),$$

where ρ is the correlation between the random variables x and y.

The first step in the approximation of the bivariate normal probability $N_2(a,b;\rho)$ involves developing a routine that evaluates the function $\phi(a,b;\rho)$ below:

$$\phi(a, b; \rho) \approx .31830989\sqrt{1-\rho^2}\sum_{i=1}^{5}\sum_{j=1}^{5} w_i w_j f(x_i, x_j), \tag{1}$$

where

$$f(x_i, x_j) = exp[a_1(2x_i - a_1) + b_1(2x_j - b_1) + 2\rho(x_i - a_1)(x_j - b_1)], \tag{2}$$

the pairs of weights (w) and corresponding abscissa values (x) are:

i, j	w	x
1	.24840615	.10024215
2	.39233107	.48281397
3	.21141819	1.0609498
4	.033246660	1.7797294
5	.00082485334	2.6697604

---

[1] The Gaussian quadrature method for approximating the bivariate normal is from Drezner (1978), and the Gaussian quadratures for the intergral are from Steen, Byrne, and Gelbard (1969). For a contingency table approach to this problem, see Wang (1987).

and the coefficients a_1 and b_1 are computed using

$$a_1 = \frac{a}{\sqrt{2(1-\rho^2)}} \quad \text{and} \quad b_1 = \frac{b}{\sqrt{2(1-\rho^2)}}.$$

The second step in the approximation involves computing the product, $ab\rho$.

If $ab\rho \leq 0$, compute the bivariate normal probability, $N_2(a,b;\rho)$, using the following rules:

1. If $a \leq 0$, $b \leq 0$, and $\rho \leq 0$, then $N_2(a,b;\rho) = \phi(a,b;\rho)$.
2. If $a \leq 0$, $b > 0$, and $\rho > 0$, then $N_2(a,b;\rho) = N_1(a) - \phi(a,-b;-\rho)$.
3. If $a > 0$, $b \leq 0$, and $\rho > 0$, then $N_2(a,b;\rho) = N_1(b) - \phi(-a,b;-\rho)$.
4. If $a > 0$, $b > 0$, and $\rho \leq 0$, then $N_2(a,b;\rho) = N_1(a) + N_1(b) - 1 + \phi(-a,-b;\rho)$.

If $ab\rho > 0$, compute the bivariate normal probability, $N_2(a,b;\rho)$, as:

$$N_2(a, b; \rho) = N_2(a, 0; \rho_{ab}) + N_2(b, 0; \rho_{ba}) - \delta,$$

where the values of $N_2(\cdot)$ on the right-hand side are computed from the rules for $ab\rho \leq 0$,

$$\rho_{ab} = \frac{(\rho a - b)\text{Sgn}(a)}{\sqrt{a^2 - 2\rho ab + b^2}}, \quad \rho_{ba} = \frac{(\rho b - a)\text{Sgn}(b)}{\sqrt{a^2 - 2\rho ab + b^2}},$$

$$\delta = \frac{1 - \text{Sgn}(a) \times \text{Sgn}(b)}{4},$$

and

$$\text{Sgn}(x) = \begin{cases} 1 & x \geq 0 \\ -1 & x < 0. \end{cases}$$

$N_1(d)$ is the cumulative univariate normal probability. An approximation for $N_1(d)$ is contained in Appendix 11.2.

Finally, to assist those who may attempt to code this algorithm, sample computations for the bivariate normal probabilities are shown on page 340:

a	b	ρ	$N_2(a, b; \rho)$
-1.00	-1.00	-.50	.003782
-1.00	1.00	-.50	.096141
1.00	-1.00	-.50	.096141
1.00	1.00	-.50	.686472
-1.00	-1.00	.50	.062514
-1.00	1.00	.50	.154873
1.00	-1.00	.50	.154873
1.00	1.00	.50	.745203
.00	.00	.00	.250000
.00	.00	-.50	.166667
.00	.00	.50	.333333

EXAMPLE 13.A

Compute the risk-neutral probability that IBM and GM will have stock prices above $120 and $60, respectively, at the end of two months. The current price of IBM is $107 and the current price of GM is $48. Assume the riskless rate of interest is 10 percent annually, IBM and GM returns are bivariate normally distributed, IBM has a return volatility of 33 percent annually, GM has a return volatility of 36 percent annually, and the correlation between the returns of the two stocks is .6. Neither stock pays a dividend during the next two months.

The first step in finding this probability is to compute the upper integral limits for the standardized normal bivariate density function.

For IBM, the computation is

$$a = \frac{[\ln(107/120) + (.10 - .5(.33)^2)(2/12)]}{.33\sqrt{2/12}} = -.7948$$

and, for GM, the computation is

$$b = \frac{[\ln(48/60) + (.10 - .5(.36)^2)(2/12)]}{.36\sqrt{2/12}} = -1.4784.$$

The next step is to apply an approximation method to compute the bivariate normal probability. Applying the procedure described above, the probability is

$$N_2(a, b; \rho) = N_2(-.7948, -1.4784; .6) = .0463.$$

The probability that in two months IBM will have a stock price above 120 and that GM will have a stock price above 60 is slightly more than 4.6 percent.

It is instructive to note that the individual probabilities of each stock realizing its crtitical future value are

$$N_1(a) = N_1(-.7948) = .2134 \text{ and } N_1(b) = N_1(-1.4784) = .0697,$$

for IBM and GM, respectively. Thus, if the returns of IBM and GM were independent (i.e., their return correlation is 0), the probability that in two months IBM will have a stock price above 120 and that GM will have a stock price above 60 is .2134 × .0697 or about 1.49 percent. The reason that this probability is less than the 4.6 percent where the correlation is .6 is that, with high positive return correlation, an upward movement in IBM's stock price implies that GM's stock price will tend to move upward also. In the extreme case where these two stocks have perfect positive correlation (i.e., $\rho = +1$), the probability that in two months IBM will have a stock price above 120 and that GM will have a stock price above 60 is the lower of the two univariate probabilities, 6.97 percent.

14 STOCK INDEX AND STOCK INDEX FUTURES OPTION CONTRACTS

In Chapter 7, we discussed the use of stock index futures contracts in the management of stock portfolios. We saw how fund managers could quickly and inexpensively hedge the market risk of their portfolios by selling index futures contracts. In this chapter, we look at another means of tailoring the risk/return characteristics of stock portfolios by using options on stock indexes and stock index futures. We begin with a description of current index option and index futures option contracts. In sections 2 and 3, arbitrage price relations and valuation equations for index option are described. For the most part, we maintain the assumption that the dividend yield rate on the stock index portfolio is a constant, continuous rate. In section 4, we discuss the effect that discrete cash dividends have on the valuation of the American-style S&P 100 index options, and we address the wildcard option embedded in the S&P 100 index option contract. Section 5 contains a discussion of a popular application of index option contracts—portfolio insurance. The chapter is summarized in section 6.

14.1 STOCK INDEX AND STOCK INDEX FUTURES OPTION MARKETS

The first stock index options to trade in the U.S. were the Chicago Mercantile Exchange's S&P 500 and the New York Futures Exchange's NYSE Composite futures option contracts. They began trading on January 28, 1983. The Chicago Board Options Exchange followed quickly with the introduction of the S&P 100 option contract on March 11, 1983. The American Exchange introduced an option on the Major Market Index on July 1, 1983, and the New York Stock Exchange introduced options on the NYSE Composite Index on September 23, 1983. Since that time, a number of option contracts on more narrowly based stock indexes have been introduced, but most of these have failed.

Tables 14.1 and 14.2 contain *Wall Street Journal* listings of the currently active index option and index futures option contracts, respectively. The index options in Table 14.1 are all cash settlement contracts. When the option expires,

TABLE 14.1 Stock index option contract prices.

INDEX TRADING

Wednesday, November 13, 1991

OPTIONS

CHICAGO BOARD

S&P 100 INDEX-$100 times index

Strike	Calls–Last			Puts–Last		
Price	Nov	Dec	Jan	Nov	Dec	Jan
335	....	....	....	1/16	....	....
340	30	31½	31¼	1/16	⅝	1½
345	23	27	28	1/16	⅞	2⅛
350	21½	21⅛	....	1/16	1 3/16	3
355	16⅜	19	19⅝	1/16	1¾	3⅞
360	11¼	14¾	17	⅛	2½	4½
365	6⅜	10⅝	13½	5/16	3⅝	6
370	2 5/16	7⅜	10½	1 1/16	5¼	7¾
375	⅜	4⅜	7⅜	4⅛	7⅝	10⅞
380	1/16	2 7/16	5⅛	9¼	10⅞	13¾
385	1/16	1¼	3⅛	....	15¼	....
390	1/16	⅝	1⅞	18⅝	20	20¾

Total call volume 142,982 Total call open int. 387,114
Total put volume 128,390 Total put open int. 421,693
The index: High 371.22; Low 367.54; Close 371.21, +0.92

S&P 500 INDEX-$100 times index

Strike	Calls–Last			Puts–Last		
Price	Nov	Dec	Mar	Nov	Dec	Mar
325	....	71	....	....	....	1⅜
345	....	....	....	....	3/16	....
350	....	....	....	....	¼	2⅞
355	....	....	....	....	½	....
360	35¾	....	....	....	½	4
365	....	....	....	1/16	¾	4½
370	25½	25⅝	....	1/16	1	....
375	22⅝	....	....	1/16	1¼	7⅜
380	14¼	19¾	....	1/16	1¾	8
385	12¾	15⅞	....	⅛	2½	10
390	7⅜	11¾	19	¼	3⅝	10¾
395	2⅞	8⅜	17	⅝	5	11¾
400	½	5¼	....	4	7	....
405	⅛	3	....	....	10⅛	....
410	....	1½	....	12¾	13⅛	....
415	....	⅞	....	....	....	....
420	....	....	5½	....	....	27
425	....	3/16	3⅜	....	27⅝	28½

Total call volume 16,870 Total call open int. 400,742
Total put volume 17,372 Total put open int. 536,302
The index: High 397.42; Low 394.01; Close 397.41, +0.67

LEAPS-S&P 100 INDEX

Strike	Calls–Last			Puts–Last		
Price	Dec 92	Dec 93		Dec 92	Dec 93	
30	....	....	....	11/16	....	....
32½	....	....	....	1¼	....	....
35	....	....	....	2	2 11/16	....
37½	....	....	....	....	3⅝	....

Total call volume 0 Total call open int. 25,487
Total put volume 81 Total put open int. 86,284
The index: High 37.12; Low 36.75; Close 37.12, +0.09

LEAPS-S&P 500 INDEX

Strike	Calls–Last			Puts–Last		
Price	Dec 92	Dec 93		Dec 92	Dec 93	
30	....	....	....	....	¾	....
35	....	....	....	....	1 9/16	....
37½	....	....	....	1⅞	....	....
40	....	....	....	....	3	....

Total call volume 0 Total call open int. 26,809
Total put volume 366 Total put open int. 72,715
The index: High 39.74; Low 39.40; Close 39.74, +0.07

INSTITUTIONAL INDEX

Strike	Calls–Last			Puts–Last		
Price	Nov	Dec	Jan	Nov	Dec	Jan
335	....	....	....	....	1/16	....
340	....	....	....	....	⅛	....
360	....	....	....	....	....	11/16
370	....	....	....	....	....	1 5/16
375	....	....	....	....	½	1 5/16
380	....	32⅞	....	....	¾	....
385	....	....	....	....	13/16	2⅛
390	....	....	....	1/16	1 5/16	2 11/16
395	....	....	....	1/16	1⅝	4⅜
400	....	15	....	⅛	2 9/16	4⅜
405	7½	....	....	3/16	....	....
410	4⅛	9⅛	....	11/16	4¾	....
415	15/16	4⅞	....	2½	6½	....
420	⅛	3	5⅞	6½	....	....
425	....	1⅞	....	....	....	....
430	....	1 1/16	....	....	....	....
435	....	....	1 13/16	....	....	....
440	....	....	1 1/16	....	....	....
450	....	....	¼	....	....	....

Total call volume 1,079 Total call open int. 89,395
Total put volume 2,605 Total put open int. 104,291
The index: High 413.62; Low 410.30; Close 413.62, +0.56

JAPAN INDEX

Strike	Calls–Last			Puts–Last		
Price	Nov	Dec	Jan	Nov	Dec	Jan
225	....	....	....	....	⅜	....
230	....	....	....	....	13/16	....
235	....	....	....	....	....	2¼
240	....	....	....	¼	....	....
245	....	6⅛	9⅜	1¼	4¼	....
250	3/16	....	....	4¾	6⅝	....
260	....	1	....	....	....	....

Total call volume 220 Total call open int. 7,624
Total put volume 531 Total put open int. 21,223
The index: Close 245.50, –2.52

PHILADELPHIA

GOLD/SILVER INDEX

Strike	Calls–Last			Puts–Last		
Price	Nov	Dec	Jan	Nov	Dec	Jan
70	....	....	11⅞	....	....	....
80	½	2⅞	....	....	....	....
85	⅛	1⅜	....	....	....	....
90	....	¾	....	....	....	....

Total call volume 67 Total call open int. 1,657
Total put volume 0 Total put open int. 1,160
The index: High 80.61; Low 79.06; Close 79.53, –0.03

VALUE LINE INDEX OPTIONS

Strike	Calls–Last			Puts–Last		
Price	Nov	Dec	Jan	Nov	Dec	Jan
315	9¾	....	....	⅛	....	....
320	6½	....	12¼	5/16	3½	....
325	2½	....	....	1½	5	7⅝
330	....	4½	....	....	....	....

Total call volume 307 Total call open int. 6,387
Total put volume 397 Total put open int. 5,140
The index: High 326.47; Low 324.48; Close 326.47, +0.24

UTILITIES INDEX

Strike	Calls–Last			Puts–Last		
Price	Nov	Dec	Jan	Nov	Dec	Jan
250	4¼	....	....	....	....	....

Total call volume 11 Total call open int. 1,359
Total put volume 0 Total put open int. 78
The index: High 255.00; Low 254.24; Close 254.95, +0.63

continued

TABLE 14.1

| AMERICAN | | | | | | PACIFIC | | | | | |

AMERICAN

MAJOR MARKET INDEX

Strike	Calls—Last			Puts—Last		
Price	Nov	Dec	Jan	Nov	Dec	Jan
270	....	....	....	....	1/16	....
280	45	....	46	....	....	7/16
295	....	....	....	....	1/2	....
300	25⅛	25½	....	....	9/16	1½
305	....	21	....	1/16	7/8	....
310	16½	16½	....	1/16	1⅜	....
315	10	14⅛	....	⅛	1¾	....
320	7½	8½	12¾	⅛	2¾	5⅝
325	3⅛	6⅝	8	11/16	4	....
330	7/16	4	5½	3⅜	....	....
335	1/16	2	4⅛	....	....	....
340	....	15/16	15¼	....	....	....
345	....	⅜	1 5/16	....	....	....

Total call volume 7,617   Total call open int. 39,158
Total put volume 5,569   Total put open int. 49,128
The index: High 327.25; Low 323.58; Close 327.25, +1.28

LT-20 INDEX

Strike	Calls—Last		Puts—Last	
Price	Dec 92	Dec 93	Dec 92	Dec 93
25	....	....	⅜	....

Total call volume 0   Total call open int. 125,331
Total put volume 230   Total put open int. 134,501
The index: High 32.72; Low 32.36; Close 32.72, +0.12

PACIFIC

FINANCIAL NEWS COMPOSITE INDEX

Strike	Calls—Last			Puts—Last		
Price	Nov	Dec	Mar	Nov	Dec	Mar
260	10	....	....	....	....	....
270	⅞	....	....	1 15/16	....	....
275	....	....	....	....	6¼	....

Total call volume 19   Total call open int. 2,549
Total put volume 44   Total put open int. 374
The index: High 270.32; Low 267.77; Close 270.32, +0.94

NEW YORK

N.Y. Stock Exchange

NYSE INDEX OPTIONS

Strike	Calls—Last			Puts—Last		
Price	Nov	Dec	Jan	Nov	Dec	Jan
210	⅛	10¼	....	....	....	....
215	4⅜	6½	....	¼	1 13/16	....
217½	2⅛	....	....	3/16	....	....
220	5/16	....	....	1⅜	4⅜	....
225	....	....	....	....	....	7⅞

Total call volume 115   Total call open int. 2,843
Total put volume 162   Total put open int. 2,447
The index: High 219.37; Low 217.64; Close 219.37, +0.37

Source: Reprinted by permission of *Wall Street Journal*, © (November 14, 1991) Dow Jones & Company, Inc. All Rights Reserved Worldwide.

TABLE 14.2   Stock index futures option contract prices.

INDEX TRADING

FUTURES OPTIONS

S&P 500 STOCK INDEX (CME) $500 times premium

Strike	Calls—Settle			Puts—Settle		
Price	Nov-c	Dec-c	Ja-c	Nov-p	Dec-p	Jan-p
390	8.50	11.60	15.50	0.20	3.35	4.25
395	3.90	8.15	12.05	0.60	4.85	6.75
400	0.85	5.35	9.00	2.55	7.05	....
405	0.10	3.20	6.45	6.80	9.85	....
410	.0000	1.65	4.35	11.70	13.30	....
415	.0000	0.80	2.75	....	17.40	....

Est. vol. 6,929; Tues vol. 4,989 calls; 8,151 puts
Open Interest Tues; 36,719 calls; 69,190 puts

OTHER FUTURES OPTIONS

NYSE COMPOSITE INDEX (NYFE) $500 times premium

Strike	Calls—Settle			Puts—Settle		
Price	Nov-c	Dec-c	Jan-c	Nov-p	Dec-p	Jan-p
220	0.80	2.95	4.80	0.75	3.05	4.00

Est. vol. 136, Tues vol. 116 calls, 121 puts
Open Interest Tues 985 calls, 1,075 puts

NIKKEI 225 STOCK AVERAGE (CME) $5 times NSA

Strike	Calls—Settle			Puts—Settle		
Price	Nov-c	Dec-c	Jan-c	Nov-p	Dec-p	Jan-p
24500.	260	550	....	60	350	....

Est. vol. 185, Tues vol. 0 calls, 20 puts
Open Interest Tues 265 calls, 666 puts
CBT—Chicago Board of Trade. CME—Chicago Mercantile Exchange. NYFE—New York Futures Exchange, a unit of the New York Stock Exchange.

Source: Reprinted by permission of *Wall Street Journal*, © (November 14, 1991) Dow Jones & Company, Inc. All Rights Reserved Worldwide.

usually at the close of trading on the third Friday of the contract month, the option seller pays the option buyer an amount of cash equal to the difference between the closing index price and the exercise price of the option, assuming the option is in-the-money. No delivery takes place. When the index futures options in Table 14.2 expire, the option holder receives a position in the underlying futures contract.

Stock Index Options

All index options, except the CBOE's S&P 100 contract, are European-style. For the S&P 100 index options, exercise may occur at any time prior to expiration. If an option buyer exercises early, she receives the difference between the closing index level on that day and the exercise price of the option. The offsetting option seller, who is obliged to make the cash payment to the buyer, is randomly chosen from all of the open short positions in that option.

The prices reported in Table 14.1 are quoted in the same units as the underlying stock index, although the value of the contract is 100 times the reported price. For example, the January 360 call option on the S&P 100 index had a reported closing price of 17 on November 13, 1991, and the S&P 100 index closed at 371.21. To buy this call, one would pay 17 × $100 or $1,700. The call would provide us with the right to buy 317.21 × $100 or $37,121 worth of the S&P 100 stock portfolio for an amount of cash equal to 360.00 × $100 or $36,000 at any time between November 13, 1991, and the third Friday of January 1992. Again, the contract is cash-settled, so delivery does not actually take place. If the S&P 100 index level is, say, $380.50 at exercise, the call option buyer would receive in cash an amount equal to (380.50 − 360.00) × $100 or $2,050.

The figures in Table 14.1 show that there is a wide disparity in the trading activity of different index option contracts. The CBOE's S&P 100 contract, for example, is by far the most active. The CBOE's S&P 500 contract and the AMEX's MMI contract are moderately active. The rest of the index option contracts are fairly inactive. Given the substitutability of the broad-based index option contracts, it is not surprising that the broad-based contracts introduced earliest have been the most successful. The lack of success of the options on narrow indexes reflects the smaller market for these options.

The compositions of the stock portfolios that underlie each of the indexes with the most active option contracts were discussed in Chapter 7, except for the S&P 100. The S&P 100 index has a fairly short history. When the CBOE was considering an index option contract in the early 1980s, it decided on a value-weighted index of the one hundred largest stocks for which CBOE stock options existed. Originally, the index was called the "CBOE 100." Later, the CBOE reached an agreement to have Standard & Poors track the portfolio composition, at which time the index was renamed the S&P 100.

Stock Index Futures Options

Table 14.2 contains the two active index futures option contracts. These options are American-style, denominated as 500 times the current index value, and written on the index futures contract. Unlike index options, index futures options are delivery contracts in a sense. For example, ownership of the December 390 call on the S&P

500 futures would give one the right to buy the underlying December 1991 futures contract at a price of 390.00 at any time between November 13, 1991, and the close of trading on the third Thursday of December 1991. This option is currently in-the-money since the current price of the December S&P 500 futures is 398.30 as seen in Table 14.3. If this call were exercised on November 13, one would receive a long December S&P 500 futures position at a price of 390.00. A seller of the option, selected randomly, would receive the offsetting short position in the futures contract. When the futures contract is marked-to-market on that day, the long is allowed to withdraw 8.30 × $500 or $4,150, and the short pays in $4,150, but both would still have open futures positions. To withdraw fully from the market, the futures contracts established as a result of exercise would have to be sold.

An exception to the above exercise procedure occurs on the expiration date of the futures contract. Because the December futures option contract expires at the same time as the December futures contract and because the December futures contract is cash-settled to the index value at expiration, exercising the option at expiration amounts to cash settlement in that no futures position is left open.

Table 14.2 also shows futures option contracts with a November expiration, while Table 14.3 reveals that there is no November futures contract. The November index futures options, as well as the December futures options, are written on the December futures contracts. When an in-the-money November futures option expires on the third Friday of November, for example, a position in the underlying December futures is assumed. Again, to exit the market fully, the option holder must reverse the futures position that he receives upon exercising his option.

14.2 LOWER PRICE BOUNDS AND PUT-CALL PARITY

The arbitrage price relations for stock index and stock index futures options follow straightforwardly from the results of Chapter 10 if the underlying index is assumed to pay a constant proportional dividend yield rate. Recall that this was the assumption made in the discussion of stock index futures contracts in Chapter 7. In this case, the cost-of-carry rate, b, of the underlying stock index is the difference between the riskless rate of interest, r, and the dividend yield rate, d, on the index. Substituting $r - d$ for the cost-of-carry rate provides us with the arbitrage relations for stock index options. The cost-of-carry for a futures contract is zero, and substituting zero for the cost-of-carry rate, b, provides us with the arbitrage relations for stock index futures options.

Stock Index Options
The lower price bounds for European stock index options are

$$c(S, T; X) \geq \max[0, Se^{-dT} - Xe^{-rT}] \qquad \textbf{(14.1a)}$$

and

$$p(S, T; X) \geq \max[0, Xe^{-rT} - Se^{-dT}], \qquad \textbf{(14.1b)}$$

TABLE 14.3   Stock index futures contract prices.

INDEX TRADING

FUTURES

S&P 500 INDEX (CME) 500 times index

	Open	High	Low	Settle	Chg	High	Low	Open Interest
Dec	395.00	398.50	394.30	398.30	+ 1.00	401.50	316.50	139,341
Mr92	396.80	400.50	396.50	400.35	+ 1.00	404.00	374.70	7,544
June	398.30	402.35	398.30	402.20	+ 1.10	407.00	379.00	1,102

Est vol 42,125; vol Tues 41,413; open int 148,048, +916.
Indx prelim High 397.42; Low 394.01; Close 397.42 +.68

NIKKEI 225 Stock Average (CME)—$5 times NSA

Dec	24690.	24700.	24600.	24700.	− 340.	28900.	22380.	10,869
Mr92	25250.	25250.	25170.	25230.	− 340.	26725.	23000.	2,423

Est vol 1,107; vol Tues 1,132; open int 13,292, +467.
The index: High 24814.35; Low 24416.23; Close 24416.23 − 251.50

NYSE COMPOSITE INDEX (NYFE) 500 times index

Dec	218.00	220.10	217.75	220.05	+ .70	220.10	175.50	5,026
Mr92	218.80	221.00	218.80	221.00	+ .80	221.00	207.60	746
June	....	....	....	222.00	+ .80	220.10	208.90	172
Sept	....	....	....	223.00	+ .89	221.00	217.50	123

Est vol 5,057; vol Tues 5,996; open int 6,067, +344.
The index: High 219.37; Low 217.64; Close 219.37 +.37

MAJOR MKT INDEX (CBT) $500 times index

Nov	323.70	327.40	323.25	327.25	+ 1.55	327.40	315.20	2,819
Dec	323.50	327.70	323.50	327.70	+ 1.50	327.70	315.75	746

Est vol 2,500; vol Tues 1,163; open int 3,598, +122.
The index: High 327.25; Low 323.58; Close 327.25 +1.28

MGMI BASE METAL INDEX (FOX) 100 times index

Nov	....	....	....	134.50	....	140.50	132.50	2,246
Dec	....	....	....	134.80	....	182.70	133.00	8,662
Ja92	....	....	....	134.90	....	137.10	132.30	120
Mar	....	....	....	135.30	....	160.20	132.60	2,643
June	....	....	....	136.00	....	155.90	134.50	962
Sept	....	....	....	136.80	....	146.60	134.60	149

Est vol 0; vol Tues 0; open int 14,712, .
The index: High 134.52; Low 133.58; Close 134.03 +.81

OTHER FUTURES

Settlement price of selected contract. Volume and open interest of all contract months.

KC Mini Value Line (KC)—100 times index
Dec 328.60 +.85; Est. vol. 100; Open int. 254
KC Value Line Index (KC)—500 times index
Dec 328.30 +.70; Est. vol. 250; Open int. 1,722
The index: High 326.47; Low 324.48; Close 326.47 +.24
CRB Index (NYFE)—500 times index
Dec 214.90 +.35; Est. vol. 206; Open int. 1,221
The index: High 214.43; Low 213.94; Close 214.20 +.26

CBT—Chicago Board of Trade. CME—Chicago Mercantile Exchange. KC—Kansas City Board of Trade. NYFE—New York Futures Exchange, a unit of the New York Stock Exchange.

Source: Reprinted by permission of *Wall Street Journal*, © (November 14, 1991) Dow Jones & Company, Inc. All Rights Reserved Worldwide.

for the call and the put, respectively. The lower price bounds for the American call and put options on stock indexes are

$$C(S, T; X) \geq \max[0, Se^{-dT} - Xe^{-rT}, S - X] \qquad \textbf{(14.2a)}$$

and

$$P(S,T;X) \geq \max[0, Xe^{-rT} - Se^{-dT}, X - S],$$ **(14.2b)**

respectively. The put-call parity relation for European stock index options is

$$c(S,T;X) - p(S,T;X) = Se^{-dT} - Xe^{-rT},$$ **(14.3)**

and the put-call parity relation for American stock index options is

$$Se^{-dT} - X \leq C(S,T;X) - P(S,T;X) \leq S - Xe^{-rT}.$$ **(14.4)**

Note that in all of these relations, there is an implicit assumption that the dividend income received (or paid) while the arbitrage portfolio is held is automatically reinvested in the stock index portfolio.

Stock Index Futures Options

The lower price bounds for European stock index futures options are

$$c(F,T;X) \geq \max[0, e^{-rT}(F - X)]$$ **(14.5a)**

and

$$p(F,T;X) \geq \max[0, e^{-rT}(X - F)],$$ **(14.5b)**

for the call and the put, respectively. The lower price bounds for the American call and put options on stock index futures are

$$C(F,T;X) \geq \max[0, F - X]$$ **(14.6a)**

and

$$P(F,T;X) \geq \max[0, X - F],$$ **(14.6b)**

respectively. The put-call parity relation for European stock index futures options is

$$c(F,T;X) - p(F,T;X) = e^{-rT}(F - X),$$ **(14.7)**

and the put-call parity relation for American stock index futures options is

$$Fe^{-rT} - X \le C(F,T;X) - P(F,T;X) \le F - Xe^{-rT}. \tag{14.8}$$

In all of these relations, there is an implicit assumption that the futures position is the rollover position originally described in Chapter 3.

Index Options Versus Index Futures Options

For some of the stock indexes, like the S&P 500, index futures contracts, index option contracts, and index futures option contracts trade simultaneously. For example, if the index options and the index futures options have the same expiration date and if they are both European, it follows that

$$c(S,T;X) = c(F,T;X) \tag{14.9a}$$

and

$$p(S,T;X) = p(F,T;X). \tag{14.9b}$$

In this case, index options and index futures options are perfect substitutes for one another. If the options are American, and if the dividend yield rate is below the riskless rate of interest, the price relations are

$$C(F,T;X) \ge C(S,T;X) \tag{14.10a}$$

and

$$P(S,T;X) \ge P(F,T;X). \tag{14.10b}$$

Violation of the conditions (14.9a) through (14.10b) implies that costless arbitrage profits may be earned.

It is also important to recognize that stock index options may be priced in relation to the futures contracts. The put-call parity equations, (14.3) and (14.4), can be expressed in relation to the price of the index futures contract (rather than the underlying index) by using the cost-of-carry relation, $F = Se^{bT}$, to substitute for S. For European index options, (14.3) becomes

$$c(S,T;X) - p(S,T;X) = e^{-rT}(F - X), \tag{14.11}$$

and, for American index options, (14.4) becomes

$$Fe^{-rT} - X \le C(S,T;X) - P(S,T;X) \le Fe^{-(r-d)T} - Xe^{-rT}. \tag{14.12}$$

These relations are particularly important for index option market makers who use index futures as a way of laying off the risk of index option portfolios they hold. It is considerably less expensive to buy and sell futures contracts on the index than it is the index portfolio itself.

Likewise, index futures options may be priced in relation to the underlying index. For European index futures options, the relation is

$$c(F,T;X) - p(F,T;X) = Se^{-dT} - Xe^{-rT},$$ (14.13)

and, for American index futures options, the relation is

$$Se^{-dT} - X \le C(F,T;X) - P(F,T;X) \le Se^{(r-d)T} - Xe^{-rT}.$$ (14.14)

14.3 VALUATION EQUATIONS

European Stock Index Options

Under the assumption of a constant, proportional dividend yield rate of the stock index portfolio, valuation equations for European stock index options follow directly from equations (11.25) and (11.28) in Chapter 11. The *pricing equation of a European call option on a stock index*[1] is

$$c(S,T;X) = Se^{-dT} N(d_1) - Xe^{-rT} N(d_2),$$ (14.15)

and the pricing equation for a European put option on a stock index is

$$p(S,T;X) = Xe^{-rT} N(-d_2) - Se^{-dT} N(-d_1),$$ (14.16)

where

$$d_1 = \frac{\ln(S/X) + [(r-d) + .5\sigma^2]T}{\sigma\sqrt{T}}, \quad d_2 = d_1 - \sigma\sqrt{T}.$$

American Stock Index Options

With a constant proportional dividend yield rate, both the American call and the American put options on stock indexes may be rationally exercised early. As was noted in Chapter 11, pricing equations for these options have not been derived, and approximation methods must be used to price such options. Many different approximation methods are possible. We discussed the binomial method in Chapter 13. It

---

[1] This model is called the constant, proportional dividend yield model and first appeared in Merton (1973).

is well suited for American-style options where the underlying commodity makes cash disbursements during the option's life. The simplest and quickest approximation method for pricing American-style options with a constant, continuous cost-of-carry rate, however, is the quadratic approximation method of Barone–Adesi and Whaley (1987). Below their method is adapted to the stock index and stock index futures option valuation problems.

For an *American call option on a stock index*, the quadratic approximation is

$$C(S,T;X) = \begin{cases} c(S,T;X) + A_2(S/S^*)^{q_2} & \text{if } S < S^* \\ S - X & \text{if } S \geq S^*, \end{cases} \tag{14.17}$$

where

$$A_2 = \frac{S^*\{1 - e^{-dT}N[d_1(S^*)]\}}{q_2}, \quad d_1(S) = \frac{\ln(S/X) + [(r-d) + .5\sigma^2]T}{\sigma\sqrt{T}},$$

$$q_2 = \frac{1 - n + \sqrt{(n-1)^2 + 4k}}{2}, \quad n = \frac{2(r-d)}{\sigma^2}, \quad k = \frac{2r}{\sigma^2(1 - e^{-rT})}.$$

S^* is the critical index level above which the American call should be exercised immediately and is the solution to

$$S^* - X = c(S^*,T;X) + \{1 - e^{-dT}N[d_1(S^*)]\}S^*/q_2, \tag{14.17a}$$

where $c(S,X;T)$ is the European call option formula (14.15). For an *American put option on a stock index*, the quadratic approximation is

$$P(S,T;X) = \begin{cases} p(S,T;X) + A_1(S/S^{**})^{q_1} & \text{if } S > S^{**} \\ X - S & \text{if } S \leq S^{**}, \end{cases} \tag{14.18}$$

where

$$A_1 = -\frac{S^{**}\{1 - e^{-dT}N[-d_1(S^{**})]\}}{q_1}, \quad q_1 = \frac{1 - n - \sqrt{(n-1)^2 + 4k}}{2}.$$

S^{**} is the critical index level below which the American put should be exercised immediately and is the solution to

$$X - S^{**} = p(S^{**},T;X) - \{1 - e^{-dT}N[-d_1(S^{**})]\}S^{**}/q_1, \tag{14.18a}$$

where $p(S,X;T)$ is the European put option formula (14.16). All other notation is as defined for the American call option.

EXAMPLE 14.1

Compute the price of a 90-day S&P 100 index put option with an exercise price of 350. The current S&P 100 index level is 355.00, the dividend yield on the index is 3.50 percent annually, and the volatility rate is 25 percent annually. The riskless rate of interest is 6 percent.

The S&P 100 index option is an American-style option, but, since the quadratic approximation requires the value of the corresponding European option, we will compute it first. Applying

$$p = 350e^{-.035(90/365)} N(d_1) - 355e^{-.06(90/365)} N(d_2),$$

where

$$d_1 = \frac{\ln(355/350) + [.06 - .035 + .5(.25)^2](90/365)}{.25\sqrt{90/365}} = .2260,$$

$$d_2 = d_1 - .25\sqrt{90/365} = .1018.$$

The values of $N(-d_1)$ and $N(-d_2)$ are .4106 and .4594, respectively, so the European put option price is

$$p = 344.860(.4594) - 351.949(.4106) = 13.918.$$

Applying the quadratic approximation (14.18), we find that the critical index level, S^{**}, below which the index put should be exercised immediately is 285.347. Since the index level is currently 355.00, we are not in the early exercise region. The value of A_1 is 1.778; the value of q_1 is -11.335. The approximate value of the S&P 100 option is, therefore,

$$P(S, T; X) = p(S, T; X) + A_1(S/S^{**})^{q_1}$$

$$= 13.918 + 1.778(355.00/285.347)^{-11.335}$$

$$= 14.068.$$

The value of the S&P 100 index put is 14.068, and the value of the right to early exercise is .15.

European Stock Index Futures Options

The cost of carrying a futures contract is zero, independent of whether it is a stock index futures, a foreign currency futures, and so on. Using equations (11.25) and

(11.28) from Chapter 11, the *value of a European call on an index futures contract* is

$$c(F, T; X) = e^{-rT}[FN(d_1) - XN(d_2)],$$ **(14.19)**

and the *value of a European put option on an index futures contract* is

$$p(F, T; X) = e^{-rT}[XN(-d_2) - FN(-d_1)],$$ **(14.20)**

where

$$d_1 = \frac{\ln(F/X) + .5\sigma^2 T}{\sigma\sqrt{T}}, \quad d_2 = d_1 - \sigma\sqrt{T}.$$

American Stock Index Futures Options

American options on stock index futures contracts can also be valued with the help of the quadratic approximation. In the case of the *American call option on stock index futures*, the approximation is

$$C(F, T; X) = \begin{cases} c(F, T; X) + A_2(F/F^*)^{q_2} & \text{if } F < F^* \\ F - X & \text{if } F \geq F^*, \end{cases}$$ **(14.21)**

where

$$A_2 = \frac{F^*\{1 - e^{-rT}N[d_1(F^*)]\}}{q_2}, \quad d_1(F) = \frac{\ln(F/X) + .5\sigma^2 T}{\sigma\sqrt{T}},$$

$$q_2 = \frac{1 + \sqrt{1 + 4k}}{2}, \quad k = \frac{2r}{\sigma^2(1 - e^{-rT})}.$$

F^* is the critical futures price above which the American call should be exercised immediately and is the solution to

$$F^* - X = c(F^*, T; X) + \{1 - e^{-rT}N[d_1(F^*)]\}F^*/q_2,$$ **(14.21a)**

where $c(F, T; X)$ is the European call option formula (14.19). For an *American put option on a stock index futures contract*, the approximation is

$$P(F, T; X) = \begin{cases} p(F, T; X) + A_1(F/F^{**})^{q_1} & \text{if } F > F^{**} \\ X - F & \text{if } F \leq F^{**}, \end{cases}$$ **(14.22)**

where

$$A_1 = -\frac{F^{**}\{1 - e^{-rT}N[-d_1(F^{**})]\}}{q_1}, \qquad q_1 = \frac{1 - \sqrt{1 + 4k}}{2}.$$

F^{**} is the critical futures price below above which the American put should be exercised immediately and is the solution to

$$X - F^{**} = p(F^{**}, T; X) - \{1 - e^{-rT}N[-d_1(F^{**})]\}F^{**}/q_1, \qquad \textbf{(14.22a)}$$

where $p(F, T; X)$ is the European put option pricing formula (14.20). All other notation is as defined for the American call option.

EXAMPLE 14.2

Compute the price of a 90-day call option on the S&P 500 futures contract. Assume the call has an exercise price of 380 and the current futures price is 400.00. The riskless rate of interest is 6 percent annually and the volatility rate of the futures contract is 25 percent annually.

The S&P 500 futures option contract is an American-style option, so we use the quadratic approximation. As an intermediate step, however, we first compute the value of the corresponding European-style futures option contract using equation (14.19).

$$c = e^{-.06(90/365)}[400N(d_1) - 380N(d_2)],$$

where

$$d_1 = \frac{\ln(400/380) + .5(.25)^2(90/365)}{.25\sqrt{90/365}} = .475,$$

$$d_2 = d_1 - .25\sqrt{90/365} = .351.$$

The values of $N(d_1)$ and $N(d_2)$ are .683 and .637, respectively, so the European call option price is

$$c = 394.126(.683) - 374.419(.637) = 30.68.$$

Applying the quadratic approximation (14.21), we find that the critical index level, F^*, above which the call should be exercised immediately is 491.458. Since the futures price is currently 400.00, we are not in the immediate early exercise region. The value of A_2 is 1.270, the value of q_2 is 11.945. The approximate value of the S&P 500 futures option is, therefore,

$$C(F, T; X) = c(F, T; X) + A_2(F/F^*)^{q_2}$$
$$= 30.68 + 1.370(400.00/491.458)^{11.945}$$
$$= 30.80.$$

The value of the call option on the S&P 500 futures is 30.80. Hence, the value of the right to early exercise is about 12¢.

14.4 DISCRETE DIVIDENDS AND THE S&P 100 INDEX OPTION

Discrete Dividends

For many stock indexes, the assumption that dividends are paid at a constant, continuous rate is unrealistic. To value S&P 100 index options precisely, for example, it is necessary to account for the fact that the dividends on the index are discrete and seasonal in their nature. Firms tend to pay dividends in quarterly cycles and generally use a December 31 fiscal year-end. For these reasons, monthly seasonality in index dividend payments is expected.

Figure 14.1 summarizes the monthly dividend patterns of the S&P 100 index during the period March 1983 through December 1989.[2] The figure shows that the most popular ex-dividend months are February, May, August, and November. The average daily dividend payments are higher in these months, and the frequency of zero-dividend days is lower. Of these four months, the average daily dividend during the month of February is highest, 6.09¢, probably as a result of the fact that extra dividend payments are typically declared in the last quarter of the fiscal year. Of the total number of February trading days in this sample, less than 32 percent have zero dividends. The least popular months are January, April, July, and October. During these months, the average daily dividend is less than half of the average dividend across all days. In addition, the frequency of zero-dividend days during these months exceeds 55 percent of the total trading days.

Figure 14.1 also shows that average dividends have generally increased over the seven-year sample period. In August 1983, for example, the average daily payout was 4.45¢, and, in August 1989, the average payout was 6.70¢. The growth in the payouts also occurred in non-peak months. In April 1983, the average daily dividend was 0.43¢, and, in April 1989, the average dividend was 2.15¢.

Aside from the monthly seasonal pattern in S&P 100 dividends, there is also a daily seasonal pattern. Figure 14.2 presents average dividends by day of the week. Monday has the largest average payment, 4.94¢. In addition, of the total number of Mondays in the sample period, only 18 percent are zero-dividend days. At the other extreme, Wednesday appears to be the least popular day to pay dividends. In more than 55 percent of the total number of Wednesdays during the sample period, no dividends are paid. The average dividend payment across all Wednesdays is 1.76¢. Moreover, Wednesday's popularity as an ex-dividend day appears to be

---

[2]This figure and the dividend information were obtained from Harvey and Whaley (1992b).

FIGURE 14.1   Average daily dividend on S&P 100 index by month and
year: March 1983–December 1989.

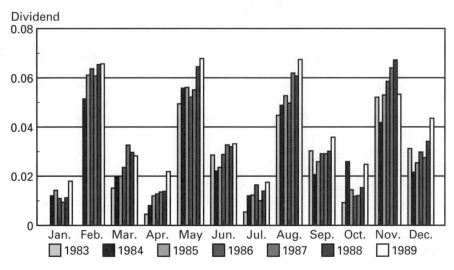

Source: Harvey and Whaley (1992b).

FIGURE 14.2   Average daily dividend on S&P 100 index by day and
year: March 1983–December 1989.

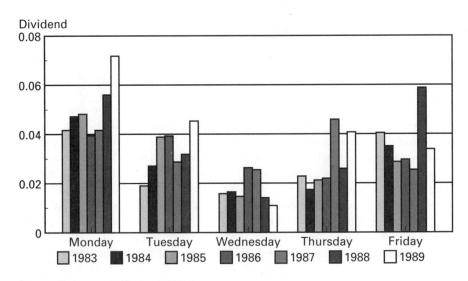

Source: Harvey and Whaley (1992b).

declining over the sample period. Regarding the remaining days of the week, Friday is more popular than Tuesday, which, in turn, is more popular than Thursday. For Tuesdays and Thursdays, there are more zero-dividend days than non-zero-dividend days.

The above dividend descriptions are written in terms of average dividend amounts. The importance of dividends in S&P 100 index option valuation has to do not only with the average level of dividends but also the magnitudes of individual daily dividend payments. Many cash dividends on the S&P 100 index are quite large. The largest cash dividend on the index during the March 11, 1983–December 29, 1989, sample period was 55.13¢ on Thursday, November 5, 1987. On Friday, December 23, 1983, the cash dividend on the S&P 100 index was 46.83¢, and, on Thursday, May 7, 1987, it was 46.10¢. The holder of an S&P 100 index call, for example, may find it optimal to exercise her option the day immediately before such a large dividend is to be paid, and the holder of an S&P 100 index put may find it optimal to exercise his option just after.

S&P 100 Index Option Valuation

Assuming that the cash dividend series for the S&P 100 index is known, call and put options on the S&P 100 index can be quickly and efficiently valued using the dividend-adjusted binomial method described in the last chapter. The binomial method accounts for the possibility that large cash dividends may induce exercise of the option prior to expiration. Since the approximation method was described in detail in the last chapter, no further description is provided here.

While the dividend-adjusted binomial method accounts for the possibility of early exercise from a theoretical perspective, it is useful to know that early exercise is a practical matter. Figures 14.3 and 14.4 show the number of call and put options on the S&P 100 index that were exercised early during the period March 12, 1983, through November 30, 1989. Figure 14.3 shows that considerable early exercise activity for calls occurs in the last week before expiration, although exercise activity extends out to as much as 134 days prior to expiration. It is doubtful that the early exercise activity thirty days or more before expiration is rational. However, the sheer number of exercises in the weeks prior to expiration indicate that early exercise of index call options is not uncommon. Indeed, it may be likely if a large dividend is paid during the option's remaining life.

Figure 14.4 shows the number of S&P 100 index put contracts exercised prior to expiration. Early exercise of index puts is more frequent than calls. Early exercise activity for puts in the weeks prior to expiration appears commonplace and extends as far out as 109 days.

The Wildcard Option

While some of the early exercise activity shown in Figures 14.3 and 14.4 may be dividend-induced, some may also be attributable to the wildcard option embedded in the S&P 100 option contract. The wildcard option arises because the proceeds from exercise are based on the difference between the index level established at 3:00 PM CST when the NYSE closes and the exercise price of the options. However, the index option market stays open until 3:15 PM, giving the option holder

FIGURE 14.3   Exercise history of S&P 100 index call options: March 12, 1983, through November 30, 1989.

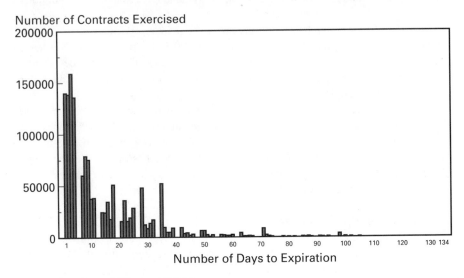

Source: Harvey and Whaley (1992b).

FIGURE 14.4   Exercise history of S&P 100 index put options: March 12, 1983, through November 30, 1989.

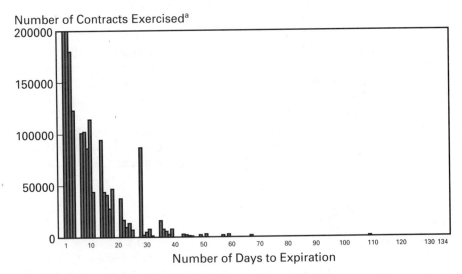

a. 422,604 and 208,981 puts exercised one and two days prior to expiration.

Source: Harvey and Whaley (1992b).

until 3:15 PM to decide whether to exercise the option. The fact that stock prices can move during the fifteen-minute interval after the NYSE close gives the option holder a "wildcard option," that is, in the case of a put, an option providing the right to put the index option to the writer after 3:00 PM for cash proceeds established at 3:00 PM.

14.5 PORTFOLIO INSURANCE

Portfolio insurance protects the principal value of a portfolio against price declines. In effect, a portfolio insurance policy is a put option for which the exercise price of the put is the principal value of the portfolio. The portfolio being insured may consist of any number of assets or securities, although it is most usually discussed in terms of stock portfolios. The discussion in this section focuses on stock portfolio insurance.

Portfolio insurance may be purchased directly in the form of exchange-traded options or indirectly through dynamic trading strategies. The first is *static portfolio insurance,* where the fund manager simply purchases exchange-traded put options. The second is *dynamic portfolio insurance,* where the fund manager mimics the payoffs of the put by dynamically rebalancing the composition of the portfolio between stocks and short-term debt as the market goes up or down.

Static Portfolio Insurance

Static portfolio insurance of a stock portfolio involves the purchase of a protective put option. If the value of the stock portfolio is S and the price of a European put option with exercise price X and time to expiration T is $p(S, T; X)$, the terminal value of the insured portfolio is as depicted in Table 14.4. Note that with portfolio insurance, the value of the overall portfolio does not fall below X, the exercise value of the put or, in the context of this application, the face amount of the insurance policy. The dividend income on the stock portfolio is assumed to be zero for the sake of simplicity.

To illustrate static portfolio insurance, consider an index portfolio with a current value of 100. Suppose the riskless rate of interest is 8 percent, the standard

TABLE 14.4   Terminal value of stock portfolio with static portfolio insurance.

| | | Terminal Value | |
Position	Initial Value	$\tilde{S}_T \leq X$	$\tilde{S}_T > X$
Own Stock Portfolio	$-S$	$\tilde{S}_T$	$\tilde{S}_T$
Buy Index Put	$-p$	$X - \tilde{S}_T$	0
Net Portfolio Value	$-S - p$	X	$\tilde{S}_T$

TABLE 14.5   Insured stock portfolio value at alternative stock index levels, using static portfolio insurance.[a]

Index Level S	Put Option p	Portfolio Value $S + p$
59.87	36.21	96.08
63.02	33.06	96.08
66.34	29.75	96.09
69.83	26.29	96.13
73.51	22.70	96.21
77.38	19.03	96.41
81.45	15.38	96.83
85.74	11.87	97.61
90.25	8.67	98.92
95.00	5.94	100.94
100.00	3.79	103.79
105.00	2.29	107.29
110.25	1.27	111.52
115.76	0.65	116.42
121.55	0.31	121.86
127.63	0.13	127.76
134.01	0.05	134.06
140.71	0.02	140.73
147.75	0.01	147.75
155.13	0.00	155.13
162.89	0.00	162.89

a. In the valuation of the European put, the index is assumed to pay no dividends, the riskless rate of interest is 8 percent, and the standard deviation of the index return is 20 percent. The put option has an exercise price of 100 and a time to expiration of six months.

deviation of the instantaneous rate of return of the index portfolio is 20 percent, and the stock portfolio pays no dividends. To insure the value of this portfolio, the fund manager would buy a European put option on the index (we are assuming such an option exists), where the exercise price of the put is 100 and the time to expiration of the put is six months. Note that the insurance policy that the manager is choosing insures that the value of the overall fund is at least 100 at the end of six months.

Now, let us consider both the existing value of the insured portfolio as well as the value of the portfolio if the index level rises or falls immediately. These values are represented in Table 14.5. The current position is where the index level is 100. The increments up (down) from 100 in the first column of the table are 5 percent of the preceding (succeeding) index level. The second column is the value of the European put at the different index levels. Note that the original price of the portfolio insurance is 3.79. Finally, the last column is the overall value of the insured portfolio. Note that the overall portfolio value never goes below 96.08. This value is the present value of 100 over the six-month interval, that is, $96.08e^{.08(.5)} = 100.00$. Recall that the policy the manager purchased insured a portfolio value of at least 100 at the end of six months.

Dynamic Portfolio Insurance

Dynamic portfolio insurance does the same thing as the static insurance, except a put option is not purchased directly. Instead, the fund manager dynamically rebalances a portfolio consisting of stocks and short-term riskless debt such that the payoff contingencies of the portfolio are exactly the same as the payoff contingencies of the portfolio with static insurance.

To be more precise, under the static portfolio insurance scheme above, the value of the insured portfolio is $S + p$. If we substitute the value of a European put option on the index (14.16), we get

$$S + p = S + Xe^{-rT}N(-d_2) - SN(-d_1)$$
$$= S[1 - N(-d_1)] + Xe^{-rT}N(-d_2)$$
$$= SN(d_1) + Xe^{-rT}N(-d_2)$$
$$= Sw_1 + Xe^{-rT}w_2, \qquad\qquad\text{(14.23)}$$

where $w_1 = N(d_1)$ is the number of units of the index and $w_2 = N(-d_2)$ is the number of units of T-bills. Note that both w_1 and w_2 will change as the index level, S, and the time to expiration, T, change. In fact, in theory, the weights must change as soon as we have an infinitesimal change in either variable.

To demonstrate the dynamic portfolio insurance scheme more clearly, consider Table 14.6. The first column is the index level and the second column is the price of the short-term debt instrument. The third and fourth columns are the portfolio weights w_1 and w_2, and the final column is the portfolio value. Note that as the index level falls, funds are removed from stocks and placed in T-bills, and, as the index level rises, funds are moved from T-bills and placed in stock. Note also that the portfolio values are identical to the values in Table 14.5, showing that the two portfolio insurance schemes provide identical results in theory. The problem with the dynamic approach is that, from a practical perspective, continuous rebalancing is not possible.

Table 14.7 gives some perspective on what happens when the portfolio is not rebalanced. The weights are established when the index level is 100 and are held at that level independent of the direction the index moves. Note that when the index falls, we do not remove funds from stocks to place in T-bills, so the portfolio value falls below the present value of the 100 we want to have on hand in six months. On the other hand, if the index level rises, we do not profit by as much because we continue to hold a large proportion of T-bills.

TABLE 14.6   Insured stock portfolio value at alternative index levels, using dynamic portfolio insurance with continuous rebalancing.[a]

Index Level S	T-Bill Price Xe^{-rT}	Stock Portfolio Weight w_1	T-Bill Weight w_2	Portfolio Value
59.87	96.08	0.001	1.000	96.08
63.02	96.08	0.002	0.999	96.08
66.34	96.08	0.005	0.996	96.09
69.83	96.08	0.014	0.990	96.13
73.51	96.08	0.034	0.975	96.21
77.38	96.08	0.072	0.945	96.41
81.45	96.08	0.136	0.892	96.83
85.74	96.08	0.231	0.809	97.61
90.25	96.08	0.355	0.696	98.92
95.00	96.08	0.496	0.560	100.94
100.00	96.08	0.638	0.416	103.79
105.00	96.08	0.758	0.289	107.29
110.25	96.08	0.852	0.183	111.52
115.76	96.08	0.918	0.106	116.42
121.55	96.08	0.959	0.056	121.86
127.63	96.08	0.981	0.026	127.76
134.01	96.08	0.992	0.011	134.06
140.71	96.08	0.997	0.004	140.73
147.75	96.08	0.999	0.001	147.75
155.13	96.08	1.000	0.000	155.13
162.89	96.08	1.000	0.000	162.89

a. In the valuation of the European put, the index is assumed to pay no dividends, the riskless rate of interest is 8 percent, and the standard deviation of the index return is 20 percent. The put option has an exercise price of 100 and a time to expiration of six months.

As a compromise between continuous rebalancing and no rebalancing, dynamic portfolio insurers usually rebalance when the index level moves by a certain percent from the time the portfolio was last rebalanced. In Table 14.8, we simulate this activity using a 5-percent trigger point. When the stock index is at a level of 100, we have the original portfolio weights seen in the previous tables. If the index moves down by 5 percent, for example, the new portfolio value will be 100.59 (i.e., 0.638 × 95.00 + 0.416 × 96.08), and the portfolio will be rebalanced with the new weights, 0.495 and 0.558, for stocks and T-bills, respectively. Note that this scheme does not completely insure downside protection. If the stock index level falls 15 percent, the portfolio value falls below the 96.08 necessary to insure

TABLE 14.7   Insured stock portfolio value at alternative stock index levels, using dynamic portfolio insurance with no rebalancing.[a]

Index Level S	T-Bill Price Xe^{-rT}	Stock Portfolio Weight w_1	T-Bill Weight w_2	Portfolio Value
59.87	96.08	0.638	0.416	78.18
63.02	96.08	0.638	0.416	80.19
66.34	96.08	0.638	0.416	82.31
69.83	96.08	0.638	0.416	84.53
73.51	96.08	0.638	0.416	86.88
77.38	96.08	0.638	0.416	89.35
81.45	96.08	0.638	0.416	91.95
85.74	96.08	0.638	0.416	94.68
90.25	96.08	0.638	0.416	97.56
95.00	96.08	0.638	0.416	100.59
100.00	96.08	0.638	0.416	103.79
105.00	96.08	0.638	0.416	106.98
110.25	96.08	0.638	0.416	110.33
115.76	96.08	0.638	0.416	113.84
121.55	96.08	0.638	0.416	117.54
127.63	96.08	0.638	0.416	121.42
134.01	96.08	0.638	0.416	125.49
140.71	96.08	0.638	0.416	129.76
147.75	96.08	0.638	0.416	134.25
155.13	96.08	0.638	0.416	138.97
162.89	96.08	0.638	0.416	143.92

a. In the valuation of the European put, the index is assumed to pay no dividends, the riskless rate of interest is 8 percent, and the standard deviation of the index return is 20 percent. The put option has an exercise price of 100 and a time to expiration of six months.

that 100 is on hand in six months. On the other side, because we are slow to rebalance when the index level is going up, the upside potential is not as great as it was in the continuous rebalancing case.

14.6 SUMMARY

This chapter focuses on stock index option contracts. Options on stock indexes and on stock index futures are traded in the U.S. In sections 2 and 3, we discuss the pricing principles for these options, where the cash index is assumed to pay dividends at a constant, continuous rate through time.

TABLE 14.8   Insured stock portfolio value at alternative stock index levels, using dynamic portfolio insurance with discrete rebalancing.[a]

Index Level S	T-Bill Price Xe^{-rT}	Stock Portfolio Weight w_1	T-Bill Weight w_2	Portfolio Value
59.87	96.08	0.001	0.985	94.65
63.02	96.08	0.002	0.984	94.66
66.34	96.08	0.005	0.982	94.67
69.83	96.08	0.014	0.976	94.72
73.51	96.08	0.034	0.961	94.85
77.38	96.08	0.071	0.933	95.12
81.45	96.08	0.135	0.882	95.67
85.74	96.08	0.229	0.802	96.65
90.25	96.08	0.353	0.691	98.24
95.00	96.08	0.495	0.558	100.59
100.00	96.08	0.638	0.416	103.79
105.00	96.08	0.755	0.288	106.98
110.25	96.08	0.847	0.183	110.94
115.76	96.08	0.911	0.105	115.61
121.55	96.08	0.951	0.055	120.89
127.63	96.08	0.973	0.026	126.67
134.01	96.08	0.984	0.011	132.87
140.71	96.08	0.988	0.004	139.46
147.75	96.08	0.990	0.001	146.42
155.13	96.08	0.991	0.000	153.73
162.89	96.08	0.991	0.000	161.41

a. In the valuation of the European put, the index is assumed to pay no dividends, the riskless rate of interest is 8 percent, and the standard deviation of the index return is 20 percent. The put option has an exercise price of 100 and a time to expiration of six months. Rebalancing occurs if the index level moves by 5 percent.

Section 4 examines the effect of discrete cash dividend payments. The cash dividend payments on the S&P 100 index portfolio are shown to be discrete and seasonal. Some of the cash dividends are large enough to induce early exercise. The wildcard option embedded in the S&P 100 option contract is also discussed.

The final section deals with portfolio insurance. Both static portfolio insurance using index put options and dynamic portfolio insurance using portfolio rebalancing are discussed.

15

INTEREST RATE AND INTEREST RATE FUTURES OPTION CONTRACTS

Options on Treasury instruments began trading in October 1982. These instruments offer important new ways for managing the interest rate risk of fixed-income portfolios. In particular, interest rate options provide an effective means of managing the convexity risk—a subject first discussed in Chapter 8. In the first section of this chapter, we describe the interest rate option and futures option markets that are currently active in the United States. Of the exchange-traded option contracts, the T-bond futures option is clearly the most popular. Options on T-bonds and T-notes are not as actively traded, although OTC markets for these contracts continue to proliferate. We then proceed, in section 2, with a discussion of short-term interest rate option valuation. Short-term interest rate options provide an interesting new valuation challenge. Using the standard lognormal price distribution assumption from the previous chapters is clearly inappropriate because the underlying asset value cannot exceed a predetermined level.[1] In its place, we substitute the assumption that yield is lognormally distributed and then rederive the European option valuation equations. The third and the fourth sections discuss T-bond and T-bond futures option valuation under the lognormal price and the lognormal yield assumptions, respectively. Section 5 is a detailed discussion of duration/convexity risk management.

---

[1] Recall that the assumption of a lognormal price distribution permits the price to rise without limit.

15.1 INTEREST RATE OPTION MARKETS

The first interest rate option contracts to trade in the United States were the Chicago Board of Trade's (CBT's) Treasury bond futures option contract and the Chicago Mercantile Exchange's (CME's) Eurodollar futures option contract on October 1, 1982. The Chicago Board Options Exchange (CBOE) introduced options on Treasury bonds, and the American Exchange introduced options on Treasury notes and bills on October 22, 1982. Other interest rate options have been introduced subsequently.

Table 15.1 contains a listing of interest rate instruments from the *Wall Street Journal*. Options on Treasury bonds and notes are traded at the CBOE. These contracts expire on the Saturday after the third Friday of the contract month, are American-style, and require the delivery of a specific Treasury bond or Treasury note. Exchange-traded options on T-bonds and notes are not very active, however. In fact, no active contracts are listed in Table 15.1. The table reports only prices of relatively inactive CBOE options on short-term and long-term bond indexes.

The most active interest rate options are those written on interest rate futures contracts. Of these, the CBT's Treasury bond futures option and the CME's Eurodollar futures option contracts have the greatest trading volume and open interest, as shown in Table 15.1. Upon exercising a T-bond futures option, a long or short position in the nearby T-bond futures contract is assumed. These options are American-style and thus may be exercised at any time up to and including the expiration day. The last day of trading is the Friday preceding, by at least five business days, the first notice day for the corresponding T-bond futures contract. In general, the first notice day of the futures is the first business day of the contract month.

The Eurodollar futures option is also American-style. The expiration day of the Eurodollar futures option contract is the second London business day before the third Wednesday of the contract month, the same as that of the underlying Eurodollar futures. Exercise of the Eurodollar option results in delivery of a position in the Eurodollar futures contract of the same maturity. The Eurodollar futures contract, in turn, fixes the price (or, equivalently, the yield) on a three-month Eurodollar deposit.

Table 15.2 on pages 370–371 shows the large number of Treasury issues outstanding on a given date. Not all of these, nor even the majority of these, have exchange-traded options. If individuals want to buy or sell options on particular bond issues, they usually go to OTC markets where bond option contracts can be tailored in any manner. It is commonplace to see both European- and American-style OTC bond options, including ones with times to expiration of several years.

In Chapter 8, we discussed a number of conventions regarding T-bonds and T-bond price reporting. For example, the decimal part of the reported price represents 32nds. Thus, the reported bid price (in Table 15.2) of 107:07 for the $8\frac{1}{2}$s of May 1997 is actually $107\frac{7}{32}$. Two other conventions are that the face value of a Treasury bond is $100,000 and the bond price is reported as a percentage of par. Thus, the bid price of the $8\frac{1}{2}$s of May 1997 is actually $107\frac{7}{32} \times \$1000$ or $107,218.75. Finally, the reported bond price does not include the accrued interest for the current coupon period. For the $8\frac{1}{2}$s of May 1997, this means that from the

TABLE 15.1   Interest rate options and futures.

INTEREST RATE INSTRUMENTS

Wednesday, November 13, 1991
For Notes and Bonds, decimals in closing prices represent 32nds; 1.01 means 1 1/32. For Bills, decimals in closing prices represent basis points; $25 per .01.

OPTIONS
CHICAGO BOARD

OPTIONS ON SHORT-TERM INTEREST RATES

Strike	Calls–Last			Puts–Last		
Price	Nov	Dec	Jan	Nov	Dec	Jan
45	....	....	1 5/16	....	....	....

Total call volume 45   Total call open int. 1,787
Total put volume 0   Total put open int. 130
IRX levels: High 47.50; Low 46.20; Close 46.20, unch

OPTIONS ON LONG-TERM INTEREST RATES

Strike	Calls–Last		.	Puts–Last		
Price	Nov	Dec	Jan	Nov	Dec	Jan
75	....	1 5/16	....	....	7/16	....
77½	....	½	....	....	....	....

Total call volume 17   Total call open int. 2,012
Total put volume 6   Total put open int. 1,470
LTX levels: High 75.40; Low 74.08; Close 74.73, +0.58

FUTURES

	Open	High	Low	Settle	Chg	Yield Settle	Chg	Open Interest
TREASURY BONDS (CBT)–$100,000; pts. 32nds of 100%								
Dec	101-04	101-05	99-15	100-03	− 29	7.991	+ .095	280,722
Mr92	100-08	100-10	98-20	99-07	− 30	8.079	+ .095	31,420
June	99-12	99-12	97-30	98-10	− 30	8.173	+ .097	10,197
Sept	98-13	98-13	97-06	97-14	− 31	8.264	+ .101	2,717
Dec	97-19	97-19	96-10	96-20	− 31	8.350	+ .102	4,487
Mr93	96-00	96-05	95-28	95-28	− 32	8.430	+ .107	511

Est vol 370,000; vol Tues 245,191; op int 330,091, +8,975.

TREASURY BONDS (MCE)–$50,000; pts. 32nds of 100%

| Dec | 101-02 | 101-02 | 99-15 | 100-04 | − 32 | 7.987 | + .100 | 13,542 |

Est vol 6,600; vol Tues 6,396; open int 13,641, −132.

T–BONDS (LIFFE) U.S. $100,000; pts of 100%

| Dec | 101-02 | 100-09 | 99-21 | 100-05 | − 0-23 | 101-03 | 96-24 | 5,443 |

Est vol 2,273; vol Tues 4,086; open int 5,480, +721.

GERMAN GOV'T. BOND (LIFFE)
250,000 marks; $ per mark (.01)

| Dec | 86.23 | 86.25 | 86.02 | 86.19 | + .02 | 86.44 | 83.73 | 75,176 |
| Mr92 | n.a. | n.a. | n.a. | n.a. | n.a. | 86.70 | 85.39 | 6,879 |

Est vol 47,392; vol Tues 51,218; open int 82,055, −2,487.

TREASURY NOTES (CBT)–$100,000; pts. 32nds of 100%

Dec	103-23	103-23	102-18	103-06	− 14	7.540	+ .061	86,289
Mr92	102-29	102-29	101-26	102-13	− 14	7.651	+ .062	12,194
June	....	....	....	101-18	− 13	7.772	+ .058	418

Est vol 30,000; vol Tues 25,215; open int 98,902, +4,714.

5 YR TREAS NOTES (CBT)–$100,000; pts. 32nds of 100%

| Dec | 04-275 | 104-28 | 104-12 | 04-215 | − 5.5 | 6.880 | + .040 | 91,919 |
| Mr92 | 04-015 | 04-015 | 103-19 | 03-275 | − 6.0 | 7.071 | + .045 | 10,105 |

Est vol 19,429; vol Tues 16,648; open int 102,024, +2,602.

2 YR TREAS NOTES (CBT)–$200,000; pts. 32nds of 100%

| Dec | 103-26 | 103-26 | 103-17 | 03-255 | − ¼ | .... | .... | 13,800 |
| Mr92 | 103-11 | 103-11 | 03-057 | 03-105 | − ½ | .... | .... | 3,553 |

Est vol 1,500; vol Tues 885; open int 17,353, +153.

30-DAY INTEREST RATE (CBT)–$5 million; pts. of 100%

Nov	95.14	95.14	95.13	95.14	− .01	4.86	+ .01	1,254
Dec	95.12	95.12	95.08	95.09	− .05	4.91	+ .05	1,232
Ja92	95.16	95.17	95.15	95.17	− .05	4.83	+ .05	1,100
Feb	95.23	95.27	95.23	95.26	− .04	4.74	+ .04	962
Mar	95.18	95.21	95.18	95.21	− .05	4.79	+ .05	570
Apr	95.20	95.20	95.20	95.20	− .05	4.80	+ .05	107
June	95.10	95.11	95.10	95.11	− .04	4.89	+ .04	189

Est vol 725; vol Tues 529; open int 5,464, +185.

TREASURY BILLS (IMM)–$1 mil.; pts. of 100%

	Open	High	Low	Settle	Chg	Discount Settle	Chg	Open Interest
Dec	95.38	95.38	95.31	95.34	− .03	4.66	+ .03	21,996
Mr92	95.52	95.52	95.42	95.50	− .02	4.50	+ .02	29,371
June	95.23	95.34	95.23	95.32	− .03	4.68	+ .03	3,892
Sept	95.09	95.09	95.05	95.08	− .02	4.92	+ .02	338
Dec	94.64	94.64	94.64	94.64	....	5.36	....	156

Est vol 6,328; vol Tues 5,830; open int 55,771, +261.

LIBOR-1 MO. (IMM)–$3,000,000; points of 100%

Nov	95.05	95.05	95.02	95.02	− .04	4.98	+ .04	6,950
Dec	94.60	94.60	94.50	94.55	− .10	5.45	+ .10	7,336
Ja92	95.11	95.11	95.02	95.08	− .05	4.92	+ .05	9,651
Feb	95.01	95.08	94.99	95.06	− .05	4.94	+ .05	2,515
Mar	94.96	95.01	94.94	95.00	− .05	5.00	+ .05	1,390
Apr	....	....	....	95.01	− .04	4.99	+ .04	163

Est vol 1,577; vol Tues 2,063; open int 28,005, +300.

	Open	High	Low	Settle	Chg	High	Low	Open Interest
MUNI BOND INDEX (CBT)-$1,000; times Bond Buyer MBI								
Dec	95-23	95-23	95-01	95-08	− 15	95-25	88-16	12,542
Mr92	95-04	95-04	94-07	94-13	− 19	95-04	88-00	827

Est vol 2,500; vol Tues 2,607; open int 13,370, +850.
The index: Close 95-09; Yield 6.82.

EURODOLLAR (IMM)–$1 million; pts of 100%

	Open	High	Low	Settle	Chg	Yield Settle	Chg	Open Interest
Dec	94.85	94.86	94.75	94.80	− .07	5.20	+ .07	242,049
Mr92	94.99	94.99	94.84	94.94	− .05	5.06	+ .05	252,314
June	94.77	94.78	94.62	94.74	− .04	5.26	+ .04	145,943
Sept	94.48	94.50	94.34	94.46	− .03	5.54	+ .03	100,739
Dec	93.94	93.96	93.83	93.93	− .03	6.07	+ .03	71,656
Mr93	93.76	93.77	93.65	93.74	− .03	6.26	+ .03	55,423
June	93.46	93.46	93.36	93.43	− .02	6.57	+ .02	44,243
Sept	93.17	93.19	93.09	93.17	− .01	6.83	+ .01	31,658
Dec	92.79	92.82	92.72	92.82	+ .02	7.18	− .02	21,132
Mr94	92.76	92.81	92.71	92.80	+ .03	7.20	− .03	27,888
June	92.50	92.58	92.46	92.57	+ .05	7.43	− .05	17,956
Sept	92.28	92.37	92.23	92.35	+ .06	7.65	− .06	11,828
Dec	91.97	92.06	91.92	92.05	+ .07	7.95	− .07	9,816
Mr95	91.96	92.05	91.93	92.04	+ .07	7.96	− .07	7,178
June	91.84	91.93	91.82	91.92	+ .07	8.08	− .07	6,868
Sept	91.69	91.78	91.67	91.77	+ .07	8.23	− .07	6,419

Est vol 283,796; vol Tues 130,709; open int 1,053,277, +4,629.

EURODOLLAR (LIFFE)–$1 million; pts of 100%

	Open	High	Low	Settle	Change	Lifetime High	Low	Open Interest
Dec	94.86	94.87	94.75	94.83	− .02	94.94	90.58	17,546
Mr92	94.97	94.99	94.85	94.96	....	95.06	90.60	10,098
June	94.77	94.78	94.66	94.75	....	94.83	90.97	5,226
Sept	94.49	94.49	94.47	94.46	....	94.53	90.97	2,724
Dec	93.97	93.97	93.95	93.93	....	94.00	91.54	614
Mr93	93.80	93.80	93.78	93.74	+ .02	93.80	91.55	545
June	....	....	93.43	93.43	− .23	93.44	92.60	405
Sept	....	....	93.17	93.17	+ .08	93.09	92.82	137

Est vol 3,771; vol Tues 4,227; open int 37,295, +327.

STERLING (LIFFE)–£500,000; pts. of 100%

Dec	89.79	89.82	89.78	89.81	+ .02	90.35	86.52	52,369
Mr92	90.25	90.29	90.24	90.28	+ .04	90.49	86.68	45,849
June	90.34	90.37	90.33	90.36	+ .03	90.46	87.45	34,626
Sept	90.31	90.33	90.29	90.32	+ .02	90.41	87.46	10,853
Dec	90.22	90.23	90.20	90.23	+ .02	90.32	87.55	6,664
Mr93	90.07	90.10	90.07	90.09	+ .02	90.16	87.58	4,548
June	89.97	89.97	89.97	89.98	+ .02	90.09	87.58	2,095
Sept	89.93	89.95	89.93	89.95	+ .02	90.08	88.20	1,746
Dec	89.88	89.90	89.88	89.92	+ .04	90.02	88.95	1,641

Est vol 20,529; vol Tues 20,507; open int 160,391, −1,238.

LONG GILT (LIFFE)–£50,000; 32nds of 100%

| Dec | 95-17 | 95-23 | 95-09 | 95-17 | + 0-03 | 97-17 | 89-10 | 43,299 |
| Mr92 | 95-24 | 95-24 | 95-18 | 94-22 | + 0-05 | 96-06 | 94-18 | 2,524 |

Est vol 24,368; vol Tues 23,953; open int 45,823, +1,160.

continued

last coupon date, May 15, 1991, to the current date, November 13, 1991, interest of 8.5/2 × 182/184 × $1000, or $4,203.80, has accrued. Therefore, the total bid price of the bond is (107.21875 + 4.20380) × $1000, or $111,422.55.

TABLE 15.1

OTHER INTEREST RATE FUTURES

Settlement prices of selected contracts. Volume and open interest of all contract months.

Mortgage-Backed (CBT)–$100,000, pts. & 64ths of 100%
Nov Cpn 8.5 102-04 –6; Est. vol. 0; Open Int. 90
5-Yr. Int. Rate Swap (CBT)–$25 per ½ b.p.; pts of 100%
Dec 92.770 –.010; Est. vol. 50; Open Int. 707
3-Yr. Int. Rate Swap (CBT)–$25 per ½ b.p.; pts of 100%
Dec 93.490 –.010; Est. vol. 0; Open Int. 456
Treas. Auction 5 Yr (FINEX)–$250,000, 100 minus yield
Dec 93.22 –4.0; Est. vol. 100; Open Int. 4

CBT–Chicago Board of Trade. FINEX–Financial Instrument Exchange, a division of the New York Cotton Exchange. IMM–International Monetary Market at Chicago Mercantile Exchange. LIFFE–London International Financial Futures Exchange. MCE–MidAmerica Commodity Exchange.

FUTURES OPTIONS

T-BONDS (CBT) $100,000; points and 64ths of 100%

Strike	Calls–Last			Puts–Last		
Price	Dec-c	Mar-c	Jun-c	Dec-p	Mar-p	Jun-p
96	4-07	3-57	3-48	c7	0-44	1-28
98	2-08	2-31	2-40	0-02	1-19	2-19
100	0-25	1-31	1-47	0-21	2-17	3-20
102	0-02	0-51	1-06	1-60	3-32	4-42
104	0-01	0-26	0-43	3-58	5-05	6-12
106	c2	0-12	0-25	5-58	6-54	7-54

Est. vol. 100,000, Tues vol. 57,179 calls, 29,063 puts
Open Interest Tues 351,393 calls, 279,518 puts

T-NOTES (CBT) $100,000; points and 64ths of 100%

Strike	Calls–Last			Puts–Last		
Price	Dec-c	Mar-c	Jun-c	Dec-p	Mar-p	Jun-p
101	2-13	2-14	....	0-01	0-53	....
102	1-14	1-38	....	0-02	1-13	....
103	0-23	1-08	....	0-11	1-45	....
104	0-04	0-48	....	0-55	....	....
105	0-01	0-32	....	....	....	....
106	0-01	....	....	....	....	....

Est. vol. 7,500, Tues vol. 2,665 calls, 1,850 puts
Open Interest Tues 38,546 calls, 34,901 puts

MUNICIPAL BOND INDEX (CBT) $100,000; pts. & 64ths of 100%

Strike	Calls–Settle			Puts–Settle		
Price	Dec-c	Mar-c	Jun-c	Dec-p	Mar-p	Jun-p
93	2-19	2-00	1-56	0-05	0-40	1-13
94	1-26	1-26	....	0-11	1-00	....
95	0-44	....	....	0-28	....	....
96	0-18	....	0-44	1-03	....	2-57
97	....	....	....	....	....	....
98	....	....	....	....	....	....

Est. vol. 10, Tues vol. 64 calls, 2 puts
Open interest Tues 6,538 calls, 6,435 puts

5 YR TREAS NOTES (CBT) $100,000; points and 64ths of 100%

Strike	Calls–Last			Puts–Last		
Price	Dec-c	Mar-c	Jun-c	Dec-p	Mar-p	Jun-p
10350	1-11	0-62	....	0-01	0-39	....
10400	0-44	0-45	....	0-01	0-54	....
10450	0-16	0-32	....	0-05	....	....
10500	0-02	....	....	0-24	....	....
10550	0-01	0-14	....	....	....	....
10600	....	....	....	....	....	....

Est. vol. 2,500, Tues vol. 315 calls, 960 puts
Open interest Tues 5,186 calls, 6,365 puts

5 YR INT. RATE SWAP (CBT) $12.50 per ¼ b.p.; pts of 100%

Strike	Calls–Last			Puts–Last		
Price	Dec-c	Mar-c	Jun-c	Dec-p	Mar-p	Jun-p
9260	....	....	....	....	....	....
9270	....	....	....	....	....	....
9280	....	....	....	....	....	....
9290	....	....	....	....	....	....
9300	....	....	....	....	....	....
9310	....	....	....	....	....	....

Est. vol. 0, Tues vol. 0 calls, 0 puts
Open interest TTues 115 calls, 140 puts

EURODOLLAR (IMM) $ million; pts. of 100%

Strike	Calls–Settle			Puts–Settle		
Price	Dec-c	Mar-c	Jun-c	Dec-p	Mar-p	Jun-p
9425	0.56	0.72	0.56	0.01	0.03	0.09
9450	0.32	0.50	0.39	0.02	0.06	0.16
9475	0.12	0.30	0.25	0.07	0.11	0.26
9500	0.02	0.15	0.14	0.22	0.21	0.39
9525	.0004	0.07	0.08	0.45	0.38	....
9550	....	0.03	0.04	0.70	....	....

Est. vol. 62,887, Tues vol. 15,575 calls, 7,508 puts
Open interest Tues 248,142 calls, 360,020 puts

Source: Reprinted by permission of *Wall Street Journal*, © (November 14, 1991) Dow Jones & Company, Inc. All Rights Reserved Worldwide.

It is important to review these pricing conventions since similar conventions are used in bond option pricing. For example, prices of T-bond options traded at the CBOE are also reported in 32nds and as a percentage of par. Thus, a reported T-bond option price of 2-24 means that the cost of the option is $2\frac{24}{32} \times \$1000$, or $2,750. To provide a finer demarcation in option price, some OTC T-bond option dealers quote prices in 64ths. The CBOT uses a similar practice for T-bond futures options.[2]

The accrued interest convention also has an impact on T-bond option pricing mechanics. Assume, for example, that a call option with an exercise price of 107 is written on the 8½s of May 1997. If this option were to be exercised on November 13, 1991, the bond holder would pay the exercise price and receive a T-bond that she could immediately sell for $111,422.55. The exercise price, however, is *not* simply the stated exercise price times $1,000. If the call is exercised, the option

---

[2]Recall that the CBOT's T-bond futures contract is quoted in 32nds.

holder must not only pay the stated exercise price but also the accrued interest as of the exercise date. Thus, the total exercise price on November 13, 1991, is (107 + 4.20380) × $1000, or $111,203.80.

The price of the Eurodollar futures option is expressed in decimal form, representing basis points. Exercising the Eurodollar futures option implies that a futures position is assumed. The December 9475 call option contract implies that the option holder may buy a Eurodollar futures contract at an index level of 94.75.[3] Each basis point of the price of the option is worth $25, so the price of the December 9475 call is 12 × $25, or $300. (See Table 15.1.) The $25 value comes from the value of .01 percent of $1 million for three months (i.e., .0001 × $1,000,000 × 90/360 = $25).

15.2 SHORT-TERM INTEREST RATE OPTION PRICING

The assumption that the underlying commodity has a lognormal price distribution at the option's expiration works well for most commodities, but it is inappropriate for short-term debt instruments such as a T-bill or Eurodollar deposit. The lognormal distribution allows for the possibility of infinitely large prices. T-bills and Eurodollar deposits, which generally mature three months after the option expiration, have a predetermined future value. This fixed future value makes the possibility of an infinitely large price only three months before maturity unreasonable.

To circumvent this problem, we assume that the yield, rather than the price, of the short-term debt instrument is lognormally distributed at the option's expiration. Under this assumption, the yield can fall to zero, in which case the market price of the short-term debt instrument becomes its predetermined maturity value. On the other hand, if the yield rises without limit, the market price of the debt instrument converges to zero.

To make the valuation approach as specific as possible, we focus on the most popular short-term debt option—the CME's Eurodollar futures option. The pricing principles developed here, however, can easily be extended to the other options on short-term debt instruments. Aside from the assumption of lognormal yield, we invoke all of the same assumptions used in Chapter 11. In particular, the assumption of risk-neutral pricing greatly simplifies the development.

Using the risk-neutral valuation approach, the value of the Eurodollar futures option today is the present value of the expected terminal value, that is,

$$c(F, T; X) = e^{-rT} E(\tilde{c}_T).$$ **(15.1)**

The terminal value of the option is, in turn, a function of the Eurodollar futures index level, $\tilde{F}_T$, that is,

$$\tilde{c}_T = \begin{cases} \tilde{F}_T - X & \text{if } F_T \geq X \\ 0 & \text{if } F_T < X. \end{cases}$$ **(15.2)**

---

[3] The translation of the index level to the yield on the $1,000,000 Eurodollar deposit is provided in Chapter 8.

TABLE 15.2 Treasury instruments.

TREASURY BONDS, NOTES & BILLS

Wednesday, November 13, 1991

Representative Over-the-Counter quotations based on transactions of $1 million or more.

Treasury bond, note and bill quotes are as of mid-afternoon. Colons in bid-and-asked quotes represent 32nds; 101:01 means 101 1/32. Net changes in 32nds. n-Treasury note. Treasury bill quotes in hundredths, quoted on terms of a rate of discount. Days to maturity calculated from settlement date. All yields are to maturity and based on the asked quote. Latest 13-week and 26-week bills are boldfaced. For bonds callable prior to maturity, yields are computed to the earliest call date for issues quoted above par and to the maturity date for issues below par. *-When issued.

Source: Federal Reserve Bank of New York.

U.S. Treasury strips as of 3 p.m. Eastern time, also based on transactions of $1 million or more. Colons in bid-and-asked quotes represent 32nds; 101:01 means 101 1/32. Net changes in 32nds. Yields calculated on the bid quotation. ci-stripped coupon interest. bp-Treasury bond, stripped principal. np-Treasury note, stripped principal. For bonds callable prior to maturity, yields are computed to the earliest call date for issues quoted above par and to the maturity date for issues below par.

Source: Bear, Stearns & Co. via Street Software Technology Inc.

GOVT. BONDS & NOTES

Rate	Maturity Mo/Yr	Bid	Asked	Chg.	Ask Yld.
$6\frac{1}{2}$	Nov 91n	100:00	100:02	....	0.00
$8\frac{1}{2}$	Nov 91n	100:00	100:02	....	0.00
$14\frac{1}{4}$	Nov 91n	100:01	100:03	....	0.00
$7\frac{3}{4}$	Nov 91n	100:04	100:06	....	3.06
$7\frac{5}{8}$	Dec 91n	100:11	100:13	....	4.24
$8\frac{1}{4}$	Dec 91n	100:14	100:16	....	4.10
$11\frac{5}{8}$	Jan 92n	101:03	101:05	− 1	4.43
$8\frac{1}{8}$	Jan 92n	100:22	100:24	− 1	4.40
$6\frac{5}{8}$	Feb 92n	100:13	100:15	....	4.65
$9\frac{1}{8}$	Feb 92n	101:01	101:03	....	4.59
$14\frac{5}{8}$	Feb 92n	102:13	102:15	− 1	4.48
$8\frac{1}{2}$	Feb 92n	101:01	101:03	....	4.61
$7\frac{7}{8}$	Mar 92n	101:03	101:05	− 1	4.69
$8\frac{1}{2}$	Mar 92n	101:11	101:13	....	4.63
$11\frac{3}{4}$	Apr 92n	102:25	102:27	− 2	4.72
$8\frac{7}{8}$	Apr 92n	101:26	101:28	....	4.68
$6\frac{5}{8}$	May 92n	100:27	100:29	....	4.77
9	May 92n	102:00	102:02	− 1	4.78
$13\frac{3}{4}$	May 92n	104:11	104:13	− 1	4.73
$8\frac{1}{2}$	May 92n	101:28	101:30	− 1	4.83
$8\frac{1}{4}$	Jun 92n	102:01	102:03	− 1	4.82
$8\frac{3}{8}$	Jun 92n	102:03	102:05	....	4.84
$10\frac{3}{8}$	Jul 92n	103:16	103:18	....	4.88
8	Jul 92n	102:02	102:04	− 1	4.92
$4\frac{1}{4}$	Aug 87-92	98:13	99:13	− 1	5.07
$7\frac{1}{4}$	Aug 92	101:18	101:22	....	4.94
$7\frac{7}{8}$	Aug 92n	102:00	102:02	− 1	5.04
$8\frac{1}{4}$	Aug 92n	102:09	102:11	− 1	5.03
$8\frac{1}{8}$	Aug 92n	102:11	102:13	− 1	4.99
$8\frac{1}{8}$	Sep 92n	102:18	102:20	− 1	5.02
$8\frac{3}{4}$	Sep 92n	103:03	103:05	− 1	5.02
$9\frac{3}{4}$	Oct 92n	104:04	104:06	− 1	5.02
$7\frac{3}{4}$	Oct 92n	102:12	102:14	− 1	5.11
$7\frac{3}{4}$	Nov 92n	102:15	102:17	− 1	5.12
$8\frac{3}{8}$	Nov 92n	103:02	103:04	− 1	5.13
$10\frac{1}{2}$	Nov 92n	105:04	105:06	− 1	5.11
$7\frac{3}{8}$	Nov 92n	102:06	102:08	− 1	5.13
$7\frac{1}{4}$	Dec 92n	102:06	102:08	....	5.17
$9\frac{1}{8}$	Dec 92n	104:06	104:08	− 1	5.19
$8\frac{3}{4}$	Jan 93n	103:28	103:30	− 2	5.23
7	Jan 93n	101:30	102:00	− 1	5.27
4	Feb 88-93	96:22	97:22	− 1	5.94
$6\frac{3}{4}$	Feb 93	101:22	101:26	− 1	5.24
$7\frac{7}{8}$	Feb 93	103:00	103:04	− 1	5.26
$8\frac{1}{4}$	Feb 93n	103:15	103:17	− 1	5.30
$8\frac{3}{8}$	Feb 93n	103:20	103:22	− 1	5.29
$10\frac{7}{8}$	Feb 93n	106:19	106:21	− 2	5.31
$6\frac{3}{4}$	Feb 93n	101:22	101:24	− 2	5.33
$7\frac{1}{8}$	Mar 93n	102:08	102:10	− 2	5.36
$9\frac{5}{8}$	Mar 93n	105:17	105:19	− 1	5.35
$7\frac{3}{8}$	Apr 93n	102:20	102:22	− 1	5.38
7	Apr 93n	102:05	102:07	− 1	5.40
$7\frac{5}{8}$	May 93n	103:02	103:04	....	5.43
$8\frac{5}{8}$	May 93n	104:15	104:17	....	5.44

Rate	Maturity Mo/Yr	Bid	Asked	Chg.	Ask Yld.
$8\frac{1}{2}$	Jul 97n	107:07	107:09	− 5	6.92
$8\frac{5}{8}$	Aug 97n	107:26	107:28	− 6	6.94
$8\frac{3}{4}$	Oct 97n	108:16	108:18	− 4	6.96
$8\frac{7}{8}$	Nov 97n	109:04	109:06	− 7	6.97
$7\frac{7}{8}$	Jan 98n	104:06	104:08	− 7	7.01
$8\frac{1}{8}$	Feb 98n	105:13	105:15	− 6	7.03
$7\frac{7}{8}$	Apr 98n	104:06	104:08	− 5	7.04
7	May 93-98	100:16	100:24	....	6.47
9	May 98n	109:27	109:29	− 8	7.07
$8\frac{1}{4}$	Jul 98n	105:30	106:00	− 7	7.10
$9\frac{1}{4}$	Aug 98n	111:04	111:06	− 8	7.13
$7\frac{1}{8}$	Oct 98n	100:09	100:11	− 5	7.06
$3\frac{1}{2}$	Nov 98	97:24	98:24	+ 24	3.70
$8\frac{7}{8}$	Nov 98n	109:09	109:11	− 6	7.15
$8\frac{7}{8}$	Feb 99n	109:09	109:11	− 6	7.20
$8\frac{1}{2}$	May 94-99	105:00	105:08	− 4	6.20
$9\frac{1}{8}$	May 99n	110:23	110:25	− 7	7.24
8	Aug 99n	104:08	104:10	− 6	7.26
$7\frac{7}{8}$	Nov 99n	103:15	103:17	− 6	7.28
$7\frac{7}{8}$	Feb 95-00	102:15	102:19	− 1	6.97
$8\frac{1}{2}$	Feb 00n	107:01	107:03	− 9	7.34
$8\frac{7}{8}$	May 00n	109:06	109:08	− 12	7.39
$8\frac{3}{8}$	Aug 95-00	104:18	104:22	− 3	6.93
$8\frac{3}{4}$	Aug 00n	108:12	108:14	− 13	7.42
$8\frac{1}{2}$	Nov 00n	106:27	106:29	− 13	7.43
$7\frac{3}{4}$	Feb 01n	101:31	102:01	− 11	7.44
$11\frac{3}{4}$	Feb 01	128:14	128:18	− 10	7.43
8	May 01n	103:22	103:24	− 10	7.44
$13\frac{1}{8}$	May 01	138:04	138:08	− 13	7.44
$7\frac{7}{8}$	Aug 01n	102:29	102:31	− 14	7.44
8	Aug 96-01	103:19	103:23	− 15	7.07
$13\frac{3}{8}$	Aug 01	140:16	140:20	− 8	7.44
$7\frac{1}{2}$	Nov 01n*	100:19	100:20	− 11	7.41
$15\frac{3}{4}$	Nov 01	157:21	157:25	− 10	7.45
$14\frac{1}{4}$	Feb 02	147:25	147:29	− 14	7.48
$11\frac{5}{8}$	Nov 02	130:10	130:14	− 13	7.51
$10\frac{3}{4}$	Feb 03	123:31	124:03	− 12	7.54
$10\frac{3}{4}$	May 03	124:06	124:10	− 12	7.55
$11\frac{1}{8}$	Aug 03	127:04	127:08	− 15	7.58
$11\frac{7}{8}$	Nov 03	133:07	133:11	− 23	7.59
$12\frac{3}{8}$	May 04	137:30	138:02	− 29	7.60
$13\frac{3}{4}$	Aug 04	149:07	149:11	− 29	7.63
$11\frac{5}{8}$	Nov 04	132:02	132:06	− 23	7.67
$8\frac{1}{4}$	May 00-05	104:10	104:14	− 8	7.53
12	May 05	135:23	135:27	− 26	7.69
$10\frac{3}{4}$	Aug 05	125:12	125:16	− 19	7.71
$9\frac{3}{8}$	Feb 06	114:14	114:18	− 18	7.68
$7\frac{5}{8}$	Feb 02-07	99:20	99:24	− 16	7.65
$7\frac{7}{8}$	Nov 02-07	101:14	101:18	− 16	7.66
$8\frac{3}{8}$	Aug 03-08	104:28	105:00	− 12	7.72
$8\frac{3}{4}$	Nov 03-08	107:19	107:23	− 19	7.75
$9\frac{1}{8}$	May 04-09	110:21	110:25	− 24	7.76
$10\frac{3}{8}$	Nov 04-09	120:28	121:00	− 24	7.78
$11\frac{3}{4}$	Feb 05-10	132:10	132:14	− 25	7.78

Mat.	Type	Bid	Asked	Chg.	Bid Yld.
Nov 99	np	55:03	55:07	− 7	7.59
Feb 00	ci	53:28	54:00	− 8	7.64
Feb 00	np	53:22	53:27	− 9	7.68
May 00	ci	52:28	53:00	− 7	7.64
May 00	np	52:22	52:27	− 7	7.68
Aug 00	ci.	51:26	51:30	− 7	7.66
Aug 00	np	51:23	51:27	− 7	7.68
Nov 00	ci	50:24	50:28	− 8	7.68
Nov 00	np	50:24	50:28	− 7	7.68
Feb 01	ci	49:14	49:19	− 7	7.76
Feb 01	np	49:09	49:13	− 8	7.80
May 01	ci	48:14	48:18	− 8	7.78
May 01	np	48:08	48:12	− 9	7.82
Aug 01	ci	47:16	47:21	− 9	7.78
Aug 01	np	47:11	47:15	− 8	7.82
Nov 01	ci	46:20	46:24	− 7	7.78
Feb 02	ci	45:09	45:13	− 12	7.88
May 02	ci	44:11	44:15	− 11	7.90
Aug 02	ci	43:12	43:17	− 12	7.92
Nov 02	ci	42:15	42:19	− 11	7.94
Feb 03	ci	41:16	41:21	− 12	7.97
May 03	ci	40:21	40:26	− 12	7.98
Aug 03	ci	39:27	39:31	− 11	7.99
Nov 03	ci	39:00	39:05	− 12	8.00
Feb 04	ci	38:04	38:08	− 11	8.03
May 04	ci	37:09	37:13	− 12	8.05
Aug 04	ci	36:16	36:21	− 12	8.06
Nov 04	ci	35:24	35:28	− 12	8.07
Nov 04	bp	35:23	35:27	− 11	8.08
Feb 05	ci	34:31	35:03	− 11	8.09
May 05	ci	34:08	34:12	− 11	8.10
May 05	bp	34:09	34:13	− 11	8.09
Aug 05	ci	33:18	33:22	− 11	8.10
Aug 05	bp	33:19	33:24	− 12	8.09
Nov 05	ci	32:29	33:01	− 11	8.10
Feb 06	ci	32:05	32:10	− 12	8.12
Feb 06	bp	32:04	32:08	− 11	8.13
May 06	ci	31:17	31:21	− 11	8.12
Aug 06	ci	30:29	31:01	− 11	8.12
Nov 06	ci	30:10	30:14	− 11	8.12
Feb 07	ci	29:16	29:20	− 12	8.17
May 07	ci	28:29	29:01	− 12	8.17
Aug 07	ci	28:11	28:15	− 12	8.17
Nov 07	ci	27:25	27:29	− 12	8.17
Feb 08	ci	27:03	27:07	− 11	8.20
May 08	ci	26:15	26:19	− 11	8.22
Aug 08	ci	25:30	26:02	− 11	8.22
Nov 08	ci	25:14	25:18	− 10	8.22
Feb 09	ci	24:25	24:29	− 11	8.25
May 09	ci	24:10	24:13	− 10	8.25
Aug 09	ci	23:26	23:30	− 10	8.25
Nov 09	ci	23:11	23:15	− 10	8.25
Nov 09	bp	22:30	23:02	− 9	8.35
Feb 10	ci	22:28	23:00	− 10	8.25
May 10	ci	22:13	22:17	− 10	8.25
Aug 10	ci	21:30	22:01	− 10	8.26
Nov 10	ci	21:15	21:19	− 11	8.26
Feb 11	ci	21:02	21:05	− 10	8.26
May 11	ci	20:20	20:24	− 10	8.26
Aug 11	ci	20:07	20:11	− 10	8.26
Nov 11	ci	19:26	19:30	− 10	8.26
Feb 12	ci	19:12	19:16	− 10	8.27
May 12	ci	19:00	19:03	− 9	8.27
Aug 12	ci	18:20	18:23	− 9	8.27
Nov 12	ci	18:08	18:11	− 9	8.27
Feb 13	ci	17:28	17:31	− 9	8.27
May 13	ci	17:16	17:20	− 10	8.27
Aug 13	ci	17:05	17:09	− 9	8.27
Nov 13	ci	16:26	16:30	− 9	8.27
Feb 14	ci	16:15	16:19	− 9	8.27
May 14	ci	16:05	16:08	− 9	8.27
Aug 14	ci	15:26	15:30	− 9	8.27
Nov 14	ci	15:16	15:20	− 9	8.27
Feb 15	ci	15:06	15:10	− 9	8.27
Feb 15	bp	15:07	15:11	− 8	8.26
May 15	ci	14:29	15:00	− 8	8.27

TABLE 15.2 continued

10 1/8	May 93n	106:18	106:20	-2	5.46
6 3/4	May 93n	101:26	101:28	-1	5.47
7	Jun 93n	102:08	102:10	-1	5.49
8 1/8	Jun 93n	103:31	104:01	-1	5.50
7 1/4	Jul 93n	102:21	102:23	-1	5.52
6 7/8	Jul 93n	102:02	102:04	-1	5.56
7 1/2	Aug 88-93	100:20	100:24	+2	7.04
8	Aug 93n	103:30	104:00	....	5.57
8 5/8	Aug 93	104:30	105:02	....	5.55
8 3/4	Aug 93n	105:05	105:07	....	5.58
11 7/8	Aug 93n	110:11	110:13	....	5.56
6 3/8	Aug 93n	101:09	101:11	....	5.58
6 1/8	Sep 93n	100:27	100:29	....	5.61
8 1/4	Sep 93n	104:19	104:21	-1	5.60
7 1/8	Oct 93n	102:21	102:23	-1	5.61
6	Oct 93n	100:21	100:23	....	5.61
7 3/4	Nov 93n	103:27	103:29	-1	5.66
8 5/8	Nov 93	105:15	105:19	+1	5.63
9	Nov 93n	106:05	106:07	-1	5.67
11 3/4	Nov 93n	111:10	111:12	-1	5.65
7 5/8	Dec 93n	103:24	103:26	-1	5.70
7	Jan 94n	102:15	102:17	-2	5.74
6 7/8	Feb 94n	102:09	102:11	....	5.75
8 7/8	Feb 94n	106:10	106:12	-3	5.81
9	Feb 94	106:18	106:22	-2	5.79
8 1/2	Mar 94n	105:24	105:26	-2	5.84
7	Apr 94n	102:19	102:21	-1	5.81
4 1/8	May 89-94	96:24	97:24	-3	5.09
7	May 94n	102:17	102:19	-2	5.87
9 1/2	May 94n	108:06	108:08	-3	5.90
13 1/8	May 94n	116:17	116:19	-3	5.89
8 1/2	Jun 94n	106:03	106:05	-1	5.93
8	Jul 94n	104:30	105:00	-2	5.95
6 7/8	Aug 94n	102:08	102:10	-3	5.95
8 5/8	Aug 94n	106:16	106:18	-2	6.00
8 3/4	Aug 94	106:25	106:29	-2	5.99
12 5/8	Aug 94n	116:17	116:19	-2	5.99
8 1/2	Sep 94n	106:12	106:14	-1	6.03
9 1/2	Oct 94n	109:00	109:02	-2	6.06
6	Nov 94n*	100:00	100:01	-2	5.99
8 1/4	Nov 94n	105:27	105:29	-2	6.07
10 1/8	Nov 94	110:28	111:00	-3	6.06
11 5/8	Nov 94n	114:31	115:01	-2	6.07
7 5/8	Dec 94n	104:10	104:12	-2	6.07
8 5/8	Jan 95n	106:30	107:00	-2	6.16
3	Feb 95	97:00	98:00	-3	3.66
7 3/4	Feb 95n	104:17	104:19	-3	6.17
10 1/2	Feb 95	112:10	112:14	-3	6.22
11 1/4	Feb 95n	114:17	114:19	-5	6.22
8 3/8	Apr 95n	106:08	106:10	-4	6.29
8 1/2	May 95n	106:24	106:26	-2	6.30
10 3/8	May 95	112:14	112:18	-3	6.32
11 1/4	May 95n	115:03	115:05	-4	6.35
12 5/8	May 95	119:14	119:18	-2	6.31
8 7/8	Jul 95n	107:28	107:30	-4	6.41
8 1/2	Aug 95n	106:24	106:26	-4	6.43
10 1/2	Aug 95n	113:07	113:09	-4	6.46
8 5/8	Oct 95n	107:08	107:10	-4	6.48
8 1/2	Nov 95n	106:28	106:30	-4	6.50
9 1/2	Nov 95n	110:10	110:12	-6	6.51
11 1/2	Nov 95	117:12	117:16	-4	6.47
9 1/4	Jan 96n	109:18	109:20	-5	6.57
7 1/2	Jan 96n	103:09	103:11	-5	6.58
7 7/8	Feb 96n	104:18	104:20	-5	6.61
8 7/8	Feb 96n	108:07	108:09	-6	6.61
7 1/2	Feb 96n	103:07	103:09	-5	6.61
7 3/4	Mar 96n	104:03	104:05	-5	6.64
9 3/8	Apr 96n	110:08	110:10	-5	6.64
7 5/8	Apr 96n	103:22	103:24	-5	6.64
7 3/8	May 96n	102:22	102:24	-5	6.66
7 5/8	May 96n	103:21	103:23	-5	6.66
7 7/8	Jun 96n	104:18	104:20	-5	6.70
7 7/8	Jul 96n	104:19	104:21	-6	6.70
7 7/8	Jul 96n	104:23	104:25	-5	6.68
7 1/4	Aug 96n	102:06	102:08	-5	6.69
7	Sep 96n	101:06	101:08	-5	6.70
8	Oct 96n	105:06	105:08	-5	6.73
6 7/8	Oct 96n	100:26	100:28	-5	6.66
7 1/4	Nov 96n	102:04	102:06	-5	6.73
8	Jan 97n	105:04	105:06	-5	6.79
8 1/2	Apr 97n	107:07	107:09	-5	6.87
8 1/2	May 97n	107:07	107:09	-5	6.89
10	May 05-10	118:15	118:19	-23	7.75
12 3/4	Nov 05-10	141:24	141:28	-29	7.79
13 7/8	May 06-11	152:06	152:10	-30	7.79
14	Nov 06-11	154:08	154:12	-31	7.79
10 3/8	Nov 07-12	122:13	122:17	-25	7.87
12	Aug 08-13	137:25	137:29	-30	7.88
13 1/4	May 09-14	150:07	150:11	-36	7.89
12 1/2	Aug 09-14	143:13	143:17	-34	7.90
11 3/4	Nov 09-14	136:27	136:31	-35	7.87
11 1/4	Feb 15	135:01	135:05	-36	7.92
10 5/8	Aug 15	128:19	128:23	-33	7.92
9 7/8	Nov 15	120:23	120:25	-30	7.93
9 1/4	Feb 16	113:30	114:00	-33	7.94
7 1/4	May 16	92:21	92:23	-27	7.93
7 1/2	Nov 16	95:07	95:09	-28	7.94
8 3/4	May 17	108:25	108:27	-31	7.94
8 7/8	Aug 17	110:05	110:07	-31	7.94
9 1/8	May 18	113:00	113:02	-32	7.94
9	Nov 18	111:21	111:23	-32	7.94
8 7/8	Feb 19	110:09	110:11	-32	7.94
8 1/8	Aug 19	101:31	102:01	-30	7.94
8 1/2	Feb 20	106:06	106:08	-32	7.94
8 3/4	May 20	109:02	109:04	-32	7.94
8 3/4	Aug 20	109:02	109:04	-30	7.94
7 7/8	Feb 21	99:07	99:09	-30	7.94
8 1/8	May 21	102:04	102:06	-31	7.93
8 1/8	Aug 21	102:09	102:11	-30	7.92
8	Nov 21*	101:12	101:13	-28	7.88

U.S. TREASURY STRIPS

Mat.	Type	Bid	Asked	Chg.	Bid Yld.
Feb 92	ci	98:26	98:26	+ 1	4.87
May 92	ci	97:18	97:19	- 1	4.99
Aug 92	ci	96:11	96:11	- 1	5.04
Nov 92	ci	95:04	95:05	- 2	5.05
Feb 93	ci	93:19	93:20	- 1	5.38
May 93	ci	92:08	92:09	- 2	5.46
Aug 93	ci	90:26	90:27	- 3	5.59
Nov 93	ci	89:13	89:15	- 2	5.68
Feb 94	ci	87:24	87:26	- 1	5.89
May 94	ci	86:13	86:15	- 1	5.93
Aug 94	ci	84:30	85:00	- 3	6.03
Nov 94	ci	83:12	83:15	- 3	6.15
Nov 94	np	83:08	83:11	- 3	6.20
Feb 95	ci	81:18	81:20	- 4	6.37
Feb 95	np	81:24	81:26	- 4	6.30
May 95	ci	80:02	80:05	- 5	6.45
May 95	np	80:01	80:03	- 4	6.47
Aug 95	ci	78:20	78:22	- 4	6.52
Aug 95	np	78:14	78:17	- 5	6.58
Nov 95	ci	77:08	77:11	- 5	6.56
Nov 95	np	77:02	77:05	- 5	6.62
Feb 96	ci	75:14	75:17	- 5	6.74
Feb 96	np	75:09	75:12	- 5	6.79
May 96	ci	74:04	74:07	- 5	6.77
May 96	np	74:01	74:05	- 6	6.79
Aug 96	ci	72:19	72:22	- 5	6.86
Nov 96	ci	71:14	71:17	- 6	6.84
Nov 96	np	70:10	70:13	- 3	7.17
Feb 97	ci	69:20	69:23	- 4	7.02
May 97	ci	68:07	68:10	- 3	7.08
May 97	np	68:05	68:09	- 4	7.09
Aug 97	ci	66:27	66:31	- 4	7.13
Aug 97	np	66:26	66:29	- 3	7.14
Nov 97	ci	65:24	65:28	- 1	7.11
Nov 97	np	65:18	65:22	- 4	7.16
Feb 98	ci	63:31	64:02	- 8	7.28
Feb 98	np	63:23	63:27	- 4	7.34
May 98	ci	62:24	62:28	- 8	7.30
May 98	np	62:16	62:20	- 4	7.36
Aug 98	ci	61:15	61:19	- 8	7.34
Aug 98	np	61:06	61:10	- 4	7.41
Nov 98	ci	60:12	60:16	- 8	7.34
Nov 98	np	60:05	60:09	- 7	7.39
Feb 99	ci	58:19	58:23	- 7	7.51
Feb 99	np	58:14	58:18	- 8	7.55
May 99	ci	57:14	57:18	- 7	7.53
May 99	np	57:09	57:13	- 8	7.57
Aug 99	ci	56:07	56:11	- 7	7.57
Aug 99	np	56:04	56:08	- 7	7.59
Nov 99	ci	55:06	55:10	- 8	7.57
Aug 15	ci	14:19	14:22	- 9	8.27
Aug 15	bp	14:20	14:23	- 8	8.26
Nov 15	ci	14:10	14:13	- 8	8.27
Nov 15	bp	14:11	14:14	- 7	8.26
Feb 16	ci	14:00	14:04	- 9	8.27
Feb 16	bp	14:03	14:06	- 8	8.25
May 16	ci	13:23	13:27	- 9	8.27
May 16	bp	14:00	14:03	- 8	8.19
Aug 16	ci	13:15	13:18	- 8	8.27
Nov 16	ci	13:06	13:09	- 8	8.27
Nov 16	bp	13:12	13:15	- 6	8.21
Feb 17	ci	12:31	13:02	- 8	8.26
May 17	ci	12:22	12:25	- 8	8.26
May 17	bp	12:26	12:29	- 8	8.22
Aug 17	ci	12:14	12:17	- 8	8.26
Aug 17	bp	12:18	12:21	- 8	8.22
Nov 17	ci	12:05	12:08	- 8	8.27
Feb 18	ci	11:31	12:02	- 8	8.25
May 18	ci	11:24	11:26	- 7	8.25
May 18	bp	11:27	11:30	- 8	8.21
Aug 18	ci	11:16	11:19	- 8	8.25
Nov 18	ci	11:09	11:12	- 7	8.25
Nov 18	bp	11:12	11:15	- 9	8.21
Feb 19	ci	11:03	11:06	- 8	8.23
Feb 19	bp	11:08	11:11	- 8	8.18
May 19	ci	10:29	11:00	- 8	8.22
Aug 19	ci	10:22	10:25	- 8	8.22
Aug 19	bp	10:27	10:30	- 7	8.17
Nov 19	ci	10:16	10:19	- 8	8.21
Feb 20	ci	10:11	10:13	- 7	8.20
Feb 20	bp	10:14	10:17	- 7	8.16
May 20	ci	10:05	10:08	- 7	8.19
May 20	bp	10:08	10:10	- 7	8.16
Aug 20	ci	9:30	10:01	- 7	8.19
Aug 20	bp	10:02	10:05	- 9	8.15
Nov 20	ci	9:26	9:28	- 7	8.17
Feb 21	ci	9:20	9:22	- 7	8.17
Feb 21	bp	9:23	9:26	- 8	8.13
May 21	ci	9:16	9:19	- 7	8.14
May 21	bp	9:19	9:21	- 7	8.11
Aug 21	ci	9:19	9:21	- 7	8.04
Aug 21	bp	9:18	9:20	- 9	8.05
Nov 21	bp	9:19	9:22	- 6	7.97

TREASURY BILLS

Maturity	Days to Mat.	Bid	Asked	Chg.	Ask Yld.
Nov 21 '91	6	4.68	4.58	-0.02	4.65
Nov 29 '91	14	4.54	4.44	-0.01	4.52
Dec 05 '91	20	4.41	4.31	-0.03	4.39
Dec 12 '91	27	4.36	4.26	-0.08	4.34
Dec 19 '91	34	4.39	4.35	-0.05	4.43
Dec 26 '91	41	4.40	4.36	-0.04	4.45
Jan 02 '92	48	4.43	4.39	-0.02	4.49
Jan 09 '92	55	4.50	4.46	-0.02	4.57
Jan 16 '92	62	4.55	4.53	-0.01	4.63
Jan 23 '92	69	4.57	4.55	-0.01	4.67
Jan 30 '92	76	4.57	4.55	-0.01	4.67
Feb 06 '92	83	4.62	4.60	....	4.73
Feb 13 '92	**90**	**4.63**	**4.61**	....	**4.73**
Feb 20 '92	97	4.62	4.60	....	4.74
Feb 27 '92	104	4.62	4.60	....	4.74
Mar 05 '92	111	4.64	4.62	....	4.76
Mar 12 '92	118	4.66	4.64	+0.01	4.79
Mar 19 '92	125	4.66	4.64	+0.01	4.79
Mar 26 '92	132	4.64	4.62	....	4.78
Apr 02 '92	139	4.66	4.64	....	4.80
Apr 09 '92	146	4.69	4.67	....	4.84
Apr 16 '92	153	4.69	4.67	+0.01	4.84
Apr 23 '92	160	4.72	4.70	....	4.88
Apr 30 '92	167	4.68	4.66	....	4.84
May 07 '92	174	4.72	4.70	+0.02	4.89
May 14 '92	**181**	**4.70**	**4.68**	**-0.01**	**4.87**
Jun 04 '92	202	4.65	4.63	+0.02	4.82
Jul 02 '92	230	4.71	4.69	+0.01	4.89
Jul 30 '92	258	4.74	4.72	+0.03	4.93
Aug 27 '92	286	4.74	4.72	+0.02	4.94
Sep 24 '92	314	4.73	4.71	+0.04	4.94
Oct 22 '92	342	4.75	4.73	+0.03	4.98

Source: Reprinted by permission of *Wall Street Journal*, © (November 14, 1991) Dow Jones & Company, Inc. All Rights Reserved Worldwide.

If we assume the terminal futures price is lognormally distributed, we would evaluate $E(\tilde{c}_T)$ in the same manner we did in Chapter 11, and substitute this into (15.1). The valuation equation would be (11.25) with the cost-of-carry rate, b, set to zero because the underlying instrument is a futures contract.

The assumption of lognormally distributed yield requires a modification of the terminal value function, (15.2), for the call. In Chapter 8, we discussed the fact that the Eurodollar futures price is an index level computed by subtracting the yield on the Eurodollar deposit from 100. In other words, the futures price is $F = 100 - y$. If we substitute this definition into (15.2) and rearrange, we find that the terminal call price can be expressed as

$$\tilde{c}_T = \begin{cases} (100 - X) - \tilde{y}_T & \text{if } y_T \leq 100 - X \\ 0 & \text{if } y_T > 100 - X. \end{cases} \qquad \text{(15.3)}$$

But equation (15.3) looks surprisingly familiar. It is the terminal value function of a European put option, where y_T has replaced S_T and where $(100 - X)$ has replaced X. Since y_T is lognormally distributed, the European put formula (11.28) of Chapter 11 can be applied directly. Using the fact that $y = (100 - F)$, the expected terminal call price is

$$E(\tilde{c}_T) = (100 - X)N(-d_2) - (100 - F)N(-d_1), \qquad \text{(15.4)}$$

where

$$d_1 = \frac{\ln[(100 - F)/(100 - X)] + .5\sigma_y^2 T}{\sigma_y\sqrt{T}} \quad \text{and} \quad d_2 = d_1 - \sigma_y\sqrt{T},$$

and σ_y is the standard deviation of the logarithm of the yield ratios, $\ln(y_t/y_{t-1})$. Substituting (15.4) into (15.1), the *price of a European call option on a Eurodollar futures contract*[4] is

$$c(F, T; X) = e^{-rT}[(100 - X)N(-d_2) - (100 - F)N(-d_1)]. \qquad \text{(15.5)}$$

By put-call parity for European futures options, the *price of a European put option on a Eurodollar futures contract* is

$$p(F, T; X) = e^{-rT}[(100 - F)N(d_1) - (100 - X)N(d_2)]. \qquad \text{(15.6)}$$

---

[4]This approach to Eurodollar futures option valuation is described in detail in Emanuel (1985).

EXAMPLE 15.1

Using the values reported in Tables 15.1 and 15.2, compute the implied yield volatility of the March 9500 call option on the Eurodollar futures contract. According to the tables, the call price is .15, the underlying futures price is 94.94, and the riskless rate of interest is about 4.6 percent. As of November 13, 1991, the option has 124 days remaining to expiration.

The implied yield volatility for this call is computed by solving

$$.15 = e^{-.046(124/365)}[(100 - 95)N(-d_2) - (100 - 94.94)N(-d_1)],$$

where

$$d_1 = \frac{\ln[(100 - 94.94)/(100 - 95.00)] + .5\sigma_y^2(124/365)}{\sigma_y\sqrt{124/365}}$$

and

$$d_2 = d_1 - \sigma_y\sqrt{124/365}.$$

Without showing the steps of the iterative search that is used to find the implied volatility, the solution is

$$\sigma_y = 10.26\%.$$

Note that this volatility is upward biased since Eurodollar futures options are American style.

Relation Between Price Volatility and Yield Volatility

Prior to this chapter, volatility has been defined as the standard deviation of the logarithm of commodity price ratios, $\ln(S_t/S_{t-1})$, or the standard deviation of the logarithm of futures price ratios, $\ln(F_t/F_{t-1})$. The volatility parameter used in (15.5) and (15.6), however, is the standard deviation of the logarithm of yield ratios, $\ln(y_t/y_{t-1})$. Since the scale of these two volatilities appears so different, it is important to understand how these two measures are linked. The yield of the Eurodollar deposit is

$$y = 100 - F, \tag{15.7}$$

so the relation between a yield change and a price change is

$$dy = -dF. \tag{15.8}$$

Multiplying the left-hand side by y/y and the right-hand side by F/F, we have

$$y\frac{dy}{y} = F\frac{dF}{F},$$

which can be rearranged as

$$\frac{dy}{y} = \frac{dF}{F}\left(\frac{F}{100-F}\right). \tag{15.9}$$

In other words, the rate of change in yield equals the rate of change in the index level scaled by the factor $F/(100-F)$. The yield volatility, σ_y, therefore, equals the return volatility, σ_F, times the factor $F/(100-F)$, that is,

$$\sigma_y = \sigma_F\left(\frac{F}{100-F}\right). \tag{15.10}$$

EXAMPLE 15.2

In Example 15.1, the implied yield volatility rate from the March 9500 Eurodollar call is shown to be 10.26 percent. Compute the implied return volatility based on this estimate.

The implied futures price volatility is the solution to

$$.1026 = \sigma_F\left(\frac{94.94}{100-94.94}\right),$$

which implies that

$$\sigma_F = 0.55\%.$$

15.3 TREASURY BOND OPTION PRICING—PRICE-BASED VALUATION

In Table 15.1, only two options are bond options—the CBOE's short-term and long-term interest rate index contracts. These options are American-style and are written on specific Treasury issues (see Table 15.2 for the price of the underlying T-bond or T-note). If we are willing to accept the assumption that long-term bond prices are lognormally distributed at the option's expiration,[5] these options can be priced using the continuous cost-of-carry commodity option framework developed in Chapters 10 and 11.

In doing so, we must account for the treatment of accrued interest. We noted earlier that the reported bond price excludes accrued interest for the current coupon period and, to find the cost of the bond, the accrued interest must be added to the reported bond price. We also noted that the exercise price of a bond option is increased by the accrued interest. Since accrued interest is added to the reported bond price and to the exercise price, one can simply ignore it and use the reported bond price and the stated exercise price in the bond option pricing formula.

The option pricing formulas require the cost of carry for a bond, which is the short-term riskless rate of interest less the coupon yield, that is, $b = r - y$. To compute the annualized coupon yield of a bond with price B for use in the option pricing equations, recognize that a coupon payment, C, is received each half year, so

$$e^{y(.5)} = \frac{B + C}{B}$$

or

$$y = 2 \times \ln\left(1 + \frac{C}{B}\right). \qquad \textbf{(15.11)}$$

It is worth noting that bonds with high coupon yields tend to depreciate in price (since they initially sell above par) and that bonds with low coupon yields tend to appreciate in price (since they initially sell below par). The value of an option, in turn, depends on the price appreciation or depreciation. The higher (lower) the rate of price appreciation on the bond, the higher (lower) the call price and the lower (higher) the put price. We now apply the commodity option pricing results of Chapters 10 and 11 using this cost-of-carry parameter.

---

[5] For short-term options of a year or less, this assumption is plausible, particularly if the underlying bond has a long time to maturity. For long-term options and/or for short-term T-bonds and T-notes, this assumption is less tenable.

EXAMPLE 15.3

Assume there exists a European-style call option on the 8½s of May 1997 that we discussed earlier in the chapter. The call has an exercise price of 107, a time to expiration of 100 days, and a current market price of $12¹/₃₂. Assume that the riskless rate of interest is 4.6 percent. Compute the implied volatility of this option based upon the average of the bid and ask bond prices.

The average of the bid and ask prices for the 8½s of May 1997 is 107⁸/₃₂ or 107.25. The coupon yield on this bond is

$$y = 2 \times \ln\left(1 + \frac{4.25}{107.25}\right) = 7.77\%.$$

Substituting into valuation equation (11.25), we get

$$1.656 = 107.25e^{(.046-.0777-.046)(100/365)}N(d_1) - 107e^{-.046(100/365)}N(d_2),$$

where

$$d_1 = \frac{\ln(107.25/107) + (.046 - .0777 + .5\sigma^2)100/365}{\sigma\sqrt{100/365}}$$

and

$$d_2 = d_1 - \sigma\sqrt{100/365}.$$

Without showing the steps of the iterative search that is used to find the implied volatility, the solution is

$$\sigma = 8.97\%.$$

By far the most active long-term interest rate option market is the CBT's Treasury bond futures options. These options are American-style, and expire on the first Friday preceding, by at least five business days, the first notice day for the corresponding T-bond futures contract. Also, the T-bond futures option has the decimal part of its price reported in 64ths. Under the assumption that the futures price at the option's expiration is lognormally distributed, the valuation of these options is possible using the quadratic approximation described in Chapter 14.

EXAMPLE 15.4

Compare the theoretical price of a March 1992 T-bond futures put option, with a strike price of 100 to the quoted price in Table 15.1, $2^{17}\!/_{64}$. The price of the March 1992 futures is $99^{7}\!/_{32}$, and, given that the option expires on February 21, 1992, the time to expiration is 100 days. Assume the riskless rate of interest is 4.6 percent and the volatility rate is 9.00 percent.

The T-bond futures option contract is an American-style option, so we use the quadratic approximation. We begin by computing the value of the corresponding European-style futures put contract using equation (14.20).

$$p = e^{-.046(100/365)}[100N(-d_2) - 99.21875N(-d_1)],$$

where

$$d_1 = \frac{\ln(99.21875/100) + .5(.09)^2(100/365)}{.09\sqrt{100/365}} = -.143,$$

$$d_2 = d_1 - .09\sqrt{100/365} = -.190.$$

The European put option value is 2.32.

Applying the quadratic approximation (14.22), we find that the critical index level F^{**} below which the put should be exercised immediately is 90.490, considerably below the current futures price of 99.21875. Hence, the value of the early exercise premium should be small. The value of A_1 is 0.092, the value of q_1 is -29.619. The approximate value of the March 100 put option on the T-bond futures is, therefore,

$$\begin{aligned} P(F, T; X) &= p(F, T; X) + A_1(F/F^{**})^{q_1} \\ &= 2.32 + 0.092(99.21875/90.490)^{-29.619} \\ &= 2.33. \end{aligned}$$

To compare this theoretical value to the observed price, we need to transform the decimal price 2.33 to 64ths, that is, $2 + (.33 \times 64)/64 = 2^{21}\!/_{64}$. In other words, the put option appears $^{4}\!/_{64}$ underpriced.

15.4 TREASURY BOND OPTION PRICING—YIELD-BASED VALUATION

Yield-based option pricing of T-bond and T-bond futures is facilitated by using the binomial approximation method described in Chapter 13. Instead of modeling movement of the underlying commodity price over the next interval of time, we model the up and down movement of the yield. The next period up and down state yields are a proportion of the current yield. If the current yield is y_0, the yield at the end of the first interval is either uy_0 or dy_0. If the total number of time steps is defined as n, where $\Delta t = T/n$ and T is the time to expiration of the option, there are $n + 1$ yield nodes at the option's expiration, with an odd number if n is even and an even number of nodes if n is odd.

This binomial lattice is illustrated in Figure 15.1. The length of each interval or time step in the figure is Δt. The factors u and d are defined as

$$u = e^{\sigma \sqrt{\Delta t}}$$

(15.12a)

and

$$d = \frac{1}{u}.$$

(15.12b)

The risk-neutral probabilities of up and down movements are

$$p = \frac{1 - d}{u - d}$$

(15.12c)

and $1 - p$, respectively.

Once the yield lattice is computed, it is necessary to compute the bond price at each node. Bond valuation equations were presented in Chapter 8. Keep in mind

FIGURE 15.1 Possible Paths that Yield May Follow under the Binomial Model

Yield at end of time interval:

0	1	2	3	4	$\cdots$	n (even)	or	n (odd)
						$u^n y_0$		$u^n y_0$
				$u^4 y_0$	$\cdots$			
			$u^3 y_0$			$\vdots$		$\vdots$
		$u^2 y_0$		$u^2 y_0$	$\cdots$			
	uy_0		uy_0					uy_0
y_0		y_0		y_0	$\cdots$	y_0		
	dy_0		dy_0					dy_0
		$d^2 y_0$		$d^2 y_0$	$\cdots$			
			$d^3 y_0$			$\vdots$		$\vdots$
				$d^4 y_0$	$\cdots$			
						$d^n y_0$		$d^n y_0$

that as you move forward through the lattice computing bond prices at each yield node, the time to maturity of the bond decreases.

Figure 15.2 shows a binomial lattice with both yield and price computed at each node. The underlying bond is assumed to be an 8-percent coupon bond with 20 years to maturity. It currently sells at par, so the current yield to maturity, y_0, is 8 percent. The riskless rate of interest, r, is 6 percent, and the yield volatility, σ_y, is 50 percent. The time to expiration of the option, T, is 90 days, and the number of time steps, n, is 90. The size of the time increment, Δt, is, therefore, one day or .00274 years. Based on this information, the factors u and d are

$$u = e^{.50\sqrt{.00274}} = 1.026517$$

and

$$d = \frac{1}{1.026517} = .974168.$$

Also, the probabilities of up and down movements are

$$p = \frac{1 - .974168}{1.026517 - .974168} = .493458$$

FIGURE 15.2   Possible paths that yield/bond price may follow under the binomial model where the current price of the 8 percent, 20-year bond is 100, the riskless rate of interest is 6 percent annually, and the yield volatility is 50 percent annually. The time to expiration of the option is 90 days, and the number of time steps is also 90. The time increment, Δt, is, therefore, 1 day or .00274 years.

Yield/bond price at end of time interval:

0	1	2	3	4	···	90 days
						84.34/9.63
				8.88/91.93	···	
			8.65/93.93			⋮
		8.43/95.94		8.43/95.97	···	
	8.21/97.97		8.21/98.00			
8.00/100.00		8.00/100.00		8.00/100.00	···	8.00/100.00
	7.79/102.08		7.79/102.11			
		7.59/104.16		7.59/104.20	···	
			7.40/106.26			⋮
				7.20/108.36	···	
						.76/237.38

and $1 - p = .506542$. Note that, in Figure 15.2, possible yields range from $y_0 d^n = 8.00\%(.974168)^{90} = .759\%$ to $y_0 u^n = 8.00\%(1.026517)^{90} = 84.339\%$ at the option's expiration and bond prices range from 237.385 to 9.627.

With the yield/bond price lattice computed, the approximation method starts at the end of the option's life and works back to the present. At the end of the option's life (column n in the figure), the option value at each yield/bond price node is given by the intrinsic value of the option. In the case of a put option,

$$P_{n,j}(B_{n,j}) = \begin{cases} 0 & \text{if } B_{n,j} > X \\ X - B_{n,j} & \text{if } B_{n,j} \leq X. \end{cases} \tag{15.13}$$

The option values one step, Δt, back in time (in column $n - 1$) are computed by taking the present value of the expected future value of the option. At any point j in column $n - 1$, the yield can move up with probability p or down with probability $1 - p$. The value of the option at time n if the yield moves up is $P_{n,j+1}$ and if the yield moves down is $P_{n,j}$. The present value of the expected future value of the option is, therefore,

$$P_{n-1,j} = \frac{pP_{n,j+1} + (1 - p)P_{n,j}}{r^*}, \tag{15.14}$$

where $r^* = e^{r\Delta t}$. Using this present value formulation, all of the option values in column $n - 1$ may be identified.

Before proceeding back another time increment, Δt, in the valuation, it is necessary to see if any of the computed option values are below their early exercise proceeds at the respective nodes, $X - B_{n-1,j}$. If the exercise proceeds are greater than the computed option value, the computed value is replaced with the early exercise proceeds. If they are not, the value is left unchanged. Note that if this step is not performed, the procedure will produce the value of a European put option.

Once the checks are performed, we go to column $n - 2$ and repeat the steps, and so on back through time. Eventually, we will work our way back to time 0, and the current value of the American put option (in column 0) will be identified.

To complete the binomial method illustration, suppose that the bond price lattice shown in Figure 15.2 underlies a 90-day American put option with an exercise price of 100. Applying the yield-based binomial method, the value of the American put is $6.157. The value of the corresponding European-style put option using the yield-based method is $5.713. The early exercise premium of the American put is, therefore, worth about 44.4¢.

15.5 MANAGING DURATION AND CONVEXITY

In Chapter 8, we discussed the duration and convexity of a fixed-income portfolio. Modified duration measures the percentage change in the value of a bond for a given change in yield,

$$D_m = -\frac{dB/B}{dy},$$ (15.15)

and convexity indicates how duration changes for a given change in yield,

$$\text{Convexity} = \frac{1}{2}\frac{d^2 B}{dy^2}\frac{1}{B}.$$ (15.16)

The keys to these expressions are the first and second derivatives of bond price with respect to a change in yield, that is, dB/dy and d^2B/dy^2, respectively. In this sense, duration and convexity are like the delta and gamma of an option. In fact, we will now show that bond option deltas and gammas enable a fixed-income portfolio manager to control the duration and convexity of the portfolio.

To understand how to tailor the duration and convexity exposure of a fixed-income portfolio, we need to develop expressions for bond (or bond futures) option price changes as a function of yield changes. The first derivative of option price with respect to a change in yield is

$$\frac{\partial O}{\partial y} = \frac{\partial O}{\partial B}\frac{dB}{dy} = \Delta\frac{dB}{dy},$$ (15.17)

where Δ is the delta value of the option. Thus, to change the dollar value exposure of a bond portfolio, we simply combine the exposure in bonds, dB/dy, with the exposure in n bond options, $\Delta dB/dy$, that is,

$$\text{Desired dollar risk exposure} = \frac{dB}{dy}(1 + n\Delta).$$ (15.18)

To reduce the portfolio's risk exposure to zero (for small changes in yields), the optimal number of options is

$$n = -\frac{1}{\Delta}.$$

In the general case, one may use N different options to hedge a bond portfolio, that is,

$$\text{Desired dollar risk exposure} = \frac{dB}{dy}\left(1 + \sum_{i=1}^{N} n_i \Delta_i\right).$$ (15.19)

Note that the dollar risk exposure is exactly zero only at the point where the derivative is taken.

EXAMPLE 15.5

Assume that a fixed-income portfolio manager holds a 9-percent, 20-year bond whose current yield to maturity is 8 percent. Its current market value is 109.82, its modified duration is 9.606, and its convexity is 70.450. Given the uncertainty about economic events, the manager decides to hedge the interest rate risk of his portfolio by writing call options on this bond. The call has an exercise price of 110 and a time to expiration of 3 months. The current price of this option is 2.900, its delta is .472, and its gamma is .0474. Compute the number of call options to sell against this bond to immunize it from movements in the bond's yield.

The optimal number of calls to negate the duration exposure is

$$ n = -\frac{1}{.472} = -2.119. $$

If we sell this number of options against the underlying bond, the bond portfolio value for given changes in the yield is shown in Figure 15.3.

Figure 15.3 demonstrates that the delta-neutral hedge reduces the range of possible portfolio values. The unhedged portfolio ranges in value from 90 to 135 over the range of yields shown, while the hedged portfolio ranges in value from 90 to 110. But, even with the delta-neutral hedge, the range of possible portfolio values is large over this somewhat limited yield range. In addition, the hedged port-

FIGURE 15.3   Hedging Duration Exposure Using Bond Options

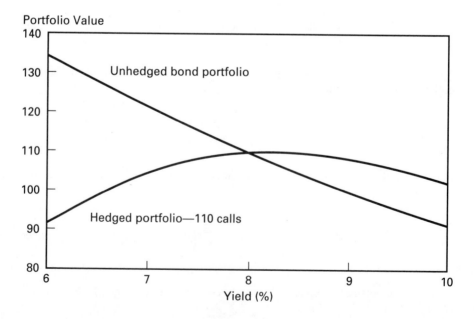

folio has reduced value if the yield rises *or* falls. To improve upon this hedge, it is possible to use more than one option to hedge both duration and convexity risk.

The zero-risk portfolio given by (15.19) is analogous to the delta-neutral portfolio discussed in Chapter 12. In that chapter, we also noted that a change in delta brought about by a commodity price change introduces gamma risk. A similar situation arises in the case of the hedged bond portfolio. Not only does the bond option delta change as the yield changes, but so does the duration of the bond portfolio. To compensate for these effects, we must consider the second partial derivative of the bond option price with respect to yield, that is

$$
\begin{aligned}
\frac{\partial^2 O}{\partial y^2} &= \frac{\partial(\frac{\partial O}{\partial y})}{\partial y} = \frac{\partial(\frac{\partial O}{\partial B}\frac{dB}{dy})}{\partial y} = \frac{\partial O}{\partial B}\frac{d^2 B}{dy^2} + \frac{dB}{dy}\frac{\partial^2 O}{\partial B \partial y} \\
&= \Delta\frac{d^2 B}{dy^2} + \frac{dB}{dy}\frac{\partial(\frac{\partial O}{\partial B})}{\partial y} = \Delta\frac{d^2 B}{dy^2} + \frac{dB}{dy}\frac{\partial \Delta}{\partial y} \\
&= \Delta\frac{d^2 B}{dy^2} + \frac{dB}{dy}\frac{\partial \Delta}{\partial B}\frac{\partial B}{\partial y} \\
&= \Delta\left(\frac{d^2 B}{dy^2}\right) + \gamma\left(\frac{dB}{dy}\right)^2,
\end{aligned}
\tag{15.20}
$$

where $\gamma = \partial\Delta/\partial B$ is the gamma value of the option. Combining the convexity exposure of the bond with a portfolio that consists of N bond options, we get dollar convexity exposure

$$
\begin{aligned}
\text{Dollar convexity} &= \frac{d^2 B}{dy^2} + \sum_{i=1}^{N} n_i\Delta_i\left(\frac{d^2 B}{dy^2}\right) + \sum_{i=1}^{N} n_i\gamma_i\left(\frac{dB}{dy}\right)^2 \\
&= \frac{d^2 B}{dy^2}\left(1 + \sum_{i=1}^{N} n_i\Delta_i + f\sum_{i=1}^{N} n_i\gamma_i\right),
\end{aligned}
\tag{15.21}
$$

where $f = \left(\frac{dB}{dy}\right)^2 / \left(\frac{d^2 B}{dy^2}\right)$.

EXAMPLE 15.6

Unsatisfied with the effectiveness of the hedge portfolio indicated in Example 15.5, the portfolio manager decides to evaluate the effectiveness of a hedge of both the duration and the convexity risk of his position. Aside from the 110 call described in the last exercise, a 105 call with three months to expiration is available. The current price of the 105 call is 5.720, its delta is .703, and its gamma is .0403. Compute the number of calls to buy/sell against this bond to immunize it from movements in the bond's yield.

To neutralize the duration and the convexity risk of the bond portfolio, we need to solve simultaneously the following equations:

$$n_1 \Delta_1 + n_2 \Delta_2 = -1$$

and

$$n_1(\Delta_1 + f\gamma_1) + n_2(\Delta_2 + f\gamma_2) = -1.$$

To compute the coefficient f, we need to know the values of dB/dy and d^2B/dy^2. These can be obtained from the modified duration and the convexity figures reported for the bond. That is, from equations (15.15) and (15.16), we know

$$\frac{dB}{dy} = BD_m = 109.82 \times 9.606 = 1,054.93,$$

and

$$\frac{d^2B}{dy^2} = 2B\text{Convexity} = 2 \times 109.82 \times 70.450 = 15,473.64.$$

The value of f is, therefore, 71.921. The deltas and gammas of the individual options are known, and the remaining task is only computational. The optimal composition of the duration/convexity hedge is to sell 3.315 105 calls and to buy 2.819 110 calls.

The effectiveness of this hedge relative to the unhedged portfolio and the duration-hedged portfolio from Example 15.5 can be seen in Figure 15.4. The range of outcomes has been further diminished. Using both calls generates a curve that is much more horizontal at 110, ranging from 103 to 116. In addition, the hedged portfolio rises if the yield falls and falls more slowly if the yield rises. Clearly, this second hedge is more effective than the hedge discussed in Example 15.5.

15.6 SUMMARY

This chapter focuses on the valuation of interest rate options. After reviewing the designs of the U.S. exchange-traded interest option contracts, we discuss short-term interest rate option valuation. Using the standard lognormal price distribution assumption is inappropriate for these options. In its place, we use the assumption that yield is lognormally distributed and rederive the European option valuation equations. In the third section, T-bond and T-bond futures option valuation under

FIGURE 15.4   Hedging Duration/Convexity Exposure Using Bond
Options Portfolio Value

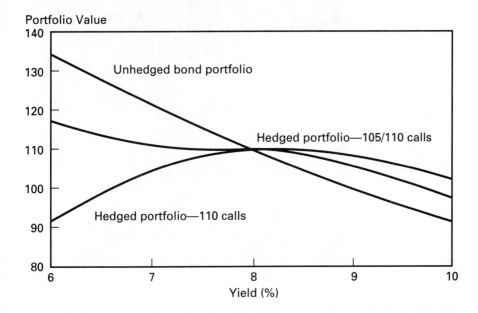

the lognormal price distribution assumption is presented. The fourth section describes the same valuation but under the lognormal yield assumption. The binomial method is also used. Finally, we show how T-bond option contracts can be used to control the duration and the convexity of a fixed-income portfolio.

16 OTHER OPTION CONTRACTS

The last three chapters have focused on specific option contracts on stocks, stock indexes, and interest rate instruments. Where the valuation procedures of Chapters 10 and 11 did not directly apply to these specific option contracts, the procedures were modified. For example, we showed how the quadratic approximation could be used to price American-style index options and how the binomial method could be used to value options on assets with discrete cash flows during the option's life. In this chapter, we discuss options on currencies and on physical commodities. Since no new valuation procedures are needed for these contracts, sections 1 and 2 review only the nature of the exchange-traded options on currencies and physical commodities, and refer the reader to the appropriate valuation equations from the previous chapters. The third section discusses some exotic OTC options that are currently traded. Examples of these are options on options, options on the maximum and the minimum of two risky commodities, lookback options and barrier options. For these four types of options, we present valuation equations. Other types of exotic options include options on the average price of a commodity, deferred-start options, deferred-payment American options, and all-or-nothing options. For these instruments, we describe only the essence of the option contracts. The chapter concludes with a summary.

16.1 CURRENCY AND CURRENCY FUTURES OPTIONS

Option contracts on spot currencies have been actively traded on the Philadelphia Exchange since late 1982. Both European-style and American-style option contracts are traded, with the American-style contracts having the greatest trading volume and open interest. The most active contracts are for British pounds, German marks, Japanese yen, and Swiss francs, although options on other currencies also trade. Table 16.1 contains a listing of the currently active, exchange-traded currency option contracts. The spot currency must be delivered upon exercise of these options. The current spot prices are also reported in Table 16.1. Currency options expire on the Saturday before the third Wednesday of the contract month.

Valuation of Currency Options

The valuation of currency options is relatively straightforward. First, all of the arbitrage pricing principles developed in Chapter 10 apply. The cost-of-carry rate equals the difference between the domestic interest rate, r_d, and the foreign interest rate, r_f. Second, all of the valuation equations and approximations discussed in Chapter 11 and the trading strategies discussed in Chapter 12 also apply, assuming that the spot exchange rate has a lognormal price distribution at the option's expiration. For

TABLE 16.1   Foreign currency exchange rates and foreign currency options.

CURRENCY TRADING

EXCHANGE RATES

Wednesday, November 13, 1991
The New York foreign exchange selling rates below apply to trading among banks in amounts of $1 million and more, as quoted at 3 p.m. Eastern time by Bankers Trust Co.and other sources. Retail transactions provide fewer units of foreign currency per dollar.

Country	U.S. $ equiv. Wed.	Tues.	Currency per U.S. $ Wed.	Tues.
Argentina (Austral) ...	.0001008	.0001008	9918.67	9918.67
Australia (Dollar)	.7860	.7870	1.2723	1.2706
Austria (Schilling)	.08681	.08681	11.52	11.52
Bahrain (Dinar)	2.6539	2.6539	.3768	.3768
Belgium (Franc)	.02966	.02966	33.72	33.72
Brazil (Cruzeiro)	.00144	.00146	694.71	685.60
Britain (Pound)	1.7730	1.7725	.5640	.5642
30-Day Forward	1.7648	1.7640	.5666	.5669
90-Day Forward	1.7504	1.7496	.5713	.5716
180-Day Forward	1.7299	1.7291	.5781	.5783
Canada (Dollar)	.8842	.8838	1.1310	1.1315
30-Day Forward	.8815	.8814	1.1344	1.1346
90-Day Forward	.8784	.8779	1.1384	1.1391
180-Day Forward	.8737	.8733	1.1445	1.1451
Chile (Peso)	.002844	.002780	351.56	359.65
China (Renminbi)	.185642	.185642	5.3867	5.3867
Colombia (Peso)	.001753	.001753	570.38	570.38
Denmark (Krone)	.1573	.1573	6.3570	6.3555
Ecuador (Sucre)				
Floating rate	.000966	.000966	1035.00	1035.00
Finland (Markka)	.24984	.24941	4.0025	4.0095
France (Franc)	.17881	.17879	5.5925	5.5930
30-Day Forward	.17813	.17808	5.6140	5.6156
90-Day Forward	.17690	.17685	5.6529	5.6545
180-Day Forward	.17510	.17504	5.7110	5.7130
Germany (Mark)	.6112	.6111	1.6362	1.6365
30-Day Forward	.6090	.6088	1.6421	1.6426
90-Day Forward	.6045	.6044	1.6543	1.6544
180-Day Forward	.5982	.5982	1.6717	1.6718
Greece (Drachma)	.005405	.005405	185.00	185.00
Hong Kong (Dollar) ...	.12884	.12884	7.7615	7.7615
India (Rupee)	.03880	.03880	25.77	25.77
Indonesia (Rupiah)	.0005056	.0005056	1978.00	1978.00
Ireland (Punt)	1.6330	1.6318	.6124	.6128
Israel (Shekel)	.4308	.4321	2.3215	2.3142
Italy (Lira)	.0008121	.0008117	1231.41	1232.01

	U.S. $ equiv. Wed.	Tues.	Currency per U.S. $ Wed.	Tues.
Japan (Yen)	.007686	.007707	130.10	129.75
30-Day Forward	.007678	.007698	130.24	129.90
90-Day Forward	.007666	.007686	130.45	130.10
180-Day Forward	.007656	.007677	130.62	130.26
Jordan (Dinar)	1.4500	1.4500	.6897	.6897
Kuwait (Dinar)	3.4965	3.4965	.2860	.2860
Lebanon (Pound)	.001134	.001134	881.50	881.50
Malaysia (Ringgit)	.3650	.3647	2.7400	2.7420
Malta (Lira)	3.1250	3.1250	.3200	.3200
Mexico (Peso)				
Floating rate	.0003254	.0003254	3073.01	3073.01
Netherland (Guilder) ..	.5423	.5422	1.8440	1.8445
New Zealand (Dollar) .	.5610	.5620	1.7825	1.7794
Norway (Krone)	.1558	.1558	6.4175	6.4185
Pakistan (Rupee)	.0405	.0405	24.72	24.72
Peru (New Sol)	1.0152	1.0051	.99	.99
Philippines (Peso)	.03839	.03839	26.05	26.05
Portugal (Escudo)	.007067	.007063	141.50	141.59
Saudi Arabia (Riyal) ..	.26663	.26663	3.7505	3.7505
Singapore (Dollar)	.5958	.5959	1.6785	1.6780
South Africa (Rand)				
Commercial rate	.3568	.3574	2.8023	2.7981
Financial rate	.3248	.3240	3.0790	3.0860
South Korea (Won)	.0013310	.0013310	751.30	751.30
Spain (Peseta)	.009723	.009699	102.85	103.10
Sweden (Krona)	.1673	.1672	5.9775	5.9815
Switzerland (Franc) ..	.6888	.6892	1.4517	1.4510
30-Day Forward	.6872	.6875	1.4552	1.4546
90-Day Forward	.6835	.6839	1.4631	1.4621
180-Day Forward	.6788	.6792	1.4732	1.4724
Taiwan (Dollar)	.038850	.037908	25.74	26.38
Thailand (Baht)	.03926	.03926	25.47	25.47
Turkey (Lira)	.0002044	.0002020	4892.01	4950.00
United Arab (Dirham) .	.2723	.2723	3.6725	3.6725
Uruguay (New Peso)				
Financial	.000425	.000425	2352.94	2352.94
Venezuela (Bolivar)				
Floating rate	.01695	.01661	59.00	60.20
SDR	1.38023	1.38189	.72452	.72365
ECU	1.24952	1.25088	....	....

Special Drawing Rights (SDR) are based on exchange rates for the U.S., German, British, French and Japanese currencies. Source: International Monetary Fund.
European Currency Unit (ECU) is based on a basket of community currencies. Source: European Community Commission.

continued

TABLE 16.1

OPTIONS
PHILADELPHIA
Wednesday, November 13, 1991

Option & Underlying	Strike Price	Calls—Last			Puts—Last		
		Nov	Dec	Mar	Nov	Dec	Mar
50,000 Australian Dollars-cents per unit.							
ADollr.....	78	0.63	0.84	r	r	r	r
78.66	81	r	r	r	r	r	3.53
78.66	83	r	r	r	r	4.56	r
31,250 British Pounds-European Style.							
BPound ..	150	r	r	23.80	r	r	r
177.12 ..	167½	r	r	r	r	r	2.20
177.12 ..	175	r	3.00	4.25	r	r	r
177.12 ..	177½	r	r	3.25	r	r	r
177.12 ..	187½	r	r	r	r	r	14.20
31,250 British Pounds-cents per unit.							
BPound ..	167½	r	10.00	r	r	0.18	r
177.12 ..	172½	r	4.90	r	r	0.92	r
177.12 ..	175	2.20	2.95	r	0.27	1.70	r
177.12 ..	177½	0.63	2.10	r	1.05	r	r
177.12 ..	180	0.07	r	r	r	r	r
177.12 ..	182½	r	0.52	r	r	r	r
177.12 ..	190	s	r	r	s	13.77	r
50,000 Canadian Dollars-European Style.							
CDollar....	87½	r	r	r	r	0.30	r
88.23	88	r	r	r	0.08	r	r
88.23	88½	r	r	r	0.25	r	r
50,000 Canadian Dollars-cents per unit.							
CDollr.....	84½	r	r	r	r	r	0.12
88.23	85	r	r	r	r	r	0.17
88.23	86	r	r	r	r	r	0.41
88.23	87½	r	r	r	r	0.24	r
88.23	88	r	0.35	r	0.07	0.55	r
88.23	88½	r	0.20	r	0.62	r	r
88.23	89	r	0.13	0.34	0.70	r	r
88.23	89½	r	r	r	r	1.48	r

62,500 German Marks-cents per unit.							
DMark	56	r	r	r	r	0.02	r
61.03	57	r	4.05	r	r	r	0.51
61.03	58	r	r	r	r	0.10	0.81
61.03	58½	2.59	r	s	r	r	s
61.03	59	2.03	2.19	r	r	0.20	r
61.03	59½	r	r	s	r	0.29	s
61.03	60	r	r	r	0.04	0.44	r
61.03	60½	0.68	r	s	0.10	0.67	s
61.03	61	0.33	0.73	r	0.23	0.90	r
61.03	61½	0.15	0.53	s	r	r	s
61.03	62	0.06	0.46	r	r	r	r
61.03	62½	r	0.30	s	r	r	s
6,250,000 Japanese Yen-100ths of a cent per unit.							
JYen......	73	r	r	r	r	0.04	r
76.99	74	2.96	r	r	r	r	r
76.99	75	r	1.98	r	r	r	r
76.99	76	r	r	r	0.04	0.43	r
76.99	76½	r	r	s	0.13	0.62	s
76.99	77	0.22	r	r	0.34	0.86	r
76.99	77½	0.08	0.46	s	r	r	s
76.99	78	0.03	0.31	r	r	r	r
76.99	79	r	r	0.82	r	r	r
76.99	85	r	r	0.09	r	r	r
76.99	86	r	r	0.07	r	r	r
6,250,000 Japanese Yen-European Style.							
JYen......	74	r	r	r	r	r	0.63
76.99	76½	r	r	s	0.09	r	s
76.99	78	r	r	1.10	r	r	r
62,500 Swiss Francs-European Style.							
SFranc....	66	r	r	r	r	r	0.94
68.85	69	r	r	1.60	r	r	r
62,500 Swiss Francs-cents per unit.							
SFranc....	65	r	r	r	r	0.07	r
68.85	68	r	r	r	r	0.58	r
68.85	68½	r	r	s	0.17	0.79	s
68.85	69	0.24	r	r	0.25	1.08	r
68.85	78½	s	r	r	s	0.33	r
Total Call Vol	14,647				Call Open Int		476,994
Total Put Vol	17,077				Put Open Int		516,307

Source: Reprinted by permission of *Wall Street Journal*, © (November 14, 1991) Dow Jones & Company, Inc. All Rights Reserved Worldwide.

European-style currency options, valuation equations (11.25) and (11.28) can be used, where $b = r_d - r_f$.[1]

For American-style currency options, the quadratic approximation from Chapter 13 is recommended. Again, the cost-of-carry rate is set equal to the difference between the domestic and foreign interest rates.

Option contracts on currency futures were developed in late 1984 and early 1985 by the Chicago Mercantile Exchange. The only such options available are American-style. Upon exercise, a long (call) or short (put) position in the futures is obtained. The expiration date of these options is the second Friday before the third Wednesday of the contract month. (The futures expires two business days before the third Wednesday.) Like the currency options, the most active currency futures options are on British pounds, German marks, Japanese yen, and Swiss francs. Table 16.2 contains current foreign currency futures and futures option contract prices.

The valuation of currency futures options is even more straightforward than the valuation of currency options. The cost-of-carry rate for any currency futures

---

[1] For an approach to foreign currency option valuation that permits interest rates to be stochastic, see Grabbe (1983).

TABLE 16.2 Foreign currency futures and futures options.

CURRENCY TRADING

FUTURES

JAPAN YEN (IMM)—12.5 million. yen; $ per yen (.00)

	Open	High	Low	Settle	Change	Lifetime High	Lifetime Low	Open Interest
Dec	.7691	.7699	.7671	.7679	− .0012	.7770	.6997	69,869
Mr92	.7666	.7684	.7659	.7665	− .0011	.7737	.7000	3,572
June	....	....	....	.7659	− .0010	.7730	.7015	917
Sept	....	....	....	.7659	− .0010	.7710	.7265	599
Dec	....	....	....	.7662	− .0009	.7700	.7512	1,290

Est vol 19,740; vol Tues 19,486; open int 76,247, +756.

DEUTSCHEMARK (IMM)—125,000 marks; $ per mark

	Open	High	Low	Settle	Change	Lifetime High	Lifetime Low	Open Interest
Dec	.6088	.6108	.6060	.6088	+ .0007	.6770	.5365	72,328
Mr92	.6012	.6045	.5998	.6024	+ .0007	.6065	.5353	6,380
June	.5965	.5970	.5960	.5963	+ .0007	.5985	.5322	715

Est vol 56,177; vol Tues 36,905; open int 79,626, −1,188.

CANADIAN DOLLAR (IMM)—100,000 dlrs.; $ per Can $

	Open	High	Low	Settle	Change	Lifetime High	Lifetime Low	Open Interest
Dec	.8771	.8817	.8763	.8812	+ .0019	.8906	.8175	20,341
Mr92	.8720	.8769	.8713	.8767	+ .0020	.8857	.8253	4,840
June	.8675	.8725	.8675	.8725	+ .0018	.8820	.8330	734
Sept	.8630	.8685	.8630	.8685	+ .0016	.8774	.8348	105

Est vol 13,890; vol Tues 7,534; open int 26,078, −782.

BRITISH POUND (IMM)—62,500 pds.; $ per pound

	Open	High	Low	Settle	Change	Lifetime High	Lifetime Low	Open Interest
Dec	1.7640	1.7696	1.7560	1.7650	+.0024	1.7900	1.5670	27,784
Mr92	1.7430	1.7490	1.7370	1.7436	+.0024	1.7570	1.5560	2,964

Est vol 13,723; vol Tues 7,681; open int 30,780, −899.

SWISS FRANC (IMM)—125,000 francs; $ per franc

	Open	High	Low	Settle	Change	Lifetime High	Lifetime Low	Open Interest
Dec	.6877	.6905	.6849	.6869	+ .0002	.8090	.6235	29,074
Mr92	.6829	.6852	.6797	.6819	+ .0004	.6995	.6225	2,196
June	.6766	.6795	.6750	.6771	+ .0004	.6840	.6426	296

Est vol 23,401; vol Tues 16,538; open int 31,566, −1,353.

AUSTRALIAN DOLLAR (IMM)—100,000 dlrs.; $ per A.$

	Open	High	Low	Settle	Change	Lifetime High	Lifetime Low	Open Interest
Dec	....	.7825	.7839	.7822	.7832	− .0006	.7960	.7380

Est vol 113; vol Tues 164; open int 1,221, −246.

U.S. DOLLAR INDEX (FINEX)—500 times USDX

	Open	High	Low	Settle	Change	Lifetime High	Lifetime Low	Open Interest
Dec	89.04	89.40	88.78	88.99	− .11	98.96	88.47	5,019
Mr92	90.07	90.30	89.90	90.08	− .10	98.90	89.60	1,045

Est vol 1,896; vol Tues 2,675; open int 6,090, −671.
The Index: High 88.86; Low 88.34; Close 88.54 −.08

OTHER FUTURES

Settlement prices of selected contracts. Volume and open interest of all contract months.

British Pound (MCE) 12,500 pounds; $ per pound
Dec 1.7650 +.0024; Est. vol. 120; Open Int. 422
Japanese Yen (MCE) 6.25 million yen; $ per yen (.00)
Dec .7679 −.0012; Est. vol. 240; Open Int. 353
Swiss Franc (MCE) 62,500 francs; $ per franc
Dec .6869 +.0002; Est. vol. 1,020; Open Int. 253
Deutschemark (MCE) 62,500 marks; $ per mark
Dec .6088 +.0007; Est. vol. 360; Open Int. 837
BP/DM Cross Rate (IMM) US $50,000 times BP/DM
Dec 2.8990 +.0005; Est. vol. 80; Open Int. 245
DM/JY Cross Rate (IMM) US $125,000 times DM/JY
Dec .7928 +.0022; Est. vol. 6; Open Int. 583
FINEX—Financial Instrument Exchange, a division of the New York Cotton Exchange. IMM—International Monetary Market at the Chicago Mercantile Exchange. MCE—MidAmerica Commodity Exchange.

FUTURES OPTIONS

JAPANESE YEN (IMM) 12,500,000 yen; cents per 100 yen

Strike Price	Calls—Settle Dec-c	Jan-c	Mar-c	Puts—Settle Dec-p	Jan-p	Mar-p
7550	1.50	1.68	....	0.21	0.54	....
7600	1.13	1.36	1.92	0.34	0.72	1.28
7650	0.81	1.09	....	0.52	0.94	....
7700	0.56	0.85	1.42	0.77	1.20	1.76
7750	0.39	0.66	....	....	....	....
7800	0.26	0.50	1.03	1.46	....	2.36

Est. vol. 9,179, Tues vol. 3,905 calls, 3,377 puts
Open Interest Tues 47,829 calls, 48,508 puts

DEUTSCHEMARK (IMM) 125,000 marks; cents per mark

Strike Price	Calls—Settle Dec-c	Jan-c	Mar-c	Puts—Settle Dec-p	Jan-p	Mar-p
6000	1.26	1.20	1.75	0.38	0.96	1.51
6050	0.94	0.97	....	0.56	1.22	....
6100	0.68	0.77	1.30	0.80	....	2.04
6150	0.48	0.60	....	1.10	....	....
6200	0.32	0.46	0.95	1.44	....	2.68
6250	0.21	....	....	1.83	....	....

Est. vol. 23,758, Tues vol. 8,623 calls, 10,510 puts
Open Interest Tues 79,104 calls, 103,796 puts

CANADIAN DOLLAR (IMM) 100,000 Can.$, cents per Can.$

Strike Price	Calls—Settle Dec-c	Jan-c	Mar-c	Puts—Settle Dec-p	Jan-p	Mar-p
8700	1.20	....	1.12	0.09	0.26	0.51
8750	0.78	0.60	0.84	0.16	0.46	0.70
8800	0.43	0.37	0.61	0.31	0.72	0.96
8850	0.21	0.21	0.43	0.59	1.06	1.26
8900	0.08	0.11	0.29	0.97	....	1.62
8950	0.02	....	0.18	....	....	....

Est. vol. 4,010, Tues vol. 913 calls, 1,284 puts
Open Interest Tues 13,838 calls, 17,860 puts

BRITISH POUND (IMM) 62,500 pounds; cents per pound

Strike Price	Calls—Settle Dec-c	Jan-c	Mar-c	Puts—Settle Dec-p	Jan-p	Mar-p
1725	4.64	....	5.54	0.66	....	3.68
1750	2.88	2.78	4.28	1.40	3.40	4.88
1775	1.60	1.80	3.24	2.60	4.92	6.30
1800	0.82	1.12	2.40	4.28	....	7.92
1825	0.36	0.68	1.74	6.34	....	....
1850	0.16	....	1.22	8.62	....	11.66

Est. vol. 1,706, Tues vol. 856 calls, 681 puts
Open Interest Tues 9,526 calls, 10,067 puts

SWISS FRANC (IMM) 125,000 francs; cents per franc

Strike Price	Calls—Settle Dec-c	Jan-c	Mar-c	Puts—Settle Dec-p	Jan-p	Mar-p
6750	1.55	....	....	0.35	0.91	....
6800	1.20	1.32	1.92	0.50	1.13	1.73
6850	0.91	1.08	....	0.72	1.39	....
6900	0.68	0.87	1.46	0.98	....	2.27
6950	0.49	0.70	....	1.28	....	....
7000	0.34	0.56	1.10	1.63	....	....

Est. vol. 1,746, Tues vol. 965 calls, 706 puts
Open Interest Tues 12,608 calls, 16,145 puts

U.S. DOLLAR INDEX (FINEX) 500 times index

Strike Price	Calls—Settle Dec-c	Jan-c	Feb-c	Puts—Settle Dec-p	Jan-p	Feb-p
87	....	3.40	....	0.27	....	....
88	1.51	2.64	....	0.52	0.59	....
89	0.92	1.97	....	0.93	0.92	....
90	0.52	1.42	....	1.53	1.35	....
91	0.27	0.98	....	2.28	....	....
92	0.13	0.66	....	3.13	....	....

Est. vol. 570, Tues vol. 60 calls, 292 puts
Open Interest Tues 12,054 calls, 16,739 puts

OTHER FUTURES OPTIONS

Final or settlement prices of selected contracts. Volume and open interest are totals in all contract months.

Australian Dollar (IMM) $100,000; $ per $

Strike	Dec-c	Jan-c	Mar-c	Dec-p	Jan-p	Mar-p
7850	0.47	....	....	0.65	....	....

Est. vol. 3. Tues vol. 55. Op. Int. 1,668.

FINEX—Financial Instrument Exchange, a division of the New York Cotton Exchange. IMM—International Monetary Market at Chicago Mercantile Exchange. LIFFE-London International Financing Futures Exchange.

is zero, so we set $b = 0$ in all of the pricing relations of Chapters 10 and 11 and the trading strategies of Chapter 12.

Uses of Currency Options

Currency options are helpful in managing foreign exchange risk that arises in international trade or in the management of international investment portfolios. Currency options allow more flexible hedging of exchange risk than is possible with currency futures alone.

As an example, consider a U.S. importer of German machinery that costs DM500,000 and is to be delivered in March 1992. Payment in German marks is to be made upon delivery. At the March futures price of $0.6024 shown in Table 16.2, the dollar cost of the machinery will be $301,200. Of course, if the price of the German mark increases, the dollar cost of the machinery will increase. One way to hedge this exchange risk is to buy four futures contracts (each contract applies to DM125,000) or to enter into an appropriate forward contract with a bank. If the price of the D-mark does increase, the increased equivalent dollar cost of the machinery is offset by the profit on the futures position. On the other hand, if the price of the D-mark decreases, the lower dollar cost is offset by the loss on the futures position.

An alternative way to hedge against D-mark price increases is to buy March call options on the D-mark spot currency or on the D-mark futures. If the D-mark appreciates, the increase in the dollar cost of the machinery is offset by the profit on the call options. On the other hand, if the D-mark depreciates, the lower cost of the machinery is a pure gain. This type of hedge provides insurance against increases in the exchange rate without an offsetting penalty should the exchange rate drop. Naturally, the call premium reflects the value of this insurance. To reduce the premium cost, one might buy out-of-the-money D-mark futures options. For example, Table 16.2 indicates it would have been possible to buy call options on the D-mark futures with an exercise price of 0.61 at a cost of 1.30 cents per mark. Since each contract at the Chicago Mercantile Exchange is DM125,000, four contracts are necessary, and the total premium is $6,500. This option position would cap the total dollar cost at $(0.61)(500,000) = $305,000$, while retaining the possibility of gain if the D-mark should depreciate. Increases in the D-mark above 0.61 would be offset by profits on the futures option position.

Options can provide a useful hedge if there is uncertainty about the underlying import or export contract. For example, consider a U.S. company that bids a price of 350,000 pounds to install a computer system in Great Britain and suppose the British company has a month in which to accept or reject the bid. The U.S. company is concerned about a depreciation of the British pound, but if it sells futures to hedge the foreign exchange risk, and the bid is not accepted, the company is left with an open currency futures position that may have to be liquidated at a loss. An alternative hedge is for the U.S. company to buy put contracts on 350,000 British pounds. By purchasing puts, the company guarantees the price at which pounds can be sold if the bid is accepted. If the bid is rejected, the put option is not exercised and is sold. In effect, the U.S. company is using an option to hedge a contract that has an option feature. The U.S. company has given the British company the put option to sell 350,000 pounds to the U.S. company in return for the computer system. The U.S. company hedges that risk by buying a put.[2]

In addition to hedging import and export contracts, currency options are useful in international investment and portfolio management. Investment in a foreign country exposes a portfolio to exchange rate risk as well as the usual risk of capital losses. Currency options can be used to modify that risk. For example, an investor in Australian bonds could hedge principal and/or interest payments by purchasing puts on the Australian dollar. Over-the-counter options written by banks are frequently used to tailor such hedges to the needs of the investor, particularly when longer maturities are necessary and/or when a sequence of options is required (as when a stream of coupon payments is hedged). Some fixed-income securities are offered with imbedded currency options. For example, a bond might offer to pay interest and/or principal in either of two currencies at a fixed exchange rate, with the investor having the option to choose the currency. Complex or exotic options, which are discussed below, are often created to deal with currency risk. For example, a bond could offer to pay principal and interest in dollars or in two other currencies at fixed exchange rates established in the bond indenture. The holder of the bond thus has a dollar bond plus the option of choosing the most valuable of the three currencies in which payment may be received.

16.2 PHYSICAL COMMODITY FUTURES OPTIONS

Markets for option contracts on physical commodity futures became active in 1982 with the introduction of sugar futures options by the Coffee, Sugar, and Cocoa Exchange and of gold futures options by the Commodity Exchange. These option contracts are American-style and settle through delivery of a position in the underlying futures. The grain contracts trade predominantly on the Chicago Board of Trade; the livestock contracts on the Chicago Mercantile Exchange; oil and oil-related products on the New York Mercantile Exchange; and metals at the Commodity Exchange. Table 16.3 contains a listing of the currently active, exchange-traded commodity options. As with all futures option contracts, the valuation principles follow from Chapters 10 through 12 once the cost-of-carry rate is set to zero ($b = 0$).

16.3 EXOTIC OPTIONS

Exotic options are complex options that typically incorporate two or more option features. A compound option, for example, is considered an exotic option. It pro-

---

[2]The hedging uses of currency options in the kind of situation described here are also discussed in Giddy (1983) and in Feiger and Jacquillat (1979).

TABLE 16.3   Commodity futures options.

COMMODITY FUTURES OPTIONS

Wednesday, November 13, 1991.

— AGRICULTURAL —

CORN (CBT) 5,000 bu.; cents per bu.

Strike	Calls–Settle			Puts–Settle		
Price	Dec-c	Mar-c	May-c	Dec-p	Mar-p	May-p
230	16	25½	....	⅛	½	¾
240	6¼	17	24	⅝	2¼	2½
250	⅞	11¼	17⅛	5	5½	5
260	c4	7	12	14⅛	11⅝	9¾
270	c2	4⅛	8	24	18½	15¼
280	c1	2⅜	5¼	34	27	23

Est. vol. 8,000, Tues vol. 4,078 calls, 3,862 puts
Open Interest Tues 112,688 calls, 73,185 puts

SOYBEANS (CBT) 5,000 bu.; cents per bu.

Strike	Calls–Settle			Puts–Settle		
Price	Jan-c	Mar-c	May-c	Jan-p	Mar-p	May-c
500	57½	65½	....	¼	1	2
525	33¼	43½	....	1½	3¾	5½
550	15⅞	26	35	8	11¾	13¼
575	6	15¼	23½	23½	25	25½
600	2⅜	9	16½	44½	43	41½
625	1	5¾	10¾	68¼	65	60½

Est. vol. 6,000, Tues vol. 4,563 calls, 1,671 puts
Open Interest Tues 51,853 calls, 19,669 puts

SOYBEAN MEAL (CBT) 100 tons; $ per ton

Strike	Calls–Settle			Puts–Settle		
Price	Dec-c	Jan-c	Mar-c	Dec-p	Jan-p	Mar-c
170	10.90	9.30	....	.05	.50	2.35
175	5.90	5.55	6.35	.30	1.75	4.60
180	2.00	3.50	4.55	1.10	4.20	7.60
185	.40	1.70	3.25	4.40	7.75	11.20
190	c3	1.00	2.20	9.10	12.00	....
195	.05	.55	1.60	14.10	....	....

Est. vol. 300, Tues vol. 405 calls, 415 puts
Open Interest Tues 6,814 calls, 6,286 puts

SOYBEAN OIL (CBT) 60,000 lbs.; cents per lb.

Strike	Calls–Settle			Puts–Settle		
Price	Dec-c	Jan-c	Mar-c	Dec-p	Jan-p	Mar-c
17	1.880	....	....	.005	....	....
18	.900	....	....	.020	.060	.220
19	.100	.400	....	.220	.470	.490
20	.010	.140	.450	1.130	1.200	1.180
21	.005	.050	.210	2.130	2.150	1.950
22	.005	.020	.130	6.130	3.100	2.850

Est. vol. 300, Tues vol. 147 calls, 58 puts
Open Interest Tues 5,687 calls, 3,020 puts

WHEAT (CBT) 5,000 bu.; cents per bu.

Strike	Calls–Settle			Puts–Settle		
Price	Dec-c	Mar-c	May-c	Dec-p	Mar-p	May-p
330	22½	26¾	21½	⅛	4	13½
340	12⅝	19¾	16	½	7	18
350	4½	14¼	12	2	10¾	24
360	⅝	10	10	10	8¼	16¼	....
370	⅛	7	6½	17½	22¾	....
380	⅛	4¾	5¼	30½	....	....

Est. vol. 3,500, Tues vol. 2,186 calls, 2,861 puts
Open Interest Tues 28,890 calls, 32,465 puts

WHEAT (KC) 5,000 bu.; cents per bu.

Strike	Calls–Settle			Puts–Settle		
Price	Dec-c	Mar-c	May-c	Dec-p	Mar-p	May-p
340	16	20½	16½	⅝	6	16¾
350	6	15	13½	1¼	10	....
360	1	11½	8¾	5¼	14¼	....
370	⅜	6½	6½	14¾	21½	....
380	....	4	5	24½	....	....
390	....	2½	3¼	....	....	....

Est. vol. 372, Tues vol. 168 calls, 1,030 puts
Open Interest Tues 6,414 calls, 7,637 puts

COTTON (CTN) 50,000 lbs.; cents per lb.

Strike	Calls–Settle			Puts–Settle		
Price	Mar-c	May-c	Jl-c	Mar-p	May-p	Jly-p
57	....	....	....	1.25	1.50	....
58	2.90	....	....	1.60	1.90	....
59	....	3.25	....	2.02	2.25	....
60	1.90	2.75	....	2.60	2.75	....
61	1.50	2.30	....	3.20	3.30	3.50
62	1.15	1.95	2.55	3.85	3.85	....

Est. vol. 1,400; Tues vol. 1,065 calls; 534 puts
Open Interest Tues; 17,101 calls; 13,990 puts

ORANGE JUICE (CTN) 15,000 lbs.; cents per lb.

Strike	Calls–Settle			Puts–Settle		
Price	Jan-c	Mar-c	My-c	Jan-p	Mar-p	May-p
165	13.25	18.05	....	1.60	7.50	11.10
170	9.65	16.40	....	3.00	9.75	13.25
175	6.65	13.85	....	....	12.20	15.50
180	4.35	11.70	....	....	....	....
185	1.95	9.65	....	....	....	....
190	1.55	....	....	....	....	....

Est. vol. 375; Tues vol. 98 calls; 116 puts
Open Interest Tues; 4,002 calls; 5,065 puts

COFFEE (CSCE) 37,500 lbs.; cents per lb.

Strike	Calls–Settle			Puts–Settle		
Price	Mar-c	May-c	Jl-c	Mar-p	May-p	Jly-p
75	9.03	11.75	14.10	0.78	0.95	0.95
80	5.38	8.20	10.40	2.25	2.40	2.25
85	3.32	5.15	6.80	5.00	4.60	4.20
90	2.10	3.45	4.95	8.78	7.65	6.80
95	1.33	2.35	3.50	13.08	11.55	10.35
100	0.90	1.60	2.53	17.65	15.80	14.38

Est. vol. 745; Tues vol. 930 calls; 68 puts
Open Interest Tues; 15,495 calls; puts

SUGAR–WORLD (CSCE) 112,000 lbs.; cents per lb.

Strike	Calls–Settle			Puts–Settle		
Price	Dec-c	Mar-c	My-c	Dec-p	Mar-p	May-p
7.50	0.83	0.98	....	0.06	0.21	....
8.00	0.42	0.68	0.75	0.16	0.40	0.51
8.50	0.19	0.45	....	0.43	0.67	....
9.00	0.07	0.30	0.41	0.79	1.00	1.11
9.50	0.03	0.20	....	1.26	1.43	....
10.00	0.02	0.12	0.20	1.75	1.85	1.94

Est. vol. 7,719; Tues vol. 1,431 calls; 498 puts
Open Interest Tues; 73,733 calls; 31,856 puts

COCOA (CSCE) 10 metric tons; $ per ton

Strike	Calls–Settle			Puts–Settle		
Price	Mar-c	May-c	Jl-c	Mar-p	May-p	Jly-p
1100	174	214	257	10	14	23
1200	96	139	184	35	39	50
1300	50	84	121	90	84	91
1400	23	48	81	159	148	147
1500	12	29	54	248	229	220
1600	5	19	44	341	319	310

Est. vol. 408; Tues vol. 519 calls; 155 puts
Open Interest Tues; 9,019 calls; 10,478 puts

— OIL —

CRUDE OIL (NYM) 1,000 bbls.; $ per bbl.

Strike	Calls–Settle			Puts–Settle		
Price	Jan-c	Feb-c	Mr-c	Jan-p	Feb-p	Mar-p
20	2.28	....	....	.06	.18	.31
21	1.38	1.33	1.25	.16	.37	.55
22	.63	.68	.69	.41	.72	.98
23	.23	.30	.35	1.01	1.33	1.62
24	.07	.13	.16	1.85	2.16	....
25	.03	.06	.07	....	....	....

Est. vol. 18,873; Tues vol. 10,016 calls; 23,569 puts
Open Interest Tues; 104,742 calls; 130,839 puts

vides its holder with the right to buy another option. Options on the maximum of two (or more) risky commodities are also considered to be exotic options. With this option, the investor has the right to buy "the better of two commodities." Because exotic options are complex and are often tailored to the needs of the customer, they are available primarily in the OTC market.

TABLE 16.3   continued

HEATING OIL No.2 (NYM) 42,000 gal.; $ per gal.

Strike Price	Calls—Settle			Puts—Settle		
	Jan-c	Feb-c	Mr-c	Jan-p	Feb-p	Mar-p
62	.0478	.0454	.0301	.0030	.0116	.0255
64	.0323	.0329	.0215	.0075	.0190	.0369
66	.0198	.0219	.0160	.0150	.0280	.0514
68	.0115	.0160	.0115	.0267	.0421	....
70	.0070	.0110	.0085	.0422	.0571	.0839
72	.0042	.0077	.0065	.0594	....	....

Est. vol. 8,615; Tues vol. 5,373 calls; 4,349 puts
Open Interest Tues; 57,423 calls; 19,720 puts

GASOLINE—Unleaded (NYM) 42,000 gal.; $ per gal.

Strike Price	Calls—Settle			Puts—Settle		
	Jan-c	Feb-c	Mr-c	Jan-p	Feb-p	Mar-p
58	.0344	.0386	....	.0030	.0060	.0065
60	.0194	.0246	.0366	.0080	.0120	.0120
62	.0095	.0145	.0246	.0181	.0219	.0200
64	.0045	.0080	.0160	.0331	.0354	.0314
66	.0025	.0043	.0100	.0511	.0517	.0454
68	.0015	.0022	.0062	....	....	....

Est. vol. 2,275; Tues vol. 4,287 calls; 3,129 puts
Open Interest Tues; 26,183 calls; 12,417 puts

—LIVESTOCK—

CATTLE-FEEDER (CME) 44,000 lbs.; cents per lb.

Strike Price	Calls—Settle			Puts—Settle		
	Nov-c	Jan-c	Mar-c	Nov-p	Jan-p	Mar-p
80	4.00	3.70	2.92	0.00	0.70	1.60
82	2.00	2.20	1.87	0.02	1.20	2.45
84	0.30	1.17	0.85	0.30	2.17	3.52
86	0.02	0.52	0.40	2.02	3.50	5.07
88	0.00	0.17	0.25	4.00	5.17	....
90	0.00	0.05	0.10	6.00	7.00	....

Est. vol. 337, Tues vol. 92 calls, 187 puts
Open Interest Tues 3,250 calls, 5,929 puts

CATTLE-LIVE (CME) 40,000 lbs.; cents per lb.

Strike Price	Calls—Settle			Puts—Settle		
	Dec-c	Feb-c	Apr-c	Dec-p	Feb-p	Apr-p
70	5.00	....	....	0.05	0.35	0.60
72	3.10	3.62	....	0.15	0.62	0.95
74	1.45	2.12	2.20	0.50	1.10	1.52
76	0.35	1.02	1.10	1.40	1.95	2.42
78	0.05	0.32	0.47	3.10	....	....
80	0.00	0.10	0.15	5.05	....	....

Est. vol. 2,527, Tues vol. 1,242 calls, 2,291 puts
Open Interest Tues 17,961 calls, 31,004 puts

HOGS—LIVE (CME) 40,000 lbs.; cents per lb.

Strike Price	Calls—Settle			Puts—Settle		
	Dec-c	Feb-c	Apr-c	Dec-p	Feb-p	Apr-p
38	3.70	4.97	....	0.05	0.15	0.60
40	1.75	3.32	1.85	0.20	0.50	1.30
42	0.55	1.87	1.00	0.90	1.05	2.45
44	0.12	0.90	0.52	2.47	2.07	3.85
46	0.05	0.42	0.22	4.40	3.60	5.55
48	0.00	0.15	0.10	6.35	5.32	....

Est. vol. 252, Tues vol. 337 calls, 177 puts
Open Interest Tues 5,053 calls, 2,941 puts

—METALS—

COPPER (CMX) 25,000 lbs.; cents per lb.

Strike Price	Calls—Last			Puts—Last		
	Mar-c	May-c	Jly-c	Mar-p	May-p	Jly-p
98	6.10	6.40	6.30	1.50	2.90	3.65
100	4.60	5.10	5.20	2.05	3.70	4.60
102	3.60	4.05	4.25	2.95	4.65	5.65
104	2.85	3.25	3.55	4.20	5.75	6.85
105	2.30	2.90	3.20	4.60	6.40	7.50
106	2.00	2.60	2.95	5.30	7.10	8.25

Est. vol. 260, Tues vol. 50 calls, 141 puts
Open Interest Tues 2,616 calls, 2,041 puts

GOLD (CMX) 100 troy ounces; dollars per troy ounce

Strike Price	Calls—Last			Puts—Last		
	Jan-c	Feb-c	Apr-c	Jan-p	Feb-p	Apr-p
340	20.20	20.50	23.70	0.20	0.60	1.50
350	10.60	11.70	15.50	0.60	1.70	3.30
360	3.30	5.00	9.10	3.20	4.90	6.70
370	0.70	1.90	5.00	10.60	11.80	12.50
380	0.30	0.80	2.70	20.10	20.50	19.90
390	0.20	0.50	1.60	30.00	30.00	28.60

Est. vol. 4,000, Tues vol. 2,387 calls, 1,392 puts
Open Interest Tues 49,979 calls, 18,110 puts

SILVER (CMX) 5,000 troy ounces; cents per troy ounce

Strike Price	Calls—Last			Puts—Last		
	Jan-c	Feb-c	Mar-c	Jan-p	Feb-p	Mar-p
350	60.7	61.0	61.7	0.1	0.4	1.0
375	36.2	37.0	39.1	0.5	1.8	3.4
400	14.4	17.5	21.0	3.7	7.0	10.3
425	3.5	7.0	21.0	3.7	7.0	10.3
450	1.1	3.0	4.8	40.3	42.0	44.1
475	0.7	1.50	2.7	64.8	65.0	67.0

Est. vol. 12,000, Tues vol. 2,739 calls, 603 puts
Open Interest Tues 34,209 calls, 8,172 puts

OTHER FUTURES OPTIONS

Final or settlement prices of selected contracts. Volume and open interest are totals in all contract months.

Lumber (CME) 160,000 bd .ft., $ per 1,000 bd.ft.

Strike	Jan-c	Mar-c	May-c	Jan-p	Mar-p	May-p
210	6.70	....	5.20		....	....

Est. vol. 10. Tues vol. 0. Op. Int. 149.

Oats (CBT) 5,000 bu.; cents per bu.

Strike	Dec-c	Mar-c	May-c	Dec-p	Mar-p	May-p
130	½	....	....	1¾	3	....

Est. vol. 5. Tues vol. 2. Op. Int. 439.

Platinum (NYM) 50 troy oz.; $ per troy oz.

Strike	Jan-c	Feb-c	Mar-c	Jan-p	Feb-p	Mar-p
360	10.00	....	....	5.50	....	....

Est. vol. 76. Tues vol. 76. Op. Int. n.a..

Pork Bellies (CME) 40,000 lbs.; cents per lb.

Strike	Nov-c	Feb-c	Mar-c	Nov-p	Feb-p	Mar-p
40	....	2.60	3.05	0.75	2.92	3.42

Est. vol. 146. Tues vol. 494. Op. Int. 5,668.

Silver (CBT) 1,000 troy oz.; cents per troy oz.

Strike	Dec-c	Feb-c	Apr-c	Dec-p	Feb-p	Apr-p
400	4.0	....	23.0	1.5	....	....

Est. vol. 5. Tues vol. 3. Op. Int. 208.

Soybeans (MCE) 1,000 bu.; cents per bu.

Strike	Jan-c	Mar-c	May-c	Jan-p	Mar-p	May-p
550	15⅞	26	35	8	11¾	13¼

Est. vol. 150. Tues vol. 179. Op. Int. 3,694.

Wheat (MPLS) 5,000 bu.; cents per bu.

Strike	Dec-c	Mar-c	May-c	Dec-p	Mar-p	May-p
340	1½	12½	15	5	13	....

Est. vol. 5. Tues vol. 16. Op. Int. 712.

In this section, we apply the lognormal price distribution mechanics used in Chapters 11 and 12 to price compound options (or, more commonly, "options on options"), options on the maximum or the minimum, lookback options, and barrier options. Illustrations are provided. Following these discussions, we describe some other types of exotic options that currently trade. Our list of exotic options is necessarily incomplete, since new option contracts are designed and traded almost every day. The descriptions included will give a flavor for the ingenuity of some current option contract designs.

Options on Options

Compound options or *options on options* fall in the category of exotic options. Call (put) options providing the right to buy (sell) call options (i.e., calls on calls or puts on calls) and call (put) options providing the right to buy (sell) put options (i.e., calls on puts or puts on puts) are the most common forms. To value these options on options,[3] we adopt the assumptions and notation used in Chapter 11. The critical assumptions are that the terminal commodity price distribution is lognormal and that the principles of risk-neutral valuation apply. The call and put options that we are valuing are assumed to be European-style with exercise prices, c_t^* and p_t^*, respectively, and with time to expiration t. The notation representing the right to buy a call at time t (i.e., a call on a call) is $c(c,t;c_t^*)$, the right to sell a call at time t (i.e., a put on a call) is $p(c,t;c_t^*)$, the right to buy a put at time t (i.e., a call on a put) is $c(p,t;p_t^*)$, and the right to sell a put at time t (i.e., a put on a put) is $p(p,t;p_t^*)$. The option received or delivered at expiration from the exercise of an option on an option has exercise price X and time to expiration T. The notation used to describe the underlying options is $c(S_t,T;X)$ and $p(S_t,T;X)$, respectively. Conditional upon knowing S_t, these European-style options can be valued using equations (11.25) and (11.28) from Chapter 11.

To demonstrate how to value a compound option, we use a call on a call. The first step in the risk-neutral valuation approach is to formulate the option's payoff contingencies. For the call on a call, the payoff contingencies at time t are

$$
c_t = \begin{cases} c(S_t, T; X) - c_t^* & \text{if} \quad c_t > c_t^* \\ 0 & \text{if} \quad c_t \le c_t^*. \end{cases} \tag{16.1}
$$

That is, if the value of the call to be received at time t, $c(S_t, T;X)$, is greater than the exercise price, c_t^*, the call option holder will exercise his right to buy the call. If the value is less, he will let it expire worthless.

The second step involves restating the contingent payoffs in (16.1) in terms of the underlying commodity price at time t, S_t, in order to make the problem more

---

[3] The models presented in this section are based on the work of Geske (1979).

tractable mathematically. The commodity price above which the call option holder
will choose to exercise his call at time t is given by

$$c(S_t^*, T; X) = c_t^*, \tag{16.2}$$

where $c(S_t, T; X)$ represents the European-style option valuation equation (11.25)
evaluated at $S = S_t^*$. Note that the value of S_t^* may be solved iteratively in the
same manner that we have computed critical commodity prices in earlier chapters.[4]
With S_t^* known, the payoff contingencies expressed in (16.1) may be written as

$$c_t = \begin{cases} c(S_t, T; X) - c_t^* & \text{if} \quad S_t > S_t^* \\ 0 & \text{if} \quad S_t \le S_t^*. \end{cases} \tag{16.3}$$

Call on Call. Under risk-neutral valuation, the value of a call on a call may
be written as the present value of the expected terminal value of the option, where
the discount rate is the riskless rate of interest, r:

$$c(c_t, t; c_t^*) = e^{-rt} E[c(S_t, T; X) - c_t^* | S_t > S_t^*] \text{Prob}(S_t > S_t^*). \tag{16.4}$$

Expressing $c(S_t, T; X)$ in terms of its terminal commodity price payoffs and isolating
the cost of exercising the option at time t, equation (16.4) becomes

$$\begin{aligned} c(c_t, t; c_t^*) = {} & e^{-r(t+T)} E(S_T | S_T > X \text{ and } S_t > S_t^*) \text{Prob}(S_T > X \text{ and } S_t > S_t^*) \\ & - e^{-r(t+T)} X \text{Prob}(S_T > X \text{ and } S_t > S_t^*) \\ & - e^{-rt} c_t^* \text{Prob}(S_t > S_t^*). \end{aligned} \tag{16.5}$$

---

[4] See, for example, the valuation of American-style call options on dividend-paying stocks in Chapter 13 or the valuation of American-style options using the quadratic approximation method in Chapter 14.

Under the assumption that future commodity prices are lognormally distributed, the *value of a European-style call on a call is*

$$c(c_t, t; c_t^*) = Se^{(b-r)(t+T)} N_2(a_1, b_1; \sqrt{t/(t+T)})$$
$$- Xe^{-r(t+T)} N_2(a_2, b_2; \sqrt{t/(t+T)})$$
$$- e^{-rt} c_t^* N_1(b_2), \qquad \qquad \textbf{(16.6)}$$

where

$$a_1 = \frac{\ln(S/X) + (b + .5\sigma^2)(t+T)}{\sigma\sqrt{t+T}}, \quad a_2 = a_1 - \sigma\sqrt{t+T},$$

$$b_1 = \frac{\ln(S/S_t^*) + (b + .5\sigma^2)t}{\sigma\sqrt{t}}, \quad b_2 = b_1 - \sigma\sqrt{t},$$

and $N_1(\cdot)$ and $N_2(\cdot)$, are the cumulative univariate and bivariate unit normal density functions described in Chapters 11 and 13, respectively.

In equation (16.6), the term $N_2(a_1, b_1; \sqrt{t/(t+T)})$ is the delta value of the call option on a call option. It describes the call option price movement for a small change in the commodity price. Recall that in Chapter 12 we showed how delta values are used for hedging purposes. The term $N_1(b_2)$ is the probability that the commodity price will exceed the critical commodity price at time t. The term $N_2(a_2, b_2; \sqrt{t/(t+T)})$ is the probability that the commodity price will exceed S_t^* at time t and the exercise price X at time $t + T$.

Put on Call. The simplest way to derive the valuation equation for a put on a call is to deduce the valuation formula from known results. In Chapter 12, we showed that a long-call/short-commodity position is tantamount to a long-put position. Here, the underlying commodity position is a call option, so a long-call-on-a-call/short-call position should be tantamount to a put on a call. Since we have the valuation equation for a call on a call (16.6) and for a European-call (11.25), the *valuation equation for a put on a call is*

$$p(c_t, t; c_t^*) = Se^{(b-r)(t+T)} N_2(a_1, b_1; \sqrt{t/(t+T)})$$
$$- Xe^{-r(t+T)} N_2(a_2, b_2; \sqrt{t/(t+T)}) - e^{-rt} c_t^* N_1(b_2)$$
$$- Se^{(b-r)(t+T)} N_1(a_1) + Xe^{-r(t+T)} N_1(a_2) + e^{-rt} c_t^*$$
$$= Xe^{-r(t+T)} N_2(a_2, -b_2; -\sqrt{t/(t+T)})$$
$$- Se^{(b-r)(t+T)} N_2(a_1, -b_1; -\sqrt{t/(t+T)})$$
$$+ e^{-rt} c_t^* N_1(-b_2), \qquad \qquad \textbf{(16.7)}$$

where all notation is defined in (16.6).

Call on Put. The risk-neutral valuation framework shown above can also be applied to value a call on a put. The value of a *European-style call on a put* is

$$
\begin{aligned}
c(p_t, t; p_t^*) =& Xe^{-r(t+T)} N_2(-a_2, -b_2; \sqrt{t/(t+T)}) \\
&- Se^{(b-r)(t+T)} N_2(-a_1, -b_1; \sqrt{t/(t+T)}) \\
&- e^{-rt} p_t^* N_1(-b_2).
\end{aligned} \tag{16.8}
$$

The critical commodity price below which the call option holder will choose to exercise the call to buy the put at time t is determined by solving

$$
p(S_t^*, T; X) = p_t^*. \tag{16.9}
$$

$p(S_t, T;X)$ represents the European-style option valuation equation (11.28) evaluated at $S = S_t^*$. All other notation is as previously defined. The term $N_2(-a_1, -b_1; \sqrt{t/(t+T)})$ is the delta value of a call option on a put option delta value. The term $N_1(-b_2)$ is the probability that the commodity price will be below the critical commodity price at time t. The term $N_2(-a_2, -b_2; \sqrt{t/(t+T)})$ is the probability that the commodity price will be below S_t^* at time t and the exercise price X at time $t + T$.

Put on Put. A put on a put has the same payoff contingencies as a long-call on-a-put/short-put position. Using equations (11.28) and (16.8), it can be shown that the *value of a put on a put* is

$$
\begin{aligned}
p(p_t, t; p_t^*) =& Se^{(b-r)(t+T)} N_2(-a_1, b_1; -\sqrt{t/(t+T)}) \\
&- Xe^{-r(t+T)} N_2(-a_2, b_2; -\sqrt{t/(t+T)}) \\
&+ e^{-rt} p_t^* N_1(b_2),
\end{aligned} \tag{16.10}
$$

where all notation is defined above.

EXAMPLE 16.1

Consider a call option that provides its holder with the right to buy a put option on the S&P 500 index portfolio. The put that would be delivered against the call if the call is exercised has an exercise price of $400 and a time to expiration of six months. The call has an exercise price of $10 and a time to expiration of three months. The S&P 500 index is currently at 390, pays dividends at a constant rate of 4 percent annually, and has a volatility rate of 28 percent. The riskless rate of interest is 7 percent.

The first step in valuating the compound option is to compute the critical commodity price below which the call will be exercised to take delivery of the put. This is done by solving

$$p(S_t^*, .5; 400) = 10.00.$$

The critical commodity price, S_t^*, is 497.814. The next step is to apply the valuation formula (16.8). Here, we get

$$
\begin{aligned}
c = &400e^{-.07(.25+.5)} N_2(-a_2, -b_2; \sqrt{.25/.75}) \\
&- 390e^{.03(.25+.5)} N_2(-a_1, -b_1; \sqrt{.25/.75}) \\
&- 10e^{-.07(.25)} N_1(-b_2) = 27.722,
\end{aligned}
$$

where

$$a_1 = \frac{\ln(390/400) + [.03 + .5(.28)^2](.75)}{.28\sqrt{.75}} = .1096,$$

$$a_2 = .1096 - .28\sqrt{.75} = -.1329,$$

$$b_1 = \frac{\ln(390/497.814) + [.03 + .5(.28)^2](.25)}{.28\sqrt{.25}} = -1.620,$$

$$b_2 = -1.620 - .28\sqrt{.25} = -1.760.$$

The probability that the commodity price will be below the critical commodity price at time t, $N_1(-b_2)$, is .961. The probability that the commodity price will be below S_t^* at time t and below the exercise price, X, at time $t + T$, $N_2(a_2, b_2; \sqrt{t/(t + T)})$, is .453. The value of a call on a call with the same terms as the put is 27.012. (The critical index price is 342.424.)

Options on the Maximum and the Minimum

Options on the maximum and the minimum of two or more risky commodities are popular exotic options.[5] For example, someone may buy the right to buy the S&P 500 index or gold for $400, depending on which commodity is worth more at the option's expiration. As in the case of compound options, options on the maximum and the minimum can be valued straightforwardly, assuming that both commodity prices have lognormal price distributions at the option's expiration. Under the

---

[5] Other names for the option on the maximum are "the better of two assets" or "outperformance options." The models presented here are on the maximum or the minimum of two risky commodities and the valuation models are based on Stulz (1982). To generalize these models to three or more risky assets, see Johnson (1987).

risk-neutral valuation approach, the value of a call option on the maximum, for example, may be written as

$$
\begin{aligned}
c_{\max}(S_1, S_2; X) = {} & \\
& e^{-rT} E(\tilde{S}_{1,T}|S_{1,T} > X \text{ and } S_{1,T} > S_{2,T}) \text{Prob}(S_{1,T} > X \text{ and } S_{1,T} > S_{2,T}) \\
& + e^{-rT} E(\tilde{S}_{2,T}|S_{2,T} > X \text{ and } S_{2,T} > S_{1,T}) \text{Prob}(S_{2,T} > X \text{ and } S_{2,T} > S_{1,T}) \\
& - X e^{-rT} \text{Prob}(S_{1,T} > X \text{ or } S_{2,T} > X). \qquad \textbf{(16.11)}
\end{aligned}
$$

Under the assumption that future commodity prices are lognormally distributed, the *value of a European-style call on the maximum* is

$$
\begin{aligned}
c_{\max}(S_1, S_2; X) = {} & \\
& S_1 e^{(b_1 - r)T} N_2(d_{11}, d_1'; \rho_1') + S_2 e^{(b_2 - r)T} N_2(d_{12}, d_2'; \rho_2') \\
& - X e^{-rT} [1 - N_2(-d_{21}, -d_{22}; \rho_{12})], \qquad \textbf{(16.12)}
\end{aligned}
$$

where

$$
d_{11} = \frac{\ln(S_1/X_1) + (b_1 + .5\sigma_1^2)T}{\sigma_1 \sqrt{T}}, \quad d_{21} = d_{11} - \sigma_1\sqrt{T},
$$

$$
d_{12} = \frac{\ln(S_2/X_2) + (b_2 + .5\sigma_2^2)T}{\sigma_2 \sqrt{T}}, \quad d_{22} = d_{12} - \sigma_2\sqrt{T},
$$

$$
d_1' = \frac{\ln(S_1/S_2) + (b_1 - b_2 + .5\sigma^2)T}{\sigma \sqrt{T}}, \quad d_2' = -(d_1' - \sigma\sqrt{T}),
$$

$$
\sigma^2 = \sigma_1^2 + \sigma_2^2 - 2\rho_{12}\sigma_1\sigma_2, \quad \rho_1' = \frac{\sigma_1 - \rho_{12}\sigma_2}{\sigma}, \quad \text{and} \quad \rho_2' = \frac{\sigma_2 - \rho_{12}\sigma_1}{\sigma}.
$$

In equation (16.12), the term $1 - N_2(-d_{21}, -d_{22}; \rho_{12})$ is the probability that one of the two commodity prices will exceed the exercise price at time T or, alternatively, one minus the probability that neither commodity will have a price greater than the exercise price at the option's expiration.

EXAMPLE 16.2

Consider a call option that provides its holder the right to buy $100,000 worth of the S&P 500 index portfolio at an exercise price of $400 or $100,000 worth of a particular T-bond at an exercise price of $100, whichever is worth more at the end of three months. The S&P 500 index is currently priced at $360, pays dividends at a rate of 4 percent annually, and has a return volatility of 28 percent. The T-bond is currently priced at $98, pays a coupon yield of 10 percent, and has a return volatility of 15 percent. The correlation between the rates of return of the S&P 500 and the T-bond is .5. The riskless rate of interest is 7 percent.

Before applying the option on the maximum formula, it is important to recognize that there are two exercise prices in this problem: $400 for the S&P index portfolio and $100 for the T-bond. What this implies is that we can buy $100,000/$400 = 250 "units" of the index portfolio or $100,000/$100 = 1,000 T-bond "units" at the end of three months, depending on which is worth more. At this juncture, we must decide whether to work with the valuation equation (16.12) in units of the S&P 500 index portfolio, in which case we multiply the current T-bond price and its exercise price by 4, and then multiply the computed option price by 250, or to work with the valuation equation (16.12) in units of the T-bond, in which case we divide the current S&P 500 price and the option's S&P 500 exercise price by 4, and then multiply the computed option price by 1,000.[6] In this exercise, we choose to work in units of the S&P 500 index portfolio, so we adjust the T-bond prices: the current T-bond price is assumed to be 392, and the T-bond exercise price is 400.

With the units of the two underlying assets comparable, we now apply equation (16.12):

$$c_{max} = 360e^{-.04(.25)}N_2(d_{11}, d_1'; \rho_1') + 392e^{-.10(.25)}N_2(d_{12}, -d_2'; \rho_2')$$
$$- 400e^{-.07(.25)}[1 - N_2(-d_{21}, -d_{22}; .5)] = 11.962,$$

where

$$d_{11} = \frac{\ln(360/400) + [.07 - .04 + .5(.28)^2](.25)}{.28\sqrt{.25}} = -.6290,$$

$$d_{21} = -.6290 - .28\sqrt{.25} = -.7690,$$

$$d_{12} = \frac{\ln(392/400) + [.07 - .10 + .5(.15)^2](.25)}{.15\sqrt{.25}} = -.3319,$$

$$d_{22} = -.3319 - .15\sqrt{.25} = -.4069,$$

$$d_1' = \frac{\ln(360/392) + [.06 + .5\sigma^2](.25)}{\sigma\sqrt{.25}} = -.5175,$$

$$d_2' = -(-.5175 - \sigma\sqrt{.25}) = .6388,$$

$$\sigma = \sqrt{.28^2 + .15^2 - 2(.5)(.28)(.15)} = .2427,$$

$$\rho_1' = \frac{.28 - .5(.15)}{.2427} = .8447,$$

$$\rho_2' = \frac{.15 - .5(.28)}{.2427} = .0412.$$

---

[6]These types of adjustments can be made freely because the option price is linearly homogeneous in both the commodity price and the exercise price. See Merton (1973).

The computed option price is 11.962, which implies the value of the option contract is $11.962 × 250, or $2,990.50. The probability that either or both components of the option are in-the-money at expiration is $1 - N_2(.7690, .4069; .5)$, or 42.72 percent.

Under the same assumptions, the *value of a European-style call on the minimum* is

$$
c_{\min}(S_1, S_2; X) =
$$
$$
S_1 e^{(b_1-r)T} N_2(d_{11}, -d_1'; -\rho_1') + S_2 e^{(b_2-r)T} N_2(d_{12}, -d_2'; -\rho_2')
$$
$$
- X e^{-rT} N_2(d_{21}, d_{22}; \rho_{12}), \tag{16.13}
$$

where all notation is as previously defined.

Lookback Options

Aside from compound options and options on the maximum and the minimum, many other exotic options trade in OTC markets. Some of the options are backward looking. A *lookback call option* provides its holder with settlement proceeds equal to the difference between the highest commodity price during the life of the option less the exercise price, and a *lookback put option* provides its holder with settlement proceeds equal to the difference between the exercise price and the lowest commodity price during the life of the option. It should come as no surprise, therefore, that these options are sometimes referred to as "no-regret options."

In a sense, lookback options are like American-style options because the option holder is guaranteed the most advantageous exercise price. Lookback call options can be valued analytically using the risk-neutral valuation mechanics.[7] The reason for this is that it never pays to exercise a lookback option prior to expiration. Independent of how low the commodity price has been thus far during the option's life, there is always some positive probability that it will fall further. For this reason, the option holder will always defer early exercise in the hope of recognizing higher exercise proceeds in the future.

Under the assumptions of risk-neutral valuation and lognormally distributed future commodity prices, the *value of a lookback call* may be written as

$$
c_{LB} = S e^{(b-r)T} N_1(d_1) - X e^{-rT} N_1(d_2)
$$
$$
+ S e^{(b-r)T} \lambda \left[e^{-b[T + \frac{2\ln(S/X)}{\sigma^2}]} N_1(d_3) - N_1(-d_1) \right], \tag{16.14}
$$

where X is the current minimum price of the commodity during the life of the option, $\lambda = .5\sigma^2/b$, $d_1 = \dfrac{\ln(S/X) + (b + .5\sigma^2)T}{\sigma\sqrt{T}}$, $d_2 = d_1 - \sigma\sqrt{T}$ and $d_3 = \dfrac{(b - .5\sigma^2)T}{\sigma\sqrt{T}}$. Note that the first two terms of the option are the value of a European-

---

[7] The pricing equations provided here are based on the work of Goldman, Sosin, and Gatto (1979).

style call option whose exercise price is the current minimum value of the under-lying commodity. This is the least the lookback call can be worth since the com-modity price may fall below X, thereby driving the "exercise price" down further.

EXAMPLE 16.3

Consider a lookback call option that provides its holder with the right to buy the S&P 500 index at any time during the next three months. The S&P 500 index is currently at a level of 390, pays dividends at a constant rate of 4 percent annually, and has a volatility rate of 28 percent. The riskless rate of interest is 7 percent.

The cost-of-carry rate is $.07 - .04 = .03$. The value of the lookback call is, therefore,

$$c_{LB} = 390e^{(.03-.07).25} N_1(d_1) - 390e^{-.07(.25)} N_1(d_2)$$
$$+ 390e^{(.03-.07).25} \lambda \left[e^{-.03[.25 + \frac{2\ln(390/390)}{.28^2}]} N_1(d_3) - N_1(-d_1) \right] = 42.583,$$

where

$$\lambda = .5(.28)^2/.03 = 1.3067,$$
$$d_1 = \frac{\ln(390/390) + [.03 + .5(.28)^2].25}{.28\sqrt{.25}} = .1236,$$
$$d_2 = .1236 - .28\sqrt{.25} = -.0164,$$

and

$$d_3 = \frac{[.03 - .5(.28)^2].25}{.28\sqrt{.25}} = -.0164.$$

Note that the price of the lookback call is considerably higher than an at-the-money index call option. The value of a European-style call (i.e., the sum of the first two terms in the valuation equation) is only 22.941.

The *value of a European-style lookback put option* is

$$p_{LB} = Xe^{-rT} N_1(-d_2) - Se^{(b-r)T} N_1(-d_1)$$
$$+ Se^{(b-r)T} \lambda \left[N_1(d_1) - e^{-b[T + \frac{2\ln(S/X)}{\sigma^2}]} N_1(-d_3) \right], \qquad \textbf{(16.15)}$$

where all notation is as defined for the lookback call. Note that a standard Euro-pean-style put option is the lower bound for the price of the lookback put option. The third term is necessarily positive. Using the same parameters as in Example

16.3, the value of a lookback put option is \$43.468, with the underlying ordinary European-style put being valued at \$20.056.

Other backward-looking options are also traded. For example, *average price* or *Asian options* are based on the average (either arithmetic or geometric) commodity price during the option's life. The average commodity price may be used as the exercise price of the option, in which case the settlement value of the call will be the terminal commodity price less the average price, or it may be used as the terminal commodity price, in which case the settlement value will be the average price less the exercise price. Unfortunately, most Asian options do not have closed-form valuation equations. Accurate pricing involves the use of numerical methods.[8]

Barrier Options

Barrier options are options whose existence depends on the underlying commodity price. A *down-and-out call,* for example, is a call that expires if the commodity price falls below a prespecified "out" barrier, H.[9] At that time, the option buyer may receive a cash rebate, R. A *down-and-in call* is a call that comes into existence if the commodity price falls below the "in" barrier at any time during the option's life. Note that if we buy a down-and-out call and a down-and-in call with the same barrier price, H, exercise price, X, and time to expiration, T, the portfolio has the same payoff contingencies as a standard call option. For this reason, we automatically know how to value a down-and-in call if we can value a down-and-out call.

Under the assumptions of risk-neutral valuation and lognormally distributed commodity prices, the valuation equation for a down-and-out call option is

$$
\begin{aligned}
c_{\mathrm{DO}} =& Se^{(b-r)T} N_1(a_1) - Xe^{-rT} N_1(b_2) \\
& - Se^{(b-r)T}(H/S)^{2(\eta+1)} N_1(b_1) + Xe^{-rT}(H/S)^{2\eta} N_1(b_2) \\
& + R(H/S)^{\eta+\gamma} N_1(c_1) + R(H/S)^{\eta-\gamma} N_1(c_2),
\end{aligned} \tag{16.16}
$$

H is the barrier commodity price below which the call option life ends; R is the rebate, if any, received by the option buyer should the option terminate,

$$
\eta = \frac{b}{\sigma^2} - 1/2, \quad \gamma = \sqrt{\eta^2 + \frac{2r}{\sigma^2}},
$$

$$
a_1 = \frac{\ln(S/X)}{\sigma\sqrt{T}} + (1+\eta)\sigma\sqrt{T}, \quad a_2 = a_1 - \sigma\sqrt{T},
$$

$$
b_1 = \frac{\ln(H^2/SX)}{\sigma\sqrt{T}} + (1+\eta)\sigma\sqrt{T}, \quad b_2 = b_1 - \sigma\sqrt{T},
$$

$$
c_1 = \frac{\ln(H/S)}{\sigma\sqrt{T}} + \gamma\sigma\sqrt{T}, \quad \text{and} \quad c_2 = c_1 - 2\gamma\sigma\sqrt{T}.
$$

---

[8]There are a number of useful background readings for those interested in pricing Asian options. Among them are Boyle (1977) and Boyle and Emanuel (1985).

[9]The valuation equation for the down-and-out call option was first provided in Cox and Rubinstein (1985, Ch. 7). The valuation equation presented here is a modified version of the formula presented in Rubinstein (1990).

The valuation equation for a down-and-in call is simply equation (11.25) less (16.16).

EXAMPLE 16.4

Consider a down-and-in call option that provides its holder with the right to buy the S&P 500 index at 380 any time during the next three months, should the index level fall below 375. The S&P 500 index is currently at a level of 390, pays dividends at a constant rate of 4 percent annually, and has a volatility rate of 28 percent. The riskless rate of interest is 7 percent.

The cost-of-carry rate is $.07 - .04 = .03$. The value of the down-and-out call is

$$
\begin{aligned}
c_{\text{DO}} =& 390e^{(.03-.07).25} N_1(a_1) - 380e^{-.07(.25)} N_1(b_2) \\
&- 390e^{(.03-.07).25}(375/390)^{2(\eta+1)} N_1(b_1) \\
&+ 380e^{-.07(.25)}(375/390)^{2\eta} N_1(b_2) = 14.817,
\end{aligned}
$$

where

$$
\eta = \frac{.03}{.28^2} - 1/2 = -.1173,
$$

$$
\gamma = \sqrt{.1173^2 + \frac{2(.07)}{.28^2}} = 1.3414,
$$

$$
a_1 = \frac{\ln(390/380)}{.28\sqrt{.25}} + (1 - .1173).28\sqrt{.25} = .3091,
$$

$$
a_2 = a_1 - .28\sqrt{.25} = .1691,
$$

$$
b_1 = \frac{\ln[375^2/(390 \times 380)]}{.28\sqrt{.25}} + .28(1 - .1173)\sqrt{.25} = -.2512,
$$

$$
b_2 = b_1 - .28\sqrt{.25} = -.3912,
$$

$$
c_1 = \frac{\ln(375/390)}{.28\sqrt{.25}} + .28(1.3414)\sqrt{.25} = -.0924,
$$

and

$$
c_2 = c_1 - .56(1.3414)\sqrt{.25} = -.4680.
$$

The value of a standard European-style call option is 28.151, using equation (11.25). The value of the down-and-in call is, therefore, $28.151 - 14.817 = 13.334$.

An *up-and-out put* and an *up-and-in put* can be valued in a similar manner. An up-and-out put is a put that expires if the commodity price rises above the "out" barrier. Its valuation equation is

$$
\begin{aligned}
p_{UO} =& Xe^{-rT} N_1(-b_2) - Se^{(b-r)T} N_1(-a_1) \\
&+ Se^{(b-r)T}(H/S)^{2(\eta+1)} N_1(-b_1) - Xe^{-rT}(H/S)^{2\eta} N_1(-b_2) \\
&- R(H/S)^{\eta+\gamma} N_1(-c_1) - R(H/S)^{\eta-\gamma} N_1(-c_2).
\end{aligned}
\tag{16.17}
$$

An up-and-in put comes into existence when the commodity price rises above H. Its valuation equation is simply (11.28) less (16.17).

Other Exotic Options

Exotic options abound.[10] Among those not yet mentioned are those involving deferred features. A *deferred-start option*, for example, is an option which is purchased before its life actually begins. A *deferred payment American option* is like a standard American-style option except, if the option is exercised early, the option buyer does not receive the exercise proceeds until the end of the option's life. Yet others involve lump sum payoffs. An *all-or-nothing call (put) option*, for example, pays a predetermined amount (i.e., the "all") should the underlying commodity price be above (below) the exercise price at the option's expiration. A *one-touch all-or-nothing call (put)* pays a predetermined amount if the commodity price touches the exercise price at any time during the option's life.

16.4 SUMMARY

This chapter concludes the presentation of option valuation principles and applications. First, we discussed currency and currency futures options. Contract specifications were provided, and we noted that the valuation of these options is a straightforward application of the constant cost-of-carry framework developed in Chapters 10 and 11. The cost-of-carry rate for currency options is the domestic rate of interest less the foreign rate of interest, and the cost-of-carry rate for currency futures options is zero. We discussed, as well, the use of currency options in hedging the currency risk that arises in international trade or investment. Second, we discussed physical commodity futures options. In general, no options on physical commodities trade, only options on physical commodity futures. Hence, the valuation principles for these options also follow straightforwardly from the constant cost-of-carry framework of the earlier chapters. The cost-of-carry rate for physical commodity futures is zero.

---

[10] For a brief review of a range of exotic options, see Hudson (1991).

The remainder of the chapter focuses on exotic options. These are not exchange-traded options but are unusual options that trade in OTC markets. We show how options on options, options on the maximum and the minimum of two commodities, lookback options, and barrier options may be valued within a log-normal price distribution framework. But, these are only four of a myriad of option contract designs that exist in the OTC markets. We discuss others; however, the list is certainly incomplete given the pace with which these new contracts are introduced.

REFERENCES

Barone–Adesi, G. and R.E. Whaley, 1987. "Efficient Analytic Approximation of American Option Values." *Journal of Finance* 42 (June), 301–320.

Barone–Adesi, G. and R.E. Whaley, 1988. "On the Valuation of American Put Options on Dividend-Paying Stocks." *Advances in Futures and Options Research* 3, 1–13.

Black, D.G., 1986. "Success and Failure of Futures Contracts: Theory and Empirical Evidence." *Monograph Series Finance and Economics.* Monograph 1986–1. Salomon Brothers Center for the Study of Financial Institutions, NYU. 68 pages.

Black, F., 1976. "The Pricing of Commodity Contracts." *Journal of Financial Economics* 3, 167–179.

Black, F. and M. Scholes, 1973. "The Pricing of Options and Corporate Liabilities." *Journal of Political Economy* 81 (May/June), 637–659.

Bodie, Z. and V.I. Rosansky, 1980. "Risk and Return in Commodity Futures." *Financial Analysts Journal* (May/June), 27–39.

Boyle, P., 1977. "Options: A Monte Carlo Approach." *Journal of Financial Economics* 4 (May), 323–338.

Boyle, P. and D. Emanuel, 1985. "The Pricing of Options on the Generalized Mean." Working paper, University of Waterloo.

Brennan, M.J. and E.S. Schwartz, 1977. "The Valuation of American Put Options." *Journal of Finance* 32 (May), 449–462.

Brennan, M.J. and E.S. Schwartz, 1990. "Arbitrage in Stock Index Futures." *Journal of Business* 63 (January), S7–S31.

Carlton, D.W., 1984. "Futures Markets: Their Purpose, Their History, Their Growth, Their Successes and Failures." *Journal of Futures Markets* 4 (Fall), 237–271.

Chicago Board of Trade, 1989. *Commodity Trading Manual.* Edited by P. Catania and others. Chicago: Board of Trade of the City of Chicago. 401 pages.

Chicago Board of Trade, 1990. "Emergency Action." Chicago: Board of Trade of the City of Chicago.

Chiras, D.P. and S. Manaster, 1978. "The Informational Content of Option Prices and a Test of Market Efficiency." *Journal of Financial Economics* 6 (June–September), 213–234.

Choie, K.S. and F. Novemstky, 1989. "Replication of Long-Term with Short-Term Options." *Journal of Portfolio Management* 15 (Winter), 17–19.

Cohen, K.J., S.F. Maier, R.A. Schwartz, and D.K. Whitcomb, 1986. *The Microstructure of Securities Markets.* Englewood Cliffs, NJ: Prentice–Hall, Inc.

Commodity Futures Trading Commission, 1988. *Final Report on Stock Index Futures and Cash Market Activity During October 1987.* 200 pages.

Cootner, P., 1960a. "Returns to Speculators: Telser Versus Keynes." *Journal of Political Economy* 68 (August), 396–404.

Cootner, P., 1960b. "Rejoinder." *Journal of Political Economy* 68 (August), 415–418.

Cornell B. and K. French, 1983. "Taxes and the Pricing of Stock Index Futures." *Journal of Finance* 38 (June), 675–694.

Cox, J.C., J.E. Ingersoll, and S.A. Ross, 1981. "The Relation Between Forward and Futures Prices." *Journal of Financial Economics* 9 (December), 321–346.

Cox, J.C. and S.A. Ross, 1976. "The Valuation of Options for Alternative Stochastic Processes." *Journal of Financial Economics* 3, 145–166.

Cox, J.C., S.A. Ross, and M. Rubinstein, 1979. "Option Pricing: A Simplified Approach." *Journal of Financial Economics* 7 (September), 229–263.

Cox, J.C. and M. Rubinstein, 1985. *Option Markets*. Englewood Cliffs, NJ: Prentice–Hall, Inc.

Drezner, Z., 1978. "Computation of the Bivariate Normal Integral." *Mathematics of Computation* 32 (January), 277–279.

Dusak, K., 1973. "Futures Trading and Investor Returns: An Investigation of Commodity Market Risk Premiums." *Journal of Political Economy* 87 (November/December), 1387–1406.

Ederington, L.H., 1979. "The Hedging Performance of the New Futures Markets." *Journal of Finance* 34 (March), 157–169.

Eiteman D. and A. Stonehill, 1986. *Multinational Financial Management*. Reading, MA: Addison–Wesley.

Elton, E., M. Gruber, and J. Rentzler, 1987. "Professionally Managed Publicly Traded Commodity Funds." *Journal of Business* 60 (April), 175–199.

Elton, E., M. Gruber and J. Rentzler, 1989. "New Public Offerings, Information, and Investor Rationality: the Case of Publicly Offered Commodity Funds." *Journal of Business* 62 (January), 1–15.

Emanuel, D., 1985. "Eurodollar Volatility and Option Pricing." *Market Perspectives* 3 (April), 1, 3–4.

Fabozzi, F.J. and T.D. Fabozzi, 1989. *Bond Markets, Analysis and Strategies*. Prentice–Hall, Inc.: Englewood Cliffs, N.J.

Fama, E., 1970. "Efficient Capital Markets: A Review of Theory and Empirical Tests." *Journal of Finance* 25 (May), 383–417.

Feiger, G. and B. Jacquillat, 1979. "Currency Option Bonds, Puts and Calls on Spot Exchange and the Contingent Foreign Earnings." *Journal of Finance* 33 (December), 1129–1139.

Figlewski, S., 1984. "Explaining the Early Discounts on Stock Index Futures: The Case for Disequilibrium." *Financial Analysts Journal* (July/August), 43–47.

Fisher, L., 1966. "Some New Stock Market Indexes." *Journal of Business* 39 (January), 191–225.

French, K., 1980. "Stock Returns and the Weekend Effect." *Journal of Financial Economics* 8 (March), 55–69.

Garcia, C. and F.J. Gould, 1987. "Using Stock Index Futures for 'Uncertain' Arbitrage." Working paper, Graduate School of Business, University of Chicago.

Garman, M. and M. Klass, 1980. "On the Estimation of Security Price Volatilities from Historical Data." *Journal of Business* 53 (January), 67–78.

Gastineau, G. and A. Madansky, 1983. "S&P 500 Stock Index Futures Evaluation Tables." *Financial Analysts Journal* (November/December), 68–76.

Geske, R., 1979. "The Valuation of Compound Options." *Journal of Financial Economics* 7 (March), 63–81.

Gibbons, M.R. and P. Hess, 1981. "Day of the Week Effects and Asset Returns." *Journal of Business* 54 (October), 579–596.

Giddy, Ian, 1983. "The Foreign Exchange Option as a Hedging Tool." *Midland Corporate Finance Journal* 1 (Fall), 32–42.

Goldman, B., H. Sosin, and M. Gatto, 1979. "Path Dependent Options: Buy at the Low and Sell at the High." *Journal of Finance* 34 (December), 1111–1127.

Gould, F.J., 1988. "Stock Index Futures: The Arbitrage Cycle and Portfolio Insurance." *Financial Analysts Journal* 44 (January/February), 48–62.

Grabbe, J.O., 1983. "The Pricing of Call and Put Options on Foreign Exchange." *Journal of International Money and Finance* 2, 239–253.

Grabbe, J.O., 1986. *International Financial Markets.* New York: Elsivier.

Harvey, C.R. and R.E. Whaley, 1991. "S&P 100 Index Option Volatility." *Journal of Finance* 46 (September), 1551–1561.

Harvey, C.R. and R.E. Whaley, 1992a. "Market Volatility Prediction and the Efficiency of the S&P 100 Index Option Market." *Journal of Financial Economics.*

Harvey, C.R. and R.E. Whaley, 1992b. "Dividends and S&P 100 Index Option Valuation." *Journal of Futures Markets.*

Hicks, J.R., 1939. *Value and Capital.* Oxford University Press.

Hotelling, H., 1931. "The Economics of Exhaustible Resources." *Journal of Political Economy* 39 (April), 137–175.

Houthakker, H.S., 1957. "Can Speculators Forecast Prices?" *Review of Economics and Statistics* 34, 143–151.

Hudson, M., 1991. "The Value in Going Out." *Risk* 4 (March).

Jaffee, D.M., 1984. "The Impact of Financial Futures and Options on Capital Formation." *Journal of Futures Markets* 4 (Fall), 417–447.

Jamshidian, F. and Y. Zhu, 1990. "Replication of an Option on a Bond Portfolio." *Review of Futures Markets* 9, 84–100.

Johnson, H., 1987. "Options on the Maximum or the Minimum of Several Risky Assets." *Journal of Financial and Quantitative Analysis* 22 (September), 277–283.

Johnston, E. and J. McConnell, 1989. "Requiem for a Market: An Analysis of the Rise and Fall of a Financial Futures Contract." *Review of Financial Studies* 2, 1–23.

Keynes, J.M., 1930. *A Treatise on Money, Volume 2.* London: MacMillan Press.

Kleidon, A., 1991. "Arbitrage, Nontrading, and Stale Prices: October 1987." Working paper, Graduate School of Business, Stanford University.

Kleidon, A., and R.E. Whaley, 1991. "One Market? Stocks, Futures and Options During October 1987." Working paper, Fuqua School of Business, Duke University.

Latane, H. and R. Rendleman, 1976. "Standard Deviation of Stock Price Ratios Implied by Option Premia." *Journal of Finance* 31 (May), 369–382.

Lessard, D. (ed.), 1985. *International Financial Management: Theory and Application.* New York: John Wiley and Sons.

Lintner, J., 1965. "The Valuation of Risk Assets and the Selection of Risky Investments in Stock Portfolios and Capital Budgets." *Review of Economics and Statistics* 47 (February), 13–37.

Lo, A.W. and A.C. MacKinlay, 1988. "Stock Market Prices Do Not Follow a Random Walk: Evidence from a Simple Specification Test." *Review of Financial Studies* 1 (Spring), 41–66.

MacKinlay, A.C. and K. Ramaswamy, 1988. "Index-Futures Arbitrage and the Behavior of Stock Index Futures Prices." *Review of Financial Studies* 1 (Summer), 137–158.

Margrabe, W., 1978. "The Value of an Option to Exchange One Asset for Another." *Journal of Finance* 33 (March), 177–186.

Margrabe, W., 1982. "A Theory of the Price of a Contingent Claim on *N* Asset Prices." Working paper, School of Government and Business Administration, George Washington University.

Merton, R.C., 1973. "The Theory of Rational Option Pricing." *Bell Journal of Economics and Management Science* 4 (Spring), 141–183.

Miller, M., J. Muthuswamy, and R.E. Whaley, 1991. "Predictability of S&P 500 Basis Changes: Arbitrage-Induced or Statistical Illusion." Working paper, Fuqua School of Business, Duke University.

Miller, M. and C.W. Upton, 1985. "A Test of the Hotelling Valuation Principle." *Journal of Political Economy* 93 (February), 1–25.

Modest, D. and M. Sundaresan, 1983. "The Relationship Between Spot and Futures Prices in Stock Index Futures Markets: Some Preliminary Evidence." *Journal of Futures Markets* 3 (Summer), 15–41.

Parkinson, M., 1980. "The Extreme Value Method for Estimating the Variances of the Rate of Return." *Journal of Business* 53 (January), 61–65.

Patell, J.M. and M. Wolfson, 1979. "Anticipated Information Releases Reflected in Option Prices." *Journal of Accounting and Economics* 8, 179–201.

Peck, A.E., 1985. "The Economic Role of Traditional Commodity Futures Markets," in A.E. Peck (ed.) *Futures Markets: Their Economic Role.* Washington, DC: American Enterprise Institute, 1–82.

Peters, E., 1985. "The Growing Efficiency of Index Futures Markets." *Journal of Portfolio Management* 11 (Summer), 52–56.

Pindyck, R.S. and D.L. Rubinfeld, 1981. *Econometric Models and Economic Forecasts.* Second Edition, McGraw–Hill Book Company, Inc.

Pirrong, S.C., D. Haddock, and R. Kormendi, 1991. *Grain Futures Contracts for the 1990s: An Economic Appraisal.* Report for the Chicago Board of Trade and the Commodity Futures Trading Commission.

Protopapadkis, A. and H.R. Stoll, 1983. "The Law of One Price in International Commodity Markets: A Reformulation and Some Formal Tests." *Journal of International Money and Finance* 5 (September), 1431–1455.

Rockwell, C.S., 1967. "Normal Backwardation, Forecasting, and the Returns to Commodity Futures Traders." *Food Research Institute Studies* 7 (Supplement), 107–130.

Roll, R., 1977. "An Analytic Valuation Formula for Unprotected American Call Options with Known Dividends." *Journal of Financial Economics* 5, 251–258.

Rubinstein, M., 1990. "Exotic Options." Working paper, University of California at Berkeley (November).

Samuelson, P.A., 1965. "Rational Theory of Warrant Pricing." *Industrial Management Review* 6, 13–39.

Schmalensee, R. and R. R. Trippi., 1978. "Common Stock Volatility Expectations Implied by Option Prices." *Journal of Finance* 33 (March), 129–147.

Shulz, G.U. and S. Trautman, 1991. "Valuation of Warrants: Theory and Empirical Tests for Warrants Written on German Stocks." Working paper, Department of Law and Economics, Johannes–Gutenberg Universität Mainz.

Shapiro, A., 1989. *International Financial Management.* Boston: Allyn and Bacon.

Sharpe, W.F., 1984. "Capital Asset Prices: A Theory of Market Equilibrium Under Conditions of Risk." *Journal of Finance* 19 (September), 425–442.

Silber, W.L., 1985. "The Economic Role of Financial Futures." in A. Peck (ed.) *Futures Markets: Their Economic Role.* Washington, DC: American Enterprise Institute, 83–114.

Smidt, S., 1965. "A Test of the Serial Independence of Price Changes in Soybean Futures." *Food Research Institute Studies* 5.

Smidt, S., 1985. "Trading Floor Practices on Futures and Securities Exchanges: Economics, Regulation, and Policy," in A. Peck (ed.) *Futures Markets: Regulatory Issues.* Washington, DC: American Enterprise Institute, 49–142.

Smith, C.W, Jr., 1977. "Alternative Methods for Raising Capital: Rights Versus Underwritten Offerings." *Journal of Financial Economics* 5 (December), 273–307.

Solnik, B., 1988. *International Investments.* Reading MA: Addison–Wesley.

Steen, N.M., G.D. Byrne, and E.M. Gelbard, 1969. "Gaussian Quadratures for the Integrals," *Mathematical Computation* 23, 661–671.

Stephan, J.A. and R.E. Whaley, 1990. "Intraday Price Change and Trading Volume Relations in the Stock and Stock Option Markets." *Journal of Finance* 45 (March), 191–220.

Stevenson, R.A. and R.M. Bear, 1970. "Commodity Futures: Trends or Random Walks?" *Journal of Finance* 25 (March), 65–81.

Stigum, M., 1990. *The Money Market.* Third Edition, Dow Jones–Irwin, Homewood, IL.

Stoll, H.R., 1969. "The Relationship Between Put and Call Option Prices." *Journal of Finance* 24, 801–824.

Stoll, H.R., 1979. "Commodity Futures and Spot Price Determination and Hedging in Capital Market Equilibrium." *Journal of Financial and Quantitative Analysis* 14 (November), 873–894.

Stoll, H.R., 1988a. "Index Futures, Program Trading, and Stock Market Procedures." *Journal of Futures Markets* 8 (August), 391–412.

Stoll, H.R., 1988b. "Portfolio Trading." *Journal of Portfolio Management* 14 (Summer), 20–24.

Stoll, H.R. and R.E. Whaley, 1985. "The New Option Markets," in A. Peck (ed.) *Futures Markets: Their Economic Role.* Washington, DC: American Enterprice Institute, 205–282.

Stoll, H.R. and R.E. Whaley, 1986. "The New Option Instruments: Arbitrageable Linkages and Valuation." *Advances in Futures and Option Research* 1, 25–62.

Stoll, H.R. and R.E. Whaley, 1986. "Expiration Day Effects of Index Options and Futures," *Monograph Series in Finance and Economics.* Monograph 1986–3, Salomon Brothers Center for the Study of Financial Institutions, NYU. 89 pages.

Stoll, H.R. and R.E. Whaley, 1987. "Program Trading and Expiration-Day Effects." *Financial Analysts Journal* 43 (March/April), 16–28.

Stoll, H.R. and R.E. Whaley, 1988. "Futures and Options on Stock Indexes: Economic Purpose, Arbitrage, and Market Structure." *Review of Futures Markets* 7, 224–48.

Stoll, H.R. and R.E. Whaley, 1990a. "Stock Market Structure and Volatility." *Review of Financial Studies* 3, 37–71.

Stoll, H.R. and R.E. Whaley, 1990b. "The Dynamics of Stock Index and Stock Index Futures Returns." *Journal of Financial and Quantitative Analysis* 25 (December), 441–468.

Stoll, H.R. and R.E. Whaley, 1991. "Expiration-Day Effects: What Has Changed?" *Financial Analysts Journal* 47 (January/February), 58–72.

Stulz, R., 1982. "Options on the Minimum or the Maximum of Two Risky Assets: Analysis and Applications." *Journal of Financial Economics* 10, 161–185.

Telser, L., 1958. "Futures Trading and the Storage of Cotton and Wheat." *Journal of Political Economy* 66 (June), 233–255.

Telser, L., 1960. "Returns to Speculators: Telser Versus Keynes: Reply." *Journal of Political Economy* 68 (August), 404–415.

Telser, L. and H. Higinbotham, 1977. "Organized Futures Markets: Costs and Benefits." *Journal of Political Economy* 85 (October), 969–1000.

Wang, Y.J., 1987. "The Probability Integrals of Bivariate Normal Distributions: A Contingency Table Approach." *Biometrika* 74, 185–190.

Whaley, R.E., 1981. "On the Valuation of American Call Options on Stocks with Known Dividends." *Journal of Financial Economics* 9 (June), 207–211.

Whaley, R.E., 1982, "Valuation of American Call Options on Dividend-Paying Stocks: Empirical Tests." *Journal of Financial Economics* 10, 29–58.

Whaley, R.E., 1986a. "On Valuing American Futures Options." *Financial Analysts Journal* 42 (May/June), 49–59.

Whaley, R.E., 1986b. "Valuation of American Futures Options: Theory and Empirical Tests." *Journal of Finance* 41 (March), 127–150.

Whaley, R.E. (ed.), 1991. *Selected Writings on Futures Markets: Interrelations Among Futures, Option and Futures Option Markets.* Chicago: Chicago Board of Trade.

INDEX